LCCN: 2024925907

"POWER IS TRUTH"

Written by

Shazadi Baig

Learning satisfies the desire one seeks, despite life's limitations. Reading and visual experiences shape thoughts and perceptions. Experience the captivating togetherness by immersing yourself in my writing with an open mind. Confidence plays a crucial role in speaking; success by reinforcing the belief in infinite truth.

BRIEF INTRODUCTION

In this presentation: Truth is revealed to be Power and the ultimate source of all knowledge and strength. Exploring Islam is a commitment to truth and distancing from lies.

This exploration helps individuals understand similarities and differences between religions, aiding them in navigating life's challenges.

Unpredictable word flow prevents guessing my next statement. Engagement fosters learning and open-mindedness in the pursuit of knowledge. Close-mindedness restricts exploration. Grasp the intensity of my words as I share unexpected insights.

Expand your knowledge by reading my book. I have a distinctive style with passionate delivery and profound words. The Quran and hadith cannot be substituted.

Comparisons broaden the mind, while decisions are predetermined by Allah, leading humans towards their destined journeys.

Insha'Allah, you will be attentive to my words. Interested readers are engaged. My book touches on various themes, offering a concise comparison between Islam and Christianity in terms of history, daily events, life, world, beneficiaries, distractions, happiness, dilemmas, and achievements.

The mind and heart defy singular focus in search of the unexpected. I explore Abrahamic faiths, giving special consideration to their beliefs and distinguishing features.

As long as the mind and heart are not in sync, predictions hold no worth, and the predetermined nature of destiny leaves one clueless about their purpose, thus making the pursuit of answers inevitable.

The dissemination of knowledge is a core belief among Muslims. Lack of profound comprehension in a field hampers progress and causes confusion.

Lack of clarity and conflicting messages only add to chaos and hinder learning. It is crucial for Muslims to share knowledge of Islam with a positive perspective.

Without conversation, there can be no impact on any relationship. If Allah had not conversed with the angels and sent the angel Gabriel to deliver messages to all prophets, there would be no revelations.

If Allah engages in conversations, then who are we as humans to disregard the vital aspect of communication? Remaining silent leads to stagnation, causing us to deviate from the essence of life and the delivery of knowledge to humanity.

My ongoing conversations promote shared knowledge and emphasize the significance of communication.

The Bible and Quran reveal contrasting aspects that require attention to fully understand. The significant episode maintains its conflicts without affecting relationships, solely appeasing inquisitive minds in search of truth.

I am committed to sharing knowledge!

The theme of most knowledgeable Muslims for centuries. The time wasted is seeking approval from humans is unnecessary for solace. Instead, finding solace in the creator's approval is sufficient and will last forever.

Those who believe are fearless towards humans, **as truth knows no limits.** Islam provides clear guidance and prepares its followers to standalone against those who deceive others and hinder societal progress.

Valuing time is the essence of life!

As **Allah** permits, I can share, but I cannot dictate the response. **Allah** possesses the power, and humans can only lead the world towards Allah's path by facing trials and seeking deliverance.

Despite the efforts of humanity, it is **Allah** who enables the reception of the words of truth and decides who ignores them; **if you have my book, it is because Allah has facilitated our connection.**

A believer can hold monotheistic or polytheistic beliefs, as I can share knowledge of **Allah.** The motto is to bring clarity and unity through communication.

Painting the truth is easy with transparency and no barriers. My presentation covers Islam and Christianity, touching Abrahamic faiths including Quran Hadiths, comparative analysis, and observations on the expanding universe.

Muslim history is part of my observations and societal norms expand curiosity about Islam. Belief comes from within and cannot be taught. My diverse and unique talents are a memorandum of distinction.

Talents are shared, not hidden. Sharing knowledge fulfills me, like a painting that is complete. I thrive with an audience to connect and evoke emotions.

"POWER IS TRUTH" focuses on positive communication, prioritizing truth and knowledge. **"DELIVERY IS POWER"** was my previous book; sharing the truth is my ongoing progress. I explore the connection between faith and global challenges.

Unveiling the reality of Allah as I navigate through my earthly journey. Belief amplifies the impact of communication. Islam's progress was aided by the acumination of truth through open communication.

The history of lineage names has always held a captivating allure for humans, satisfying our curiosity. Religion serves as the ultimate anchor for the disposition of Muslims and believers of faith.

What meaning does anything hold if we cannot embrace the knowledge of Allah in this life?

The significance of your impact on the world is determined by what you leave behind, emphasizing the importance of actions like those of the **Prophet Muhammad peace be upon him.**

Sharing my understanding of Islam, its history, comparisons, and the value of faith over worldly things gives my life meaning. Faith allows one to savor this life while also preparing for the next.

"Shazadi," my name, is rooted in generations of affluent aristocrats from both my paternal and maternal lineage, signifying **"Princess."** The name **Baig**, my surname, derives from the Turkish title **Baig**, symbolizing Turkish heritage and Muslim affiliation, denoting a rank of nobility and respect.

The title Bey, Baig, or Baeg is traditionally used by chieftains and individuals with esteemed lineage to Turkic rulers. Spellings differ, but the name remains unchanged.

Elite Muslims typically had both a formal and informal name, which showed their social status. The ism, a formal name derived from Arabic origins, was commonly used in official documents, legal matters, and formal settings.

It was a symbol of honor and respect. The informal name, was a nickname that showed personal relationships and family connections.

By using these dual names, the elites could balance their public and private lives, demonstrating their social position while preserving a personal bond.

The origin and meaning of names and family lineage do not imply arrogance, but suggest that a good name can inspire individuals to live up to its reputation

The name plays a significant role in shaping one's personality, but education forms the bedrock for upholding the name, along with character and delivery, making a profound impact on my life and the readers.

Islam emphasizes the significance of names, as they reflect heritage and balance. Therefore, many converts adopt a Muslim name to represent their new identity.

Sharing lineage or names merely reveals history, it doesn't compensate for pride or heritage.

Only Allah deserves pride, not our family, money, knowledge, appearance, or any other external characteristic. Sharing history with humility is simply that. **Allah** is the only one worthy of pride.

No matter your social position, poverty exists within every human being. Life's true meaning isn't about material possessions, but about our actions, relationships, and positive impact on the world.

Your parents and social standing are determined by Allah. Humans try. To improve ourselves, we need to reflect on our actions and seek forgiveness. **Astaghfirullah constant repentance.**

Ultimately, Allah has the final say. Without His permission, nothing can be achieved. **Insha'Allah**. If Allah wills it.

I emphasize this point because my finality is with **Allah**. Material possessions, lineage, wealth, and status are left behind. The weight of our actions carries on, reaching beyond the grave.

Muslims, not limited to Turkish people, embarked on migrations to various lands, including subcontinents of India, Western regions, Saudi Arabia, and beyond.

The world is vast, and these transitions and legacies endured. Muslims maintain their commitment to their word regardless of which continent they move to.

The word acts as an arrow, released from the speaker's command, reflecting their character.

Those who cannot keep their **word** lack integrity. Turkish people and most Muslims embody the values of Islam, speaking truthfully and keeping their word without hesitation.

The philosophy of all Muslims, regardless of their region, is ultimately to uphold the word.

Regardless of the blessings one receives from **Allah** in terms of knowledge, lineage, wealth, and health, a **humble servant of Allah** always remains **grateful and understands that sharing knowledge is the ultimate form of sharing.**

I must advocate for the truth of Islam. The core values include peace, justice, equality, and compassion. **As a Muslim woman, I constantly strive to exercise my rights given by Islam.**

Correcting misconceptions about Islam, including oppression and violence. My goal is to educate about the teachings of Islam, which emphasize knowledge and personal growth.

Open dialogue fosters unity in society.

Arrogance and pride cannot be attributed to a human who is born from dust and will return to dust.

The creator, **Allah,** can only hold pride and mercy." **POWER IS TRUTH"** is crucial to life's challenges.

Truth liberates falsehood confines!

Truth breathes without constraints in any society Open-minded reading can spark curiosity about Islam. Noted valid comparisons.

Friendships and humanity exist regardless of religion. **Allah's knowledge is all-encompassing.**

My presentation depends on Allah's will. Insha'Allah!

My book is titled **"POWER IS TRUTH"** to highlight the power inherent in truth. And, eyes are a gateway to the heart. **THE LIES DROWN TRUTH RULES.**

Quran: (Surah al-Fatir) 35:11. And Allah created you from dust, then from a sperm-drop, then He made you mates. And no female conceives, nor does she give birth, except with His Knowledge. And no aged person is granted (additional) life, nor is his lifespan lessened, but that it is in a Register.

TABLE OF CONTENTS

CHAPTER 1
MONOTHEISM INCLINES TOWARDS ONENESS NO OUTLINES

BISMILLAH HIR RAHMAN NIR RAHIM:

In the Name of Allah, the Most Glorified, the Most High, the Merciful, the Compassionate.

Arabic, as the chosen language of delivery of the Quran, holds immense significance in the Islamic faith.

Learning Arabic words not only enables individuals to understand the essence of the Quran but also allows for a deeper connection with the teachings of Islam.

Arabic is a rich and complex language that carries a unique beauty and depth, making it impossible to fully capture its essence in translation.

The Arabic words used in the Quran possess a divine quality and hold profound meanings that cannot be fully conveyed in any other language.

Therefore, it becomes imperative for those seeking a comprehensive understanding of the Quran to learn Arabic and appreciate the linguistic nuances that make it so special.

By learning Arabic, individuals gain access to the original text, allowing them to interpret and analyze the Quran in a more authentic manner. Ultimately, studying Arabic not only deepens one's understanding of the Quran, but also enriches their spiritual journey and broadens their horizons.

Allah has sent his books to guide and enlighten his messengers and their respective communities throughout history.

The **Tourat** (Torah) was revealed to the prophet Moses in the Hebrew language, as it was the language spoken and understood by him and the Israelites.

Similarly, the **Zabur** (Psalms) was given in the ancient Hebrew language to the prophet David, enabling him to communicate its teachings effectively to his people.

Jesus received the **Injeel** (Gospel) in the widely spoken Aramaic language of his time and region.

The **Quran**, the last and most complete revelation, was given to Prophet Muhammad in Arabic, the language spoken fluently by the people of Arabia.

This guaranteed that the messages of these celestial books were accessible and understandable to the prophets and their communities, making it easier for them to spread and comprehend Allah's guidance.

Jesus, like others, received a Gospel book from Allah, which was given to the obedient, disobedient and unmanageable people of Israel. If he were God, he wouldn't have been given a book by the Creator Allah or Allah-ha as Jesus referred to him.

Allah, the creator, is beyond comparison to humans, making any documented imagination flawed as no prophet can become God. God's accessibility is concealed despite being readily accessible.

Allah, in the Islamic faith, is the unseen and omnipresent one true God. Allah can perceive everything, including thoughts, prayers, and actions of every human being.

Believers find comfort in the concept of Allah's omniscience, knowing that their pleas, struggles, and achievements are not ignored.

Accountability revolves around the notion that every individual is accountable for their own choices and actions. Allah's judgment of each person is determined by their intentions, deeds, and commitment to His commandments.

The belief in accountability among Muslims drives them to pursue righteousness, be conscious of their actions, and seek forgiveness for any wrongdoings. Repenting for sins can bring a person closer to Allah as they seek betterment and closure.

The power of truth is undeniable for those who possess a deep understanding of the scriptures.

Over time, many texts and writings have surfaced claiming to be revelations, but they lack the authenticity and inherent truth that can only be found in the scriptural word of God.

These writings, authored by ordinary individuals, cannot fill the gaps or alter the course set forth by divine revelation.

Attempting to reconcile the divine and human aspects becomes a challenging and exhausting task, ultimately leading believers to make their own decisions regarding what to follow.

This belief in one God, which has persisted since the creation of humanity, transcends time and space. Even before humans arrived on Earth 50,000 years ago, their souls existed together, acknowledging and answering to their creator as the only supreme entity.

Quran: Surah Hadid: 57;22. No calamity or blessing occurs on earth or in yourselves without being ˈwrittenˈ in a Record before We bring it into being. This is certainly easy for Allah.

The essence of every human being inherently rejects the worship of other humans, as it goes against their innate nature.

However, throughout history, the practice of worshiping deities has been prevalent since pagan times.

This can be attributed to the human desire to have something tangible to worship, as the need to visually perceive what one worships often leads to the worship of false deities.

These false deities, being visible and tangible, become more accessible and easier to comprehend compared to the concept of an unseen God.

The common perception in Christendom that Jesus is God or the Son of God has been subject to historical debates and interpretations.

Some scholars argue that certain aspects of Christian theology, such as the concept of a divine being taking human form, can be traced back to pagan beliefs and mythologies.

Quran clarifies doubts. For example, the idea of a deity having a divine offspring or a divine figure descending to Earth can be found in various pagan religions throughout history.

These resemblances have led to no speculation that early Christians have borrowed and adapted these ideas when planning their beliefs about Jesus.

However, it is important to note that this theory is not universally accepted and remains a topic of ongoing scholarly discussion. As research and understanding of historical contexts continue to evolve, we may gain further insights into how these perceptions and beliefs developed in Christianity.

The common theory and belief in Abrahamic faith, which includes Judaism, Christianity, and Islam, is that God is an unseen and transcendent being.

In the story of Moses, the prophet requested to see God, but when he was granted a glimpse of His divine presence, Moses could not bear the intense radiance and fainted

This incident highlights how humans are limited in perceiving and understanding God visually, making it impossible for them to envision God in their weak state of creation.

The engagement with the beauty beyond human sight is hindered by our frailty.

It illustrates that the created human being, with all their intelligence and education, is inherently limited in their understanding of God's infinite wisdom and knowledge.

This belief leads to the notion that God is the epitome of intelligence and wisdom, surpassing the comprehension of any human being.

Jesus, a monotheistic prophet with the Jewish lineage, did not come to tell the Jews to worship him or claim to be the Son of God. From the moment of his birth, he established himself as a prophet and a Messiah.

However, the belief in Jesus as the divine Son of God is a complex theological concept that can be difficult for people to comprehend, especially those who were not present during his time.

The contradiction arises from the fact that some people witnessed God's presence while others did not, despite the belief in an ever-present God.

It is reasonable that past decades witnessed the prophets since they had a finite lifespan, received revelations, and then departed. According to Islamic belief, Jesus was raised up alive.

If he were God or a triune God, it would be impossible for only a few to witness his presence as he is for every human. The concept of the unseen God is logical since he cannot be seen but can hear and see everyone, making it a reasonable agreement of the mind.

The notion of God sending his son to die for humanity, whom he himself created, can be challenging for many to understand and accept.

It requires a deep exploration of theological teachings and a willingness to grapple with the complexities of divine revelation. People often view intelligence as the combination of knowledge and the ability to apply that knowledge effectively.

It is not simply about the accumulation of facts and information, but the ability to discern truth from falsehood and deliver that knowledge truthfully.

The allure of deceit mesmerizes many individuals, seeking to please others and gain personal advantage.

However, true intelligence lies in being immune to such deception and focusing on acquiring knowledge that is beneficial and empowering.

Some may perceive intelligence in terms of material gains or the ability to travel extensively. While these experiences can broaden one's perspective and provide valuable insights, true intelligence goes beyond superficial achievements.

Travel can indeed be a brilliant teacher, exposing individuals to different cultures, ideas, and ways of life.

However, it is the knowledge gained through these experiences and the willingness to share and learn from others that truly empowers individuals.

The Muslim community has a long history of thriving through knowledge sharing.

In the thriving businesses, often adopt a model of profit-sharing, recognizing the importance of equitable distribution and empowering their employees. This approach not only fosters a sense of community and cooperation but also ensures the long-term success of the business.

Ultimately, knowledge is not something to be hoarded or kept hidden away. It is shared, disseminated, and used for the betterment of society.

True intelligence lies in the ability to gain knowledge, understand its value, and actively engage in sharing and learning from others.

By doing so, individuals can contribute to the collective growth and progress of humanity.

The Quran acknowledges the previous scriptures, such as the Torah, Gospel, and the Psalms that were sent in the Abrahamic faith. However, it also seeks to rectify any additions or complexities that may have been introduced.

The Quran invites people of the book and all faiths to come together on common terms, emphasizing the shared beliefs and values that exist among them.

While Jews and Muslims are ancestrally related through their shared lineage with Abraham, the Quran also states that Christians are close for listening to the message of God that Muslims continually share.

Interestingly, throughout history, more Christians have been reported to be accepting Islam than followers of any other faith.

This closeness between Islam and Christianity can be attributed to a few factors. One of them is the shared figure of Jesus, who is highly revered in both faiths. However, it is important to note that the concept of Jesus in Islam is entirely different from that of the Christian faith.

In Islam, Jesus is considered a revered prophet and the Messiah, but he does not hold any divinity or claim to be God. He is the son of Mary, but not as a divine being himself.

Another shared belief in Christianity and Islam is the expectation of the second coming of Jesus. However, it is worth mentioning that the connotations and interpretations of this event differ between the two ideologies.

But history speaks. it is the disobedience that became costly after being known as the chosen people lost the title per Quran after being exiled for disobedience.

Like any religious or cultural group, there are variations in beliefs and practices among Jews. Throughout history, Jews have faced periods of both inclusion and exclusion in different societies.

Some Jewish communities have been isolated or persecuted in the past, but it is not accurate to say that they were universally secluded for a long time.

Muslims were the first to lend the Jews a hand in all aspects inviting them to share the lands and protection after they faced injustice.

Time Magazine: Jan 27, 2017 — A small exhibit in NYC will highlight the little-known stories of Muslims who risked their lives to save Jewish people during the Holocaust.

Regarding the relationship between Jews and Muslims, there have been periods of cooperation and periods of tension throughout history.

It is correct to claim that Muslims are the only ones who have invited and helped Jews during difficult times. Interactions between these two religious groups have been complex and varied over time and in different regions.

The lineage that Jews and Muslims hold indeed connects them as first cousins through the sons of Ishmael and Isaac.

According to religious texts, Ishmael was the first born son of Abraham and his wife Sarah's handmaiden, Hagar, while Isaac was the son of Abraham and his wife, Sarah.

Abraham, a prominent figure in religious texts, found himself in a difficult situation when his wife Sarah believed she could not conceive a child.

To ensure Abraham had a lineage, Sarah suggested he marry Hagar, her maidservant.

Abraham agreed and took Hagar as his second wife. Hagar eventually became pregnant and gave birth to a son named Ishmael. However, Sarah's doubts were proven wrong when she, at a later age, miraculously conceived and gave birth to a son named Isaac.

This turn of events brought joy and fulfillment to Abraham and Sarah, as their desire for a lineage was fulfilled through both Ishmael and Isaac.

The story of Abraham, Sarah, Hagar, Ishmael, and Isaac is often seen as a testament to the faith and patience of these individuals in the face of adversity.

Ishmael became the father of the Arab people, while Isaac became the father of the Jewish people.

This shared ancestry has resulted in historical and cultural connections between Jews and Muslims, as they both trace their roots back to the patriarch Abraham. This exploitation of circumstances and Western influence can be traced back to the establishment of the State of Israel in 1948.

The Zionist movement, which sought to create a Jewish homeland, gained support from Western countries, particularly the United States.

The narrative of Jews returning to their ancestral land after centuries of exile resonated with many in the West, leading to financial and political backing for the establishment of Israel.

However, religious or cultural kinship did not solely motivate this support for Israel. Geopolitical interests played a significant role as well.

Western powers saw the establishment of Israel to maintain influence and control in the Middle East, particularly given the region's strategic importance and vast oil reserves.

This led to a complex web of alliances and rivalries, with Western countries often prioritizing their own interests over the well-being and rights of both Palestinians and Muslims in the region.

The rise of evangelical Christianity in the Western world added another layer to this complex dynamic.

Many evangelical Christians believe in the concept of the End Times, where Jesus will return and establish his kingdom on Earth. This belief has led to a powerful support for Israel among some evangelicals, as they see the return of Jews to the Holy Land as a fulfillment of biblical prophecy.

Unfortunately, this support for Israel has often overlooked the rights and well-being of Palestinians and Muslims.

Those who support Israel have often overlooked the rights and well-being of Palestinians and Muslims, with a small unit of Christians disregarding the displacement and suffering.

Palestinians experienced during the establishment of Israel, as well as ongoing conflicts and human rights violations. This has only deepened divisions and fueled resentment in the region, perpetuating a cycle of violence and injustice.

In conclusion, while there may have been a sense of kinship and understanding between Jews and Muslims based on their common lineage, the exploitation of circumstances and Western influence has complicated and strained this relationship.

The establishment of Israel, driven by geopolitical interests and influenced by religious beliefs, has resulted in ongoing tensions and conflicts in the region.

It is crucial to acknowledge and address these complexities in order to move towards a more just and peaceful future for all communities involved.

The belief in the coming of the Messiah in Christian theology stems from the belief that Jesus Christ, the Son of God, will return to Earth in the Second Coming to judge both the living and the dead.

Based on biblical prophecies, especially in the New Testament, this belief holds a central position in Christian eschatology. In a similar vein, the return of Jesus, referred to as Isa, carries significant meaning in Islam.

Quran clarifies Jesus will come back to Earth before the Day of judgment to restore justice, defeat the Antichrist, and bring about peace.

Although Christians and Muslims share the belief in the return of Jesus, their approaches and beliefs regarding this event vary. Christians expect Jesus' return as the divine Son of God, while Muslims regard him as a prophet and servant of Allah.

Christian theology highlights Jesus' return as a source of redemption and salvation, while Islamic belief prioritizes the establishment of a just and peaceful society rooted in Islamic principles.

The belief in the coming of the Messiah varies among Jews.

While there are Jews who believe in a future Messiah bringing peace and redemption, others interpret the concept differently or see the Messianic Age as a period of spiritual transformation rather than a literal return of a messianic figure.

Orthodox, Conservative, and Reform Judaism are among the prominent sects in the Jewish community. These sects often interpret differently messianic concepts.

Orthodox Judaism typically believes in the coming of a Messiah who will bring about the redemption of the Jewish people and the world.

Traditional messianic prophecies, which originated from the rejection of Jesus and the anticipation of another messiah, root their beliefs.

Various interpretations reveal messianic concepts in Judaism.

When examining the rise of Christianity long after Jesus' ascension, certain Jewish individuals perceive the Messiah as a symbolic figure, symbolizing personal or societal transformation, instead of recognizing Jesus as the Messiah.

Quran: Surah Anbiya: 21;7. And We sent not before you, [O Muhammad], except men to whom We revealed [the message], so ask the people of the message if you do not know.

While there is no disagreement, the Quran affirms that Prophet Muhammad was sent as a mercy to humanity.

The Quran stands as the ultimate finality, unchangeable and uncorrupted. While understanding its directness may require a precise comprehension, the truth it holds is always direct and not hidden.

It is important to note that rudeness or harshness should not be mistaken for truth. Such behavior stems from emotions and doubts, rather than a genuine reflection of truth.

Muslims across the world use the greeting **"As-Salamu Alaykum"** as a way to show respect and goodwill towards each other.

It is a common practice to respond with **"Wa-Alaykum As-Salam"** or **"Wa Alaykum As-Salamu Wa Rahmatullah"** which means "And peace be upon you too" or "And peace and mercy of Allah be upon you too."

This exchange of greetings is considered a measure of kindness and is an important part of Muslim etiquette. The greeting is not limited to a specific country or region, but is used universally among Muslims to express warmth and welcome.

It is important to note that the greeting is not used sarcastically or in anger, but as a sincere gesture of hospitality and friendship.

The term **"Muslim"** derives from the Arabic word **"Islam,"** which means **"submission."**

A Muslim is an adherent of the Islamic faith, someone who willingly and wholeheartedly submits to the will of Allah, the one true God in Islam. Muslims believe that Allah's will is perfect and superior to their own desires and wishes.

Salvation is attained not through Jesus, but through accepting one God and declaring Muhammad peace be upon him as the final messenger of Allah for Muslims.

The concept of submission to the will of Allah lies at the core of Muslim identity and shapes their daily practices, rituals, and interactions with others. It emphasizes humility, obedience, and reliance on Allah's wisdom and guidance for leading a righteous and purposeful life.

Translating these Arabic words can be complex and should be used in specific contexts. "**SWT**" is an abbreviation that signifies reverence and devotion to **Allah.**

"**PBUH**" is a term used to show respect for deceased prophets and esteemed Muslims, signifying "peace be upon him."

Haram refers to anything that is forbidden or prohibited in Islam. It is the opposite of halal. **Halal** refers to what is permissible according to Islamic law.

Fasiqun is a term used to describe someone who openly commits sins or engages in immoral behavior. It refers to a person who is disobedient to Allah and does not adhere to religious obligations.

Munafiqin refers to hypocrites, individuals who outwardly claim to be Muslim or believers but inwardly conceal their disbelief or lack of faith.

They pretend to be righteous, but their intentions and actions do not align with their words. This act of hypocrisy is known as Nifāq.

Quran: Surah Taubah: [9:68] Allah has promised Hell-Fire to the hypocrites, both men and women, and to the unbelievers. They shall abide in it: a sufficient recompense for them...

Zina refers to the act of unlawful sexual intercourse, specifically referring to adultery or fornication. It is considered a major sin in Islam.

Mazloom refers to someone who is wronged or oppressed. It is a term used to describe someone who is treated unfairly or subjected to injustice.

Kafir is a term used to refer to a non-believer or someone who rejects or denies the truth of one God.

It is used to describing someone who is not a Muslim or a Muslim who turns on his faith. Or do not believe in one God.

Shirk refers to associating partners with Allah in worship, which is considered a major sin in Islam.

It is the act of attributing divine qualities or powers to anyone or anything other than Allah.

This includes worshipping idols, saints, or any other created beings, as well as seeking help or guidance from them instead of turning to Allah alone.

Shirk is a grave offense because it goes against the fundamental belief in the oneness of Allah (**Tawhid**), which is the core principle of Islamic faith.

Abrahamic faiths mean monotheism and avoid any form of shirk in order to maintain a pure and sincere relationship with Allah.

In Islam, **Shirk** is the gravest and unforgivable sin. **Shirk** refers to the act of associating partners with **Allah** (God) or worshiping anything or anyone other than Allah.

It directly violates the fundamental principle of **Tawhid**, which is the belief in the oneness of Allah.

The concept of **Shirk** encompasses a wide range of actions, including idol worship, belief in multiple gods, seeking intermediaries between oneself and Allah, or attributing divine qualities to created beings.

Muslims believe that Allah's forgiveness is conditional upon repentance, but Shirk is regarded as an exception.

Those who commit **Shirk** have essentially rejected the core principle of **Islam** and have therefore severed their connection with Allah. Forgiveness for **Shirk** is not granted in the afterlife, and those who die in a state of **Shirk** are destined for eternal punishment.

Quran: Surah Nisa: 4:48. "Allah forgives not that partners should be set up with Him, but He forgives anything else, to whom He pleases. To set up partners with Allah is to devise a sin most heinous indeed".

The punishment inflicted by Allah upon those who worship partners or engage in idol worship might raise questions about His alleged cruelty, particularly when considering the righteousness of these individuals.

Allah punishes no one without giving them a warning. A lifetime is more than enough time to discover the truth, and in today's world, there are no excuses, as information is readily accessible.

Islam has spread into every aspect of life. In the real world, it is impossible to replace the name CEO of a business, if an employee were to call themselves the CEO, it would not be tolerated.

Similarly, Jesus did not come to replace Allah and change his name to God.

Quran: Surah Maidah: 5:68. Say, people of the Book, you have no true basis for your religion unless you uphold the Torah, and the Gospel, and which has been sent down to you from your Lord, but what has been sent down to you prophet from your Lord is sure to increase many of them in their insolence and defiance: do not worry about those who defy Allah.

Except for the unaltered Quran, the rearrangement of past scriptures in Abrahamic religions erases any trace of originality.

Despite this, people from different faiths, including some Muslims, continue to break norms and lead others astray, using religion to justify their actions and claiming that Allah accepts their hypocrisy.

Prophet Muhammad (peace be upon him) shared three signs of a hypocrite in a hadith.

His explanation pointed out that the first sign emerges when a person habitually resorts to lying and deceit in their speech, demonstrating a lack of honesty and integrity.

When individuals make promises but consistently cannot deliver on them, it shows their unreliability and lack of commitment.

Last, the third sign arises when an individual is given with something, whether it is a responsibility, a secret, or a possession, and they betray that confidence, revealing a deficiency in loyalty and commitment. As part of this trial, Allah has created both **Jannah** (heaven) and **Jahannam** (hell) to serve as tests and evaluations of one's life.

Salat is the Arabic term for prayer. It refers to the ritualistic prayers performed by Muslims five times a day as one of the five pillars of Islam.

Astaghfirullah, which translates to "**I seek forgiveness from Alla**h," is a powerful phrase that holds great significance in Islam.

Muslims constantly recite **Astaghfirullah** to seek repentance from their Lord. It is a way of acknowledging one's sins and shortcomings, and expressing sincere remorse for them.

This act of repentance is not limited to a particular time or place; rather, it is an ongoing practice that Muslims engage in throughout their lives.

The recitation of Astaghfirullah serves as a reminder of the need for self-reflection, spiritual growth, and seeking forgiveness for any transgressions committed.

These Arabic phrases; **"Insha'Allah"**, **"Mashallah"**, **"Alhamdulillah"**, **"Subhan Allah"**, and **"Takbir"**, hold great reverence in the Arabic language and are widely used by Muslims around the world.

Each phrase carries its own significance **and is deeply ingrained in Islamic culture and tradition. "Insha'Allah" translates to "if Allah wills" and is used to express hope and reliance on Allah's guidance and decision.**

"Mashallah" is an expression of admiration and is used when praising or acknowledging someone's blessings or achievements.

"Alhamdulillah" means "praise be to Allah" and is used to express gratitude and thankfulness to Allah.

"Takbir" refers to the phrase **"Allahu Akbar,"** meaning "Allah is the greatest," and is often recited in times of celebration, during prayer, or in moments of awe and reverence.

These phrases are not only linguistic expressions but also serve as reminders of the central role of Allah in the lives of Muslims and the importance of humility, gratitude, and acknowledging His greatness.

Islamophobes often exploit the term **"jihad"** to promote a false narrative that it is solely associated with terrorism or violence.

In reality, **jihad** encompasses a broader concept of personal and collective struggle for righteousness and justice.

It can involve internal struggles against one's own ego, striving to be a better person and adhering to Islamic teachings. It can encompass efforts to help others, engage in charitable acts, and fight against social injustices.

Jihad also includes defending one's faith in the face of persecution or oppression, which may involve physical self-defense in extreme cases.

However, the overwhelming majority of Muslims understand jihad as a peaceful and spiritual concept, focusing on self-improvement and serving others rather than promoting violence.

It is crucial to separate the distorted portrayal of jihad by Islamophobes from its true essence within the Islamic faith.

The word **"Zalimun"** in Arabic can be translated as **"oppressors"** or **"wrongdoers"**.

It is derived from the root word **"Zulm"**, which refers to acts of **injustice, cruelty, or oppression.**

In Arabic, **"Zalimun"** is used to describe individuals or groups who inflict harm or injustice upon others, often through abuse of power or disregard for their rights. It is a term that carries negative connotations and is often associated with those who act unjustly or oppressively.

Islamic theology and religious discussions often make use of the term **"Mushrik"**. In Arabic, it means either "polytheist" or "idolater."

This is considered a serious sin in Islam, as the religion strongly emphasizes the belief in the oneness of God, known as **Tawhid**. Individuals or groups who worship multiple deities are referred to as **Mushrik.**

It's crucial to mention that **Mushrik's** purpose is to establish the meanings of Islamic theology in the Arabic context and the Quran, without any intention to offend or discriminate.

The Quran cannot be modified to satisfy people's preferences over time.

Quran: Surah Nisa: 4;48. Allah does not forgive associating others with Him in worship, but forgives anything else of whoever He wills. And whoever associates others with Allah has indeed committed a grave sin.

Muslims widely used the phrase **"Khalas"**, especially in the Arab-speaking world. This Arabic word has various meanings, such as "enough," "stop," or "finished."

The word **Khalas** holds a significant place in Islamic culture and is often uttered to signify the completion of a task or to bring closure to a matter. This versatile phrase captures finality and brings a sense of resolution and peace.

The Arabic language holds a unique rhythmic quality that no other language can truly capture. Its syntax is incredibly melodic, allowing for a continuous flow of meanings that not only educates the reader but also enriches the understanding of oneself.

The **Quran** exemplifies this rhythmic nature by purposefully repeating certain words and phrases, emphasizing their significance and solidifying their meaning. In the mundane world, people often dismiss information after hearing it once.

The **Quran's** unhesitating repetition highlights the unchanging nature of its message, further emphasizing the eternal truths it conveys.

The five pillars of Islam are the five fundamental acts of worship that every Muslim is expected to follow in order to show their faith and commitment to Allah. These pillars are:

1) Shahada: The declaration of faith, which involves believing and proclaiming that there is no God but Allah, and Muhammad is his messenger.

2) Salat: The performance of five daily prayers, known as Salah, which are obligatory for all Muslims. These prayers are performed at specific times throughout the day and involve specific movements and recitations.

3) Zakat: The giving of alms or charity to those in need. Muslims are required to donate a portion of their wealth, usually 2.5%, to help the poor and support charitable causes.

4) Sawm: The observance of fasting during the holy month of Ramadan. Muslims abstain from eating, drinking, and other physical needs from dawn until sunset as a means of self-discipline and spiritual reflection.

5) Hajj: The pilgrimage to the holy city of Mecca, which every able-bodied and financially capable Muslim must undertake at least once in their lifetime. It involves a series of rituals and acts of worship performed over several days, culminating in the circumambulation of the Kaaba.

Muslims worship Allah alone, not the **Kaaba**, but the circle symbolizes completion and endlessness.

The fundamental belief of Christendom is that salvation is found only through trusting in Christ alone.

This core doctrine, known as sola fide, emphasizes the belief that individuals are justified and saved by faith in Jesus Christ, rather than by their own works or efforts.

This belief is rooted in the teachings of the Bible, particularly in the New Testament, where Jesus himself proclaimed he is the way, the truth, and the life, and that no one can come to the Father except through him **(John 14:6).** Therefore, Christendom holds that faith in Jesus as the Son of God and the savior of humanity is essential for obtaining eternal salvation.

The **New Testament** is a collection of religious texts that form the second part of the Christian Bible. The New Testament comprises 27 books, written in Greek, and scholars believe it was composed over several decades in the first century CE.

Different authors are attributed to other books, including the apostles Matthew, Mark, Luke, and John, who are traditionally associated with the four Gospels.

The book of Revelation, written by the apostle John, is included in the New Testament and contains apocalyptic visions and prophecies.

So, while the New Testament does include the book of Revelation, it is important to note that not all Paul or the people directly involved in the writing process wrote the books.

Unlike Jesus, who received revelations from the angel Gabriel, Paul referred to his experiences as visions rather than direct revelations from God.

Islam does not endorse imaginary behavior. Although saints and believers may have had visions, they did not rewrite scriptures like Pauline Christianity. Allah-sent messages in the Quran and previous scriptures lack reference to Paul or Pauline Christianity.

The New Testament, comprising Paul's letters and teachings, is an essential component of Christendom known as Pauline Christianity.

It offers valuable perspectives on Jesus' teachings, the early Christian community, and the evolution of Christian theology.

Bible: NIV: John 14:6. Jesus answered, "I am the way and the truth and the life. No one comes to the Father except through me.

Clear prophecy shows that Jesus, during his time on Earth, recognized the limitations of his mission and understood that he could not handle the defiance of the Jews at that specific moment.

Each passage in the scriptures has a specific timeframe in which a human messenger can effectively fulfill their purpose.

Therefore, Jesus prophesied he would come again to complete his assigned task. In the meantime, Prophet Muhammad was sent as a successor, and the text clearly shows that Jesus will send someone else in the future.

Prophet Muhammad never claimed divinity for himself but referred to himself as the humble servant of Allah.

Moses, a prophet from the Israelites, was followed by Jesus who was also sent to the Israelites. Jesus came to fulfill the law of Moses, not to claim divinity. From the faithful,

Allah appointed prophets. **Muhammad PBUH** who later became a prophet, was renowned for his honesty.

Initially, many people rejected him, but once he gained prophethood, his enemies labeled him a madman despite previously considering him the most trustworthy and honest.

Speaking the truth invites enemies, while lying avoids them, but the consequences of downfall outweigh any gains. Pharaoh's arrogance is a prime illustration.

He proclaimed the same message as all the other prophets in the Abrahamic tradition.

Therefore, **Jesus** declaring himself as **God or the Son of God** would contradict the **laws of Moses**, which he stated he came to fulfill, not to break. By acknowledging his role as a prophet and Messiah, Jesus aligns with the clear evidence of his own words and remains distinct from the concept of divinity.

Jesus, as a central figure in Christianity, emphasized the importance of following the laws of Moses to the Jewish people. He clarified that his purpose was not to abolish or break these laws but to fulfill them.

This affirmation of the importance of the laws of Moses is deeply rooted in Judaism, which is a monotheistic religion.

Monotheism, the belief in one God, is a fundamental principle of Judaism.

Additionally, the Jewish people place great emphasis on following the commandments and laws outlined in the Torah, which includes the teachings of Moses.

While Judaism does not have a specific set of pillars like some other religions, the monotheistic belief and adherence to the laws of Moses are core principles that guide the faith and practice of practicing Jewish individuals.

Jesus, who lived in 1st-century Palestine, embraced monotheism, just like all prophets sent by Allah. He aimed to reform and revive Judaism, questioning interpretations and practices that had deviated from the core principles of the faith.

Jesus stressed the significance of compassion and justice, urging his followers to abide by God's commandments.

Jesus aimed to restore Judaism to its fundamental principles, not condemn the entire faith, despite conflicts with certain Jewish and Roman authorities.

In the Jewish faith, God is the supreme authority and the ultimate Lord. Jesus lacks reverence and is not regarded as a divine entity. In the same way, Muslims do not see Jesus as a divine figure.

Despite the complexities and uncertainties of life, the beauty of Islam lies in its unwavering delivery of the truth, which remains constant and unchanging throughout history. By embracing Islam's monotheistic beliefs and seeking solace in the divine truth, humans can find comfort and guidance in their journey towards understanding the mysteries of existence.

The changes to the doctrine of Christendom that took place in Constantinople (now known as Istanbul, Turkey) were indeed significant. However, it is important to clarify some misconceptions.

Emperor Constantine convened the Council of Nicaea in 325 AD. It made significant decisions about Christ's nature, but it didn't bear the sole responsibility for all changes in Christian doctrine.

Constantine's council primarily addressed Arianism, a theological dispute regarding the divinity of Jesus. The Nicene Creed upheld the belief in the Trinity, a cornerstone of Christianity.

While political and social factors certainly influenced the proceedings, it is accurate to claim that these changes were solely motivated by political reforms and greed.

Christianity is often associated with Western regions, such as Europe and America, but many people may not realize that its origins can be traced back to the Eastern regions of the Roman Empire, specifically in the city of Constantinople, which is now known as Istanbul, Turkey.

The birthplace of Islam is Saudi Arabia, where the faith originated. **Islam is a monotheistic religion, which means it is centered on the belief in one God.**

This faith, which was also followed by Adam and Eve, received its name gradually, just like a graduate climbing each step. **Allah presented Islam to humanity when the world was prepared for it.**

Turkey, with its unique geographical location, straddles two continents, Europe and Asia, making it the only country in the world that sits on the crossroads of Eastern and Western lands.

This position has had a profound influence on Turkey's history and culture, as it has been a melting pot of different civilizations and ideologies. The moral compass of Islam, deeply rooted in Turkish society, has played a significant role in shaping the country's values and traditions.

The Byzantine Empire and the Ottoman Empire coexisted during different periods.

The Ottoman Empire's abolition of the Byzantine Empire highlights its historical success under Muslim rule.

The destruction of lands during the Christian era spans centuries and has left a trail of devastation in its wake.

From the Crusades to colonization, the Christian powers have often capitalized on the ruins of the countries they left behind, showcasing a prolonged history of greed.

This history reveals itself through the systematic pillaging of resources, the exploitation of local populations, and the deliberate erasure of cultural heritage.

The desire for wealth and dominance has fueled the destruction of once-thriving civilizations, leaving behind scars that are still felt today.

Whether it be the looting of ancient treasures, a relentless pursuit of power and profit has marked the forced conversion of indigenous peoples or the economic exploitation of natural resources at the expense of the lands and peoples they encountered.

The consequences of this history of greed continue to shape the world, reminding us of the need for reflection and accountability.

Instead, the Ottoman Empire, with its vast territorial expanse, left a lasting legacy rather than destruction. In contrast, many European powers that occupied and reigned over vast lands have often faced turmoil.

History shows that there is no single **"Golden Age"** of Europe fully influenced by Christendom, as the continent has experienced periods of violence, power struggles, and conflicts.

The idea of violent force seeking power while espousing the teachings of Jesus is indeed harsh, as history reveals the narratives.

Constantine, the Roman Emperor, played a significant role in shaping the narrative of Christendom. He recognized that in order to unite his empire and gain widespread acceptance of Christianity, certain changes needed to be made.

The early teachings of Jesus were strategically altered to align with the existing pagan beliefs and practices.

This included presenting Jesus as a deity to be worshiped, as the concept of an unseen God would have been difficult for the pagans to comprehend.

Images and statues of Jesus, Mary, and saints were quickly introduced to provide tangible representations of godliness. This calculated plan was not impulsive but carefully plotted to ensure the smooth transition of the empire into a Christian state.

The interesting contrast lies in how other monotheistic religions, such as Islam and Judaism, worship an unseen God without the need for physical representations.

Muslims, like Jews, believe in the concept of monotheism and worship Allah, the unseen God, without the use of images or statues. However, despite this shared belief, there are distinct ideological and cultural differences between Judaism and Islam.

The Jews have a long history of defiance and resistance against various empires, while Islam has its own unique set of teachings and practices.

It is important to recognize and understand these differences when examining the various faiths and their relationship with the concept of an unseen God.

It was in this cosmopolitan city, Constantinople, known in Turkey as a significant center of trade and cultural exchange, that the concept of the **Trinity** was officially introduced and established as a fundamental doctrine of Christianity.

Constantinople, with its strategic location at the crossroads of Europe and Asia, played a crucial role in the spread of Christianity to both the East and the West. However, due to the subsequent historical developments and the influence of Western Christianity, the association of Christianity with Western regions has become more prevalent in popular perception.

Nonetheless, it is important to recognize the historical roots and diverse origins of this influential religion. Constantine, as an intelligent man, saw the potential of Constantinople as a strategic location for trade and defense.

At the crossroads of Europe and Asia, the city became a hub for commerce and cultural exchange. Its proximity to the Muslim world made it even more significant, as it allowed for connections and interactions with various cultures and religions.

However, it is important to note that Constantine's decision to move the capital was driven by more than just trade and defense. He also had a political agenda, aiming to solidify his power and establish Christianity as the dominant religion of the Roman Empire.

Constantine, the Roman Emperor, was pivotal in Christianity's development. To unify the Byzantine empire, Constantine created a religion that combined paganism and the worship of Jesus. The decision aimed to merge Christian and pagan traditions and establish a common belief system.

This blend laid the foundation for Catholicism, although its exact nature is still debated. His influence and power led to the spread and acceptance of this new religion, establishing the Catholic Church as a dominant force.

Despite controversies, Catholicism has endured, evolving into an influential global tradition. Faithless actions sustain the name, despite depletion.

It is important to approach religion with an open mind, acknowledging the complexities and different interpretations that exist within various faiths.

Examining the dogma of Christendom reveals its roots in paganism, not aligned with Jesus' teachings.

In the search for peace and one God, does Jesus, as God and Son of God, per Christendom symbolize the concept of the Holy Trinity becoming one?

This surpasses human imagination in monotheistic beliefs.

Would Jesus condone sexual abuse in the facility and doctrine? Christianity, stemming from Catholicism, has different branches, but all trace back to the same triune interest related to cultic practices or sexual abuse in churches.

Following cultic traditions with a documented history of sexual abuse would be challenging.

The ongoing battle within the Catholic regime regarding solitude and celibacy enforced by priesthood has raised concerns about the potential for molestation and the creation of breeding grounds for child abuse.

Many argue that children who enter this system are often unaware of the risks they may face. Numerous news records have shed light on these issues, making it challenging to have faith in any reform within the Catholic Church that such evil has plagued.

It is important to note that this concept of enforced celibacy and solitude has no direct connection or indoctrination from Jesus himself.

It is worth acknowledging that the formation of Christianity as a whole stems from incorporating Roman beliefs by Constantine, which have shaped the institutional structure of the Catholic Church.

These unfortunate youngsters who keep these acts secret out of fear face dire consequences and disturbances in their later lives.

They may become unsure of their sexuality or experience mental distortions requiring therapy for decades. It is important to approach this topic with sensitivity and understanding.

Abuse can have profound effects on a person's psychological well-being, including their sense of self, trust, and ability to form healthy relationships.

It is not uncommon for survivors of abuse to grapple with confusion, shame, and insecurity, regardless of their sexual orientation.

Some individuals who have experienced abuse may question their own sexuality as they navigate their identity and attempt to make sense of their experiences.

Young trauma survivors in these churches often seek therapy after confessing in Constantine's dark confession box he organized as penance.

The only thing they are aware of is that their parents exposed them to the dangers that lurk in these churches, where children cannot be left without parental guidance.

It is truly unfortunate, but the history of such cases is consistent, making them more than mere allegations.

The reported instances of inappropriate behavior within these churches persist, causing immense harm. It is crucial to recognize that these cults and their actions go against the teachings of Jesus.

Jesus, the prophet and Messiah of the Abrahamic faiths, would never condone such behavior.

To connect him to this evil and associate his name with these ideologies is not only blasphemous but also paganistic.

The teachings of Jesus emphasize monotheism, compassion, and respect for all individuals, especially the vulnerable, including children.

It is important to separate these harmful practices from the true teachings of Jesus and address the issue at hand to protect the innocent and ensure justice prevails.

New York Times: Jun 2, 2023 — More than 300 priests were found to have abused children, at least 1,000 of them, over the course of seven decades.

The abuse of children in churches for sexual play is a heinous and unforgivable act that causes immeasurable harm to the innocent victims.

It is not something that can be simply brushed aside with a small apology.

This kind of abuse shatters the trust and faith of these young individuals who have come to the church to learn about God and seek solace in their spirituality. It is particularly devastating because they are taught that Jesus forgives all sins, including the most evil ones.

This convenient strategy of offering apologies without taking appropriate action has destroyed countless lives and the erosion of faith in religious institutions.

The magnitude of the damage caused by these actions cannot be overstated.

However, Christianity has spread to various parts of the world, including the Middle East, Africa, Asia, and America. While the number of churches may fluctuate in different regions because of various factors, the faith continues to be practiced by millions of believers globally.

Regarding the mention of mosques taking over, it is important to acknowledge that Christianity and Islam are separate religious traditions with their own distinct beliefs and practices.

While the growth of Islam may have influenced the religious landscape in certain regions, it does not negate the existence or significance of Christianity.

The Council of Nicaea, which took place in 325 AD, was convened by Emperor Constantine in Nicaea, present-day Iznik, Turkey. The theological dispute concerning the Holy Trinity and the divinity of Jesus Christ remain constant dispute for monotheistic beliefs.

At the council, the bishops and theologians affirmed the equality of the Father, the Son, and the Holy Spirit, stating that they are all co-eternal and of the same substance.

This concept, known as Homoousios, was a crucial development in Christian theology.

The council affirmed the belief that only the Son, Jesus Christ, became incarnate as a human being, emphasizing his unique role as the savior and mediator between God and humanity.

These decisions, which were enshrined in the Nicene Creed, laid the foundation for orthodox Christian beliefs and played a significant role in shaping the development of Christian doctrine.

Christianity originated in Constantinople, where it merged the teachings of Jesus with pagan rituals. Constantine cleverly mixed paganism with monotheism, using Jesus as a triune god.

Jesus, as a historical figure, was a Jewish preacher who spread his message of monotheism, compassion, and salvation through deeds, not through him. The statement that Jesus was a deity and replacing God was blasphemous and the work of Satan is based on the belief misrepresented by Constantine among others.

Jesus was a monotheist, not a polytheist. These allegations against him are lies and history documents the truth.

Monotheism is the belief in the existence of only one God, while polytheism refers to the belief in multiple gods. This concept is central to the Christian faith, as it upholds the belief in the unity of triune God and not singularity of one God.

Therefore, any assertion that Jesus replaces or usurps God's position would be seen as blasphemous and contradict the core principles of Jesus.

Such a claim may be perceived as the work of Satan, who is commonly believed to oppose God and deceive humanity. Constantine embraced Christianity, but Jesus never declared himself a Christian.

However, their teachings laid the groundwork for the beliefs and principles that would shape Christianity, albeit with modifications. It had no likeness to the teachings of Jesus to the Jews.

Later, Constantine, the Roman emperor, declared his acceptance of Christianity as his faith.

However, it is important to note that the alterations he made to the words of the scripture, the Bible, and the new reforms introduced by him and the council do not align with the teachings of the monotheistic faith that Jesus preached to the Jews.

It is crucial to understand that Christianity as we know it today did not exist during Jesus' time, and the faith that was formed in the name of Jesus underwent alterations and modifications known to the world.

These changes, influenced by Constantine and subsequent councils, shaped the development of Christianity as a distinct religious tradition.

After Jesus' ascension to Allah (God), the error of Constantine, mixed with his doctrine, spread his teachings as gospel truth which was mixed with humans taking a vote to trinity not biblically and established a community of believers who came to be known as Christians.

The term "Christianity" did indeed emerge after Jesus' lifetime as a way to identify his followers.

The concept of the Trinity, however, has its roots in the early centuries of Christianity and was not directly taught by Jesus.

Facts indicate that Constantine, the Roman Emperor, can be credited with introducing the concept of the Trinity into Christian doctrine, rather than it being mere allegations.

Constantine's influence on the development of Christian theology, including the doctrine of the Trinity, is a topic of debate among scholars. It is worth noting that not all branches of Christianity embrace the concept of the Trinity, as there are denominations that interpret the teachings of Jesus differently.

The concept of worshiping Jesus and accepting the triune dogma remains the same for all affiliations in Christendom. Human corrupters not Jesus, ingrained in the caveat of teaching centuries ago.

Humanity seeks solace and understanding from God, some by adopting their own ideologies and claiming that God understands, but it is humanity who must understand His laws and regulations.

Lies told enough times can become reality for the misunderstood.

But truth will eventually override the falsehood.

Sins may be impulses or emotions but plotted schemes make up for their misconduct or adherence to their own rules. Asserting that God understands these actions only fosters additional turmoil and undermines peace.

Beware of this open-minded evil company that advocates for pleasure in evil and claims God understands. It's wise to distance oneself from such a company, as matters of the sound heart should be prioritized.

The key is repentance, not continuing to do evil. Repentance offers the opportunity for every person on earth to correct their mistakes.

Quran: Surah Baqarah: 2:105. The disbelievers from the People of the Book and the polytheists would not want you to receive any blessing from your Lord, but Allah selects whoever He wills for His mercy. And Allah is the Lord of infinite bounty.

Quran: Surah Baqarah 2:111. The Jews and Christians each claim that none will enter Paradise except those of their own faith. These are their desires. Reply, O Prophet, show me your proof if what you say is true.

Quran: Surah Baqarah 2;122. O Children of Israel! Remember My favors upon you and how I honored you above the others.

Allah forgives those who genuinely repent, but not those who promote or incite evil, or justify it by claiming God's understanding.

The key lies in recognizing the distinction. Humans cannot teach God to understand or speak on His behalf, but the angels meticulously record daily actions to track personal growth.

Upon learning the entire history of Christendom, most Bible readers and followers portray Jesus as the savior and emphasize that eternal life is possible only through him.

Jews claim to be chosen and destined for heaven, yet they were expelled from Israel for not obeying Allah.

Muslims, led by Omar bin Khattab, reached out to Jews and invited them during his era, bringing about a significant moment of peace. The rule of Muslims in history must be told, as it holds the key to achieving lasting peace.

Turmoil persists among the Abrahamic faiths unless they all agree on one God and acknowledge all prophets.

Quran: Surah Baqarah: 2:140. Do you claim that Abraham, Ishmael, Isaac, Jacob, and his descendants were all Jews or Christians?" Say, "Who is more knowledgeable: you or Allah?

All prophets except **Muhammad PBUH** were sent to the people of Israel, whereas he came from Saudi Arabia. **The land didn't play a role in the development of Islam; it was the faith itself that gave birth to the religion.**

Only those who share similar thoughts can comprehend the message, or one can choose to reflect on the decision to understand it. Islam is a monotheistic faith.

Initially, both Jews and Muslims prayed towards Jerusalem, known as the **Qibla**. Yet, Allah's infinite wisdom resulted in a change of the **Qibla** towards the **Kaaba in Mecca**, causing commotions among their communities.

Even without belief in the new delivery of Islam, this change sent an obvious message that monotheism alone couldn't absolve them of disobedience.

Allah deliberately separated the prayer and direction to emphasize that Islam was the ultimate form of monotheistic belief. This change reminded them that all prophets were sent by Allah, and it was not for humans to pick which prophet to follow.

Disobedience carries consequences, but Allah, in His mercy, always offers the opportunity for repentance and reform.

Quran: Surah Baqarah: 2;142. The foolish among the people will ask, why did they turn away from the direction of prayer they used to face? Say, O Prophet, the east and west belong only to Allah. He guides whoever He wills to the straight path.

The pagans requested to retain the statues as a reminder for prayer, while Islam forbids statues, images, and idol worship.

Different branches of Christianity have varying views on the use of statues and religious imagery, with some emphasizing their significance in worship and others choosing not to use them at all.

However, the Christian theology still maintains the concept of a triune god or son of god. **Jesus, the Messiah, was instrumental in spreading monotheistic beliefs. Jesus, like other prophets, shed light on the truth.**

The Jews rejected him as their awaited Messiah due to his poorly received message. Jesus' unconventional birth from a virgin was one reason for their rejection. Despite opposition, Jesus performed miracles with Allah's permission. He could breathe life into a clay bird, a notable miracle attributed to him. He spoke at birth he cured lepers.

These miraculous acts testified were performed by permission of the divine authority Allah during a time of widespread diseases.

The miracles sent by Allah to people of the past are recorded in the unchanged Quran. The Jews anticipate a new Messiah from David's descendants, evident in Jesus' struggle against their defiance and disregard for his teachings.

The constant approach to unify monotheism into the Abrahamic faith, specifically within the context of Christianity, requires persistent efforts and clear clarification in order to make decisive decisions.

It is crucial to explore the roots of Christendom without overlooking nuances in monotheism. Jesus, a monotheist, worshiped Allah and referred to him as **Allah-ha**. Jesus did not imply he would become a triune God.

It is important to note that the concept of the Trinity emerged later, specifically during the time of Constantine and the Council of Nicaea cannot be denied. **However, over time, repeated lies can potentially be perceived as truth, especially among those who are unwilling to seek out the truth themselves.**

Embracing and adhering to cultic beliefs that do not align with the nature of Jesus the Messiah may hinder individuals from discovering the genuine essence of his teachings.

Quran: Surah Hud: 11:18. And who is more unjust than he who invents a lie about Allah? Those will be presented before their Lord, and the witnesses will say, these are the ones who lied against their Lord. Unquestionably the curse of Allah is upon the wrongdoers.

The Quran addresses the worship of a human deity, specifically referring to the concept of Jesus being worshiped as God as blasphemous.

It emphasizes that after studying the historical context and understanding the facts, individuals who are open to pondering can find guidance in this matter.

Quran: Surah Imran: 3:64. Say, O People of the Scripture! Come to a common word between us and you: that we shall worship none but God, and that we shall ascribe no partner unto Him, and that none of us shall take others for lords beside God.

One crucial aspect highlighted in the Quran is the unequivocal affirmation that no prophet, including Prophet Muhammad and Jesus, ever proclaimed themselves to be divine

This concept of monotheism, known as tawhid, is central to Islamic belief and is repeatedly emphasized in the Quran.

The Quran presents Prophet Muhammad as a human being, emphasizing his role as a teacher and leader rather than as a deity. Similarly, Jesus, who is highly revered in Islam as a prophet, is also depicted as a human messenger of Allah, not as a divine figure.

In conclusion, the Quran's verses are considered clear and comprehensible to all, regardless of the language in which they are presented.

Such a belief goes against the fundamental principle of monotheism, which is central to Islam. The Quran, as the holy scripture of Islam, emphasizes the oneness of God, Allah, and strictly prohibits associating partners with Him.

Therefore, engaging in acts that promote the worship of multiple deities or consider Jesus as divine would be considered a grave sin in Islamic belief.

Instead, Islam teaches that true worship should be directed solely towards Allah, the one and only God. By reading, pondering, and contemplating the message of the Quran, individuals can come to a deeper understanding of this truth and align their worship practices accordingly.

The truth summarizes the case's facts, arguments, and supporting evidence.

Bible: ESV: John: 3:1:21 You *Must Be Born Again*—Now there was a man of the Pharisees named Nicodemus, a ruler of the Jews. This man came to *Jesus* by night and said to him,

Bible hub 3:3 Jesus **answered and said to him, "Truly, truly, I say to you, unless one is born *again*, he cannot see the kingdom of God." Amplified *Bible Jesus* answered him.**

The Bible teaches that rebirth and anointing are prerequisites for faith in him and for achieving salvation. **It challenges the belief Jesus was a monotheist.**

CHAPTER 2
THE IMPORTANCE OF IDENTITY

Islamic belief holds that Allah has a constant and unchanging singular identity. He is known for his exceptional compassion. The **99 names of Allah** are attributes that enhance our understanding of His nature without altering His core identity.

Allah remains constant and does not undergo any transformations or take on a human form, unlike the Trinity in Christianity.

Humans cannot comprehend Allah's identity, which remains veiled and unseen.

Islamic theology holds the belief that if Allah can be seen, then that being is not the true God. A fundamental aspect of Islam is the belief that Allah is one and transcendent.

The **99 names of Allah**, also known as **Asma-Ul-Husna**, are a compilation of various attributes and qualities that describe the divine nature of **Allah** in Islamic tradition. These names are sacred and are recited and revered by Muslims all over the world.

Each name represents a specific aspect of Allah's character and serves as a reminder of His limitless power, mercy, and wisdom. Some of the well-known names include Ar-Rahman (The Merciful), Al-Wadud (The Loving), Al-Malik (The King), Al-Hakim (The Wise), Al-Khaliq (The Creator), Al-Basir (All seeing), Ar-Razzaq (The Provider), Al-Ghaffar (The all and oft forgiving), and Al Musawir (The Fashioner).

These names provide a deeper understanding of Allah's nature and help believers strengthen their connection with Him.

Studying each name of Allah allows individuals to deepen their understanding of His nature and attributes.

When someone calls out to Allah in times of need using a specific name that resonates with their situation, it shows a personal connection and reliance on His divine qualities.

However, it is important for believers to not simply repeat the same actions that led to their need for repentance. After seeking forgiveness and repenting, one must take responsibility and actively avoid falling back into the same patterns of negligence.

This responsibility lies with the individual who seeks repentance, as one strives to change their behavior and choices. By doing so, believers of every Abrahamic faith can maintain a strong connection with Allah and experience the mercy and forgiveness that He offers.

The most important and fundamental quality of a Muslim is their Muslim identity. There is no identity more powerful than being known as a Muslim. This identity remains true to the essence of being a Muslim, with a quiet but genuine presence.

The emblem of a Muslim is the unwavering belief in monotheism, justice, clarity, and the resilience to overcome setbacks. Entry to the Kaaba in Mecca is restricted to Muslims only. Allah considers the house constructed by Abraham and his son as a holy site and a place of unity for all Muslims.

The identity clearly represents the emblem of truth, excluding anyone who does not declare themselves as Muslim from entering the sacred house of Allah, which was built by Abraham for worship and unity.

The document of acceptance of Islam mentioned in the previous statement does not exclude any humanity or impose restrictions on helping each other, regardless of faith.

It serves to regulate entry into a specific area, namely the **Ka'ba in Mecca**, which is sacred by Muslims. The restriction on entry is not alarming, as it is common for certain offices or areas to only allow allowed personnel inside.

Even in such cases, sometimes unauthorized individuals enter and disrupt the peace. However, according to the teachings of Islam, the opportunity to enter the **Ka'ba** is an honor and not merely a place for sightseeing. It is a place where individuals can seek solace and spiritual fulfillment, and visiting the Ka'ba is one of the pillars of Islam.

The **Masjid al Haram** is the only mosque that restricts entry to individuals who do not adhere to the **pillars of Islam or identify as Muslims.**

"Haram" refers to aspects or actions that are forbidden in Islam. While the term **"haram"** is used to describe things that are not in line with a righteous life, it is not extensively employed by Muslims, as not every act is considered **"haram."**

Moderation is a key principle in Islam. Overeating should be avoided as it can have detrimental effects on both health and lead to wastefulness. The purpose of prohibiting immodest dressing is to promote modesty and prevent temptation.

Zina, which encompasses illicit sexual activity, is strictly forbidden as it contradicts the values of chastity and the sanctity of marriage.

Consumption of alcohol **Khamr** is prohibited because it is thought to impair judgment and contribute to sinful actions. Finally, it's important to note that pork is not allowed to be consumed.

When an animal is mistreated or subjected to torture during slaughter, the meat becomes **haram**. Alcohol, pork, carrion, carnivorous meat, and animals that died from illness, injury, stunning, poisoning, or non-religious slaughtering are all considered forbidden food substances.

"Makruh" refers to actions that are disliked or discouraged in Islam but are not sinful in and of themselves. These actions may not be forbidden, but they are not recommended or encouraged by the teachings of Islam.

The reason behind discouraging **Makruh** actions is that they can potentially lead to **Haram** (forbidden) acts. Islam encourages believers to stay away from anything that may lead to evil or sinful behavior.

This is because every disorderly action has consequences and can pave the way for further misconduct. Discouraging actions that lead to negativity is important because they negatively impact health, self-control, and humility.

Makruh actions are less sinful compared to haram actions. To foster a stronger sense of devotion and spiritual well-being, it is advisable to abstain from **Makruh** and **Haram** actions.

It is important to note that the Arabic language, in which the Quran was revealed, is highly intricate and eloquent. Misuse of words, particularly by those who are not familiar with Arabic, can lead to misunderstanding and misinterpretation.

Therefore, it is crucial to approach the Arabic language with knowledge and respect, as it is the language chosen by Allah to convey the message of the Quran.

Ka'ba, in Mecca, was indeed the only place of truce when paganism was prevalent.

As part of Islamic belief, all statues and idols were removed from the Ka'ba, as the Muslim faith strictly prohibits the worship of any deities or idols other than Allah.

Quran: Surah Taubah: 9:28. O you who have believed, indeed the polytheists are unclean, so let them not approach al-Masjid al- Haram after this their final year. And if you fear privation, Allah will enrich you from His bounty if He wills. Indeed, Allah is knowing and Wise.

Quran: Surah Baqarah: 2;27. Who break the covenant of Allah after contracting it and sever that which Allah has ordered to be joined and cause corruption.

The identity of a Muslim encompasses various aspects with core belief in one God and the Prophet Muhammad. One fundamental aspect is the practice of cleanliness, which is considered a mandate in Islam.

Islam encourages Muslims to maintain both physical and spiritual cleanliness by regularly performing ablution (wudu) before prayer and practicing good hygiene. Modesty is also an integral part of the Muslim identity, emphasizing the importance of covering one's body respectfully.

This is evident in the attire worn by Muslim women, such as the hijab, which symbolizes their commitment to modesty. The dress code in Islam mandates modesty for both men and women, not just women.

However, the identity of a Muslim is not solely defined by these external practices. It extends to one's behavior, character, and adherence to the teachings of Islam.

Being a Muslim means striving to embody the values of compassion, honesty, patience, and justice in all aspects of life.

Participation in communal activities, such as congregational prayers, fasting during Ramadan, and performing the Hajj pilgrimage, strengthens the identity of Muslims. These various venues and practices contribute to the rich and diverse identity of Muslims worldwide.

Wudu is known as the ritual ablution performed by Muslims before performing their prayers (salat). It involves specific steps that ensure thorough cleansing of the body and spirit.

Before starting wudu, Muslims are required to have the intention of purifying themselves for prayer.

The process typically begins with washing the hands, mouth, nose, face, and arms up to the elbows. Then, one wipes the head and ears, and finally washes the feet. This meticulous washing is not only a physical act but also a spiritual one, symbolizing the purification of the body and the readiness to stand before Allah in prayer.

Wudu not only cleanses the physical body but also purifies the soul, preparing them for a more focused and meaningful connection with their Creator during worship.

Therefore, maintaining personal cleanliness and performing **Wudu** are fundamental aspects of a Muslim's identity and their commitment to practicing their faith.

In Islam, people use water for cleanliness after using the restroom instead of toilet paper, unlike in Western countries. In Islam, that is deemed impure.

Every toilet in Muslim countries is equipped with a bidet or a water spray, known as a **"shattaf."** This practice of using water for cleansing after using the toilet has been a long-standing cultural and religious tradition in many Muslim-majority nations.

When visitors from Western countries encounter this practice for the first time, it often surprises them as it differs from the use of toilet paper in their own cultures. Some Western visitors, upon experiencing the hygienic benefits of using water, choose to adopt this practice in their own personal hygiene routines.

This cultural exchange has led to a growing interest in bidets and water-based cleansing methods in Western countries. As a result, some Western countries are now actively trying to adapt and incorporate these practices into their own toilet designs and hygiene habits, recognizing the benefits and effectiveness of this tradition from the Muslim world.

The concept of negation is not applicable when it comes to understanding the restriction that those with impure hearts are not cleansed to enter the **Haram the masjid.** This allowance is specifically intended for believers who have sincerely declared their submission to the will of Allah.

The **Haram**, referring to the sacred precincts in Mecca, holds immense spiritual significance for Muslims around the world. It is a place of utmost purity, where believers are expected to approach with a state of purity in both their physical and spiritual being.

Those with impure hearts, lacking the genuine devotion and submission to Allah, are not considered fit to enter this sacred space.

The cleansing of the heart is an essential prerequisite for engaging in the rituals and acts of worship within the Haram, as it signifies a deep connection and devotion to Allah.

Those who view the discriminatory practice of declining entrance to the Kaaba, the holiest site in Islam, to non-Muslims can indeed perceive as extreme the concept of Islam.

While entrance to other mosques is allowed for people of all faiths, the restriction on entering the Kaaba may seem perplexing to some. However, it is important to understand that Islam holds the Kaaba in the highest regard, as it is believed to be the house of Allah.

The restriction on entry is not intended to be discriminatory, but a way to preserve the sanctity and reverence of the **Kaaba** for believers.

Islam teaches Allah has the authority to make laws, and these laws are compelling for those who seek entry to the **Kaaba** out of curiosity or for non-religious purposes. It is a matter of faith and respect for the sacredness of this place rather than a question of human-made laws.

This practice of removing statues and making the Ka'ba exclusive to Muslims is derived from the teachings of the Quran, the holy book of Islam.

It is important to note that this law did not originate from the Saudi government, but from the religious principles outlined in the Quran. The Quran serves as the ultimate guide for Muslims, dictating their beliefs, practices, and rituals.

During the time of the prophet Abraham, his father, Azar, was a prominent idol merchant and worshipper.

However, Abraham, guided by his unwavering faith in Allah, recognized the falsehood of idol worship and embarked on a mission to dismantle this belief system. He courageously destroyed all the idols in his father's space, except for the largest one, leaving the ax embedded in it as a symbol of his defiance.

Abraham's actions infuriated his father and the people of his community, who vehemently opposed his monotheistic beliefs. They subjected him to severe torture, attempting to force him to renounce his faith. In one instance, he was even placed on a catapult and launched into a raging fire, yet miraculously emerged unharmed.

It was through Allah's divine protection that the fire transformed into a cool and peaceful environment for Abraham, showcasing the strength of his faith.

Abraham is also renowned for his pivotal role in the construction of the **Kaaba**, the sacred mosque in Mecca. With the help of his son Ishmael, Abraham was commanded by Allah to build the Kaaba.

This significant event signifies that Abraham's faith was firmly rooted in the worship of the One true God, and Islam, as a religion, follows in the footsteps of his monotheistic teachings.

Islam, as a faith, emphasizes the principles of monotheism and the exclusive worship of Allah.

The purpose of the **Kaaba** as a place of worship is explicitly stated in Islamic teachings, and entry into this holy sanctuary is restricted to Muslims alone.

This restriction serves to maintain the sanctity and purity of the **Kaaba as a center for Muslim** worship, aligning with the core beliefs and principles of Islam.

Abraham, revered as the father of all prophets, is known for his unwavering belief in the oneness of God. Islam recognizes Abraham as a central figure in its religious history, as his faith and submission to God's will set the foundation for the monotheistic beliefs that define Islam.

Islam sees itself as the culmination and finality of the line of prophets, with Prophet Muhammad being the last messenger sent by God. However, it is important to note that the core belief of every prophet, including Abraham, was the worship of a singular God and adherence to monotheism.

Any Abrahamic faith that deviates from this principle falls short of the true Abrahamic belief system.

Therefore, the essence of Abrahamic faith lies in the acceptance of monotheism and the recognition of one God, which is a fundamental aspect of Islam. Allah, owns the worlds, does not require a house, but Muslims seek unity and a sense of faith.

As prophet Muhammad raised his hands and said, "Ya Allah, I have delivered your words and message to the world and made Allah his witness that each word was told."

That is the identity of a Muslim. A Muslim's identity is not based on worrying about insults and negativity. A Muslim has arrived with the goal of self-improvement and making a positive impact on the world.

Prophet Muhammad's vision of the world and his identity remained unchanged, even in the face of mistreatment and torment from the people of Taif and beyond.

A Muslim remains steadfast in their belief, finding strength in their vision and **Tawwakul**, even when circumstances seem implausible. Anything is possible with Allah's power. The Muslim identity extends beyond oneself.

It's meant to assist Muslims struggling with their faith. Even in a climate where falsehood is accepted and truth is rudeness, it's compelling to speak the truth about Islam.

Muslims refuse to stand idly by while others are oppressed; they are committed to using all resources to provide help. Muslims must unite and contribute to global welfare, irrespective of their religious beliefs. Show them that Muslims are known for teaching justice, not oppression.

Prophet Muhammad's impact on the world came from his demeanor, not sit-ins, making him successful both religiously and secularly as a prophet and commander.

It's both a challenge and a responsibility to be part of ummah his people. He wasn't just fair to the Muslims, but to the entire world.

It is important for Muslim countries to recognize their identity as justice-seeking Muslims and confront oppression. They need to make bold moves in order to get the attention of the world. The identity holds true to knowledge and duties that rest with Muslims.

Negative behavior should retreat while the positive traits of a Muslim thrive in the presence of excellent company. A Muslim is best identified by their commitment to truth and justice.

When Allah showers someone with honor, they experience ease and sometimes receive things without anticipation.

Being able to write and speak about Allah is a privilege, thanks to His mercy. Comparing insignificant individuals who have corrupted the world to discussing Allah is a distinct level of importance that Allah gives upon those he chooses.

If Allah doesn't like you, being liked by others is insignificant in maintaining peace. When Allah approves of someone, their identity is raised.

He informs angel Gabriel, who then spreads the news to all the angels. Then most people like such a person and see the light one sheds on others.

Taw-Akul belief, though unseen, is meant only for those who believe in the teachings of Islam, not applicable to everyone or every narrative.

Both Muslims and non-Muslims perceive individuals who embody light as a source of enjoyment and envy, as their presence holds a captivating aura that softens hearts and invokes Allah's mercy.

Allah has the ability to select and decide, and it's evident that His mercy extends beyond those He favors. In the present day, regions with Islamophobia are implementing rules that go against Islam.

Speaking truth has become impolite because of the dismissal of morality and the acceptance of rules demanded by secularism, causing conflicts between those who oppose bad and strive for good.

A Muslim's identity lies in expressing gratitude to Allah for even the smallest blessings, causing their heart to tremble. Without a bank to fulfill the deeds, planning for retirement is not complete.

Story of Qazi Abu Bakr:

Qazi Abu Bakr was known for his piety as a Muslim. His unwavering reliance on Islam surpassed any personal strength he had, and he remained true to his Muslim identity. He recounted his own narrative.

People were so impressed by his beautiful Quran recitation that they asked him to teach and offered payment. Tough circumstances led him to sell his writings, recognizing that speaking about Allah yields lasting revenue and promotes understanding.

One day, feeling hungry, he went to the Kaaba to seek help from Allah, unwilling to ask anyone else. While walking, he stumbled upon a sewn pouch and searched for its owner, but found no one around. Taking it home, he opened the pouch and the pearls illuminated his room. In a brief moment, his hunger was forgotten as he enthusiastically searched for the owner, suspecting the pearls were pricey.

Before long, he learned that a pouch had been lost and someone was in search of it. The old man was delighted and offered him money; he hoped his daughter would marry someone as devout as him. He couldn't understand being rewarded for something that was rightfully his, so he politely declined.

Prior to giving it back, he requested a description of the lost item, which was so accurate that there was no doubt it belonged to the older man who had it for his daughter.

Because of increasing financial difficulties, he migrated to another town, as Allah's land is vast. He received a job offer and encountered ship problems that caused him to be thrown overboard.

Eventually, he regained consciousness and found himself in a mosque, where people nursed and cared for him.

He generated income through teaching Quran and writing. When he was prepared to depart, people felt discouraged and devised a plan.

The proposal was made to marry a beautiful girl who had lost her father, with confidence in his commitment. Mistakenly, the people believed he disliked her, but his emotions were overwhelming. Unable to express himself, he glanced down, aware of the power of Allah.

Upon noticing her, he realized that she was wearing the necklace he had discovered and gifted to her father.

Her father wanted a pious man, and her caretakers were suggesting marriage to her. He was conscious of Allah's unbeatable and precisely calculated plan.

The chances of him finding the necklace and later being asked to marry the girl who was wearing the same necklace are all part of Allah's precise plans for the believers. The plan of Allah exceeds human comprehension. The reasons behind why He does what He remains unknown to humanity, which may be challenging to fully grasp as humans, are inherently weak.

However, Allah's plan is superior to that of any human in every aspect. If humans could only comprehend the bigger picture, there would be no hesitation or worry.

Those who truly understand the power of Allah have faith instead of worry. Every incident is meticulously planned; nothing happens by chance or accident.

The Creator's intricate planning encompasses everything, making it a simple task for Him, as He is the ultimate Creator.

In Islam, it is important to clarify the nature of a heterosexual relationship because of the current liberal environment.

Some women who are divorced or single in Christianity refer to Jesus as their husband. This practice stems from their deep spiritual connection with Jesus and the belief that he provides them with love, guidance, and support.

However, it is important to note that Islam views assuming the identity of Jesus's wife in Christianity as blasphemous. In Islam, Prophet Jesus (known as Prophet Isa) holds a revered position as a prophet and messenger of God, but he is not considered divine or a husband figure.

Similarly, in Islam, unmarried Muslim women cannot refer to Prophet Muhammad as their husband, as this would be seen as disrespectful and against the teachings of Islam.

Islam emphasizes humility and the importance of maintaining appropriate boundaries and behaviors in matters of faith and self-worth.

If Jesus is known as the husband to those who are unmarried and they refer to Jesus as "my husband," it raises the question of who would be considered the wife of unmarried men.

Bible: NKJV: Isaiah 54:5:8. For your Maker is your husband, The LORD of hosts is His name; And your Redeemer is the Holy One of Israel; He is called the God of the whole earth. For the LORD has called you Like a woman forsaken and grieved in spirit, like a youthful wife who is cast off," says your God.

Bible: NKJV: Corinthians: 7:34. There is a difference between a wife and a virgin. The unmarried woman cares about the things of the Lord, that she may be holy both in body and in spirit. But she who is married cares about the things of the world—how she may please *her* husband.

However, according to this concept, the idea itself makes little sense. These ideologies primarily exist in revised editions and newly formed societies, where individuals are adopting unconventional beliefs and interpretations of religious figures.

In Islam, divorce is permitted in cases of infidelity, uncertainty, lack of intimacy, and irreconcilable differences.

Divorce is only allowed in Christianity in cases of infidelity, and most divorces occur in western states. Consummating the marriage is an essential aspect of the husband-and-wife relationship in Islam.

If one spouse refuses to engage in sexual relations, divorce can be pursued as the other no longer desires intimacy.

The bond of marriage is formed by enjoying physical intimacy and sharing spirituality.

In Islam, the idea of marrying God is unequivocally rejected. These distinctions are inevitable and vary significantly, contradicting Islamic beliefs.

According to the Bible, marriage discourages women by placing them in a subordinate position to their husbands, while unmarried women can fully devote themselves to serving God. The Bible shows submission to husbands while Quran puts a degree of responsibility over men for Muslim women.

Islam strongly promotes marriage to strengthen one's faith. The blessings received from a marriage are believed to come from Allah's guidance and help.

The teachings of the Bible and the Quran have significant differences, which makes it challenging to reconcile these beliefs.

In Islam, it is blasphemous to describe Allah as a husband or a father because of His transcendence and dissimilarity to His creation. In Islamic belief, Allah is non-human and Jesus is regarded as a human prophet created by Allah.

Although Jesus is acknowledged in both Islam and Christianity, he is not regarded as divine or a deity in the Islamic faith. Comparing the identities of Jesus in Islam and Christianity reveals stark differences. Most Jewish individuals do not recognize Jesus because of their belief in a virgin birth scar that restricts their acceptance of Allah's capabilities.

In Judaism, as well as in Judeo-Christian beliefs, women are subordinate to men. Islam regards both men and women as equal, despite the false narratives propagated by Islamophobes. Men have a certain level of responsibility towards women.

Islam promotes inclusivity and encourages Muslims to extend their kindness and hospitality to all, regardless of their background or circumstances.

It is a religion that emphasizes the importance of sharing and caring for others, fostering a sense of unity and compassion among its followers. Also extending the same kindness to all of humanity. Muslims identify Islam as their faith and their actions create discussions about Islam globally. Islam will endure regardless of the actions of Muslims.

A genuine Muslim can make grave errors, yet find solace in Allah's protection, learning from their mistakes and embracing the weight of their Muslim identity. It is the responsibility of a fellow Muslim to assist one who is falling short when another Muslim openly engages in inappropriate behavior.

No matter what any one does, a Muslim cannot lose his identity as a Muslim. It's a title that holds responsibility not vengeance.

Identity allows individuals to establish their place in the world and form connections with others. It helps shape one's sense of self and provides a foundation for personal growth and development.

Identification serves as a tool for accountability and responsibility. Through identification cards, licenses, and other forms of official documentation, individuals can access essential services, exercise their rights, and participate in various aspects of society.

The greatest responsibility one can bear is proudly proclaiming "I am a Muslim". This identity holds immense significance, encompassing much more than superficial concerns or mere agreement.

It carries within it, qualities of character, truth, honor, and representation. Understanding the depth of this identity reveals that it surpasses any other honor or position one may hold. Being a Muslim is like having a key to **"Jannah"** heaven, the abode of those who truly comprehend the essence of being a Muslim and the rewards it brings.

In the Quran, specifically in **Surah Al-Qiyyama** (Chapter of the Resurrection), it mentions the significance and uniqueness of the fingertips as identification. It states that on the Day of judgment, Allah will resurrect humanity and recreate them from their very fingertips.

This highlights the divine knowledge and attention to detail displayed by Allah, as even the smallest part of a person's body, such as their fingertips, holds a distinct and individualistic pattern.

The Quran mentioned fingerprints as identification centuries before their scientific discovery and human utilization. It showcases the Quran's foresight and its ability to provide guidance and knowledge in various aspects of life, including the understanding of human identity.

Quran: Surah Qiyyama: "Does the Man think we shall not assemble his bones (and raise him up alive from grave)?? Verily we are powerful enough to restore his very fingertips!"

Fingerprints develop in the embryo at around four months of gestation. This intricate pattern is formed through the fusion of the epidermis and dermis layers of the skin.

The unique curvatures and ridges found in fingerprints differ between individuals, making them highly distinctive. It is fascinating to note that these patterns do not universally correspond or align with any specific characteristic or trait.

Scientists and the Quran acknowledge the distinctiveness of fingerprints. It was first mentioned in the Quranic text. Allah, the creator, informs humans of life's intricacies; searching requires time and exploration.

The study of fingerprints by humanity is a testament to our innate curiosity and desire for self-discovery. It is a fascinating field of study that delves into the unique patterns and ridges on our fingertips, which are distinct to each individual.

This study not only helps in forensic investigations and identification, but it also reveals the intricate nature of the human body.

Similarly, the Quran, revered by Muslims, is believed to contain guidance and knowledge about all aspects of human existence. The identification of fingerprints in the Quran serves as evidence that everything the Quran has foretold is accurate.

Therefore, when we examine the history of biblical changes and reforms, the identity of Jesus described in the Quran is undeniable.

He is indeed the son of Mary, not the son of God. The Quran, being a divine revelation, is free from any imperfections or alterations that human hands may have caused. It is a testament to the power of Allah, as no miracle is too great for Him. The preservation of the Quran ensures its descriptions are flawless and uncorrupted.

It is often seen as a comprehensive guide that addresses various aspects of human life, including spiritual, moral, social, and legal dimensions.

It is clear that the Quran has not neglected any part of human existence, and that it provides a vast scope for exploration, self-discovery, and understanding of the world and oneself.

This extends to animals as well, where identification tags and licenses help ensure their well-being and safety, while also providing crucial information about their owners.

Overall, identity and the markers associated with it are vital in establishing and maintaining a sense of belonging and contributing to the functioning of a civilized society. In a civilized society, the act of identity forgery is a breach of trust and a threat to the integrity of the community.

There have been efforts to prevent such deceptive behaviors and protect individuals' rights.

However, it is important to acknowledge that despite these measures, sometimes humanity seeks to deceive others for personal gain or ulterior motives.

This pursuit of deceit occurs worldwide and poses a significant challenge to maintaining a just and harmonious society. In view of this, it is essential to consider the concept of accountability beyond the human realm. From a spiritual perspective, many believe in the existence of a higher power, such as Allah, who is the supreme and only creator.

According to various religious beliefs, Allah the creator possesses omniscience and is aware of every action, thought, and intention of humanity. Nothing escapes the vigilant scrutiny of Allah's divine knowledge.

Allah keeps a meticulous record of every individual's action and intention, which forms part of the daily regimen of records. This belief serves as a reminder of the ultimate accountability that transcends human interactions and societal measures.

Therefore, while society continues to tackle identity forgery and deceit, the notion of divine accountability offers a perspective that surpasses human limitations. It emphasizes the importance of personal integrity and the understanding that ultimately, all actions and intentions are subject to a higher judgment.

Identity is deeply connected to self and society. Assuming different identities and deceiving others with various names and pictures reflects a loss of character and deceitful nature.

This behavior damages trust and has serious consequences when the truth comes out.

Sometimes, the discovery of multiple identities may completely shatter the trust others had in that person, leading to isolation and ostracization. If the individual acknowledges and displays their alternative identity alongside their legal name, it can serve as transparency and legal documentation.

This practice helps establish accountability and ensures that the person's true identity is known and recognized in any country.

The importance of identity becomes even more apparent when it is used to establish the authenticity of a person's actions, determining whether they are driven by truth or mischief.

Thus, identity plays a crucial role in understanding a person's character and standing, influencing how they are perceived and trusted by others.

In Islam, modesty in clothing is not just a cultural practice, but a core principle that reflects the spiritual values of the religion. It emphasizes the importance of modesty in both appearance and behavior, to preserve one's dignity and protect the soul from corruption.

Islamic teachings encourage individuals, both men and women, to dress in a manner that covers their bodies modestly, without drawing unnecessary attention to themselves.

This includes wearing loose-fitting garments that do not cling to the body, as well as covering the hair, the face covering is not mandated its optional.

The concept of covering the physical being is a means to protect the inner self, allowing individuals to focus on cultivating their spirituality and connection with God.

During the days of decadence, pagans embraced a lifestyle of minimal clothing, often choosing to be completely naked or barely covered. This act of calling out to their gods while in a state of nudity became a common practice.

As this trend gained popularity, it influenced societies, particularly in the Western world.

The Western lands, fascinated by the allure of nudity, started embracing nudism to express their freedom and explore their inner selves. This movement, influenced by Eastern cultures such as India, where Hindus traditionally embrace simplicity in clothing, has gradually made its way into Western society.

The influence of Eastern religions and their dress codes can be seen in various aspects of Western fashion and style. While Western society may not fully adopt the dress code of Hinduism, elements of it have certainly made an impact.

In recent times, there has been a heightened fascination with nudity in Western society, pushing boundaries and exploring the concept of the human body.

This has led to the rise of nudist practices, where individuals express themselves by embracing nudity or less clothing as self-expression.

While some may argue that this exploitation of the soul is taking things to an extreme, others see it as an exploration of personal freedom and breaking societal norms.

The influence of Eastern cultures and the increasing acceptance of nudity in Western society have undoubtedly shaped the way people express themselves through clothing or lack thereof.

The era of the 1960's in US. had a significant impact on Western society as women challenged traditional gender roles and took off in various aspects of life. The feminist movement gained momentum during this time, advocating for women's rights, equality, and liberation from societal constraints.

To challenge societal norms and assert their autonomy, some women symbolically removed their undergarments and took part in sit-ins, refusing to conform to the rules dictated by men.

This bold act aimed to show that they would not be silenced or controlled by patriarchal authority.

However, it is important to note that open sexuality and illegitimate children were not only associated with flower children conceived outside of wedlock. These aspects were broader reflections of the sexual revolution and changing attitudes towards relationships and family structures during that time.

The change in moral compass of the Western climax in the US and around Western regions has led to a progressive decline in moral ethics associated with the faith of Christendom.

Throughout history, the influence of Western culture has dominated the principles and values of Christianity. However, it is important to note that this dominance has resulted in a patriarchal system where men hold the majority of power and authority within the faith.

This imbalance has often suppressed the independence and agency of women, the Bible itself acknowledging women's fault and blame as significant from the very beginning.

In the beginning of creation, both Adam and Eve were tempted by Satan, yet it is commonly believed within Christendom that Eve was the primary temptress, leading Adam to follow suit.

This narrative, places the blame on women for the act of eating from the forbidden fruit, perpetuating a view that women are inherently sinful or easily influenced.

However, it is crucial to approach these interpretations critically, recognizing the need for a more balanced and inclusive understanding of gender roles and responsibilities within the faith.

The role and identity of women in Western cultures following Christendom has indeed undergone significant changes.

While certain interpretations of Christianity have historically restricted women's leadership and authority over men, it is essential to note that there is a wide range of beliefs and practices within the Christian faith.

Many Christian denominations and individuals have embraced more egalitarian perspectives, recognizing the equal worth and capabilities of women.

In recent decades, there has been a growing movement within Christianity that promotes women's empowerment and encourages their participation in all areas of church and society. These progressives challenge the traditional limitations placed on women and open up avenues for their progression and leadership.

While there may still be pockets of resistance, it is accurate to assert that Christianity as a whole uniformly denies women the opportunity to rule over men or rejects their quest for progression.

The movement being referred to is the ongoing push for gender equality and women's rights.

The idea proposed is that in order to resist this movement, the script or narrative that guides societal norms and values is rewritten continually and set forth as teachings of the Bible which are human and Divine. By doing so, women would be uplifted and given equal status and opportunities.

The Quran, already promotes the upliftment of women. Unlike the Bible, which historically blames women for original sin, believers suggest the Quran has consistently elevated the status of women since the rise of Islam.

The reference to Adam and Eve in Christendom's history highlights the idea that women have been blamed historically for the downfall of humanity.

Even if both Adam and Eve were active participants in the story, it is commonly believed that Eve is held solely responsible in the Bible. This narrative perpetuates the notion of women's inferiority and contributes to the need for script rewrites that challenge these gendered power dynamics.

Ultimately, the argument posits that adapting religious teachings to reflect contemporary values is necessary to keep up with the changing times and promote equality for women.

Women started to actively participate in the workforce, pursuing careers and breaking barriers in previously male-dominated industries. Introducing the birth control pill revolutionized reproductive rights and allowed women to have more control over their bodies and choices.

The 1960's in U.S saw a rise in the popularity of the women's liberation movement, with protests and demonstrations demanding equal pay, reproductive freedom, and an end to gender discrimination.

This period marked a significant shift in societal attitudes towards women, paving the way for future advancements in gender equality. This includes inviting those who may not be comfortable with the idea of nudity, and exposing them to the fitnah (temptation) of going against their own beliefs and values.

The influence of nudity has even extended to social media, where fashion runways showcase increasingly revealing outfits, promoting the idea that showing less clothing is acceptable and fashionable.

In today's society, the rise of social media has allowed disturbed individuals to expose themselves, inviting more evil and fitnah.

These individuals often express their faith while simultaneously working to destruct the very fabric of society.

They exploit the ignorance and naivety of those who are unaware of their deceitful intentions. Therefore, it is crucial to live with a single identity, facing the challenges and difficulties head-on, rather than adopting multiple identities to corrupt one's inner soul.

Stripping away one's clothing, both metaphorically and literally, to exploit the vulnerable souls of others ultimately brings no satisfaction and only serves to further damage one's own soul.

The phenomenon of men embracing drag and nudism adds another layer of complexity to this societal dilemma.

Many individuals now switch between multiple personalities, presenting as men during the day and women at night. This dual identity perpetuates the nature of deceit and unfortunately, it has become widely acceptable in our society.

However, if one dares to voice the truth, it is often labeled as discrimination because of the prevalence of secularism and the diminishing value placed on modesty, which is a fundamental aspect of faith in all Abrahamic religions.

The vastness of secularism has distorted the truth, turning it into discrimination rather than acknowledging it as a virtue.

CNN: Apr 29, 2023 — To many, the stereotypical image of a drag queen is one of a gay man dressed in exaggerated feminine getup, oversized wigs and heavy makeup.

ABC News: Aug 3, 2023 — Fab and fearless drag queens take on small-town America ... male or female sexual characteristics" which ... drag artist, in a statement to ABC News ...

This imposition of identity crisis is prevalent in secular states that preach the belief in the prophet Jesus. It is a hypocritical stance, as these states claim to promote independence and individuality, yet they impose their own set of beliefs on young minds in public schools.

This imposition forces the youth to grapple with their identity and conform to corrupted ideas, rather than allowing them the freedom to explore their unique selves. The adults responsible for this imposition perpetuate these ideas through social media and create an environment that fosters conformity.

Unfortunately, this environment often leads them to indulge in substances that are detrimental to their brain development, causing further chaos and misery. This toxic cycle can cause individuals to experience depression, contemplate suicide, or pretend to be happy when, in reality, they are not.

In Islamic doctrine, certain implications and cross-identities are not acceptable.

These include concepts such as same-sex relationships and gender fluidity, which are going against the traditional understanding of gender roles and relationships in Islam. Not exclusive to all Abrahamic faiths. Muslim countries adhere to Islamic teachings and laws, which do not recognize or accept these forms of equality.

While it is important to note that there is diversity within the Muslim community and differing interpretations of Islamic teachings, the consensus in most Muslim-majority countries is that these concepts are not permissible.

It is crucial to respect the beliefs and values of different cultures and religions while promoting understanding and dialogue on issues of equality.

In Islam, the core teachings of the Quran do not support the concept of entertaining cross-identities. Muslims believe that their faith provides guidance on how to live a righteous and fulfilling life, and this includes adhering to certain moral and ethical principles.

These principles discourage actions that are sinful or contrary to the teachings of Islam.

Therefore, they may not shy away from addressing issues or practices that they perceive as harmful or contradictory to their faith.

The Trevor Project: Nearly 1 in 5 transgender and nonbinary youth attempted suicide and LGBTQ youth of color reported higher rates than their white peers.

The Guardian: More than 50% of trans and non-binary youth in US …Dec 17, 2022 — The alarmingly high rates of depression, anxiety and suicide attempts are spread across liberal and conservative regions.

Those who constantly declare their happiness are often seeking validation and recognition from others, showing a lack of inner contentment.

Their actions and behavior often betray their true state of unhappiness, as they may reject or dismiss the gifts of happiness given to them by genuinely happy individuals.

In contrast, the Prophet Muhammad exemplified a different approach. He did not proclaim his happiness verbally, but let the radiant smile on his face express the inner light and abundance of his soul.

This inner light and wealth of happiness were so palpable that there was no doubt or need for him to vocalize it. The warmth emitted by his genuine happiness became a source of inspiration and joy for others, allowing them to experience and feel the same happiness within themselves.

In the world of fashion, there is a growing concern about how some designers who may struggle with their sexuality are using their platforms to exploit the industry.

This exploitation is not only reflected in the emptiness of the designs but also in how the clothes barely hang on to the body, prioritizing shock value over elegance and modesty.

There is a troubling trend on social media where shameless men and women expose themselves, disregarding the Islamic principles of modesty and decency that prohibits such behavior in public.

This display of nudity or the promotion of explicit content goes against the teachings of Islam. It contributes to the widespread **fitnah** (evil) that is increasingly becoming public rather than remaining private.

It is not just men who engage in these actions, as women have been affected by the Western world's exploitation of their bodies for decades.

Some feminists have reacted to this dilemma and are attempting to combat it, but their values often clash with religious beliefs and cannot resonate with those who hold faith as their guiding principle.

While these feminist efforts may create more chaos and division, they struggle to find acceptance within religious communities that adhere to their concepts of modesty, morality, and faith.

This necessitates an understanding that Muslims are living in a society where there may be opposing beliefs and practices to Islam.

In Islam, such behavior is not accepted, and there are consequences for those who deviate from the teachings. Muslims believe in the concept of accountability, where punishment for wrongdoing is believed to exist, both in this life and in the hereafter.

Hell is seen as a result for those who persist in behavior that is sinful in Islam. Therefore, it is important for Muslims to navigate this challenging climate while upholding their faith and promoting the teachings of Islam and repentance.

The worst part of this existence of different identities is the stigma and taboo surrounding them in all Abrahamic faiths. While many faiths are encouraged to show tolerance and understanding towards the ills perpetrated by society, there is often a reluctance to address or openly discuss these issues.

Islamophobia is a deeply rooted issue that unfairly targets and stereotypes Muslims, often based on misinformation and prejudice. However, it is important to distinguish between legitimate criticism and false accusations.

Addressing evil and promoting good should not be viewed as discrimination or prejudice, but as a call for justice and ethical behavior.

It is crucial to recognize that Islamic ideologies will not resemble the backward times and Islam is front and center matches every decade as the performance is pristine.

The followers of Islam may have flaws but constant efforts can be made towards progress.

While some individuals may choose to express their identities through different clothing styles, fashion statements should not be used to judge the entire religion. It is also important to note that certain practices or designs may not be permissible in Islam, as well as in other Abrahamic faiths.

It is essential to approach these matters with understanding and respect, rather than perpetuating stereotypes or making baseless assumptions about Islam and its followers.

However, Islam remains firm in its stance and does not accommodate behaviors that are not permitted by Allah.

When Allah prohibits something, it is for a reason, and the consequences of defying these prohibitions are greater than any temporary enjoyment that may be derived from such behavior.

In fact, indulging in activities that are forbidden by Islam often leads to feelings of guilt, emptiness, and ultimately, depression. The Islamic perspective on sexual conduct is rooted in the teachings of the Quran and Hadiths, which outline the boundaries and guidelines for intimate relationships.

Islam promotes the idea of a monogamous, lawful marriage between a man and a woman as the ideal setting for sexual expression.

Engaging in extramarital or promiscuous relationships, regardless of the sexual orientation, is considered sinful and detrimental to both physical and emotional well-being.

Islam places a strong emphasis on the preservation of health and the prevention of harm. This includes avoiding behaviors that may lead to the spread of diseases, such as engaging in sexual activities with multiple partners.

By adhering to the teachings of Islam, individuals are encouraged to prioritize their own well-being and the well-being of their community.

While technological advancements have brought many benefits to humanity, they have also given rise to new challenges. The misuse of technology for immoral purposes, such as promoting harmful sexual practices, can have devastating effects on society.

It is important to recognize the dangers of such experimentation and uphold the values and principles that protect the physical, emotional, and spiritual well-being of individuals.

In conclusion, Islam prohibits engaging in illicit behaviors that may spread diseases and emphasizes the importance of maintaining physical and emotional well-being within the boundaries set by Allah.

Islam promotes the concept of sexual purity and encourages individuals to engage in sexual relations solely within the framework of a monogamous marital relationship.

This promotes a sense of trust, loyalty, and commitment between spouses, fostering a healthy and harmonious family life. Islam acknowledges the existence of various gender identities but upholds the principle that sexual relations should occur within the confines of a lawful marriage between opposite genders.

Islam discusses the dynamics of heterosexual relationships within marriage and the context of sexual interactions.

It does not endorse or support bisexuality, transgender relationships, or same-sex relationships, regardless of societal norms or progressiveness.

The Quran remains unchanged despite societal changes, just as history has shown the consequences of disregarding divine warnings. Cities have been destroyed, new generations have emerged, and the wicked may thrive temporarily, but they will ultimately be held accountable by Allah.

However, it is vital to remember that all sexual activities, regardless of the individual's gender or sexual orientation, come with risks of disease transmission if adequate precautions are not taken.

Muslims acknowledge that giving a country or town the freedom to engage in illicit sex and immoral activities is a primary reason for its downfall.

The need for external intervention or the use of arms becomes unnecessary, as the country will eventually destroy itself from within.

The negative consequences of such behaviors are evident in the rising levels of unhappiness, mental health issues, and the increased reliance on psychiatric medication.

Suicide and depression have become ongoing issues in countries that deviate from the laws and teachings of the biblical text, acting in opposition to the divine laws of Allah. Studies on sexually transmitted infections consistently highlight the importance irrespective of one's gender and especially compromised sexual orientation.

Overall, Islam promotes responsible and consensual sexual behavior within the bounds of a lawful marriage, emphasizing the well-being and protection of individuals.

Prophet Muhammad's hadiths state that when individuals sin during the night or in seclusion, Allah shields them.

When a individual openly admits his transgressions and makes them appealing to others in this current time, this person lacks compassion. The act of inviting deviance is not impulsive, but a deliberate evil.

Allah will not forgive such a person unless they change and repent. This person not only exposes their sins but also exposes the sins of others. According to hadiths, they consider such a person a tyrant of evil and deem them unforgivable unless they change and repent.

In Islam, the duty of strength lies in safeguarding moral character, while those who boast about their sins are flawed, not those who sin and seek repentance. Those who expose sins of others end up promoting the worst.

Quran: Surah Imran: "Take on only as much as you can do of good deeds, for the best of deeds is that which is done consistently, even if it is little."

Constant delivery of truth and existence among the morally corrupt is not only necessary but also the most effective way of saving our identity as a society. In a world where deception and dishonesty prevail, it becomes imperative to identify and uphold truth without fear.

Islam takes the concept of hell, referred to as **Jahannam**, seriously. It is commonly believed that this place is intended for unbelievers and rebels, acting as a stark contrast to the clear and bright world that awaits justice.

In Islam, individuals will be held accountable for their actions in this temporary world, and they will be rewarded or punished accordingly in the afterlife.

In this world, believers or disbelievers can alter their identities and continue their journey of portraying help to humanity. However, it is important to acknowledge that genuine help stems from within oneself.

Help can manifest in various forms, and the inherent kindness that exists within every human being transcends religious beliefs.

When extending help, individuals do not check the belief system of others before offering help. Belief in Allah and adherence to the teachings of Islam do not negate the importance of providing help.

In fact, Allah has emphasized the exploration of truth as a vital aspect of humanity. While Islam has made its presence known in various avenues, there remains a significant number of individuals who are unaware of its true essence.

Therefore, it becomes the duty of Muslims to explain and educate others about the fundamentals of Islam as a monotheistic religion.

Quran: 3:12 Surah Imran: O Prophet! Tell the disbelievers, soon you will be empowered and driven to hell what an evil place to rest.

The identity crisis that some individuals face can be a challenging and transformative experience. It can cause them to question their beliefs and values, leading to a period of uncertainty and self-reflection.

During this time, it is important for others to offer support and understanding, as these individuals navigate their own personal journey.

Comments like **"I will see you in hell"** should never be taken lightly, as they can contribute to the emotional distress and confusion that someone in an identity crisis may already be experiencing.

In this world, each person's existence is unique, and they face their own individual trials and challenges.

While Allah has chosen and perfected Islam as a religion, it is important to respect that others may have different beliefs and practices. It does not diminish the importance of being compassionate towards all of humanity.

The question of why Allah did not perfect and choose Islam as the religion for the entire world is complex. As the creator, Allah has given humanity free will and the ability to choose their own path.

Islam teaches Muslims must submit to Allah's will and follow the teachings of the Quran, but this requires conviction and understanding.

If everyone were automatically Muslim, there would be no genuine submission or choice involved. Trials and challenges play a crucial role in shaping individuals and testing their faith.

These trials are necessary for personal growth and development. Islam encourages believers to spread the message of truth to all of humanity, but ultimately, it is up to each individual to accept or reject it.

In a world plagued by Islamophobia, it becomes even more important for Muslims to reach out, educate, and share knowledge in order to dispel misconceptions and build bridges of understanding.

The responsibility of Muslims extends beyond their own community; they are called to help and serve all of humanity, spreading light and truth wherever they go. By embracing this civic duty, Muslims can contribute to a more enlightened and harmonious world.

The prophet Muhammad was known for his compassion, wisdom, and dedication to justice. He tirelessly worked to uplift the oppressed and spread the message of unity, peace, and love. Muslims look up to him as an example of how to live a righteous life and emulate his teachings.

It is crucial to understand that accepting a Muslim name or converting to Islam does not erase one's lineage or disregard the importance of their previous identity. Rather, it represents a new identity rooted in faith and belief.

Those who are genuinely interested in learning and understanding the differences fully understood the intricate details and nuances of these concepts.

It does not diminish the importance of being compassionate towards all of humanity. However, it is also important to acknowledge that there is a fundamental difference in the belief of replacing the one and only creator and calling out to someone else.

Allah's mercy extends to every human being, regardless of their beliefs, and He answers prayers based on the sincerity and faith of the individual.

It is crucial to understand that accepting a Muslim name or converting to Islam does not erase one's lineage or disregard the importance of their previous identity. Rather, it represents a new identity rooted in faith and belief.

Those who are genuinely interested in learning and understanding the differences fully understood the intricate details and nuances of these concepts.

For those who view the world as a continuous arena of challenges and mishaps, it is important to recognize that even the worst of humans might transform into the best if Allah wills it.

The **sharing of knowledge** itself is considered an act of **charity in Islam and is rewarded by Allah.** It is unfortunate that some people label Muslims as extreme or terrorists, but the true delivery of Islam lies in the pursuit of truth and the spreading of peace and justice.

Haya, which translates to shame in Arabic, holds great significance in Islamic culture. It is an essential aspect of faith and is deeply rooted in the teachings of Islam.

Haya encompasses modesty, humility, and a sense of shame for committing sins or engaging in behaviors that go against the principles of Islam. It encourages individuals to not discuss their past sins or boast about negative aspects of their lives, such as engaging in relationships outside of marriage, excessive drinking, smoking cigarettes, or indulging in shisha (hookah).

This cultural norm is widespread among individuals who aim to progress and make personal improvements, as they strive to uphold their dignity and safeguard their reputation as Muslims or believers.

The idea of **Haya** shame self-protection fosters accountability, self-discipline, and reverence for oneself and others.

When individuals make mistakes, it is important to acknowledge that these errors do not account for regression or lack of discipline. Mistakes are part of being human and can serve as reminders for self-improvement.

However, it is crucial to note that repeated and intentional wrongdoing goes beyond mere mistakes. Continual engagement in evil actions reflects a habit rather than an occasional lapse.

This persistent evil behavior shows a loss of the mercy and forgiveness of Allah. Individuals need to recognize their faults, seek correction, and strive to break free from harmful habits to regain the blessings of divine mercy.

Writing about the people of Lot brings a somber atmosphere to a Muslim's perspective. His identity was compromised and false allegations were made to damage his reputation.

The Bible presents a different perspective on the event where Allah punished the people of Lot for engaging in same-sex relationships, which went against their established norms. The drawback of this philosophy is that Lot's relationship with his daughters, as portrayed in the Bible, represents a moral deterioration.

In the Bible, the prophets are held responsible for their shortcomings as they are accused and attributed with allegations.

Lot, a revered figure in Islam, dedicated the entire night to prayer and seeking forgiveness from Allah, refraining from any involvement with his daughters.

The Quran, which does not allocate evil to prophets. He did not impregnate his daughters, contradicting the claim that he slept with both his daughters, as depicted in the Bible.

It becomes difficult to respect prophets mentioned in the Bible when there are conflicting accounts.

Despite being Abrahamic faiths, the Bible and Quran have distinct yet similar stories, with the Quran providing corrected versions rather than copied ones from the Torah or the Bible.

Quran: Surah Araf: 7:81. You approach men lustfully in place of women. You are a people who exceed all bounds.

The narrative of Lot and the people of Sodom and Gomorrah appears in both the Quran and the Bible.

The Quran states that the people of Lot were involved in severe acts of homosexuality and wickedness, resulting in their destruction by Allah. Lot, a righteous prophet, begged his people to give up their sinful behavior and cautioned them about the coming punishment.

Lot offered his daughters in marriage to protect them unaware they were disguised angels from harm, hoping it would deter the people from their evil desires.

Despite his warning, the people ignored it and continued their wrongdoing.

Islam and Christianity both teach that same-sex relationships go against their scriptures. Lot's actions in the Quran do not depict any immoral behavior, except for his plea to punish these people.

The Bible mentions the incident with Lot's daughters, but it does not explicitly condemn Lot for his actions.

It is difficult to comprehend why Allah did not punish a prophet who crossed boundaries and had sexual relations with his daughters, as described in the Bible, after they got him drunk and became pregnant by him.

Bible: NIV: 19:30:38. One day the older daughter said to the younger, "Our father is old, and there is no man around here to give us children—as is the custom all over the earth.

Non-religious individuals would not approve of such actions, and such stories in the Bible raise doubts about whether the justice system aligns with biblical teachings.

The Quran considers these actions to be punishable. The biblical and Quranic figures of Prophet Lot are distinct individuals.

The fundamental idea conveyed in both religious texts is that homosexuality is a sin and violates the laws of Allah. There is no justification for blaming Lot according to the Bible's account.

The Western push for acceptance of same-sex relationships has extended beyond societal acceptance and has infiltrated various aspects of life, including schools, social media, and even pornography.

This widespread acceptance has caused significant turmoil in the moral compass of individuals who adhere to the ethical teachings of Abrahamic faiths, namely Judaism, Christianity, and Islam.

Many argue that the government's interference in matters of sexuality is a deliberate attempt to showcase independence and disregard the moral beliefs of those who hold strong religious convictions.

The open and vocal dialogue surrounding sexuality and LGBTQ+ rights has reached unprecedented levels, causing distress for individuals who believe that discussing such matters openly contradicts their religious teachings.

Unfortunately, expressing dissenting views on this issue is often labeled as prejudice, leaving no room for differing opinions or religious perspectives.

However, the portrayal of Islam and the promotion of Islamophobia are not seen as taboo, and most Western social media platforms depict Islam as being backward.

In reality, it is the Western world that has not progressed beyond primitive times, while Islam has clearly provided guidelines on the likes and dislikes of Allah, along with the concept of free will and its consequences.

The primitive immorality is revised and called progression is a reach for deceiving masses who don't understand the lucid concept and nature of evil.

Islam does not label or allocate blame to the prophets who came to teach, unlike the altered false presentations of their identities.

The concern lies not in the existence of diverse sexual orientations, but in the public and explicit display of sexuality, which can be found in both public spaces and pornographic content. This exposure can be confusing and influential for young minds, potentially leading to a state of moral confusion.

However, it is important to note that this dilemma is not prevalent in Muslim-majority countries, as their cultural and religious beliefs often prioritize modesty and privacy regarding matters of sexuality.

While corruption exists globally, it is not as prevalent or obvious in Muslim countries; however, it is still possible to find whatever you are looking for.

Islam is a faith of monotheism, followed by all prophets who have existed since the beginning of humanity.

It teaches that there is only one God, Allah, who is the creator and sustainer of the universe. Islam believes that throughout history, Allah sent many prophets to guide and deliver His message to humanity.

The concept presented in the Bible about Lot, the prophet who engaged in inappropriate acts with his daughters, raises questions about why Allah would choose him as a prophet and encourage homosexuality and incestuous relationships.

This seems illogical when considering the teachings of the Bible.

If prophets are depicted as being morally corrupt, then it would imply that homosexuality and incestuous relationships are acceptable and that open sexuality has become more normalized in these societies.

Atheists also argue that once an individual reaches adulthood, typically at 18, personal choices should be respected.

They further question why Lot was not punished according to the Bible, but in Islam, such actions would cause public execution. The legacy of actions persists as individuals interpret biblical text to create new stigmas that serve their own agendas.

This concept of submission to Allah is central to Islam, which is why followers of Islam are known as Muslims. Islam teaches that there is only one true God, Allah, and that all other deities or objects of worship are false idols.

These prophets acted as messengers of Allah, delivering His teachings and guiding people towards the path of righteousness. Each prophet, including Moses, Jesus, and Muhammad, demonstrated complete submission to the will of Allah and served as examples for their followers to emulate.

Thus, in an Islamic sense, they are considered Muslims. They rejected polytheism and emphasized the importance of worshiping and obeying Allah alone.

The term "Muslim" signifies one who surrenders their own will to the will of Allah and seeks to live under His teachings.

As we delve deeper into the historical differences between the two, introducing polytheistic beliefs contrasts with Jesus' monotheistic teachings. However, it is important to highlight that knowledge should not be perceived as a hindrance, but as a decisive factor in making informed decisions.

Understanding is a gift given upon individuals by Allah, and it holds great significance in a person's spiritual journey. Not everyone possesses the ability to comprehend the intricacies of complex ideas and concepts, which can often lead to doubts and confusion.

The importance of education in Islam cannot be overstated.

While the prophet Muhammad was unlettered, his lack of formal education did not hinder his ability to grasp and understand the truth.

Monotheistic concepts and submission to God have existed throughout human history, and they are indeed fundamental aspects of Islam.

The identity of the prophets was not based on legal documents or worldly titles, but on their mission to convey the word of Allah and guide people towards righteousness. They never claimed divinity for themselves, as they knew fully that they were human beings chosen by Allah to fulfill a specific role in guiding humanity towards the truth.

During the time of Constantine in Constantinople, Christianity underwent a significant transformation.

As the religion gained prominence and became the official religion of the Roman Empire, various theological debates and disagreements arose.

These debates often led to misrepresentations and misinterpretations of Jesus' identity. The merging of Christian beliefs with existing pagan practices and beliefs further contributed to the distortion of Jesus' true nature.

Jesus didn't explicitly mention Christianity during his earthly ministry. He prophesied his own ascension at birth, as Allah granted him speaking credentials per Quran.

The Quran does not believe in the resurrection of Jesus. According to Islamic teachings, Jesus was not crucified but was rather raised to heaven by God.

However, in Christian belief, the resurrection of Jesus plays a central role and is a confirmation of his divinity and the basis of the Christian faith.

Bible: ESV: John: 14:28. John 14:28: "If you really loved me, you would have been glad, because I am going to the Father; for the Father is greater and mightier than I am."

In John 14:28, Jesus expresses his desire to go to the Father without mentioning his crucifixion. He also acknowledges the Father's superiority over him. According to the Bible, Jesus was questioned about his identity as the Son of God or the evolving God.

Bible: ESV: Matthew 5:17, "Do not think that I have come to abolish the Law or the Prophets; I have not come to abolish them but to fulfill them."

Why didn't he reveal the truth to the Jews when he was sent to guide them and encourage them to follow the laws of Moses?

He came to uphold the law of Moses, not establish his own law. These examples pose a challenge to surpass.

If the entire belief of Christianity rests on the resurrection of a mortal prophet, then it becomes contradictory when that prophet denies it in the Bible by saying "the father is greater than I". How can a God who is evolving have a unique status?

There is only one god, and no one is co-equal unless we are referring to pagan gods in Hinduism, where they are all seen as equal but in different metaphors.

It is important to note that the Quran describes Mary and Jesus, recognizing them as important figures in Islam.

Mary, or Maryam in Arabic, is highly revered in the Quran and is considered a pious and chaste woman. Jesus, or Isa in Arabic, is also recognized as a prophet in Islam, but his divinity and resurrection are not accepted.

However, it is clear that Constantine's motivations were driven by political interests and a desire for control rather than purely religious conviction. Despite the efforts of the council, controversies and misunderstandings about Jesus' true identity continued to persist.

These misconceptions were fueled by various factors, including cultural influences, theological disagreements, and the spread of heretical teachings.

As a result, misconceptions and divergent interpretations of Jesus' identity have persisted throughout history, leading to the development of different Christian denominations and theological traditions.

The history of Jesus and the development of Christianity is a complex topic that has been subject to various interpretations and debates among scholars and religious followers.

While there have been instances of distortion and manipulation of Jesus' identity for personal gains throughout history, it is essential to differentiate between historical analysis and theological beliefs.

The representation of Jesus' identity in various churches has indeed been subject to distortion and alteration throughout history.

In Roman Catholic churches, Jesus is often depicted as having blond hair and blue eyes, while in other churches, he is portrayed as black or brown.

These depictions reinforce the idea of Jesus as a divine figure and to attract followers to the church. However, it is important to note that there is no authentic historical evidence regarding Jesus' physical appearance, as no photographs or detailed descriptions exist.

The continuous deception surrounding his identity is a significant observation, particularly considering the impact of religion on global chaos.

The Roman Empire played a significant role in shaping the Christian faith, but many aspects of this religion align with historical truth, and are at odds with the delivery of Jesus.

Despite the undeniable connection between the Torah and Christianity, the alterations and misrepresentations of Jesus' identity are a part of history that deserves to be recognized and discussed.

Jesus did not call himself Christian because Christianity as a distinct religion did not exist during his time. Jesus was born into a Jewish family and identified himself as a Jew.

However, after his ascension, not resurrection, by newly formed religious beliefs indoctrinated by the Roman Empire with alterations to Jesus' delivery and his teachings, it was not his followers that formed a separate movement that eventually became known as Christianity.

In the early centuries of Constantinople, the game changers were the intellectuals, theologians, and rulers who sought to shape the empire of Constantine.

They recognized the significance of Christianity as a unifying force and sought to mold it to appeal to a broader audience.

These individuals started a series of theological changes that deviated from the traditional teachings of Jesus and his followers thus compromising the identity of Jesus.

One of the most significant changes was the re-identification of Jesus.

He was seen as the divine Son of God, but not as the son of Mary, a human figure who embodied the qualities of compassion, love, wisdom and through him salvation was attained.

These alterations to the understanding of Jesus' identity had far-reaching consequences for the development of Christianity in Constantinople and beyond.

They skillfully manipulated the narratives and teachings of Jesus, merging elements of existing religions and incorporating their own ideologies.

They spun tales of miracles, divine messages, and a grand purpose for humanity's salvation.

The newly formed religion was carefully crafted to appeal to both the wealthy and the poor, promising solace, redemption, and a pathway to eternal bliss.

They propagated a distorted version of Jesus, presenting him as the long-awaited Messiah, the son of Mary, and the embodiment of divine power.

This fabricated identity was a potent tool for control, as it provided a central figure for the masses to venerate and obey.

The mix of truth and lies created a mesmerizing allure, captivating the minds and hearts of countless believers.

As history dimmed and the search for a supreme authority intensified, this new religion emerged, shaping the course of human spirituality for centuries to come.

The distortion of Jesus' identity and introducing paganistic reforms can be traced back to the early days of the Christian church, when it was influenced by various political and cultural factors.

The consolidation of power and greed among some leaders led to the adoption of certain practices and beliefs that deviated from the original teachings of Jesus.

Understanding this history is crucial in order to differentiate between the genuine message of Jesus and the distortions that arose.

It is important to note that not all Christians handle these distortions, as many follow the teachings of Jesus with sincerity and compassion.

Similarly, the Quran acknowledges the existence of the **"People of the Book,"** referring to Jews and Christians, while the Bible does not specifically mention the term "Christian."

These factors play a role in shaping the identities of individuals and communities in relation to their religious beliefs. The concept of Jesus' divinity manipulated the masses and led to different interpretations of his nature and relationship with God, resulting in various Christian doctrines, such as the belief in Jesus as the Son of God.

Quran: Surah Maryam: (19:33) Peace be upon me the day I was born and the day I will die, and the day I will be raised up alive."

It establishes a common understanding of Christianity. However, even after the council, controversies and misunderstandings persisted, leading to the perpetuation' true identity.

The roots of this distortion can be traced back to the inherent nature of humanity, which is prone to manipulation and deceit.

Throughout history, not only theology but even recorded historical events have been reshaped and altered to manipulate the masses.

However, amidst this sea of falsehoods, the Quran stands as a beacon of truth.

Quran: Surah Hijar: Verse 1 and 2. "Alif 'A', Lam 'L', Ra 'R'. These are the verses of the Book and (of) a clear Qur'an (that makes things manifest)."

"Often will those who disbelieved wish that they were Muslims."

Quran: Surah Hijar: Verse 3. "Leave them (alone) so that they may eat and enjoy themselves, and that they may be bemused by hope for they will soon know."

Continuous clarity is crucial in a world of misinformation. Clear and accurate understanding of truth and facts is crucial. Reliable information is paramount.

To address theological climate change effectively, we must avoid falsehoods and misinformation. Maintaining clarity ensures informed decisions, effective policies, and evidence-based actions. Through transparency and a culture of truth, we can confidently face the challenges of theological history.

It is crucial to note that the concept of Jesus as a prophet is primarily associated with monotheism, which emerged centuries after his time.

Additionally, the spread of Christianity into different regions and cultures also led to the incorporation of local customs and traditions into Christian practices.

For example, the celebration of Christmas on December 25th was influenced by pagan winter solstice celebrations. These adaptations and influences from pagan and cultic practices were not solely driven by monotheism, but rather reflect the complex and diverse history of Christianity.

The continuous effort to exemplify the truth necessitates the explanation of Jesus' role in both Islam and Christendom. In Islam, Jesus is regarded as a revered prophet, but not as the son of God or a deity himself. This distinction is crucial, as monotheism rejects the idea of Jesus evolving into a god or being born as the son of God.

The concept of monotheism is central to both religions and needs to be understood in order to navigate the complexities of their theological beliefs.

It is important to clarify that God, being a transcendent being, does not possess a physical image, and therefore the notion of creating man in His image is not applicable.

The concept of humans created in God's image raises questions about their complexity.

If humanity were the reflections of a divine being, we would all be the same or similar in demeanor. Humanity includes diverse characteristics, beliefs, and behaviors. This diversity challenges the notion of a single divine entity reflecting on all of us.

Evil and the human capacity for harm raise doubts about being created in God's image. If humans were made in God's image, they would be inherently good and incapable of evil actions.

Mortality separates humans from the divine. Humans, being mortal, have imperfections and limitations, contrasting with the divine essence attributed to God.

The concept of humans made in God's image doesn't explain human diversity, complexity, evil, and mortality.

Yet, we see different races, cultures, languages, and beliefs across the globe. This suggests that the concept of being made in God's image is more metaphorical than literal.

Being created in God's image can lead to a dangerous sense of superiority or entitlement.

If humans believe they are inherently divine, they may feel justified in imposing their beliefs and values onto others, leading to intolerance and conflict.

History is filled with examples of religious wars and persecution, all stemming from this misguided belief in our own godlike nature. Additionally, the concept of being created in God's image cannot address the complexities of human nature.

Humans are not only capable of noble acts of kindness and compassion but also of cruelty and selfishness.

Bible: NIV: Genesis: 1:27. So God created mankind in his own image, in the image of God he created them; male and female he created them.

If humanity were truly reflections of a perfect and moral deity, why do humans possess such contradictory traits?

This raises questions about the nature of God and our relationship to divinity. Examining Christian beliefs and biblical concepts.

In conclusion, while the idea of being created in the image of God may have been intended to instill moral values and guide human behavior, it falls short in explaining the realities of human existence and behaviors.

The diversity, imperfections, and complexities of humanity cannot be easily reconciled with this concept.

It is important for individuals to examine and question these beliefs critically in order to seek a deeper understanding of truth and morality.

First surah: In the Quran is Surah Fatiha.

Surah Fatiha, also known as the **Opening Chapter of the Quran,** serves as a concise and comprehensive summary of the fundamental principles and values upon which the Quran and Islam are based. Its explicit meaning is straightforward and leaves no room for doubt.

It emphasizes the importance of recognizing that the Quran is a guide that provides clear directions for leading a righteous and fulfilling life.

The **Surah** highlights the significance of adherence to divine laws, which encompass mercy, kindness, justice, and truth.

It conveys the message that passiveness has no place when justice is aligned with truth, urging believers to actively seek justice and stand up against injustice.

Surah Fatiha emphasizes the significance of repentance in strengthening the bond between a believer and their Creator. It serves as a reminder that sincere repentance solidifies and deepens one's connection with God, allowing for personal growth and spiritual development.

Overall, **Surah Fatiha** encapsulates the core principles of Islam, urging believers to seek guidance, follow divine laws, and strive for justice and repentance.

Quran: Surah Fatiha: In the name of Allah, the Entirely Merciful, the Especially Merciful. [All] praise is [due] to Allah, Lord of the worlds – The Entirely Merciful, the Especially Merciful, Sovereign of the Day of Recompense. It is You we worship and

You we ask for help. Guide us to the straight path—the path of those upon whom You have bestowed favor, not of those who have evoked [Your] anger or of those who are astray.

This **Surah** is recited in every **Salat**, and **Salat** cannot be performed without **Surah Fatiha**.

The angel Gabriel would visit Muhammad peace be upon him and recite verses he would then memorize and share with his companions. The precision and beauty of the Quran's language, its impeccable grammar and syntax, and the poetic nature of its verses are evidence of its divine origin.

Prophet Muhammad, peace be upon him, was indeed an unlettered prophet, meaning he did not receive a formal education or possess the ability to read and write.

However, Allah, in His infinite wisdom, bestowed upon him the extraordinary ability to transmit the divine revelations exactly as they were delivered to him.

This unique gift allowed Prophet Muhammad to convey the message of Allah accurately, with no distortion or alteration. It is important to note that most people, even those with exceptional memory or eloquence, would struggle to relay a conversation with the same precision and exactness as the prophets.

This exceptional measure of preserving the divine message in its original form was a manifestation of Allah's divine will and was specifically designed for delivering the Quran to humanity.

The Quran, therefore, stands as a remarkable testament to the miraculous nature of Prophet Muhammad's prophethood and the divine preservation of the last revelation.

Its eloquence and coherence have astounded scholars throughout history, and its message continues to resonate with millions of people around the world.

The Quran's status as a divine revelation, rather than a human creation, is a fundamental belief in Islam and contributes to the deep respect and veneration Muslims have for this sacred text.

The smallest surah of the Quran is Al-Kawthar.

In the hot Arabian desert, the smallest Surah of the Quran presented a challenge to the poetic, literary Arabs. The Arabs showcased their precise literary prowess by devoting extensive time to reading and writing.

The heightened precision of the Quran led people to falsely label Prophet Muhammad as a madman, possessed, or magician.

They were convinced that the smallest Surahs flawless precision was evidence of Allah's craftsmanship.

The beautiful melody and recitation of the Quran have moved non-Muslims have been moved to tears, even without understanding the language. Many Muslims have the skill of fluent Arabic reading, leading to a strong Quranic appreciation.

Even if all the Qurans were burned, the ability to reproduce them persists because of the quantum realm of knowledge surpassing ignorance.

Islam means submission to the will of Allah.

Quran: Surah Baqarah: 2.269. Allah grants wisdom to whoever He wills. And whoever is granted wisdom is certainly blessed with a great privilege. But none will be mindful ˈof thisˈ except people of reason.

Allah, Elohim, Allah-ha, and Bhagwan are all names for an unseen entity transcending human perception. Only one God runs this world, and the next, which is why he is known as the owner of the "worlds". **Beyond human comprehension, Allah is transcendent.**

Allah is above the material realm. Beyond time, space, and physical attributes, Allah exists. He is an all-powerful and all-knowing being beyond human comprehension. Muslims gain knowledge of Allah's attributes through the Quran.

Surah Nur describes him as a light, which is the closest description until meeting Allah on judgment day. If he walked the earth as a human, he is not Allah.

Quran: Surah Nur: 24;35. Allah is the Light of the heavens and the earth. The example of His light is like a niche within which is a lamp, the lamp is within glass, the glass as if it were a pearly white star lit from the oil of a blessed olive tree, neither of the east nor the west, whose oil would almost glow even if untouched by fire. Light upon light. Allah guides to His light whom He wills. And Allah presents examples for the people, and Allah is knowing of all things.

In Islamic belief after death; On this day, Allah will resurrect all individuals and hold them accountable for their actions in their earthly life.

The concept of resurrection and judgment of each individual that will rise on day of judgement is central to Islamic beliefs, as it determines the eternal fate of each person. Islam rejects the idea of reincarnation, as it contradicts the belief in a single, permanent death followed by resurrection.

Instead, the focus is on the individual's actions and deeds in this life, which will determine their place in the afterlife. Accounting holds a central place in the Islamic faith. In the Day of Judgment as per the Quran, each person will face the consequences of their deeds in this life.

Allah, the ultimate judge, conducts accounting that is both swift and fair, as expected.

Muslims hold the belief that the soul lives in a state of waiting, known as **Barzakh,** which signifies separation from the physical world, a concept that differs from some Christian beliefs.

Unlike Islamic beliefs, which judge the afterlife based on actions, Christians view death as a passage to heaven.

Islam emphasizes individual actions rather than reliance on others, and belief in one God and the last prophet, Muhammad, as well as belief in all prophets sent by Allah in Abrahamic religions.

The concepts found in the Bible were introduced well after Jesus' ascent. Understanding belief involves truth, not changes. Both divine and human elements exist within the Bible.

The Christian faith asserts that Jesus, by giving up his life on the cross, triumphed over sin and death, granting salvation to those who have faith in him. Christians see physical death as a transition to the eternal realm, despite its undeniable existence.

The belief is that individuals who live righteously and have faith in Christ will receive eternal life in Heaven, with God. Islam, which is based on monotheism, does not believe in giving Jesus the prophet and Messiah authority over sin and judgment. The Jesus in Islam differs from the Jesus in Christianity.

Allah will evaluate each person on this day, considering their actions and adherence to Islam. One's eternal fate, paradise or hell, depends on the judgment's outcome.

The belief in a fair and comprehensive accounting system reminds Muslims to fulfill their obligations to Allah and other people, and to lead righteous lives.

The contrasting beliefs of Christianity and Islam are evident in their defining voices, with Jesus serving as a figure of reverence for both faiths.

Explaining differences is crucial for understanding because unanswered questions demand explanations.

Humanity doesn't discriminate based on faith, but those who want to understand can explore theological differences. Considering the various ways dead bodies can be disposed of; some may raise doubts about the resurrection of bodies on judgment day.

However, if Allah can create life from a mere sperm and cells, it is not a challenge for Allah to resurrect the dead. Every person in the world has a purpose and will be answerable to their creator.

Islam represents the concept of **Barzakh,** an intermediate state between death and resurrection, where the soul remains until the Day of judgment.

Islam rejects the belief that Jesus exists in three bodies because it contradicts the fundamental principle of **Tawhid,** which is the belief in the oneness of God. In Islamic theology, Jesus (known as Isa in Arabic) is a prophet and a messenger of God, not divine.

Islam breeds only monotheism, that God is absolutely one and has no partners or associates.

Quran: Surah al-Baqarah: 2:256. Let there be no compulsion in religion, for the truth stands out clearly from falsehood. So, whoever renounces false gods and believes in Allah has certainly grasped the firmest, unfailing hand-hold. And Allah is All-Hearing, All-Knowing.

The Islamic tradition places great emphasis on seeking knowledge and gaining education.

The Quran itself encourages Muslims to seek knowledge and to reflect upon the signs of God in the universe. Islamic history is filled with examples of scholars and thinkers who have made significant contributions to various fields of knowledge, such as philosophy, science, mathematics, and literature.

Muslims have established renowned educational institutions, libraries, and centers of learning throughout history, fostering an environment conducive to intellectual growth and development.

While formal education is highly valued in society, it is also acknowledged that learning can take place in various settings and through different means.

Education can be formal or self-research, but Muslims have shared knowledge instead of keeping it secret, impacting the world through learning and sharing.

Fez, Morocco, in 859. This university, known as the University of Al Quaraouiyine, is considered to be the oldest existing degree-granting university in the world. Fatima Fihri, a devout Muslim woman, founded the university, intending to educate both men and women.

The establishment of this university marked a significant milestone in the history of education and played a crucial role in the spread of knowledge and learning throughout the Muslim world.

The university's curriculum focused on various subjects such as Islamic studies, theology, mathematics, and astronomy, attracting scholars from different parts of the world.

The Introduction of this formal educational institution by Fatima Fihri laid the foundation for future developments in education and continues to be a symbol of the rich intellectual heritage of the Muslim civilization. The sharing of its achievements and invitations to the world.

There are individuals who spend their entire lives in pursuit of truth, patiently waiting for moments of enlightenment and progression. It is during these opportune moments that the truth reveals itself, calling out to those who seek the path of Islam.

Quran: Surah Baqarah: 2.270. Whatever charities you give or vows you make are surely known to Allah. And the wrongdoers will have no helpers. God knows what you contribute or what you vow.

The act of sharing knowledge in Islam is regarded as charity, specifically called **Sadaqah.**

Allah rewards all good deeds in Islam, including sharing knowledge. The rewards for such acts are multiplied as they affect countless individuals. Sharing knowledge in Islam is a means of seeking blessings and closeness to the Creator.

A Muslim's word is rooted in their character, but valuing one's word is not limited to Muslims. Truth-seekers and those with moral values also prioritize their word. The concept of keeping one's word is deeply ingrained in Islam and is a measure of one's character and reliability

Allah, in the Quran, has assured that He will protect His last revelation, the Quran, from any alterations. Allah, who knows His creation's capabilities, is known for showing mercy and forgiveness to those who seek the truth.

CHAPTER 3
THE GOAL IS NOT SURVIVAL.

The concept of strength encompasses both masculine and feminine energies in equal measure.

It embodies the harmonious balance between yin and yang. True strength not only requires the ability to tame and pacify unruly forces, but also causes deep self-awareness. To hand over your rights to something greater and more formidable than yourself, it is essential to have unwavering faith in your own inner power.

While strength is occasionally linked to physical prowess, it encompasses various forms.

Interestingly, the mightiest individuals can also exhibit the utmost gentleness. So, where do your personal strengths reside? Is up to the faith and integrity one holds.

Survival as a goal can be necessary in dire circumstances, such as when faced with a life-threatening situation or extreme adversity. However, it is important to recognize that merely surviving is not enough to create meaningful change or progress.

Merely focusing on survival without seeking the truth or understanding the underlying causes of the challenges we face can lead to a stagnant existence.

Quran: Surah Anam: 6:114"it is He Who has sent down unto you the Book (the Qur'an), explained in detail"

The Quran, which was revealed to Prophet Muhammad, took 23 years to be completed.

At 40, he was given prophethood after spending 23 years completing the Quran. He passed away at 63. With the transient nature of this world, his work was completed, and it was inevitable for him to return.

Generations have meticulously preserved and passed down the text of the Quran, ensuring that its script remains unchanged, with no alterations or modifications.

This preservation is a miraculous aspect of the Quran, as it has remained unchanged for over 14 centuries. The teachings of Islam from the Quran are perennial and applicable in all times and places. Islam remains constant and offers guidance to its followers.

Survival in the altered text refers to adapting and evolving with the changing trends and societal norms. However, Islam is not just a trend or a survival strategy; it is a comprehensive way of life based on the teachings of the **Quran** and the example set by the **Prophet Muhammad (peace be upon him).**

Islam offers a sense of certainty and simplicity to its followers, guiding them in every aspect of life. It emphasizes the importance of adhering to the truth and staying steadfast in the face of challenges.

The concept of survival, as understood by those who don't comprehend the true essence of Islam, may involve compromising one's principles or conforming to societal pressures. However, Islam does not condone such behavior.

In contrast to the constantly changing and often regressive trends of society, Islam remains steadfast in its values and principles.

It does not indulge in the rhetoric of moral relativism or conform to the whims and fancies of the times. Instead, Islam stands alone as a beacon of truth, offering guidance and solace to those who seek it.

While some regions may claim to be progressive, they may actually revert to practices and beliefs that are rooted in their pagan past.

Islam remains firm in its teachings, unchanged by the fluctuations of societal norms. It does not condone or engage in acts that go against its principles of justice, compassion, and righteousness.

In a world where truth is often distorted and values are compromised,

Islam stands as a refuge for those seeking absolute truth and guidance. It is not swayed by the ever-changing tides of society, but offers a timeless and unwavering path towards righteousness.

Islam's goal is to establish truth and justice, ensuring that it will be the only one standing in its purest form. True growth and transformation occur when we go beyond mere survival and actively seek the truth, confront our circumstances, and strive for improvement.

Embracing a proactive approach unlocks our full potential for development.

Abrahamic faiths emphasize belief in a single, all-powerful, and supreme being. God's nature transcends human understanding, encompassing attributes like all-knowing, all-present, and all-powerful. To fall short of this belief held by all prophets of Allah is to fall short of the Abrahamic faiths.

The story of Mary, the mother of Jesus, is one of devotion and faith. When she was given to the temple by her mother, it was a testament to her commitment to fulfilling her vow to Allah.

Despite her old age, she remained steadfast in her belief that Allah would grant her a child. And indeed, Allah answered her prayers and blessed her with Mary

Quran: Surah Imran verse 3. The wife of Imran said, "My Lord, I have vowed to You what is in my womb, dedicated, so accept from me; You are the Hearer and Knower.

Allah did not punish this family or make the salvation of others dependent on Jesus. This notion goes against the principles of justice and fairness that Allah upholds.

The concept of crucifixion highlights the punishment faced by the family of Imran. Initially, Mary endured humiliation from the Jews because of her virgin birth, which tarnished her character.

However, her steadfast belief in her virtuous nature allowed her to survive.

Allah permitted the crucifixion because of the scriptures being altered for selfish reasons. This concept is impossible to grasp. The concept could lead people to believe Allah is unjust, by punishing those who do good and rewarding evil, but this is absolutely untrue.

In fact, Allah rewards the good, as evidenced by the blessings given upon the family of Imran.

Therefore, that the crucifixion was carried out for the sake of the Jews and Romans to witness his humiliation holds no valid meaning. The Quran completely denies this episode, and it is not the Muslims, but Allah himself, who asserts the unchangeable nature of the Quran.

It was not Jesus is factual for Muslims per Quran.

The Quran stresses individual accountability for actions, with judgment based on those actions. Holding one person accountable for the wrongdoings of others is unjust.

The Quran emphasizes Allah's special provisions and care for Mary. She had a comfortable life and food whenever she wanted. Her devoted worship of Allah brought her bliss, not punishment.

If Allah used the son of a devout woman as a means of salvation for others, but allowed the non-believers to harm him, it would be unjust to the mother who faithfully served Allah and her family, who followed their faith devotedly.

In Islam, Allah ensured the protection of Jesus' rights and called him to Himself while he was still alive, not dead. The Quran does not state that he died or bore the sins of others, nor does it suggest that he can take on the sins of others for salvation through his death. It should be observed that the concepts are different.

Allah is a fair and just God, who rewards those who do good and benefit others.

The divergence between Christianity and Islam lies in the necessity of Jesus' death for human sins. In Islam, salvation comes from repentance, good deeds, and submission to Allah. Allah's will is carried out. Sacrificing one person isn't necessary for atonement in Islam.

Overall, the Quran presents a clear and consistent message about Jesus and his role as a prophet. Like the other prophets before him, he delivered the same message of monotheism and devotion to Allah.

Islam rejects the notion of Jesus being punished for the sins of humanity.

By delving deeply into these religious texts and seeking guidance from religious authorities, believers can gain a better understanding of their creator's nature and the distinction between humans and the divine.

If the goal in life is solely survival, then a human can survive without researching the truth of the Abrahamic faiths, which have been consistent since the time of Adam and Eve, according to religious texts.

Survival, in this context, refers to meeting one's basic physical needs for sustenance, shelter, and safety. However, it is important to note that humans are not solely driven by the goal of survival.

They possess intellectual curiosity, a desire for meaning and purpose, and a quest for understanding the world around them.

For many individuals, exploring religious beliefs and seeking truth in the Abrahamic faiths can provide guidance, moral values, a sense of community, and a deeper understanding of the human experience.

While survival may be a fundamental goal, humans often strive for more than mere existence, and positing truth and spiritual fulfillment is a significant aspect of many people's lives.

Religion can provide a sense of purpose in life and a feeling of connection to a larger community. It can also give individuals a sense of comfort and hope in times of difficulty.

Truth is a core principle in Islam. Muslims are encouraged to maintain truth in beliefs and actions.

The religion emphasizes the importance of truth for spiritual growth and a moral society. Islam opposes survival mode and manipulation for personal gain.

It encourages honesty, integrity, and transparency. Muslims are encouraged to seek knowledge, question assumptions, and analyze information critically for the truth.

This includes addressing uncomfortable truths and acknowledging the consequences of one's actions.

Neglecting the truth while embracing one's own ideologies is frowned upon in Islam.

Islam seeks a community grounded in truth, justice, and compassion. Truth leads to personal growth, spiritual fulfillment, and a harmonious society.

Islam did not stand still once it came gushing as a force of water; it spread throughout the world from the scorching desert of the Arabian Peninsula.

The true meaning of Islam goes beyond mere survival or achieving material success without faith. This faith transforms and motivates individuals to excel and surpass their limits. Islam encourages followers to seek knowledge, develop skills, and contribute meaningfully to society.

Islam, a religion that originated in the 7th century in the Arabian Peninsula, highlights compassion, justice, and righteousness as its core values. The teachings of Islam emphasize the importance of showing empathy and kindness towards others, especially the less fortunate.

It advocates for fair treatment and equal rights for all individuals, regardless of their social status, gender, or ethnicity. Islam encourages believers to strive for righteousness in their actions and to uphold the principles of honesty, integrity, and moral uprightness.

The religion challenged oppressive systems and sought to bring about social justice by promoting equality and fairness. Through its teachings, Islam has inspired countless individuals to work towards creating a more just and compassionate society.

During the era of segregation, many minorities faced harsh treatment and discrimination based on their race.

Seeking solace and acceptance, some individuals turned to Islam, as it provided an inclusive and egalitarian environment where people of all races and colors were welcomed.

In contrast to the prevailing notions of racial superiority and the justification of segregation, Islam emphasized the equality of all individuals, regardless of their race or background.

Mosques became spaces of togetherness, where people of different colors and races could come together to worship and support one another.

This acceptance and unity offered by Islam provided a refuge for those who were marginalized and excluded by society.

While the term "racism" may not have been used in that specific historical context, the principles of equality and acceptance promoted by Islam challenged the very foundations of segregation and served as a powerful tool against racial discrimination.

Wikipedia: Racial segregation of churches in the United States is a pattern of Christian churches maintaining segregated congregations based on race. As of 2001, as many as 87% of Christian churches in the United States were completely made up of only white or African-American parishioners.

The most oppressed black race in Western societies sought Islam, because of Christianity's discrimination against them, is a complex and multifaceted issue.

While some individuals from African backgrounds may have found solace in Islam because of its emphasis on equality and the absence of racial distinctions, it is important to recognize that the reasons for converting to Islam are varied and personal.

Historically, the transatlantic subordinate trade and the subsequent enslavement of Africans in America had a profound impact on the racial dynamics in Western societies.

European and Anglo-Saxon Christianity often served as a tool for justifying and perpetuating slavery. Despite slavery being widespread in pre-Islamic times, slaves had certain rights under Islamic law.

This association between Christianity and the oppression of black people undoubtedly influenced some individuals to seek alternative religious identities, such as Islam.

Many Christian communities actively promote racial equality and social justice. The black churches are still growing, suggesting that segregation is still ongoing.

Therefore, while some black individuals in Western societies may have turned to Islam as a response to discrimination within Christianity, it is essential to approach this topic with nuance and avoid generalizations.

A wide range of factors shapes the experiences and choices of individuals within any religious group, and it is important to respect and acknowledge this diversity.

Washington Post: Aug 29, 2023 — A new survey from Pew Research reveals once again how deeply divided religious Americans are on matters of race.

USA Today: June 17, 2023 — New poll shows racial issues divide Americans. But people of faith can help unite us. · Religion has been a baton of oppression in America, but...

Wikipedia: However, segregated black churches have also become a positive space for community issues like civil rights, in addition to offering a respite for black...

During the era of segregation in the Western lands, many black individuals sought solace and liberation by embracing Islam.

This trend was observed in both the olden days and continues to the present times. The appeal of Islam to black individuals experiencing discrimination and segregation can be attributed to several factors.

First, Islam emphasizes the equality and brotherhood of all believers, regardless of their race or ethnicity. This message resonated deeply with those seeking an escape from the oppressive systems of racial segregation.

Second, Islam provided a sense of community and support for black individuals, offering a space where they could find acceptance and solidarity. The teachings of Islam encouraged self-respect, self-reliance, and self-improvement, empowering black individuals to challenge the discriminatory norms prevalent in society.

Overall, the adoption of Islam by many blacks during times of segregation served as a means of resistance and a pathway towards freedom and equality.

In Islam, the concept of unity and equality among believers is deeply ingrained. This is reflected in the design and functioning of mosques worldwide.

Regardless of race, color, or social status, Muslims gather in mosques to worship together, demonstrating the fundamental principle of equality in Islam. Mosques are sacred spaces where individuals come together to pray, learn, and foster a sense of community.

The absence of color-coded divisions within mosques emphasizes the universality of Islam and the importance of unity among its followers.

This inclusive approach has attracted individuals from diverse backgrounds, including the black community, who have found solace and acceptance in the Islamic faith.

Islam promotes a belief in spiritual and moral values rather than focusing on material success or discrimination based on race or color.

Abu Bakr, being a close companion of the Prophet Muhammad and a man of great wealth, was determined to secure Bilal's freedom at any cost. He knew that Bilal's faith and resilience were invaluable, and he couldn't bear to see him suffer under the cruelty of Umayyah.

Despite Umayyah's sarcastic remark, Abu Bakr remained steadfast in his resolve and offered an even larger sum of money to ensure Bilal's independence.

Bilal was a young black man with solid faith in his creator. He understood the importance of standing up for justice and equality, regardless of one's race or social status. Abu Bakr's unwavering determination eventually convinced Umayyah to reluctantly sell Bilal, granting him the freedom he so desperately deserved.

This act of compassion and solidarity showcased Abu Bakr's character as a righteous and compassionate leader within the early Muslim community.

Despite obstacles, Abu Bakr persisted in his efforts to free Bilal and approached to negotiate their release. Using his wealth, he secured the freedom of Bilal and many others.

This act of compassion and solidarity showed the Islamic principles of justice and equality, as Abu Bakr recognized the inherent dignity of all individuals, regardless of their social status. Bilal, a black man of African descent, faced discrimination and persecution in pre-Islamic Arabia. However, his faith as a Muslim was not a hindrance to Abu Bakr's decision to rescue him.

Despite enduring such immense suffering, Bilal remained steadfast and continued to proclaim his faith, repeating the word **"Ahad"** (meaning "One") as a testament to his unwavering devotion to Allah. This incident showcases Bilal's incredible resilience and serves as a powerful example of faith under persecution in the early days of Islam.

His oppressors, hoping to break his spirit, subjected him to unimaginable pain, yet Bilal's love for his faith and his trust in Allah gave him the strength to endure.

He understood that protecting his faith meant protecting the very essence of his existence, and he refused to compromise his beliefs, even if it meant sacrificing his own life.

Bilal's unwavering dedication to his faith serves as an inspiration to believers throughout history, reminding them that true faith requires a willingness to face persecution and adversity with courage and conviction.

In the story of Bilal, a genuine believer in Allah, he faced many trials and challenges. Despite the difficulties he faced, Bilal never wavered in his faith and continuously relied on Allah for guidance and support.

This unwavering trust and reliance on Allah's will, allowed Bilal to remain patient and steadfast in the face of adversity. Ultimately, Allah's intervention came, and Bilal received the help he needed, proving once again the perfect timing and choice of helpers that are beyond human comprehension.

Mentioning such stories can restore lost faith.

This act exemplified the Islamic principle of equality, which transcends racial or ethnic differences. Islam teaches that all individuals, regardless of their background, are equal in the sight of Allah and should be treated with justice and respect.

Abu Bakr's rescue of Bilal showcased the genuine spirit of Islam, where humanity and fairness take precedence over racial or color distinctions. Islam provides a threshold for those who seek to uphold and promote equality among all people.

He was the companion of Prophet Muhammad, known for his unwavering loyalty and commitment to the teachings of Islam.

He would often use his wealth to support and uplift the marginalized in society, advocating for justice and equality. Abu Bakr's steadfast support of Prophet Muhammad during times of persecution and hardship showcased his deep belief in the principles of compassion and solidarity.

He understood that it was not enough to merely witness oppression; action was required to bring about positive change and alleviate the suffering of others Abu Bakr's example serves as a reminder that it is our innate nature to assist and uplift one another, standing against injustice and promoting a society built on empathy and mutual support.

The liberation of Bilal served as a significant milestone in the prior history of Islam, challenging the prevailing notion of slavery and highlighting the values of freedom and human rights.

It set a powerful precedent for the abolition of slavery in later centuries, inspiring many Muslims to strive for a more equitable society.

Bilal ibn Rabah al-Habashi was born into slavery in Mecca, but he found freedom and liberation through his unwavering belief in Islam. Despite facing persecution and torture for his faith, Bilal remained steadfast and refused to renounce his beliefs.

He became a symbol of resilience and stood as a shining example of the values of equality and justice in Islam.

Bilal's loyalty to Prophet Muhammad was unwavering, and he played a crucial role in the early years of Islam.

He was chosen by the Prophet himself to be the first muazzin, tasked with calling the Adhan, the Islamic call to prayer. Bilal's beautiful voice echoed through the streets of Mecca, inviting people to submit to the will of Allah and embrace the teachings of Islam.

His significance as the first person of known African ancestry to become a Muslim cannot be understated.

In a time when racial prejudice and discrimination were prevalent, Bilal shattered stereotypes and proved that Islam transcends racial and social barriers.

He demonstrated that true faith and devotion are not contingent upon one's background or ethnicity but are rooted in the purity of one's heart.

Bilal's profound lesson of the freedom and supremacy of conscience resonates across time and religions. He taught that true freedom lies in staying true to one's beliefs and principles, even in the face of adversity.

Bilal's unwavering commitment to his faith serves as an inspiration for people of all ages and religions, reminding them of the importance of standing up for what is right, regardless of the consequences.

His legacy lives on, not only in the annals of Islamic history but also in the hearts of those who admire his courage and unwavering faith. Bilal's story serves as a reminder that true greatness is not measured by wealth or power but by the strength of one's convictions and the impact they have on the world.

Another reason for not abolishing slavery outright in the Quran may be attributed to the gradual nature of societal change.

The Quran acknowledges the existence of slavery but encourages believers to treat their slaves with kindness and fairness. Later it was removed as every episode is a test for those who endure hardships and for those who help those in need of help.

It emphasizes the importance of freeing slaves as an act of righteousness, but it does not impose an immediate and total abolition. This approach can be seen as a practical step towards societal transformation, as sudden abolition could have led to economic instability and social unrest.

There were several reasons the idol worshipers in Makkah vehemently opposed the spread of Islam, despite the good intentions of the Muslims. First, the idol worshipers saw their religious beliefs and practices threatened by the message of the Oneness of Allah.

Islam challenged the prevalent polytheistic beliefs and exposed the falsehood of idol worship, which posed a direct threat to their religious and social order.

Second, the idol worshipers held a significant economic interest in the polytheistic practices. Makkah was a thriving center of trade, and the idol worshipers benefited from the pilgrims who visited the city to worship the idols.

The spread of Islam threatened the lucrative business associated with idol worship, as it called for monotheism and discouraged the worship of idols, leading to a decline in the income of the idolaters.

The leaders of Makkah, who were primarily from the Quraysh tribe, held a position of power and authority, which was closely tied to the prevailing polytheistic system.

Embracing Islam meant challenging their authority and traditional power structures. Therefore, they felt threatened by the message of Islam and sought to suppress its followers to maintain their control and influence over the people.

Tribal and societal pressures influenced the idol worshipers. The acceptance of Islam meant breaking away from the tribal customs and traditions that were deeply ingrained in their society. This change was a betrayal of their ancestral beliefs and a threat to their social fabric.

The idolaters saw the spread of Islam as a direct challenge to their beliefs, practices, and societal order, leading them to resort to persecution and suppression of the Muslims. The Quran's teachings aimed to gradually shift attitudes towards slavery, promoting compassion and ultimately paving the way for its eventual eradication.

Islam is a factual faith that attracts a diverse range of followers, including many minorities and converts who have not found acceptance or belonging in other religious institutions.

One of the reasons why these individuals are drawn to Islam is its emphasis on equality and the absence of a hierarchical structure within the mosque.

Unlike some other religions that have dignitaries or clergy with elevated status, Islam promotes a sense of egalitarianism where all individuals, regardless of their background or social standing, are considered equal in the eyes of God.

This notion of equality within the mosque creates a welcoming and inclusive atmosphere that resonates with those who have felt marginalized or excluded in other religious settings.

Islam recognizes that men and women have distinct roles and responsibilities based on their biological and psychological differences. However, this does not imply that one gender is superior or has more authority over the other.

Some interpretations of certain biblical texts have been used to justify the oppression of women. For instance, passages in the Bible state that women should not have authority over men.

However, it is crucial to approach religious texts with a nuanced understanding, considering historical context, cultural factors, and different interpretations

Bible: 1 Timothy 2;12. I do not permit a woman to teach or to assume authority over a man; she must be quiet.

If the Bible is clear that women must not have authority over men, then perhaps women running for office who identify as Christian should carefully study and understand the teachings of the Bible. In doing so, they may need to reconcile their beliefs and actions with the scripture.

Some may argue that these women should either denounce their faith in Christianity if they find conflict between their political ambitions and biblical teachings, or they may question whether certain passages have been altered or misinterpreted.

Ultimately, it is up to individuals to interpret the Bible and determine how it aligns with their personal convictions and beliefs.

It is important to note that interpretations and practices within any religion can vary among individuals and communities. While some may adhere strictly to certain interpretations, others may have more inclusive or progressive beliefs.

The Bible contains many passages that are often interpreted as placing women in a subordinate position to men

Bible: Ephesians 5:22-24: "Wives, submit yourselves to your own husbands as you do to the Lord. For the husband is the head of the wife as Christ is the head of the church."

These verses mentioned in the Bible have had a significant influence on the changing and evolving world, especially in societies where women are traditionally subordinate to men. In this current climate, women are fighting for their rights and striving to gain power and equality.

The Bible and the Quran are both religious texts that have been influential in shaping the beliefs and practices of their respective faiths.

However, the Bible has undergone different processes of interpretation and adaptation in response to the changing needs and values of humanity.

The Bible, composed of multiple books written by different authors over centuries, has indeed experienced various changes and reforms.

Throughout history, translators, interpreters, and editors have made different translations, interpretations, and revisions to make the teachings of the Bible more accessible and relevant to different societies.

The changes reflect the evolving understanding of the Bible's message in response to history.

The Quran is the eternal and unchanging word of Allah, revealed to the Prophet Muhammad through the angel Gabriel. It is the ultimate source of guidance and perfection, requiring no alteration or modification.

The Quran is a timeless and universal guide for all aspects of life, as its teachings are to be directly from Allah and, therefore, flawless. The Muslims may have imperfections, but the Quran remains unblemished, unaltered, and unchangeable in any circumstances. Whether one follows, it is solely up to the individual believers.

The belief in the perfection and immutability of the Quran stems from the conviction that Allah, being all-knowing and all-wise, is incapable of making any mistakes or flaws in his divine revelations.

Therefore, the Quran is the ultimate and unchangeable source of truth and guidance for Muslims.

It is important to acknowledge that in certain Muslim-majority countries, many women have held offices and even ruled nations. This is not an exaggeration, but rather a testament to the truth that women can overcome societal limitations and achieve greatness.

Nevertheless, many women choose to move forward and challenge these notions, disregarding the biblical teachings that place them in an inferior position. They advocate for gender equality and work towards creating a more inclusive and just society.

In the same token, it is important to recognize that there are women who do not read the Bible and yet still hold misconceptions about Muslim women, considering them to be backward.

However, it is crucial to understand that Islam actually grants Muslim women rights and respect that are unparalleled in comparison to other faiths.

These rights, bestowed upon women by Allah, were not obtained through a fight for equal rights, as women in America did. Islam recognizes the inherent value and dignity of women, granting them rights such as the right to education, the right to own and inherit property, the right to choose their spouse, and the right to engage in business and participate in society.

It is essential to dispel the notion that Muslim women are oppressed or backward, as they are beneficiaries of a faith that actively promotes their rights and dignifies their existence.

Islamophobia creates an environment where individuals fighting for their rights often face more hurdles.

Women in feminist areas which preach equality are still advocating for fairer wages and treatment. They also address common issues like sexual harassment in the workplace, which often forces them to keep these incidents hidden to further their careers.

This unjust reality is later revealed through lawsuits and exposure on social media when these brave individuals finally come forward. While it is important to note that not all situations adhere to these parameters, numerous cases have demonstrated the existence and recurrence of such struggles.

The fight for women's rights in America was indeed a long and arduous battle that spanned several decades. Women faced many challenges and barriers in their quest for equality, and it is important to understand the complexities of these struggles.

While some men played a role in perpetuating gender inequalities, it is crucial to recognize that individuals often used the Bible as a tool to justify and reinforce traditional gender roles and male authority.

Many religious teachings interpreted passages in the Bible as giving man's dominion over women, which further entrenched societal norms and hindered progress towards gender equality.

The fight for women's rights in America involved challenging both societal norms and religious beliefs, ultimately leading to significant advancements in women's equality.

The region witnessed incidents that extended beyond just burning bras in the U.S. There was a broader movement for women's liberation, which aimed to challenge traditional gender roles and fight for equal rights.

Women burned bras as a symbol of their rejection of societal expectations that confined them to domestic roles.

Birth control was a significant step towards women's sexual liberation and autonomy. It is important to note that the liberation movement sought to address inequality and give women the same opportunities as men, rather than being solely about being sexual equals.

However, this movement faced criticism from those who believed it was a moral decline and a departure from religious teachings. Some individuals interpreted the newfound freedom and love-centric lifestyles as a defiance of traditional values, particularly those rooted in religious beliefs.

The term "flower children" emerged to describe a countercultural group that embraced peace, love, and nonconformity, often rejecting societal norms and institutions. This movement was a revolution, primarily calling for change and challenging societal norms rather than deliberately defying religious teachings.

Islam grants women's rights and independence. Belief is independent of culture. The Quran values men and women equally and emphasizes respect for women. Women in Islamic societies have held authority and played important roles. Muslim women did not need to march in parades to fight for independence.

Defying the Bible's instructions to rule over men is a significant offense; you must choose between the Bible, the Torah and your authority.

Those who advocate for equality, uphold the Bible, and support female leadership might appear contradictory. This is because the Bible forbids women from having authority over men.

The Bible suggests women shouldn't hold leadership roles. Islam differs from Christianity and Judaism in its promotion of a unified role for both men and women. Placing more responsibility on men compared to women.

In today's world, many church-going women may challenge certain interpretations of these texts and seek to gain power and equality within their religious communities. Their actions reflect a desire to address potential inconsistencies or inequalities in religious teachings, or straightforward defiance of the Biblical text.

Dialogue and understanding in religious communities prevent discriminatory scripture interpretations, but rectifying the ever-changing Bible is challenging.

Quran: Surah Baqarah 2:228. And women shall have rights similar to the rights against them, according to what is equitable; but men have a degree (of responsibility) over them.

NBC New York: A Yale professor has filed a federal gender discrimination lawsuit against a prominent Harlem church after it did not hire her for its senior.

While certain passages in the Bible suggest male authority over women, it is important to consider the broader context and interpretation of these verses.

Many Christians today believe in the concept of biblical equality, which recognizes the inherent worth and equal rights of both men and women. They argue the Bible should be read in light of its cultural and historical context, acknowledging that societal norms and perspectives have evolved over time.

Consequently, there have been efforts to reexamine and challenge traditional interpretations, highlighting women's roles and leadership in the early Christian church.

While it may be difficult for women to reconcile their desire for leadership and authority with certain biblical passages, many individuals and Christian denominations have navigated these tensions.

They may emphasize the overarching themes of love, equality, and justice found throughout the Bible, interpreting it in a way that supports gender equality and women's leadership. The fact is the Bible gives no authority to women over men.

Ultimately, the question of women's authority in Christendom is a complex and multifaceted issue, with various interpretations and perspectives within the Christian community.

It is an ongoing dialogue that continues to evolve as society progresses and as individuals grapple with interpreting biblical teachings.

It is correct to claim that Islamophobic regimes are solely responsible for portraying Muslim women's backwardness in Islam. Islam holds people from diverse societies, but cultures are not the same as religious interpretations and practices, with some individuals or groups advocating for regressive gender roles.

However, it is crucial to note that these interpretations do not represent the entirety of Islam or its followers. Similarly, the Bible does not advocate for the rule of women over men.

While some religious texts may have passages that can be interpreted in different ways, it is essential to approach religious teachings with an open mind and recognize the inherent equality and direction of the text instead of readjusting text which has been the issue all along with Biblical text.

The Quran is unchangeable and will not change with the passage of time.

The faith of Islam and the Quran provide Muslim women with independence and rights, but there are certain limitations within the religious practices.

While women may not call men to prayer or lead men in prayer in the mosque, this does not imply that women are segregated or deemed inferior.

It is a matter of maintaining a respectful and focused atmosphere during worship. The separation of men and women during congregational prayers is a logical arrangement that promotes full compliance and attentiveness to Allah. It is not negligence or discrimination.

Despite these restrictions, women in Islam have played significant roles in teaching and contributing to Islamic scholarship.

Aisha, the wife of Prophet Muhammad, is known for her extensive knowledge and hadiths attributed to her.

Many other women have also excelled in various fields, but they have achieved success by upholding the laws and teachings of the Quran rather than challenging or fighting against them.

The misconception often fuels this fear that Islam is a monolithic entity seeking to take over the world.

However, the reality is far from this distorted view. Muslim women have been at the forefront of progress and empowerment within the Islamic faith for centuries.

An incident involving Prophet Muhammad's daughter, Fatima, exemplifies support of her decision:

When she received an invitation to a Jewish wedding, she sought her father's permission to attend.

Prophet Muhammad, known for his progressive views, left the decision entirely up to her, acknowledging her agency. However, Fatima faced a predicament as she did not possess suitable attire for the occasion.

Undeterred, she turned to Allah in prayer, seeking guidance and help. Miraculously, her prayers were answered, and angels were sent to provide her with beautiful clothes.

The stunning transformation she underwent left the guests in awe, with some even fainting upon seeing her radiant presence.

Fatima, deeply connected to her spirituality, recognized the power of her purity and prayed to Allah, believing that the crowd's initial reaction was due to their misconception of her presence as evil.

True to her faith, the guests and the bride eventually regained consciousness, dispelling any doubts about Fatima's virtuous nature.

This incident serves as a testament to the influential impact of a woman's beauty and presence, both in the past and present. Prophet Muhammad's empowering stance on women's independence is further highlighted by his granting Fatima the freedom to make her own choices.

Hafsa Bint Omar, the daughter of Omar ibn al-Khattab, was indeed the wife of Prophet Muhammad.

However, it is important to clarify that she was the first woman to become a Hafiz, which refers to someone who has memorized the entire Quran by heart.

Hafsa played a significant role in preserving the Quran as she was entrusted with safeguarding a copy of the scripture during the caliphate of Uthman ibn Affan.

Waraqah was a wealthy and influential women during the time of Prophet Muhammad. She was known for her dedication to learning about her Creator and sought to create a space in her home where she could worship and seek knowledge.

Recognizing the importance of the call to prayer, she requested the Prophet Muhammad to send someone to give the **adhan** (call to prayer) in her home, demonstrating her commitment to the teachings of Islam.

Her devotion to Islam extended beyond the confines of her home. She took on a leadership role among women. Although women cannot lead mixed **Jamah** in prayer prophet told her to lead her family in prayer its unknown they could be children.

This showcases the selflessness and dedication of Muslim women, who not only served their communities but also actively participated in humanitarian efforts.

The Arabs had a strong admiration for poetry and were knowledgeable about Arabic literature. She was an affluent woman who possessed both literacy and Quranic memorization skills.

Umm Waraqa was a woman known for her dignity, not arrogance.

With great fervor, she implored Prophet Muhammad to accompany her on the battleship, desiring to be of help.

During the night, Omar would patrol to protect his people, and as the 2nd caliph, he would listen to her recitation of the Quran from outside her home.

Instead of committing suicide, she aspired to care for the soldiers and achieve martyrdom, a revered concept in Islam.

The prophet told her to stay at home, promising that one day she would achieve martyrdom, fulfilling her desire.

When Omar passed by her home one day, he realized she wasn't reciting the Quran. Despite being alive, she had gained the reputation of a Shaheda among many, including Prophet Muhammad.

When Omar entered her house, she was taken aback to find out that two of her servants had murdered her in pursuit of her wealth, despite her advanced age.

Omar asserted that she was truly a Shaheda, a martyred women just as the Prophet Muhammad had foreseen. She died as a martyr, as she had implored Allah to grant her this status. Allah invites believers to approach Him with a pure and sincere heart as He examines every believer's heart.

It is essential to understand that the rights of Muslim women are firmly rooted in the Quran and bestowed upon them by Allah. Islam recognizes the inherent value and equal worth of women, and the Quran provides guidance on their rights and responsibilities.

Muslim women have the right to education, property ownership, marriage, divorce, and inheritance, among others.

Waraqah among other Muslim scholars, teachers, and learners showcases the role of Muslim women as knowledge seekers and community participants.

Their Quranic rights enable them to excel and contribute positively to society. Dispelling misconceptions is important to understand Muslim women's true status. The attitude a person exhibits reflects their deep love and desire for something.

The attitude of a person determines whether they encourage others towards goodness or exhibit evil. In this digital era, individuals can use social media to either promote positive or negative content.

Aisha, the wife of Prophet Muhammad, was not only known for her wisdom and knowledge but also for her prolific contribution to the collection of hadiths.

She played a pivotal role in transmitting and documenting the sayings, actions, and approvals of the Prophet. Aisha's narrations are widely recognized and respected by scholars and students of Islam.

Her meticulous attention to detail and remarkable memory allowed her to preserve a significant number of hadiths, covering various aspects of daily life, religious practices, ethics, and jurisprudence.

Her hadiths became an essential part of the vast body of Islamic teachings and continue to serve as a crucial source of guidance and inspiration for Muslims around the world.

In the time of Prophet Muhammad, alliances and bonds were often formed through marriage, and this was no different for Aisha, the daughter of Abu Bakr, who was a close companion of the Prophet.

Aisha's marriage to Prophet Muhammad solidified a strong connection between their families and further strengthened the ties between Abu Bakr and the Prophet. However, it is important to note that in the present day, while marriages can still foster alliances, the climate of shared faith often plays a more significant role.

In communities where faith is a central aspect of individuals' lives, the bonds formed through shared beliefs and values hold greater importance than mere marital connections built on different venues.

These shared religious commitments create a sense of unity and mutual support, transcending the boundaries of familial ties. Therefore, many times, the shared faith becomes the driving force behind the formation and maintenance of alliances, surpassing the significance of mere attractions.

This discrepancy in the age of Aisha prophet Muhammad's wife has been a topic of debate and criticism, particularly among non-Muslims.

Some argue that marrying a young girl was a common practice during that era, while others condemn it as unethical. It is important to note that cultural norms and practices have evolved significantly since then.

Ultimately, the exact age of Aisha at the time of her marriage to Prophet Muhammad remains uncertain, as historical records from that period are limited and often conflicting.

In medieval times, the age of marriage was not determined by a specific legal requirement but by societal norms and customs. It was common for parents to arrange marriages for their children, especially among the wealthy, to secure alliances and maintain or increase their wealth.

Sometimes, girls were even engaged at birth, ensuring the preservation of family fortunes through strategic unions. However, as time progressed, societal attitudes towards marriage changed.

In Islam, for instance, consummation of marriage was permitted after the girl reached the age of puberty, usually shown by the onset of menstruation.

This was a sign of physical readiness for marriage. These historical practices and traditions highlight the evolving nature of marriage customs over time.

This skepticism leads them to prioritize spirituality over organized religion, often expressing their belief in a higher power without conforming to specific dogmas.

When questioned about their religious beliefs, they may simply state that they are "spiritual, but not religious. "The spread of alteration to the Bible is a topic that has been historically studied and documented.

It is not an allegation made by individuals who do not follow this faith, but rather a recognition of the changes that have occurred over time. However, it is important to note that the conception of truth and the rejection of certain Biblical texts can also come from followers of the faith themselves.

Some individuals may reject certain passages or interpretations of the Bible under the acceptance of spirituality, seeking a deeper understanding or connection with their own beliefs.

In contrast, Islam has a different approach and perspective on the preservation of its teachings.

It is believed by Muslims that the message of Islam, delivered through prophet Muhammad, has remained constant throughout time. The core principle of Islam is the worship of one God, and this message has been reiterated through the Quran, which has remained unchanged since its inception.

While it is true that all humans, regardless of their religious beliefs, seek peace and fulfillment in their lives, the means and methods of achieving this peace may vary.

Each person's spiritual journey is unique and influenced by their cultural and personal experiences.

In conclusion, while the spread of alteration in the Bible has been historically recognized, it is important to acknowledge that followers of the faith can also contribute to the rejection of certain texts.

For Muslims, religion is not a loose concept or a personal interpretation; it is a precise and concise force that governs all aspects of life.

Islam is a complete way of life, with rules and regulations that are comparable to legislation in secular jurisdictions. One of the essential practices in Islam is the daily prayer, known as Salat

This practice is considered a gift bestowed upon Prophet Muhammad during his miraculous journey on the Buraq, a winged horse, in a single night. Muslims view this gift from Allah with utmost reverence and do not take it lightly. The Salat serves as a source of peace and a means of connecting with the divine.

In Islam, the legislation surrounding Salat and other religious practices is contractual, with logical laws and regulations.

Just as in any legal system, there are consequences for non-compliance.

However, it is important to understand that the concept of respite exists, even for those who may deviate from the prescribed path. Satan, too, is given respite, but will ultimately face the consequences of his actions, as every beginning has an end.

In summary, while contempt and accusations may arise from the rejection of organized religious beliefs and the preference for spirituality, it is crucial to recognize the different perspectives and understand the significance of religious practices within each faith tradition.

Islam views its laws as strict and binding, considering prayer (Salat) a precious gift from God. Respite exists for those who deviate, but ultimately, everyone will face the consequences of their actions. Islam is a well-structured religion with clear guidelines on how to worship and connect with Allah.

The legislation and contractual aspects of Islam are precisely defined to ensure that Muslims understand the importance of Salat, the Islamic prayer. If every Muslim truly comprehended the value of Salat, they would not neglect it for worldly affairs.

In Islam, the separation of genders during worship is rooted in the belief of maintaining a pure and focused environment for spiritual connection with Allah. The mosque is considered a sacred space where individuals come to engage in prayer and seek spiritual solace.

This practice emphasizes modesty, requiring both men and women to dress modestly, and women cover their heads with a hijab, symbolizing humility and respect.

It does not mean this separation of genders in mosques to diminish the value or role of women in Islam, but to ensure an atmosphere conducive to worship and spiritual growth for both genders.

Islam strongly emphasizes the importance of self-discipline, self-control, and the preservation of one's spiritual and emotional well-being.

By encouraging separate spaces for men and women, Islam aims to create an atmosphere of purity, tranquility, and devotion within places of worship.

The intermixing in the churches have led to arousal of meetings and staring at opposite genders leading to personal interest instead of focus on attendance to Allah.

Understanding the concept of truth, legislation, and contracts is crucial for individuals to navigate and thrive in society. People who study contracts are equipped to interpret and apply the laws of their respective societies, states, or countries.

Even seemingly trivial actions like running a red light while driving have legal implications and consequences for negligence.

Allah, in His wisdom, has endowed humans with an exceptional level of intellect and reasoning.

Bible: 1 Timothy 2:13-14. Paul describes how in the church, God assigns different roles to men and women as a result of the way mankind was created and entered the way in which sin entered the world.

The continuous blame on women in Christianity can be seen in various biblical narratives.

The story of Eve in the Garden of Eden is often interpreted as portraying women as temptresses who led humanity astray.

This perpetuates the harmful stereotype that women handle the downfall of humanity. Christianity often depicts God as weak and inferior to the evil he created, such as Satan.

The quest for understanding this philosophy is ongoing, as the concepts presented in religious texts often lack clarity and cannot provide satisfactory answers.

It is crucial to note that questioning or critiquing religious beliefs does not lead to chaos or conflicts between faiths or humanity.

Individuals have the freedom to worship any deity, even themselves, as some in this changed society claim to be divine.

This change in perspective reveals a deficiency in theological understanding and an overreliance on simplistic concepts. True satisfaction in life depends on having inner peace and harmony.

Bible: Genesis 3:1-24 NIRV. The serpent was more clever than any of the wild animals the LORD God had made. The serpent said to the woman, "Did God really say, you must not.

It would be a waste if humans do not fully utilize their faculties. Ignorance of the laws and disregarding the jurisdiction of Allah can lead to a tiresome existence, devoid of the simplicity and coherence that comes from following the laws.

However, those who understand and adhere to the laws find a sense of purpose and hope in facing life's trials, as they believe in the possibility of better days ahead.

There is a continuous stream of questions regarding which Bible to believe in, as the concept is not always clear. It is important to note that the church was invented with its regulations stemming from Catholic venues.

Such heinous acts should never taint the pursuit of peace and a genuine connection with God.

If the concept of the search for peace and one God is true, then the question arises: would Jesus, whom they declare to be following, approve of sexual abuse in the facility and doctrine of faith?

Christianity, which stems from Catholicism and has various branches, all traces back to the same triune interest, which Jesus had nothing to do with cultic practices or sexual abuse in churches in the name of Christendom.

The concept of monotheism, which is central to the Abrahamic faiths, emphasizes the belief in one God. This belief is significant, as it provides an unambiguous path for individuals to follow.

In the analogy of someone going on the wrong road and getting lost, the importance of one God can be seen as offering a guiding light to those who may have strayed from the right path.

Thus, the belief in one God serves as a reminder that there is always hope for redemption and a way to rectify one's spiritual journey.

In many countries, Christians often go door-to-door to invite people to salvation through Jesus and the teachings of Christianity.

Similarly, if people are aware of the historical roots of their faith, it becomes easier to understand and appreciate the process of history marked by greed and power struggles.

However, understanding is not a force that cannot be imposed on others; it is simply the truth that stands on its own.

Regardless of one's faith or lack thereof, every human possesses an inherent nature that is ingrained within them, and this nature is believed to be a mercy from the creator, Allah

It is important to note that Allah is the creator and not human, and unlike humans, Allah did not create humanity in his own image.

Allah is often described as an indescribable light that encompasses the universe, and it is believed that every individual will ultimately face Allah on the Day of Judgment.

When it comes to prayer, monotheistic believers direct their prayers solely to this one God. This act of prayer serves as a means of communication, submission, and seeking guidance from the divine.

This indicates that Jesus' teachings were in line with the monotheistic beliefs of Judaism, where Moses prayed to one God, known as Allah in Arabic.

Furthermore, Jesus never claimed divinity for himself during his earthly ministry.

Instead, he emphasized the worship of the one true God and taught his disciples to do the same. Jesus' teachings and actions were consistent with the monotheistic beliefs of Judaism, as he did not portray himself as God walking the earth in human form.

It is important to recognize that monotheism is Abrahamic faiths. It asserts the belief in one supreme God while acknowledging the diversity of religious practices and beliefs.

Having a sense of purpose and direction helps individuals to avoid the chaos and confusion that often arise when they are disconnected from their spirituality.

By integrating the facets of life, such as family, community, and personal growth, Islam offers a holistic approach to achieving peace and fulfillment.

In a world filled with chaos and uncertainty, Islam provides a timeless and relevant guide to living a purposeful and consistent life.

The Quran explicitly states that Allah does not beget nor is He begotten. It reiterated this notion to emphasize the uniqueness and absolute independence of Allah.

Accusations that Allah fathered a son are baseless and offensive because they undermine the fundamental principles of Islamic monotheism.

The **Surah Al-Ikhlas**, also known as **Surah Tawheed**, is the 112th chapter of the Quran. It is a concise yet powerful **Surah** that declares the oneness of Allah, emphasizing that there is no god but Allah.

Muslims recite this surah frequently in their daily prayers, reaffirming their belief in the absolute unity and uniqueness of Allah.

Surah Ikhlas:

In the name of Allah, the Entirely Merciful, the Especially Merciful

Say, "He is Allah, [who is] One,

Allah, the Eternal Refuge.

He neither begets nor is born,

Nor is there to Him any equivalent.

The benefits of reciting **Surah Al-Ikhlas** are manifold. First, it serves to seek forgiveness for sins. When recited sincerely and with devotion, it is believed to cleanse the heart and soul, granting forgiveness and purification.

Another remarkable benefit of reciting this surah is the protection it offers.

The Arabic language in which the Quran is revealed is sublime and unparalleled in its precision and eloquence. Even non-Arabic speakers can memorize and recognize the beauty and clarity of the Quranic verses.

This unifying factor of reciting the Quran in Arabic during the **Salat** (prayer) showcases the unity and respect among Muslims worldwide. It serves as a reminder of the shared faith and the importance of following the Quran as a source of guidance.

TRUTH OVERSHADOWS LIES!

Barsisa the monk's story of losing to Satan is mirrored in the 20th century, where it transforms disbelief into belief among Muslims.

The story of Barsisa the monk offers valuable insights into the challenges faced by individuals in a complex society, even in the 20th century.

It highlights the dilemmas that pious individuals encounter when trying to navigate their religious beliefs in a world that often views religion as a cult or a backward practice.

Reading and reflecting upon this story can help us understand the struggles faced by those who are sincerely trying to adhere to their faith while also grappling with societal pressures and temptations.

In Western cultures, people often accept immoral behavior as modernity.

Faith encourages us to examine our own personal behaviors and make positive changes, fostering empathy and understanding in today's diverse and interconnected world.

Quran: Surah Nur: 24:19. Verily those who love that indecency should spread among the believers deserve a painful chastisement in the world and the Hereafter.

Quran: Surah Qasas: 28:56. You surely cannot guide whoever you like ˹O Prophet˺, but it is Allah Who guides whoever He wills, and He knows best who are ˹fit to be˺ guided.

Quran: Surah Anfal: 8:48. And (remember) when Shaytan made their (evil) deeds seem fair to them and said, "No one of mankind can overcome you this day (of the battle of Badr) and verily, I am your neighbor (for each and every help)." But when the two forces came into sight of each other, he ran away and said "Verily, I have nothing to do with you. Verily, I see what you see not. Verily, I fear Allah for Allah is severe in punishment."

Muslims have not been foreign to battles throughout history. One of the most significant battles in Islamic history is the Battle of Badr.

It took place in the year 624 CE and was fought between the early Muslim community, led by Prophet Muhammad, and the powerful Quraysh tribe of Mecca.

Despite being outnumbered and having limited resources, the Muslims emerged victorious in this battle. The Battle of Badr holds immense significance as it marked a turning point for the Muslims, boosting their morale and establishing their presence as a formidable force.

It also solidified the early Muslim community's faith and conviction in their cause, laying the foundation for subsequent battles and the eventual spread of Islam.

Omar Bin Khattab, a prominent figure in Islamic history, was not only a convert to Islam but also played a crucial role in strengthening the convictions of faith among the Muslim community.

As Islam faced opposition and many battles throughout its early years, Muslims stood united in the face of adversity.

The importance of seeking justice is not negated in Islam, despite the Christian concept of turning the other cheek. Many wars have been greatly influenced by Christendom, which encompasses Christians and nations with Christian majorities.

The historical impact and dominance of Christian nations explain this primarily. Take the Crusades as an illustration, where Christian armies fought between the 11th and 13th centuries to regain sacred territories in the name of Christianity.

Religious motivations are often intertwined with conflicts like the Thirty Years' War, colonization of the Americas, and other European conflicts involving Christian nations.

Muslims have fought in various conflicts throughout history to defend their lands, faith, and communities from external dangers. Muslim forces battled invading Christian armies during the Crusades to safeguard their territories.

Muslims in the Ottoman Empire fought against European colonialism to protect their sovereignty. Despite Muslim defense, most wars fought by Muslims have been defensive, aiming to protect their way of life rather than impose their beliefs.

The forced belief of Christendom refers to the historical period when Christianity was imposed on societies, often through political and social pressure.

Despite the shift towards secularism in many Western countries, the influence of Christianity is still prevalent.

However, it is important to note that the support for Israel by superpowers is not solely based on religious beliefs but also has geopolitical considerations.

The threat of terrorism is a complex issue that cannot be solely attributed to any one religion, as acts of terrorism can be perpetrated by individuals of various religious backgrounds.

A movement has been growing in Western countries, advocating for acceptance of Christianity and religious diversity, but unfortunately, Islamophobia remains prevalent because of social media.

It's important to recognize that Islam doesn't impose its beliefs on others. In Islam, people have the freedom to choose their beliefs, and coexistence with non-Muslims has been existent for decades in Muslim countries.

Politico: Feb 20, 2024 — An influential think tank is developing plans to infuse Christian nationalist ideas in his administration.

The ongoing endeavor to Christianize the country prompts reflection on the relationship between religion and politics.

The immense hypocrisy undermines the values and erodes faith, while the stories they spread through social media dismantle all belief systems, obstructing moral ethics.

In countries where secularism is a prominent principle of ethics, it can indeed be challenging to reconcile faith with the prevailing societal norms.

Secularism, which advocates for the separation of religion and state, often prioritizes neutrality and equality among different beliefs.

While this approach ensures a fair and inclusive society, it can pose difficulties for individuals who place a strong emphasis on their religious beliefs.

The clash between personal faith and secular ideals can lead to a sense of tension and conflict for those seeking to live out their religious convictions in a public sphere that may not fully accommodate or recognize their beliefs.

Balancing faith and secularism requires individuals to navigate complex discussions, engage in interfaith dialogue, and advocate for religious freedom and expression while respecting the principles of a secular society.

Some focus on influencing legislation to align with their religious values, such as pushing for restrictions on abortions. However, this stance can be seen as contradictory when considering their support for same-sex marriages, as it raises questions about consistency in their beliefs and priorities.

The issue of Christianizing the country also raises concerns about inclusivity and diversity. Critics argue that privileging one religion over others goes against the principles of religious freedom and equality.

It can create a sense of exclusion for individuals who do not identify as Christian or practice different faiths, potentially leading to divisions and discrimination.

Another aspect of this movement is the ongoing debate over the separation of church and state. Advocates for a strict separation argue that the state should remain neutral on matters of religion to ensure fair treatment for all citizens.

They believe public policies should not be influenced by any specific religious perspective.

Proponents of Christianization Evangelicals argue for a more active role of religion in public life, advocating for integrating religious principles into governance and policy making.

Concerns have been raised about the public-school systems in some areas promoting Islamophobia and hypocrisy.

While advocating for Christian values, these systems may not provide an inclusive and diverse education that respects the beliefs and cultures of all students.

The promotion of secularism is ongoing in these settings. This ongoing process of addressing these issues requires open dialogue, understanding, and a commitment to upholding the principles of inclusivity, diversity, and the separation of church and state.

In some Jewish and Muslim communities, there is a religious belief that allows for abortions should be permitted if the mother's life is in danger.

However, in certain jurisdictions, laws or regulations were introduced that restricted access to abortion, even where the mother's life was at risk.

This was seen by some members of the Jewish community as discrimination and a violation of their religious rights.

They challenged these restrictive laws and regulations in court, arguing that they infringed upon their freedom of religion and denied them the ability to decide based on their religious beliefs.

Ultimately, belief systems are personal choices that should not be imposed on others. Muslims view neglecting to help a fellow Muslim in need as a betrayal of the principles of Island hypocrisy.

Islam teaches its followers to speak the truth and stand up against injustice, even in a society that may prioritize personal interests or turn a blind eye to others' suffering.

The surah in the Quran that emphasizes Allah will bring better people and demolish lands is **Surah Al-Anfal** (The Spoils of War). In this surah, Allah reassures the believers that He is in control of all affairs and has the power to replace those who disbelieve and disobey with better individuals who have faith and righteousness.

Allah also warns those who oppose His guidance and spread corruption that He will destroy their lands and bring about justice and retribution.

This surah serves as a reminder of Allah's sovereignty and His ability to bring about positive change and justice into the world.

Quran: Surah Anfal: 8:70. O Prophet! Tell the captives in your custody, if Allah finds goodness in your hearts, he will give you better than what has been taken from you and forgive you. For Allah is all forgiving and merciful.

Quran: Surah Taghabun: 64:11. "No calamity befalls, but by the Leave of Allah, and whosoever believes in Allah, He guides his heart [to true Faith with certainty]. And Allah is the All-Knower of everything."

No calamity, separation, destruction, or disapproval of faith can occur without the knowledge of Allah.

Although Satan may promise to divert humanity from the right path, he is ultimately a weak being with no power over a genuine believer. Every aspect of existence, down to the falling of a single leaf, requires the approval of Allah.

His divine knowledge encompasses every event and circumstance, ensuring that nothing happens without His will.

Believers trust in His wisdom and rely on His strength to navigate through the trials of life, knowing that nothing happens without His knowledge and approval.

Allah, as described in **Surah Nur**, is beyond human comprehension and cannot be likened to any physical or spiritual entity. The Quran emphasizes Allah is not bound by the limitations of human form or nature. While humans are weak, Allah is infinite in power, knowledge, and perfection,

CHAPTER 4
BELIEVERS, DOUBTFUL, FEARFUL, OR ATTENTIVE.

In times of doubt, faith can indeed be different for believers. Doubts can arise from various sources, such as external influences, personal experiences, or philosophical questions.

These doubts can shake the equilibrium of a person's belief system, causing them to question their faith and seek answers.

Amidst shifting ideologies, the importance of having a true confidant to guide and correct struggling believers is often underestimated. Muslims have a responsibility to support those struggling with their faith actively, rather than remaining silent.

This act of friendship and support at its highest peak is a testament to the strength of the Muslim community.

Unfortunately, in the age of social media, it has become more prevalent to outsource and further the turmoil by engaging in conflicts and spreading conflicting ideologies that do not align with Islam or any Abrahamic faith.

Speaking the truth becomes more important than keeping up appearances or perpetuating fake words. By actively helping those who are doubtful, Muslims can contribute to a stronger and more united community based on true faith and understanding.

They are part of the broader human community and strive to live according to the principles and laws of Islam. However, doubts can pose challenges even for the most devout believers, and impatience can sometimes overshadow their strength.

It is important to acknowledge that Muslims, like everyone else, are prone to making mistakes.

In the era of prophet Muhammad, individuals confessed to him about the increasing proximity of doubts and disbelief, along with the overwhelming sense of guilt.

Prophet Muhammad emphasized that doubts gain no strength when actions are not taken. Only actions can be punished, not thoughts, and Satan's plan is built on whispers.

Satan's evil nature leads him to sow doubts about the creator of Allah in your mind.

The question of who created Allah has been asked, as Allah created Jesus.

The answer lies in the virgin's concept birth of Mary. Referring to Jesus as the son of God is seen as blasphemous by people of the book in Islam. Eventually transforming into a triune deity.

Negativity breeds doubt and fear, perpetuating more negativity.

Abraham went to see his son and observed the first wife sharing all the negatives while the second wife presented everything in a glamorous way, despite no change in material circumstances.

Every situation has the potential for both misery and positivity; it is up to us to seek the good. The answer lies in optimism, not pessimism, as it has the power to change one's life.

This highlights the complex dynamics and diverse perspectives within the Muslim community. Ultimately, the focus should be on self-improvement and striving to be better Muslims, rather than being overly concerned with external judgments.

The Abrahamic books, including the Gospel, Torah Psalms and the Quran, can provide solace to seekers who are seeking peace. However, when delving into the questions and exploring the texts, confusion may arise due to the historical context of changes made to other biblical texts.

It is widely known that human hands have intervened to correct and modify the divine word, leading to a fragmented and altered narrative.

Most Bibles are color coded to explain the word of divine and the word of human. The color coding helps readers distinguish between passages that are considered being directly inspired by God and those that reflect the perspectives and experiences of human authors.

If a human book, such as the one containing your words, were mixed with the divine text, the context and meaning would undoubtedly be altered.

Each human possesses a unique mind, perspective, and understanding, making it impossible to fully align with the divine message especially if its been altered to suit personal agendas.

Those who seek shelter in truth may find themselves more confused, as they struggle to discern the true intent and message of the Bible within its biblical context.

Many individuals depend on pastors, priests, and other religious authorities to interpret and select which verses to emphasize and teach in religious gatherings, as they possess the knowledge and authority to guide others in understanding and applying the scriptures.

Hope plays a crucial role in the life of a believer. It becomes their driving force, pushing them to overcome uncertainties and challenges.

Even in the face of adversity, believers can find solace and inspiration in their hope for a better future. This hope aligns their minds with positivity, allowing them to navigate through turbulent waters with resilience and determination.

It is important to note that even disbelievers can have hope. The human mind is naturally inclined towards hope, as it seeks purpose and meaning in life.

However, if negativity becomes the dominant force in one's life, it can overshadow hope and hinder personal growth. Positivity has the potential to lift even the most unsure individuals out of deep waters, providing them with strength and clarity to navigate through difficult times.

Quran: Surah Imran: 3: 175. It is Satan who urges you to fear his followers; do not fear them, but fear Me, if you are true believers.

The continuous effort of the contained society in the regions, such as the Western civilization, is a facade that promotes individualism. However, this is actually an impact of a collective society and a mindset that influences people who do not understand the workings of evil.

This mindset draws individuals away from the rules of Allah and instead conforms to the rules of Satan, leading to decadence. This decadence is now spreading from the Western regions and reaching the rest of the world, causing a constant struggle against the system.

Interestingly, some individuals from the Western civilization travel to Muslim lands in the Middle East and return with a newfound love for the Muslim culture and hospitality.

They may even seek interfaith marriages with Muslim men and women. However, it is important to note that such unions are governed by rules set forth by Islamic law, which adds a layer of complexity to each episode.

It is worth mentioning that the Western civilization also pushes for independence within its collective society, particularly targeting the young generation in public schools, where the corrosion of traditional values often begins.

PolitiFact: The United States Department of Education has introduced an Islamic indoctrination program for the public schools, called 'Access Islam.' "

The intention to introduce Access Islam into schools is a way to distort the true teachings of Islam. Instead of providing an accurate and comprehensive understanding of the religion, it is a means to manipulate and misrepresent the fundamentals of Islam.

This manipulation made it easier to propagate false beliefs and stereotypes, portraying Islam as a religion associated with terrorism.

The perpetrators behind this agenda aimed to instill doubt and fear in the minds of people, ultimately tarnishing the image of Islam.

However, it is important to recognize that the chaos and conflict in the Middle East are driven by various factors, including greed and geopolitical interests.

Some individuals harbor envy towards the Muslim lands and may use their greed as motivation to create unrest and instability.

However, it is significant to note that these actions are not representative of the true teachings of Islam.

Sometimes, individuals who initially held prejudice and disbelief towards Islam have experienced a transformation. They realize the fallacy of their previous beliefs and have embraced Islam as their faith, becoming actively involved in its practice.

This serves as a testament to the weakness of the plan orchestrated by those who seek to deceive and mislead.

Imam Ghazali, also known as Abu Hamid al-Ghazali, was a prominent figure in the golden age of Islam.

He made significant contributions to Muslim theology and philosophy during this period. Initially, Ghazali had doubts about the teachings of Islam and embarked on a journey of seeking truth and understanding. However, through his profound intellectual exploration, he ultimately embraced Islam and became a devout Sunni Muslim.

Do not allow your heart to take pleasure with the praises of people, nor be saddened by their condemnation. Al-Ghazali. ·

Desires make slaves out of kings and patience makes kings out of slaves. Al-Ghazali.

During the Golden age of Islam, Imam Ghazali's knowledge and learning played a crucial role in the spread of theology.

What good is education and knowledge without proposed actions?

Knowledge without action is wastefulness and action without knowledge is foolishness. A-Ghazali.

His writings and teachings became highly regarded among Muslims, who considered him an authority in matters of faith.

Ghazali's emphasis on adhering to the **Sunnah (the way of life and teachings of Prophet Muhammad)** resonated with Sunni Muslims, as they believe in following the example of the Prophet.

It is important to note that the Sunni-Shia divide did not exist during the time of Prophet Muhammad.

This division arose after the Prophet's death regarding the issue of leadership and succession. Shia Muslims believe that the lineage of authority to rule should have been through Ali, who was the son-in-law of the Prophet.

However, Abu Bakr was chosen as the first Caliph, and his leadership was accepted by Omar bin Khattab, the second Caliph.

In terms of knowledge and dignity, Islam places great importance on evidence and learning. Abu Bakr, who was chosen as the first Caliph, was known for his extensive knowledge and wisdom.

He was a close companion of Prophet Muhammad and possessed a deep understanding of Islamic teachings. Eventually, Ali did become the Caliph, but it was during his rule as the fourth Caliph.

The Guardian: Losing their religion. In 1972 92% of Americans said they were Christian, Pew reported, but by 2070 that number will drop to below 50% – and the number of "religiously unaffiliated" Americans – or 'nones' will probably outnumber those adhering to Christianity.

CBS news: Sep 14, 2022 — A new report finds that the number of people choosing to disaffiliate from Christianity is increasing – and could overtake the nation's …

NPR: Sep 17, 2022 — America's Christian majority is on track to end as more leave religion A new study shows that America's Christian majority has been shrinking…

The crucifixion can be a source of doubt for those who were not present, much like the concept of God walking on earth. It is important to understand that God is for everyone, not just a select few.

If God took on human form, one might wonder why He is not readily visible, considering that humans naturally prefer tangible and visual experiences.

This inability to physically see God raises questions for those who desire to have a visual encounter with Him. That Jesus was seen by those who were defiant and did not listen also raises further inquiries.

By this logic, perhaps clarity per the Quran establishes Jesus is not God or the son of God. These thoughts and doubts do not diminish our curiosity, as Allah, being an unseen God, remains veiled from our physical senses.

The answer and explanation may be troublesome for some, but Islam sees it as explanatory rather than aggressive or forceful, as the shared prophet Jesus.

These questions are what Islam considers for those with a curious mind. Where is God if he refused to show himself to Moses, but later walked around in the body of Jesus?

We need answers, not more doubts. Clearing these doubts is easy, as God never walked on earth, as it is beneath him.

Why didn't Jesus tell the Jews that he was God? Why did he refer to Jonah as an example, who also lived on earth for three days and three nights? The clarity of answers in Islam is why people are drawn to it, not as a passing fad, but to find answers for their doubts.

The voice of truth mentioned by Jesus was none other than the prophet Muhammad, who would continue the legacy of prophethood.

As a prophet of God, Jesus did not explicitly speak about his crucifixion or the concept of him being worshiped as God in the future by a new religion known as Christendom.

The Quran explicitly states that those who follow Jesus' message of monotheism will be in submission to Allah, showing a path towards Islam, which is a religion that upholds the belief in the oneness of God.

Thus, this verse points to the Muslims, as they adhere to the teachings of Jesus that were centered on the worship of Allah alone.

Quran: Surah Imran: 3:55. [Mention] when Allah said, "O Jesus, indeed I will take you and raise you to Myself and purify you from those who disbelieve and make those who follow you [in submission to Allah alone] superior to those who disbelieve until the Day of Resurrection. Then to Me is your return, and I will judge between you concerning that in which you used to differ.

While some may find these distinctions tiresome or insulting, it is important to acknowledge that they do not inherently deface the truth of monotheism.

Christianity's fading presence in society does not negate the central tenets of monotheism, which assert the belief in a singular, supreme entity.

These distinctions merely highlight the diverse interpretations and practices within monotheistic religions, fostering a deeper understanding and appreciation of religious pluralism.

The first testament, known as the Tourat in Arabic or Torah in Hebrew, is believed to have been given to the prophet Moses by Allah.

It contains the laws and teachings that were revealed to Moses and serves as a fundamental scripture in Judaism. Similarly, the Psalms, or Zabur in Arabic, are attributed to the prophet David.

According to Islamic belief, David received the Psalms as divine revelations from Allah, rather than writing them himself.

It is widely believed that the prophets, including Muhammad, received the scriptures they conveyed from Allah through angelic revelations.

Muhammad, the last of the prophets, holds a unique position compared to other prophets. Each prophet was chosen by Allah with specific credentials and a divine message tailored to the needs of their respective times and people.

However, the Quran, revealed to Muhammad, remains timeless and applicable to all humanity.

Muhammad emerged as the voice of humanity, reaching out to all nations, colors, and people, spreading the message of monotheism and guiding them towards a righteous path.

Business Insider: Nov 15, 2015 — The Bible has been changed and altered over the years.

The translators have removed the word "begotten" and say "one and only" Son. ... Here is John 3:16 from both the KJV and the NIV: For God so loved the world ...

The concept of Jesus being the begotten son is blasphemous by those who understand the meaning, as it implies a physical relationship between God and Mary. This belief has led to debates and disagreements among different religious groups.

The Bible used "**begotten**" to describe Jesus but later changed it to "**only son**". Allah guaranteed the preservation of the Quranic text. The term "only begotten son" held significant theological value for many Christians, representing the unique relationship between Jesus and God the Father.

However, during the Reformation period, there was a backlash against the use of the word "**begotten**" because of its potential for misinterpretation or confusion.

As a result, King James, Revised Standard Version and subsequent translations opted to use the phrase "**only son**" instead.

These changes caused a level of chaos and disagreement among believers, as the constant modifications to scripture can make it difficult to fully grasp and appreciate its teachings.

The interference of humans in the divine word has led to altered stories and interpretations, making it a challenge for those seeking accuracy and a true understanding of the scriptures of the Bible.

Throughout history, human hands have played a role in altering and manipulating religious scriptures, which is why Allah has warned about the changes made by humans.

However, it is challenging to determine the original and unaltered scriptures of the Bible because of the passage of time and the absence of Jesus during the compilation of the texts.

Jesus, not mentioning Paul, raises questions about his role in the continuation of the Old Testament. If Paul was the author of the New Testament, it is peculiar that Jesus did not speak about him.

The Jewish people were seeking answers, not doubts, so why did Jesus not inform them about the emergence of a new religion called Christianity after his ascension?

Despite the prophets delivering messages and dispelling doubts, none of this was foretold. It is puzzling that Jesus, if he truly was God incarnate, did not reveal many things, which seems illogical to the average person.

The inadequate answers leave lingering doubts cause a reevaluation of faith.

While Christendom, commonly known as Judeo-Christianity, can be seen as an extension of earlier Abrahamic faiths with new stories from Paul and adjustments, it is important to note that the Quran, although sharing similarities with these faiths, does not simply copy their stories.

Instead, it corrects the versions and delivery of the stories, as Allah would not allow any alterations to his divine message.

If a story aligns with the Quran, Muslims believe in it; otherwise, the story is dismissed. This reflects the unchangeable nature of Islam, which stems from the previous books and the adjustments made to the words or revelations sent to prophets by Allah.

The Quran clarifies Muhammad is a servant, not a god, and affirms that every prophet sent was just that - a prophet, not a deity.

Accepting this concept can be challenging, as faith often discourages questioning. However, Islam encourages individuals to read, reflect, and then believe.

Multiple authors wrote the New Testament from around 49 CE to the mid-2nd century CE. It is highly likely that Paul the apostle wrote seven of the New Testament Epistles (Romans, 1 Corinthians, 2 Corinthians, Galatians, Philippians, 1 Thessalonians, Philemon).

Jesus, not informing the Jews, raises doubts, as Muhammad, the last prophet, did not mention having a successor but claimed to be the final one.

According to historical accounts, Paul of Tarsus, also known as Saul, was initially a Jewish Pharisee who persecuted early followers of Jesus. However, his dramatic conversion took place around 4-7 years after Jesus' crucifixion.

The theological divergence between Islam and Christianity reflects the differing interpretations and doctrines of these two major religions.

The discrepancy of the crucifixion is indeed a significant factor that sets Islam apart from the dogma of Christianity and Judaism.

In Christianity, the crucifixion of Jesus is considered a pivotal event in human history, representing the ultimate sacrifice for the redemption of humanity's sins.

The concept of a divine being having a son is incompatible with both Judaism and Islam, as both religions emphasize the oneness of God and reject the idea of multiple deities or partners. Christianity views Jesus as the incarnation of God, which is perceived as polytheism by adherents of Judaism and Islam.

The Quran refutes the notion that Jesus was killed by the Jews through crucifixion, stating that his death was only an illusion. The Quran's story indicates another person was crucified in Jesus' stead, while Jesus ascended to heaven with Allah's help.

This viewpoint clashes with the traditional Christian belief that Jesus' death on the cross was the means of redeeming humanity. Notably, the Quran recognized the Jews' anticipated gloating over Jesus' crucifixion, but highlights the disparity between their actions and the true outcome of Jesus' destiny.

Quran: Surah Nisa: 4;157 And for their saying, "Indeed. We have killed the Messiah, Jesus, son of Mary, the messenger of Allah". And they did not kill him, nor did they crucify him: but another was made to resemble him to them. And indeed, those who

differ over it are in doubt about it. They have no knowledge of it except the following assumption. And they did not kill him for certain.

Some will question the validity of this verse, which refers to the miraculous birth of Jesus by a pious woman, Mary, through the power of Allah. However, if Allah can give such a miraculous event, it leaves no doubt for those who believe in the power of God.

Many Christians have already found resonance in this belief and have embraced Islam. The numbers of converts from Christianity to Islam are growing, as the Islamic faith does not center on the concept of resurrection, which is a fundamental belief of Christianity.

The idea of embracing Islam is not just about a change in faith, but an acknowledgment of the continuity and unity of God's message throughout history.

Instead, Islamic doctrine maintains that God raised Jesus to heaven, sparing him from the fate of being killed on the cross.

This discrepancy in the crucifixion's understanding is a fundamental theological difference that distinguishes Islam from the dogmas of Christianity and Judaism.

The discussion surrounding the highly sensitive issue of Jesus' resurrection requires a dedicated effort to explain and clarify the different theological perspectives. Each individual is entitled to their own beliefs and should be respected for their personal convictions.

While theological differences can be informative and help us understand various viewpoints, it is important to remember that these differences should not diminish the humanity of any individual, regardless of whether they follow a religion.

Every human being deserves respect and understanding, and their beliefs, or lack thereof, should not be used to devalue their worth or exclude them from meaningful discussions.

It is crucial to approach these sensitive topics with empathy and open-mindedness, fostering an environment that promotes dialogue and mutual understanding among individuals of diverse beliefs. The theory of crucifixion is rejected by Islam. Although both faiths acknowledge Jesus, differentiating between them is straightforward.

In Islam, Allah is the primary figure, serving as the only creator. Islam does not negotiate the threads of the Quran, making this solidifying distinction unresolvable through negotiation.

Theological differences don't desensitize friendships.

Separating Islam and Christianity as the bases of Christendom is important because they are distinct religions with different beliefs and practices. While both Islam and Christianity have roots in the Abrahamic tradition, their theological doctrines and foundational figures differ significantly.

The entire foundation of Christianity lies in Jesus' salvation and the forgiveness it offers. If Jesus were to deny this, how would the faith hold up against the truth? Faith is unquestioned in the heart and soul, but differences in explanations may not align with faith or truth.

Islam rejects relying on others and emphasizes personal responsibility for justice. The miracles of Allah transcend time and have been a consistent occurrence throughout the lives of all the prophets, each according to their era. These miracles continue to happen, and those who have faith in Allah do not question them.

However, disbelief often leads people to search for flaws in miracles in order to make them fit within the confines of the human mind. Both Jews and Christians struggle to comprehend the idea of a virgin birth.

The Jews resorted to name-calling and blaming Mary, while Christians proclaimed Jesus as the son of God, denying the miraculous nature of Allah. Muslims acknowledge Allah has the power to do anything and did not assign Jesus the status of the son of God.

This is because Allah is not a human being, but Jesus is. Allah neither gives birth, eats, sleeps, nor dies, so it is impossible for Jesus to be His son. Instead, Jesus is regarded as a miracle, just as many miracles occurred prior to the last revelation, the Quran.

The history of Christianity also encompasses various reformations and developments over time, leading to different denominations and interpretations of the faith.

Ultimately, it is important to recognize the unique characteristics and teachings of each religion to understand their significance within the broader context of religious diversity.

According to the Book of Acts, Paul experienced a vision of Jesus on the road to Damascus, which led to his transformation and subsequent mission to spread the teachings of Jesus. Paul played a significant role in the formation of early Christianity, writing many letters that became part of the New Testament.

The Bible is a sacred text known as the Gospel sent to **Isa Ibn Maryam** known as Mary's son.

The formation of Christendom, the religious movement that emerged after Jesus, indeed marked a significant shift in the understanding and interpretation of his teachings.

As Christianity spread throughout different regions, it became intertwined with local customs, traditions, and beliefs, resulting in a blending of gospel teachings with human writings and pagan influences. This amalgamation gave rise to various sects and denominations, each developing their own versions of Christian beliefs.

Within this diverse landscape, there were groups that deviated from the original teachings of Jesus, elevating him to a divine status beyond what was intended. They emphasized his miracles, teachings, and his role as the Son of God, often equating him with God the Father.

This departure from the concept of Jesus as a human being with a unique relationship to God led to a theological divergence from the virgin birth narrative.

Some followers of Christ in this new religious landscape struggled to fully grasp the idea of a miraculous birth without a human father. The notion of God being the father of Jesus in a supernatural capacity seemed plausible to comprehend and acceptable for some.

Muslims believe in the concept of tawhid, which means the oneness and uniqueness of Allah. This means that Allah does not have partners and is the ultimate creator and sustainer of everything in the universe.

The Quran interpret miracles as a connection with God, it is not to imply that God has a partner or depends on anyone or anything. Rather, it is a recognition of His power and ability to manifest His will in extraordinary ways.

Torah and the Quran cite the example of parting the sea to highlight the limitless power of Allah. If Allah can perform such a miraculous act, it is easy for Muslims to understand that He can also create a child without the exchange of sperm and eggs.

Muslims do not see this concept as difficult or doubtful because they have faith in the limitless capabilities of Allah as the ultimate creator.

Quran: Surah Ash Shura: 26:63. So We inspired Moses: "Strike the sea with your staff," and the sea was split, each part was like a huge mountain.

Quran: Surah Ash Shura: 26:66. Then We drowned the others.

Allah's mercy is indeed boundless and incomparable. It encompasses all of creation, and He is always ready to forgive those who sincerely repent and seek His forgiveness.

However, it is important to understand that Allah is also a just God. Those who continuously disobey His commands and persist in their wrongdoing may face dire consequences in this life or the next.

These consequences serve as a means of accountability and a reminder for individuals to rectify their actions and turn back to Allah. The more knowledge one gains about the consequences of their choices, the easier it becomes to navigate through life and make decisions that are in line with a righteous and fulfilling thesis.

There were those who rejected or downplayed the virgin birth of Jesus seeking alternative explanations or interpretations that aligned more closely with their existing beliefs and cultural understandings. Jews rejected it.

This gradual assimilation of Christianity with pagan practices and the reinterpretation of Jesus teachings and nature marked a significant turning point in the development of Christendom.

It led to the establishment of new rituals, traditions, and theological frameworks that incorporated elements of both Christianity and paganism.

Thus, the evolution of Christianity in this period can be seen as a fusion of various influences, resulting in a religious landscape that differed significantly from the original teachings of Jesus and the early Christian community.

However, as time passed and the texts were copied and translated, alterations and additions were made, leading to potential distortions in the original message. Cultural and political influences also played a role in shaping the interpretation of the scriptures.

These factors, combined with human error, have resulted in multiple changes and variations in the Bible as it exists today. The true message of the Gospel, as originally conveyed to Isa ibn Maryam (Jesus), may have been obscured over time.

However, these accounts were believed to be inspired by the Holy Spirit and were considered authoritative by the early Christian communities. It is important to note that the New Testament is not a comprehensive record of everything Jesus said or did during his ministry.

Quran: Surah Imran: 3:64. "O People of the Scripture, come to a word that is equitable between us and you - that we will not worship except Allah and not associate anything with Him and not take one another as lords instead of Allah." But if they turn away, then say, "Bear witness that we are Muslims [submitting to Him]."

The influence of pagan beliefs and practices on early Christianity can be seen in certain aspects of Roman culture, especially during the period of transition. As Christianity spread throughout the Roman Empire, there was a blending of polytheistic beliefs and Christian teachings.

This syncretism is evident in the incorporation of pagan festivals and rituals into Christian celebrations, as well as the veneration of saints and relics.

However, this does not mean that Christianity as a whole embraced polytheism; rather, it reflects the complex process of cultural assimilation and adaptation, which removes it from monotheistic beliefs. Monotheism is the belief in the existence of a single, supreme entity.

In Islam, the core belief of monotheism is centered around Allah, who is understood as the one and only God, with no partners, associates, or offspring.

According to Islamic teachings, Allah is the unseen, omnipotent, and omniscient creator of the universe.

Jesus referred to Allah as **"Allah-ha,"** an Arabic term that signifies the oneness and uniqueness of God. Jesus is the fulfillment of the promises made to Abraham, Moses, and other prophets, emphasizing the continuity between the Torah and the Gospel.

Surah Imran, also known as **"The Family of Imran,"** is the third chapter of the Quran. This Surah primarily focuses on the story of the family of Imran, which includes the Prophet Moses (Musa), the Virgin Mary (Maryam), and Jesus (Isa) peace be upon them.

The **Surah** delves into the lineage and virtuous characteristics of **Imran's** family, highlighting their devotion to God and their significant roles in shaping the course of history.

It mentions the miraculous birth of Maryam and her upbringing in the temple, as well as the divine selection of Maryam as the mother of Jesus.

> **Quran: Surah Imran: 3:175. It is Satan who urges you to fear his followers; do not fear them, but fear Me, if you are true believers.**

Those who are influenced by Satan may fear rejection and judgment from others, causing them to hesitate in speaking the truth. However, it would be hypocritical for those who possess a knowledge of the truth to simply let humanity unquestioningly embrace narratives and belief systems that have been altered to cater to the prevailing societal influences.

What is needed is not a revision of the creation itself, for only Allah is the ultimate creator.

Who handled the world's well-being when the son was being killed? Why would a father not offer help but witness his son suffer, especially when he is considered God the Father?

Making his son a sacrificial human for the sins of others seems blasphemous and akin to a cultic practice, as no Abrahamic faith has ever condoned human sacrifice to appease others.

The idea of a triune God sacrificing himself to save humanity's sins is incomprehensible to those who seek answers and seek to dispel doubts.

If he truly was God, why couldn't he protect himself?

There is a theological aspect and interference associated with this concept that does not align with the pursuit of truth.

That God is both Jesus and simultaneously three in one, thereby sacrificing himself rather than his son, and becoming one with three, is difficult to reconcile with the Abrahamic faith.

However, it may make more sense within the context of mythology. As a result, Islam completely rejects this ideology.

This distinction is not meant to insult, but to explain truth. It is only natural for humans to seek truth and strive to understand the concepts that govern our existence on this earth.

Therefore, the Quran eliminates any traces of doubt and clarifies that he is a living prophet who will return to address those who harbor doubts and refute the notion that he was sacrificed for their sins.

In the world of humans, it is instinctual for parents, whether they be mothers or fathers, to protect their children. This concept is deeply rooted in the principles of life.

A father diligently watches over his suffering son, while a mother seeks solace elsewhere. Example would be Jesus father putting him through suffering for the sinners impossible to belief such concept.

According to the Bible, God, the father of all creation, made humans in his image.

It is quite puzzling to contemplate why humans frequently display more empathy towards others than God did towards his own son or even towards himself, considering that he created humanity, became three in one according to Christendom, and ultimately sacrificed himself for the very beings he brought into existence.

It is indeed a tough concept to grasp. However, Islam rejects this notion and encourages individuals to seek the truth rather than falsehood.

The Quran emphasizes the importance of finding common ground, as intended by all prophets, with the same message of one God, Allah.

This contradiction only adds to the confusion and raises doubts about this episode. Fortunately, Islam offers answers to these inquiries.

The story goes that just as Jonah was in the stomach of a fish, Jesus is said to be alive. This example, given by Jesus himself, shows that God, being a compassionate entity, would not allow the son of Mary to be tortured by the Romans or the Jews.

This explanation clears any doubts, and additional verses from the Quran can further clarify questions regarding this analogy of torture.

It may seem impossible for a common mind to believe that God, who has the power to stop anything, especially his own son, would allow such suffering.

Many individuals who initially embrace the Christian faith often transition into atheism after seeking unanswered questions.

An example of this is Charles Darwin, who was originally a Christian but became a critic when his inquiries remained unresolved. As a result, he developed his own theories, which are now considered mere hypotheses.

Those who dare to challenge such ideas often face dismissal by the church without receiving satisfactory responses to their queries.

On the other hand, Islam provides answers to all questions, as the prophet of Islam addressed and answered those who questioned.

In Islam, asking questions is not seen as losing faith but rather gaining faith in the correct order after understanding. Many people seek Islam and find the answers they are looking for.

The Quran encourages questioning and pondering before belief. It is understood that no one can believe without some level of understanding, which is why Islam has no problem clarifying the episode of the son of Mary and the nature of his birth.

The **Surah Maryam** and **Surah Imran** serve as testaments to provide answers and clear any doubts.

Each individual will face the consequences of their actions, as they will reap what they sow.

It is the duty of a Muslim to guide others and demonstrate the distinctions in reverence, particularly when it comes to protecting the rights and fulfilling the duties of the family of Imran, a reference to a specific family lineage within Islam.

Allah chose Mary, known for her unwavering devotion and piety, to bear Jesus as a mother. She was deemed worthy of giving birth to the Messiah, and thus received a divine blessing from Allah.

God granted this unique privilege to Mary, not for Jesus to impersonate Him or become part of a trinity, but to fulfill the prophecy and bring truth to humanity. Allah sent Jesus as a messenger to guide people towards righteousness and establish the truth of monotheism.

Mary's role as the mother of Jesus was a testament to her faithfulness and righteousness, making her an exemplary figure in the eyes of believers.

The perception of Islam as a religion associated with terrorism and the spreading of Islamophobia is contradictory and illogical.

The colorful paint on Islam represents its core teachings. The concept of forgiveness, salvation, and the belief in a savior who offers redemption is Christianity. If redemption is through a human prophet, belief is simply accepting the savior who sacrificed their life for unknown people's sins.

It's humiliating to be in front of those who didn't accept Jesus as the Messiah or see him as a prophet. Sacrificing one's life of a prophet for the demeaning individuals who rejected him as the Messiah is illogical.

If Allah did not want humans to question anything, he would make a human without a brain to not think for themselves yet believe what is told and not question.

But Islam has insisted on questioning reading, understanding, pondering and then belief for some the belief is instant but some have questions.

These individuals who fear the rise of Islam often engage in spreading Islamophobia by perpetuating negative stereotypes and promoting fear and hatred towards Muslims.

However, their actions inadvertently draw attention to the religion and spark curiosity among others. People who may have had no previous knowledge or interest in Islam are now compelled to learn more about it due to the controversies and discussions surrounding it.

This unintentional promotion of Islam can be seen as a paradoxical outcome of their attempts to tarnish the faith. Islam places great importance on self-correction through repentance, promoting a message of peace and compassion.

It teaches its followers to seek forgiveness from Allah and from others, promoting a sense of humility and empathy.

However, those who propagate Islamophobia often fail to recognize these fundamental teachings and focus solely on perpetuating negative stereotypes. In conclusion, the paradoxical nature of those who fear the rise of Islam inadvertently spreading awareness of the faith highlights the importance of questioning beliefs and seeking understanding.

Islam emphasizes the values of peace, compassion, and forgiveness, which are often overshadowed by the actions of those who perpetuate negative stereotypes.

It is through open dialogue and genuine efforts to understand that misconceptions can be challenged and a more inclusive society can be fostered.

Find centered balance by restraining chaotic desires. Islam's fundamentals are simple and relevant to daily life. Understanding Islam is crucial. Islam, a monotheistic faith revealed through Muhammad as the Prophet of Allah.

Millions of Muslims worldwide pray five times a day. Salat includes physical and spiritual subservience, Quranic recitations, and specific postural positions. Studies confirm **Salat's** positive effects on health.

The call to prayer, known as Azan, holds significant importance in the Islamic faith. It serves as a reminder for Muslims to come together and engage in the act of worship, which ultimately leads to success in both this life and the.

The words **"Hayya Alas Salah"**, **"Hayya Alal Falah"**, translate to "come to prayer, come to success" in English. This powerful call resonates throughout Muslim countries, reverberating in the air and reaching every corner, inviting Muslims and those who wish to join to partake in the five daily prayers.

Salat, also known as prayer, is a mandatory practice for Muslims and it is the second pillar of Islam. It is a voluntary act with great spiritual significance.

Those who attend spiritual well-being focus on their spiritual well-being understand and appreciate the many benefits it brings to their lives.

However, it is crucial to acknowledge that there are consequences for defying this mandated act, whether in this world or the next.

Islam teaches that judgment is not written off as unconditional love, rather it is a contractual faith where Muslims have obligations and mandates to follow.

Allah has always provided a warning before punishing anyone. He sends prophets and individuals to deliver these warnings.

Quran: Surah Mulk: 67:9. They will say, "Yes, a warner had come to us, but we denied and said, 'Allah has not sent down anything. You are not but in great error.'"

Those who invite others to hell are already living in hell in this world and are aware of the consequences in the next. One's perception of the world determines whether they live in misery or happiness.

Accusations rely on the way one lives, with no evidence except for how one's life is projected onto others.

Teaching truth and valuing the transient world's circumference is imperative.

Just as humans live by regulations imposed upon them by other humans, it is reasonable to accept that Allah, the owner of the universe, sets regulations for believers to adhere to. It is essential to recognize that the power of the unseen, that which cannot be seen, holds more influence and authority than one may expect.

The **Azan's** loud call to prayer in Muslim countries is a melodious and soul-stirring nature creates an atmosphere of unity, devotion, and divine connection, fostering a sense of community among Muslims worldwide.

The sound and call to prayer five times a day mesmerized the newcomers and travelers to the Islamic faith and Allah is aware of the dedication of those who respond to the call and recognize that those who attend are blessed with rewards.

Those who never attend Salat in Jamah congregation have yet to experience the beauty of this call. Muslims who rarely pray often make it a point to attend the Jummah Friday prayers, treating it like a festive occasion

Ramadan, the sacred month, holds deep significance for Muslims, as it represents a sacrament of faith and devotion.

The bounds of this faith are indescribable, as the dedication to understanding is marked by simplicity, consistency, and effort.

Islam stands apart from other faiths in the world, as it is a contractual relationship between the believer and Allah, guided by mandated laws and a firm belief in Allah.

The gesture of opening the hands by the ears at the beginning of **Salat**, which is the Muslim prayer, is known as the **Takbir.**

It is a symbolic action that signifies the declaration of the greatness and oneness of Allah. The phrase **"Allahu Akbar"** is recited while performing this gesture, which translates to "Allah is the Greatest" in English.

This expression serves as a reminder to the worshiper that Allah is above all, supreme and worthy of praise. By raising the hands and proclaiming this phrase,

Muslims acknowledge their submission to Allah and their readiness to engage in prayer.

It is a moment of reverence and devotion, as believers prepare themselves to enter a spiritual connection with their Creator. In **Rukku**, a Muslim recites **"Subhaan Rabbi al-Adheem,"** with straight back, hands on knees, and head down.

The Muslim benefits both spiritually and scientifically from this position daily. **Rukku** stretches lower back, thighs, legs, and calves and improves upper torso blood circulation.

Sujood, also known as the prostration, is a fundamental position in Muslim prayers. It involves placing the frontal cortex of the head on the ground, with the hands resting on the sides and the lower body raised.

During prayer, Muslims regard this posture as the most submissive and humble position one can assume.

It symbolizes complete surrender and submission to the Almighty. When performed in congregation, the sight of many individuals simultaneously in the position of **Sujood** sends a powerful message of unity, devotion, and peace.

The watchful eye of Allah witnesses this array of peaceful prostrations, fostering a deep sense of spirituality and connection among the worshippers.

This increased blood supply to the brain during Sujood stimulates the brain's frontal cortex, which handles higher cognitive functions such as decision-making, problem-solving, and concentration.

The act of prostration in **Sujood** also helps to improve posture and spinal alignment.

Placing the body in a submissive position with the forehead on the ground stretches and straightens the spine, alleviating any tension or discomfort. This can provide relief from back pain and promote better spinal health.

he act of prostration in **Sujood** promotes a sense of humility and surrender to Allah, fostering a deeper spiritual connection and a feeling of peace and tranquility.

Studies have shown that **Sujood**, the act of prostration during prayer in Islam, has various health benefits.

One significant finding is that Sujood helps restore the health of the heart. When individuals perform **Sujood**, there is a decrease in both systolic and diastolic blood pressures.

This reduction in blood pressure is beneficial for individuals with hypertension or those at risk for cardiovascular diseases. **Sujood** leads to an increase in pulse rate at different time points during the prostration.

This increase in pulse rate shows improved cardiovascular function and blood circulation.

Overall, the act of **Sujood** contributes to the maintenance and improvement of heart health. Sujood in Muslim prayer has physical and psychological benefits. Surrendering to the divine brings peace and freedom from worries.

In **Sujood**, Muslims recite **"Subhan Rabiya Ala"** 3 times. This phrase translates to "Glory be to my Lord, the Most High." It is praise and acknowledgment of Allah's greatness and supremacy. Muslims strive to humble themselves before Allah in this position of prostration, expressing their complete submission and devotion to Him.

The recitation of **"Subhan Rabiya Ala"** in **Sujood** is a fundamental part of the daily prayers, serving as a reminder of the believers' dependence on Allah and their recognition of His infinite power and majesty.

After reciting **"Sami 'Allahu Leman Hamidah,"** which means "Allah hears those who praise Him," the individual would slowly rise from the bowing position known as Rukku. As they stand upright, they would utter **"Rabanna Lakel Hamd,"** which translates to "Our Lord, all praise is due to You."

This phrase expresses gratitude and acknowledgment of Allah's greatness and blessings.

The act of standing up signifies the completion of the bowing portion of the Muslim prayer, known as Salah or Salat, and the transition to the next position, known as **Sujood** (prostration). This transition represents the physical and spiritual movements involved in worshiping and submitting oneself to Allah.

The Muslim prayer, known as **Salat**, is indeed a unique form of worship that emphasizes the alignment of the body, mind, and heart. Unlike any other prayer in the world, **Salat** requires the continuous recitation of specific verses from the Quran, as well as various physical actions such as standing, bowing, and prostrating.

This combination of verbal and physical engagement allows individuals to fully immerse themselves in prayer, creating a deep connection between their thoughts, intentions, and physical movements.

The mandatory attendance of both body and mind in Salat is a fundamental aspect of Islamic practice, as it signifies the holistic nature of worship and the necessity of engaging one's entire being in devotion to God.

During **Salat**, when a person stands up and recites continuous **Surahs** and words to praise **Allah**, the hands are folded in a specific manner.

This physical act helps to focus the mind and engage both the body and the mind in the prayer.

By folding the hands, one brings a sense of stillness and concentration to the prayer. The continuous recitation of surahs and words of praise keep the mind occupied, preventing it from wandering and allowing for a deeper connection with Allah.

This engagement of both the physical and mental aspects during Salat helps to create a more meaningful and fulfilling prayer experience.

Hadith: Number 0758: Narrated Tawus: The Apostle of Allah (peace be upon him) used to place his right hand on his left hand, then he folded them strictly on his chest in prayer.

During performing **Salat**, Muslims are required to sit down with their knees together and their hands resting on their thighs. This position signifies humility and submission before God. In every prayer, Muslims recite various surahs from the Quran.

These Surahs connect with God and seek His guidance. The name of the Prophet Abraham (peace be upon him) and the Prophet Muhammad (peace be upon him) are mentioned in every prayer.

This highlights the significance of these prophets in the Abrahamic faiths. Prophet Abraham is considered the father of all Abrahamic faiths, including Islam, Judaism, and Christianity. By doing so, Muslims express their acknowledgement and affirmation of the fundamental Islamic creed, **"there is no god except Allah."**

This gesture serves as a visual representation of the unity and uniqueness of God in Islamic belief. In the last position of ending Salat, Muslims turn the head to the right and left to acknowledge two angels.

These angels record and document daily deeds. Muslims send salaams to express gratitude and seek blessings from Allah, acknowledging recording angels. This act reminds us to be accountable and lead a virtuous life.

When Muslims raise their hands in prayer after finishing **Salat**, they do so with open hands, not closed. This gesture is known as the **du'a'** position, which signifies humility and a sense of supplication to Allah.

The open hands symbolize an act of reaching out to the Almighty, expressing sincere gratitude and seeking blessings.

Unlike a beggar who may approach with closed hands, Muslims raise their open hands as a sign of complete surrender and dependence on Allah's mercy and guidance.

This posture serves as a reminder that, just as a beggar seeks help with open hands, believers approach their Creator, seeking spiritual fulfillment and divine intervention with a similar gesture of openness and humility.

In Islam, the act of prayer, known as **Salat**, is an integral part of a Muslim's daily life and is performed in a specific manner. One unique aspect of **Salat** is that it is always conducted in Arabic, regardless of the country or continent where the Muslim lives.

This practice ensures a sense of unity among Muslims worldwide, as they all recite the same verses from the Quran and perform the same physical movements during prayer.

This unified structure of Salat reinforces the belief in the oneness of God and the universal nature of Islam. The Quran remains unchanged throughout history, regardless of cultural or regional differences.

Thus, Islam maintains a unique and cohesive identity, with its closed hands of prayer and the preservation of the Quran serving as universal symbols of unity and solidarity among its followers. Muslims refer to the five daily prayers in Islam as Salah or Salat. They are mandatory for every Muslim who is between the ages of seven and ten, or even earlier.

Children typically follow their parents' lead in attending these prayers, as they are one of the fundamental pillars of Islam. Muslims perform the five daily prayers at specific times throughout the day and night.

The first prayer is **Fajr**, which is performed before sunrise. **Duhr**, the second prayer, is performed after the sun has passed its zenith, typically around midday. The third prayer is **Asr**, performed in the afternoon. **Maghrib**, the fourth prayer, is performed immediately after sunset. And finally, the fifth prayer is **Isha**, performed after twilight has completely disappeared.

Each prayer comprises a specific number of units, or **Rak'as**, and includes recitation of verses from the Quran, bowing, prostrating, and supplicating to **Allah.**

The daily prayers connect with Allah, seeking guidance and forgiveness, and expressing gratitude and devotion.

Quran: Surah Isra: 17:78. Establish prayer at the decline of the sun [from its meridian] until the darkness of the night and [also] the Qur'an of dawn.

Each prayer in Islam comes with its own blessings and benefits. The fajr prayer offers protection from Allah.

During the Duhr prayer, the gates of heaven open up. Asr prayer brings success in life and serves as a prevention from hellfire.

Maghrib prayer is associated with success in wealth and family matters. The Isha prayer ensures a peaceful night's sleep and signifies the closure of the day. Allah rewards those who attend prayers.

The recitation of the Quran in the morning, after the fajr prayer, is heard by the angels. Those who recite it receive substantial rewards.

Believers can also face trials, sometimes even more than disbelievers. Allah tests the faith of those who believe, just as He tested the prophets in the past and will test His people. Keeping your faith intact during times of trials makes one a genuine believer, a Momin.

A Muslim is someone who believes in Islam, but a Momin, an Arabic word, goes beyond that and believes in all circumstances. In this world, death is an inevitable reality that every individual will face. It is a finality, marking the end of our journey on Earth.

People prepare for the future in this worldly life, such as planning for retirement, believers prepare for the next and this life on earth.

Those who believe in the existence of a higher power and actively strive to prepare for the afterlife understand the importance of their actions and the consequences they will face.

This life is a temporary phase, a test, where we are given the opportunity to prove our faith and dedication to our Creator. It is through this preparation and obedience to the teachings of our religion that we can ensure we do not miss out on the rewards and blessings that await us in the next.

This world is not eternal, it is transient, and therefore, we must take the steps to meet our Creator with a clean heart and a righteous life.

Quran: Surah Imran; 3:185. Every soul will taste death, and you will only be given your full compensation on the day of resurrection. So, he who is drawn away from the fire and admitted to Paradise has attained his desire. And what is life in this world except the enjoyment of delusion.

In Islam, life and death are closely tied to belief in Allah's power and control. Humans lack ultimate control over their lives, as everything rests with Allah.

This understanding humbles and submits one to the faith.

Salat is a physical and mental expression of humility. Muslims pray together, standing side by side, to symbolize equality and unity before Allah. Bowing down during prayer emphasizes humility and submission.

Bible: Psalm 143:6, which states, "I spread out my hands to you; I thirst for you like a parched land."

If Jesus is indeed God, there would be no need for him to pray to **Allah-ha** except to explain his divine nature. He mentioned nothing like this, and he certainly did not deceive his followers or leave them to guess or create their own religion after his ascension.

Jesus, just like the prophets before him, came to guide and lead people towards a belief in monotheism. Many statues of Jesus were removed from churches although belief and idolizing a human being is consistent, as a Trinitarian God.

Islam denies the concept of the trinity, considering Allah as the only God and Jesus as a human prophet. But why didn't Jesus reveal his godhood to the Jews?

Jews did not adopt polytheism, remaining faithful to monotheism. Christianity is a modified version of Judaism, with political changes and the addition of Pauline theology.

While humans may be weak and fallible, the emulation of the Prophet Muhammad is a means of drawing closer to God and living a righteous life. Following Jesus and other prophets is similar, but it is impossible to follow Jesus if he is divine, as humans cannot match the qualities of a god like Allah.

Therefore, we cannot believe that he is God. Jesus is the Prophet Messiah. The belief in the Incarnation, where God takes on human form, is a unique aspect of Christian theology and may differ from the Islamic understanding of God's transcendence.

However, it is important to approach these theological differences with respect and understanding, as religious beliefs and interpretations can vary among individuals and faith traditions.

The clarity is Jesus was praying to Allah not himself no one in right senses can pray to themselves if they know they will evolve to God.

Psalm 63:4 says, "I will bless you as long as I live; at your name, I will lift up my hands." It is when we put down our idols and lift our hands to God that our worship is restored to the One who is worthy of devotion. As we remain open-handed in worship to God, we will not feel the need to pick up other things.

Belief is a powerful force that extends far beyond the realms of religion.

It encompasses a wide spectrum of ideas, values, and convictions that shape our perspectives and actions. Belief can be found in various aspects of life, such as personal goals, relationships, career aspirations, and even societal change.

It is not limited to any specific shade or color; it is as diverse as the human experience itself.

When one truly believes in something, their mind becomes electrified with determination and confidence, creating a sense of certainty that what they believe in will come to fruition. This unwavering conviction fuels their actions, propelling them forward towards their desired outcome.

Whether it is a spiritual faith, a belief in oneself, or a cause worth fighting for, believers are not deceivers but individuals driven by the power of their convictions.

Zayd ibn Haritha: The Beloved Adopted Son of Prophet Muhammad

Zayd Ibn Haritha's story being revealed in the Quran, despite his non-prophet status, is both amazing and an honorable mention. While traveling with his mother, a gang of tribes raided and stole belongings.

They forcibly separated him from his mother and sold him as a slave.

Later, Khadija bought him for four hundred dirhams in the subordinate market and brought him to Mecca.

Prophet Muhammad instantly liked Zayd upon marrying Khadija. Khadija and Muhammad PBUH treated him like family. Zayd ibn Harith holds a significant place in the life of Prophet Muhammad, as he was gifted to him by his wife, Khadija.

This act of generosity from Khadija showcased her deep love and respect for her husband. Prophet Muhammad, in turn, grew fond of Zayd and treated him as his own son, even before he gained prophethood.

Zayd's remarkable intelligence and unwavering loyalty made him an integral part of the Prophet's life, as he accompanied him wherever he went and found solace and contentment in his presence.

Khadiga's gift of Zayd to Prophet Muhammad was a testament to the strong bond shared between the couple.

Zayd, originally from the tribe of Banu Kalb, quickly became an integral part of Prophet Muhammad's household. Their bond was not just that of an adopted son, but something much deeper.

The Prophet treated Zayd with the utmost love, care, and respect, creating a strong attachment between them. Zayd's presence brought comfort and tranquility . showcasing prophet Muhammad's compassion and kindness towards others.

One day, Zayd's father finally found him after an exhaustive search. He had written tearful poems, uncertain of his son's fate. Upon learning that Zayd was with Muhammad, peace be upon him, he offered anything to bring his son back.

Despite being a young man, about ten years younger than Prophet Muhammad, Zayd stayed with him, disregarding the emotional decision of his parents.

Haritha, Zayd's father, said you would choose freedom over slavery. He couldn't leave because he found something special in Muhammad PBUH. He felt a special bond and peace with him.

Upon hearing that comment, Prophet Muhammad referred to him as his son. He was not very senior. He treated him as family. The relationship grew stronger.

This act of seeking Zaynab's consent for marriage showcased the progressive nature of Islam in addressing societal norms and emphasizing the importance of individual choice and consent. It challenged the prevailing attitudes towards adoption and marriage, as it was not only acceptable but also encouraged in this instance.

Zaynab's agreement to the marriage after rethinking the ayah from the Quran, which emphasizes listening to Allah and the Prophet, further highlights the significance of personal reflection and understanding in deciding within the Islamic faith.

This story serves as a powerful example of how Islam promotes agency and the freedom to make choices based on one's own understanding and beliefs.

It reminds us that Islam is a religion that values consent, individual autonomy, and the critical interpretation of religious teachings.

When prophet Muhammad proposed marriage to Zaynab, she thought he was proposing for himself.

She was taken aback by the proposal to his adopted son Zayd, causing her to say no at first, but eventually changed her mind when the prophet intervened.

Quran: Surah Muhammad: 47:33. O believers! Obey Allah and obey the Messenger, and do not let your deeds be in vain.

After much deliberation, she believed that accepting the proposal from the prophet Muhammad to marry Zayd was the right decision.

As a faithful and devout woman, she understood the importance of following Allah's guidance and obeying the prophet's teachings.

The logistics of the Quran emphasized the significance of listening to Allah and the prophet, further strengthening her conviction to say yes.

However, little did she know that this marriage would have its own set of challenges and difficulties that would prove hard to reconcile.

These trials tested her faith and resilience as she navigated through the complexities and tried to find a balance in her relationship with Zayd.

It was a journey filled with emotional turbulence and introspection, as she sought guidance from Allah and the prophet to guide her through this difficult period. Zayd, who was a close companion of Prophet Muhammad, indeed faced several challenges in his marriage.

Despite his best efforts to maintain a harmonious relationship, there were persistent issues that caused imbalance and discord.

However, it is important to note that Allah's divine plan often works in mysterious ways. Zayd's Intelligence and Devotion grew.

After prophet Muhammad gained prophethood Zayd accepted Islam whole heartedly he found the sense of belonging with prophet Muhammad and Khadija.

Zayd's remarkable intellect and sharp mind were evident from an early age. He quickly grasped the teachings of Islam and actively participated in discussions alongside Prophet Muhammad.

Zayd's unwavering devotion to the Prophet was reflected in his willingness to follow him wherever he went, whether it was during peaceful times or in the midst of challenging situations.

This loyalty and dedication made Zayd an integral part of the Prophet's life, as he served as a trusted companion, confidant, and advisor.

The Quran shows Allah is the one who plans everything, but having emotions and feelings is a characteristic of being human. However, a true believer, or Momin, is someone who does not act upon those emotions. Only Allah has knowledge of what is in the heart.

In this context, it is mentioned that the Prophet visited the house of Zayd, his adopted son, but upon discovering that he was not present, he respectfully left. Prophet Muhammad, known for his exemplary character and piety, respected the privacy and boundaries of others.

While leaving, he quietly offered praise to Allah, acknowledging His ability to touch hearts and the exquisite beauty of His creations.

Zayd inquired with his wife Zainab whether she had invited him as expected, and if Muhammad had entered.

Zaynab replied he had left without entering, but she noticed him murmuring softly to himself.

Zaynab's beauty was renowned and had captivated many, yet the Prophet, guided by his divine mission, resisted any temptations and left without engaging further.

Allah had a distinct plan prepared. Prophet Muhammad and Zaynab were not initially attracted to each other, but it was Allah's plan for them to unite. Zaynab and Prophet Muhammad were cousins, they shared a familial bond.

Only Allah knows what the prophet held in his heart. The delivery of revelations reveals the prophet's honesty, even discussing his own self. If given the chance, he would conceal this verse as it pertained to the prophet.

However, his commitment to honesty and sharing revelations left no room for keeping anything to himself. He faithfully delivered every truth as it was revealed to him.

This verse recognizes that the prophet is a human being with emotions, highlighting that he, a person, experiences feelings.

However, he did not accept the invitation and instead expressed his praise and gratitude to Allah silently.

Zayd, perplexed by Zaynab's statement, inquired why she did not invite the Prophet inside. Zaynab explained she extended the invitation, but the Prophet chose not to enter the house. He was a man who felt emotions, finding her beauty captivating. He left, praising Allah, without acting on his desires.

This aligns with Islamic principles. Hearts won't be in sync unless Allah's plan allows it. He brings them together, except for forbidden relationships, which are controlled by Satan.

Zayd dissolved his marriage to Zaynab because of ongoing issues rooted in social conflicts. Zainab's way of speaking was quite distinct as well.

Despite her gentle demeanor, she seemed assertive, as the disparities were irreconcilable. However, the beauty of faith lies in the ability to control and restrain oneself from acting upon every passing feeling.

The plans and arrangements made by Allah are clear in the story, clarifying that Allah himself orchestrated the marriage between Zaynab and Prophet Muhammad from above.

Prophet Muhammad revealed the ayah of **Surah Ahzab**, where what he had hidden in his heart was yet to be fully described in simple terms.

The delicacy of mentioning the feelings of humans expresses the difference in human emotions, which exists in contrast to the divine nature of God. Indeed, humans cannot compare themselves to God, as He is not human and will never demean Himself to inhabit a human body, even though He created them from mere sand.

Zayd's marriage to Zaynab held milestones of understanding relationships that every relationship is not compatible. Prophet Muhammad, played a significant role in the marriage of Zayd ibn Haritha and Zaynab Bint Jahsh.

It was Prophet Muhammad himself who proposed the idea of their union, vouching for Zayd's impeccable character and suitability as a husband.

Zaynab, a wealthy widow from the Quraysh tribe, eventually agreed to the marriage. However, despite the initial hopes, the marriage faced insurmountable challenges because of stark cultural differences.

Zaynab, coming from a privileged background, found it difficult to fully embrace the idea of being married to a former subordinate like Zayd.

The discord arising from these cultural contrasts eventually led to the dissolution of their marriage.

Interestingly, despite having known Zaynab for his entire life, Prophet Muhammad had no intention of marrying her himself.

It was only through the divine revelation that he was instructed to marry Zaynab after her divorce from Zayd.

This incident serves as a reminder that even with the best intentions, marriages can falter because of incompatibility and the inability to bridge cultural divides.

Quran: Surah Nisa:4;59."O you who believe! Obey Allah and obey the Messenger (Muhammad SAW), and those of you (Muslims) who are in authority. (And) if you differ in anything amongst yourselves, refer to Allah and His Messenger (SAW), if you believe in Allah and in the Last Day. That is better and more suitable for final determination".

Zaynab, being a pious woman who believed in obeying the Prophet, made the ultimate decision to marry Zayd. However, despite her efforts, there were irreconcilable differences between Zayd and Zaynab, leading to the dissolution of their marriage.

Allah instructed Prophet Muhammad to marry Zaynab. Although Zayd was not Prophet Muhammad's biological son, the decision to marry his ex-wife was a difficult one for the Prophet.

He knew that people in the Arabian Peninsula would criticize and gossip about him, but he prioritized following the command of Allah above the opinions of humans.

This incident highlighted a significant aspect of Islam, namely that a person who is regarded as a son but is not biologically related does not possess the same rights as a biological son.

For example, while inheritance is a compulsory right for a biological son, it is not obligatory for a son who is designated as such but is not biologically related.

Thus, these two individuals do not share equal rights. It is permissible to marry the ex-wife of a son who is not biologically related, but the biological father may not marry the wife of one's biological son.

These distinctions were established through the prophets to bring clarity and uphold the principles of contracts in Islam. In Islam, the concept of adoption differs slightly from that of many other cultures.

Islam encourages the act of caring for and raising orphaned or abandoned children, but it does not allow for the complete erasure of a child's lineage or the assumption of a false identity.

Instead, Islam emphasizes the importance of maintaining the child's connection to their biological lineage and informing them about their true parentage when they can understand.

This transparency ensures the child grows up with a clear understanding of their origins and identity.

However, Islam allows for the changing of a person's name during conversion to Islam, as converts may choose to adopt a Muslim name as an informed choice. This practice is a way of embracing their new faith and identity while still knowing their lineage and heritage.

Islam does not endorse adoption, but supports foster care with the understanding of parentage and name preservation.

Zayd Ibn Haritha arrived at Khadija's as a young boy, yet his name remained unchanged to ibn Muhammad. Nonetheless, the rules clarified the Islamic context of adoption.

Inheritance is possible for fostered children from their biological parents. Gifts and inheritance are accepted but inheritance not forced to non-biological offspring—it's a choice.

Islam covers all areas of life comprehensively. This incident educates about care, trust, adoptions, foster care, and rights in Islamic doctrine.

Muhammad peace be upon him didn't receive prophethood until he turned forty. During their time together, Zayd ibn Haritha found him to be honorable, loving, honest, humorous, and trustworthy.

He recognized his uniqueness, but never foresaw his role as a prophet. But he was engaged in Islam after the prophets prophethood. The word "ibn" consistently means son or daughter in Arabic. The father's name is crucial in describing lineage, which is upheld in the Muslim world.

Zayd's freedom was granted, and he became the first freed slave to accept Islam. Zayd quickly became one of the Prophet's closest companions and played a significant role in the early development of the Muslim community.

He took part in several key battles, such as the Battle of Badr and the Battle of Uhud, displaying great bravery and loyalty.

Zayd's conversion to Islam and his subsequent contributions to the faith exemplify the inclusive and egalitarian nature of Islam, which emphasizes the equal worth and dignity of all individuals, regardless of their social status or background.

Zayd was referred to as the Prophet's son and was treated with love and care. At eleven, Zayd expressed his eagerness to join the battles in the spread of Islam.

However, Prophet Muhammad, understanding the age of maturity in Islam to be around fifteen years old, advised Zayd to wait until he reached that age. Later, when Zayd reached the age, he accompanied the Prophet on various battles, playing an active role in the propagation of Islam.

Zayd ibn Haritha possessed not only remarkable but also extraordinary proficiency in the Arabic language. He committed himself to attaining mastery in the complexities of Arabic grammar, vocabulary, and literature.

Through his diligence in studying and comprehending the language, he became an expert in both spoken and written Arabic.

Zayd's linguistic abilities played a vital role in his position as a scribe for Prophet Muhammad, as he diligently transcribed and safeguarded the divine revelations given upon the Prophet.

His deep understanding of Arabic enabled him to accurately record and compile the verses of the Quran, ensuring the preservation of the teachings of Islam in a written form.

Zayd's commitment to safeguarding the words of God played an essential role in the compilation of the Quran, which has remained unchanged since its inception, along with his meticulousness and dedication to his task.

While Zayd's efforts to salvage his marriage may not have yielded the desired outcome, it was all part of a greater plan set forth by Allah.

Through these trials, Prophet Muhammad provided guidance and support to Zayd, teaching him valuable lessons about perseverance, patience, and reliance on Allah's wisdom.

This mention occurs in verse 37 of Surah al-Ahzab, which recounts the tale of Zayd's union with Zaynab Bint Jahsh.

Ultimately, this experience served as a catalyst for significant changes in Zayd's life, leading him to play a crucial role in the history of Islam.

The disparities in their social status and cultural backgrounds made their marriage unsuitable. Zayd, originally a slave, was employed by Khadija and was treated as a son by Prophet Muhammad.

Zayd's opportunities were limited, and he didn't have the privileges that Zaynab enjoyed as a member of the influential Quraish family. Despite the belief that social status doesn't matter, history proves otherwise.

Their relationship was strained by power imbalances and societal pressures. Their diverse cultural upbringings led to contrasting values, traditions, and lifestyles.

Zayd's view on freedom and independence was influenced by his time as a slave, whereas Zaynab was used to a contrasting lifestyle. These differences frequently led to misunderstandings and conflicts in their everyday existence.

Their diverse backgrounds posed ongoing challenges that made it hard to overcome, ultimately impeding their marital success. Despite prophet Muhammad's attempts to reconcile the marriage, no improvement was observed.

The relationship couldn't survive because of conflicting lineages and social status. Zayd finally surrendered, acknowledging it as Allah's divine plan. Zayd and Zaynab's union crumbled because of insurmountable differences.

This story highlights the profound inclination of human emotions that surpasses desires or physical beauty, as the command of Allah takes precedence.

According to **Surah Al-Ahzab** of the Quran, Allah arranged the marriage between Zaynab Bint Jahsh and Prophet Muhammad. Prior to their marriage, to Zaynab Prophet Muhammad adhered to the iddah period, a waiting period for divorced or widowed women before they can remarry.

Women usually experience this period for three menstrual cycles or three months and ten days. The waiting period has several purposes, such as eliminating paternity confusion and allowing emotions to calm before making new commitments.

Prophet Muhammad followed these rules, showing his commitment to the guidance and principles of the Quran.

This divine intervention is explicitly mentioned in the Quran, affirming that this marriage resulted from Allah's decree. Zaynab herself often mentioned that while families may have arranged marriages, it was Allah who united her with the prophet.

This unexpected occurrence served as a reminder of Allah's supreme control and divine plan. Not only did this marriage challenge societal norms, but it also showed the wisdom of Allah's decisions.

Zaynab, a woman who was both pious and self-assured, held the belief that Prophet Muhammad's past marriages extended friendships and alliances. The marriage of Prophet Muhammad and Zaynab caused controversy, as some accused him of marrying his adopted son's wife. It was Allah who had orchestrated their union.

Quran: Surah Ahzab: 33:37. And [remember, O Muhammad], when you said to the one on whom Allah bestowed favor and you bestowed favor, "Keep your wife and fear Allah," while you concealed within yourself that which Allah is to disclose. And you feared the people, while Allah has more right that you fear Him. So, when Zayd had no longer any need for her, we married her to you in order that there not be upon the believers any discomfort concerning the wives of their adopted sons when they no longer have need of them. And ever is the command of Allah accomplished.

It served as evidence that Allah's designs are beyond human grasp and that He exercises complete dominion over the destinies of His creatures. Prophet Muhammad's union with Zaynab served as a symbol of Allah's guidance for His followers.

The facts are clear why Allah married him to Zaynab is beyond perception but the laws become clear adopted sons' wife after the divorce is permissible but the biological son's wife in Islam is not permitted for marriage.

Thus, Islam leaves no doubts and prophet Muhammad was used to show the people laws and regulations to come forth.

If prophet Muhammad wanted to marry Zaynab he could have before suggesting him to Zayd but the marriage between Zayd and Zaynab was not successful; they also came from different backgrounds which they did not adjust to and divorce took place.

Then prophet Muhammad married Zaynab as Allah commanded the marriage.

The Prophet's marriage to Zaynab Bint Jahsh (RA) is explicitly prescribed in the Qur'an, in Surah Al-Ahzab (33:37). This verse clearly states that Allah commanded the Prophet ﷺ to marry Zaynab, who was previously married to his adopted son Zayd ibn Haritha (RA).

Despite this explicit prescription in the Qur'an, the Prophet's marriage to Zaynab remains a topic of controversy among some individuals.

Some argue that it was a marriage of convenience or political strategy, while others question the appropriateness of marrying one's adopted son's ex-wife.

However, it is important to understand the context of this marriage to fully comprehend its significance and the wisdom behind it.

The marriage abolished the pre-Islamic Arab custom of adoption and to establish clear guidelines for kinship and marriage in Islam.

It showed the equality of all believers in the eyes of Allah, regardless of lineage or social status.

The controversy surrounding this marriage often arises because of a lack of understanding of the historical and cultural context, as well as a limited interpretation of the Qur'anic verses pertaining to it.

Prophet Muhammad gave Walema, which is a traditional Islamic reception, after the consummation of his marriage to Zaynab. This Walema was significant not only because it celebrated their union but also because it was a large and grand affair.

It was attended by numerous guests, including family members, friends, and members of the community. The event was characterized by joyful festivities, feasting, and expressions of happiness and gratitude.

Prophet Muhammad's decision to hold such a grand Walema for his marriage to Zaynab exemplified the importance of celebrating and sharing happiness with others in Islamic tradition.

After the marriage of Prophet Muhammad to Zaynab, Allah implemented the practice of hijab.

It is important to note that while Prophet Muhammad paid the Mahr (dowry) to Zaynab, it was Allah who ordained and blessed their union.

The concept of hijab, which refers to the modesty and covering of women, was not directly linked to their marriage, but it was a broader commandment from Allah that was revealed after his marriage to Zaynab.

Quran: Surah Ahzab: 33:59. O Prophet, tell your wives and your daughters and the women of the believers to bring down over themselves [part] of their outer garments. That is more suitable...

Implementing hijab was a means of safeguarding the dignity and honor of women, promoting modesty in society, and establishing guidelines for interaction between men and women.

The teachings of the Quran were becoming clearer when Prophet Muhammad set an exemplary example.

Despite facing challenges, he did not let the opinions or rumors of others override the law and commandments of Allah.

The relationship between Zayd and prophet Muhammad remained the same perhaps even stronger he was relieved from separation and dissolution from Zaynab which had many cracks due to cultural setback.

In 629 CE, the Battle of Mut'ah took place. The region of Mut'ah in present-day Jordan was the site of this battle. To counter the Byzantine assault on a Muslim ally, prophet Muhammad entrusted Zayd with leading a small army of about 3,000 men.

Despite the odds and a formidable foe, Zayd showed incredible courage and strategic prowess. He fought valiantly on the battlefield, and was martyred during the intense fighting.

Zayd's leadership and sacrifice in the Battle of Mut'ah are highly revered in Islamic history, and he is remembered as a courageous and dedicated commander.

The Battle of Yarmouk took place in 636 AD and marked a significant turning point in the Rashidun's history Caliphate.

The Muslim forces, led by Khalid ibn Al-Walid, faced an overwhelming Byzantine army. Despite being outnumbered by a ratio of approximately 3 to 1, Khalid's strategic brilliance and tactical prowess proved instrumental in their success.

He devised a plan that capitalized on the weaknesses of the Byzantine forces, exploiting their disarray and lack of coordination. Under his command, the Muslim army executed swift and coordinated attacks, using cavalry charges and archery to devastating effect.

Khalid's ability to inspire and motivate his troops further boosted their morale and determination.

In the end, the Muslim forces emerged victorious, inflicting heavy casualties on the Byzantine army and securing control over the region.

The Battle of Yarmouk not only solidified the position of the Rashidun Caliphate, but also paved the way to expand Islamic territories in the Near East.

The Battle of Yarmouk, took place in 629 CE near the village of Yarmouk, in present-day Jordan. This battle was a significant event in the early Islamic history and is considered a pivotal moment in the expansion of the Islamic empire.

The success of the Battle of Yarmouk is a subject of debate among historians. While the Muslim forces, led by Zayd ibn Haritha, fought valiantly against the Byzantine army, they ultimately faced overwhelming numbers and were forced to retreat.

Despite not achieving a decisive victory, the battle showcased the bravery and resilience of the Muslim warriors and marked a turning point in the relations between the Muslims and the Byzantines. Zayd ibn Haritha, the renowned companion of Prophet Muhammad, played a crucial role in the Battle of Yarmouk.

He was a trusted general and a close confidant of the Prophet. Zayd led the Muslim forces with great courage and strategic acumen during the battle.

However, tragically, Zayd ibn Haritha was fatally wounded in the midst of the intense fighting. He fought valiantly until his last breath, displaying immense bravery and unwavering dedication to the cause of Islam

Zayd's death was a significant loss for the Muslim community, as he was highly respected and admired for his unwavering commitment to the faith and his exceptional military leadership skills.

His sacrifice in the Battle of Yarmouk is remembered as a testament to the devotion and sacrifice of the early Muslims in the pursuit of spreading the message of Islam. He was martyred his legacy still lives.

The incident of Zayd Ibn Amr, who carried the same name in search of faith, found his faith and answers in Syria, which is known as Bilad al-Sham in Arabic.

Zayd Ibn Amr was a pre-Islamic Arab poet and a prominent figure in the Jahiliya period of ignorance. He was known for his quest for monotheism and rejection of idol worship.

In his search for truth, Zayd traveled to various lands, including Syria, where he encountered Christian monks and scholars. It was in Syria that he found the answers he was seeking and embraced a monotheistic faith.

The influence of his journey and experiences in Syria played a significant role in shaping his beliefs and convictions. Syria is known for its resilience and is blessed by Allah. The historical significance of Syria in Islam dates back to the time of Prophet Muhammad, who engaged in trade in the region.

The belief amplifies the spiritual importance of Syria for Muslims that Jesus will descend there during the end times.

Unfortunately, the current conditions in Syria have been marred by conflict and the invasion of foreign forces driven by greed and political agendas.

These invaders have manipulated the Muslim lands, causing immense suffering and displacement for the people of Syria. Despite these challenges, the resilience and strength of the Syrian people have persisted, and they continue to hold on to their faith and the sacredness of their land.

False accusations and propaganda further exacerbate the situation, but the truth remains that the land of Syria is blessed, and those who survive and endure on this land are considered to be blessed as well.

The propaganda and lies against Syrians and Islam are not only heinous but also baseless. Islam does not force itself upon anyone, as religion is a matter of choice.

Muslims understand that faith should be embraced willingly, without coercion.

The Islamophobic individuals who spread false information take pleasure in instigating hatred and circulating derogatory content on social media.

Their intentions are driven by a desire to gain access to the rich resources of Muslim lands, causing nothing but destruction.

The history of their actions in Syria speaks for itself, as they have shown a complete disregard for human life, targeting hospitals and other essential infrastructure.

Hadith: Al-Bukhari. The authority of Saleem ibn 'Abdullah ibn 'Umar, who narrated from his father, that he said: "Zayd ibn 'Amr went to Syria asking about the (true) religion.

He held up his hand and said, he had accepted Islam when prophet Muhammad received prophethood. Islam is the religion of Ibraheem the prophet known as Abraham.

"O Allah! I make you my witness that I am upon the religion of Ibraheem.'"

The theological debates and power struggles within the Christian church in Constantinople during the Byzantine Iconoclasm were complex and multifaceted.

In order to maintain control over their diverse territories, Roman rulers often assimilated local religious beliefs and practices into their own. This led to incorporating pagan elements into the portrayal of Jesus, such as his association with sun gods or his depiction as a Roman emperor.

These political motivations aimed to appease and unify different religious communities under Roman rule.

Political and power struggles within the early Christian community fueled some theological debates. Politics, culture, and theology influenced the distortion of Jesus' identity, not any Muslim country.

Identifying these distortion sources helps us understand Christianity's historical development and the influence on religious beliefs. The Byzantine Empire, also known as the Eastern Roman Empire, indeed had its own internal dynamics, including religious tensions.

One of the significant divisions within the Christian church was the conflict between the Eastern Orthodox Church and the Latin (Roman) Catholic Church.

These factions had ideological differences and engaged in power struggles, with each seeking to exert influence over the Byzantine state. Christianity emerged from manipulation and political greed to control the masses.

Different interpretations led to various Christian denominations. Jesus, a monotheist of Abrahamic lineage and faith, had no role in the formation of Christendom.

While political interests influenced Christianity's history, it is too simplistic to attribute it solely to greed and politics. Humans seek faith, but truth is the ultimate decision-maker.

Jesus' identity cannot be portrayed as divine to associate him with pagan rituals unrelated to his teachings.

Later, the Evangelicals emerged and rejected the act of worshiping statues, emphasizing the importance of a direct relationship with God. However, their fundamental principles remained unchanged. They continued to uphold the belief in the divinity of Jesus Christ and the teachings of the Bible. The only significant difference was the removal of the practice of displaying statues of Jesus.

Despite this change, the concept of revering and following Jesus as the central figure of their faith remained firmly intact within the Evangelical movement.

The focus shifted towards a more personal and spiritual connection with Jesus, highlighting the importance of faith, prayer, and scripture in their worship practices.

Jesus himself identified as a Jew and taught within the Jewish tradition.

Islamic faith maintains that the Quran denies Jesus' crucifixion on the cross. Muslims believe that the crucifixion was a divine deception or illusion. Jesus was born east of Jerusalem, near Judea. This place is now part of Palestine. The explanation highlights Jesus' Palestinian identity.

It is important to note that countries may undergo changes in name and experience periods of war and occupation, but the actual land of Jesus' birth remains unchanged in terms of its location. This understanding is not a source of no confusion for Muslims who clearly understand the Quranic teachings on this matter.

Surah Maryam in the Quran clearly explains the identity of Jesus from Allah.

It highlights the implications and additions made by certain individuals and groups in order to distort the true nature of Jesus as a prophet and the Messiah.

These distortions were made to serve the interests of those who sought to benefit from the chaos and confusion surrounding Jesus' identity. The Roman Empire, with its desire to maintain control and suppress any threat to its power, played a significant role in this.

By promoting the idea of Jesus as divine, they sought to divert people away from the genuine message of monotheism and keep paganism alive.

This manipulation and distortion of Jesus' identity was driven by greed, chaos, and a continuous effort to maintain their power and control over the masses.

Just as a human who creates a robot does not become the robot itself to demonstrate its functionality. To critically evaluate claims and distinguish between truth and falsehood is essential.

This belief is the foundation of monotheism, which rejects any faith or person falling short of a monotheistic belief and any additions to the original belief of Abraham.

Any deviation from the pure monotheistic belief is considered paganism.

Abraham, being the father of all Abrahamic prophets, holds a significant position in this context. Jesus, as part of the lineage of Abrahamic prophets, is recognized within this framework.

However, this contentious issue continues to spark debates and conflicts in the region, with different perspectives on the motivations behind the partitioning of Palestine.

The goal is to find a peaceful and fair resolution that respects the rights and aspirations of all parties involved, while also ensuring the security and well-being of the affected individuals and communities.

Over the years, the super power has provided significant military and economic aid to Israel, cementing their partnership and ensuring Israel's security in a volatile region.

However, this close alliance has also faced challenges and controversies, particularly regarding Israeli settlement policies in the occupied territories and the Israeli-Palestinian conflict.

As a result, Islam is now a truly global religion, with diverse Muslim communities contributing to its richness and diversity. Muslim countries need unity not separation to help the world.

CHAPTER 5
SPIRITUALITY VERSUS SEXUALITY

Understanding is a concept that is reserved for those who possess the ability to comprehend various sources of information. It is not a universal quality that can be attributed to every individual.

When spirituality is stripped away and replaced solely with a focus on sexuality, the consequences can be dire.

Sexuality, while a fleeting aspect of human nature, can be transformed through passion and desire. However, spirituality serves as the wellspring from which each soul draws its essence.

Removing spirituality from one's life leaves behind a void that engulfs the individual and spreads like wildfire across entire continents. This phenomenon can be observed in the Western world, where sexual desires are often mistaken for love, creating a poignant hypocrisy.

True love, in its purest form, is built upon respect and trust. Without trust, love cannot exist.

It is imperative to recognize the significance of spirituality and the role it plays in fostering genuine connections and meaningful relationships.

People universally acknowledge that food, water, air, and shelter are essential for human survival, but there is ongoing debate regarding the inclusion of sexuality as a basic need.

While sexual activity is a natural and instinctual aspect of human life, it is not essential for individual survival in the same way as the aforementioned needs.

However, it is important to note that companionship and intimacy are vital for emotional well-being and overall happiness.

In a heterosexual relationship, religious doctrines, such as those found in the Abrahamic faiths, promote the idea of sexuality as a means of companionship and procreation.

In Islam, marriage is considered a union that completes one's faith. It is believed that through marriage, a person fulfills their religious duties and responsibilities.

The Quran emphasizes the importance of marriage in finding tranquility, love, and companionship.

Quran: Surah Nur: 24:32. Marry those among you who are single, or the virtuous ones among yourselves, male or female: if they are in poverty, Allah will give them means out of His grace.

Bible: Genesis: 2:24. Marriage involves spiritual, emotional, and physical closeness. Therefore, shall a man leave his father and mother, and shall cleave unto his wife.

Bible: Mark 10-6-9. "But at the beginning of creation God 'made them male and female.' 'For this reason, a man will leave his father and mother and be united to his wife, and the two will become one flesh.' So, they are no longer two, but one flesh. Therefore, what God has joined together, let no one separate."

Believing in the Bible's concept of two bodies merging as one would cause sharing hunger sensations and much more.

Challenging it may be, but breaking a spiritual connection is difficult, even when it contradicts nature's laws.

The union of spiritual and physical realms makes it illogical for marriages within this union to break up, as they are intertwined as one. The reader is left contemplating the concept. However, despite this firm belief in the permanence of marriage many marriages in Western societies end in dissolution.

Divorce, although not permitted in the Bible except in cases of infidelity, has become a common occurrence. This discrepancy between the ideal and the reality can be challenging for believers to reconcile.

Bible: KJV: Corinthians 7:12. But to the rest speak I, not the Lord: If any brother hath a wife that believeth not, and she be pleased to dwell with him,...

Bible: NIV: 19:9. I tell you that anyone who divorces his wife, except for sexual immorality, and marries another woman commits adultery."

If divorce is only allowed for immorality according to the verse, what does that mean for divorces based on irreconcilable differences?

Are Christians who get divorced for this reason living in adultery? The logic is not in line with the present times or doesn't align with Western lifestyles.

In the Bible, the clarity of the verses regarding marriage can be seen as limiting free will in certain circumstances. According to biblical teachings, marriage is considered a lifelong commitment, and divorce is only permissible in cases of infidelity.

In such cases, the innocent party has the option to divorce but is not obligated to do so. However, once a marriage is dissolved, the Bible maintains the individuals involved are still considered married in the eyes of God.

The Bible indeed contains verses that speak about remarriage and adultery. Some passages, such as **Matthew 19:9**, state that those who divorce and remarry, except in cases of infidelity, are committing adultery.

These verses can have a significant impact on the psyche of individuals who adhere to the teachings of the Bible. They may struggle with feelings of guilt or internal conflict if they find themselves in a situation that goes against these teachings.

In countries that follow the Bible as a religious guide, the interference of political regimes can sometimes create tension between religious beliefs and civil laws. This can lead to situations where the political regime imposes laws that may contradict certain biblical teachings.

This can create a dilemma for individuals who desire to adhere strictly to the Bible, as they may feel torn between following their religious beliefs or complying with the laws of the land.

In the current climate where divorce rates are consistently high and irreconcilable differences, excluding infidelity, can persist, the Bible does not allow divorce in these circumstances.

However, people who follow Christendom find themselves unable to continue living in such turmoil. The regimes that govern these continents have faded laws, eradicating the principles outlined in the Bible and overruling them to accommodate the desires of the people.

This not only extends to divorce but also delves into the fabric of domestic lives, such as allowing for LGBT rights. While personal choices should be respected, it is important to note that these decisions go against the teachings of the Bible and other Abrahamic faiths.

The clash between societal changes and religious beliefs has created a significant divide among individuals and has led to ongoing debates and discussions.

In contrast, Muslim countries often have legal systems based on the Quran. While Muslims, like followers of any faith, can be flawed, the laws in these countries align more closely with the teachings of the Quran.

This can provide a sense of consistency and stability for those who wish to follow their religious teachings without conflict between religious beliefs and political regimes.

It is important to note that interpretations of religious texts can vary, and different individuals and communities may have different understandings of these verses.

The relationship between religion and politics is complex and can differ significantly across countries and cultures.

The Quran provides a more flexible approach to marriage and divorce. It grants individuals the right to enter marriages, the right to divorce, and even the right to remarry the same spouse twice, should they choose to do so.

However, if the relationship does not work out after the second attempt, the person must marry another individual before they can remarry their former spouse.

This approach acknowledges the complexities of human relationships and allows for second chances while also promoting accountability and ensuring that individuals are not trapped in unhappy marriages.

In Islam, marriage is regarded as a contractual event, similar to any other legal agreement. While it is considered an important aspect of completing the Deen (faith), it is not forced upon anyone.

Islam recognizes the importance of a harmonious relationship between a man and a woman, as they are believed to complement and support one another

However, it is essential to note that consent and mutual understanding are vital components of a successful and fulfilling marriage in Islamic teachings. In contrast, Islam approaches marriage as a contractual agreement that can be dissolved under certain circumstances.

While the belief is that pairs are made in heaven, Islam recognizes that there may be situations where a relationship becomes unsustainable or harmful. In such cases, Islam allows for divorce to resolve the issues and protecting the well-being of both parties.

Islam permits divorce when there is chaos or discord in a marriage. Islam recognizes that, despite encouraging marriage, it doesn't force couples to remain together if their relationship becomes beyond repair.

This approach allows for the possibility of starting anew and finding happiness in a unique relationship. In summary, the concepts of marriage and divorce differ between Christianity and Islam.

Christianity emphasizes the lifelong commitment of marriage, allowing divorce only in cases of infidelity, while Islam recognizes the potential need for dissolution in certain circumstances. The concept of marriage is often regarded as an institution rather than a mere promise.

If someone cannot have faith and embrace change, how can they guarantee a union without faith? Both Islam and Christianity have distinct approaches for addressing challenges and difficulties within a marital relationship.

For instance, Prophet Muhammad's daughter experienced divorce, which shows that lack of compatibility is not a reason to force two individuals to live together.

In Islam, marriage completes faith, as Allah knows the sanctuary of marriage and faith together is bliss, and it does not grant men the authority to deny women their rights, as it is sometimes perceived in Christianity.

Despite the misrepresentation of Islam in Islamophobic societies, Islamic laws apply to all of humanity and do not oppress women or men within a marriage.

In contrast to the Bible, which discourages divorce, both the European Union and the United States have legalized divorce through governmental reforms. These reforms were necessary to address the changing societal dynamics and to provide individuals with the option to end their marriages legally.

While divorce goes against the teachings of the Bible, it was deemed essential to accommodate the needs and rights of individuals in modern society. However, in Islam, divorce is permitted and regulated by the laws of the Quran.

Wikipedia: With a law adopted in 1969, California became the first U.S. state to permit no-fault divorce. California's law was framed on a roughly contemporaneous effort ...

Prior to 1937, divorce laws in the US were significantly stricter, making it incredibly difficult for individuals to end their marriages. Individuals could only get a divorce in cases of adultery, which demanded substantial evidence and often caused public humiliation.

However, the laws underwent a significant change in 1937, broadening the grounds for divorce. This revision allowed individuals to seek divorce based on bigamy, desertion, insanity, and drunkenness, provided they could provide sufficient proof.

These amendments marked a significant step forward in granting individuals the right to dissolve their marriages, where serious issues were present, facilitating a more fair approach to divorce.

During the time of the Prophet Muhammad, Islam introduced a revolutionary concept of equitable rights in marriage and divorce, ensuring the participation and agency of both men and women.

Islamic teachings emphasized the importance of mutual consent and understanding in a marital relationship. If a marriage became untenable and efforts for reconciliation failed, Islam granted the right of divorce to both parties.

This ensured that no one was held hostage in an unfulfilling or abusive relationship. These principles were rooted in the core values of Islam and were not introduced through regimes or political systems.

It is important to distinguish between the principles of the faith itself and the way they may have been distorted or misused by certain rulers or governments throughout history.

The Western world, which adhered to Christendom, allowed divorce rights much later, and these rights were mainly a result of political changes rather than being supported by the Bible.

The Bible supports the concept of maintaining a committed relationship and advises against divorce. With the evolution of societal norms and values, political movements emerged that questioned the rigid religious perspectives on divorce and advocated for legal changes.

The recognition of the importance of individual autonomy and the pursuit of personal happiness and fulfillment played a significant role in driving these changes.

As a result, laws pertaining to divorce were slowly introduced, providing individuals with the option to dissolve their marriages under specific circumstances.

While the Bible did not directly endorse divorce rights, the changes adapted from legal system. As a result, some religious communities have embraced more flexible approaches to divorce, based on their own interpretations of scripture.

Islamic law acknowledges that sometimes marriages may become untenable, and it provides guidelines and procedures for divorce. Unlike the Bible, Islam does not require governmental intervention to permit divorce.

Instead, the rights and obligations of divorce are already outlined in the Quran, allowing Muslim men and women to exercise their contractual rights granted by Allah.

However, it is important to note that while the Bible is followed by Christians, the interpretation and application of its teachings have evolved over time to suit the changing societal norms and values.

This recognition of the need for adaptability and flexibility in interpreting biblical laws has allowed Christianity to adapt to the changing times.

The laws and regulations of the Quran, as followed by Muslims, are believed to be divine and unchangeable. Muslims view the Quran as the literal word of Allah and consider its laws to be perfect and timeless.

While Muslims, are also susceptible to flaws and defiance, the rules and regulations outlined in the Quran are considered to be flawless and non-negotiable.

The contrasting interpretations of divine laws in Christianity and Islam result in distinct degrees of adaptability in their respective belief systems and contrasting perceptions and portrayals of Jesus, the shared prophet.

In Islam, marriage is a union where both people acknowledge the belief in one God. Without this belief, marriage immediately focuses on differences and worldly aspects.

Islam recognizes the importance of sexual satisfaction for both men and women. It emphasizes the rights and responsibilities of both parties in a marriage, including the right to seek sexual pleasure.

If a spouse constantly denies or neglects their partner's sexual needs without any legitimate reason, it can lead to marital dissatisfaction and may eventually justify the dissolution of the marriage.

However, it is important to note that Islam also promotes mutual respect, communication, and understanding in marital relationships.

If a couple is experiencing difficulties in their sexual relationship, Islam encourages them to seek guidance and counseling to address the issue rather than resorting to divorce immediately.

The aim is to foster a healthy and fulfilling sexual relationship within the boundaries of Islamic teachings. Overall, Islam values sexual intimacy within the context of marriage and recognizes its significance in maintaining a strong and harmonious relationship.

However, it also emphasizes the importance of consent, mutual satisfaction, and open communication between spouses to ensure a healthy and fulfilling sexual relationship.

While sexual intimacy cannot be forced, it is important to note that in Islam, a wife who consistently refuses her husband's advances without valid reasons is considered to violate her marital duties or the husband disagreeing to show affection.

Foreplay is important in Islam not relationship is forced. Prophet Muhammad encouraged foreplay prior to sexual intimacy which is not talked about but an important aspect of marriage.

However, Islam also recognizes that there may be valid reasons for a spouse to refuse intimacy, such as physical or emotional health issues.

In such cases, divorce is a better solution rather than forcing the couple to stay in an unhappy or unfulfilling marriage.

Unlike the concepts found in the Bible, Islam considers the complexities and dilemmas faced by individuals in different eras and understands the evolving nature of human relationships.

It aims to provide guidance that applies and is relevant in any decade.

Although Christianity has had conflicting messages over time, it's important to distinguish Jesus' actions as a prophet and Messiah not divine per Islam.

In Islam, sexual intimacy is considered an essential aspect of marriage and is highly valued. It is a means of strengthening the bond between husband and wife and fulfilling their physical and emotional needs.

The consummation of marriage is not only encouraged but also necessary for the validity of the marriage contract. If a couple cannot engage in sexual relations after marriage with no valid reason, it can be grounds for annulment or divorce.

In Islam, the bond of sexuality is considered an important aspect of marriage, but it is not the only factor that determines the strength of the relationship.

If one partner refuses or cannot perform sexually, Islam recognizes that this is a natural aspect of human nature and does not force them to stay together against their will. If one spouse falls ill and cannot engage in sexual activity, Islam allows for understanding and compassion in such situations.

In Islam, it is not permissible to deprive a husband or wife of sex. If irreconcilable differences exist, divorce is allowed. Seclusion and disinterest in sexuality are also grounds for problems in a marriage, along with other factors such as addictions, financial issues, and disinterest in appearance.

The list goes on, but it is best to avoid coexisting in an alienated environment, as loneliness is better than being lonely in a marriage. Islam does not support injustice; instead, a union is built on trust and justice. It is important to emphasize that trust and faith are the foundations of a strong relationship.

Therefore, Islam recommends that both husband and wife adorn themselves for each other. Every action is recorded by the angels, and a woman who deprives her husband is cursed, while a man who mistreats a woman will have to answer to Allah.

Islam acknowledges that attraction and desire are innate qualities in humans, and if the bond of attraction or desire has diminished or eluded itself, the marriage can be dissolved.

Infidelity or the involvement of one spouse outside the marriage is also considered a valid reason for divorce in Islam. Islam values the happiness and well-being of both parties involved in a marriage, and if staying together leads to unhappiness or infidelity, divorce is a better option.

It's crucial to acknowledge that emotions can override rationality in relationships and intimate encounters.

Western societies, known for their independence and openness, have a contrasting culture to Islamic beliefs. Surprisingly, even the most faithful believers and Muslims can face unforeseen challenges. The environment plays a crucial role.

In certain incidents, especially among ethnic women or couples, there can be challenges in disclosing personal issues that have led to a separation from sexuality.

This is true when living in Western societies or in a continuously evolving world, where breaking social or cultural norms may cause judgment or stigma.

The individuals involved may choose to keep these issues private, as only they truly understand the complexities involved.

Those who may have violated laws or societal expectations are unlikely to admit to their actions, often portraying themselves as victims and framing the other party in a negative light.

The involvement of family, as recommended by Islamic teachings, can sometimes exacerbate the issues further.

The current climate, however, allows for more informed decision-making, as individuals are increasingly empowered to assert their independence and challenge traditional norms.

Despite this, Islamic laws remain unchanged and offer guidance in such situations.

Recognizing the importance of sexuality in fostering closeness and intimacy within a marriage, Islam acknowledges the rights of individuals and proposes alternatives to either work on fixing the issues, finding a solution, or seeking dissolution of the marriage.

It is important to note that Islam allows for the possibility of returning and remarrying if circumstances change. This flexibility and adaptability make Islam relevant in any decade, as its teachings are considered the direct word of Allah.

Oxytocin is released during various social interactions, such as hugging, holding hands, and even positive interactions with friends and family members.

It promotes feelings of trust, empathy, and closeness, which are essential for healthy relationships of all kinds, including friendships and familial bonds.

In Islam, it holds great significance to highlight that sexual relations are only deemed permissible between a husband and wife. Islam emphasizes the negative consequences and disharmony that arise from engaging in illicit relationships.

It is taught that a person who indulges in fornication should marry someone who has also committed this act, while a believer should seek a partner who shares their faith.

It is important to note that a believer cannot sustain a relationship with a non-believer unless one of them changes their path.

It is worth mentioning that two wrongs cannot coexist, but it is possible for wrong to be corrected and transformed into right, as right holds more power.

In various cultural and religious contexts, such as the teachings of Prophet Muhammad, there is an emphasis on considering different factors when choosing a life partner.

The Prophet Muhammad advised individuals to prioritize qualities such as lineage, beauty, wealth, and faith when selecting a spouse. However, he also acknowledged that these external attributes are not the sole indicators of a successful marriage.

If these factors cannot align, he advised prioritizing faith, as is the most crucial aspect of a lasting and fulfilling relationship.

In Islam, heterosexual marriages are encouraged, and the notion of two bodies becoming one is not recognized. Each individual is accountable for their own physical and spiritual welfare.

In Islam, sexual satisfaction after a permissible marriage is recognized as a source of bliss, but it does not merge the individuals into one body. Islam allows divorce but emphasizes the importance of both parties attempting to salvage the marriage. In Islam, a corrupted relationship does not need to be prolonged.

Separating the two bodies would be impossible if they were one in Christendom. Despite being part of the Abrahamic faith, Christianity and Islam have contrasting ideologies.

Bible: Genesis 2:24:"A man leaves his father and mother and is united to his wife, and they become one flesh".

In certain situations, economic conditions may arise that deter individuals from staying or allow disbelievers to dominate.

If someone embraces Islam, or Christianity it is advisable to leave behind and instead follow the teachings of choices. The Quran, which emphasize justice. It is important to note that one cannot effectively serve others if they neglect themselves and remain stagnant.

Bible: Mark 10:8-9. "And the two shall become one flesh'; so, then they are no longer two, but one flesh. Therefore, what God has joined together, let not man separate.

The concept of one flesh is not something easy to comprehend. In Islam, the responsibility for intimate relations lies solely with each individual soul, particularly when it involves two believers.

This is pleasing to Allah, and it is believed that angels are sent to bestow blessings and protect such unions. Fornication is condemned and disliked by Allah. Islam does not grant any individual the authority to merge their flesh with another.

Instead, it emphasizes the importance of being true to oneself and finding joy in the companionship of another soul in a permissible relationship.

It is important to remember that this world is temporary, and no marriage is guaranteed. However, the faith of a believer is something that they must hold onto steadfastly. The Prophet Muhammad also encouraged his followers to marry and establish families, as it is a way to strengthen the Muslim community and preserve moral values.

Marriage in Islam is not only a physical and emotional bond between a husband and wife but also a spiritual connection. It is a partnership based on mutual love, respect, and support, with the goal of seeking the pleasure of Allah.

Through marriage, Muslims strive to build a harmonious and righteous family, raising children in an environment of love, faith, and piety.

Even without children, people still abide by Islamic principles and view marriage as a contractual commitment tied with Nikah, two witnesses and Mahr bridal gift and permission of the responsible adult to marry the young women.

Non-Muslim women marrying Muslim men cannot impose their beliefs on Islam, as Muslim laws supersede the wishes of non-Muslim women. Muslim women marry Muslim men to honor their faith and create a fulfilling family unit.

Any gender that divides or forces compromising the faith of Islam turns the home into an empty place devoid of angelic visits. Jews and Muslims share the closest monotheistic beliefs, while Christianity varies in its idolization of Jesus as a prophet and messiah across different countries.

Illicit sexual encounters in Western environments are spreading worldwide, leaving many feeling empty and deeply traumatized, with some opting for discreteness and repentance rather than openly discussing multiple partners.

Their spiritual yearning remains unfulfilled despite their pursuit of satisfaction through a series of sexual mishaps. Certain individuals in modern society may discover that traditional heterosexual relationships do not fully satisfy their desires, prompting them to explore bisexuality.

Wikipedia: The first American bisexual newsletter published at national scale was edited in 1988 by Gary North, and it was called Bisexuality: News, Views, and Networking.

Dissatisfaction with inner selves in Western countries leads to a pursuit of sexual exploration through music, drugs, and nightlife, resulting in increased unfulfillment. Islam does not waver in its principles, no matter what others may say.

The younger generation is being influenced negatively in public settings and schools. Moral codes of behavior are being eliminated by these institutions, while promoting open sexuality.

Countries in the Western world with less than three hundred years of history are going through a destructive phase that affects both the young and the old.

The evolution of music, particularly in the realm of rap, has seen a shift from melodies, romantic lyrics, and meaningful rhymes to a more explicit and degrading portrayal of women and bad language.

This trend, which originated on the streets of New York City, has left many who seek solace and happiness through music feeling empty and unsatisfied, even after listening to every note.

The commercialization and glorification of derogatory content has overshadowed the shared values of those who turn to music as a source of joy and inspiration.

As a result, the once profound impact of music on emotional well-being has been compromised, leaving listeners longing for the days when melodies, lyrics, and rhymes were more uplifting and respectful. This issue is not limited to just a few musicians, but a pervasive problem across the industry.

Many artists, from various genres and backgrounds, have tragically taken their own lives because of the intense pressures and struggles they face.

The music they create often reflects their inner turmoil, with lyrics and language that reveal their battles with depression, anxiety, and even their struggles with sexuality. Unfortunately, these expressions of pain can inadvertently influence vulnerable individuals who seek solace and comfort in music.

Nightclubs, fueled by alcohol, drugs, and a culture of indulgence, become the backdrop for these individuals to drown their sorrows and find temporary escape.

The cycle continues as these musicians, trapped in their own misery, use social media platforms to share their struggles, inadvertently inviting others into their torment.

It is a sad reality that this industry, driven by influence and mass appeal, can perpetuate a culture of despair instead of providing the upliftment and contentment that many seek.

Quran reading has a profound impact on individuals, creating a sense of spiritual connection and inner peace.

The verses of the Quran are filled with wisdom, guidance, and reminders of the temporary nature of worldly pleasures. As one delves into the teachings of the Quran, they find their heart and mind focused on the profound messages it conveys.

The allure of music, with its often superficial lyrics, becomes less appealing to those engrossed in the depths of the Quran.

Quran reading promotes a sense of solitude and reflection, encouraging individuals to detach from the distractions of the materialistic world.

This detachment includes avoiding environments that promote a hedonistic lifestyle, characterized by painted faces, nudity, and illicit behavior.

New converts and Muslims seeking a true understanding of Islam must realize that this faith is progressive and will not allow the influence of pagan practices to affect its teachings.

Dating in Western countries has progressed beyond the conventional dinner date. Clear expectations exist for both dinner and online platforms for sexual encounters. Society's regression to paganistic era caused by reliance on personal desires.

History.com. Feb 26, 2019 — Dec. 10, 1869: The legislature of the territory of Wyoming passes America's first woman suffrage law, granting women the right to vote and hold ...

NBC news: In 2020, Women's Equality Day marks the 100th anniversary of women's right to vote. But the fight for equality didn't stop with the 19th...

The women's suffrage movement in the U.S began in the late 19th century and culminated in the 19th Amendment, which granted women the right to vote in 1920. The movement fought for equal political rights and recognition of women's contributions to society.

Similarly, the fight for LGBTQ+ rights in the U.S has gained momentum in recent decades. Advocates for LGBTQ+ rights seek equal treatment and acceptance of individuals of all sexual orientations, including homosexuality and bisexuality.

They aim to challenge societal prejudices and discriminatory laws that restrict their rights.

However, these efforts often face resistance from certain religious groups, particularly within Abrahamic faiths, whose beliefs may not align with the full acceptance of LGBTQ+ individuals.

The ongoing struggle to advocate for equal rights for different sexual orientations and same-sex relationships is a complex issue that often clashes with certain religious beliefs, particularly within the Abrahamic religions.

While many secular belief systems promote the values of equality and acceptance, they may not align with the doctrines and teachings of these religious traditions.

Quran: Surah Al Isra: 17;81. And declare, "The truth has come and falsehood has vanished. Indeed, falsehood is bound to vanish."

However, Abrahamic religious doctrines hinder the progress towards equal rights, leading to ongoing debates and challenges in finding an imbalance between religious freedom and LGBTQ+ rights.

Islam remains progressive by not adjusting rights as time progresses. This faith has already given rights to women, men, animals, plants, and even the body itself. In Islam, women are granted equal rights to education, inheritance, and employment, challenging traditional gender norms.

Men are encouraged to treat women with respect and kindness, emphasizing the importance of gender equality.

Islam also teaches the importance of animal rights, promoting compassion and care towards all living creatures. Islamic teachings emphasize environmental stewardship, recognizing the rights of plants and the need for ecological balance.

Islam's recognition of the body's rights includes the prohibition of harmful practices, such as self-harm, substance abuse, and neglecting one's physical well-being. By upholding these rights, Islam remains progressive and relevant in a changing world

Women fought for independence in Western countries, only to compromise the dignity that underpins the beliefs of all Abrahamic faiths, while men ensured they were constantly reminded of their independence and women, for years, sacrificed their dignity by acquiescing to the whims of these men.

One who can disregard Allah for a human can easily discard that human as well, as time is not on their side. The core principles of all Abrahamic faiths do not condone illicit relationships, as they are cursed in Islam.

Dating became prevalent in western society in the 20th century, as societal norms began to shift and people started seeking romantic relationships outside of traditional courtship. Western countries made these changes intending to favor men.

This novel courtship method disregards religious principles and enables people to select partners based on personal preferences. The rise of dating also brought about the widespread use of the term to describe a woman in a romantic partnership.

Within Islam, premarital or extramarital relationships are haram (prohibited). It is strongly discouraged to commit **Zina**, sexual intercourse which comprises adultery or fornication, as it has a detrimental effect on marriage and the family.

Not only does this behavior go against religious principles, but it also weakens the significance of commitment, fidelity, and mutual respect in a relationship. Ultimately, these actions undermine both spiritual well-being and the trust and integrity of the relationship.

Unfortunately, no one can escape the influence of this society, and many Muslims fall victim to its allure of freedom and self-indulgence, finding it more appealing than the restrictions imposed by Islam.

In these countries, Christianity offers a tempting escape, as the forgiveness of Jesus seems to provide a way out of all evil, with the understanding of a compassionate Jesus.

However, in Islam, rewriting the laws of the Quran is strictly prohibited. Muslims who have been exposed to this environment undoubtedly face setbacks, but eventually, they come to realize that the essence of their faith is far stronger than the transient allure of a deceptive lifestyle that only brings anxiety, depression, and doubt.

Muslim women may not live in wedlock, nor can Muslim men. However, society has become so hypocritical that even Muslim parents are learning to accept it if the man of the family steps out of bounds.

If a girl crosses these lines, she faces dire consequences. Allah's punishment is the same for all genders - he sees no distinction.

This option is more widely accepted in Western societies, due to the influence of political regimes that promote open-mindedness and inclusivity.

Manipulators often exploit Islam to pressure those who don't comply and make them feel guilty for underperforming, whether in business or personal matters. Those who manipulate faith are Islamophobias.

Even the most devout believers may stumble in this test, but they can regain their strength through sincere repentance, even if they had to halt their participation.

However, it is crucial to approach these situations with understanding. Demeaning or belittling one another is not the response; it is a manifestation of negativity and harmful behavior.

One can view emotions taking precedence over judgment as a betrayal or defamation of character, but as a human experience. It is unfortunate that some individuals, particularly those with less education or a narrow mindset, may resort to insults and derogatory labels to satisfy their own egos when they do not get what they want.

Muslim women often face cultural and religious pressures, but it is important to address any wrongs constructively, rather than repeatedly voicing them in a negative light.

Ultimately, turning to Allah for guidance and seeking to fulfill marital rights with mutual respect and understanding is the Islamic motto.

The prevalence of these behaviors and advancements might be higher among individuals living in the Western world who practice Islam. The crucial aspect of reformation and repentance is self-reflection and making a conscious effort to alter one's behavior.

Muslim women, and men like any other individual, experience a range of emotions and desires. People in Western culture freely express their desires.

The clash between Western culture and Islam creates a dilemma, as Muslims, like everyone else, have emotions but restrictions.

The complexity of reconciling personal desires and religious limits emphasizes the need to prioritize the emotional well-being of Muslims within their faith and cultural norms, Islamic doctrine and unchangeable principles.

Islam views both Muslim men and women as equals, despite societal distinctions. Islam appears constricting to individuals who have changed their beliefs to align with contemporary values, resurrecting a period of excess, particularly in Western cultures.

Abu Dawud: 4781 Al-Bukhari: 6115. I seek refuge with Allah against Satan, the outcast.

Quran: Surah Al Muminun: 97-98. And say, "My Lord! I seek refuge in You from the temptations of the devils. And I seek refuge in You, my Lord, that they ˈevenˈ come near me...

The accurate perception of Muslims is often twisted and weakened by those with hidden motives. Islam is discredited by manipulators who exploit emotions, misunderstandings, and cultural differences.

As long as there is a believer fighting for truth, the reign of Islam will endure. Allah shows mercy to those who seek repentance.

Western countries made these changes intending to favor men. Privacy holds great significance in Islam, leading to the potential escalation of gossip beyond the initial wrongdoing.

Quran: Surah Maidah: 5:54. O believers! Whoever among you abandons their faith, Allah will replace them with others who love Him and are loved by Him. They will be humble with the believers but firm towards the disbelievers, struggling in the way of Allah: fearing no blame from anyone. This is the favor of Allah. He grants it to whoever He wills. And Allah is all-bountiful, all Knowing.

By maintaining faith, seeking forgiveness, and remaining steadfast, Muslims and believers can resist the manipulative tactics of those who seek to undermine their worth and perpetuate negative stereotypes.

Mistakes are an inevitable part of the human experience, and even the most devoted believers are not exempt from making them.

However, what sets them apart is their ability to learn and grow from their mistakes. Rather than eroding their faith or knowledge, mistakes actually serve as powerful catalysts for growth.

Mistakes present believers with an opportunity to reflect, introspect, and reassess their beliefs and practices. This process of self-examination deepens their understanding of their faith and enhances their knowledge.

By acknowledging their mistakes and taking responsibility for them, believers show humility and a genuine commitment to personal growth.

Their faith becomes more resilient and their knowledge more refined, as they incorporate the lessons learned from their mistakes into their spiritual journey. Ultimately, mistakes do not weaken the faith of the best believers, but strengthen it, empowering them to navigate challenges with greater wisdom and resilience.

Islamic teachings emphasize the importance of maintaining chastity and purity before marriage. Premarital intimacy known as Zina is (forbidden) in Islam and is discouraged as it is seen as a violation of the sanctity of marriage.

Islam encourages individuals to practice self-restraint and to engage in sexual relations only within the confines of a lawful marriage.

Quran: Surah Isra: 17:32. Do not go near adultery. It is truly a shameful deed and an evil way.

Regarding homosexuality, Islamic teachings hold that same-sex relationships are not permissible. The Quranic story of the people of Lot (known as the people of Sodom and Gomorrah) is often cited as evidence of the prohibition of homosexual acts.

Islam condemns homosexual acts and views them as sinful, according to its teachings and principles. Islamic scripture, including the Quran and Hadith, clearly state that same-sex relationships are forbidden.

Allah created humans as male and female, and the purpose of sexual relationships is within the bounds of marriage between a man and a woman. Therefore, engaging in homosexual or bisexual acts as a deviation from the natural order is non permissible.

Islam emphasizes the importance of repentance and reformation for those who have engaged in such acts, encouraging them to seek forgiveness and strive towards righteousness.

Exclusion from societies that promote and encourage such desires is necessary to maintain the moral integrity and purity of the community.

However, it is important to note that while Islam condemns homosexual acts, it also teaches its followers to treat all individuals with respect, compassion, and fairness, regardless of their sexual orientation.

Committing wrong actions is bad, but spreading negative rhetoric is even worse, as Allah forgives. In a contaminated society, where secularism and self-desires are promoted, there is a constant reminder for those living in Western countries about the interference in marriages and courtship.

The promotion of same-sex marriages and the encouragement for Muslims to abandon Nikah (Islamic marriage) can be seen as a misguided attempt at modernization.

Muslims highly value the institution of marriage as a familial bond and contract between a man and a woman, completing their faith.

Courtship and marriage should occur in the presence of Allah and be witnessed by two Muslim individuals. The importance of faith in the union is clear, as it underscores the necessity of Allah's blessings and guidance for a satisfying marriage.

As a result, it is highly unlikely that a practicing Muslim would have their marriage performed by a secular court in Western countries that does not uphold Islamic principles.

The Quran's teachings emphasize the importance of Nikah, which is the Islamic marriage contract, as a vital component of the Muslim way of life.

If a Muslim has no choice but to be exposed to non-Muslim courts, Islam acknowledges the necessity and validity of this need.

Muslims in every country should not have to compromise their principles for non-Muslims, as the influence of academia and secularism is causing some Muslims to view Islam negatively and secularism positively, resulting in widespread destruction and power struggles.

Allah knows the nature of this episode and whether it will cause destruction or restoration is up to His will.

In Muslim-Christian marriages, **Nikah** (Islamic marriage) arises when a Muslim man desires to marry a Christian woman. In this scenario, if the Christian woman insists on a church marriage and requests the Muslim man to be baptized, he may choose to opt for a civil marriage instead.

According to the **fatwa** issued by **Al Azhar Mosque**, in Egypt two witnesses and the offering of a mahr (a mandatory gift from the groom to the bride) are required for this type of marriage.

She has the option to accept or reject, but she must be given the opportunity. The agreement must be mutually agreed upon by both parties before signing the marriage contract for it to be valid.

Nikah is typically a **Sunnah**, but in this case, two witnesses and the payment of **Mahr** become compulsory. A key aspect of Islamic marriage is mutual agreement, including accepting **Mahr** even if it's refused after being proposed.

These are not adjustments to accommodate but accepting without violating Islamic law. It is important to note that two Muslims intending to marry would strictly adhere to the **Nikah** ceremony. However, the question of Nikah arises primarily in Muslim-Christian marriages, where the Christian party may request a church marriage, which is not permissible in Islam.

According to Islamic law, a Muslim man may marry a Christian woman, but any children resulting from the marriage would be Muslim.

Conversely, Christian law dictates that a Christian woman cannot marry a Muslim man unless he is baptized, and the children are to be raised as Christians. Therefore, the Muslim man is not breaking Islamic law by marrying a Christian woman, but it is the Christian woman who would contravene biblical law if he and she refuses baptism.

These laws and considerations become necessary to clarify and address the increasing prevalence of interracial marriages.

It is important to note that Muslim women are only permitted to marry Muslim men, and in such cases, **Nikah** would be performed, assuming both parties are Muslim and have agreed upon the **Mahr.**

In Islamic law, it is stated that the children of a Muslim man are Muslim by progeny. This means that regardless of the religious affiliation of the mother, the children will be recognized as Muslims.

Similarly, the children of a Jewish woman are Jewish by progeny, meaning that their religious identity follows the lineage of their mother.

However, for children of Christian women, their religious affiliation is not automatically determined. In order for them to be Christian, they must be baptized into the faith. This requirement highlights the importance of the sacrament of baptism within the Christian tradition.

These religious laws play a significant role in determining the permissibility of marriage within the Islamic faith. According to Islamic teachings, believing Muslim women must marry Muslim men.

This requirement is based on the belief that the religious identity of the children will be preserved and their upbringing in the Islamic faith will be ensured.

Islam allows interracial marriages, but with certain conditions. According to Islamic teachings, a Muslim man may marry a chaste believing woman Jewish or Christian

These conditions are in place to ensure the compatibility of the spouses in terms of their religious values and to safeguard the religious upbringing of their future children.

Overall, these laws and conditions are necessary within Islamic teachings to maintain the religious identity of the offspring and to address concerns that some parents may have regarding civil and interracial marriages.

Islamic tradition deeply roots it and sees it as a strength in Islamic values. Therefore, a practicing Muslim would typically seek a Muslim officiant and conduct their marriage ceremony within a Muslim setting, adhering to the teachings of Islam and honoring their religious beliefs.

In Islam, marriage is the union of a man and a woman, symbolizing the creation of Adam and Eve as the first couple.

The goal of marriage in Islam is to establish a family and fulfill emotional, physical, and spiritual needs. In Islam, having children is a gift, but not everyone is fortunate enough to have them. Similarly, Islam views material possessions and children as a test.

Non-Muslims rarely take part in unions performed by Muslims, as common sense would suggest. Non-Muslim institutions are not appropriate for Muslims seeking to formalize marriage.

Global diversity allows for better choices unless there is no other option. Neglecting the creator and indulging in selfish desires can be detrimental to our overall well-being and spirituality.

Quran: Surah Anfal: 8:28. And know that your properties and your children are but a trial and that Allah has with Him a great reward.

The laws of Allah primarily connect the religious perspective of Islamic beliefs. Recognizing the diversity in Western societies is crucial, as they comprise multiple religious and cultural traditions.

Continuously condemning Islamic beliefs and portraying Islam as backward is a key aspect of supporting Islamophobia.

The narrative of modernity is based on backward laws connected to pagan days and secularism, which attracts those who are ignorant of the beliefs and driven by self-desires.

Certain religious beliefs are not in line with the laws of Western countries, even Christianity, which is being pushed to conform to secularism.

Newly formed Western societies are effectively shaping the mindset of many individuals as a cohesive whole.

The phrase "pagan days" might seem unclear, but it encompasses the varied historical and cultural influences that have influenced Western societies.

Certain continents are attempting to eradicate all religions in order to promote secularism and adept practices that are not aligned with any Abrahamic faith.

It is important to acknowledge the potential negative effects of Western influence on global society, such as consumerism and cultural homogenization, but we must approach these discussions with nuance and avoid blaming all societies for global issues or the suppression of intelligence and morality.

Despite the influence of promoting false independence, every person possesses a mind and is ultimately responsible for their own actions. Ultimately, the world is an intricate and interdependent sphere, shaped by various forces.

To avoid falling into the trap of simplistic narratives, it is vital to critically analyze and actively engage with the multiple forces shaping our societies.

Regarding LGBT rights, Islamic teachings prioritize the preservation of traditional family structures and uphold the belief that marriage is a heterosexual institution.

Some advocate for inclusivity and respect for the rights of LGBT individuals, while others hold more traditional interpretations of Islamic teachings.

The views on this issue can be diverse but the Quran will not change to accommodate societal changes or decadence.

However, the acceptance of bisexuality varies in different countries, including Western countries. While the acceptance of bisexuality in the U.S. is politically influenced, it is important to note that societal attitudes towards bisexuality have been evolving over time.

It is not accurate to label bisexuality as a mere fad. The portrayal of explicit content and pornography in the media is a complex issue influenced by various factors.

While it is true that pornography is a thriving industry, it is crucial to approach this topic with nuance and recognize the diverse opinions and perspectives within society.

Bible: Leviticus 18:22 ~ You shall not lie with a male as with a woman; it is an abomination.

Bible: Leviticus 20:13 ~ If a man lies with a male as with a woman, both of them have committed an abomination; they shall surely be put to death; their blood is upon them.

Bible; Jude 1:7 ~ Just as Sodom and Gomorrah and the surrounding cities, which likewise indulged in sexual immorality and pursued unnatural desire, serve as an example by undergoing a punishment of eternal fire.

Bible: Romans 1:26-28 ~ For this reason God gave them up to dishonorable passions. For their women exchanged natural relations for those that are contrary to nature; and the men likewise gave up natural relations with women and were consumed with passion for one another, men committing shameless acts with men and receiving in themselves the due penalty for their error. And since they did not see fit to acknowledge God, God gave them up to a debased mind to do what ought not to be done.

The country attempts to enforce Christianity as the dominant religion while simultaneously implementing laws that contradict the principles outlined in the Bible.

Doing so would be a disservice to the system, as it would undermine the separation of church and state. It is important to respect the diversity of beliefs and ensure that individuals have the freedom to practice their own religion or no religion at all.

Advocating for laws solely based on biblical accounts and pushing Christianity with advocating the bounds of societal progress and secular advancements is inherently illogical.

While the Mosaic law prohibited certain cultic practices, modern society in Western countries has evolved to promote religious freedom and diversity, including the practice of Christianity.

However, the mixing of Church and State in these regions can be confusing for individuals seeking the truth, as it can blur the lines between religious beliefs and governance.

It is important to balance respecting different faiths and promoting societal progress, but Western society pushes Christianity and promotes secular principles, while one is contradictory to the other.

The rise of LGBT rights and acceptance in society is not solely because of political interference or a dominant regime. It results from a long and ongoing struggle for equality and recognition of diverse sexual orientations and gender identities.

While some political regimes have played a role in promoting LGBT rights, it is important to recognize that societal attitudes and cultural shifts have also contributed significantly.

The push for inclusion and acceptance of LGBT individuals has been driven by grassroots movements, activism, and a growing understanding of human rights. It is important to acknowledge that including LGBT perspectives in public schools is open to all the young and expressive.

This is challenging for conservative parents who hold traditional beliefs, find it difficult to reconcile their beliefs to allow their child to explore their gender preference at a young age. In many conservative households, the upbringing of children often involves adhering to strict gender roles and expectations.

Allowing children to decide their own gender is a direct contradiction to these traditional values. Conservative parents feel concerned about the potential long-term consequences of their child's exploration, leading to confusion and regret later in life.

The upbringing often influences the involvement of nature in sexual behavior and its moral and ethical implications within a household. Different cultures and religious beliefs have varying perspectives on what is acceptable behavior.

Western regimes, in their pursuit of secularism, have introduced a more liberal approach to sexuality that may not align with the teachings of the Abrahamic faiths such as Christianity, Islam, and Judaism.

This has resulted in a clash between traditional values and modern societal norms. While some argue that nature itself plays a role in shaping sexual behavior, others contend it is the responsibility of the household and religious teachings to guide individuals in their moral and ethical choices.

The tension between these two perspectives has sparked ongoing debates and discussions about the world.

Muslim countries are moving forward and not experiencing a resurgence of ancient pagan practices. If the truth is spoken, those who disagree may respond with backlash, labeling the speaker as a Muslim extremist or cultic. Or needing therapy.

Hadith; Abu Hurairah reports that the Holy Prophet said: "Four types of people are, when they begin their day, under the wrath of Allah and when they reach their evenings they are under the rage of Allah." I asked: "Who are they, O Messenger of Allah?" He said: "Men who imitate women and women who imitate men and he who goes unto animals and he who goes unto men".

Hadith: As narrated by Abu Hurairah ؓ the Holy Prophet said: "Allah has cursed seven types of his creatures from above the seven heavens. He has cursed one of them

thrice, while has cursed the others one time which is enough for them. He has said, "Cursed is he who did what the people of Lot did (cursed 3 times).

Hadith: Ibn `Abbas ؓ narrates that the Holy Prophet said: "Allah Almighty does not look (mercifully) at the person who commits anal intercourse with a man or woman."

Hadith: Abu Hurairah ؓ narrates that the Holy Prophet ﷺ said: "Cursed is he who goes unto women anally."

In many Western societies, and spreading globally it is not uncommon for individuals to explore and express their gender identity in various ways, including adopting the appearance traditionally associated with the opposite gender.

This phenomenon is perceived as a sign of progressiveness and personal freedom. Individuals may also invite others to engage in inappropriate acts by encouraging and sharing explicit images or content.

Those who believe it goes against traditional values and can lead to societal unrest criticized this lack of privacy and the promotion of such behavior.

In contrast, Muslim societies often place a strong emphasis on modesty and discouraging actions that may lead to fitnah, evil or social discord.

If similar acts were to occur in Muslim countries, there would likely be stricter consequences because of the cultural and religious values held by most of the population.

By focusing on political conversations as mere spectators or individuals who don't actively contribute to societal change, they cannot recognize and address their own emotional needs, hindering personal growth and genuine success.

In today's society, where gender equality is being increasingly emphasized, the success of women can sometimes trigger feelings of insecurity in men. Some men may feel threatened by a successful woman and resort to belittling her intelligence or dismissing her accomplishments.

However, it is crucial for the younger generations to choose their company wisely and seek advice from individuals who have tangible evidence of progress and success.

Judging someone's character, integrity, and honor based solely on material possessions is not accurate.

Prioritizing the protection of rights and benefits everyone's interests. Engaging in gossip is inappropriate because it frequently seeks to diminish and sabotage others. Prohibited in Islam without exceptions.

In Islam, spirituality and sexuality are integral aspects of human nature and are given utmost importance. Islam recognizes humans are created with natural desires for intimacy and companionship, including sexual desires.

In certain societies, sexuality is viewed as an expression of love or a recognition that God understands the needs of human beings. However, in Islam, the desires of human nature are not considered being needs that should be indulged without limits.

The Quran is an unchangeable and contractual document, and the laws regarding sexuality and relationships are clearly outlined within it. These laws cannot be dismissed or ignored.

While mistakes can be made, they should not be shared or discussed openly, especially if they involve two Muslims. For those who never leave the comfort of their home or nest, the search for satisfaction and fulfillment becomes a constant struggle.

Loneliness becomes their constant companion, pushing them to seek venues and avenues to fulfill their needs. In their desperation, they may even attempt to engage in behaviors that go against their own moral code.

The absence of a family or a life partner is a heavy burden to bear, and one can't help but wonder why some individuals are destined to walk this path.

Only Allah knows the secrets of each individual's heart and the reasons behind their circumstances.

Marriage is now happening later in life as independence and personal growth, particularly among women, have been prioritized.

This has led to both negative and positive outcomes, with some relationships suffering and others serving as inspirational models.

Despite being a natural part of life, some parents find it difficult to let go of their grown children, unintentionally impeding their path to happiness.

The best parents are the ones who prepare their nest for fearless flying, embracing the best of life with confident wings. Islam imparts teachings on morality, ethics, sexuality, justice, and religion, leaving no aspect untouched.

Sometimes, the pursuit of revenue becomes a hindrance to exploration and growth. The fear of stepping out of the comfort zone and facing the unknown can paralyze individuals, trapping them in a cycle of misery.

They choose to stay in their familiar but unsatisfying circumstances, opting for the safety of routine rather than taking risks and embracing new experiences.

Ultimately, it is a complex interplay of emotions, circumstances, and personal choices that keep individuals confined within the walls of their homes.

Loneliness, doubt, fear, and even laziness can all contribute to the decision to remain stagnant and isolated.

Each person's journey is unique, and only they can decide whether breaking free from their confinement is worth the effort and uncertainty that exploration entails.

Individuals who partake in emotional erosion may be surprised, as it is an unfamiliar territory for them.

Unplanned incidents can occur during meetings with different genders or even with the same gender, fostering relationships through visits, social media, and other means.

Progress and change are crucial when surrounded by positive influences, as negative influences can lead to unhealthy habits.

Quran: Surah Araf 7:29. And when they commit an immorality, they say, "We found our fathers doing it, and Allah has ordered us to do it." Say, "Indeed, Allah does not order immorality. Do you say about Allah that you do not know?"

If one demeans or blames the other who stopped themselves, it is important to remember that Allah knows that the most intimate act did not take place and this can serve as an opportunity for self-correction and growth.

Clarifying the importance of addressing the erosion of emotions or connections becomes essential during these unprecedented moments, and openness can provide support for Muslims and believers.

Muslims living in Western societies often face challenges because of the differing cultural norms and expectations surrounding sexual relationships, as these societies view acts of intimacy as expressions of love or personal needs.

Therefore, for a Muslim to recognize their mistake, self-correct, and resist societal pressures can be seen as a blessing.

Disbelievers or the bruised egotistical advice is often rooted in a cult-like mentality that promotes a free-form of sexuality, disregarding the moral boundaries set by Islam.

They may even blame the one who resists their prescriptions of illicit sex, calling them backward and sheltered. They seize upon any weaknesses or past indiscretions to manipulate and control.

This is prevalent among women, who are often targeted emotionally. It serves as a stark warning for believers to be cautious and vigilant in such a challenged society.

The exploiters can exploit the situation further by unfairly labeling those who resist temptation after indulging as extremist Muslims or cult members who strictly adhere to Quranic laws.

Exploiters show religious fanaticism by utilizing this label. It is not rare for Muslims to be branded with derogatory names like terrorists or extremists.

These misguided perceptions within Western society lump all Muslims together, which has become a trend of Islamophobia.

Emotions have the potential to cloud judgment and lead to unintended consequences. However, it is important to note that emotions typically come into play after a period of prolonged sweet talks and romance, leading to a sense of passion, particularly among women, and sometimes men.

In Islam, sodomy is a sinful act and is not permitted, even within the context of a marriage. It violates the natural order and a deviation from the purpose of sexual relations.

Engaging in sodomy can be a breach of the marital contract, and it may provide valid grounds for divorce.

Islam promotes sexual intimacy and pleasure between spouses, but within the boundaries set by religious teachings.

Any sexual acts that are unnatural or go against Islamic principles are strongly discouraged and may have consequences within the marital relationship.

The subject of sexuality is indeed a crucial aspect within any society, as it encompasses the dynamics of attraction between individuals of opposite genders.

Allah rewards those who exercise self-control and follow His teachings, rather than condemning them for their desires.

Giving Sadeqa, or acts of charity, even if close intimacy did not take place, is also encouraged to seek forgiveness. Changing course and redirecting one's attractions towards marriage is seen as the only way to comply with the rules of Islam.

This topic is relevant in Western societies where open expressions of sexuality are normal. Muslims often find it challenging to navigate these societal norms while maintaining their faith.

Slip-ups are often scrutinized by non-believers, perpetuating Islamophobia. However, it is crucial for Muslims and believers of the Abrahamic faith to not fall short and to strive for improvement.

It is important to keep sins hidden, as Allah covers the sins of those who keep them concealed.

Satan tempts individuals to expose their own sins and the sins of others, especially to disbelievers who eagerly await such news.

Understanding the intricacies of human emotions and attractions is a natural part of being human. If the attraction is between two believers, there are avenues within Islam to make actions permissible, such as through marriage.

In order to make these actions permissible per Islam it is necessary for individuals involved to enter a committed relationship through Nikah marriage.

Marriage, as encouraged by Allah, holds a significant place in Islamic belief. In an open society, where love is often expressed through sexuality outside the confines of marriage, the foundations of relationships can be shaken.

However, the true bliss and fulfillment lie in the union of marriage, where two believers come together in a sacred bond.

The beauty of this union is such that even the angels, known for their purity and grace, are said to shy away during sexual acts and give blessings upon the couple.

This is especially problematic when one is labeled as a Muslim, as it makes it easy for non-Muslims to note derogatory actions. However, it is important to remember that in Islam, correction and repentance can rectify even the worst scenarios.

Living in wedlock is highly valued and celebrated in a sticky climate, and unfortunately, this perspective is spreading worldwide.

It is crucial to acknowledge that Muslim countries have strict cultural and religious norms governing relationships and sexuality, which rarely approve or permit such actions. But hidden agendas lie in most places humans exist.

The rise of industrialization and urbanization in the 19th century. As traditional social structures began to shift and individuals had more freedom to choose their partners, men took the lead in formalizing the concept of dating.

This was clear in Western lands, where patriarchal norms prevailed and men held more power in society. Men played a crucial role in shaping the rules and expectations of dating, from initiating the process to setting the terms of courtship.

They introduced practices such as asking women out, planning and paying for dates, and establishing guidelines for behavior. While women certainly took part in dating, men who defined the rules and expectations based on their own desires and societal ideals largely influenced and controlled it.

The girlfriend-boyfriend relationship in the Western world has undergone significant changes over the past few decades. Previously, these relationships were often seen as more conservative, with a focus on commitment, loyalty, and traditional values.

However, as time has progressed, the dynamics of these relationships have shifted, and the concept of "free emission" has become more prevalent.

This refers to a more open and casual approach to intimate relationships, with a focus on personal freedom and exploration. While some may argue that this newfound freedom has led to a loss of morality and elasticity in relationships, others see it as a natural evolution of societal norms.

The rise of technology and social media has introduced new challenges, such as the prevalence of dishonesty and the creation of false identities.

This has further complicated the notion of independence and morality within relationships, as individuals may feel more inclined to code lies or present themselves in a way that is not entirely truthful.

Overall, the concept of independence in relationships has evolved over time, but it is important to consider the potential consequences and impact on morality.

Western women seeking independence from the confines of the Bible, which historically relegated them to a subordinate position, found a new sense of empowerment.

Muslim women found this in Islam. Unlike Christianity, which often saw women as inferior to men, Islam gave women a newfound respect and recognition. Prior to the advent of Islam, women were often marginalized and treated as property, with limited rights and freedoms.

However, Islamic teachings emphasized the dignity and honor of women, granting them rights and responsibilities previously unheard of.

Islam brought about a significant shift in societal attitudes towards women, granting them the right to education, property ownership, and the ability to participate in public life.

This newfound independence within the confines of Islam allowed women to maintain their dignity while also asserting their rights and achieving a level of autonomy that was previously unimaginable.

In Western society, it became the norm for women to be submissive and adhere to the societal expectations set by men. These expectations were often rooted in traditional beliefs and religious texts, such as the Bible, which upheld the idea of women being submissive to men.

This created a backward and oppressive environment for women. However, as women in the West experienced newfound independence and autonomy, they started to question and challenge these societal norms.

They sought liberation from the confines of traditional gender roles and expectations. Islam, as a religion, does not advocate for the backwardness or submissiveness of women. It emphasizes the dignity and equality of all individuals, regardless of gender.

Islam grants women independence, knowledge, and rights that are often still being fought for by Western women. However, exposure to Western society can sometimes lead to a false sense of independence, where women conform to societal pressures without truly understanding the principles and values that Islam promotes.

In contrast to how western media portrays Islam, the fight for women's independence in a male dominant society remains constant. The Bible does not explicitly grant the independence that women are seeking, which poses a challenge to secularism as it does not align with biblical teachings.

The concept of promoting independence for women contradicts the teachings of the Bible.

However, Islam offers women independence, dignity, equality, and responsibility over themselves, alongside men. Many women appreciate the sense of responsibility and care that Islam encourages, rather than negligence.

The portrayal of Muslim women as backward by Western social media is often based on uninformed assumptions. It is important to note that Christianity does not grant women equal rights or decision-making power within the religion.

Bible ESV: Timothy 2;12. I do not permit a woman to teach or to exercise authority over a man; rather, she is to remain quiet.

It is not alarming to encounter a contradiction between the Bible and those who advocate for Christianity as a dominant force alongside secularism, as these two concepts are at odds with each other.

Therefore, it seems illogical for women who identify with the Christian faith to enter positions of power, as the Bible does not permit them to rule over men. In contrast, Islam has granted women rights, and many women in Muslim countries have held positions of leadership.

Recognizing the ongoing fight for women's rights is vital, as western societal advancements challenge the often-adjusted biblical principles to meet current demands. Western society debates the Bible's lack of authority for women, with the theme constantly evolving.

The blending of biblical principles and secularism limits theological ideas. Islam has helped to ensure equal rights for both genders. Contrary to Western society's misinformation, Islamic principles have elevated women's status and created new opportunities for them.

It is essential for individuals to educate themselves on the various aspects and true nature of Islam before making judgments or spreading misinformation.

The Islamophobic society cannot continue without a Muslim or Muslims voicing the truth and challenging the misconceptions and stereotypes that fuel discrimination and hatred.

Remaining silent would not only be hypocritical but also detrimental to the progress of society. Muslims have a responsibility to stand up for truth, not only for themselves but also for the larger Muslim community and the principles of justice and equality.

By speaking out against Islamophobia, they can help educate others, break down barriers, and foster understanding and acceptance. It is through their courage and determination that positive change can be achieved, ensuring a more inclusive and harmonious society for all.

Prophet Muhammad's wife, Khadija, is indeed a perfect example of breaking traditional norms.

In a society where it was customary for men to propose in marriage, Khadija, a successful and influential businesswoman, took the initiative and proposed to Prophet Muhammad.

This act not only showed her confidence and assertiveness but also showcased the progressive nature of Islam in empowering women. Khadija's proposal was accepted by Prophet Muhammad, highlighting the importance of mutual consent and the recognition of a woman's agency in decision-making.

Khadija holds the distinction of being the first female Muslim, as she embraced Islam after Prophet Muhammad received the first revelation. Her courage, faith, and leadership continue to inspire Muslim women around the world, serving as a reminder that they too can actively pursue their desires and make significant contributions to society.

There is a pressing need to continue efforts to educate people in Western lands about the women of Islam and the progressive secularism that Muslims face.

It is important to shed light on the empowering aspects of Islam, such as the story of Khadija, who served as an example of independence for women.

Islam grants women the freedom to propose to a man they believe in, and it encourages them to take charge of their own lives.

This narrative challenges the misconception that women in Islam are oppressed or submissive.

By sharing stories like the one mentioned, where a woman prophet Muhammad's wife Khadija covers her husband with a blanket as he witnesses the awe-inspiring angel Gabriel, with approximately 600 wings that can cover the vast portion of the sky, we can emphasize the spiritual experiences and profound faith that exist within the religion.

It is crucial to promote understanding and open dialogue to counter stereotypes and promote a more inclusive and accurate representation of Islam in Western societies.

However, it is important to understand that the concept of haram and halal (permissible) is specific to Muslims and their religious obligations. Other faiths have their own set of laws and guidelines.

In Islam, these laws are a contractual agreement between the individual and their Creator. Non-compliance with certain rules or unintentional acts that are deemed impermissible does not automatically remove one from the fold of Islam.

Instead, repentance and acts of charity (Sadeqa) play a crucial role in seeking forgiveness for these unintended transgressions. It is essential to clearly understand Islamic teachings and consult knowledgeable scholars to avoid unnecessary blame or confusion.

In a society conducive to Islamic principles, it is important to address certain behaviors that may go against these principles. Some individuals, in order to maintain peace, may apologize to an abusive person.

However, it is crucial to emphasize that this behavior should be explained within the context of a diverse society, where many people have found themselves in similar situations. The portrayal of gender dynamics in the Bible can indeed be controversial and challenging to understand in a modern context.

One particular example often cited is found in **Bible: Deuteronomy 22:28-29**, which states that if a man rapes a virgin, he must pay a fine to her father and marry her, with divorce not being allowed.

This passage has been interpreted as oppressive towards women as it seems to prioritize the rights of the perpetrator over the victim.

Bible: NIV: 22:28;29 If a man happens to meet a virgin who is not pledged to be married and rapes her and they are discovered, he shall pay her father fifty shekels[a] of silver. He must marry the young woman, for he has violated her. He can never divorce her as long as he lives.

In contrast, Islamic law, as interpreted by some scholars, prescribes severe punishments, including death, for those found guilty of rape. This approach is based on the principle of upholding justice and protecting the rights of the victim.

Islamic teachings emphasize the importance of consent and the dignity of individuals, particularly women, in matters of sexuality and personal autonomy. The wide range of narratives in Bible teachings necessitates meticulous notation. The Quran maintains a consistent approach.

Societal and cultural contexts influence the interpretation and application of religious texts. Delving into the intricacies of these religious traditions demands meticulous study and an examination of diverse perspectives.

In Christianity, women have long fought for equality, challenging traditional gender roles and advocating for their rights. However, within the Christian faith, there are still remnants of a patriarchal system that does not view women as equal to men.

This can be seen in certain interpretations of biblical texts that reinforce male dominance and restrict women's roles within the church.

Islam has a specific chapter in the Quran called Surah An-Nisa that addresses women's rights and emphasizes their dignity and equality.

However, it is important to note that even within the Muslim community, there are instances where women's rights are not fully understood or respected.

Similarly, when men convert to Islam from Christianity, they may bring with them certain beliefs and attitudes rooted in male egoism, unless they are educated about Islam's teachings on gender equality.

Therefore, it is crucial to engage in open and informed discussions about Islam and its principles regarding the rights and dignity of women, so that both Muslim and non-Muslim men can develop a more egalitarian mindset.

Sometimes, individuals may choose to hide their own personal struggles by blaming others, hindering the principles of morality.

To truly understand Islam and its teachings, the pursuit of knowledge is essential. Only through knowledge can one grasp Islam at its best and make informed decisions that align with its principles.

In Islam, it is believed that mistakes are a natural part of human existence and should not hinder a Muslim's progress.

However, it is important for Muslims to be cautious of those who seek to exploit their weaknesses for personal gain or to portray themselves as victims.

In Islam, gossip is a grave sin that must be avoided, while Allah is forgiving.

Temporary conflicts and rumors can change to lasting friendships or even marriages when blame dissipates and both parties find emotional balance. It's important to recognize that both parties handle their actions and to listen to the inner voice that tells the truth.

For men who are sensitive to rejection of their masculinity, it becomes a constant struggle to prove themselves and assert dominance. The impact of a challenge to masculinity can lead to different defensive responses.

To compensate, it could resort to aggressive or hyper-masculine behavior, seeking validation from others or constantly asserting dominance. This is especially crucial for individuals transitioning from a faith like Christendom, where women are perceived as inferior, to receive additional education in Islam, particularly converts to Islam.

When faced with rejection or criticism, they may respond defensively, angrily, or by withdrawing.

The fragile ego that men often have results from societal expectations and stereotypes about masculinity, which create significant pressure to meet certain ideals.

If their sense of masculinity is endangered, they view it as a personal affront and become more susceptible to rejection. Education is essential for someone transitioning from Christianity to Islam, especially in Western countries influenced by Western society.

Islam encourages individuals to seek spiritual fulfillment through the practice of their faith, while also acknowledging and addressing their sexual needs within the framework of a lawful and committed relationship.

By recognizing the importance of both spirituality and sexuality, Islam aims to provide a balanced approach to human desires and promote a harmonious and fulfilling life.

Believers often prioritize their faith and strive to adhere to its teachings, including those related to sexuality. However, human emotions are complex and can sometimes overpower even the most devout individuals.

Intimate contact and romantic involvement with someone of the opposite gender can trigger unexpected and intense emotions that believers may not have expected. These emotions can potentially create a conflict between their faith and their desires.

The erosion of expected emotions can be a challenging and confusing experience for believers, as they may find themselves grappling with conflicting feelings and questioning their beliefs.

It is important to acknowledge that human nature and emotions can influence individuals, regardless of their religious convictions.

Many individuals living in western civilizations find it easier to accept various spheres of life compared to those in other parts of the world.

However, it is important to acknowledge that Muslims residing in western societies often face unique challenges in navigating these spheres. In every act, there are typically two participants involved, each with their own intentions and motivations.

However, in some cases, one participant may be driven by feelings of jealousy or insecurity, or they may eagerly wait for an opportunity to exploit the perceived weakness of the other.

This destructive behavior can be seen as a manifestation of the evil plot of Satan, as it aims to manipulate, divide, and undermine the genuine connection and trust between individuals.

The transparent nature of this ploy highlights the need for vigilance and discernment to protect oneself from such harmful influences.

Society, which disregards their personal boundaries and autonomy burdens those who choose not to engage in certain activities.

This challenge is faced by both women and men in western society, as societal norms often perpetuate victim-blaming and cannot hold perpetrators accountable for their actions.

Forgiveness holds great importance in Islam, and sincere repentance to Allah leads to forgiveness. Mentioning the mistakes or flaws of others only compounds the wrongdoing, as with accounting in Islam.

Islam teaches that if Allah has forgiven someone, it is not for others to judge or demean them based on actions that they are not aware of whether they have been taken to Allah.

Sexuality is a complex and diverse aspect of human nature that encompasses a wide range of desires and attractions. It is influenced by a multitude of factors, including personal experiences, cultural influences, and individual preferences.

In today's society, there is a growing recognition and acceptance of different sexual orientations and identities, challenging traditional beliefs and norms.

This shift has led to an increased understanding and exploration of sexuality, as individuals feel more empowered to express their desires openly without filter.

The climate of sexual exploration and freedom. In ancient pagan societies, such as those in Greece and Rome, sexual relationships were often seen as a means of personal and spiritual fulfillment.

The Roman emperors, known for their lavish lifestyles, openly indulged in same-sex relationships and even had relationships with all genders.

This acceptance and openness towards various forms of sexuality continued to influence societal attitudes, even as Christianity spread.

However, with the rise of Christendom, attitudes towards sexuality underwent a significant transformation.

The Church, seeking to establish a moral order, viewed sex primarily within the confines of marriage and for procreation.

This shift led to a more restrictive and regulated approach to sexuality, which persisted for centuries.

In Islamic mosques, there is a strict adherence to gender separation, with separate prayer areas for men and women. This segregation ensures that there is limited interaction between the sexes within the mosque premises.

This separation is highly respected and maintained to create an environment of modesty and focus on worship. Unlike in Catholic confessions, where individuals privately disclose their sins to a priest in a secluded confessional booth, there is no such practice in Islamic mosques.

Muslims are encouraged to seek forgiveness from Allah directly, with no intermediaries.

In recent years, there has been a significant shift in societal attitudes towards diverse sexual orientations and identities. This shift can be attributed to several factors, including the increasing influence of secularism and liberalism.

As societies have become more open-minded and accepting, individuals have felt more empowered to explore and express their true selves, free from the constraints of traditional norms.

This re-emergence of exploration and acceptance mirrors the pagan roots of sexual freedom, which celebrated a wide range of sexual practices and identities.

It represents a departure from the more rigid traditions that historically imposed strict moral codes and stigmatized anything outside of the heterosexual, monogamous norm.

The acceptance of diverse relationship structures and open sexuality has gained popularity in many societies, but some see it as a failed form of liberalism that enforces secularism.

This mirrors the practices of ancient pagan societies and contradicts traditional religious values.

Prophets, from an Islamic standpoint, are human beings chosen by God to transmit His message to mankind. They have attributes like righteousness, wisdom, and divine guidance, yet they are not divine beings.

Understanding and imitating the actions and teachings of prophets is relatively easier because they possess the same human nature as us.

God is believed to be transcendent and beyond human comprehension. He is the creator of the universe and everything in it, including humans.

As such, God is unique and incomparable to any of His creations. He has no partners, associates, or offspring, as He is self-sufficient and independent. This concept, known as Tawheed, is central to Islamic theology and highlights the distinction between the Creator and the creation.

While prophets serve as role models for humans to emulate in their actions and beliefs, attempting to mimic God would be impossible and inappropriate.

Liberals are often matched by having an affinity for pagan customs, which may seem acceptable within their ideology. The concept of "shacking up," where individuals live together without a formal marriage contract but still refer to each other as husband or wife.

In these societies, it is increasingly deemed acceptable to raise families and have children outside of wedlock.

This shift challenges the traditional institution of marriage and raises concerns about the implications it may have on family structures and societal norms.

Despite the unchanging nature of religious beliefs and interpretations, individuals still maintain autonomy and agency over their sexual identities and expressions.

It is vital to acknowledge that the principles and traditions of Islam cannot be replaced, even though some individuals may feel dissatisfied or restricted by religious practices. Understanding this distinction is crucial for those who perceive religion as an accomplishment in attaining success.

However, Islam does not shy away from addressing this issue and provides guidance on how to maintain moral and ethical boundaries within the realm of sexuality.

Islam denounces the political charade that uses sexuality to manipulate and control people. It believes that such distortions of values, which disregard the teachings of the Quran and the prophets, are false and destined to fail in the long run.

Islam encourages adherents to respond to the rules and commandments of Allah with patience, understanding, and adherence rather than aggression or alterations. It teaches that genuine success lies in aligning one's actions and desires with the teachings of Islam and living a righteous life.

The annulment of beliefs and experimentation with Satan, such as engaging in forbidden desires and actions, becomes vital for those who disobey Allah.

In societies that lean towards progressive modernization, there is a noticeable trend in the changing landscape of sexuality. What was once concealed and deemed forbidden is now openly embraced and acknowledged in different settings. Many view this change in societal views on sexuality as a deceitful tactic to control the masses.

This modernization can lead to the deception of individuals, as the allure of newfound freedom and acceptance, while possibly straying further from the teachings of Allah, swayed them.

This continuous cycle of sin and dissatisfaction is often seen as the play of Satan, as he tempts individuals into exploring forbidden pleasures and experimenting with their sexuality.

Those who engage in a promiscuous lifestyle may initially find some pleasure in their pursuits, but over time, they become desensitized and no longer find satisfaction in their actions.

Whether it's trying out adrenaline-pumping activities like skydiving or bungee jumping, or experimenting with mind-altering substances, individuals driven by the need for new experiences are constantly pushing boundaries.

They thrive on the thrill of the unknown and the rush of stepping outside their comfort zones.

This insatiable curiosity drives them to seek uncharted territories, whether it's exploring unexplored destinations or engaging in unconventional hobbies. As they indulge in increasingly extreme behaviors, they constantly challenge themselves to go further, faster, and higher.

This relentless pursuit of novelty and excitement not only provides them with an exhilarating life, but also fuels their personal growth and self-discovery.

While it is perfectly acceptable to explore and challenge oneself in various sports and activities to test the limits of the body and mind, the same principle does not apply to sexuality.

Engaging in sexual activities should always prioritize consent, respect, and the well-being of all parties involved.

Rape is a heinous crime that goes against the principles of consent and respect for individual autonomy, regardless of the societal attitudes towards sexuality.

It is essential to distinguish between consensual sexual expressions and the violation of one's rights through acts of sexual violence.

Statista: Oct 20, 2023 — In 2022, about 442,754 women were raped or sexually assaulted in the U.S. - an increase from the previous year. In that same year, 89,053 men.

Wikipedia: The 2018 Uniform Crime Report (UCR), which measures rapes that are reported to police, estimated that there were 139,380 rapes reported to law enforcement in.

Datasets: Dec 18, 2023 — In 2022, the rate of forcible rapes in the United States stood at 40 per 100,000 inhabitants. As the FBI revised the definition of rape in 2013, the 2022 rate is a slight decrease from 199.

However, despite their efforts, they cannot find true fulfillment, as the pleasure they seek is devoid of any deeper meaning or connection. This constant quest for gratification ultimately leaves them feeling even more dissatisfied than before, trapped in a never-ending cycle of fruitless pleasure.

It is a reminder of the temptations and deceptions that Satan employs to lead individuals astray and away from the true satisfaction that can only be found in a life aligned with moral and spiritual values.

Many people in these societies choose cohabitation as a practical solution to the pressure of maintaining financial stability. The combination of soaring living expenses, stagnant wages, mounting student debt, and scarce job prospects has made it increasingly challenging for individuals to cover their costs.

Some challenge the religious boundaries and adapt to the secular lifestyle, which operate within different limits that may not align with Islamic principles.

As a result, cohabitation has become a more viable option for couples to share the financial burden and achieve a level of economic stability. The societal acceptance of cohabitation results from a broader cultural shift that promotes a secular mindset and diminishes traditional values.

Forces that seek to undermine religious beliefs influence this trend, leading individuals to fall into the trap of Satan and abandon the sanctity of marriage.

This perspective views cohabitation as weakening the institution of marriage and promoting a morally compromised lifestyle.

While all religious Abrahamic texts state that sexual relationships should only be between a man and a woman, it is crucial to recognize that not everyone adheres to the same religious doctrines or interprets them in the same way.

The level of western authorities' engagement in matters of sexuality and gender discretion with the LGBT community differs from country to country. In nations that are dedicated to sexual diversity and inclusivity, they actively endorse and advocate for LGBT rights.

The legalization of same-sex marriage, implementing anti-discrimination laws, and the formation of LGBT organizations have led governments in these countries to promote discussions and representation of LGBT issues on social media and other platforms.

This approach aims to raise awareness and cultivate acceptance. The unit advocating for these laws cannot support Christianity while conflicting with it and other Abrahamic religions.

Social platforms in Muslim countries do not encourage the promotion or advocacy of LGBT rights, and the government does not actively support it.

These countries often adhere to the laws and principles outlined in the Quran, which play a significant role in shaping societal norms and values.

The story of Lot in the Bible differs from the story in the Quran. In the Bible, Lot asks for the men who were engaging in sexual relations with each other to be punished. However, he ultimately ends up impregnating his daughters, who were with him.

Bible: KJV: Genesis: 19:31:35. And the firstborn said unto the younger, our father is old, and there is not a man in the earth to come in unto us after the manner of all the earth: come, let our father drink wine and we will lie with him, that we may preserve seed of our father.

Bible: NIV: Genesis: 19:35:36. So they got their father to drink wine that night also, and the younger daughter went in and slept with him. Again, he was not aware of it when she lay down or when she got up. So, both of Lot's daughters became pregnant by their father.

Bible: NIV: Genesis 19:30:38. So both of Lot's daughters became pregnant by their father... The older daughter had a son, and she named him Moab; he is the father of the Moabites of today.

Given that incest is portrayed in the Bible without repercussions for Lot and his daughters, what would prevent an ordinary person from engaging in similar actions if a biblical text includes such narratives?

Bible: KJV: Genesis 19:26. But his wife looked back from behind him, and she became a pillar of salt.

What's difficult to understand is that Lot sleeps with his two daughters, gets drunk, and acts without awareness. Despite being a prophet according to the Bible, he faces no punishment, but his wife does and turns into a pillar of salt as she looks back at the land.

There is no such story in the Quran.

Quran sees Lot as a righteous man who begged Allah to punish those who sought men. He left with his two daughters and his wife stayed back.

The Quran depicts Lot as a righteous man who was saddened by the immoral acts of his community. He implored Allah to penalize individuals involved in same-sex relationships and seeking pleasure with men, as it contradicted Allah's ordained natural order.

Allah commanded Lot to leave the city along with his two daughters, as they were the only believers who obeyed Allah's teachings. Despite the warnings, Lot's wife stayed.

This event shows the repercussions of deviating from the correct course and emphasizes the significance of adhering to Allah's guidance.

At the southwestern edge of the Dead Sea lies Har Sedum, also known as Jabal Usdum in Arabic, a prominent geographical feature.

The name is a direct reference to the notorious biblical city of Sodom. Near the Dead Sea, close to the presumed ancient cities of Sodom and Gomorrah, is the industrial site of Sedum in Israel.

The historical and archaeological importance of the area is heightened by its closeness, as it is thought to be the real location of the biblical story of Sodom and Gomorrah's destruction.

Mount Sodom and the nearby industrial site of Sedum make this region a captivating destination for biblical history enthusiasts and those fascinated by the geological wonders of the Dead Sea area.

It is important to note that while the Bible mentions the wickedness of the men of Sodom, it does not explicitly state that Lot asked Allah for punishment.

This specific detail may be attributed to Islamic traditions and interpretations of the story.

Bible: Genesis 19:33. Lot was innocent of this sin, but was guilty of another sin. He was innocent because "He perceived not when she lay down, nor when she arose"

Bible: Luke 17:26-32. This certainly demonstrates God's wrath against sin, His mercy in rescuing the godly from destruction, and the certainty of the final judgment to come

Bible: Peter 24:10. The angels said they were going to destroy Sodom, but in this passage the LORD rained brimstone and fire. Even though God works through His messengers, it is still His work.

God overthrew all the inhabitants of the cities, and what grew on the ground. It was a total destruction including all the residents and the surrounding vegetation.

No matter how sensitive the issue, it is absolutely reprehensible and inexcusable for a father to impregnate his daughters, especially if he is considered a prophet of Allah.

That the daughters of a prophet would conspire against their own father, especially when they were raised in the teachings of the Biblical text, seems highly implausible.

It is deeply troubling that any society would deem these actions acceptable, and it is even more disturbing to blame Jesus for their sins to rationalize their behavior.

Despite the continuous alterations, the ongoing trend in the altered bible is to consistently blame prophets. The stories are impossible to believe, regardless of the followers' faithfulness.

These actions not only contradict the moral principles that a prophet teaches, but they also undermine the integrity and reputation of the prophets, as depicted in biblical stories.

How can anyone in good conscience follow a prophet who shows such a lack of moral character? Lot was tasked with selecting a path, while Abraham directed himself towards his own path.

The relevance of sensitive subjects such as rape and incest is increasing. The story of Lot and his daughters in the Bible is a complex and morally troubling one.

After the destruction of Sodom and Gomorrah, Lot and his daughters sought refuge in a cave, as described in the Bible.

Fearing they were the only survivors, the daughters felt desperate and believed it was necessary to continue their family line.

They devised a plan to get their father drunk and engage in sexual relations with him, resulting in both daughters becoming pregnant.

While the actions of Lot's daughters can be considered morally wrong and incestuous, it is important to note that the Bible does not explicitly condemn or punish them for their actions.

However, it is crucial to remember that the Bible comprises ancient texts that reflect the cultural and societal norms of their time.

While it contains valuable moral teachings, it cannot be seen as a complete and exhaustive moral guide.

As for Lot's involvement, the Bible portrays him as an unwitting participant, unaware of the events because of his intoxication.

The narrative does not excuse his actions, but highlights the consequences of his choices and the moral complexities surrounding the story.

Interpreting and understanding biblical narratives requires careful consideration of cultural context, historical background, and the intended message of the text.

The Quran provides a different account and perspective that differs from the story. Highlighting the truth of divine justice by showing the punishment inflicted on those who defied Allah and purity of Prophet Lot.

Bible: Genesis: 13;10-13. And Lot lifted his eyes, and beheld all the plain of Jordan, that it was well watered everywhere, before the LORD destroyed Sodom and Gomorrah, even as the garden of the LORD, like the land of Egypt, as thou come unto Zoar. Then Lot chose him all over the plain of Jordan; and Lot journeyed east: and they separated themselves, the one from the other. Abram dwelled in the land of Canaan, and Lot dwelled in the cities of the plain, and pitched his tent toward Sodom. But the men of Sodom were wicked and sinners before the LORD exceedingly.

Lot, the nephew of Prophet Ibrahim, resided in Palestine alongside his uncle. However, because of prevailing circumstances, Lot undertook a journey and migrated to parts of Jordan by the will of Allah.

This migration, known as hijra, occurred during a significant period in history.

Lot settled in the region on the eastern bank of the Jordan River, which belongs to Jordan.

The southern portion of the western bank, where Lot's journey led him, falls within the Palestinian West Bank and has been under Israeli occupation since the 1967 Arab Israeli war.

This intricate geopolitical situation underscores the historical and contemporary importance of the region where Lot sought refuge and established his new home.

Hadith: Abu Dawood 4463. Narrated Abdullah ibn Abbas: "If a man who is not married is seized committing sodomy he will be stoned to death."

Quran: Surah Araf: 7:80 And remember when We sent Lot [as a Messenger to his people and he said to them: 'Do you realize you practice an indecency of which no other people in the world were guilty of before you?

Quran: Surah Araf: 7:81 You approach men lustfully in place of women. You are a people who exceed all bounds.

Quran: Surah Araf: 7:82 Their only answer was: 'Banish them from your town. They are people who pretend to be pure.'

Quran Surah Araf: 7:83. Then We delivered Lot and his household to save his wife who stayed behind.

Quran: Surah Araf 7:84. We let loose a shower [of stones] upon them,[67] Observe, then, the end of the evildoers.

Similar to a delicious dinner plate that loses its appeal once it's fully eaten and all that remains are empty remnants, individuals who engage in actions that are not permissible by Allah and the scriptures find themselves unfulfilled and empty.

These temporary sources of satisfaction provide a quick fix, offering people a momentary sense of pleasure or accomplishment. However, chasing fame, success, or engaging in illicit sex can become obsessions that lack depth and emotional connection, ultimately leaving individuals unsatisfied.

In our fast-paced world, many people overlook the importance of pursuing lasting happiness.

They mistakenly believe that these pursuits will bring them fulfillment, only to find that the happiness they provide is fleeting and leaves them feeling empty and disconnected from their true purpose.

This spiritual disconnect stems from the fact that true fulfillment can only be found by connecting with a higher power and aligning one's actions with a higher purpose

In Islam, the Quran regards sodomy as a grave sin and forbids it. It is one of the major sins with severe consequences. Islamic teachings consider the act itself a grave violation, although forgiveness can be achieved through sincere repentance and behavioral change.

In Islam, the production, distribution, and consumption of pornography are sinful because of their promotion and involvement in sexual immorality. Viewing or promoting forbidden activities is an offense. Islamic beliefs remain unchanged regardless of the era.

The punishment imposed by God is a concept that is difficult to reconcile. Fear and repentance can transform into mercy, and the history of the people of Lot serves as a reminder that Allah punishes those who ignore His warnings.

The Bible's portrayal of Lot and his daughters raises perplexing questions about incest and its consequences. Various religious texts condemn and view homosexuality as a sinful act, resulting in punishment or societal exclusion. The dead sea in Sodom, where nothing grows, was destroyed by God.

The blending of Christianity and secularism, driven by higher authorities, creates a complex narrative around the influence of sexuality. Officials in these regimes promote false independence to collude and manipulate the masses.

The Quran, as the central religious text in Islam, is sacred and provides guidance on various aspects of life, including matters related to gender and sexuality.

As a result, the general stance in these countries is to maintain traditional interpretations of Islamic teachings, which does not support or endorse homosexuality.

Accusations of hypocrisy are often directed towards the countries that simultaneously promote Christianity while embracing ideas that contradict most Biblical texts. Some groups in these countries are more traditional than others.

The tension between conservatism and progressivism in these countries often leads to debates and disagreements over issues related to sexuality, privacy, and individual rights.

These weak and narrow-minded individuals cannot see the detrimental effects of engaging in open sexuality and seeking validation through social media acceptance.

While they may initially view it as progressive and a way to fit in, they are merely succumbing to societal pressures without considering the consequences.

It is also important to note that the Quran advises it is better for a man to have only one wife if he fears he cannot maintain justice among them.

Thus, while Islam permits polygamy, it also emphasizes the importance of fairness and responsibility in such relationships.

The practice of allowing women to have only one husband at a time has historical and cultural roots. One reason is the concern over determining the paternity of a child.

Islamic teachings promote a different approach. Islam encourages individuals to seek contentment within the framework of a lawful and committed relationship. In Islam, the teachings of Allah serve as a guide to lead a purposeful life.

The allowance of polygamy, for example, is explicitly mentioned in the Quran. However, it is crucial to understand that this permission comes with certain conditions and responsibilities.

Polygamy is not encouraged for personal desires or to build harems, but to fulfill specific social and familial obligations.

Islamic teachings emphasize the importance of fair treatment and equality among a man's multiple wives, including meeting their physical, emotional, and financial needs. While a man can choose up to four wives, it is recommended to choose only one.

The practice of polygamy in Islam aims to address specific circumstances, such as caring for widows, orphans, or women struggling to find suitable partners, rather than exploiting or oppressing women. Most Muslim men are married to just one woman, as maintaining one household is challenging enough and having responsibility for four is unattainable.

Prophet Muhammad's marriage to Khadija was indeed a significant period in his life, lasting for twenty-five years. Khadija played a crucial role in supporting and standing by him during the early years of his prophethood.

However, upon her passing away, the dynamics of Islam shifted. Muhammad's mission of spreading Islam gained momentum, and he married other women, many of whom played vital roles in various aspects of his life and the development of Islam.

Prophet Muhammad entered various marriages for a range of reasons, including the establishment of alliances with influential tribes and the promotion of peace and unity among diverse communities.

These women played a significant role in advancing the message of Islam by providing support to the Prophet and actively taking part in community matters.

They embraced Islam and educated many Muslims. Aisha, the wife of the prophet, authored many hadiths, and people referred to his wives as the mothers of believers.

Marrying the wives of the prophet Muhammad was prohibited for everyone.

The prophet of Islam, Muhammad, was indeed a powerful and influential figure, successful in both secular and religious matters. However, it is important to note that his relationships and marriages were not driven by personal desires or a quest for power.

In Islam, marriage is a commitment and a way to establish a stable and harmonious family structure. The Islamic faith upholds marriage to protect the dignity and rights of both women and men, rather than promoting promiscuity or illicit relationships.

However, in Muslim-majority countries where Islamic law is recognized, marriage is typically conducted through the court system, as it aligns with the Islamic legal framework.

Introducing polytheistic beliefs into a household that follows monotheism can create conflicts and contradictions in terms of religious practices and values. Such unions can lead to a loss of spiritual harmony and a weakening of faith.

It is important to note that Islam promotes tolerance and respect for people of different faiths, but with marriage, compatibility of beliefs is highly valued among Muslims. The goal is to create a home where both partners can spiritually grow and support each other's journey towards God.

Navigating interfaith marriages or households in this context can be challenging, as societal pressures may clash with religious beliefs.

However, it is essential to emphasize that successful navigation relies on open communication and a willingness to accommodate each other's practices.

For Muslims, the belief in Christianity as a prophet serving as God, while Islam sees an unseen god and the last prophet is Muhammad, can pose a hindrance in accommodating other practices.

The Quran mentions Christianity as the Gospel given to Jesus, emphasizing the importance of finding common ground in the belief of one God.

The belief in the oneness of one God was present in all religions, but it was after Jesus' ascension that Christianity emerged, gaining its name and significance.

Christianity is experiencing a significant decline as changes and a loss of faith have caused many to leave.

Statista: Decline of Christianity in U.S. Mar 28, 2024 — New data from Gallup shows that church attendance has dropped across all polled Christian groups. As the following chart shows, the biggest drop...

Pew Research Center: Dec 21, 2022 — In coming decades, Muslims are expected to grow faster than any other major religious group, rivaling or surpassing Christians as the world's...

While challenges may exist; the excitement of welcoming something new is always inviting but if the invitation is not in line with Islamic beliefs the offspring will hold no faith seeing the discrepancy of beliefs in the household. Islam does not say the people of the book can change the faith of the household for instance the offspring.

This episode focuses on moving towards secularism in a Western world where faith is uncertain, and academia and material takes precedence over religion. This system is inclined towards doctrines that do not conform to any Abrahamic faith.

Despite the attacks from Islamophobes, on social media, Islam remains the fastest growing religion in the world. Joining Islam leads to personal reform and improvement; it is not about changing Islam to fit individual needs.

The push to introduce discussions about sexuality in public schools aims to include young individuals, put doubts in young minds and question their own identities, allowing them to explore ideas that were once practiced in ancient pagan times.

This effort is being led by societies that consider themselves modern, using it to reshape young minds and remove traditional beliefs. While other religious texts have evolved over time, Islam has remained steadfast and unchanging.

NBC News: Aug 30,2023. Seventeen states enacted more than 30 new LGBTQ-related education laws in 2023, which will all be in effect for the 2023-24 school year unless they are blocked in court, according to the American Civil Liberties Union.

U.S News and World Report: Aug 14, 2019 — California became the first state to pass a law requiring schools to teach LGBT history in 2011, followed by Colorado and New Jersey in 2019.

The constant influence on young minds to indulge in their own desires instead of adhering to traditional religious beliefs is a concerning issue.

This primarily affects vulnerable individuals who come from strict or broken families, searching for acceptance. Even in adulthood, these individuals may struggle to form their own identities if their upbringing was overshadowed by darkness.

Some overcome these circumstances, while others become lost in confusion. Therefore, Islam emphasizes the importance of knowing and understanding one's faith, as evil has persisted for years.

It originates from regions that claim independence driven by self-indulgence, hoping that God will still love them.

However, true love from God requires respect and repentance, not defiance. Therefore, in this climate, it becomes crucial to learn and comprehend the truth. Islam is a religion that upholds the principles of equality, justice, and freedom for all individuals, including women.

It denounces any form of domination or coercion in matters of faith. In Islam, women may practice their religion freely and decide regarding their faith with no interference from men.

The Quran, explicitly emphasizes the importance of consent and autonomy, stating that there is no compulsion in religion but for Muslims who follow Islam regulations have no exemption.

Quran: Surah Baqarah: 2:256. Let there be no compulsion in religion, for the truth stands out clearly from falsehood. So, whoever renounces false gods and believes in Allah has certainly grasped the firmest, unfailing hand-hold. And Allah is All-hearing, All-knowing.

Islam recognizes Allah is the one and only God. Worshiping anyone outside of this belief is shirk. All prophets, including Jesus, worshiped Allah. Therefore, Islamic laws cannot be altered to please the people of the book or their women.

Islam supports the empowerment and safeguarding of rights, enabling individuals to choose and practice their faith freely without imposition or dominance. Laws are not interchangeable.

Allah, in His infinite wisdom, recognized the importance of creating a safe and harmonious environment for Muslim women to raise their families.

Mixed interfaith marriages have existed since the time of Prophet Muhammad, albeit with restrictions. However, compromising one's faith for any kind of interaction, be it friendships or unions, results in many losses.

Those who invite others to discover truth never falter, as truth prevails and there is only one God.

Marrying within the same faith ensures that the couple can jointly instill Islamic teachings and principles in their children, promoting a cohesive upbringing that aligns with their religious values. The prophets of the Quran maintain their dignity.

Lot was not punished despite the allegations made against him in the Bible, nor were his daughters punished for their actions. These stories are perplexing, as they challenge the teachings of scripture and may not resonate well with believers or non-believers. Most individuals, irrespective of their religious beliefs, have a moral code of ethics.

The selection of stories in the Bible raises questions for those seeking to study scripture and explore similar narratives. This curiosity may lead them to contrast with the Quran, which presents stories in a different dialect.

The Quran is unchanged and preserved in its original form, which adds to the certainty that the portrayal of Lot's story remains true.

It is a last attempt to seek clarity amidst a society that promotes interference in matters of sexuality by the current legislations and challenges religious teachings.

The white parade, which promotes acceptance of acts not condoned by biblical text, has become a societal norm. However, it is concerning that there is no equivalent parade for heterosexuals.

This push on society to embrace all acts and genders is alarming and goes against the teachings of Abrahamic faiths. Islam is unafraid to deliver what Allah has said about the creation of man and women.

Although it is recognized by this society that women can be in lesbian relationships, it is crucial to highlight that this contradicts Islamic teachings.

Those who adhere to Allah's laws are not easily deceived by the portrayal of relationships as art on social media and the promotion of all acts through technology.

The truly broad-minded individuals are those who understand the difference between what is permissible and what is not, while the narrow-minded ones are constrained by a belief system that appears progressive but distorts the truth and confuses those who are easily swayed.

The belief that Allah created a man and a woman as his first creation is deeply rooted in Islamic teachings. The Quran and Hadith and all Abrahamic faiths state Allah created Adam and Eve as the first human beings, leading to this understanding among Muslims.

The story of the people of Lot serves as a cautionary tale in Islamic history:

The people of Lot engaged in immoral practices, including homosexuality. Because of their transgressions, Allah trounced them and destroyed their land. This narrative serves as a reminder of the consequences of indulging in forbidden desires and straying away from the path prescribed by Allah.

In the Quran, the story of Prophet Lot (or Lut in Arabic) is mentioned multiple times, emphasizing his role as a prophet sent to guide his people away from engaging in immoral acts, particularly homosexuality.

The Quran portrays the people of Lot as committing grave sins and transgressions, including engaging in same-sex relationships. However, the Quran does not provide specific details about Lot's daughters being involved in any inappropriate acts with him. Prophets of God were sent to teach not to commit worse crimes.

Instead, it focuses on the punishment that befell the people of Lot because of their disobedience and refusal to heed the prophet's warnings. The Quran's stance on homosexuality is clear, considering it a sinful act, just like other Abrahamic faiths.

Muslim-majority countries, guided by Islamic principles derived from the Quran, uphold this perspective and do not recognize same-sex marriages or promote homosexuality as acceptable behavior.

Sexuality in Islam is indeed considered a private matter between a husband and wife. It is viewed as an intimate aspect of their relationship. Islam recognizes sins exist among all genders, but it emphasizes the importance of seeking repentance privately and maintaining one's privacy with the Creator.

Social media and pornography are the two major factors that undermine the integrity of those who promote evil.

The senses of many are being distorted by indulging in and promoting filth. Those who promote evil and live in decadence cannot guide others towards the light.

The remedy lies in reading the Quran or books that elucidate the true nature of the soul, countering the negative influence of society. Allah shows mercy to those who seek answers and rewards those who seek. The Quran's narratives of truth outshine any Islamophobic news outlets to provide answers and clarity.

Islam intervened in pagan societies with its own set of principles and reforms, which are final and unchangeable. It is important to note that Islam rejects hypocrisy and encourages Muslims to explain their beliefs and principles with clarity and honesty.

Quran: Surah Nisa: 4;145. Surely, the hypocrites will be in the lowest depths of the Fire—and you will never find for them any helper—

While a person may initially seem kind and compatible, differences in faith can significantly affect the relationships as life progresses. It is important to prioritize compatibility in belief systems to create a stronger and more harmonious match.

By building a firm foundation rooted in spiritual and emotional connection, humanity can discover stability and guidance when facing life's challenges. Travel, without a doubt, is one of life's most profound teachers.

The Quran itself encourages exploration and the exploration of lands, as they hold stories waiting to be discovered. Particularly in the Middle Eastern lands, where history echoes loudly, one can delve into the origins of it all. By observing the differences found in Western lands, one can savor the enriching experience of learning.

Quran: Surah Ank abut: 29:20. Say, O Prophet. Travel throughout the land and see how Allah originated the creation, then Allah will bring it into being one more time. Surely Allah is most capable of everything. Say, travel throughout the earth and observe how HE brings life into being.

CHAPTER 6
ERRORS DON'T IMPEDE PROGRESS.

Errors of life cannot impede progress; instead, they have the potential to strengthen individuals and propel them forward.

Mistakes should not be seen as hindrances, but as opportunities for growth and learning. Every mistake made is a chance to reflect, analyze, and understand where improvements can be made.

By acknowledging and learning from these mistakes, individuals can enhance their skills, knowledge, and overall abilities.

This process of learning and self-improvement ultimately leads to becoming a better version of oneself. Therefore, rather than being discouraged by mistakes, individuals can embrace them as steppingstones on the path to progress.

Throughout history, sometimes individuals who initially made mistakes in their understanding or practice of the faith of Islam eventually became exemplary figures in the teachings of the religion.

There have been cases where individuals who initially opposed or fought against Islam eventually became strong supporters and advocates of the faith.

Gratefulness is a fundamental characteristic of a believer, as it reflects humility and recognition of the blessings given to them by Allah.

Those who cannot express gratitude upon receiving these blessings may find that their blessings diminish. Allah, in His wisdom, is not hesitant to discipline those who lack gratitude.

The many manifestations of this discipline serve as a reminder for believers to value what they have. It's important to recognize that both believers and non-believers can lack gratitude, but those who believe they're entitled often fall short of expressing appreciation.

In contrast, those who give generously and express gratitude for what they have received are more likely to continue receiving blessings from Allah.

It is a reminder for all to appreciate and value the gifts given to them, as failing to do so may result in the reduction of these blessings.

Quran: Surah Baqarah: 2;152. Remember Me: I will remember you. And thank Me, and never be ungrateful.

Allah the Almighty has given many blessings and favors, ranging from small to large. It's important to recognize and value even the smallest acts of kindness from others. Islam places great emphasis on gratitude, as it signifies faith and humbleness.

Even though animals don't have the same level of intellect as humans, they still show gratitude in their own ways. Refusing gratitude and rejecting acts of kindness consistently indicates a mindset of ego and arrogance, which goes against Islamic teachings.

Satan's influence can divert attention, but he is not solely responsible for the attitude that opposes Allah's values of gratitude and humility. It is crucial for believers to keep in mind that Allah abhors ingratitude and encourages us to foster gratitude in every area of our lives.

A story about belief:

With his newfound understanding of Islam, the man fueled his challenge against the beliefs and practices of the disbelievers he was surrounded by. He engaged in debates and discussions, trying to convince them of the truth of Islam. However, instead of being receptive, they mocked and ridiculed him, fueling his disapproval even further.

As he continued to resist their influence, he found solace in the knowledge and teachings that the believer had shared with him.

It served as his anchor and guiding light during challenging times. He continued to face challenges in fully embracing all the Islamic laws, which were highly restrictive compared to his previous lifestyle, and he struggled to show gratitude towards Allah for guiding him to Islam.

The newfound faith faded as poor company became a comforting distraction, causing actions to deviate.

Amidst the chaos of loud noise, a negative atmosphere, and a rowdy crowd, music became the solace for him and for those who were revealed in the havoc.

Allah does not bless evil or any environment of empty crowds and noisy distractions that cannot fulfill the soul hindering a place that celebrates wickedness.

Despite the believer's unwavering support, the involvement turned into a constant advocate for evil as the beat echoed.

Over time, he faced the challenge of pleasing the disbelievers and his ego, leading him to uncover flaws in the believer.

The believer spoke extensively about Islam, providing information on its principles, beliefs, and practices.

Despite facing disapproval from the company he kept, he returned as a believer remained engaged and dedicated to sharing knowledge. around as Allah knows the hearts that stray but yearn to return do return to the path of righteousness.

His disturbing behavior persisted for a while until he rejected his chaotic life and realized that someone had replaced his spirituality.

He saw no other option but to return to what brought him joy: freedom and worshiping the creator, knowing that his soul was content. The return of a believer surpasses their departure in strength.

The highlight of Allah's power to change hearts as HE wills it.

The Quran, Allah emphasizes the importance of gratitude and promises to give more to those who are grateful.

His lack of gratitude towards Allah had caused him to stray from the path he was invited to. Gratitude becomes scarce and desires take precedence, leading to complications for new converts or Muslims raised in Islam.

The influence of poor company can lead the weak astray towards chaos.

Like the believer, the grateful person finds their way to the duly noted path. The believer's transformation serves as a shining example for those who doubted, showing that the search for truth leads to illumination.

Any one person does not define Islam, but by the actions of those who follow it. While the behavior of believers and non-believers may vary, Islam itself remains constant and unchanging.

This concept applies to the faith of Islam, which is monotheistic and unchangeable. When Muslims share their faith with friendships it creates a strong bond that anything of importance or material cannot replace. This exchange of faith and spiritual growth is sacred and valuable.

However, there are certain Islamophobic disbelievers who constantly try to sow doubts and challenge the faith of Muslims.

Their persistent approach becomes activism for those who engage with them. It is important for Muslims to be discerning and protect their progress and spiritual growth by surrounding themselves with those who complement and support their journey.

In the Quran, there are many verses that emphasize the significance of even the smallest creatures and their role in the grand scheme of things. These verses highlight the importance of paying attention to the intricate details of life as they carry profound messages of truth.

The verse in **Surah "Al-Ank abut"** draws a powerful analogy between those who take allies other than Allah. It highlights the delicate and intricate nature of the spider's web, which serves as the spider's home and means of survival.

Despite the complexity of its web, the verse emphasizes that the spider's home is weak and easily breakable.

Male and female spiders have a weak bond because of the extreme behavior of sexual cannibalism. Female spiders of certain species may kill and consume the male spider after mating.

This behavior has multiple functions, including providing the female with nutrition for her reproductive efforts and reducing competition for her offspring's survival. Although it may appear harsh, this behavior is a natural and adaptive strategy that has evolved in specific spider species.

The home that distorts a believer's belief also destroys the soul seeking spirituality. While spiders can offer multiple examples, they also serve a purpose.

This analogy serves to remind believers of the fragility and vulnerability of relying on anything other than Allah. Just like the spider's web, which can be destroyed in an instant, the alliances and support sought from other than Allah can prove unreliable and ultimately weak.

In a world where Islamophobia is prevalent and misconceptions about Islam are widespread, it is crucial to have friends who remind us of the true teachings and principles of Islam.

The friends are a source of guidance and support, reminding us to strive for righteousness and adhere to the values of our faith.

The friendship brings immense joy and contentment, as they encourage us to lead a life that aligns with our religious beliefs.

While there are many types of friendships that enhance our lives, it is important to discern between those that contribute positively and those that promote evil or cannot correct us when we stray from the right path.

Such friendships can be detrimental, as they may lead one astray and hinder spiritual growth. These individuals may disguise themselves as friends, but in reality, they are enemies who seek to exploit and manipulate the weak for their own gain.

It is crucial to educate ourselves and others about the true teachings of Islam, in order to combat the spread of Islamophobia and counter the negative narratives perpetuated by those with ulterior motives.

Surah Qaaf also recounts the story of a spider:

The spiders amazing ability to weave a stunning web. The spider's exceptional skills are showcased by this web, with its intricate design and delicate threads

This aspect of the spider's abilities serves as a metaphor for the ephemeral nature of worldly possessions and the transient nature of life itself. It reminds us that even the most intricate creations can be destroyed or rendered insignificant in an instant.

The story emphasizes the significance of humility and gratitude, as it is the smallest creatures like the spider that can protect and aid humans when the need arises.

This serves as a reminder one cannot underestimate the potential impact of even the most seemingly insignificant beings in our lives.

It serves as a reminder of the talent and craftsmanship present in all of Allah's creations. However, a comparison is made between the home of a spider and the home of a Muslim, who neglects their prayers.

Just as the web of a spider can be easily broken by enviers or external factors, the home of a Muslim who does not prioritize prayer is weak and vulnerable. The act of prayer, known as Salat, is not just a ritual but a means of protection for the believer.

It strengthens their faith, safeguards their home and family, and shields them from the negative influences and envy of others.

Understanding the value of Salat and regularly performing it is essential for a Muslim's spiritual well-being and the security of their household.

Quran: Surah Ank abut: 29:41. The case of those who took others than Allah as their protectors is that of a spider who builds a house: but the frailest of all houses is the spider's house: if they only knew.

The Quran tells the remarkable story of young believers seeking refuge in a cave to escape persecution. Using His infinite wisdom, Allah sent a spider to create a web at the cave entrance, giving the illusion of abandonment.

This seemingly insignificant web acted as a shield, preventing their enemies from entering unnoticed.

Despite being in a dark cave, the sun's rays miraculously veered away from the entrance, ensuring the safety and comfort of the young hiding within.

This story serves as a powerful reminder that Allah has the power to create extraordinary circumstances, even in the face of seemingly insurmountable obstacles.

It highlights the omnipotence and mercy of Allah, teaching us that nothing is impossible for Him, and that He can provide protection and guidance to those who put their trust in Him.

The loyal dog rested beside the children, slumbering for 309 years. These factors converged to safeguard the children and preserve them, enabling them to awaken unscathed in a transformed world, ready to embark on their journey. Guided by Allah, the spider played a crucial role in diverting the enemy's attention away from the children.

When the children woke up, they were unaware that the world around them had drastically changed. They were astonished to discover that they had been asleep for 309 years.

This miracle showcased Allah's power and protection, as He used a simple creature like a spider to preserve the safety of His devoted followers.

The intricate details highlight the precision and perfection in Allah's creation. It serves as a reminder for us to be vigilant and grateful for the blessings given upon us.

Throughout the Quran, Allah has shown many miracles to guide and inspire humanity. These miracles are a testament to His limitless power and mercy.

By reflecting upon the story of the spider, we are reminded of the importance of being grateful for the blessings we have been given and to always remain vigilant in our faith.

The benefits of a spider are many and often overlooked. First, spiders play a crucial role in controlling insect populations. They are voracious predators, feeding on a wide range of insects, including flies, mosquitoes, and crop pests.

By keeping the insect population in check, spiders help to maintain the ecological balance in their habitats and reduce the need for pesticides. Spiders are skilled web-builders, creating intricate and strong silk webs to catch their prey.

These webs can also act as natural indicators of environmental health, as they can be affected by pollution levels and changes in insect abundance. Spider venom has shown potential in the development of medical treatments.

Some compounds found in spider venom have been used to create painkillers and blood thinners, while others have shown promise in fighting cancer cells. Overall, spiders are an essential part of ecosystems, contributing to pest control, environmental monitoring, and even medical advancements.

The Quran indeed highlights the significance of even the smallest creatures, such as spiders, to emphasize the divine wisdom in every aspect of creation.

"Indeed, Allah does not neglect even the weight of an atom; and there is no creature on earth or within the heavens that is not known to Him." This verse reflects the divine care and attention given to all creatures, regardless of their size or significance.

Quran: Surah Zal Zalah: 99:7. So whoever does an atom's weight of good will see it.

The recording of human actions is not performed by Allah himself, but by his angels. These angels are tasked with meticulously recording every single deed, both good and bad, committed by individuals.

Although Allah does not directly perform the recording, he possesses complete knowledge and awareness of every action carried out by each person.

The accounting system in the afterlife is fair and transparent, favoring the accumulation of either good or evil deeds. This serves as a reminder for individuals to strive for righteousness and be mindful of their actions, as they will be held accountable in the divine judgment.

The Islamic belief is that living in this world is a test, where individuals must adhere to the teachings of the Quran and the Prophet Muhammad's example.

Regardless of whether they are good or bad, the Day of Judgment will reckon the actions we take in this life. The conviction of accountability motivates Muslims to seek righteousness and steer away from sinful actions.

Salvation in Islam is to be obtained through genuine repentance, acts of kindness, and surrendering to Allah's rules. While having faith in Allah is crucial, it is equally important to live a morally upright life and actively engage in righteous actions.

Muslims are motivated to always seek forgiveness for their sins and work towards self-improvement by practicing charity, kindness, honesty, and justice.

This emphasis on personal responsibility highlights how Islamic beliefs hold individuals accountable for their actions and subject to judgment.

Allah sent all prophets, including Jesus, to teach the same message without deviation from the path. The attainment comes from individual efforts to please Allah and live a virtuous life.

Those who comprehend that God is not human also comprehend that the unseen God is not visible to some and invisible to others.

It is implausible for God to make himself known to only a certain group and not make his presence known to the entire human race.

Given that God is just and timeless, it makes perfect sense the prophets had a specific lifespan in this world and shared the revelations they received.

God does not vanish and leave behind stories; he is an unseen God. Any assertion of witnessing God, even in religious texts, is false because God has never been seen, not even by prophets.

The Quran teaches that ultimately; it is these details and adherence to them that hold greater importance than the collective humanity itself.

When one departs from this world, they will leave behind the entirety of humanity, but their deeds, both good and bad, will accompany them like baggage.

A friendship based on the ethical code of truth rather than being swayed by superficial distractions holds value. Those who embraced Islam during the time of the Prophet Muhammad did not turn back to the polytheistic beliefs of the past, showing the strength and purity of their faith.

While friendships may come and go, believers can only discover true spirituality on the battlefield of unwavering belief, where they remain steadfast and devoted to their monotheistic faith.

Exploring the reasons behind why Allah sent every creature to this world becomes essential, as the Quran constantly emphasizes their magnitude and importance.

The Quran indeed mentions a surah that specifically refers to a bee, known as **Surah An-Nahl (Surah 16)**. This chapter highlights the incredible creation and importance of bees in the natural world.

The bee is recognized for its remarkable ability to produce honey and its role in pollination, which contributes to the growth and diversity of plant life.

In the Quran, the bee serves as an example to highlight Allah's wisdom, and the lessons present. The presence of the bee in the Quran highlights the vast amount of knowledge encompassed in the scripture.

The Qur'an mentions the organization and hard work of bees, as they gather nectar from various sources and transform it into honey. This serves as a valuable lesson for human beings to adopt a similar lifestyle of productivity, cooperation, and harmony with the environment.

By emulating bees, humanity can cultivate strong social relationships and respect the environment. The small creatures mentioned in the Quran serve as daily life examples.

The Quran mentions the bee and the benefits of honey in several verses, highlighting its significance in both the natural world and for human health.

It emphasizes the importance of balance in life and encourages Muslims to reflect on the wonders of creation.

Honey is renowned for its numerous health benefits, as it is a natural source of vitamins, minerals, antioxidants, and antibacterial properties. Consuming honey regularly can boost the immune system, improve digestion, promote wound healing, and provide an energy boost.

Many Muslims incorporate honey into their daily routine by consuming it every morning before breakfast, either on its own or as an ingredient in various dishes and beverages. This practice is not only rooted in religious teachings but also based on the observed benefits of honey for overall well-being.

Quran: Surah Nahl: 68:69. And your Lord inspired the bees: "Make ʾyourʾ homes in the mountains, the trees, and in what people construct, (69) and feed from ʾthe flower of any fruit you please and follow the ways your Lord has made easy for you. From their bellies comes forth liquid of varying colors, in which there is healing for people. Surely this is a sign for those who reflect.

The teachings of the Prophet Muhammad (peace be upon him) further emphasize the significance of honey. He advised his followers to consume honey for its many health benefits and healing properties.

Honey has long been recognized for its antibacterial, antiviral, and anti-inflammatory properties, making it a natural remedy for a variety of ailments. The Prophet himself used honey for medicinal purposes and recommended its use as a treatment for various illnesses.

Overall, the verses in the Qur'an and the guidance of the Prophet Muhammad highlight the importance of adopting the characteristics of bees in our social and environmental interactions. They emphasize the therapeutic value of honey, encouraging its consumption for the promotion of good health and well-being.

The fly, an often overlooked and seemingly insignificant creature, has found its way into the pages of the Quran, Allah emphasizes the extraordinary level of detail in His creation by mentioning the fly.

This serves as a reminder of Allah's infinite power and wisdom, which extends to even the tiniest aspects of life.

Reflecting on Allah's creation, the Quran highlights the significance of even the smallest living beings, like the fly, as a testament to their intricate balance and purpose. Humans protect themselves from flies by using screens, highlighting the disturbance even a small creature can cause in their lives.

Quran: Surah Hajj: 22:73. O people, a parable is set forth: pay heed to it. Those who call upon aught other than Allah shall never be able to create even a fly, even if all of them were to come together to do that. And if the fly were to snatch away anything from them, they could not recover from it.

Flies have been found to provide many benefits, according to scientists. The pollination process heavily relies on flies, as they assist in the reproduction of different plants. They play a role as decomposers, breaking down organic matter and recycling nutrients back into the ecosystem.

Flies also act as a food source for other organisms, playing a role in the delicate food chain balance. Every creature created by Allah has a purpose.

Hadith: Bukhari: Prophet Muhammad said, if a fly falls in the vessel, any of you, let him dip all of it in the vessel and then throw it away, for one of its wings has the ailment and the other has the cure.

In the Quran, there are teachings about various aspects of human life, including diets that are beneficial to the human body. It provides guidance on the intricacies of small creatures, highlighting the wonders of Allah's creation.

These teachings are available for those who will explore and seek knowledge. However, for those who choose to ignore these teachings and deviate from the path, they are assigned a Jinn as per their own wish, which can lead them further astray.

It is important to note that Allah guides those whom He wills, not necessarily those whom one loves. In Islam, the concept of rights and justice is fascinating.

Every part of one's body has rights over the individual who possesses the mind. This emphasizes the importance of taking care of oneself and treating the body with respect and justice, as prescribed by Islamic teachings.

Quran: Surah Anam: 6:125. Whoever Allah wants to guide- He expands his breast to contain Islam: and whoever He wants to send astray He makes his breast tight and constricted as though he were climbing into the sky. Thus does Allah place defilement upon those who do not believe.

The concept of responsibility in Islam is complex and multifaceted. While Allah is the ultimate authority and has complete control over everything, including the fate of individuals, Islam also emphasizes the importance of free will and personal accountability.

Each person has been endowed with the ability to make choices, and they will be held responsible for those choices on the Day of judgment.

Allah, being the All-Knowing, is aware of the intentions and innermost thoughts of every individual. He knows the sincerity of one's faith and the true nature of their actions.

Therefore, while the ultimate judgment lies with Allah, humans are still accountable for their deeds. Good actions will be rewarded, and bad actions will have consequences.

Regarding the scriptures, Islam believes in the divine revelation of several books, including the Quran, Torah, Psalms, and Gospel. However, it is recognized that over time, some of these scriptures have undergone alterations and revisions.

Therefore, the Quran is unique and infallible, as it is believed to be the final and uncorrupted revelation from Allah. The Quran has remained unchanged since its revelation, and its message is consistent across all countries and cultures.

For those who are new to Islam or have been exposed to Islamophobia, it is essential to provide them with accurate teachings from the Quran. This will help dispel any misconceptions and provide them with a clear understanding of the true teachings of Islam.

The Quran's unaltered nature emphasizes the importance of following its teachings with no compromised or adulterated versions.

The influence of women in Islam has been profound, as women were previously marginalized in society.

In contrast to the Bible and Torah, the Quran emphasizes the importance of women's rights in Islam, without resorting to violence as seen in Islamophobic regions that disregard independence. Before the Quran was revealed.

The role of Khadija, the first woman to embrace Islam, was crucial to the life of Prophet Muhammad. Despite being wealthy and intelligent, she was the pioneering woman who embraced Islam and stood by the Prophet on his mission.

Her unwavering faith and prayers served as a source of strength and guidance for him. The Prophet, recognizing Khadija's wisdom and deep understanding of Islam, sought her advice and valued her input.

Their mutual respect and gratitude fostered a harmonious and loving relationship. The tale of Khadija and Prophet Muhammad emphasizes gratitude, humility, knowledge, and time appreciation.

The genuine success is found in faith, wisdom, and meaningful connections, not material wealth or inflated egos.

Undoubtedly, this love story is remarkable. Khadija, a thriving and self-reliant entrepreneur, was deeply impressed by Muhammad's noble character and integrity before they got married.

Acknowledging his extraordinary attributes, she proposed marriage to him. Khadija's confidence, assertiveness, and belief in equality were highlighted by her highly unusual act of proposing to a man.

Muhammad (PBUH) acknowledged Khadija's significance and the possibility of a harmonious collaboration, so he accepted her proposal. This choice exemplified his respect for her independence, intelligence, and the importance of women's involvement in society.

Their union not only established a loving and supportive marriage, but also served as a powerful model for future generations, emphasizing the equal importance of women in Islam and humanity overall.

The best relationship is built on spirituality, trust, and belief in Islam for Muslims, and this applies to all faiths.

Khadija, the first wife of Prophet Muhammad, played a pivotal role in the independence of Muslim women. She was a successful businesswoman, and a highly respected figure in her community.

Khadija's accomplishments and demeanor became an example for Muslim women, inspiring them to pursue their own entrepreneurial endeavors and contribute to society.

Her marriage with Prophet Muhammad was marked by love, trust, and mutual respect, setting a precedent for successful and egalitarian marriages within the Muslim community.

Khadija's legacy continues to inspire Muslim women to strive for independence, empowerment, and self-determination in various aspects of their lives.

In the evolving society it is not uncommon to see marriages built on superficial desires and lustful attractions. These relationships often lack the foundation of trust and spirituality, which are crucial for a lasting and fulfilling union.

While physical attraction may initially spark the flame of love, it is trust that sustains the relationship through the trials and tribulations of life.

A marriage based on trust means having faith in one another's words, actions, and decisions. It involves open communication, honesty, and the ability to rely on each other in times of need.

Similarly, spirituality plays a vital role in a lasting marriage. It goes beyond religious beliefs and encompasses a shared sense of purpose, values, and beliefs about the world and one's place in it.

When a couple is spiritually connected, they find strength and guidance in something greater than themselves, allowing them to weather any storm that comes their way.

These marriages built on trust and spirituality are indeed rare to find, but their rarity makes them incredibly precious and enduring.

They provide a solid foundation for love, growth, and mutual support, making them more likely to stand the test of time.

The reminders to others that they have strayed can be seen as the worst because the person doing the reminding is often in a worse position themselves.

They may not be strayed, but they are plagued by deep waters of distrust and hidden agendas.

The multiple personalities can become tiresome. However, time will ultimately reward each individual for the duties they have performed, and those who battle within themselves to fix their woes and seek repentance are the true believers.

It is better to have strayed and make corrections than to never acknowledge one's mistakes. It is also better to have loved, than to never experience love at all. The love felt by believers differs from that of disbelievers, as it is accompanied by a sense of discontentment that falls shy of inner peace.

The expression of care and love in friendships is strongest when there are shared spiritual beliefs and trust. Sharing similar spiritual beliefs or practices strengthens the bond and fosters deeper understanding and support. Learning becomes the ally of those who venture beyond societal norms.

Common habits and a dedication to personal growth often result in shared interests and companionship.

Consistency creates a smooth flow, while stagnation becomes obsolete in the journey of daily life or learning. My book transports me to an unanticipated world. Safe travels as you embark on a journey beyond your imagination.

Jonah's story encompasses inspirational truth, belief, and repentance:

The story of Jonah serves as a powerful reminder of the consequences of impatience and the importance of forgiveness. Jonah, a prophet, became frustrated with his people and left them. However, upon his return, he was amazed to discover that they had not only missed him, but they had also grown and improved in his absence.

This realization was a humbling experience for Jonah, especially as he had endured a harrowing ordeal in the depths of the sea, swallowed by a whale.

Despite his initial disappointment and impatience, Jonah's people welcomed him back with open arms, expressing their joy and gratitude for his return.

Jonah, also known as Yunus in Islamic tradition, was a prophet sent by Allah to the people of Nineveh. Initially, Jonah faced difficulties in making his people believe in his message.

However, after being swallowed by a whale and spending time in its belly, Jonah repented and sought forgiveness from Allah. Subsequently, he was saved and returned to his people.

To his surprise, he found that his people had become believers in Allah. This miraculous transformation of the people's hearts was a testament to the power of Allah and the effectiveness of Jonah's teachings.

The people had turned away from their previous evil ways and remembered the teachings and lessons imparted by Jonah.

This event serves as a reminder to **Muslims** and the **people of the book (Jews and Christians)** of the power of faith, repentance, and the ability of Allah to change hearts. It is considered a profound example of divine intervention and the transformative nature of belief.

The story of Jonah is a well-known example of a miraculous event recorded in religious texts. Despite being swallowed by a large fish, Jonah miraculously survived inside its stomach for three days and three nights.

Believers believe that this event, which may seem impossible, is actually a divine intervention from Allah. It's essential to note that the miracle didn't elevate Jonah to the level of a god; it was simply one of the many miracles given by Allah on the people of that time.

Miracles are extraordinary events that defy the natural laws and are believed to be manifestations of divine intervention. Throughout history, miracles have been reported in various religious traditions and have served as evidence of the existence and power of a higher being.

Miracles still occur as answered prayers, blessings, and other acts of divine intervention, but they are not considered to be on the same level as the miracles witnessed during the time of the prophets.

Many prophets have been granted miracles by the will of Allah, but none transformed the prophet into a god except Christendom.

Prophets possess knowledge that surpasses the boundaries of Allah's creation. Similarly, saints also possess a greater understanding compared to ordinary individuals. However, even they encounter challenges in comprehending the nuances between faith and genuine belief, as this is an integral part of knowledge.

This distinction between miracles and prophets highlights the belief in the oneness of Allah and the understanding that prophets are mere messengers chosen by Him to convey His message to humanity.

In Islam, Jesus (**Isa**) is revered as a prophet and a righteous figure. The Qur'an portrays him as a pure and sinless soul, chosen by God to deliver His message to humanity. The story of Jesus being strayed and then returning, as mentioned in the Bible, serves no purpose in Islam because it contradicts the belief in his infallibility.

The Quran depicts Jesus, born of Mary, as a pure and righteous figure, untouched by sin, stemming from a line of devout family.

The contradictory messages in the Bible concerning Jesus being swayed present a challenge to the belief that he is God. According to the Bible, God is described as the creator of Satan, implying that Satan cannot have any power or influence over God or his son, Jesus.

Bible: NKJV: 4:1;11. Then Jesus was led up by the Spirit into the wilderness to be tempted by the devil. And when He had fasted forty days and forty nights, afterward He was hungry. Now when the tempter came to Him, he said, If You are the Son of God, command that these stones become bread. Jesus answered him, 'Do not put the Lord your God to the test.'

But He answered and said, Man shall not live by bread alone, but by every word that proceeds from the mouth of God. Then the devil took Him up into the holy city, set Him on the pinnacle of the temple, and said to Him, If You are the Son of God, throw Yourself down.

He shall give His angels charge over you, and, In their hands they shall bear you up,
Lest you dash your foot against a stone. Jesus said to him, You shall not attempt the Lord your God

Again, the devil took Him up on an exceedingly high mountain, and showed Him all the kingdoms of the world and their glory. And he said to Him, All these things I will give You if You will fall down and worship me.

Then Jesus said to him, Away with you, Satan! You shall worship the Lord your God, and Him only you shall serve. Then the devil left Him, and behold, angels came and ministered to Him.

According to Islam, it is impossible for Satan to have any authority over Jesus. The claim that Jesus was God, despite his perceived weakness, as stated in the Bible, is unfounded.

Quran clarifies Jesus is not God nor an imperfect prophet; rather, he is the sinless son of Mary,

It is important to note that there is no mention in the Quran of Satan ever tempting the prophet. Any such claims are fabricated lies. In fact, the Quran describes Jesus as a sinless character.

Throughout the history of Abrahamic faiths, no prophet has ever followed Satan, except in the Bible, which also elevates Jesus as the son of God and is part of a triune God. It is simply not possible to follow a weak person, let alone a personification of a weak God.

A blasphemous lie against this revered prophet, the Messiah Jesus. It is the responsibility of Muslims to safeguard his honorable identity, treating it with utmost respect and guarding against any malicious intentions.

If Jesus, being the one they named as the son of God or the triune God, was not spared from false accusations, it is easy to imagine that others would also face similar untrue allegations. With this mindset, no one can escape from the unfounded accusations made by those who falter.

There is no sign of repentance that Jesus made to Allah the father for swaying to the darker side it makes no sense if he is a prophet why did he not repent as Jonah did there is no way he could follow the Satan when common people who pray to God know the difference and here is Jesus who is son of God or soon to be god himself following a weak Satan is impossible and blasphemous as Islam sees Jesus as pure and sinless and following Satan is a sin.

In Islam, Jesus **(Isa)** is one of the greatest prophets and messengers of Allah. According to Islamic belief, Jesus was born to Mary (Maryam) through a miraculous birth, conceived by the will of Allah with no a human father. This emphasizes his purity and special status.

The Quran mentions Jesus possessed extraordinary qualities and performed miracles by the permission of Allah, including healing the sick, raising the dead, and speaking as an infant.

However, Islam denies the concept of Jesus being the literal son of God or part of a divine Trinity.

Instead, Jesus is a human prophet, chosen by Allah to deliver the message of monotheism and righteousness to the people. Islam emphasizes the oneness of Allah and the belief that no human can be divine or part divine. Jesus is revered and respected in Islam, but his role and nature differ from the Christian understanding.

The theological differences surrounding the verses of the Bible mentioned above are indeed significant, and addressing them is crucial to clarify any allegations made against Jesus the Messiah.

These verses may pertain to various topics, such as Jesus' divinity, his role as the Savior, or his fulfillment of prophecies.

By examining and interpreting these verses, theologians and scholars aim to shed light on Jesus and his purpose in the Christian faith. This clarification is essential not only for believers seeking a deeper understanding of their faith, but also for those who may have misconceptions or doubts about Jesus' identity and mission.

His birth was miraculous ensuring his purity from the beginning. Therefore, it is refuted in the Islamic context that Jesus could be led astray by evil forces.

In the verses of the Bible, it is an exasperation to encounter teachings that seem to contradict the moral code attributed to Jesus. For instance, there are references to Satan who, according to Islamic beliefs, has knowledge of Allah.

The mention of Jesus going through reincarnation, as suggested in Hinduism, and becoming one in three, alludes to a concept that deviates from the monotheistic belief upheld in Christianity.

This raises questions and concerns, as it seems to move away from strict monotheism and potentially align more closely with polytheistic beliefs that incorporate multiple divine aspects, rather than monotheism.

It is important to understand the Islamic perspective on Satan (known as 'Shaitan'). In Islamic theology, Satan is a Jinn, a separate creation from humans, who was expelled from paradise because of his defiance and arrogance.

Although Satan possesses knowledge and awareness of Allah, he still disobeyed Him. As a result, humanity considers him a sworn enemy, constantly seeking to misguide and lead people astray.

For the encounter between Jesus and Satan, Islamic belief holds that Satan did not question Jesus' nature by saying, "If you are the Son of God." Instead, Satan never tempted Jesus by questioning his piety and testing his faith.

Jesus, being a prophet and a chosen servant of Allah, was pure and Satan could not tempt him being born pure. He was not inclined to evil upholding his devotion to God alone. It is essential to note that Islam categorically denies the concept of God having any biological offspring. God, in Islamic belief, is beyond human attributes and does not have any progeny.

Therefore, Jesus never claimed to be the biological son of God. Instead, he consistently emphasized his role as a servant and messenger of Allah, calling people to worship the one true God.

Satan was the only Jinn in heaven. Jesus rebukes him, not questioning his awareness of his future divinity per Bible.

If Jesus was indeed considered the son of God, it would indeed seem contradictory for him to be tempted by Satan or driven into the wilderness to be shown the temptations of the world.

It is impossible to believe the verse in the Bible where Jesus says to Satan that he cannot tempt his Lord. According to the Quran, Satan is weak and was created by Allah.

If Jesus was truly God, it goes against reason that he could be tempted by something that God himself created.

The accusations against Jesus in Muslim doctrine are blasphemous, as they portray him as weak and uncertain about his sinlessness, which he is believed to have been born with according to Islam.

Therefore, the statement that he cannot be tempted is a factual attempt to highlight the differences between the Bible and the Quran.

It is important for beliefs to align with logic, as Allah has given humans the ability to reason and cannot be tempted by something he created, such as Satan from the jinn family.

The idea of Jesus being both human and divine does not align with the belief that God does not die, is not born, and does not disappear. He is present for everyone, not just some.

If Jesus is God, why did he leave? It's not like a fairy tale.

Even Moses, who was Jewish, could not see God, so it is not possible for ordinary people to view God. There is no consistency in the previous text, and the Quran states God cannot be seen. Jesus was a prophet, not divine, and he prayed to Allah.

This contradicts the idea that Jesus, being God, could be swayed or influenced by external forces. The Quranic belief system does not contain these discrepancies.

It presents a consistent narrative where God is depicted as being fully in control and not susceptible to any external influence.

These discrepancies are not minor and have significant implications for individuals seeking to make informed decisions about their faith.

Understanding and recognizing the differences between these belief systems is essential for individuals to make valid decisions about their spiritual beliefs.

The worst of humans is the one who not only commits sins themselves but also actively encourages and entices others to partake in sinful behavior.

This is clear in the realm of technology, where individuals can use various platforms to spread negativity, hatred, and immoral actions.

Whether it be through cyberbullying, hacking, or engaging in illicit activities or misleading online, through spreading lies these individuals actively contaminate others with their negative influence.

Those who sin and try to lure others into hearing about their sinful acts are equally reprehensible.

However, it is important to remember that change is possible if one's heart will cleanse itself.

Through introspection, self-reflection, and seeking forgiveness, individuals can transform their ways and strive to make amends for the harm they have caused.

It is crucial to recognize the potential for redemption and growth, as humans are capable of change and improvement.

Story of two believing women:

The pious woman, named Aisha, was known for her unwavering devotion to her faith. She diligently followed all the regulations and rituals prescribed by Islam, spending her days in prayer and acts of charity.

However, she had a tendency to judge others and keep a mental tally of their sins, particularly for her neighbor, Zara, who worked as a prostitute to earn a living.

Zara had a hard life. She was forced into the profession because of desperate circumstances and had always longed for a way out. Despite her actions not aligning with the teachings of Islam, she still held belief in her heart and sought forgiveness from Allah for the choices she had made.

As time went on, Aisha's obsession with Zara's sins grew, and she couldn't help but share her judgment and gossip about her with others. Unbeknown to Aisha, Allah was watching their every interaction, including Aisha's spreading of rumors and gossip.

Allah, the Most Merciful, did not condone Zara's actions but forgave her as she continually repented and asked to return back to him from harsh trials of life.

In this scenario, Zara is struggling with a source of income that she believes is not bringing her any joy or fulfillment.

She turns to Allah daily, seeking forgiveness and asking for relief from this situation. Aisha, instead of offering support or help, engages in gossip about Zara's predicament, which goes against the principles of a genuine believer.

This highlights the different responses that people have in their daily lives. Some individuals openly spread evil and engage in harmful behaviors, while others recognize their weaknesses and repent in private.

However, there are also those who exploit these negative aspects of life as a means of income, which ultimately has detrimental effects on their souls.

It is important to remember that Allah is aware of all the different avenues and paths that individuals take. He allows these events to occur, and only Allah knows the future destiny of each soul.

On a fateful day, a tragedy unfolded, leading to the unfortunate demise of both Aisha and Zara. The news that Allah granted forgiveness to Zara, a prostitute, took aback the community while Aisha, a righteous woman, faced consequences for her habit of spreading rumors and meticulously recording her deeds.

Allah placed more importance on a heart that seeks forgiveness and repents, rather than one that judges the sins of others.

The story acted as a reminder for both the community and the gossip-mongers. Islam emphasizes the importance of not talking about others and urges individuals to abstain from gossip. If one engages in such behavior, seeking forgiveness becomes necessary. Giving proper attention is necessary in order to address the weaknesses present in humans.

The motto of Islam is to guide believers who may stray from the right path, while avoiding spreading gossip. It is the duty of a believer to assist fellow believers.

Different cultures may say **"I don't judge"** and watch someone go astray, but a believer in Islam invites others to the right path, understanding that judgment ultimately lies with Allah.

Instead, it is our duty to focus on our own repentance, seek forgiveness from Allah, and guide others with kindness and compassion.

The tale taught them the importance of restoring relationships, rectifying wrongs, and avoiding the pitfalls of gossip and judgment.

Surah Maryam in the Quran narrates the remarkable story of Maryam (Mary) and her experiences with the Jewish community.

Despite facing potential judgment and ridicule, Maryam's unwavering faith and commitment to her chastity enabled her to return with her son, Jesus after his birth.

If Mary had feared the Jews, she would not have returned to them, fearing that her character would be dislodged. However, she had no fear. She gave birth to a prophet and a Messiah, not a god or a son of God. It is not possible for a human to give birth to a god.

The concept of Jesus being half divine and half human, and then eventually becoming God, is incomprehensible within the Abrahamic faiths of monotheism.

God does not evolve; He is an unseen god, not a human. He did not create humans in His image, as stated in Islam.

Allah is Nur, an unseen light that will only be revealed on the day of judgment. Mary giving birth to Jesus without a husband is a miracle of Allah. He is capable of anything, as nothing is hard for Allah. With a mere command, something can come into existence.

Quran: Surah Baqarah: 2;117. "He is the One Who has originated the heavens and the earth, and when He wills to (originate) a thing, He only says to it: 'Be', and it becomes"

The phrase **"Kun Fa-Yakūn"** meaning **"be, and it is"** in Arabic, is mentioned eight times in the Quran as a depiction of Allah's act of creation.

Quran mentions Jesus, even as an infant, spoke miraculously, confirming his prophethood and servitude to Allah. However, Jesus never explicitly stated that he would sacrifice himself for the sins of humanity.

This concept of atonement through blood sacrifice emerged later in Christian theology.

Muslims, during the holy month of Ramadan, break their fast by consuming dates, which holds significance as Maryam was provided a stream and a date tree to sustain her during her challenging time.

Eid al-Adha is one of the most important celebrations in Islam, commemorating the willingness of Prophet Ibrahim (Abraham) to sacrifice his son, Ismail (Ishmael), as an act of obedience to Allah, which ultimately resulted in the substitution of a ram as a sacrifice.

In Islamic faith, Allah is regarded as a compassionate God who does not endorse or demand human sacrifice. The oneness of Allah is a key focus in Islamic teachings, and the concept of associating partners with Him is firmly rejected.

The belief among Muslims is that Allah is self-sufficient and does not require sacrifices for appeasement. Instead, Islam emphasizes Allah is forgiving and compassionate, urging believers to seek His forgiveness and mercy through sincere repentance and righteous acts.

Human sacrifice is not supported by the teachings of the Islamic faith and is foreign to its concept.

According to Islamic teachings, Jesus' purity and righteousness are inherent to his being, and he cannot be led astray by Satan or any other temptations.

This distinction is crucial as it emphasizes the uniqueness of Jesus as a prophet, rather than associating him with the concept of a triune God or the literal son of God.

Islam teaches that Jesus (**Isa**) is a revered prophet and messenger of God, but not divine. The Quran reveals Jesus was born to the Virgin Mary, who is regarded as a virtuous and pious woman.

By Quranic doctrine, Jesus was born with no sin and led a sinless life, serving as an exemplary figure for humanity.

Islam emphasizes that prophets, including Jesus, are sent by God to guide and teach humanity, and they are not prone to committing sins or straying from the righteous path.

The story of Jonah, mentioned in the previous sentence, is an example of impatience rather than defiance, or straying from the right path; disbelievers will name it straying but it's important to note it was impatience and leaving without Allah's will highlight the importance's plan.

This is a reminder to Muslims that even the most revered individuals in Islam, like Jesus, demonstrate steadfast commitment to God, inspiring believers to pursue spiritual progress and redemption.

In Islam, believers are reminded that evil can manifest in various ways, triggered by different impulses. It could result from physical attraction, where one may be tempted to engage in sinful actions.

However, intention to commit a sin is discouraged, as the angels record this intention as a point for the individual if he refrains from indulging.

Islam emphasizes personal accountability, with each person being responsible for their own actions before Allah.

The accounting of one's deeds is a private matter between the individual and Allah, not for others to judge or manipulate. Engaging in sinful acts intentionally and continuously, while also encouraging others to do the same, is considered a deliberate spread of evil.

The modifications made to the Bible do not alter his status as a monotheist or the rejection he faced from the Jews, who did not recognize him as a prophet.

The Quran contains specific chapters, **Surah Maryam and Surah Imran**, that delve into the details of this family, which are not found in any other book and provide clarifications on this matter.

In the Quran, it is explicitly stated that Jesus (**Isa**) is a prophet and a servant of God, not God Himself or the literal son of God. The Quran emphasizes the sinlessness and purity of the prophets, including Jesus.

It is inconceivable for a being, such as Jesus if he were God, to follow Satan or commit any sin. Satan is considered the ultimate symbol of evil and disobedience, and the nature of Jesus per Quran is inherently free from any wrongdoing.

Therefore, there is no contradiction in the Quran.

Religious texts employ metaphors to depict God's qualities and traits, recognizing our limited grasp of the divine.

God's knowledge of the seen and unseen, and ability to discern human hearts, is a core belief in multiple faiths. The holy land has enduring religious significance worldwide.

It's a place for solace, divine guidance, and deeper faith connection. According to the Bible, there are passages that describe Satan taking Jesus to a high mountain to tempt him.

Therefore, the dogma that denies the purity of Jesus is unequivocally rejected by the Quran. Surah Imran, in particular, provides compelling evidence of Jesus' immaculate character and emphasizes his status as a continuous declaration within the Quran.

This declaration stands in direct contradiction to the belief that accuses Jesus, a pure and righteous soul, of following Satan and declaring himself a prophet at birth.

Such an accusation is not only blasphemous but also goes against the broader teachings of the Quran, which emphasize Jesus' righteousness and prophethood.

It is important to understand the Quran's message in its entirety and not misinterpret or misrepresent its teachings regarding the pure nature of Jesus.

It is indeed a challenging concept to grasp the idea of a weakened god who is tempted by Satan. This notion goes against the traditional belief in a divine being who is all-powerful and untouchable by evil.

In today's world, where Satan's influence seems pervasive and humanity is inherently flawed with both good and evil, it becomes even more perplexing to understand.

If Jesus were to come and assist the Jews in their disobedience today, without the aid of social media to spread his message, it is challenging to predict how he would respond based on the portrayal of his vulnerability in the Bible.

If he was tempted in a time without social media, imagine what the biblical prophets like Lot, Noah, Moses, and Jesus would do. It is illogical to belittle the prophets or accuse them of evil in order to satisfy the limitations of human nature, as Allah sent them as examples to humanity, not to cause disruption.

This clear explanation in the Quranic text highlights a difference between the Bible and the Quran. While humanity exists in all cultures, learning about religious differences only enhances our spiritual journey and decision-making process.

Hence, it is improbable for him to associate with Satan and succumb to temptation. Rather, his inclination would be towards leading humanity towards righteousness and spiritual advancement.

According to the Quran, salvation is attained through one's deeds and not through a human prophet like Jesus.

Bible NIV: John. 6:33-63. Whoever eats my flesh and drinks my blood has eternal life, and I will raise them up on the last day. For my flesh is real food and my blood is real drink.

Quran: Surah Maidah: 5:15. O people of the book! Now our messenger has come to you, revealing much of what you have hidden of the scriptures and disregarding much. There certainly has come to you from Allah a light and a clear book.

In contrast, Christianity interprets the act of consuming the body and blood of Jesus as a symbolic representation of communion with him and his sacrifice on the cross. This belief, known as the Eucharist or Holy Communion, is a central sacrament in Christian worship.

It is a way for believers to partake in the spiritual presence of Jesus and to remember his sacrifice for the forgiveness of sins

While the language used in the Bible may seem graphic or unsettling, it is important to understand the symbolic nature of these teachings within the context of Christian theology.

Comparing this practice to pagan rituals is an oversimplification that acknowledges the theological significance and distinctiveness of Christian beliefs.

The concept of consuming the flesh and blood of Jesus, as depicted in certain Christian rituals such as the Eucharist, raises theological and religious concerns from various perspectives.

...

From a monotheistic standpoint, the act of physically eating the flesh of a prophet like Jesus can be seen as contradicting the fundamental belief in the oneness of God.

In Islam, this notion is considered haram, meaning forbidden, as it goes against the teachings of the Quran and the principles of tawhid (the oneness of God).

The idea of consuming flesh and blood also carries associations with pagan rituals and practices, which were prevalent in pre-Christian cultures.

This connection with pagan concepts and practices can be attributed to the historical development of Christendom, where various cultural influences and traditions merged with Christian beliefs.

Bread and wine in Christian rituals represent the body and blood of Jesus symbolically.

Different Christian denominations and individuals have varying interpretations of this concept. The blending of divine and human aspects reflects the belief in the incarnation of Jesus.

Jesus would disagree with the blasphemous words said about him in the Bible. It makes no sense to ask monotheistic Jews to drink his blood and eat his flesh.

Monotheism was practiced by the Jews. Christianity is a development from Judaism.

Islam came to correct the altered previous books. Allegations must match the Quran for Muslims to believe them, but these stories do not. Islam is a doctrine without polytheism, believing in one God.

Quran: Surah Imran: 3:189. To Allah ˹alone˺ belongs the kingdom of the heavens and the earth. And Allah is Most Capable of everything.

Quran: Surah Baqarah: 2:62. Indeed, the believers, Jews, Christians, and Sabeans —whoever ˹truly˺ believes in Allah and the Last Day and does good will have their reward with their Lord. And there will be no fear for them, nor will they grieve.

Quran: Surah Maidah: 5:5. Today all good, pure foods have been made lawful for you. Similarly, the food of the People of the Book. It is permissible for you and yours is permissible for them. And permissible for you in marriage are chaste believing women as well as chaste women of those given the Scripture before you—as long as you pay them their dowries in wedlock, neither fornicating nor taking them as mistresses. And whoever rejects the faith, all their good deeds will be void ˹in this life˺ and in the Hereafter they will be among the losers.

Quran: Surah Maidah: 5:19. O people of the scripture, there has come to you Our messenger to make clear to you the religion after a period of suspension of messengers lest you say. There came not to us any bringer of good tidings or a warner. But there has come to you a bringer of good tidings and a warner. And Allah is over all things competent.

Quran: Surah Maidah: 5:77. Say O Muhammad, O people of the Scripture Jews and Christians! Exceed not the limits in your religion by believing in something other than the truth, and do not follow the vain desires of people who went astray in times gone by, and who misled many, and strayed themselves from the Right Path.

Quran: Surah Maidah 5:64, The Jews say: Allah's Hand is tied up (i.e. He does not give and spend His Bounty. Be their hands tied up and be cursed for what they uttered.

Nay, both His Hands are widely outstretched. He spends of His Bounty as He wills. Verily, the Revelation that has come to you from Allah increases in most of them their obstinate rebellion and disbelief. We have put enmity and hatred amongst them till the Day of Resurrection. Every time they kindled the fire of war, Allah extinguished it; and they ever strive to make mischief on earth. And Allah does not like the *Mufsidun* mischief-makers.

The verses of the Quran can serve as a source of clarity for those who seek understanding. However, monotheistic principles do not align with concepts such as redemption, salvation, and the idea of blood and flesh, which are considered being polytheistic beliefs.

It is essential for individuals to refrain completely from such actions to prevent the growth of the hole of evil within oneself. Islam discourages blaming others for one's own sins, as each person handles their own choices.

Expressing the truth is easy, but it requires an interest in learning about the principles and directness of Islam.

Their stories emphasize the transformative power of Islam and highlight the ability of individuals to change their perspectives and embrace a faith that they once opposed.

Before Prophet Muhammad gained prophethood, he was known for his remarkable reputation as an honest man.

He was frequently referred to as **"Al-Ameen,"** which means **"The Trustworthy"** in Arabic. **Muhammad PBUH** was known for his integrity, sincerity, and truthfulness in his dealings with others. His honesty was widely recognized by the people of Mecca, where he lived, and he was often sought as a mediator to resolve disputes.

Prophet Muhammad's reputation as a trustworthy individual extended beyond his personal life; he was also known for his honesty in his profession as a merchant. People trusted him with their belongings and sought his advice on business matters because of his impeccable character.

This reputation of honesty and integrity laid the foundation for his acceptance and credibility when he later received the divine revelation and became the Prophet of Islam.

Before receiving prophet hood, Prophet Muhammad's character was established through a series of divine interventions and signs. Even before his birth, miraculous events were said to have occurred. During the time of pregnancy, his mother, Amina, experienced extraordinary sensations and visions.

She felt a divine light and something truly exceptional. During his childhood and adolescence, Muhammad continued to have spiritual experiences, and people could not ignore his noble character, honesty, and wisdom.

People in his community recognized his exceptional qualities long before he received the revelation from Allah and became the final messenger of Islam.

The preparation for his role as the prophet was not limited to a specific period but encompassed his entire life, shaping him into the ideal vessel for delivering the divine message to humanity.

Halima, the wet nurse, took in young Muhammad and brought him to her home. She first hesitated because of the obvious reason he came from a single mother and she may not pay enough.

Despite her own economic struggles, she found that after the infant Muhammad arrived, her household seemed to overflow with abundance.

It was as if blessings poured in from every corner. The presence of Muhammad brought about a transformation in Halima and her husband's lives, leaving them amazed. His presence brought joy, tranquility, and prosperity to their previously difficult circumstances.

The couple felt a deep sense of gratitude for being chosen to care for this special child, and they lovingly nurtured him as if he were their own. She grew to love him more than ever, along with her son.

As **Muhammad PBUH** grew older, his innate wisdom and extraordinary character shone, leaving an indelible impact on those who crossed his path.

Halima did not know at the time that she had been entrusted with the upbringing of the last and final prophet of Allah, a responsibility that would forever change the course of history.

Angel Gabriel opened young Muhammad's heart twice, which scared the little boy who played with him. These heart surgeries with **ZAM –ZAM** water cleansed his heart of any evil a human is born with. The story highlights the importance of this episode.

Halima brought him back to his mother, Amina, who saw the sadness in her eyes and extended their stay. As a young boy, he moved back in with his mother, went on a road trip together, and she passed away.

Muhammad's first experience of death as an adolescent, was his mother's passing in the scorching desert of Saudi Arabia. As he stood by her side, helpless and waiting for help to arrive, he felt the immense weight of grief and loss.

It was during this painful moment that Allah began testing his strengths and weaknesses. How Allah prepares individuals for their life's journey is unknown to humanity.

Through this testing, Muhammad's character and resilience were being shaped, as he learned to lean on his faith and trust in Allah's plan.

This experience marked the beginning of a series of trials and tribulations that would ultimately shape Muhammad into the Prophet he would become.

The experiences and trials faced by each prophet are distinct and tailored to their specific mission and purpose.

For example, Prophet Moses faced the challenge of leading the Israelites out of bondage in Egypt and guiding them through the wilderness, while Prophet Muhammad faced establishing the Islamic faith and uniting the Arabian tribes.

These experiences were unique to each prophet and cannot be compared or equated.

Similarly, every individual faces their own set of trials and challenges that are personal and specific to their circumstances. These trials may vary in nature and intensity, depending on factors such as personal strengths, weaknesses, and life circumstances.

Therefore, it is not fair or appropriate to compare one person's trials to another, as each individual's journey is unique and cannot be fully understood or appreciated by others.

After all, if God created the world, it would appear illogical for him to be enticed by something he himself brought into existence.

This concept challenges the common understanding of God's all-knowing and all-powerful nature. It raises doubts and questions, as even in fairy tales, the plot and beliefs are typically questioned and analyzed before being accepted as a basis of belief.

Story of two thieves:

The two men, who had a reputation for looting unsuspecting individuals, found themselves in dire need of sustenance. They had exhausted all their options and were now hungry beyond belief.

In a moment of desperation, one of them suggested knocking on the door of a Muslim, believing that they would be met with compassion, generosity, and a warm welcome.

The other, however, took a different route and opted to knock on the door of a non-Muslim, unsure of what kind of response they would receive.

The man, who had been a thief for years, had never experienced such kindness and compassion before. As he sat at the table, surrounded by the Muslim family, he couldn't help but be moved by their genuine concern for his well-being.

They not only fed him but also engaged in meaningful conversation, asking about his life and sharing their own stories. The man felt a sense of belonging and acceptance that he had never felt before.

It was in that moment that he realized the true essence of Islam - a religion that emphasizes compassion, generosity, and love for humanity.

Regardless of one's faith, humanity continues to progress without hindrance.

Inspired by the actions of the Muslim family, the man made a firm decision to change his ways and seek a more righteous path. He vowed to not only abandon his life of crime but also to dedicate himself to helping others in need.

The transformative power of a single act of kindness had completely shifted his perspective and ignited a desire for positive change within him.

From that day forward, the man became an advocate for charity and kindness, spreading the teachings of Islam and showing the impact it can have on a person's life.

Besides providing food, Muslims also attempted to make him feel comfortable and at home. They went beyond just meeting his basic needs and created a sense of community and togetherness.

This hospitality is ingrained in Muslim culture and is a common practice, despite the circumstances of society that may discourage such openness.

Even in situations where distrust is prevalent, Muslims still offer a plate of food to a sincere and hungry person, regardless of whether it is served indoors or outdoors.

This gesture exemplifies their generosity and compassion, as they prioritize the well-being of others above societal norms or limitations.

Whether it was a simple meal shared on a doorstep or a more elaborate feast, the Muslims' willingness to open their doors to strangers created a warm and welcoming atmosphere that made the narrator, the former thief, feel at ease and grateful for their kindness.

The man who knocked on the door of a non-Muslim did not receive the same warm reception. He was turned away, possibly because of his appearance or unfamiliarity.

This experience left him hungry and disappointed. It highlights the stark contrast in attitudes towards hospitality. During this remarkable time, individuals sought personal reformation and change through the teachings of Islam.

The religion emphasizes the importance of humanity, encouraging its followers to display kindness, compassion, and respect towards others.

However, in the current climate, discretion has become necessary when discussing Islam, because of the widespread use of social media and the potential for misinterpretation or misrepresentation of its teachings.

These stories serve as a reminder of a time when true findings were sought by those genuinely interested in personal growth and transformation, rather than being influenced by the noise and biases often found on social media platforms.

The transformative power of Islam is clear in the thief's story. Intrigued by the kindness and generosity he witnessed from Muslims; he embraced Islam and changed his way of life. This shows the profound impact that the principles of Islam, such as compassion and forgiveness, can have on individuals.

Story of a believing women who questioned if Allah was just:

A woman who firmly believed in Allah had a question about His justice. The believers were eager to respond to her question in the most satisfactory manner.

She recounted her tale, explaining that she knits every day and sells her knitted items at the market. My income barely covers our needs, so I stay up knitting to provide for my family. She was clearly by herself responsible for her family.

As I entered the market, she said finally, the bird flew away with what I had knitted to sell. With sadness, she expressed her belief in Allah but also questioned His justice, causing the crowd at the mosque to look at her.

Someone arrived at the mosque with bags of gold, claiming to be shipwrecked and saved by a knitted piece dropped by a bird.

They pledged to donate their wealth to Allah. They proposed donating it to someone in need. While standing, she was handed the bags of gold.

As she spoke, tears streamed down her face, explaining that the bird had taken what I had knitted to feed my family. Your knitting was credited with saving our lives, so here are some bags of gold for you.

She asserted that nobody should feel obligated to answer my question as Allah is the ultimate judge. Those who worry and lack **"taw Akul"** belief are unaware of his plans.

Believers understand that questioning Allah during difficult times can be natural response, but they also recognize that Allah tests them for a reason.

In Islam, Allah is the ultimate giver and taker of blessings. The Quran teaches one should turn to Allah alone to share their inner turmoil or bliss. This is because Allah is the only being who has complete knowledge and understanding of our hearts and minds.

Allah's actions are not bound by human accountability, meaning that He can give or take back blessings with no obligation to explain or justify His decisions. Therefore, it is more beneficial and meaningful to confide in and seek solace from Allah, as He is the ultimate source of comfort and guidance.

The trials faced by believers, including revered figures like Prophet Abraham and the prophets, strengthen their faith and character.

No believer is exempt from tests; it is a fundamental part of their spiritual journey. In contrast, disbelievers may find a simple life without the burden of faith, relying solely on their own rules and ways.

However, they cannot understand that true peace and fulfillment cannot be achieved through worldly possessions or physical well-being alone. The intricacies of life and its uncertainties highlight the importance of surrendering to a higher power.

In a poignant moment, a lady who received bags of gold tearfully advised the crowd not to question Allah, but to instead seek enough faith as believers to trust in His justice, even during the harshest of times.

Believers perceive these challenges as hidden blessings, knowing that there are rewards and lessons within them.

The mindset of a believer is profoundly different from that of a non-believer; even in the face of suffering, a believer remains steadfast, firmly believing that Allah has something better in store for them.

In Islam, prophets, including the Prophet Muhammad, as well as previous prophets, have faced many tests and challenges in their lives. These tests strengthen their faith and prove their devotion to Allah.

Similarly, believers in Islam are also subjected to various tests throughout their lives. These tests may come as disbelievers who try to disrupt their thoughts and beliefs or through challenging life circumstances.

Quran: Surah Muhammad: Verse 31. "We will certainly test you ˈbelieversˈ until We prove those of you who ˈtrulyˈ struggle ˈin Allah's causeˈ and remain steadfast, and reveal how you conduct yourselves".

CHAPTER 7
RESPECT TO THE WISE AND CONSCIOUS.

Respect begins with acknowledging and honoring the creator who brought you into existence, recognizing the simple act of being a human on earth, and appreciating the necessities of life, such as water, food, relationships, and materials.

Self-respect is also an essential aspect of respect. It means valuing what Allah thinks, even in the unseen realms of the conscious mind, rather than attaching importance to others' opinions, which may hold little or no significance.

Dreams of Allah to a believer are respect for the seen and the unseen. The promise of Allah will come true. What are the conditions of its gratefulness?

It's not just about academia, gym workouts, or eating healthy to maintain desired material possessions, looks, or status. It's about Allah - without Him, there is nothing.

That's why enemies are piling up against Muslim lands. Muslims need to remember Allah and be grateful.

A genuine believer is not a deceiver. Why does someone not follow through on their word? Either they are a liar or they are afraid of the consequences.

A Muslim's word reflects their character. Don't say something you can't deliver, because Allah always keeps His promises. Take the example of Pharaoh, who repeatedly killed newborn boys every other year.

But the year he didn't kill, Musa's mother hid her pregnancy and trusted in Allah's promise to save her son. She placed him in the waters, as her dream had instructed, and had unwavering belief.

Allah returned Musa to her, and she became his wet nurse - no one else. This is the power of Allah's promise. If you have doubts, seek clarity to receive Allah's promise.

Quran: Surah Baqarah: 2:152. Remember me; I will remember you. And thank me, and never be ungrateful.

The ruler, owner of this world and the next, emphasizes the importance of gratitude and remembrance to his creation. It is a kind act to remind others, while it is ungrateful to read and forget.

Only a tyrant to oneself would lack self-respect, as respect for oneself aligns with respect for the creator.

The Quran holds the answers to what humans need, and it is not just about exploring the world without belief, but exploring it with belief and receiving more than expected. Insha'Allah and Alhamdulillah for everything.

Courage is not just about speaking one's mind, but also about going beyond the immediate desires and temptations that may hinder personal growth and progress.

It involves taming the fierce lions of impulse and passion with the strength of ingenuity and self-control. A courageous individual understands disappointments are a part of life, but they do not let them deter their determination to try again.

They possess the bravery to express their true thoughts and desires, even when it may be difficult or unpopular.

By speaking the truth and acknowledging differences, they can break free from the need to please others and remain true to themselves.

This ability to express oneself without contradicting their own thoughts is a testament to their unwavering courage.

The prophets faced immense challenges as they delivered their messages. They were often mocked, ridiculed, and rejected by the very people they were sent to guide.

Despite this, they displayed unwavering courage and determination to convey the truth. Their unwavering desire to fulfill their divine duty fueled their actions, even in the face of adversity.

This same spirit of unwavering dedication to truth continues to exist in the present day. There are individuals who strive to deliver truth and shed light on important matters, even when faced with skepticism, criticism, and denial.

Before he died, Yaqub, the prophet and father of sons, gave his children a warning and asked them to make a promise. He asked them to declare their belief in someone after he passed away.

In response, his sons expressed their faith in the Lord, Allah. Them not mentioning the Trinitarian God concept or state that Jesus was to come as God, as Allah never gives His place to His creation, serves as a constant reminder for believers in the oneness of Allah.

Their commitment to spreading truth and promoting understanding serves as a testament to the timeless importance of honesty and enlightenment in our society.

According to the Quran, previous scriptures mention the names of these prophets as well.

This highlights the consistent presence of monotheism and the prophetic tradition in history. The Quran emphasizes God selected these prophets and esteemed them as righteous examples.

The Quran mentions the names of twenty-five prophets, but believers estimate Allah sent over 124,000 prophets.

These prophets played a crucial role in disseminating the word of Allah and guiding their people towards the path of righteousness and moral conduct.

While the Quran highlights the stories and teachings of a select few prophets, it acknowledges the existence of many others who have contributed to the spiritual growth and enlightenment of humanity.

The prophets serve as a source of inspiration and guidance for Muslims, demonstrating the importance of faith, morality, and devotion to Allah.

They were not sent to demean degrade themselves or belittle people, but to rectify their behavior and teach them the proper context of how to live a righteous life.

Each prophet had a unique message and set of examples that they left behind for people to learn from.

These examples inspire and bring about positive change in the lives of individuals and societies. The stories of these prophets serve as a source of guidance and motivation for believers, showing them the importance of faith, patience, perseverance, and righteousness.

By following the life-changing behaviors of these prophets, individuals can strive to become better versions of themselves and fulfill their purpose in this world.

Moses, also known as Musa in Arabic, holds a significant position in the Abrahamic faiths, including Islam. He is revered as a prominent prophet and messenger of God, and his teachings and legacy are highly respected.

In the Quran, Moses is mentioned by name 136 times, making him the most frequently mentioned individual in the Quran. His life story is extensively narrated and recounted, surpassing that of any other prophet.

Moses' journey from being raised as a prince in Egypt to leading the Israelites out of slavery is a tale of courage, faith, and divine intervention.

His encounters with Pharaoh, the miracles he performed, and the delivery of the Ten Commandments are all detailed in the Quran, solidifying his importance in the religious scriptures.

As a revered prophet, Moses serves as a role model for believers, and his teachings continue to guide and inspire millions of people around the world.

Some prophets were granted miracles to demonstrate the truth of their message, while others were given scriptures, such as the Torah, the Psalms, the Gospel, and the Qur'an, to convey Allah's guidance to humanity.

Despite facing many challenges and opposition, these prophets remained steadfast in their mission, inviting people to worship Allah alone and adhere to His commandments.

Their teachings formed the basis of monotheism and laid the foundation for the major religions that exist today.

The list of prophets in Islam includes Adam, the first human and prophet; Idris (Enoch), known for his wisdom; Nuh (Noah), who built the ark to save believers from the Great Flood; Hud, sent to the people of 'Ad; Saleh, sent to the people of Thamud; Lut, who was sent to the people of Sodom and Gomorrah; Ibrahim (Abraham).

The patriarch and father of many prophets; Ismail (Ishmael) and Ishaq (Isaac), the sons of Ibrahim; Yaqub (Jacob), the father of the twelve tribes of Israel; Yusuf (Joseph), known for his story of patience and perseverance; Shu'ayb, sent to the people of Madyan.

Ayyub (Job), who endured immense suffering with patience; Dhulkifl (Ezekiel), about whom less is known; Musa (Moses), who led the Israelites out of Egypt; Harun (Aaron), the brother of Musa; Dawud (David), the king and prophet; Sulayman (Solomon), renowned for his wisdom and kingdom; Ilyas (Elias), a prophet who preached against idol worship; and Isa (Jesus), a central figure in Islam and the Messiah.

The last prophet of Islam is Muhammad, who is considered the seal of the prophethood, meaning that no new prophets will come after him. Muhammad is also known as Muhammad in other languages.

These prophets played significant roles in delivering the message of Islam and guiding their respective communities towards righteousness.

Their names may have variations in different languages, but their teachings and contributions remain consistent across religious scriptures.

Muhammad, in particular, is a universally recognized name in both Arabic and English, highlighting his importance as the last prophet in Islam.

In Jewish scripture, they also refer to him as Mohammadian, further emphasizing his recognition in different religious traditions.

The prophets mentioned in the Quran and the previous scriptures are integral figures in Islamic theology, with their stories and teachings serving as a foundation for understanding and practicing the faith.

The acceptance of mistakes without recrimination or repentance creates an environment of acceptance of ills not understanding.

However, simply accepting mistakes without seeking to understand them can be fruitless.

It is through understanding the reasons behind our mistakes that we can truly learn and grow. By analyzing our actions and their consequences, we can identify the areas of our life that need improvement.

This understanding becomes conducive to growth because it allows us to make positive changes and avoid repeating the same mistakes.

By embracing a mindset of self-reflection and learning from our mistakes, we can transform setbacks into opportunities for personal development and success.

The prophets mentioned in the Bible and the Quran share similar names, such as Moses, Abraham, Noah, and Jesus, but their portrayal and role in their respective scriptures differ significantly.

The Quran presents the prophets as righteous individuals who were chosen by God to guide humanity. While it acknowledges the challenges and tests that the prophets faced, it does not depict them engaging in immoral or sinful behavior.

The Quran upholds the dignity and respect of the prophets, as they are seen as role models for believers to emulate.

It would contradict the purpose of following the prophets if they were portrayed as committing worse sins than the people they were sent to guide.

Therefore, the Quran does not tolerate any demeaning or disrespectful depiction of the prophets. While the Bible presents Moses as having committed murder, it is important to consider the context and circumstances of the event.

The Bible is a religious text that holds great significance for millions of people around the world.

However, for some individuals, it can be challenging to engage with the Bible after encountering disrespectful remarks about certain prophets.

One example of this is the portrayal of the prophet Moses as a murderer.

This depiction can be deeply offensive and disrespectful towards the prophets of Allah, as they are revered figures in Islam.

The encounters and temptations of the prophet Jesus in the Bible are truly awe-inspiring. They shed light on the fact that even these revered prophets faced false accusations.

Every faith in the world has contributed something positive.

However, we cannot simply ignore allegations, as they can tarnish the credibility. Skeptics become even more skeptical if interpreting Biblical text is distorted.

It becomes challenging to maintain belief when those who delivered the message don't pack an excellent reputation. This is detrimental to faith, and it is not the case with the Quran.

Quran: Surah Maidah: 5;114. Jesus, son of Mary, prayed, "O Allah, our Lord! Send us from heaven a table spread with food as a feast for us—the first and last of us—and as a sign from You. Provide for us! You are indeed the Best Provider."

Deadline: Aug 4, 2024 — The Vatican responded Saturday to the controversial drag performance that depicted Leonardo da Vinci's "Last Supper" painting during the 2024 Paris Olympics' ...

The display of disrespect knows no boundaries for the illiterate individuals who lack respect for religion. They indulge in showcasing disrespectful pictures, pornography, and derogatory content that deviate from reality and promote satanism.

The 2024 Paris Olympic Games' opening ceremony caused controversy with a performance that some interpreted as a mockery of Leonardo da Vinci's The Last Supper, involving drag queens and dancers.

At the event, a group of drag queens and dancers gathered around a lengthy table, with one performer donning a star crown positioned at the center while the dancers surrounded her.

Certain individuals interpreted this setup as the performer, symbolizing Jesus and the dancers embodying the disciples.

Faith skeptics mock what they don't understand, and those who convert to Islam require education because of the boundlessness of paganism.

The authority of Allah is irreplaceable, while the unseen entity observes all evil and the visible deities are unaware of it. Satan flees from the wicked and focuses on exciting believers, as unbelievers already belong to him.

Disrespectful language and derogatory remarks regarding the prophets can hinder the ability to engage with the Bible and appreciate its wisdom or lessons.

The portrayal of prophets in the Quran emphasizes their role as messengers of Allah, chosen to convey His divine message to the people.

They are individuals of exemplary character and righteousness, who call people to monotheism and moral rectitude.

The Quran highlights their unwavering faith, perseverance in the face of adversity, and dedication to their mission.

Overall, although the names of the prophets in the Bible and the Quran may match, the concepts surrounding their actions, presentations, and roles in their respective scriptures are distinct.

The Bible delves into the lives and experiences of the prophets, emphasizing the derogatory actions of Moses, Noah, Lot, and Jesus, while the Quran focuses more on their divine mission and the message they convey.

The mismatch between the Bible and the Quran in their presentation of prophets is extensive and can be seen with more examples.

Quran: Surah Nisa: 4:18. However, repentance is not accepted from those who knowingly persist in sin until they start dying, and then cry, now I repent! Not those who die as disbelievers. For them WE have prepared a painful punishment.

The verse in **Surah Nisa** of the Quran justifies the actions of persistent sinners who view life as a series of mishaps and seek to control the world.

Pharaoh's defiance serves as a reminder that arrogance pales compared to Allah's anger. With a ratio of 99 percent mercy to 1 percent anger, his mercy far surpasses his anger, yet the anger has caused havoc in once prosperous cities.

Although forgiveness is ample, the absence of spiritual contentment leads to eventual loss.

The mindset of the Western ideology often emphasizes the importance of acknowledging and addressing past wrongs in order to heal and move forward.

They believe that healing cannot occur without acknowledging the damage that has been done.

Therefore, they create platforms for people to admit openly their wrongdoings and assume responsibility for their actions. This concept extends to church, where confessions take place in a dark box to another individual.

Islam teaches a more private and direct approach to repentance. Muslims are encouraged to seek forgiveness from Allah and make efforts to conceal their sins, rather than attesting them.

In Islam, forgiveness means letting go of the past and not bringing up past mistakes.

The clash of ideologies and ways of thinking between the West and Islam is significant, with vast differences in how forgiveness and healing are understood.

Learning from Muslims can be valuable, as their mindset is often grounded in a balance between the mind and the heart.

It is important to note that the concept of "forgive but don't forget" is not found in any Abrahamic book, and it does not align with the teachings of Islam.

Story of Amr bin Al-As:

Amr bin Al-As, a prominent figure and believer, was initially known for his opposition to Islam. He fought against Muslims in various battles, causing concern among the believers.

Prophet Muhammad, being the final messenger of Allah, understood the power and significance of supplication.

Despite his concerns about Amr bin Al-As, a strong and fearless warrior who fought against the Muslims, Prophet Muhammad turned to Allah for guidance.

He raised his hands in prayer, seeking Allah's forgiveness and questioning how someone like Amr bin Al-As could be pardoned.

Throughout the episodes of his life, Allah consistently clarified that no prophet has control over His mercy or forgiveness. This emphasized the limits set for all prophets, highlighting Allah's supremacy and the fact that only He truly knows what lives in people's hearts.

It is important to note that even though Prophet Muhammad was the last testament to the Abrahamic faiths, Allah maintained His ultimate authority.

Amr bin Al-As eventually became a devoted believer after previously being a disbeliever, further emphasizing that Allah is the knower of both the seen and unseen.

This continuous understanding reinforces the Islamic belief that Jesus is not God, but a prophet who, like the others sent by Allah, did not possess knowledge of the unseen.

Allah's response came in **Surah Al-Imran**, emphasizing that the ultimate judgment lies with Him alone. This incident highlighted the profound role of Prophet Muhammad as a messenger, while also emphasizing that Allah is the ultimate decision-maker.

Quran: Surah Imran: 3:128. You ˈO Prophetˈ have no say in the matter. It is up to Allah to turn to them in mercy or punish them, for indeed they are wrongdoers.

The transformation of Amr bin Al-As astonished many, as he experienced a complete change of heart and embraced Islam.

The man who had once fought against Muslims, now fought alongside them, displaying the immense power of Allah to transform individuals.

This remarkable transformation serves as a testament to the mercy and guidance of Allah, demonstrating that His ability to change hearts is limitless.

It also serves as a reminder that Allah's wisdom surpasses human understanding, and He can bring about profound changes in even the most unlikely of individuals.

Amr ibn As, a prominent figure in the battle of Khandaq, showcased his astute political acumen during this crucial event. As the battle raged on, he keenly observed the changing tides and recognized the signs of divine intervention.

He understood Allah had sent the strong winds, which hindered the opponents' progress and fortified the Muslims' position. As the favorable outcome of the battle became apparent, Amr's heart underwent a transformative shift.

His previous opposition to the Muslims wavered, and he started contemplating a change in allegiance.

Recognizing the inevitable triumph of the Muslims, Amr ibn As saw an opportunity to align himself with the victorious side, thus embarking on a new political course.

Amr, a prominent figure among the Quraysh, moved to Abyssinia (modern-day Ethiopia) after the defeat in Mecca. He believed that if the Muslims were victorious, they would be treated with respect in Abyssinia, and if they were to lose, they would still have their dignity intact to return.

Seeking to preserve his own dignity, Amr sought protection from Nagashi, the Christian king of Abyssinia, who had previously granted protection to Muslims.

Prophet Muhammad, upon gaining victory in Mecca, sent Jafar ibn Abi Talib to Najashi to thank him and to request the return of the Muslims who had sought asylum.

Najashi agreed to protect Amr and allow him to stay. However, when Amr realized that the man who came to visit him was against his team, he felt the need to give up his protection and engage in a one-on-one fight.

It was during this encounter that Amr discovered Najashi had secretly accepted Islam, and his anger towards the man who came from the Prophet, receiving revelations from Allah, reflected his own faith.

Nagashi, revealing his Muslim identity, admonished Amr and urged him to convert to Islam before facing destruction. Amr paid close attention to the words of the king and converted to Islam.

This unexpected turn of events showcased Allah's plan and how even those who opposed Islam could be guided towards it.

Upon his conversion, Amr held a high status among the Muhajiroun (migrants) and was warmly welcomed by Prophet Muhammad himself.

He pledged his allegiance to support Islam both politically and spiritually, and in a symbolic gesture, he held the Prophet's hand and recited the shahada, the testimony of faith.

Prior to this, Amr had requested Allah's forgiveness for all his past sins, and the Prophet assured him that accepting Islam meant a clean slate for him.

Amr proved to be a strong and dedicated believer, entrusted with certain responsibilities within the Islamic community. His journey from opposing Islam to becoming a devout Muslim serves as a testament to the transformative power of faith and the mercy of Allah.

Amr bin Aas played a major role after the passing of Prophet Muhammad as a military commander appointed by Prophet Muhammad in the Battle of Yarmouk in Syria.

This battle was a significant turning point in Islamic history, as it marked the expansion of the Muslim empire into new territories.

Amr's strategic skills and leadership abilities were instrumental in the victory of the Muslim army.

He demonstrated great courage and determination on the battlefield, inspiring his troops and leading them to success. Amr's deep understanding of politics and diplomacy also proved valuable in negotiating with local tribes and establishing alliances.

His efforts in spreading the message of Islam in Oman were equally successful, as he could effectively communicate the principles of the faith and win over many converts.

Amr's close relationship with Prophet Muhammad allowed him to witness firsthand the Prophet's kindness, compassion, and wisdom. Despite hoping to be the Prophet's favorite, Amr realized that Prophet Muhammad treated everyone in his company with equal love and respect.

This experience taught Amr the importance of inclusivity and the power of unity within the Muslim community.

Amr ibn As Aas, a prominent Muslim military leader, indeed played a significant role in the conquest of modern-day Palestine.

When Omar bin Khattab, the second caliph of the Rashidun Caliphate, arrived in Jerusalem to receive the keys to the city, Amr ibn Aas advised him on the strategic importance of Egypt for the Muslims.

Recognizing the potential benefits, Amr emphasized the necessity of conquering Egypt to ensure Muslim control over the region.

He believed that without Egypt under Muslim rule, the Romans would continue to exert influence and pose a threat to the Muslim territories.

Thus, Amr's counsel played a crucial role in convincing Omar bin Khattab to prioritize the conquest of Egypt for the benefit and security of the Muslim community.

The dedication of those who converted to Islam and left legacies is indescribable.

Muslims who were born into this faith still discuss the convoys of belief and hope for more to come, as they learn the true stories of faith and commitment to Islam with sincere belief.

Egypt is widely considered the cradle of civilization, as it is home to some of the world's oldest and most influential civilizations, such as the ancient Egyptians and their pharaohs.

Throughout history, Egypt has been a center of learning, attracting scholars, philosophers, and scientists from all over the world.

The control of Muslims in this land has played a significant role in shaping its cultural, intellectual, and architectural landscape.

Islam in the 7th century brought a new era of growth and development, as Muslim rulers established universities, libraries, and centers of knowledge, making Egypt a hub for intellectual exchange and scholarship.

Islamic influence can be seen in the magnificent mosques and Islamic architectural masterpieces that dot the Egyptian landscape, such as the Great Mosque of Cairo and the Al-Azhar Mosque, one of the oldest universities in the world.

The Muslim control of Egypt has left an indelible mark on the country, making it a rich and diverse tapestry of history, culture, and learning.

During the ancient times, Egypt served as a flourishing hub of intellectual activity and learning. The city of Alexandria housed the renowned. The Library of Alexandria, which was the largest library in the world.

This magnificent institution attracted scholars from all over, serving as a center for research, education, and the preservation of knowledge.

The library contained a vast collection of books, manuscripts, and scrolls, covering a wide range of subjects including mathematics, astronomy, philosophy, medicine, and literature.

During the Islamic Golden Age, which spanned from the 8th to the 14th century, Muslim scholars in Egypt and other parts of the Muslim world made significant contributions to various fields of knowledge.

They actively sought knowledge and were known for their openness and willingness to share their discoveries with the rest of the world.

This spirit of collaboration and dissemination of knowledge played a crucial role in the advancement of science, mathematics, medicine, and other disciplines during that time.

Under the leadership of Amr, Omar bin Khattab sent a well-trained army of 4000 men to conquer Egypt. The conquest of Egypt by the Muslims took place in the year 639 CE.

The Egyptian forces, led by the Byzantine commander, were no match for the disciplined and determined Muslim army.

Amr and his troops swiftly advanced, capturing key cities and territories along the Nile River.

The Egyptians, impressed by the military prowess of the Muslims, eventually surrendered, and Egypt came under Islamic rule.

This conquest marked a significant turning point in the expansion of the Islamic Empire and laid the foundation for the spread of Islam throughout North Africa.

He appointed Amr Ibn Aas the governor of Egypt, recognizing his exceptional military strategy and leadership skills. Under Amr's rule, Egypt flourished as a Muslim country, with the implementation of Islamic laws and principles.

Amr Ibn As established a strong administrative system, ensuring justice and fairness for all. He also focused on the development of agriculture and trade, harnessing the fertile lands of the Nile to boost the economy.

Omar bin Khattab's visit to Egypt further solidified the bond between the Muslim rulers and the people of Egypt. During his visit, he listened to the concerns and needs of the locals, implementing reforms and improvements accordingly.

This strengthened the trust and loyalty of the Egyptian population towards the Muslim leadership.

Overall, Amr Ibn Aas and Omar bin Khattab's combined efforts ensured the successful establishment of Islam in Egypt, leaving a lasting impact on its history and culture.

Alexandria, on the northern coast of Egypt, is not only famous for its historical significance as an ancient city but also for its strategic location on the Mediterranean Sea.

The city's port, known as the White Sea, has played a crucial role in facilitating trade and maritime connections with various countries that can sail.

However, it is important to note that by the time Alexandria was established, Egypt had already been conquered by Muslim armies in the 7th century.

The Muslim conquest of Egypt brought significant changes to the region, including the introduction of Islam as the dominant religion and the establishment of a new political and social order.

Despite this, Alexandria's geographical advantages and its connection to the Mediterranean Sea have continued to make it an important hub for international trade and cultural exchange throughout history.

The **"Iman"** faith was a driving force behind the conquests of Muslim armies. The concept of Tawhid, which refers to the belief in the oneness of Allah, instilled a deep sense of unity and purpose among the Muslim soldiers.

While other armies may have had trained militants, the Muslims fought with a conviction and dedication that went beyond mere military training.

Their faith provided them with a sense of divine guidance and protection, giving them the strength and determination to overcome obstacles and emerge victorious in these wars.

These Muslim soldiers were not just fighting for political or territorial gains, but for the establishment of an Islamic state governed by Islamic law.

Their unwavering belief in the principles and teachings of Islam fueled their determination and resilience on the battlefield.

This deep-rooted commitment to their faith and the desire to establish a Muslim country became a driving force in their struggle for independence.

While some may argue that the skills of trained militants played a role in the success of the Egyptian revolution, it was ultimately the unyielding faith and dedication of the Muslim soldiers that led to the establishment of Egypt as a Muslim country.

Amr ibn As, a prominent figure in Islamic history, not only played a significant role in the conquest of Egypt but also founded the city of Fu stat, known today as old Cairo.

It was in this city that he first pitched his tent, marking the spot where the iconic masjid (mosque) of Amr ibn As now stands. This mosque holds great historical and cultural importance, attracting visitors from all over the world.

Similarly, Omar bin Khattab, the second caliph of the Rashidun Caliphate, is widely revered in Egypt. His leadership and justice are celebrated, and his legacy is deeply ingrained in the hearts of the Egyptian people.

Both Amr ibn As and Omar bin Khattab continue to be highly respected figures in Egyptian history. Cairo, the capital city of Egypt, holds a deep meaning and is widely known as **Al Qahira** in Arabic.

The name **"Al Qahira"** translates to **"The Victorious"** in English, reflecting the city's rich history and its resilience throughout the centuries.

Cairo is not only a bustling metropolis but also a significant cultural and historical center, boasting iconic landmarks such as the Great Pyramids of Giza, the Sphinx, and the Egyptian Museum.

With its vibrant markets, known as souks, and ancient mosques, including the majestic Al-Azhar Mosque, Cairo showcases a blend of Islamic, Coptic, and Pharaonic influences.

The city's significance goes beyond its architectural marvels, as it has been a hub for trade, education, and innovation in the region for centuries.

Today, Cairo remains a dynamic city, representing the heart and soul of Egypt and captivating visitors with its timeless charm and profound significance.

Not only did this city talk about prominent figures and learning, but it also has a deep history connected to Prophet Muhammad.

In Cairo, there is a place known as the House of Fatima, the daughter of Prophet Muhammad, where she visited during her lifetime.

Her son Hussain, who was martyred, has a significant presence in the city. The Mosque of Hussain, where he is buried, stands as a revered site for Muslims and attracts pilgrims from all over the world.

The mosque of Imam Hussain holds great significance for Muslims, as it is the burial place of Imam Hussain, the grandson of Prophet Muhammad.

After the passing of Prophet Muhammad (PBUH), Islam split into different sects, with Sunni Muslims being one of them.

While Sunni Muslims hold the same respect for the family of Prophet Muhammad (PBUH) and acknowledge that he would not permit worship except to Allah, they also recognize that he experienced personal pain and loss in his life.

This includes the tragic deaths of his family members, such as two of his grandsons who were martyred and the death of his son at a young age.

Despite these hardships, Prophet Muhammad (PBUH) maintained his unwavering devotion to Allah. It is important to note that while crying is a natural emotion, it should not be elevated to the level of a cultic practice for Muslims when visiting graves.

While some Muslims engage in practices, such as crying at graves and requesting prayers to be accepted at the mosque, these actions are considered by scholars to be bid 'ah (innovation) and forbidden in Islam.

According to the teachings of Islam, Muslims are encouraged to direct their prayers and supplications solely to Allah, as He is the only one who has the power to respond to their requests.

However, it is important to note that not all Muslims interpret these practices in the same way, and there are varying opinions and cultural traditions within the diverse Muslim community. At the core of Islam is the belief in monotheism, emphasizing the worship and devotion to Allah alone.

Propaganda has indeed been present throughout history, including after the divisions among Islamic sects. These divisions, particularly between Sunni and Shia Muslims, have often been exploited by various groups to further their own agendas.

However, it is important to note that Sunni Muslims, like any other religious group, seek guidance and knowledge from authentic sources.

Placing great importance on verifying the authenticity of these Hadiths through rigorous scholarship and analysis.

By adhering to the authentic Hadiths, Muslims must strive to find the truth and reality of stories, enabling them to learn from the wisdom and teachings of the Prophet and endure the challenges they face in their lives.

This commitment to seeking truth and knowledge helps Muslims navigate through the complexities of propaganda and misinformation that may arise within their communities.

The mosque holds great historical and religious significance, serving as a reminder of the sacrifices made by Hussain and his family in the name of Islam.

Cairo's rich heritage intertwines with the life and legacy of Prophet Muhammad, making it a destination of great importance for those interested in Islamic history and culture.

The history of Egypt is deeply intertwined with its vibrant spice markets, which have been a hub of trade and commerce for centuries

These markets, filled with a rich assortment of aromatic spices like cardamom, cinnamon, and saffron, have not only attracted merchants from all over the world but have also become a source of fascination for tourists.

Alongside the bustling markets, Egypt is adorned with magnificent masjids (mosques) that showcase the country's rich Islamic heritage.

The melodious call to prayer, known as the azan, echoes through the streets, inviting worshippers to the masjids for their daily prayers.

These masjids are not just places of religious significance but also serve as peaceful sanctuaries for those seeking solace and tranquility.

As the majestic Nile River flows through Egypt, it serves as a constant reminder of the importance of water for sustaining life. The serene and calm nature of the river aligns with the peaceful atmosphere found within the masjids, emphasizing the importance of worshiping Allah and finding inner peace through devotion.

The White Sea in Alexandria, Egypt is a body of water that connects to several different countries and borders. It is in the northern part of the country and is considered an extension of the Mediterranean Sea.

The sea connects to the countries of Libya to the west and Israel to the northeast. It is connected to the Suez Canal, which allows for access to the Red Sea and further connections to the Indian Ocean.

The White Sea in Alexandria serves as an important hub for maritime trade and transportation, facilitating the movement of goods and people between Egypt and its neighboring countries.

Sharm El-Sheikh, in Egypt, is a renowned tourist destination known for its vibrant entertainment offerings. Tourists flock to this city to experience a wide range of recreational activities and attractions.

One of the most iconic features is the stunning view of the Red Sea, which holds historical significance as the sea that Moses famously parted according to biblical accounts.

Sharm El Sheikh's proximity to the Red Sea allows visitors to indulge in various water activities such as snorkeling, diving, and boat tours to explore the vibrant marine life and coral reefs.

While Sharm El Sheikh is in Egypt, it is relatively close to the country of Palestine, making it a convenient base for tourists looking to explore the cultural and historical landmarks of the region.

The history of Islam is indeed filled with rich teachings and profound truths. It draws those who seek answers to the fundamental questions of life, guiding them towards a deeper understanding of spirituality and morality.

Islam has a long and illustrious history, with its roots in the Arabian Peninsula where it emerged as a response to the prevailing polytheistic beliefs of the time.

The transformation of the once pagan land into a vibrant Muslim land is a testament to the power and influence of Islam. The call to prayer, known as the **Azan**, reverberates five times a day, serving as a reminder to Muslims of their connection to God and their duty to worship.

It is a powerful symbol of unity and devotion, as millions of Muslims worldwide respond to its call, regardless of their geographic location.

Additionally, the Quran is recited and studied daily in Muslim communities, providing a wealth of wisdom, guidance, and knowledge.

In this Muslim land, which was once steeped in magical and pagan beliefs, the achievements of the Islamic civilization are remarkable.

Muslims have made significant contributions to various fields, including science, mathematics, medicine, philosophy, and architecture.

The preservation and advancement of knowledge during the Islamic Golden Age paved the way for many scientific and intellectual breakthroughs that continue to shape our world today

Muslims can contribute to the progress and development of society, promoting peace, compassion, and justice.

The principles and values found within Islam can serve as a guiding light for individuals seeking truth and enlightenment in a world that is often filled with uncertainty and confusion.

CHAPTER 8
CONSISTENCY IS THE THEME

Consistency in life is a crucial factor that often separates those who achieve success from those who don't. When individuals maintain consistent behavior, they can develop positive habits and routines that contribute to their progress and growth.

By consistently working towards their goals, they are more likely to overcome obstacles and setbacks, as they persistently strive for improvement.

Consistency allows individuals to build momentum and maintain focus, leading to a higher chance of reaching their desired outcomes. In contrast, inconsistency can lead to a lack of progress and hinder personal and professional development.

Those who lack consistency may struggle to stay motivated, easily get discouraged, and frequently abandon their goals. Therefore, consistent behavior acts as a barrier between losing and success, as it ensures dedication, persistence, and a greater likelihood of achieving desired results.

Allah, being the omniscient creator, had deep knowledge and understanding of human nature before bringing them into existence.

Islam mandates five daily prayers, known as Salat, to establish consistency and discipline in the life of a believer.

The act of regularly performing these prayers not only shows devotion and obedience to Allah, but also serves as a reminder of the importance of maintaining a spiritual connection throughout the day.

By adhering to a structured prayer routine, individuals are constantly reminded of their duties and responsibilities towards their Creator, fostering a sense of discipline and commitment.

Allah, in His wisdom, knew that consistency in worship and remembrance of Him would ultimately lead to success and spiritual growth for humanity.

While some individuals may argue that they do not require mandated Salat (Islamic prayer), claiming that they pray constantly, it is important to note that Salat is a unique form of worship with distinct characteristics.

Salat involves ritualistic physical movements, such as bowing and prostrating, which demonstrate humility and submission before a higher power.

The recitation of specific verses from the Quran during Salat sets it apart from other forms of worship. This repetitive recitation serves as a constant reminder of the teachings and guidance found in the holy scriptures.

Therefore, while personal prayers and supplications are encouraged and valued in Islam, the prescribed Salat holds a significant place in the faith as a distinct and essential act of worship.

Regular physical exercise is a crucial component for individuals seeking to achieve a toned and appealing physique. Both men and women recognize the importance of going to the gym as a consistent and dedicated practice.

They understand that attending the gym in a ritualistic manner yields the best results in terms of muscle growth, strength, and overall physical fitness.

Complementing their exercise routine with healthy eating habits further enhances the desired outcomes. By engaging in this holistic approach, individuals witness significant transformations in their bodies, leading to a more attractive and sculpted appearance.

There is a rush of adrenaline when a dance or aerobic exercise takes place, causing an increase in the heart rate. This surge of adrenaline is a natural response to physical activity and serves to prepare the body for action.

As the body engages in dynamic movements and intense cardio exercises, the heart pumps blood at a faster rate, supplying oxygen and nutrients to the muscles.

This increased circulation, coupled with the release of adrenaline, results in heightened alertness, improved focus, and a surge of energy. The release of endorphins during exercise contributes to a sense of euphoria and overall well-being.

Engaging in dance or aerobic exercise not only elevates heart rate but also triggers a cascade of physiological responses that enhance physical and mental performance.

Increased strength. When you lift weights, your muscles are required to exert force against resistance, which leads to micro-tears in the muscle fibers.

As these fibers repair and rebuild themselves, they become stronger and denser, resulting in improved muscle tone and definition. Weightlifting promotes the growth of lean muscle mass, which can increase your metabolic rate and help burn calories even at rest.

This not only helps in achieving a more toned appearance, but also enhances overall body strength and functional fitness.

Regular weightlifting sessions, combined with proper nutrition and rest, can lead to significant improvements in muscle definition, tone, and overall physical performance.

Prophet Muhammad emphasized the importance of physical exercise and swimming as part of a healthy lifestyle. He recognized the many benefits of swimming as an excellent form of exercise that engages the entire body and promotes cardiovascular health.

The Prophet himself took part in swimming and recommended it to others. He provided guidance on mindful eating habits, advising his followers to consume small portions and chew their food thoroughly for better digestion.

The Prophet Muhammad taught the importance of maintaining a balanced diet by suggesting that one should keep their meals divided into thirds: one-third for food, one-third for water, and one-third to leave the stomach empty.

This practice promotes moderation and prevents overloading the body with excessive food or water, aligning with the Sunnah teachings.

Overall, Prophet Muhammad's teachings emphasized the significance of engaging in regular physical activity, adopting mindful eating habits, and maintaining a balanced lifestyle for optimal health.

Certain fruits, vegetables, and grains gain importance, as the Quran mentions some of them.

Not only are lentils mentioned in the Quran, but they also hold a significant place in the culinary traditions of Muslim countries. Lentil soup, in particular, is highly regarded and widely consumed in these regions.

One country renowned for its delicious lentil soup is Turkey. Turkish cuisine is known for its rich flavors and diverse dishes, and lentil soup is a staple in many households and restaurants.

It is typically made with red lentils, onions, garlic, and various spices, resulting in a hearty and nutritious soup.

The popularity of lentil soup in Turkey is clear in its presence on menus across the country, from humble street food stalls to upscale restaurants.

So, if you ever find yourself in Turkey, trying a bowl of their famous lentil soup is a must-do culinary experience.

The Quran describes the fruits of Jannah, or Paradise, as abundant and delightful. They are a reward for the righteous believers who will enter Jannah.

The Quran mentions these fruits come in various kinds, such as dates, pomegranates, grapes, and figs.

They are always available and easily accessible to the inhabitants of Jannah. The Quran emphasizes these fruits are of the highest quality, perfectly ripe, and free from imperfections or blemishes.

They provide nourishment, pleasure, and satisfaction to the dwellers of Paradise, symbolizing the eternal blessings and rewards that await the believers in the hereafter.

Cucumbers, onions, garlic, and their benefits are also mentioned in the Quran, as they are known for their alkalinity and many health benefits.

The importance of consistency remains evident and cannot be overlooked. Success is achieved by those who maintain consistency, even in the smallest actions. The Quran also emphasizes this principle.

The consistency of dreams or daily life can become so striking that one questions whether it is merely a coincidence.

A young person may not initially realize the significance of this realization. However, as time passes and experiences accumulate, the patterns become undeniable.

Whether it is witnessing certain actions being performed consistently or experiencing recurring dreams that seem beyond one's control, these occurrences hold deeper meanings.

The story of Prophet Yusuf (Joseph) in the Quran serves as an example of how consistent events and dreams played a pivotal role in his life.

It emphasizes the importance of paying attention to the consistent patterns that unfold around us, as they may hold significant messages and guidance for our own journeys.

In Islam, dreams are believed to hold significant value and can provide insights into various aspects of a person's life. According to Islamic teachings, there are three types of dreams.

The first type is a straightforward dream that requires no interpretation because it is shown in its actuality.

These dreams are believed to be a direct message from Allah and may serve as guidance or warnings.

The second type is a dream that requires interpretation as it may not be direct but still carries a pleasant message.

These dreams often contain symbols or metaphors that need to be deciphered to understand their meaning. Scholars and knowledgeable individuals are often consulted to interpret such dreams.

The third type of dream is not considered formative and is believed to be from Satan. These dreams are often associated with evil thoughts or negative influences and should be disregarded or rejected.

Muslims are encouraged to seek positive dreams and to seek protection from Allah against any negative or harmful dreams.

Overall, dreams hold a significant place in Islam and are considered as a means of communication between the individual and Allah, providing guidance, warnings, or insights into one's life.

The dream of Prophet Yusuf, also known as Joseph, was a vivid and significant vision that he had as a child. Despite his father's advice to keep it to himself, Yusuf couldn't contain his excitement and eagerly shared his dream with his brothers.

In the dream, Yusuf saw eleven stars, the sun, and the moon all bowing down to him, symbolizing his future greatness and leadership.

However, this revelation sparked intense jealousy among his brothers, who felt threatened by the idea of Yusuf being superior to them. Consumed by envy, they hatched a plan to get rid of Yusuf and tossed him into a deep well, abandoning him to a seemingly tragic fate.

This act of betrayal set in motion a series of events that would ultimately shape Yusuf's destiny and test his unwavering faith in God.

Zulekha, who had raised him since childhood, found Yusuf to be incredibly attractive and became infatuated with him. She falsely accused him of a crime he did not commit, resulting in his unjust imprisonment.

However, Zulekha eventually realized her mistake and acknowledged her wrongdoing. She turned to Allah in repentance, seeking His forgiveness and guidance.

In her prayers, she asked Allah to bless her with a marriage to Yusuf and to preserve her beauty.

Allah, in His infinite wisdom, responded to her plea, promising to preserve her beauty. Yusuf, too, found Zulekha attractive, but their union would be in the next life, where beauty and desires are fulfilled indefinitely.

This life, as Allah has ordained, is a test for all beings, and the rewards and blessings are reserved for the everlasting world that lies beyond.

Yusuf (Joseph), a prophet, possessed the remarkable ability to interpret dreams, which was a gift bestowed upon him by Allah.

While he was imprisoned unjustly, Yusuf utilized this divine talent to guide fellow inmates towards Allah and provided solace through his interpretations.

Eventually, news of his exceptional skill reached the king, who was troubled by a perplexing dream. Yusuf was summoned to interpret the dream, which led to his release from prison.

Yusuf the prophet interpreted the dream as a divine caution, showing seven years of bountifulness, followed by seven years of scarcity. To prepare for the famine, he recommended that the king store extra grain during years of plenty.

Subsequently, he was appointed as a trusted advisor to the king and was eventually elevated to the position of kingship and prophethood.

This miraculous turn of events highlights the mercy of Allah and serves as a profound reminder that everything occurs according to His divine timing.

Humans cannot dictate or control the actions of Allah, as He is not bound by the constraints of human desires and commands.

Despite these challenges, Yusuf never lost faith in his dream and remained steadfast in his belief that he was meant for something greater.

While in prison, his ability to interpret dreams caught the attention of the king, leading to his eventual release and appointment as a trusted advisor.

Yusuf's wisdom and guidance proved invaluable as he helped the kingdom navigate through a severe famine, ultimately solidifying his position of power and influence.

His dream of greatness became a reality as he rose to become one of the most respected and revered figures in his time.

This journey of struggle and triumph serves as a powerful reminder that even in the face of adversity, one's destiny can still be fulfilled.

Yusuf's long-held dream finally materialized after years. The dream required interpretation and was fulfilled.

Surah Yusuf is the only surah in the Quran that presents a complete narrative from beginning to end.

While the Quran contains various revelations and teachings, it primarily focuses on delivering guidance, principles, and moral lessons, presenting a consistent storyline.

However, Surah Yusuf stands out as it recounts the detailed story of the Prophet Yusuf (Joseph), beginning with his childhood and ending with his rise to power in Egypt.

This surah delves into themes such as jealousy, betrayal, patience, and forgiveness, providing valuable insights and lessons for believers to contemplate and apply in their lives.

In both the Bible and the Quran, the story of Yusuf (Joseph) depicts his brothers' jealousy and their ultimate defeat. However, there are significant differences in the narrative between the two texts.

While both religious texts mention Yusuf's triumph over his brothers, the Quran does not mention Mary being with Joseph or having any children with him.

In the Bible, Joseph is portrayed as the husband of Mary and the earthly father of Jesus, whereas the Quran presents Mary as a chaste and virtuous woman chosen by God to bear Jesus with no human intervention.

This difference in the storyline reflects the varying theological perspectives and emphasis of the two religious texts.

It is indeed important to note that there are multiple individuals named Joseph in the Bible. Dut Ripon's Latin Bible concordance, published in Paris in 1838, identifies 16 people named Joseph in the Bible.

Out of these, the New Testament mentions nine of them. The first Joseph mentioned in the Bible is Joseph, the son of Jacob, who appears in the book of Genesis.

He is the eleventh son of the patriarch Jacob and his wife Rachel, and the brother of Benjamin.

The New Testament presents Joseph of Nazareth as Mary's husband and Jesus' foster-father. Through Jacob's other son, Judah, his lineage is believed to extend all the way back to Abraham, making him a direct descendant of Jacob.

The Quran doesn't mention any Christian teachings, but it's important to note that the Quran has remained unchanged, with a consistent lesson and story line.

Yusuf, a ruler and prophet, had no affiliation with Mary or any other Yusuf mentioned in the Bible. Mary is depicted as weak in the Bible, requiring a husband to care for her son, whom she conceived without a man, but God showed His miracle when an angel infused her garment with the spirit.

According to the Quran, Mary did not marry or require help in raising her son. If she could endure labor pains on her own, she could certainly raise her son. The Quran portrays her as a determined and devout woman, with a whole surah named after her - Surah Maryam.

However, it is worth mentioning that the Quran only mentions one Joseph. According to the Quran, Mary (also known as Maryam) was a chaste and devout woman who never married nor engaged in any intimate relationship.

She remained pure and devoted to her faith throughout her life. The Quran states that Maryam only bore one child, Jesus (Isa in Arabic).

She miraculously conceived Jesus through the divine intervention of Allah without the involvement of any human father or divine father.

This unique birth is emphasized in Islamic belief, highlighting Jesus' significance as a prophet and a messenger of God.

Canonical writings such as the Bible do not name Joachim and Anna as the parents of Mary the mother of Jesus. However, in Islamic tradition, the Quran provides explicit details about the lineage and story of Mary's parents.

According to the Quran, Joachim (known as Imran in Arabic) was a righteous and devout man, blessed with wealth and piety.

He was a descendant of the Prophet David and a respected member of the community. Anna (known as Hannah in Arabic) was his wife, who longed for a child despite her old age.

One day, while observing a bird feeding its offspring, Hannah made a supplication to Allah to grant her a child. In response to her sincere prayer, Allah blessed her with a child, Maryam (Mary).

As a gesture of gratitude and devotion, Anna vowed to dedicate her child to the service of the temple. Subsequently, they raised Mary in the temple, where she grew in purity and righteousness. The Quran provides a clear and comprehensive account of the story, leaving no room for ambiguity or confusion.

Quran: Surah Rum: 30:7. They only know the worldly affairs of this life, but are totally oblivious to the hereafter.

Quran: Suran Rum: 30:8. Have they not reflected upon their own being? Allah only created the heavens and the earth and everything in between for a purpose and an appointed term. Yet most people are truly in denial of the meeting with their Lord.

Quran: Surah Rum: 30:10. Then most evil was the end of the evildoers for denying and mocking the signs of Allah.

Bible NIV: Matthew: 1:16. and Jacob the father of Joseph, the husband of Mary, and Mary was the mother of Jesus who is called the Messiah.

In the Bible, Joseph is depicted as the earthly father figure to Jesus, who provided him with love, guidance, and a nurturing home.

While if he was God the incarnate or God's son, being divine, does not require nurturing or provision, the role of Joseph in Jesus' life highlights the human aspect of Jesus' not incarnation.

According to the Bible, Joseph fully embraced his role as Jesus' father figure, despite not being his biological father. He passed on his carpentry skills, instilling a strong work ethic and practical knowledge. Joseph was given the task of naming Jesus by an angel in a dream.

According to the Quran, Mary (known as Maryam in Islamic tradition) was never married to Joseph (known as Yusuf in Islamic tradition). Instead,

Joseph, although mentioned in the Quran as a righteous man, is not depicted as Maryam's husband or as playing a role in the upbringing of Jesus.

Therefore, Maryam raised Jesus on her own, with the support and guidance of Allah per Islamic doctrine.

This narrative emphasizes the unique and miraculous nature of Jesus' birth and highlights Maryam's exceptional status as a devoted and virtuous woman in Islamic tradition.

The Bible passage Matthew 1:16 says, "Jacob was the father of Joseph, the husband of Mary, and the father of Jesus, who is called Christ."

However, it is important to note that Joseph was not Jesus' biological father, as Jesus was conceived through the Holy Spirit.

The Quranic belief asserts that God is not born nor does He give birth. This goes against the Bible's portrayal of Jesus as the begotten Son of God.

Jesus is regarded as the solitary Son of God in Christian teachings, sent to Earth to accomplish the mission of salvation.

The exclusion of "begotten" in **John 3:16** demonstrates the Bible's ongoing adaptation to contemporary society. The Quran remains steadfast, capable of withstanding the test of time, while time itself was created by Allah.

Jesus, a central figure in Christianity, prayed to **Allah-ha**. This supports the belief in a single God, he did not pray to himself. Jesus consistently emphasized his relationship with God the Father and instructed his followers to pray, aligning with this concept.

The Abrahamic faith emphasizes the unity and oneness of God, which is a central tenet across all three religions. Christianity is not mentioned in the Bible, but the Quran does and warns people to come to fair agreements as prescribed since the beginning of time.

The concept of the Trinity, which is central to Christian belief, posits that Jesus is both fully human and fully divine. This means that while Jesus experienced human characteristics and relied on earthly figures like Joseph for support, he also possessed the divine nature of God one contradicts the other.

The Quran presents a different perspective on God's characteristics, emphasizing His transcendence and uniqueness, which may differ from human qualities. Ultimately, the portrayal of Jesus in the Bible highlights the mystery and complexity of his nature as both human and divine.

Quran: Surah Rum: 30:58. We have certainly set forth every ˈkind ofˈ lesson for people in this Quran. And no matter what sign you bring to them ˈO Prophetˈ, the disbelievers will definitely say ˈto the believersˈ, "You are only a people of falsehood."

Convincing individuals who possess a basic understanding of logic and reasoning is a relatively straightforward task. These individuals are open to new ideas and will engage in meaningful discussions to expand their knowledge.

However, comprehension goes beyond mere awareness; it requires effort and a genuine desire to learn. Those who actively seek knowledge and ask questions are more likely to gain a deeper understanding of complex concepts.

There are those who reside in a state of perpetual confusion. Their minds are entangled in a web of uncertainty and doubt, creating a fertile ground for manipulation and deception.

It is believed that these dilemmas are orchestrated by malevolent forces, such as Satan, to keep individuals trapped in a cycle of confusion and misinformation. For these individuals, clarity is a precious gift that can liberate them from their cognitive entrapment.

The presentation of clarity is crucial for those who are ready to grasp it. It is a beacon of light in the darkness, illuminating the path towards understanding and truth.

However, it is important to note that not everyone may be willing or able to embrace this clarity. Some individuals may choose to remain in their state of confusion, either out of fear, stubbornness, or a lack of motivation to explore new ideas.

In conclusion, the comprehension of complex concepts goes beyond simple knowledge and understanding. It requires effort, curiosity, and a willingness to question the status quo. Clarity is not easily attained, but for those who actively seek it, it serves as a powerful tool to break free from the dilemmas imposed upon them and navigate through the complexities of life.

The tale of a man who defended his convictions:

The man, who was originally from a Christian family, had a strong sense of loyalty towards them, his culture, and his previous confidants. However, his journey to Islam resulted from Allah's invitation to faith, and he embraced it.

Despite claiming to be a Muslim, he lacked true loyalty to the faith, often demeaning Islam and failing to represent it well.

Instead of serving as an ambassador of Islam, he became known for his poor behavior, which even made the disbelievers smile, as they eagerly awaited to see if he would abandon his newfound faith.

His focus was primarily on protecting the obvious, such as the political climate and the pride associated with one's citizenship or heritage, particularly in certain cultures and countries.

Unfortunately, he disregarded the importance of representing Islam with dignity, whether he was born into the faith or accepted it later in life, as all invitations to Islam come from Allah.

Later, he underwent a transformation as life took its toll on him. The constant support of a believer had become a habit, one that he had ignored.

However, he eventually realized that his path was unfolding before him every day, despite his negligent behavior.

Although his actions may have satisfied the disbelievers and left him feeling empty, he sought fulfillment and fully embraced Islam.

By leaving behind the company that had hindered his decisions, he paved the way for success in his ventures and ultimately became the **ambassador of Islam.**

Straying in Islam can also imply a strong return, which was a testament to his unwavering faith.

These stories of today are reminiscent of those from yesterday, and they serve as a reminder that the company we keep influences our actions. Islam places great importance on surrounding oneself with good company.

The company of social media plays a significant role in perpetuating Islamophobia. Through their platforms, false narratives and misinformation are spread, often targeting Islam and Muslims.

This has led to the creation of an environment where political regimes capitalize on Islamophobia to gain support and further their own agendas. They manipulate the fears and ignorance of the illiterate and misinformed, distorting the truth about current events and influencing public opinion.

This deliberate campaign of misinformation and fear mongering not only hinders progress but also creates a society that lacks proper information and understanding about Islam.

Society's focus on individualism and sexual desires is often used as a distraction to compensate for the injustices and discrimination they perpetuate through Islamophobia.

This further marginalizes and excludes the Muslim community, contributing to a society that is lacking in empathy, understanding, and factual knowledge about Islam.

The travel opportunities for these individuals are limited due to their financial constraints. While they work long hours, their income is primarily allocated towards paying off debts and interest, leaving little room for leisurely pursuits.

However, it is important not to overlook the fact that Muslims did not attain victory during the Golden Age of Islam solely through material wealth. Instead, they uplifted others by showcasing the path to success through the teachings of Islam.

It is crucial to note that success came not from indulging in worldly desires, but from the harsh reality of conquest and fearlessness.

With a firm belief in Allah, conquering the world becomes attainable, as He has provided ample opportunities for those who have succeeded and left a lasting impact in the Muslim Empire.

To ensure the future generation's understanding of Islam, it is imperative that they receive proper education, allowing them to comprehend its teachings accurately.

This will safeguard them from being swayed by the distorted narratives propagated by Islamophobes on social media, who aim to misguide the masses with their misguided attempts.

A Muslim union, similar to the European Union, can potentially address the misunderstandings and misconceptions surrounding Islam.

By coming together, Muslim countries can promote unity, cooperation, and understanding among themselves and the rest of the world. The Gulf countries and the Turkish republic, known for their significant Muslim populations and economic power, can play a crucial role in this endeavor.

These countries possess vast resources and expertise that, if combined, can contribute to the betterment of humanity.

By collaborating and supporting one another, the Muslim countries can address common challenges and work towards mutual growth and development.

This unity could also counteract the predatory actions that take advantage of divisions among Muslim nations.

Ultimately, the focus should be on embracing the shared humanity that transcends religious differences and working towards a more inclusive and harmonious world

Muslims have a rich history of preparation and exploration, leaving behind a lasting legacy for future generations. By focusing on the symbolism of preparation, individuals can open doors to new discoveries and opportunities.

It is crucial to shift our attention away from dwelling on failures, as this mindset does not align with the principles of Islam or positivity.

Instead, it is the minor victories and accomplishments that empower individuals to push boundaries and explore the impossible.

Unfortunately, the rise of Islamophobia poses a significant obstacle to intelligence and understanding. Implying that Islam is a threat or promotes fear and prejudice towards Muslims hinders progress and restricts the potential for mutual growth and learning.

It is essential for society to recognize and combat Islamophobia to foster an environment that encourages intelligence, empathy, and understanding.

Islam is a religion that emphasizes continuous growth and development. It recognizes that change is an inherent part of life and therefore encourages individuals to adapt and evolve.

The Quran, considered the last divine document sent by Allah, encompasses timeless principles and guidance that apply to any society or era.

It acknowledges the changing nature of the universe and provides a framework that allows Muslims to navigate the complexities of a constantly evolving world.

This adaptability and flexibility have been key factors in Islam's growth and appeal to individuals seeking a religion that can resonate with their changing needs and circumstances.

By embracing change and remaining relevant to the diverse societies it encounters, Islam has attracted a growing number of followers.

The idea of separation is not the primary concern; it is the advancement and sharing of the benefits that Muslims have brought to society.

Unfortunately, there are individuals who seek to dumb down the youth and exploit their minds. These Islamophobes try to sway independence by using sexuality as their only weapon.

Their actions only lead to more chaos and erode the fabric of morality. The shame brought upon the country by these individuals is worse than any weapon used in war.

It is important to understand that the truth portrayed in Islam must be taken at face value.

The depth of the rules in the Quran should not be seen as restrictions but to provide independence and stability to both the unstable and stable minds and hearts of individuals.

Saladin, a historical figure known for his military prowess and leadership during the Crusades, made an insightful observation about the societal impact of adultery and nudity.

He believed that if these behaviors become prevalent among the younger generation, it could lead to the destruction of a nation with no warfare.

Today, with the widespread availability and acceptance of explicit content, this issue has indeed become common.

To address this problem, several steps can be taken. First, there should be increased awareness and education about the negative consequences of such behaviors on individuals and society.

Schools, families, and religious institutions can play a crucial role in promoting healthy relationships and values. Stricter regulations can be implemented to limit the accessibility and distribution of explicit content, especially to minors.

Engaging in open conversations about sexuality, consent, and respect is also essential.

Ultimately, it requires a collective effort from individuals, communities, and policymakers to combat the normalization of adultery and nudity and foster a culture that upholds moral values and healthy relationships.

The shift in societal attitudes towards clothing and adornment has indeed had a profound impact on the values and principles upheld by Abrahamic faiths. In many traditional cultures, clothing served as a symbol of wealth, modesty, and respectability.

It was a means of covering one's aura and maintaining a sense of dignity. However, with the emergence of Western influence, particularly in the media and popular culture, there has been a deliberate attempt to challenge these established norms.

The emphasis on freedom and individualism has led to a widespread disregard for modesty and a celebration of what was once considered forbidden in Islam and other Abrahamic faiths.

One significant example of this shift can be seen in the portrayal of Mary, the mother of Jesus, who is revered in both Christianity and Islam.

Mary mother of Jesus is often depicted as modestly covered, serving as a role model for women in these faiths. However, in today's society, there is a growing trend towards immodesty and a departure from the principles espoused by Abrahamic faiths.

This not only goes against the teachings of these religions but also undermines the cultural and moral fabric that has been upheld for centuries.

It is not only women who are affected by this phenomenon; men too are drawn into this deviation from traditional values.

By disregarding the rules and guidelines set forth by their respective faiths, they contribute to the normalization of nudity and other behaviors that are contrary to the teachings of Abrahamic faiths.

The consequences of this Western influence are far-reaching, as the younger generation and those easily swayed by popular trends have lost sight of the importance of modesty and the preservation of moral values.

The introduction of modernity, in its backward and chaotic form, has disrupted the very essence of Abrahamic faiths.

It has eroded the dignity and respect that was once inherent in the way individuals presented themselves to the world. As a result, there is a persistent war between those who cling to the traditional values of their faiths and those who have succumbed to the allure of Western ideals.

The consequences of this clash are evident in the fragmentation and deterioration of the moral fabric that once held these faiths together.

In Muslim countries, the adherence to modest attire and observing Islamic laws, particularly in the Gulf countries, remains strong.

However, Turkey stands out as a country that is more open to change and influenced by trends from both the Western and Eastern cultures.

This can be attributed to its thriving tourism industry, which attracts visitors from various parts of the world. It is important to note that the origins of Islam and Turkey can be traced back to central Asia, where Muslims migrated and conquered new territories.

The principles of Islam emphasize the preservation of dignity and the rejection of actions that compromise its consistency. Islam teaches its followers to uphold their cultural values while combating evil, as the Quran asserts, Satan is weak.

In contrast, the Bible presents a different belief, stating that Satan has control over the world. However, in Islam, it is firmly believed that the world is governed solely by Allah.

Bible: NCV:2 Corinthians 4:4 The devil who rules this world has blinded the minds of those who do not believe. They cannot see the light of the Good News -- the Good ...

The Quran indeed does not grant Satan the power to rule the world, as his only ability is to invite people towards evil.

Satan, also known as Iblis, was initially a firm believer, but his arrogance and disobedience led to his downfall. Although he was created from fire and lived among the angels, he belongs to the Jinn family.

It is important to note that Satan does not have control or power over the righteous individuals. In fact, believers who may temporarily stray from the right path often return even stronger, as Satan holds no influence over them.

The Quran portrays Satan as weak, just like the Jinn and humans, who have the capacity for both good and bad actions. To protect oneself from evil, the Quran emphasizes the practice of consistent behavior, including personal hygiene and performing ritual ablution (wudu) and prayer (salat).)

By establishing these consistent habits and surrounding oneself with good company, one can keep evil at bay. The influence of one's friends is significant, as their companionship leaves a lasting impact.

Those who associate with evil individuals are likely to adopt their traits, while those who choose to befriend those who strive to follow the principles of Islam experience consistent growth and adherence to these principles.

Islam, being a unique and distinct faith, introduced laws and regulations that were previously unknown to humanity. The Prophet Muhammad, through his exemplary and consistent behavior, left behind a legacy that continues to inspire both Muslims and non-Muslims alike.

CHAPTER 9
THE IMPORTANCE OF COMPANIONSHIP.

Companionship plays a crucial role in shaping character as it exerts influence. The people we choose to surround ourselves with have a significant impact on our thoughts, behaviors, and values.

When we surround ourselves with individuals who possess positive qualities such as kindness, empathy, and integrity, we are more likely to adopt these traits ourselves. If we associate with individuals who exhibit negative traits, such as selfishness, dishonesty, or laziness, we may mirror these behaviors.

Most individuals tend to perceive others based on how they perceive themselves. It is more beneficial to focus on self-improvement rather than trying to fix others. The process begins with oneself.

The value of companionship lies in its ability to mold and shape our character based on the qualities and values of those we choose as companions.

In Islamic culture, while there is an emphasis on faith and compatibility, it is important to note that Islam does not enforce segregation between people.

However, historical practices of autocrats and the upper class have often discouraged mingling between different social classes. This was done to preserve their own influence and power, as they believed that exposure to different mindsets could potentially challenge their authority.

The minds of autocrats held a significant value in their pursuit of success, as they recognized the importance of careful planning and strategizing.

They were wary of the influence of individuals from different social classes, as they believed such individuals would not understand or appreciate the importance of their methods and the bureaucracy they had put in place.

Therefore, they prioritized educating their children to ensure that they would possess the knowledge and skills to maintain their power and continue their legacy.

In their eyes, knowledge was the ultimate source of power, surpassing even lineage and inheritance.

The elites, understanding the transformative power of travel, embarked on extensive journeys to broaden their horizons and learn from different cultures and perspectives.

Islam, as a religion, also encourages travel as a means of education and personal growth.

However, travel was often seen as a luxury reserved for the wealthy, highlighting the persistent class system that continues to be challenged in the modern world.

While Islam promotes democratic principles, it also acknowledges that certain qualities, like beauty, lineage, and wealth, can play a role in the selection of life long partners, as stated by Prophet Muhammad.

In order to preserve their wealth and heritage, the upper crest often practiced endogamy, marrying within their own family. This practice ensured the consolidation of wealth and the maintenance of their esteemed heritage.

It is through firsthand experience and exposure to diverse settings, combined with extensive travel, that comprehension and understanding become easier.

The Bible, too, emphasizes the importance of being equally yoked, suggesting that individuals should seek partners who share their values and goals.

Similarly, believers within the Islamic community have traditionally been cautious about allowing their children to associate closely with those who compromise the fabric of faith.

In Islam, there is no discrimination based on class, wealth, education, or lineage. Islam promotes equality and emphasizes that all individuals are equal in the eyes of Allah.

Prophet Muhammad was born into the Banu Hashim clan of the prestigious Quraish tribe, known for their prominence and influence in Arabian society.

However, he never boasted about his lineage or used it to assert his authority.

Instead, he emphasized the importance of treating all humans with fairness and compassion, regardless of their social status or lineage. His teachings of equality, justice, and honesty were not just a passing trend, but a defining characteristic of his beliefs.

Throughout his life, he advocated for equal rights for all individuals, regardless of their race, gender, or social status. He firmly believed that justice should be the cornerstone of any society, and he fought tirelessly against discrimination and oppression.

His commitment to honesty and integrity was clear in both his personal and professional life, as he always prioritized truth and transparency.

These teachings became his trademark, as he consistently emphasized the importance of these values in creating a fair and just world for everyone.

Despite facing many trials and hardships throughout his life, Prophet Muhammad remained steadfast in upholding the values of equality and justice that his lineage held.

He believed that true nobility was not determined by one's lineage, but by their character and actions.

This exemplified his humility and commitment to treating all individuals with dignity and respect, irrespective of their background. Prophet Muhammad's teachings and actions continue to inspire people to this day, emphasizing the importance of fairness, justice, and equality for all.

While societal class systems may exist in certain cultures, they are not inherent to Islamic itself. The teachings of Islam encourage believers to treat one another with fairness, kindness, and respect, regardless of their social status.

This is especially evident during the act of prayer, known as salat, where Muslims stand side by side, shoulder to shoulder, in the mosque.

During this time, there is no segregation or differentiation based on any worldly factors. All Muslims, regardless of their background or social standing, come together as equals to worship and seek the pleasure of Allah.

This unity and inclusivity are essential aspects of Islamic faith and demonstrate the democratic nature of Islam.

In Islam, servants and slaves were indeed recognized as human beings with rights and were to be treated with fairness and kindness.

Islam encouraged treating servants well and instructed believers to be compassionate towards them. Islamic teachings emphasized the importance of respecting the dignity and humanity of all individuals, regardless of their social status.

The Prophet Muhammad himself set an example by treating his own servants with kindness and respect.

While slavery existed during the early years of Islam, the religion laid down guidelines for the just and humane treatment of slaves. Islam encouraged freeing slaves as an act of righteousness and placed great emphasis on their liberation and integration into society.

Over time, as Islamic teachings spread and societies evolved, the institution of slavery gradually diminished and was eventually abolished in many parts of the Muslim world.

However, the principles of respect and fair treatment for those in servitude remained central to Islamic teachings and continue to influence Muslim perspectives on labor and social justice today.

While culture may influence the way Islam is practiced in different regions, it is crucial to distinguish between cultural practices and religious obligations.

Some cultural practices may be mistakenly attributed to Islam, leading to a blend of traditions and religious beliefs. However, it is essential to address these differences and ensure that Islamic teachings are correctly understood and followed.

Force is not a reflection of Islam's teachings of democracy, but a cultural practice that has persisted for generations.

It is important to recognize that these practices can vary widely across different Muslim-majority countries and communities, and that Islam itself promotes inclusivity and understanding among people of different backgrounds.

Atheism, as a lack of belief in a higher authority or deity, did not become prominent until later in history. Most people throughout history held a belief, whether in pagan worship of deities or in the concept of a single god.

The concept of not believing in any superior authority seemed unfounded initially.

However, as time went by, atheism started gaining traction, particularly with the emergence of scientific and philosophical thought and many who questioned the ideology of Christendom and being saved which did not address the monologue of the inquisitive minds.

While the belief in a single god can be viewed as a factual theory, it is crucial to acknowledge that the hypothesis of atheism challenges this belief.

Atheist scholars have engaged in debates with Muslim scholars to persuade them of their viewpoint, but so far, they could not convince those who possess a profound understanding of Islam.

In the search for companionship, individuals strive to find a connection that fulfills their purpose not only in this world but also in the hereafter.

The story holds its truth in the present day:

Two women, one from a Middle Eastern aristocratic background and the other a Westernized woman, asked the Middle Eastern educated woman if she was close to her mother.

She replied, "No, I was mostly with my nannies, teachers, schools, grandmother, sometimes my mother and father and lots of family. Growing up in elaborate quarters taught me about life and prepared me for the future."

The girl from aristocratic family asked the commoner are you close to your mother. She replied, "No, I disliked her because the living quarters were small. She was overbearing, and economic conditions always took a toll."

The story clearly highlights that preparation in any situation is more valuable than merely expressing love, which holds little significance without trust and actions. Preparation meets opportunity is factual.

Consistency is key, and developing good habits through daily repetition is crucial for success.

For Muslims, the structure starts with Salat and the companionship of good company. Islam emphasizes teaching by instructing parents to teach Islam to their children rather than asking them if they want to learn.

Guide your children towards strength and preparedness to face the world, rather than fostering dependency is Islam.

Lead by example, demonstrating that strength comes from within and is not reliant on external factors.

Ensure that knowledge and learning are imparted to those who are fortunate enough to spend time in privileged environments, without neglecting the importance of education and teaching for all.

Such confidence may be cultivated from an early age through exposure to affluent and intellectually stimulating family backgrounds, or with attentive mothers and exemplary fathers.

The surroundings in which children grow up and the influence they have on them during their formative years can significantly shape their future.

Love requires more than just words; actions are the key to success. Trust is essential in all relationships, including our connection with Allah; without trust, our prayers lack meaning.

Allah's perception of us reflects our own thoughts, while expectations lead to success and doubts hinder progress. Building a sturdy base can empower people to venture beyond their limits and pursue the unimaginable.

In Islam, the concept of the Day of judgment is of utmost importance. Allah, in the Quran, emphasizes the significance of the company we keep and how it will affect us on that fateful day.

It is a reminder that the people we surround ourselves with can influence our actions and the overall state of our hearts. On the Day of Judgment, when everyone will be held accountable for their deeds, those who have chosen poor companions will witness the consequences of their choices.

The sight of the worst of people, who may have led them astray or encouraged sinful behavior, will be distressing and a source of regret.

The companionship of the best of people, those who were righteous and guided others towards goodness, will bring immense joy and tranquility to those who were fortunate enough to be in their company.

Does anyone want to experience the consequences of being surrounded by negative influences in this temporary world? Or would it be wiser to seek the company of fit companions in order to improve oneself and make proper preparations for the future? Answer lays with the one who comprehends.

It serves as a reminder to choose our friends wisely and seek the company of those who will uplift us spiritually and morally, leading us towards eternal bliss in the Hereafter.

Straying and coming back is preferable to being lost. The person who reminds others of faults, even though they were also involved, is astray, not stray.

Western societies flaunting independence poses challenges for Muslims, who often find themselves in situations they cannot change but repent.

However, when people disregard proper etiquette and freely express their sexual desires, they often face a sense of emptiness and dissatisfaction.

This trend, predominantly observed in Western regions, is an experiment and a self-destructive pursuit of personal gratification.

The demands of Western society, which emphasize individualism, consumerism, and material success, often clash with the teachings of Christianity, which stress selflessness, spiritual fulfillment, and the pursuit of God's will i.e. attaining salvation through Jesus.

This conflict can create a dilemma for believers who are trying to navigate their faith within a secular world.

Many people who struggle to reconcile these opposing forces end up leaning towards secularism and embracing the newfound freedom and independence it offers.

However, this shift can come at a cost, as it can lead to a loss of moral grounding and a disconnect from spiritual values.

There are Muslims in this climate who find themselves caught between two conflicting ideologies. On one hand, they feel the pressure to assimilate and fit in as Westerners, adopting certain elements of the Western lifestyle.

However, they also strive to maintain their Muslim identity, deeply rooted in their faith. In this struggle, they may inadvertently embrace distorted forms of independence that are not in line with Islamic teachings.

The Western world, despite its progress and advancements, still keeps remnants of paganistic beliefs and practices. Many of its ideas and reforms are borrowed from these ancient cults.

In contrast, the laws of Islam, as revealed in the books sent by Allah, offer a more advanced and structured system that aims to benefit humanity.

However, the allure of false independence and the emptiness of the soul that comes with it can be a high price to pay for those Muslims who find themselves torn between these two worlds.

The clash of cultures for Muslims in Western society can indeed be a significant challenge, as their moral code and religious beliefs may not always align with those of the Western world.

However, Muslims have proven to be highly adaptable and have succeeded in various aspects of life in any region they settle in.

Despite differing theological beliefs, friendships between the most devout Christians and Muslims can remain strong over the years.

This is because the foundation of these friendships is based on shared values of humanity, progress, and personal growth, rather than religious ideology alone.

The sharing of factual information about theology, history, and daily events, particularly regarding Muslim history, is often neglected in both Western social media and Muslim countries.

Through the revival of events, one can gain insight into the mentality of Muslims harboring no ill will towards non-Muslims.

The study of Islam and comparative religion, while acknowledging the shared Jesus with unique identities, is to maintain clarity.

The belief that the Western climate and social media platforms are hostile towards Islam and promote Islamophobia is based on the observation of many instances where the ideology of Islam is misused and misrepresented.

However, Islam itself is a progressive and unchanging faith that has stood the test of time. It is important to recognize that the political backlash and negative portrayal of Islam by some individuals or groups should not be conflated with the true essence of the religion.

Both Muslims and non-Muslims can benefit from a deeper understanding of Muslim history and the core principles of the faith.

It is understandable that Muslims living in Western regions, who lead hectic lives, may be susceptible to the allure of Western ideologies that appear to offer more independence and freedom.

However, it is crucial for Muslims to recognize that breaking moral codes that are strict in Islamic teachings can ultimately compromise their core values and principles.

Many Muslims who struggle to navigate the clash between Western cultures and their religion eventually come to realize the importance of adhering to the boundaries set by Islam.

Although some individuals may initially be drawn towards Western lifestyles, they often return to their faith, realizing that the threads that hold their beliefs are stronger than expected.

Regardless of one's faith, the ability to maintain friendships and collaborate with people from diverse backgrounds is crucial for fostering a society that continually progresses and excels in various aspects of life.

Most Muslims and Jews have been exposed to the liberated Western society dominated by Christians and the new preachers and teachers who advocate their own rules and evangelize their beliefs.

This exposure to a society that values individual independence and personal freedom can challenge the traditional beliefs and practices of these religions.

Many Muslims have found themselves caught in this predicament, where the influence of their surroundings tempts them away from their faith. However, they recognize that distancing themselves from evil companionship is the better choice.

Christianity, and Evangelization of various forms has historically influenced most.

While many individuals may not actively practice their faith, society often categorizes them as Christians based on their cultural background or nominal affiliation.

Similarly, in Muslim countries, individuals may be classified as Muslims even if they do not strictly adhere to Islamic principles. In Western societies, the influence of Christianity has waned over time, and many people have shifted towards secularism or alternative belief systems.

However, the ethical code of behavior, which emphasizes doing good to others and following a moral compass, still holds importance in these societies.

Evangelicals, a specific branch of Christianity called born again Christians, highly value the observance of religious teachings and may occasionally have confrontations or debates with people who have a different understanding, including those who are knowledgeable about Islam.

The inconsistency between actions and words in this cultic behavior creates more confusion for those trying to grasp this ideology.

The prevalence of hypocrisy within is alarming, as many of these individuals engage in mocking Islam hold behaviors that contradict the principles they claim to uphold.

The same applies to Muslims – they would earn much more respect from others if they prioritize the guidelines, they hold dear over conforming to a culture that can feel suffocating when it contradicts Muslim beliefs. Mistakes are private exposing them is not acceptable in Islam.

It is possible to be a proud Muslim while embracing your cultural identity and sharing it with the Western world. Muslims have illuminated dark cities and enlightened the world through their teachings.

It is difficult to be born again, as birth only happens once. However, in Islam, converting to the faith can cleanse one of their previous sins. It is important to remember that birth occurs only once in a lifetime, just like death.

These dynamics can serve as an eye-opener, highlighting the complexities and diversity within religious belief systems and how they interact within contemporary societies.

In any organization, regardless of faith, there can be instances where mistakes are made that may inadvertently undermine one's beliefs.

However, it is important to differentiate between a company or individual that simply makes an initial mistake and one that actively encourages further wrongdoing.

The latter is a sign of an unethical or morally corrupt entity that may wait to witness the downfall of others. In these situations, it is important to understand the importance of having a plan to leave in order to protect your own values and well-being.

It is often more beneficial to address and correct the person or company responsible for disrupting lifestyles, rather than simply walking away.

Constructive criticism and guidance can serve as a catalyst for positive change, allowing for growth and improvement. However, it is important to note that repeating the same mistakes without remorse or repentance is a detrimental habit.

True repentance involves refraining from continuing the harmful behavior and actively working towards making amends and rectifying the situation.

While it may be difficult to resist the allure of the liberated society, they understand that there are resources available to help them strengthen their faith and make better choices.

These resources can include religious communities, scholars, and educational opportunities that provide a deeper understanding of their faith and support their spiritual growth.

By availing themselves of these opportunities, Muslims can navigate the challenges of the modern world while remaining true to their beliefs.

Those who have never engaged in halal, permissible relationships may not have experienced the true bliss of sexuality, as giving oneself to an immoral companion proves to be challenging.

Personal non restraints can only satisfy physical desires, while neglecting the spiritual aspect, which goes against the teachings of Allah.

The companionship found within this realm is not comparable to the standards set by Islamic faith, or any other faith for that matter.

It is the secular society that promotes such companionship, attracting individuals who are inherently inclined towards evil or law breakers is not success.

It can be incredibly challenging to isolate oneself from such temptations, as they are prevalent in Western culture. However, Islam emphasizes the importance of finding good companionship and avoiding the company of those who encourage evil actions.

Loneliness may seem like a daunting alternative, but it is far better than being influenced by those who lead one astray.

Unfortunately, there are individuals who claim to be friends but turn out to be the worst destroyers. It often takes years of turmoil and struggle before a person realizes it was the influence of their evil companions that wasted their time and prevented them from observing the truth.

Without realizing it, one can spend decades in the company of those who are detrimental to their spiritual well-being, lacking genuine friendship.

The rush to reach out to Salat, known as prayer, is not the same for many as the adrenaline rush experienced is in other situations. Prayer is a sublime and sacred act, a time to connect with Allah in a state of submission and humility.

It is a moment of tranquility and reflection, where the individual seeks solace and guidance from the divine. Unlike the adrenaline rush, which often accompanies excitement or fear, the experience of prayer is serene and deeply personal.

It allows individuals to detach themselves from the chaos of the world and find peace in their connection with Allah. The effects of prayer are profound, bringing a sense of tranquility, clarity, and spiritual nourishment to the believer.

Quran: Surah Rum: 30:29. In fact, the wrongdoers merely follow their desires with no knowledge. Who then can guide those Allah has left to stray? They will have no helpers.

People who inhale drugs, such as substances like marijuana or cocaine, are engaging in a completely different activity than those who engage in prayer.

While drug inhalation is a recreational or addictive behavior that alters one's state of mind, prayer is a spiritual practice rooted in a deep longing to connect with the divine.

Prayer does not provide a "high" like a euphoric feeling, but it represents a constant desire to establish a connection with Allah, the creator, humans were subservient to a higher power before they were sent to earth.

Through prayer, individuals seek guidance, solace, and a sense of purpose in their lives. It is a deeply personal and meaningful practice for many, providing a sense of peace, fulfillment, and a means to express gratitude and seek forgiveness.

An American scientist recently made a controversial statement comparing prayer to a drug, which is clearly untrue as he lacks knowledge of the subject.

It's important to acknowledge that moral differentiation is possible for the state of affairs in different regions, especially regarding religious practices.

For instance, certain regions have facilities where individuals attest to their sins, while in Islam, there is no structured facility for such confessions. Instead, Islam encourages individuals to emphasize repentance in private to Allah alone.

However, if others know about someone's wrongdoing, it is crucial to correct it instead of just reminding them of their actions. It is also important to consider the context and individuals involved, as not everyone may forgive or be receptive to a reminder.

Confessing sins to a priest or pastor is viewed as a sacrament in many Christian traditions, such as Catholicism and Orthodox Christianity.

The Islamic faith teaches that salvation is not solely dependent on one's faith, but is shaped by their actions and deeds. These deeds comprise worship acts, such as prayer, fasting, and pilgrimage, alongside acts of kindness, charity, and justice towards others.

To achieve salvation, Muslims motivate themselves to live a life of piety, righteousness, and submit to Allah. In Islam, individuals handle their actions and will face rewards or punishments on the Day of judgment.

Not all Muslims actively practice the teachings of Islam, but at the core of their belief is the existence of one God and the recognition of Prophet Muhammad as the last and final messenger of God.

Unfortunately, there is a widespread lack of understanding about Islam, leading to a climate of inadequacy in comprehending its true essence.

It is crucial to educate people Muslims, and strive to uphold the dignity and respect of Prophet Muhammad.

However, deliberate instigation of Islamophobia is often used by certain individuals or political regimes to gain control and create fear among non-Muslims.

This fear-mongering is effective among those who rely heavily on social media as a source of information, often taking unfounded claims and biases as gospel truth.

It is important to clarify that there is no such thing as being "culturally Muslim." Islam is a faith that comes with specific obligations and practices, while culture is a separate entity that should not be confused with religion.

Unfortunately, some illiterate individuals about Islam may indoctrinate others with their distorted views, further perpetuating misunderstandings and prejudices.

Achieving eternal happiness in the afterlife in Islam is based on personal accountability and living a virtuous life.

Muslims are taught to strive for balance in their lives, constantly correcting their actions and seeking forgiveness for their sins. Seeking repentance is essential in Islam, as it helps individuals purify their souls and maintain a strong connection with Allah.

The faith emphasizes the importance of personal effort and accountability, rather than relying solely on the sacrifice of someone else.

Muslims believe that if Allah can create a human from a sperm drop, he can also create a human without a sperm, which is easily comprehensible because of the role of faith.

Quran: Surah Insan: 76:1. Is there not a period of time when each human is nothing yet worth mentioning?

Quran: Surah Insan: 70;2. For indeed, We alone created humans from a drop of mixed fluids, in order to test them, so We made them hear and see.

Quran: Surah Insan: 76:3. We already showed them the Way, whether they 'choose to' be grateful or ungrateful.

Quran: Surah Insan: 76:4. Indeed, We have prepared for the disbelievers chains, shackles, and a blazing Fire.

In Islam, it is believed that Allah possesses qualities of mercy and justice. While it may seem contradictory, a merciful God also enforces punishment to teach us the repercussions of our actions.

Punishment is often the result of defying established rules and guidelines, just like in any organization or worldly affair.

It's important to distinguish defiance from ignorance. When someone acts unknowingly, without understanding the repercussions, it's considered a lack of knowledge, not deliberate rebellion.

Conversely, arrogance is displayed when intentionally disobeying Allah's teachings and guidance. Human courts typically impose fines or penalties in response to arrogance.

Likewise, in Allah's court, there is a prolonged duration and an extensive procedure that includes warnings to encourage introspection, seek redemption, and discover the truth.

This procedure offers abundant opportunities for individuals to fix their wrongdoings and embrace morality.

Quran: Surah Insan: 76:5. Indeed, the virtuous will have a drink ˹of pure wine˺— flavored with camphor—

Quran: Surah Insan: 76:6. ˹from˺ a spring where Allah's servants will drink, flowing at their will.

In Islam, the concept of rewards and balance is deeply rooted in the belief that individuals are held accountable for their own actions. It emphasizes the idea that good and bad deeds are directly compensated or punished by the Creator.

This means that each person fulfills their obligations and performs righteous acts. The concept of personal responsibility is central, as it holds no one, including Prophet Muhammad or Jesus, accountable for one's deeds except for oneself.

Islam teaches that even the cessation of an evil deed is considered a good deed. This understanding promotes a sense of fairness and justice within the Islamic justice system, where individuals are rewarded or penalized according to their own actions.

Quran: Surah Insan: 76:14. The Garden's shade will be right above them, and its fruit will be made very easy to reach.

Quran: Surah Insan: 76:17. And they will be given a drink ˹of pure wine˺ flavored with ginger

Quran: Surah Insan: 76:18. from a spring there, called Salsabîl.

Heaven, as depicted in the Quran, is described with intricate detail that captivates the imagination. In the scriptures, you can find a vivid depiction of magnificent palaces embellished with shimmering glasses crafted from gold and silver.

The righteous inhabitants of this celestial realm are served with utmost care and devotion, their every desire fulfilled. Mortal beings in this world can grasp the concept that their stay here is temporary and fleeting thanks to the exquisite descriptions.

The trials and tribulations faced in this earthly existence are seemingly transparent, serving as a test for the eternal bliss of the hereafter.

The delay in experiencing the rewards of the next world holds great significance, as it allows for the process of repentance and redemption

Islam, as a faith, guarantees the consequences of deviating from its teachings after the truth has become clear.

Islam does not compel individuals to practice the religion forcefully, but rather guarantees the consequences of deviating from its teachings after the truth has become evident.

One reason for the continuous growth of Islam is its ability to provide a sense of purpose and guidance to individuals. The global Muslim community plays a significant role in spreading the message of Islam. Through mosques, Islamic centers, and various organizations,

The principles of Islam, such as justice, compassion, and equality, hold universal appeal. In a world that is often marred by conflict, inequality, and injustice, the message of Islam offers hope and a vision for a better society.

Many individuals are drawn to the values and teachings of Islam, seeing it to create a more just and harmonious world.

It is important to note that Islamophobia, the fear or prejudice against Islam and Muslims, persists in various parts of the world.

However, the growth of Islam is a testament to the resilience and determination of Muslims to practice and propagate their faith despite these challenges.

Muslims can strive to educate others about the true teachings of Islam, challenging stereotypes and fostering dialogue and understanding.

In conclusion, while it may be impossible for any individual to see the entire world, the impact of Islam can be felt across continents.

The continued growth of Islam is driven by its ability to provide guidance and purpose, the efforts of the global Muslim community in spreading its message, and the universal appeal of its principles.

Despite the obstacles it faces, Islam continues to thrive, offering a path to clarity of the soul and a prescription for a better world.

As the designer of humanity, Allah knows what can truly benefit a human being. One might question why other faiths, such as Judaism, did not have a similar practice of Salat.

It is important to note that Islam is considered a closing document among the Abrahamic faiths, with the Quran serving as the last revelation. Hence, the specific practices and rituals, including Salat, are unique to Islam.

New converts or strayed and uninformed Muslims may face challenges and obstacles as they navigate their new faith in the current society. It is important for new converts and easily influenced to remember that accepting Islam is not the end of their journey, but the beginning.

Continuous education, reflection, and seeking knowledge will allow them to deepen their understanding of the faith and fully embrace its teachings.

For helping new converts to Islam, Muslims are encouraged to provide guidance and support to those who are newly embracing the faith.

This help can take various forms, such as teaching them the basics of Islam, helping them understand and practice its principles, and answering questions they may have.

By offering knowledge and experience, Muslims can play a crucial role in helping converts navigate their new spiritual journey. Marrying a new convert to Islam is a virtuous act with abundant blessings.

Marrying a convert is believed to be a way for Muslims to contribute to their growth in faith, provide emotional support, and establish a loving and nurturing environment for them to thrive in their newfound religion.

This act of marriage is considered a means of fulfilling one's religious duty to support and uplift fellow believers, while also strengthening the Muslim community. Ultimately, both helping new converts and marrying them are acts of immense reward and blessings in Islam.

The Islamic civilizations expanded from the Arabian Peninsula (specifically Saudi Arabia) to central Asia, Africa, and beyond, reaching as far as Spain in the west.

This expansion occurred primarily through military conquest and trade networks. The early Islamic caliphates, such as the Umayyad and Abbasid caliphates, established a vast empire that encompassed diverse regions and cultures.

Through trade, Islamic merchants traveled along the Silk Road, spreading Islamic ideas and practices to places like Central Asia and China. Islamic scholars also played a crucial role in the dissemination of knowledge, translating Greek, Persian, and Indian texts into Arabic, which further facilitated the spread of Islamic civilization.

In Africa, the spread of Islam was facilitated by Muslim traders and missionaries, leading to the establishment of Islamic states and the conversion of local populations.

This expansion not only brought Islam as a religion but also contributed to the transmission of various scientific, artistic, and philosophical ideas, leaving a lasting impact on the societies it touched.

The Turkish Empire of the Ottomans began its origins in the 13th century as a small Turkic state in central Asia.

Led by the charismatic Osman I, the empire gradually expanded its territories, eventually reaching the borders of modern-day Turkey.

Prophet Muhammad, peace be upon him, indeed prophesied the conquest of Turkey. He informed the Muslims of this event, although it occurred several years later.

The Quran also mentions the defeat of the Romans, stating that if this prophecy did not come to pass, the disbelievers would have used it as an opportunity to discredit the Quran.

However, Allah's words are not bound by time, and when He declares that something will happen, it undoubtedly will.

This fulfillment of prophecies serves as a testament to the divine nature of the Quran and the truthfulness of Prophet Muhammad's message.

Quran: Surah Rum: 30:2. The Byzantines have been defeated

Quran: Surah Rum: 30:3. In the nearest land. But they, after their defeat, will overcome.

Quran: Surah Rum: 30:4. Within three to nine years. To Allah belongs the command before and after. And that day the believers will rejoice

The Quran clearly states in Surah Rum that the Eastern Roman Empire witnessed its defeat and the Muslims emerged victorious in Turkey.

It further mentions that after the Byzantines' defeat, they will eventually reclaim Jerusalem. This prophecy has already been fulfilled.

However, ultimately, the righteous will take possession of Jerusalem. Currently, righteousness seems to be absent as humanity suffers from deliberate massacres.

They will govern the city of Jerusalem, previously entrusted to Muslims by choice rather than coercion under Omar bin will be governed by them again in due time.

It is important to note that temporary setbacks are not victories, but deviations.

Their belief will guide the rule of Muslims in one Allah and all His prophets. Muslims must prioritize seeking closure, uniting in the pursuit of truth and justice, and working together towards a successful resolution by attempting to bring justice to those experiencing oppression.

Allah is fair, and trials are tests rather than tribulations. Victory will come in due time.

With the conquest of Constantinople in 1453, the Ottomans established their capital in the city, which became a symbolic bridge between Europe and Asia.

Turkey serves as a central hub for the Muslim world, connecting various regions and serving as an extension of its core.

The significance of Turkey serving as a central hub for the Muslim world cannot be overstated. Saud possesses the historical significance of Islam, while Turkey embodies the courage to speak the truth.

This pivotal moment marked the empire's expansion into the European continent, as it continued to conquer and incorporate various European territories into its dominion.

As a result, the boundaries of the Ottoman Empire encompassed both the Asian and European sides of modern-day Turkey, making it a unique transcontinental power.

This geographical position not only contributed to the empire's strategic importance but also influenced its rich cultural heritage, blending elements from both continents.

The Ottoman Empire would shape the history of the region for centuries, leaving a lasting impact on Turkey's identity and its position as a crossroads between East and West.

The Ottoman Empire, based in modern-day Turkey, indeed held great wealth and power during its peak. It controlled vast territories across three continents, including Anatolia, the Balkans, the Middle East, and North Africa.

The empire's wealth came from its control over major trade routes, such as the Silk Road, which facilitated the flow of valuable goods and resources.

The empire had a sophisticated taxation system that generated significant revenue. However, as the empire grew in size and influence, it also attracted envy and hostility from neighboring powers.

This led to a series of betrayals and consequences that ultimately contributed to the decline and eventual dissolution of the Ottoman Empire.

During his rule, Mustafa Kemal Atatürk implemented several reforms to modernize Turkey and promote secularism. He believed that separating the state and religion was crucial for the country's progress.

Under his leadership, Islamic influence was reduced, and the government actively discouraged religious practices in public life. However, in recent years, there has been a shift in Turkey towards re-establishing a stronger Islamic identity.

Despite Atatürk's reform, the influence of Islam persisted in Turkish society, as the call to prayer (azan) continued in mosques and religious practices remained a part of people's lives.

Western influence, which Atatürk had embraced, became increasingly strong, shaping various aspects of Turkish culture, lifestyle, and governance.

However, the desire for a more pronounced Islamic identity has gained momentum in recent years, leading to a change in the country's political landscape and a re-emergence of religious conservatism.

Religion was not something he leaned towards, but he did not actively discourage people from worshiping Allah. His beliefs were his own, and he respected the personal choices of others. However, during his rule, Islam was not at the forefront of his agenda.

The younger generation embraced the newfound independence and sought to explore different ideologies. As a result, the importance of Islam in society seemed to diminish, although the mosques remained a symbol of religious practice.

The semantics of the Muslim world were undergoing a significant transformation because of various reforms and changing social dynamics.

Despite the shifting landscape, there is a pressing need for young individuals to learn about Islam and make their own informed decisions about their faith.

The Republic of Turkey has been gradually growing. Implementing Quranic studies in schools is a way to ensure that the younger generation understands and appreciates the importance of their faith.

There is nothing that can succeed by discarding the laws of Islam. Success in this context is temporary, as failure is inevitable when the rules set by Allah are disregarded.

Force is not the ideology of Islam, nor is the removal of its laws. Instead, understanding is the key to achieving success. Therefore, it is important to explain the relevance of history, as history often repeats itself. Islam is not a repetition, but the ultimate truth of existence.

Initially, many reforms in Turkey drew inspiration from Western ideals, but Islam has its own principles to uphold. Democracy is an integral part of Islam, and the idea of forcing individuals to follow the faith goes against its teachings.

Instead, education plays a crucial role in helping Muslims make informed decisions and keep their faith intact.

The hope for the future of Muslims lies in embracing the beauty, elegance, and history of Islam, and using it to revive the youth and strengthen their connection to the faith.

The statue of Atatürk stands in Turkey as a symbol of the country's founder, Mustafa Kemal Atatürk. While Turkey is a predominantly Muslim country, people do not consider the statue of Atatürk as an object of worship or idolatry in the Islamic context.

Instead, it represents the secular and modern ideals that Atatürk promoted during his leadership, such as democracy, nationalism, and progress.

Islamic rulings discourage the creation of statues or images that might be venerated or worshiped, as this goes against the concept of monotheism and the worship of Allah alone.

Therefore, the Muslim world rarely has statues of leaders or individuals, as it may blur the boundaries between reverence for human figures and idolatry.

Muslims believe that Prophet Muhammad is the last and final messenger of God, and therefore hold him in the highest regard. In Islam, any form of idol worship or the creation of images that could be worshiped is prohibited.

Depicting Prophet Muhammad in any form, including cartoons or drawings, violates this principle and a disrespect towards the Prophet. Muslims know such depictions can perpetuate negative stereotypes, promote hatred, and incite violence against them.

This belief has led to widespread protests, boycotts, and even violent reactions sometimes.

It is important to note that while these reactions may not represent all Muslims; they reflect the deep reverence and sensitivity that many Muslims have towards the Prophet Muhammad.

NBC: Sep 2, 2020 — Charlie Hebdo republished controversial caricatures of the Prophet Muhammad on Wednesday to coincide with the start of the terror trial.

AP News: Oct 29, 2020 — The paper drew ire for reprinting caricatures of the Muslim Prophet Muhammad originally published by a Danish magazine in 2005 and republished...

Throughout history, Muslims have faced many provocations and challenges, but the decision to retaliate or respond is ultimately influenced by the emotions and circumstances of the individuals involved.

The intense fear and spread of Islam affect not only those who fear it, but also reaches into the homes of Muslim family members that resent Islam.

Showing disrespect and discord in such situations shows ignorance and a deep-seated hatred towards Islam. Is vile. This fear arises from the belief that Islam is taking over, even within the closest circles, where individuals initially sought peace.

Instead of trying to understand the reasons behind this arrogance and failing to respect and honor the choices of those who embrace Islam, it often leads to conflict and opposition, fueled by this hatred towards the religion.

Such companionship becomes toxic and does not foster endurance, even if it involves a relative. The solution lies in separating oneself from the hostile environment in order to find peace within Islam, the faith that one has chosen.

It is important to support and assist family members who despise Islam, once they have gained knowledge about the faith, as this can help in resolving conflicts.

Sometimes, these conflicts cannot be resolved, but it is crucial to recognize them as tests from Allah to determine the significance of the newly chosen faith. This same principle applies to a Muslim who compromises their faith for the sake of a non-Muslim, as they ultimately lose out.

However, it is important to delve into the rich history of Muslims to truly appreciate their achievements. Muslims have made significant contributions in various fields, including science, mathematics, literature, and philosophy.

Their advancements in these areas have left a lasting impact on human civilization.

The lands they conquered during various periods, such as the Islamic Golden Age, witnessed the establishment of Islam and the promotion of knowledge and education.

These lands became centers of learning and intellectual exchange, fostering a vibrant intellectual and cultural heritage that continues to influence our world today.

Understanding and acknowledging these achievements can provide a broader perspective and contribute to a more nuanced understanding of the Muslim world.

The exploration of Central Asia holds great significance in the history of human civilization. It is a region that has witnessed the convergence of various cultures, including the spread of rich Turkish traditions and customs.

As humans, our inherent curiosity and thirst for knowledge drive us to partake in adventurous explorations, and the exploration of Central Asia provides a wealth of insights into the interconnectedness of different civilizations and the diversity of human experiences.

It is important to recognize that implementing Islamic principles in Muslim countries does not mean the imposition of a rigid and oppressive system.

Islam encourages individuals to seek knowledge, engage in critical thinking, and take part in decision-making processes.

The Quran emphasizes the concept of **Shura**, or consultation, where leaders are advised to seek the opinions and advice of the people in matters of governance.

This highlights the democratic nature of Islam, where the voice of the people is valued and their participation in decision-making is encouraged.

Islam promotes the idea of justice and equality for all individuals, regardless of their social status, race, or gender.

The principles of Islam reject discrimination and advocate for the fair treatment of all members of society. This inclusivity and emphasis on justice form the foundation of a democratic system.

It is also crucial to distinguish between cultural practices and Islamic teachings. While cultural practices may vary across different Muslim countries, they should not be conflated with the core principles of Islam.

Islam is a universal religion that transcends cultural boundaries and can be practiced by individuals from diverse backgrounds.

Therefore, it is essential to separate cultural traditions from the fundamental teachings of Islam when discussing democracy and governance.

In conclusion, Islam is not only compatible with democracy, but also provides a framework that promotes justice, equality, and consultation.

Implementing Islamic principles in Muslim countries should aim to revive the true essence of Islam, while also respecting the diversity of cultural practices.

By understanding the true teachings of Islam and keeping culture separate, Muslim societies can create a harmonious balance between their religious values and democratic principles.

Company is vital for success as it can have a profound impact on our demeanor and overall well-being. Good company has the power to inspire, motivate, and uplift us, leading to personal growth and achievement.

Poor company can have a detrimental effect, draining our energy and diverting our focus from important tasks. It can steal our valuable time and hinder our progress towards our goals.

Therefore, it is crucial to choose our company wisely, as it ultimately determines the direction of our lives. Distinguishing between right and wrong company is a choice, guided by our values and principles.

However, destiny, or Qadr in Islam, plays a role in determining the choices we make and the consequences we face. Ultimately, Allah, as the all-knowing, has knowledge of what his servants will choose and the impact it will have on their lives.

There are many sins, stories, and examples, but the true benefit of learning lies in embracing the clarity of Islam.

Consistency is the key to distinguishing between good and evil.

In this vast world, with countless galaxies, seas, and oceans, it is important to recognize that our existence is minuscule. If converts to Islam continues to associate with non-believers, they cannot truly embrace the essence of Islam.

Similarly, Muslims who compromise their faith by surrounding themselves with those who have no connection to Islam are not staying true to their beliefs.

It may be easy to conform to the ways of this world, but striving for righteousness in the next life is a challenging endeavor. Time is of the essence, not just in exploring the physical world, but also in seeking inner balance.

Marrying a faithful Muslim is preferable to being with a wealthy individual who lacks faith. The company we keep reflects who we are as individuals.

Whether born into it or converting, the true beauty of Islam is found in uncovering its essence.

While it's a choice to identify as a Muslim, the genuine beauty is in delving deep and understanding this faith. The opportunity to embrace Islam is a blessing, and only those who are Muslim can fully grasp its richness.

The most powerful entreaty a believer can make to Allah is to not be under the control of disbelievers.

CHAPTER 10
OPPRESSION NEEDS ADDRESS

Oppression is a grave injustice that goes against the principles of Islam, which emphasize fairness, justice, and compassion for all individuals.

Recognizing the crucial role in society and as part of humanity is essential. Actively confronting and combating oppression in all its manifestations is of utmost importance.

Oppression can happen anywhere if the weak allow it to thrive. In religious beliefs, new Muslims can often face various forms of oppression and discrimination in societies where Islam is not accepted.

Exclusion, not inclusion, is necessary for those who cannot respect the choices of others beyond a certain age, in order to support the choice made by the person.

Prophet Muhammad migrated from Mecca to Medina because of aggression and disagreement, returning as a victorious leader that caused fear among the hypocrites.

Oppressors and aggressors are afraid of Islam, seeking turmoil instead of contentment, as it threatens their pagan beliefs.

Paganism is not considered a threat by Muslims, except for the potential disorder it may bring. The grounds of previous religious beliefs can sometimes be a breeding ground for prejudice and bias against individuals who have converted to Islam.

It is crucial to address and challenge these oppressive attitudes and create inclusive environments that respect and value the diversity of religious beliefs.

The key to becoming a winner is to first discover oneself and then extend help to others. This is the ultimate remedy. In contrast, a weak person will endure the chaos, hoping it will eventually subside.

The tests given upon us by Allah prepare us for a brighter future. However, failing to acknowledge our weaknesses is akin to succumbing to the subtle whispers and fears instilled by Satan.

This is true for those who have yet to grasp the true essence of Islam. It is essential for Muslims to fear Allah, not mere mortals.

It is crucial to support and assist individuals facing oppression, regardless of their race, religion, gender, or any other identifying characteristic.

The duty to raise awareness and educate others about the presence and impact of oppression, lies in humanity in order to foster a society that is fair to all.

In Islam, we are guided by the teachings that emphasize the significance of standing up for justice and speaking out against injustice.

If the entire world stands for injustice, one Muslim who speaks out against it can indeed make a significant impact and contribute to the prevalence of justice.

Quran; Surah Nisa: 4:134. O believers! Stand firm for justice as witnesses for Allah even if it is against yourselves, your parents, or close relatives. Be they rich or poor, Allah is best to ensure their interests. So do not let your desires cause you to deviate

How can a Muslim who humbly bows down to Allah on the ground, be afraid of those who oppress Islam, Muslims, imprison new converts or compromised Muslims. Fear exiles as truth ventures in hearts, of those who belief.

There are no excuses for the tyrant, except for their desire to exert control and deceive believers, whether they are relatives or acquaintances. Islam makes no excuses and remains steadfast in its first position.

This noble act holds the utmost importance and will not yield to any other action or trust. The first trust deed in Islam is like the primary loan in Real Estate, where the one that withholds more at stake takes precedence.

Similarly, Islam gives a lifetime of devotion and holds the top position. No one can claim this position as it is solely from Allah. The faith of Islam has already triumphed over oppression 600 years ago during prophet Muhammad's time, so there is no room for disrespect.

We can only continue to move forward. These words are relevant to those who follow trends and new converts facing family opposition. True believers have the power to disregard others' opinions and choose for themselves.

Throughout history, this is not a fictional notion but a witnessed fact. The act of one Muslim bowing in Sujood (prostration) is a powerful symbol of faith and submission to a higher power.

It represents a deep connection with God and a commitment to righteousness. Such a person, driven by their belief and understanding of the truth and reality, can inspire others and ignite change.

The power of belief, combined with the courage to speak out against injustice, has the potential to awaken the conscience of humanity and mobilize a collective effort towards justice and equality.

Those who were once oppressed and received help from Muslims are now oppressing the Muslims themselves.

Palestine continues to survive regardless of the hardships placed upon them. However, the oppression experienced in Palestine, aided by certain regimes, surpasses any other form of oppression.

Muslims have left behind a rich legacy that we can learn from and revive in order to succeed, as Islam promotes religious freedom and values the dignity of all human beings before any form of oppression.

The Ottoman Empire left a significant cultural and architectural legacy, with iconic landmarks such as the Hagia Sophia, Blue Mosque and Topkapi Palace, symbolizing its grandeur and influence.

During the Ayyubid period, which lasted from the late 12th century to the mid-13th century, Salah ad-Din (Saladin) successfully united the Muslim forces and recaptured Jerusalem in 1187.

This marked a turning point in the Crusades, as the Crusader states gradually lost their territories, including major cities like Acre and Tyre, to Muslim forces.

The Ayyubid dynasty ruled over the region, promoting Islamic culture and architecture, and establishing stability in the Levant.

Following the Ayyubid period, the Mamluks came to power in Egypt and Syria. The Mamluks were a military caste of subordinate soldiers who eventually gained political control. Under their rule, which lasted from the 13th to the 16th century, the Crusader states were extinguished.

The Mamluks successfully defended against several Crusader attempts to regain control, and their dominion extended from Egypt to modern-day Syria and Palestine. They further solidified the Islamic culture in the region, constructing grand mosques and madrasas, and fostering intellectual and artistic advancements.

In the 16th century, the Ottoman Empire emerged as a dominant force in the Middle East. The Ottomans expanded their empire, conquering Egypt and Syria, and absorbing the former Crusader territories.

Islamic culture continued to flourish during the early Ottoman period, with the empire embracing the existing Arabic and Islamic traditions of the region.

The Ottomans built upon the architectural and cultural legacy left by their predecessors, leaving their mark on cities such as Jerusalem, where significant monuments like the Dome of the Rock were renovated and expanded.

Overall, the fall of the Crusader states in 1291 marked a turning point in the region's history, leading to an extended period of Muslim rule and the consolidation of Islamic culture during the Ayyubid, Mamluk, and early Ottoman periods.

To grasp the Muslim conquests and the ultimate triumph of Islam as the world's dominant faith, it is essential to recount history. This is the very reason the world fears monotheism since the beginning of humanity. The essence of Islam lies not in blind obedience or rebellion, but in the eventual realization by Muslims that they possess a precious gem.

This era witnessed the flourishing of Islamic art, architecture, and intellectual pursuits, leaving a lasting impact on the cultural landscape of the Levant.

Later, the foreign invasions and greed led the foreign regimes to expand their territories, not intending to explore and bettering themselves, but to disrupt the peace established by Muslim empires.

This resulted in a distortion of the magnificent buildings, hospitals, and the overall humanity that had flourished under Muslim rule.

These invasions also led to the establishment of puppet regimes and fueled conflicts between different Muslim factions, pitting Muslims against each other.

Unfortunately, this turmoil continues to persist, as history has shown that Christendom has fought a significant number of wars throughout the ages, further exacerbating the tensions and conflicts within the Muslim world.

However, it's crucial to consider the multifaceted factors that contribute to conflicts, such as political, economic, and social elements, rather than attributing them solely to religious beliefs.

Christianity's teachings also emphasize love, compassion, and forgiveness, and many Christians actively strive for peace, reconciliation, and support humanitarian causes.

Although the pace of history and ongoing support for oppressors remains a concern, justice is not prevalent among those who support oppressive regimes.

Over time, many social movements and revolutions have challenged oppressive systems, leading to the recognition of fundamental human rights and the establishment of democratic societies.

The global community has shown an increased awareness and condemnation of oppressive regimes, often imposing economic sanctions and diplomatic pressure on such governments.

International organizations and non-governmental organizations tirelessly work to protect and advocate for the rights of oppressed individuals, providing them with resources and support.

Despite the persistent existence of oppression, there is a growing momentum towards dismantling oppressive systems and creating a more inclusive and fair world.

Yemen, Syria, and Iraq have all been plagued by years of turmoil and devastation. In Yemen, the ongoing conflict between the intervention of foreign powers, has resulted in a humanitarian crisis of unimaginable proportions.

The people of Yemen have been subjected to relentless airstrikes, widespread famine, and a crumbling healthcare system. Similarly, Syria and Iraq have been torn apart by long-standing conflicts, fueled by political, sectarian, and ethnic divisions.

The continuous indulgence in power struggles and the desire for territorial control has led to the massacre of innocent lives and the displacement of millions.

These Muslim lands, rich in history and culture, are facing immense challenges that require unity and cooperation, rather than further separation and discord.

It is crucial for the Muslim world to come together, support one another, and work towards peace, stability, and the well-being of all its people.

Only through unity can the true potential and beauty of these lands be restored, and the oppression and suffering be alleviated.

This ongoing greed is perpetuated by foreign powers who have no legitimate claim or relevance in the Muslim world, yet they seek to exploit and seize control of the resources and wealth that belong to Muslim lands.

These powers view the Muslim world as a source of economic and geopolitical advantage, and they employ various tactics to ensure their dominance.

They often manipulate political situations, support corrupt regimes, and engage in economic exploitation, all to further their own selfish interests.

This interference not only hinders the progress and development of Muslim countries but also fuels resentment and perpetuates a cycle of exploitation and injustice.

It is a constant challenge for the Muslim world to assert its sovereignty and protect its resources from the relentless greed of these foreign entities.

It is the greed that drives certain people to advance their own interests, while hoping for salvation from Jesus, despite their involvement in massacres.

These foreign interventions in Afghanistan have resulted in many devastating consequences, leaving countless Afghan civilians displaced and homeless.

The country has been embroiled in conflict for decades, with various countries and armed groups intervening in its internal affairs.

The Soviet Union's invasion in 1979 marked the beginning of a brutal and protracted war, causing widespread destruction and displacing millions of Afghans from their homes.

Following the Soviet withdrawal, Afghanistan plunged into a civil war, further exacerbating the humanitarian crisis. The 2001 US-led invasion, aimed at ousting the Taliban regime, brought a recent wave of instability and displacement.

The ongoing conflict, combined with the rise of extremist groups and political instability, has forced many Afghans to flee their homes in search of safety and shelter, exacerbating the already dire situation.

Evil cannot be repaid with good. Jesus' message is coherent in the Bible when he says, "I don't know you" to evildoers.

This should serve as a warning to those who cause trouble and unrest, as the turmoil within their hearts is even worse than the death faced by the martyred Muslims.

Bible Hub: Matthew: 7:23. Get away from me, you evil people.' ... Then I will say to them, 'I never knew you. Get away from me, you wicked people!' ... Then I will tell them plainly, 'I never knew you. Away from me, you evildoers!'

Attendance and support for human rights are necessary for evangelicals and literal Bible interpreters. Ensuring the avoidance of reenacting the rules of the current and previous regime is crucial, and it is imperative to cultivate the land with fertile soil.

Muslims should unite to support the world instead of imitating those who are causing destruction to the very planet they inhabit.

Quran: Surah Zumar: 39:33. The one who has brought the truth they believed in it - those are the righteous.

Speaking the truth requires belief those who fear people more than they fear Allah please people. Those who truly fear Allah do not harbor any fear towards human beings.

None other than Satan instils fear in them. However, prayer and submission to Allah grants liberation to those who engage in it.

This is not just an observation, but a stark reality that envelops the entire globe. Authoritarian Allah will question Muslims.

They can influence regime change and reduce the supply of impactful petrol in particular. The flashy display of wealth in gold and petrodollars can be utilized to benefitting the Muslim world and humanity, rather than being focused on superficial appearances.

It's the actions and contributions that truly matter, not just superficial displays of wealth.

The arms lift referred to in the statement is the U.S. decision to provide military aid to Israel during the Arab-Israeli conflict, which angered King Faisal. In response, he declared an oil embargo on the United States on October 20, 1973.

Other oil-producing Arab states supported this embargo, excluding Iraq and Libya. King Faisal believed that addressing the rights and oppression of the Palestinian people, particularly in Palestine, was of utmost importance.

He saw this as a necessary step towards achieving justice and equality in all countries involved in the conflict.

This conflict cannot be stabilized by simply blaming regimes that lack the equipment to combat the ongoing jeopardy and unrest. Muslim countries have a responsibility to actively address the situation.

One potential solution is for these countries to change their currency and establish a unified Muslim currency, such as the reals or dinars. By doing so, they can solidify their economic strength and promote the principles of humanity.

It is important for Muslim countries to come together and collectively work towards helping humanity, rather than focusing on individual interests.

Unfortunately, very little has been done although the dinar, the currency used in some Muslim countries, is one of the highest-valued currencies in the world.

To effectively address the challenges at hand and show the true nature of Muslim unity and compassion towards humanity, we require more action and collaboration.

Non-Muslims who are interested in addressing the stagnant situation and oppression against Muslims, as well as the few Christians in Palestine.

There are individuals who deeply care about human rights and social justice. They understand the significance of fighting against discrimination and standing up against prejudice in any form.

It is worth mentioning that not all non-Muslims participate in this oppression, and there are many who actively endorse and stand in solidarity with the Muslim community.

In terms of history, Muslims have a long-standing tradition of helping and protecting Jews. During the Holocaust, sometimes Muslims risked their own lives to save Jewish individuals from persecution.

These acts of compassion and bravery should be acknowledged and celebrated.

In the present day, orthodox Muslim communities are aware of the current situations and are actively working to help alleviate the challenges faced by Muslims.

One notable example is the Muslim community in New York City, where they have been at the forefront of various initiatives to support their fellow Muslims and combat discrimination.

News: Al Jazeera: Nov 7, 2023 — Hundreds of US Jewish activists have peacefully occupied New York's Statue of Liberty to demand an end to Israel's "genocidal bombardment" of...Jewish New Yorkers occupy Statue of Liberty to demand Israel-Gaza ceasefire.

Throughout history, Jews and Muslims have shared a belief in one God, rather than worshiping pagan deities. They have coexisted in harmony, fostering cultural exchange and mutual respect.

Unfortunately, the hatred and prejudice towards them have been fueled by various sources that have left a lasting mark.

Presently, some of these sources have caused chaos within their own countries, leading to widespread poverty and unprecedented inflation.

Ironically, the help and support often go to those who perpetuate oppression and discrimination, further exacerbating the suffering of Jews and Muslims who have historically lived side by side in peace.

Zionism, the political ideology centered around establishing and supporting a Jewish homeland in the historical land of Israel, has often been a contentious subject.

Some regimes in the West claim loyalty to Zionism, which can sometimes lead to accusations of prioritizing the interests of Israel over other considerations.

However, it is important to note that not all but most Jews reject Jesus, as religious beliefs and practices vary among individuals and communities.

While some Jews may adhere to their traditional faith, others may hold different religious views, but most Jews are close to families.

Many individuals, regardless of their religious or cultural background, support the principles of justice, equality, and humanity, even if they do not subscribe to specific religious beliefs.

Therefore, it is possible for people who are familiar with humanity to stand for these principles while maintaining their own unique perspectives.

The Gaza cruelty and massacre are sustained by supporting evil through sending revenue, which perpetuates these crimes.

Meanwhile, severe poverty is kept hidden, and the homeless seek shelter in harsh climates. As revenue continues to fuel the destruction of humanity, this harsh regime's existence is unsustainable. Good cannot thrive in the presence of evil.

Significant impact on raising awareness and promoting activism is impactful. These passionate individuals have organized protests, created online campaigns, and initiated meaningful discussions on campus and beyond.

Columbia University, in particular, has been a hotbed for activism, with student-led organizations hosting events, inviting guest speakers, and mobilizing the student body to take action.

The collaboration between these college students has resulted in increased visibility for the cause, attracting media attention and garnering support from various communities.

Their dedication and relentless efforts have not only sparked conversations about the issue, but have also prompted policy changes and institutional reform. With their unwavering commitment, these young activists have undoubtedly made a lasting impact on the cause they believe in.

AP News: Apr 30, 2024 — Student protests over the Israel-Hamas war have popped up at many college campuses after being inspired by demonstrators at Columbia University.

NBC news: May 1, 2024 — Protests over Israel's assault on Gaza have rocked college campuses in the U.S. and drawn condemnation from Israeli leaders, but students in the ...

These students have taken a courageous stance to advocate for the rights of humanity and to confront the consequences of their actions.

Humanity with understanding and Muslims firmly believe that in an advanced society, every human being deserves help and should not be subjected to displacement and homelessness without warning.

While many people speak out against oppression, it is crucial to address the channels and institutions in order to truly foster humanity in individuals.

Delivering a message is not enough; it requires direct communication and exposing and condemning those who shame and exploit others, especially those who claim to fight for justice but prey on the vulnerable.

The Quran even refers to such individuals as munafiq Un, or hypocrites. It is important to remember that Allah has a divine plan and his timing may not align with ours.

However, those who raise their hands in prayer for the oppressors will be heard by the creator. It is wiser to accept the prayers of those who suffer rather than face the consequences of their curses, for Allah hears them all.

This irony underscores the need to address the root causes of prejudice and to promote unity and understanding among all people.

During the days of Jahiliya, ignorance before Islam, the Jews faced their own conflicts and divisions. However, amidst the turmoil, there were instances of enduring friendships between Jews and Muslims that transcended religious differences.

These friendships were built on mutual respect, trust, and shared values. Unfortunately, the destructive force of greed eventually infiltrated these relationships, eroding the common core of humanity that once bound them together.

Greed, with its insidious influence, fueled animosity, jealousy, and a disregard for the well-being of others. As a result, the once-strong friendships between Jews and Muslims were strained and, sometimes, irreparably damaged.

This serves as a poignant reminder of the destructive power of greed and the importance of nurturing and preserving the common bonds that unite us as human beings.

It is ironic that the nation which claims to support Christianity and accuses Jews of killing their god is also supporting countries that oppress humanity. Some Muslim countries are stepping up to help both the oppressed and non-Muslims alike.

Those who truly understand humanity recognize that there should be no religious bias for addressing oppression; the focus should solely be on humanity.

Allah is aware of the oppressors, and history has shown that lands tainted by evil eventually suffer destruction and become barren.

Prophet Muhammad (peace be upon him) himself championed social justice and fought for the rights of the marginalized and oppressed. Therefore, it is incumbent upon us to follow his example and actively engage in efforts to combat oppression wherever we encounter it.

There are various ways in which we can take action. Through our actions and by spreading awareness, we can contribute to a world where oppression is confronted and ultimately eliminated.

Islam teaches us to stand up against oppression and support the rights of the oppressed, regardless of their religion, race, or social status.

Prophet Muhammad (peace be upon him) himself exemplified this by advocating for the rights of the marginalized and oppressed during his lifetime. Therefore, it is incumbent upon Muslims to actively engage in efforts to ease oppression and help those in need.

These oppressors, whether they are individuals or institutions, lack a conscience or choose to disregard it in their actions. They are driven by a self-centered desire for personal satisfaction or to fulfill their own beliefs, even if those beliefs are misguided or harmful.

They may justify their actions by convincing themselves that they are acting in the best interest of others or for a greater cause, such as the preservation of a particular ideology or belief system.

However, their motivations ultimately stem from a lack of empathy and a willingness to exploit or harm others for their own gain.

Whether it be for political power, economic dominance, or social control, these oppressors perpetuate a climate of injustice and inequality, disregarding the rights and well-being of those they oppress.

This form of oppression often involves powerful individuals or institutions using their influence and resources to manipulate information and control narratives.

By monopolizing media outlets, spreading misinformation, and silencing dissenting voices, these oppressors create a distorted reality that serves their own interests and maintains their grip on power.

They exploit the vulnerabilities of the system, such as loopholes in regulations or weak oversight mechanisms, to further their agenda and suppress the truth.

This type of oppression not only limits people's freedom and autonomy, but also undermines the foundations of a just and democratic society.

It perpetuates inequality, injustice, and systemic discrimination, as the truth becomes obscured and marginalized voices are silenced.

Muslims have a rich history of contributions and progress when they have achieved success. Instead of diminishing conquered lands, they focused on establishing freedom, justice, and learning.

They faced obstacles and found cures for medicine, instead of causing havoc. Throughout history, they have never lost control of the situation.

However, the current situation in Gaza is spiraling out of control. Muslim countries need to unite and form a powerful union to restore justice.

There is no time for separation; it is essential to come together for the greater good. Each Muslim will be held accountable by Allah for their actions, and simply posting pictures of unrest is not enough.

It is crucial to take tangible actions and make a difference. The allure of western society should not be the driving force behind decision-making; instead, it is the soul's quest for truth that should guide Muslims.

GREED CANNOT OVERPOWER THE TRUTH.

JUSTICE AND UNITY OVER PERSONAL GAIN.

The Qur'an emphasizes the importance of treating all individuals with respect, honor, and kindness, irrespective of their faith, race, gender, ethnic origin, or social status.

The Prophet Muhammad also stated that it is our duty to assist both the oppressed and the oppressor. When questioned about how to support an oppressor, the Prophet responded, "By preventing them from oppressing others."

The tale of Omar bin Khattab's son:

The son of Omar bin Khattab, Abdullah ibn Omar, was not only a believer like his father, but he also possessed a deep devotion to Islam and a strong sense of justice.

He inherited his father's traits of piety, knowledge, and wisdom, making him a respected figure in the early Muslim community.

Abdullah ibn Omar was known for his strict adherence to Islamic teachings and his unwavering commitment to the principles of equality and fairness.

He actively participated in the battles fought during the time of Prophet Muhammad, demonstrating his bravery and loyalty to the faith.

His dedication to learning and preserving the teachings of Islam led him to become one of the most knowledgeable scholars of his time.

Abdullah ibn Omar's faith and righteousness earned him a prominent place in Islamic history, as he continued to serve the Muslim community and contribute to the growth of the religion even after the passing of his father.

During the civil war, though he did not directly take part in the conflict, he remained steadfast in his beliefs and displayed a profound devotion to Islam.

Despite the surrounding turmoil, he consistently engaged in tawaf, the act of circumambulating the Kaaba, the most sacred site in Islam.

This religious practice resonated deeply with many who saw him as a leader in teaching and exemplifying the principles of Islam. His unwavering commitment to his faith served as an inspiration for others to emulate his actions and embrace his teachings.

He braced the belief that the life of a believer, particularly during times of hardship and oppression, held immense value in the eyes of Allah, surpassing that of all non-believers.

This conviction fueled his determination to adhere to his religious practices, even amidst the chaos and uncertainty of the civil war.

Quran: Surah Maidah: 5:32. Because of that, we decreed upon the Children of Israel that whoever kills a soul unless for a soul or for corruption [done] in the land - it is as if he had slain mankind entirely. And whoever saves one - it is as if he had saved mankind entirely. And our messengers had certainly come to them with clear proof. Then indeed many of them, [even] after that, throughout the land, were transgressors.

In this verse of the Quran, the children of Israel are directly addressed, with the message that killing one person is tantamount to killing all of humanity.

The presence of evil is not something new; the Quran clearly acknowledges the existence of injustice and oppression. Some disbelievers or questioners may wonder why Allah allows it.

Just as during a test in human exams, someone may fail despite being taught, why does a human allow it? The rules are clear and sublime, and understanding the consequences is guaranteed.

This world is not permanent; it is a test, and each person has their own unique test suited to them.

This is a chance for humanity to realign its course and prioritize justice, particularly in supporting the oppressed.

Muslims have a responsibility to resist the allure of this artificial world and instead focus on aiding their fellow Muslims and humanity at large, who are suffering in Palestine and other regions where oppression is rampant.

There is no succession for those who shed the blood of believers, or humanity as questioning and punishment lies with Allah. The regimes that support this evil find themselves trapped in a state of dependency, desperately seeking happiness.

Those who kill to gain lands and claim them as their own can never find true happiness, only a hollow emptiness. The Prophet Muhammad and the Quran have both warned humanity about this.

Those who support this regime of injustice and oppression do so for various reasons, including material gain and a belief in the religious significance of the region.

Evangelicals and Christendom, for example, view the establishment and preservation of Israel as a fulfillment of biblical prophecy and a sign of the imminent return of Jesus as the savior.

However, it is important for us to acknowledge that Jesus himself hailed from Palestine and is regarded as a prophet of Allah in Islam.

The worship of any prophet is forbidden, and it is essential to prioritize addressing the ongoing unrest and displacement of people instead of idolizing religious figures.

The regimes that support this oppression may have their own laws and regulations, but forcibly evicting people from their homes, even for non-payment of mortgages, is unjust and goes against the principles of fairness and compassion.

In today's technologically advanced world, people are uprooted and displaced without proper notice, causing immense suffering.

Those who support and enable this injustice will face dire consequences, as Allah gives Muslims the wealth and faith to discern right from wrong and expects them to take action to help the oppressed.

It is not a matter of religious affiliation but a universal duty for all of humanity to stand against oppression and assist those in need, particularly Muslims who are facing immense challenges.

It is crucial to address the plight of all the oppressed individuals with a resolute sensitivity.

This includes those who are unjustly thrown out of their homes and those who actively contribute to their oppression, for they are both responsible for perpetuating a destructive cycle.

The daily facade, often exploited by social media, further exacerbates this issue by blaming the weak while supporting the strong. Such an imbalance of power is the embodiment of evil.

Despite their hope to be saved, it is important to recognize that even Jesus himself acknowledges he does not know the evildoers, as stated in the Bible.

Therefore, it is our duty to work actively towards dismantling these systems of oppression and advocating for justice and equality for all.

During the Golden Age of Islam, which spanned from the 8th to the 14th century, Muslim scholars made significant contributions to various fields, including science, medicine, mathematics, philosophy, and literature.

While Europe was experiencing the Dark Ages, characterized by political instability and limited intellectual progress, Islamic scholars thrived in centers of learning, such as Baghdad, Cairo, and Cordoba.

These scholars translated and preserved ancient Greek and Roman texts, conducting groundbreaking research and advancements in various disciplines. Spain, known as Al-Andalus, was under Muslim rule for several centuries and became a hub of intellectual exchange and cultural prosperity.

Muslim rulers in Spain fostered an environment that promoted tolerance, diversity, and the pursuit of knowledge, attracting scholars from different backgrounds.

The achievements of Muslim scholars during this time not only laid the foundation for the Renaissance in Europe but also had a lasting impact on the development of global knowledge and civilizations.

One of the most notable advancements during the Golden Age of Islam was in the field of mathematics. Muslim scholars, such as Al-Khwarizmi, developed the concept of algebra and introduced Hindu-Arabic numerals to the world, which revolutionized mathematics and laid the foundation for modern arithmetic.

They also made significant contributions to astronomy, with scholars like Al-Battani accurately calculating the length of a year and improving astronomical instruments.

In the field of medicine, Muslim physicians like Ibn Sina (Avicenna) compiled and expanded upon the medical knowledge of ancient civilizations, creating influential medical encyclopedias that were used for centuries.

They conducted groundbreaking research and experiments, developing new surgical techniques and understanding the anatomy of the human body.

Islamic philosophers, such as Ibn Rushd (Averroes) and Al-Farabi, made important contributions to the field of philosophy. They synthesized a philosophical idea with Islamic theology, leading to the development of new philosophical schools of thought.

These philosophers also played a crucial role in preserving and translating the works of ancient Greek philosophers, which would later have a profound impact on European Renaissance thinkers.

Literature also flourished during this era, with poets like Rumi and Omar Khayyam producing timeless works of poetry that continue to be celebrated today.

Islamic literature encompassed various genres, including epic poetry, historical chronicles, and philosophical treatises.

These literary works not only reflected the intellectual and cultural richness of the Islamic civilization but also influenced later literary traditions in Europe and the Middle East.

Overall, the Golden Age of Islam was characterized by a thirst for knowledge and a commitment to intellectual progress.

Muslims built upon the teachings of the Quran, which encouraged seeking knowledge, to create a vibrant and innovative intellectual environment.

Their advancements in various fields laid the groundwork for future scientific and intellectual developments, leaving a lasting legacy that still impacts the world today.

Muslim scholars translated and preserved ancient texts, conducted extensive research, and developed new theories and practices.

These advancements eventually reached Europe during the Middle Ages, a period often referred to as the "dark ages," where knowledge and progress were limited.

European scholars eagerly absorbed the knowledge brought by Muslims, sparking a period of intellectual awakening known as the Renaissance.

However, it is true that as Europe began to regain its balance and grow stronger, it also sought to suppress and persecute those who were instrumental in the transmission of knowledge from the Islamic world.

This unfortunate turn of events led to the marginalization and persecution of many Muslim scholars and contributors to the knowledge that had illuminated Europe during its darkest times.

During the reign of Muslims in Spain, a rich intellectual and cultural atmosphere flourished. Muslim scholars encouraged people from all walks of life to seek knowledge and engage in intellectual pursuits.

The influence of Muslim rule in Spain can be seen in the streets, architecture, and cultural practices that still exist today.

Cities like Cordoba, Granada, and Seville are known for their stunning Islamic architecture, such as the Alhambra and the Great Mosque of Cordoba.

These cities are also home to many streets and neighborhoods with names of Arabic origin, serving as a reminder of the rich heritage left behind by the Muslims.

The Spanish language itself has borrowed many words from Arabic, further reflecting the lasting impact of Islamic culture.

In recent years, there has been a growing interest among the Spanish population in learning about Islam and understanding the faith of their historical rulers.

Many people are turning to Islamic teachings and practices to find solace and answers in the face of life's challenges. This thirst for knowledge and the search for truth is a behavior that resonates with a significant portion of the population, leading to the increasing embrace of Islam as a way of life in Spain.

They established centers of learning, such as universities and libraries, where scholars from various disciplines would gather to exchange ideas and advance knowledge.

These scholars diligently preserved and translated the works of ancient Greek and Roman philosophers, mathematicians, and scientists, thus contributing to the preservation and development of knowledge.

The Islamic civilization in Spain made significant advancements in fields such as mathematics, astronomy, medicine, and architecture, leaving a lasting imprint on the land.

During the rise of Christendom in Europe, conflicts and power struggles were prevalent among different Christian kingdoms and the Church itself.

The Crusades, for example, were a series of military campaigns driven by a desire to reclaim the Holy Land from Muslim control.

These conflicts were not only motivated by religious zeal but also by political and economic interests, further highlighting the pursuit of power and territorial expansion.

The emphasis on military might and political dominance overshadowed intellectual pursuits and the promotion of knowledge during this period.

Unlike the Islamic Golden Age, where scholars made significant advancements in fields such as mathematics, astronomy, and medicine, Europe lagged in intellectual development.

The incorporation of polytheistic beliefs into Christianity, such as the veneration of saints, deviated from the core teachings of monotheism found in the Abrahamic faiths.

This practice raised concerns among some theologians and religious thinkers who believed it to be a departure from the true essence of Christianity.

In Islamic belief, Jesus is revered as a prophet, emphasizing his role as a messenger of God rather than being considered the literal son of God.

This theological difference between Christianity and Islam influenced the way Jesus was understood and portrayed in both religions.

Overall, the rise of Christendom in Europe was characterized by power struggles, territorial expansion, a lack of emphasis on intellectual pursuits, and introducing beliefs that deviated from the core teachings of Christianity.

In contrast, Islamic belief emphasized the importance of knowledge and saw Jesus as a revered prophet rather than the son of God.

Islam marked a significant golden age and renaissance in history, with Muslims making remarkable contributions in various fields, such as science, mathematics, art, and philosophy.

This period witnessed immense progress and intellectual growth, fostering an environment of knowledge and innovation.

However, it is disheartening to see that the same breed of Muslims who once led the world in intellectual pursuits are now being counteracted by those who have forgotten or deliberately ignored this glorious past.

These individuals, lacking knowledge and understanding, unjustly portray Muslims as terrorists and ignorant individuals.

It is indeed a shame if Muslims themselves are unaware of their rich history and can be easily deceived and oppressed by those who manipulate facts and exploit their lack of knowledge.

It is crucial for Muslims to reclaim their heritage, educate themselves about their past achievements, and stand firm against deceit and oppression.

Omar-e-Farooq, a prominent political figure and respected leader, was invited to take the keys to Jerusalem due to his reputation for fairness, wisdom, and diplomatic skills. His rule was characterized by a commitment to justice and religious tolerance, which earned him the trust and support of various religious and ethnic communities in the region.

Recognizing his ability to bridge divides and find peaceful solutions, the people of Jerusalem believed that his leadership would bring stability and prosperity to the city.

With great honor and humility, Omar-e-Farooq accepted the invitation and embarked on his journey to assume the responsibility of governing Jerusalem.

Jerusalem indeed experienced a period of great prosperity and significance during the reign of the second caliph of Islam, Omar ibn al-Khattab.

Under his leadership, Jerusalem was conquered by Muslim forces in 637 CE, marking the beginning of Muslim rule in the city.

Omar's approach to governance in Jerusalem was characterized by religious tolerance, respect for the existing religious communities, and the establishment of a framework that ensured the safety and security of all residents.

This era saw the construction of the Al-Aqsa Mosque and the Dome of the Rock, two iconic structures that continue to define the city's skyline.

The history of Jerusalem during this time serves as a continuous reminder of the rich Islamic heritage and the significance of the city to Muslims worldwide.

It is crucial to remember and acknowledge this history to foster understanding, promote dialogue, and ensure the preservation of Jerusalem's cultural and religious diversity.

During Omar bin Khattab's reign as the second caliph of the Rashidun Caliphate, Jerusalem was indeed handed over to Muslim control in a peaceful manner.

After the conquest of Jerusalem in 637 CE, Omar bin Khattab entered the city and negotiated a treaty with the Christian patriarch Sophronius.

This treaty guaranteed the safety and rights of the Christian inhabitants, as well as the protection of their holy sites, including the Church of the Holy Sepulcher.

Furthermore, Omar bin Khattab's policies towards Jews and Christians extended beyond Jerusalem. Throughout his caliphate, he implemented a fair and inclusive system, known as the Pact of Umar, which allowed non-Muslims to live under Islamic rule with their religious freedoms preserved.

This pact granted them the right to practice their faith, maintain their places of worship, and be governed by their own religious laws.

Under Omar's leadership, Jews and Christians were not eradicated or forced to convert to Islam. Instead, they were invited to live in peace and coexist with Muslims, contributing to the diverse society of the time.

Omar bin Khattab's administration ensured the protection and well-being of the people of the land, fostering an environment where different religious communities could thrive and flourish.

Sepulcher church, also known as the Church of the Holy Sepulcher, was under the supervision of Muslims during certain periods in history.

This arrangement was requested by the church authorities themselves, as they believed that the fighting and conflicts between different churches and Christian sects posed a threat to the safety and sanctity of the site.

The Muslims who controlled the region were impartial mediators who could ensure the security and preservation of the church.

This arrangement allowed for the peaceful coexistence of various Christian groups within the church, preventing further violence and bloodshed.

The Sepulcher church, also known as the Church of the Holy Sepulcher, is a significant religious site in the Old City of Jerusalem.

The old city of Jerusalem is a historically significant area in the region known as Palestine. It holds great religious and cultural importance for multiple faiths, including Judaism, Christianity, and Islam.

The city is home to iconic sites like the Western Wall, the Church of the Holy Sepulcher, and the Dome of the Rock.

However, it is important to note that the status of Jerusalem is a highly contentious issue, with conflicting claims and disputes between Israelis and Palestinians.

The political and legal status of the city is still unresolved, and there are ongoing discussions for a peaceful resolution.

Christians believe that this is the place where Jesus Christ was crucified, buried, and resurrected, while in Islam, it is believed that he was raised alive, which presents an important contrast in belief systems.

Since its construction in the 4th century, the church has been cared for by various Christian denominations, such as the Greek Orthodox, Armenian Apostolic, and Roman Catholic churches.

As conflicts persisted, they were compelled to rely on trustworthy Muslims to maintain the church for centuries, and the keys have remained in the hands of Muslims.

Muslim families have been entrusted with the keys to the church for centuries. The Nusseibeh family, in particular, has shouldered the responsibility of opening and closing the church doors every day for over 1,000 years.

This unique arrangement serves as a testament to the historical coexistence and mutual respect between Muslims and Christians in Jerusalem.

During the time of the Romans, the holy site of Muslims, Masjid al-Aqsa, was unfortunately being used as a dumpster for trash disposal. This was deeply disrespectful considering the significance of the site.

According to Islamic tradition, it is believed that the Prophet Muhammad was miraculously taken on a journey known as the Isra and Miraj, where he ascended to the heavens on the back of a winged horse called Buraq.

It was during this journey that he was gifted many precious blessings, including the gift of Salah (prayer) as a central pillar of Islam.

Recognizing the importance of Masjid al-Aqsa, Omar bin Khattab, the second caliph of Islam, took on cleaning the mosque.

He understood the immense value and sanctity of this holy place and felt compelled to restore it to its rightful state of reverence.

With his own hands, Omar bin Khattab diligently cleaned the masjid, setting an example of humility and devotion to the Muslim community.

His actions serve as a reminder of the significance of Masjid al-Aqsa and the need to preserve and respect it as a sacred place of worship.

The continuous battles staged by Christendom have been a recurring theme throughout its existence.

This portrayal of a passive and loving God, referred to as Jesus, has allowed individuals to hide behind a charade, making it easier for them to commit sins and engage in acts of violence driven by greed.

Countless wars throughout history demonstrate this phenomenon, where Christians, driven by their interpretation of faith, fought and killed in the name of their religion.

Muslims have also engaged in warfare, but Islam does not adopt a passive stance towards those who oppress others. Fairness and justice are integral to Islam in every aspect.

Islam does not advocate turning the other cheek or condone the hypocrisy of fighting against the weak.

It is important to note that the actions of individual Muslims do not reflect the teachings of Islam as a whole. However, Islamic laws are impeccably designed to uphold justice for all of humanity, not just for Muslims.

This manipulation of religious teachings has perpetuated a cycle of violence and conflict, often in pursuit of power, resources, or the expansion of territories.

The consequences of these battles have been devastating, leading to the loss of countless lives and causing immeasurable suffering for those caught in the crossfire.

Islam did not indulge in wars solely for the sake of expansion or greed. While engaging in wars, Islam primarily fought these conflicts to protect the rights and well-being of Muslims.

The distinction between Muslim wars and wars driven by greed or conquest is clear and well-documented.

The Prophet Muhammad himself served as the commander-in-chief during these wars that were waged during his time as a prophet. These wars were defensive, aiming to safeguard the Muslim community from persecution, oppression, and external threats.

The Prophet Muhammad emphasized the importance of justice, mercy, and restraint in warfare, and he ensured that innocent civilians, places of worship, and property were spared from harm.

The purpose of these wars was to establish a just and harmonious society, where all individuals could freely practice their religion and live in peace.

The commander-in-chief, Prophet Muhammad, led many wars during his time in order to fight for the rights of Muslims, rather than being driven by greed or personal gain.

Prophet Muhammad, the commander-in-chief, fought these wars to defend the freedom of worship, protect the Muslim community, and ensure justice and equality for all.

His commitment to upholding the principles of Islam characterized the prophet, promoting peace, and establishing a just society.

He emphasized the importance of self-defense and protecting the rights and dignity of all individuals, regardless of their religion or background.

The wars led by Prophet Muhammad were not conquests for land or wealth, but a means to secure the fundamental rights and freedoms of the Muslim community and establish a just and harmonious society.

The wars in Islam, known as defensive wars, were not initiated by Prophet Muhammad, but were fought in defense of the Muslims and their rights.

In Islam, it is hypocritical to sit back and watch as the rights of the oppressed are taken away. Muslims are encouraged to stand alone, if necessary, in order to uphold the truth and stand against the enemy.

However, it is important to note that there are rules of engagement in Islamic warfare. Muslims are prohibited from fighting with the weak, destroying trees, and involving women and children in warfare.

Those who fight against oppressors as Muslims are well aware of the rights and principles that guide their actions in war. By adhering to these rules, Muslims aim to maintain a just and fair approach in their defensive actions.

The wars that Prophet Muhammad participated in were known as the Islamic wars or the military campaigns of the Prophet. These wars took place during the early years of Islam in the 7th century.

Some of the notable wars include the Battle of Badr in 624, where a small Muslim force defeated a larger Meccan army; the Battle of Uhud in 625, which resulted in a partial victory for the Muslims; and the Battle of the Trench in 627, where a coalition of Arab tribes attacked the Muslim city of Medina but was ultimately unsuccessful.

Prophet Muhammad also led expeditions such as the Conquest of Mecca in 630, which marked the peaceful surrender of the city to the Muslims.

These wars played a crucial role in establishing and spreading the Islamic faith in the Arabian Peninsula.

Although Saudi Arabia is flourishing with material wealth and the grandeur of the Kaaba, another significant holy site, Masjid al-Aqsa, and the Dome of the Rock, are under constant threat.

These sacred sites, located in Jerusalem, hold immense religious and historical significance for Muslims worldwide.

Despite their importance, they face ongoing challenges due to political unrest and conflicts in the region. The oppressors, aware of the unequally equipped Muslims, continue to target and jeopardize the safety of these holy places.

It is a reminder that the struggle for safeguarding these sites is a continuous battle for the Muslim community. However, the Muslims draw strength from their faith in Allah, believing that victory ultimately comes from Him.

Throughout history, the faith that preaches passiveness and turning the other cheek, namely Christianity, has been involved in many wars driven by greed rather than the protection or defense of Christian rights.

This contradiction between doctrine and practice can be observed in various instances.

For example, during the Crusades, Christians embarked on military campaigns primarily motivated by the desire to conquer and control valuable lands in the name of Christianity.

The acquisition of wealth, power, and resources often took precedence over any genuine concern for the well-being of fellow believers.

The colonization efforts of Christian nations, such as Spain and Portugal, can be seen as driven by a thirst for wealth, resources, and domination rather than the propagation of Christian values.

During the Muslim rule, which lasted from the 8th to the 15th century, Portugal and Spain experienced a period of cultural and intellectual enlightenment. The Muslim rulers, known as the Moors, brought with them advanced knowledge in various fields such as mathematics, astronomy, medicine, and architecture.

They established great centers of learning and built impressive structures like the Alhambra in Spain and the Great Mosque of Cordoba.

The Moors also introduced new agricultural techniques, bringing crops like citrus fruits, rice, and cotton to the region.

Their influence can still be seen today in the intricate geometric patterns and architectural styles found in many historical buildings across both countries.

It is important to note that although the Muslim rulers held power, they did not oppress the local populations. Instead, they fostered an environment of cultural exchange and education, leaving a lasting legacy as teachers rather than oppressors.

These historical events highlight how the faith's teachings have been disregarded in pursuit of self-interest and material gain, undermining the notion of Christianity as a religion of peace and selflessness.

The nation that supports Israel, armed and proficient in controlling arms and humanity, continues to extend its support to a nation that is accused of oppressing Palestine. This hypocrisy is not only prevalent but also intricate.

While every human may commit sins in private, the act of contributing to the massacre of the weak goes beyond mere oppression; it taints the very land upon which it occurs.

It is not a question but an answer of how humanity has taken a shift towards greed, allowing it to perpetuate such injustices.

One reason for this support could be rooted in religious beliefs. Some may argue that the support for Israel stems from the belief that Jesus, who was rejected as the Messiah by the Jews but embraced by Christians as the incarnate God, lived in the land of Israel.

However, it is important to note that Jesus hailed from Judea, which is now recognized as part of Palestine. This raises further complexities and contradictions within the geopolitical landscape surrounding the Israeli-Palestinian conflict.

Blaming the weak and marginalizing their struggles, while conveniently ignoring a long history of lies and greed, is an unjust and ineffective tactic.

This turmoil is disproportionately affecting most Muslims and the Christian population, the ongoing Israeli-Palestinian conflict has led to a dire humanitarian crisis in Gaza.

Among the challenges that the region has encountered are a blockade that severely limits the entry of essential goods, a crumbling infrastructure, and a lack of access to clean water and electricity.

Enduring high unemployment rates, limited healthcare services, and restricted movement, the people of Gaza face an incredibly challenging task of rebuilding their lives and securing a better future.

The restrictions on basic rights and freedoms, such as the freedom of movement and the right to live, further exacerbate the suffering of the people in Gaza.

The international community must recognize and address these oppressive conditions, advocating for a peaceful resolution to the conflict and supporting initiatives that promote the well-being and fundamental rights of all individuals in the region.

This oppression is not exclusive to Gaza but is also prevalent in other Muslim countries.

The systematic violation of human rights, lack of religious freedom, and restrictions on basic liberties are common issues faced by Muslims in various nations.

In some countries, oppressive regimes suppress dissent, curtail freedom of expression, and impose strict social and cultural regulations that disproportionately target the Muslim population.

Discrimination, marginalization, and inequalities are deeply rooted in the socio-political fabric of these nations, hindering the progress and well-being of their Muslim citizens.

The struggle for justice, equality, and freedom extends beyond Gaza, encompassing a broader global context. Greed serves as the driving force for those who engage in foreign invasions in the Middle East, making it a significant issue.

The international community must recognize the oppressive situation in Gaza and work towards finding a just solution that addresses the root causes of this ongoing humanitarian crisis.

It is crucial to shift the focus away from blaming the weak and instead focus on holding accountable those responsible for perpetuating oppression and inequality.

Considering the current global political climate, it is crucial for Muslims to address the issues facing Islam and speak out against oppression.

Muslims have the right to use their knowledge and education to inform and educate the masses about the political shift in Christendom that approves of Zionism.

In contrast to the passiveness often associated with Jesus in Christian teachings, there is a perception of hypocrisy in how Christendom supports oppressive actions against the weak Palestinians.

These actions portray them as warmongers, incapable of fighting against advanced technologies, and kept in a state of deprivation.

The essence of humanity resides in most individuals, and an increasing number of advocates are acknowledging the inequity and injustice inherent in the weak forces they oppose.

The unity of Muslim countries is the sole solution to support the cause of humanity.

Gallup News: Jun 21, 2024 — Protestants and highly religious Americans, traditionally Israel's most sympathetic supporters, are shrinking in size.

Gallup News: Mar 27, 2024 — A majority of U.S. adults now disapprove of Israel's military action in Gaza, a shift from the prior survey in November.

It is ironic how the oppressors or those driven by greed supply arms and then try to solve issues. If they didn't provide harmful aid to opposing forces, there would be no need to address humanity's problems.

It's like feeding a lion and then expecting it to peacefully resolve matters. The very land that provides funds and goods is the same land plagued by abundant poverty and depression.

It's important to prioritize self-help before extending assistance to others. Muslims during the golden age not only helped themselves but also contributed to the betterment of the world. They didn't destroy it; they made it better.

However, it is important to recognize the falsehood of this portrayal, as throughout history, Muslim rule has not been characterized by oppression or forced conversion.

Islamic doctrine upholds principles of liberty and justice, which allow people to worship as they choose freely and protect their families.

Rather than exiling individuals from their homes, Islamic rulers have often provided them with shelter, emphasizing the importance of humanity and justice within their faith.

However, it is important to note that the process of Christianization was complex and multifaceted. While Constantine's influence certainly played a significant part, it would be inaccurate to solely attribute the establishment of Christianity to him.

Christianity had already been spreading and gaining followers for centuries prior to Constantine's reign.

Regarding the adoption of paganistic beliefs, in an effort to unite his diverse empire, Constantine incorporated some elements of pagan rituals and practices into Christianity.

This syncretism aimed to ease the transition for the predominantly pagan population and facilitate the acceptance of the new religion. However, it is crucial to distinguish between incorporating certain cultural practices and the core teachings of Jesus.

Jesus, who emerged from the family of Imran (known as the family of Amram in Christian tradition), preached a message of monotheism and love for God and humanity.

His teachings emphasized spiritual purity, compassion, and a personal relationship with God.

These teachings were indeed overshadowed by political influences and the subsequent development of various sects within Christianity.

The formation of Catholicism and the emergence of different Christian sects throughout history were often driven by political factors, power struggles, and theological debates.

The influence of emperors, councils, and religious leaders certainly shaped the trajectory of Christianity, sometimes deviating from the original teachings of Jesus.

It is indeed ironic that Jesus, initially rejected by some segments of Jewish society, found acceptance among the followers of Christendom after the religion was shaped and established by a non-prophetic human emperor.

This historical irony highlights the complex interplay between faith, politics, and human agency in the development of religious traditions.

Mithraism and the Isis cults, while not directly part of Christendom, did have some influence on the development of early Christianity.

Mithraism was a popular mystery cult in the Roman Empire, particularly among the military, and its rituals and symbolism bore similarities to certain aspects of Christianity, such as the concept of a dying and resurrecting god.

Some scholars argue that certain Christian practices, such as the celebration of Christmas on December 25th, are influenced by Mithraic traditions.

Similarly, the Isis cults, which centered on the worship of the Egyptian goddess Isis, were also prevalent in the Roman Empire during the early centuries of Christianity. The cult's emphasis on motherhood, fertility, and divine protection resonated with many people.

Some Christian imagery, such as the depiction of Mary as a mother figure, has been suggested to have been influenced by the veneration of Isis. The idea of a divine child, born of a virgin, shares similarities with both the Isis cults and Christianity.

In Islam, the belief in the virgin birth of Jesus is indeed acknowledged. However, it is important to note that Islam does not align with the concept of Jesus being the literal son of God cannot be overstated.

Islam emphasizes the oneness and uniqueness of Allah, who is believed to be beyond human attributes and does not have any partners or offspring.

This belief is rooted in the Islamic concept of monotheism, which strictly rejects any form of association or partnership with Allah. Therefore, the idea of Jesus being the son of God is blasphemous in Islam.

However, it is important to note that while these pagan religions may have influenced certain elements of Christian tradition; they did not directly shape or play a significant role in the establishment of Christendom as a whole.

Jesus' teachings, disciple efforts, and Emperor Constantine's conversion influenced the rise of Christianity. The message of Jesus shifted from monotheism to polytheism, accepting him as a deity and forgetting his creator.

Islam, Judaism, and the prophets of Abrahamic faith all reject polytheism in favor of monotheism.

Those unfamiliar with history may not understand the concept of not having God's pictures or dying for sins. The message of Jesus was altered to serve political greed and conquest.

The Quran does indeed discuss the exile of the Jews in various verses. It highlights instances where the Jewish community disobeyed God's commands and faced the consequences of their actions, including exile.

One such example mentioned in the Quran recounts the story of the Israelites who were punished and turned into apes for violating the Sabbath. Additionally, the Jews' disobedience and their constant violation of the laws and covenants established by God.

These instances serve as reminders of the importance of obedience and adherence to God's guidance in order to avoid the pitfalls of exile and punishment.

During the time of persecution of Jews, Muslims played a significant role in helping and sheltering them.

Many Muslims, guided by the principles of compassion and justice in Islam, provided refuge to Jews and even disguised them as Muslims to protect them from harm.

These acts of solidarity were not only based on religious teachings but also on the recognition of the historical bond between Muslims and Jews.

Indeed, both communities share a common ancestry and are considered descendants of the prophet Abraham. This familial connection fostered a sense of kinship and mutual support, leading Muslims to stand up for the rights and well-being of their Jewish counterparts.

These instances of cooperation and protection during times of adversity highlight the potential for harmony and coexistence between Muslims and Jews, emphasizing the importance of nurturing these shared values in the pursuit of peaceful coexistence.

After the Jews were exiled from Israel by the Romans in 70 CE, they faced a long period of dispersion and persecution. However, it was indeed under Muslim rule that Jews were granted permission to re-enter and settle in the land of Israel.

During the early Islamic period, particularly under the Umayyad and Abbasid Caliphates, Jews were allowed to return to Jerusalem and other parts of the region.

Muslim rulers, such as Omar ibn al-Khattab and Saladin, ensured the rights and protection of Jews within their territories.

This policy of tolerance and acceptance towards Jews contributed to the flourishing of Jewish communities in various parts of the Islamic world, including Israel.

It is important to note that this period of Muslim rule facilitated the reestablishment of Jewish presence in the land, which laid the foundation for the eventual establishment of the modern state of Israel.

Jesus, as a historical figure, was indeed Jewish and his teachings often reflected the principles and laws of the Torah, which is the foundation of Jewish religious practice.

He emphasized he did not come to abolish the law of Moses but to fulfill it. Jesus upheld and respected the religious traditions of his faith.

It is important to note that the belief in Jesus as a prophetic figure was not a part of a godhead, developed later within the context of Christian theology.

While this belief is central to Christian doctrine, it is blasphemous according to the strict monotheistic regulations of Abrahamic faith, which emphasize the singularity of God.

Different sects of Christendom and traditions within the broader Abrahamic faith indeed interpret Jesus differently, each with their own unique perspectives and beliefs.

Within Christianity, there are many denominations, such as Catholicism, Protestantism, and Eastern Orthodoxy, Evangelicals, each with their own distinct interpretations of Jesus and his role as the Messiah.

These interpretations vary in terms of theological emphasis, rituals, and traditions.

Islamic doctrine acknowledges Jesus as a prophet, but not as the Son of God or the Messiah. According to Islamic belief, Muslims highly revere Jesus as a prophet, but they do not consider him divine or the savior of humanity.

Regarding Judaism, most Jews do not recognize Jesus as the Messiah. This is because of a variety of reasons, including the rejection of the concept of a virgin birth and the lack of fulfillment of messianic prophecies according to their interpretation.

Jewish beliefs hold that the Messiah is yet to come and will be a descendant of King David, ushering in an era of peace and redemption. The allegations and mischaracterizations of Jesus, as perceived by some Jews, further fueled the rejection of his messianic claims.

As a result, within the Jewish faith, the anticipation for a future prophet from the lineage of David remains.

The broad spectrum of truth regarding Jesus the Messiah encompasses various historical accounts and interpretations that have been passed down through different religious traditions and scholarly research.

While the fundamental belief among Christians is that Jesus is the Messiah, there are differing perspectives on his life, teachings, and significance.

Some view Jesus as a divine figure who performed miracles and was resurrected, while others may interpret him as a moral teacher or a revolutionary leader.

There are debates and differing theories about the historical context in which Jesus lived, the authenticity of biblical texts, and the influence of cultural and political factors on the development of his story.

Understanding the truth and history of Jesus the Messiah involves examining these various perspectives and critically evaluating the evidence to form a comprehensive understanding of his life and impact.

Bible: Matthew 5:17-18, Jesus says, Do not think that I have come to abolish the law or the prophets; I have not come to abolish them but to fulfill them.

Multiple individuals throughout history. It is composed of two main sections: the Old Testament and the New Testament. The Old Testament contains various books that were written by different authors, including prophets, kings, and scholars, such as Moses, David, Isaiah, and Jeremiah, among others.

Despite these variations, the core teachings and messages of the Bible remain central to the beliefs of millions of people worldwide.

The Abrahamic faiths encompass religious traditions that trace their origins back to the patriarch Abraham. These faiths include Judaism, Christianity, and Islam.

While they all believe in the existence of one God, there are significant differences in their understanding of the divine and the role of Jesus.

In Islam, Jesus is respected as a prophet and messiah, but not as the Son of God or a divine figure. Muslims emphasize the absolute oneness of God, highlighting that God is beyond human comprehension and cannot be fully understood or seen.

CHAPTER 11
DEFEAT UNSPOKEN FEARS AND BASELESS ALLEGATIONS.

The ultimate failure in life is failing to acknowledge the inevitable trajectory of human existence, which begins and ends with helplessness.

Some individuals are granted lengthy lives while others have shorter ones. According to Prophet Muhammad, the expected lifespan of his ummah is between 60 and 70 years, although many people have surpassed this time period.

It is now the time for repentance and deep contemplation about the offerings of this earthly life and the life after death. It can crush even those who have walked proudly on the earth, as the earth itself reminds us we are walking upon it.

Allah has allowed the earth to tantalize the bodies of those who have misused their time on earth, reminding them of their mortality.

It is important to remember that even though disbelievers may appear to be flourishing in this life, they will have no share in the hereafter.

The internal defeat begins prior to acknowledging the fleeting nature of youth, and as one grows older, even the healthiest individuals may experience sickness. Youth is the most precious time, and many waste it without guidance.

These individuals may have stories of deterioration that are told with grandeur, but those who appreciate the value of this time feel sympathy for their unfortunate narratives.

While there are individuals who prioritize and achieve success in academics and material gains, it is important to acknowledge that genuine success goes beyond these aspects and includes spiritual fulfillment.

It is not a matter of choosing one over the other, but finding a balance that encompasses all aspects of life.

Our collaboration and deeds with our creator are what we ultimately carry with us. Hence, the transformative journey of life should not be disregarded, as it is undeniably significant.

To embrace Islam is primarily through the invitation of Allah, as no one is compelled to become a Muslim against their will.

The decision to convert is willingly made, with various circumstances influencing each individual's journey.

However, it is crucial to maintain certain aspects throughout this journey, such as companionship, learning, knowledge, and unity.

It is a fact that Islam is the religion of birth, and not following Islam is a dilemma rooted in ignorance.

However, it is Allah who has the power to change hearts and reveal the functionality and truth within the heart of a believer. The core principle is to worship one God.

These elements play a crucial role in laying a strong groundwork for new converts, as well as providing guidance for Muslims to comprehend and navigate their faith.

Merely identifying oneself as a Muslim without genuinely embracing its teachings is a futile endeavor.

It is essential to comprehend the boundaries and find peace within the framework of conformity and detachment from one's past, as Allah forgives and offers a fresh start to new Muslims.

Choosing Islam and being rewarded for it is truly an honor.

Many people in middle age struggle to preserve their youth, leading to a lucrative industry for cosmetic centers and doctors. Is it a significant loss to be born a Muslim but not understand the essence of spirituality.

Breaking down barriers and reconciling the mind is important for individuals to grasp the spiritual essence of Allah as the one God, separate from any creation or deity.

One of the main reasons behind the spread of Islamophobia is the lack of knowledge and understanding of Islam among the public. The media often portrays a distorted and negative image of Islam, associating it with terrorism and extremism.

In many areas, there is violence, poverty, distortion of human rights, and illicit activities.

However, the portrayal of Muslim countries or Muslims often fall victim to a distorted view, compromising the values that Islam upholds, perpetuated by those who harbor hatred towards Islam.

The nearest a servant can be to Allah is while in Sujood. The position of utmost humility. It is important to acknowledge that good and bad exist in all societies, but the choice to focus on either aspect lies within each individual's soul.

Unfortunately, there are continuous efforts by ignorant individuals continue to expose and magnify the evils within Muslim communities, spreading fear and promoting hate.

It is crucial to recognize that such rhetoric is a double-edged sword, as it aims to weaken society and perpetuate misconceptions about Islam.

This long-standing effort to use Islam as a tool and exploit the vulnerable is further exacerbated by filming in less fortunate areas, reinforcing the notion of inequality.

The root of this havoc lies in the greed-driven actions of invaders, seeking to exploit the rich lands of the Middle East that lack resources.

The control exerted by these incompetent forces extends beyond mere tabloid lies, as they actively work to manipulate and dumb down a society that lacks proper knowledge and understanding of Islam.

As a result, many people have developed prejudice and fear towards Muslims and their faith. It is the responsibility of Muslims who possess knowledge about Islam to educate the masses and dispel these misconceptions.

By engaging in open and respectful dialogue, sharing accurate information about Islamic teachings, and promoting the true essence of Islam, Muslims can contribute to breaking down the barriers of ignorance and fostering a more inclusive and tolerant society.

It is not only a duty but also an opportunity to bridge gaps, build connections, and promote understanding among people of different backgrounds and beliefs.

Through education, Muslims can actively challenge Islamophobia and promote a more peaceful coexistence.

Bible: NIV: Matthew: 5;38;40. You have heard that it was said, 'Eye for eye, and tooth for tooth.' [But I tell you, do not resist an evil person. If anyone slaps you on the right cheek, turn to the other cheek also. And if anyone wants to sue you and take your shirt, hand over your coat as well.

Embracing the teachings in this verse of the **Bible, Matthew 5:38-40,** would prevent exploiters from resorting to wars in order to sustain a system driven by greed. The flawed nature of humanity, which cannot appreciate the importance of truth, is the root cause of the deep-rooted hypocrisy exhibited by those who engage in such actions.

However, by choosing to follow a path that aligns with one's beliefs, it becomes imperative to remain well-informed about the Abrahamic faiths.

The hypocrisy extends not only to the political realm of greed, but also to the personal sphere. The concept of word and honor holds importance for those who appreciate the significance of keeping one's promises.

In Islam, great importance is placed on the words we use and the way to address others. Respecting others and showing respect to oneself is the guiding principle.

The role of a company is always significant in directing the various aspects of one's life within the company's domain.

The Byzantine Empire did indeed play a significant role in the spread of Christianity throughout its territories.

The Byzantine Empire employed a variety of strategies to promote and establish Christianity as the dominant religion. One key approach was the conversion of rulers and their subsequent adoption of Christianity as the state religion.

This top-down approach often led to the conversion of their subjects as well, as the ruling elite's religious practices heavily influenced the population.

The Byzantine Empire engaged in missionary work, sending monks and clergy to spread the teachings of Christianity to neighboring regions.

In today's world of Christendom, the tradition of door knocking and spreading religion through invitations continues. Neither Islam nor Judaism practices this approach.

The empire used a combination of political, cultural, and religious strategies to spread Christianity throughout its territories.

The Byzantine Empire, which had its capital in Constantinople, fell to the Muslim Ottoman Empire in 1453. The Ottomans, led by Sultan Mehmed II, successfully conquered Constantinople, marking the end of the Byzantine Empire.

This event fulfilled a prophecy that had been circulating in Islamic circles for centuries, which foresaw Muslims eventually ruling and conquering Turkey.

The Ottoman Empire went on to become a significant Muslim power, expanding its territories across the Middle East, North Africa, and Southeast Europe.

The empire lasted for several centuries, until its decline and eventual dissolution in the early 20th century. Muslims have made significant contributions to various fields of knowledge and learning throughout history.

Scholars such as Al-Khwarizmi, Ibn Sina, and Al-Farabi made important discoveries and advancements that greatly impacted modern science and influenced civilizations beyond the Islamic world.

Contrary to popular misconceptions, the achievements of the Muslim world during this period were not limited to religious or theological matters.

A spirit of intellectual curiosity, open-mindedness, and a thirst for knowledge characterized the Islamic Golden Age.

Muslim scholars translated and preserved ancient Greek, Roman, and Persian texts, making them accessible to a wider audience.

They also developed new theories, conducted experiments, and made significant contributions to fields such as algebra, optics, and medicine.

However, in recent times, the contributions and achievements of Muslims have been overshadowed by negative stereotypes and misrepresentations. It's not about simply reviving history or condoning the legacy of past Muslims.

Islam encourages Muslims to excel in all aspects of life and create their own history that will be remembered. Muslims cannot let our principles and morality decay in order to be accepted by a society that may be more corrupted than an iron rusting outside.

The goal is not only to repeat ancient stories but also to strategically implement growth from within and leave a lasting impact for future generations.

These messages serve as eye-openers, reminding us that history is a testament to the advancements Muslims have made in various fields, often unknown to others.

The timeless Quran requires deep understanding and should not be left on a shelf gathering dust.

There are no excuses for those who view learning as a burden, as the afterlife is a long journey. It is wiser to invest in knowledge, which provides a reliable foundation for both this world and the hereafter.

The one who is envied is the one who possesses knowledge and a spiritual understanding of life.

Beauty is not something that others envy, as it eventually fades away. Zulekha, however, recognized the value of beauty and prayed to Allah to preserve her beauty for Yusuf.

Money is tangible; it can come and go. Allah gives to whom He wills and there is responsibility and questioning of its usage.

Islam does not consider money evil or the root of evil; it matters how it is put to use.

Having the upper hand and giving is gratitude, not a burden.

In Islam, several prophets were blessed with wealth. One of them was Abu Bakr, a companion of Prophet Muhammad, who was known for his prosperity. Prophet Muhammad himself experienced a period of wealth after his marriage to Khadija

However, his life was also filled with tests, including times of riches, poverty, and the tragic loss of his family.

He faced these challenges with remarkable strength and resilience, leaving behind a timeless legacy for the world to cherish. Following his teachings is a timeless practice for those who truly comprehend the essence of Islam.

But what about preserving knowledge if Allah were to take away one's intellect? Everything ultimately belongs to Allah, and time is the most precious of all.

Wasting time in the hope of a better future is futile, as time cannot be reclaimed. It is constantly moving forward at a rapid pace. The Quran is a timeless text, and it becomes timeless when it is truly understood.

The people who follow the teachings of the book can attempt to comprehend that Jesus' message was continued through the comforter, who would praise him as brethren.

According to the Bible, Jesus had to depart in order to send this comforter. It is perplexing how anyone could challenge his words, considering he is a respected prophet. Portraying him as a sinner who fights against sins and overcomes them is deemed blasphemous.

It is important to clarify that the misinterpretation in the understanding of the Holy Spirit, and each person's spirit is unique and carries its own significance.

Failing to believe in the extension of Jesus' words and stopping at him alone shows a lack of understanding. Muslims believe in every prophet sent by Allah without assigning divinity to any of them.

Islam continues to thrive, as the word of Allah is unchangeable and cannot be misinterpreted or misrepresented to cater to the masses. Islam does not force anyone to convert, but it welcomes those who seek to understand it.

Some individuals and groups with destructive ideologies have distorted the image of Islam and its history, perpetuating ignorance and misunderstanding.

It is, therefore, crucial for Muslims to actively engage in educating the masses about the rich intellectual heritage of Islam and its profound impact on human civilization.

Muslims have a duty to promote knowledge, dispel misconceptions, and foster dialogue to bridge the gap of understanding.

This can be done through various means, such as organizing educational programs, writing books, participating in academic conferences, and utilizing online platforms to share accurate information.

By proactively educating others, Muslims can contribute to a more informed and tolerant society, fostering mutual respect and appreciation for the diverse intellectual and cultural contributions of different civilizations throughout history.

The Ottoman Empire, which emerged in the 13th century, indeed expanded far beyond its initial boundaries and became one of the most influential and powerful empires in history.

At its height, it spanned three continents, stretching from southeastern Europe, through Anatolia, and into the Middle East.

Its extensive territorial reach included regions such as present-day Turkey, Greece, Egypt, Iraq, Syria, and parts of southeastern Europe.

The Ottoman Empire's longevity is also remarkable, lasting for over six centuries, from 1299 to 1922.

Various factors, including adept military strategies, diplomatic alliances, efficient administration, and cultural assimilation, contributed to the exceptional endurance of the Ottoman Empire.

The Ottoman Empire, which existed from the late 13th century to the early 20th century, not only extended its reach across much of Europe and Asia but also expanded into Africa.

The empire established a significant presence in North Africa, particularly in the regions of Egypt, Algeria, Tunisia, and Libya. Ottoman control over these territories brought about political, cultural, and economic changes, as the empire integrated these areas into its administrative system.

The Ottomans also sought to expand their influence further south into sub-Saharan Africa, establishing commercial and diplomatic relations with various states along the Red Sea and the East African coast.

This African expansion allowed the empire to tap into the resources and trade routes of the continent, contributing to its overall prosperity and power.

However, the Ottoman Empire's control in Africa was not without challenges, as local resistance movements and rival European powers often contested their authority.

Throughout its existence, the empire left a lasting impact on the regions it controlled, shaping their political, social, and cultural landscapes.

The Ottoman Empire did indeed use the merits of Islam as a tool for expanding its territories. However, it is important to note that the empire did not force Islam upon its subjects.

Instead, the Ottomans employed a policy known as "millet system," which allowed non-Muslim communities to maintain their own religious and legal practices under the empire's rule.

This approach not only ensured religious freedom but also facilitated the empire's expansion by appealing to diverse populations.

Islam played a central role in the empire's administration, legal system, and cultural practices, but conversion to Islam was not a prerequisite for inclusion or advancement within the Ottoman Empire.

During Constantine's rule over Constantinople in the Byzantine Empire, he indeed used religion to exert control over the minds of the people.

This exploitation of religion has had a lasting impact on the teachings of Jesus, resulting in a distorted and altered version of his message.

As a result, individuals who have been exposed to this manipulated theology often question and ultimately leave Christianity, as their own understanding and beliefs do not align with what is being taught.

These same individuals, who may have limited knowledge about Islam, lump it together with other faiths, further contributing to the misunderstanding and misrepresentation of Islam.

This collusion of minds perpetuates misconceptions and leads to an inaccurate portrayal of Islam, hindering any opportunity for genuine interfaith dialogue and understanding.

Islam is a monotheistic religion that believes in the oneness of Allah, the creator and sustainer of the universe.

In Islam, the belief system is organized around the concept of a contractual relationship between Allah and humans, where individuals willingly submit to the will of Allah and follow His guidance as outlined in the Quran.

Islam emphasizes the importance of logic and reason in understanding and interpreting religious teachings.

Islam does not view the relationship between Allah and humans as a battle or conflict.

Instead, it emphasizes the concept of submission and surrender to the divine will. Muslims believe Allah is all-powerful and cannot be tempted or influenced by anyone, including Satan.

In Islamic theology, Jesus is revered as a great prophet and messenger of Allah, but not as God Himself. Muslims reject the idea that Jesus could be tempted by Satan, as it contradicts the concept of the divine nature of Allah.

The temptation of Jesus by Satan is blasphemous in Islam because it implies a weakness or vulnerability by Jesus that is inconsistent with the belief in his prophethood.

Muslims believe that Jesus, like other prophets, was a human being chosen by Allah to convey His message to humanity. Jesus is highly respected in Islam, but he is not considered divine or part of the Godhead.

This understanding is based on the Islamic principle that God is transcendent and cannot be encompassed or limited by human attributes or vulnerabilities.

In conclusion, the Islamic perspective rejects the notion that Jesus is God based on the belief that God cannot be tempted by Satan.

This is a fundamental theological difference between Islam and Christianity, highlighting the contrasting understandings of the nature of God and the role of Jesus in the two religions.

Quran: Surah Taha: 20:98. Then Moses addressed his people, "Your only god is Allah, there is no god 'worthy of worship' except Him. He encompasses everything in 'His' knowledge."

These differing perspectives reflect the distinct teachings and doctrines of Christianity and Islam.

In discussions surrounding his divinity, Satan cannot tempt Jesus because he was born sinless in Islamic doctrine.

However, it is important to understand that Jesus, while fully divine, also took on human form during his time on Earth per Bible. This means that he experienced the same physical and emotional limitations that humans do.

Satan, as a fallen angel per Bible, but a jinn, per Quran, possesses free will and the ability to tempt others. Within the Christian faith, Satan is an adversary who intends to mislead humans.

In Islamic belief, Satan (**Iblis**) is a jinn made of smokeless fire who refused to bow to Adam and was cast out of paradise.

In Hinduism, the story of Rama rescuing Sita from the wilderness after she was tempted by evil bears resemblance to the concept of Jesus being tempted in the wilderness per Bible

However, within Christianity, Jesus is widely considered to be the Son of God or even God Himself. As a result, his temptation can be seen as a challenge to his divine essence, as upheld by the Christian faith.

Despite his sinless nature because of his divinity, he could still undergo temptation by embracing his human side.

This serves as a testament to the fact that although Jesus faced temptation, he triumphed over it and remained steadfast in his devotion to God's will.

This bears resemblance to the mythological tale in Hinduism where Rama rescued Sita, and this narrative appears to align more closely with the beliefs of Indian mythological religions as opposed to Islam and monotheism.

Both stories highlight the idea of a righteous and obedient figure overcoming temptation and sin.

Christianity and Hinduism have some similarities that can appeal to Westerners who are drawn to the colorful beliefs and traditions of the East, particularly in India.

Both religions have rich mythologies and believe in the divine's presence in the world.

In Hinduism, the concept of avatars allows humans to take on the form of gods, while in Christianity, Jesus is the incarnation of God.

This idea of divine manifestation in human form can intrigue for Westerners who seek a deeper spiritual connection.

The diverse and vibrant rituals, festivals, and sacred sites in India provide a unique experience that can captivate those who are looking for an alternative perspective on spirituality.

However, it is important to acknowledge that the subjective nature of Islam mentioned in the original text may not be a determining factor for Westerners who are attracted to Hinduism, as individuals have different preferences and reasons for exploring different belief systems.

Islam may not be as colorful as Hinduism, Christianity, or Judaism. Unlike these religions, that focus on candles and deities, Islam adheres to a simple monotheistic belief.

If Muslims engage in any cultural practices that resemble pagan interventions, it is not in line with Islam.

The essence of Islam lies in its simplicity, emphasizing submission to the will of Allah rather than elaborate rituals.

This stark contrast sets Islam apart from other religions and their specific rituals. The central ritual of Islam is the act of submission, known as Salat, along with the observance of the other pillars of Islam.

The Quran emphasizes that God is not tempted by anyone or anything, including jinn (supernatural beings created by God).

The jinn are considered to be weak and incapable of tempting God, as they are subservient to His will. Thus, the Quran does not present Jesus as being tempted by a jinn, or any other being.

Neither is Jesus accepted as a godhead or son of God except the Messiah son of Mary. This distinction in theological belief regarding the nature of Jesus and the concept of temptation is one of the major differences between the Bible and the Quran.

The claim that a human body cannot survive for 40 days and nights without food and water is accurate, as the body usually requires nourishment to sustain itself.

The Quran does not mention any fasting or temptation that would allow the body to survive without water for forty days, emphasizing the importance of water for survival.

Historical records show instances of individuals fasting for long periods. People often credit these events to extraordinary circumstances or divine intervention.

However, the significance of events and its connection to human separation from food and water. These differences are not minor and contradict a whole story, which is not in line with Quranic belief. Jesus was pure he was not lured by Satan per Quran.

Quran: Surah Nisa: 4:76. The believers fight for God's cause, while those who reject faith fight for an unjust cause. Fight the allies of Satan: Satan's strategies are truly weak.

There aren't many subjects that social media platforms thrive on, especially those that involve spreading Islamophobic lies about Islam, a subject that is completely foreign to many.

Unfortunately, those who engage in this behavior are often uneducated about the beliefs and laws of Islam, leading to a constant stream of negativity being poured into regions that predominantly profess Christendom.

It is disheartening to see that these individuals do not seem to follow the teachings of Jesus, except for the altered truths they choose to believe.

They often resurface during times of argument or conflict, exacerbating the situation because of their ignorance.

This ignorance not only hinders daily life but also prevents the potential for simple and pleasant interactions between humanity, which should be the norm rather than the exception.

It is a sad truth that this sense of harmony and understanding is not consistently present in our society.

These few individuals who use social media platforms to promote Islamophobia are exploiting the power of technology and the reach of the internet to spread hate and fear.

Their actions go against the principles of unity and understanding that most humanity desires. However, we should acknowledge that their actions have limited influence.

The youth of this generation, including those from Muslim heritage, have already made significant contributions to society and will continue to do so in the future.

They possess the knowledge and the courage to stand up for the truth and challenge the societal norms that suppress individuality. It is crucial for society to overcome the fear that is instilled and to embrace diversity and independent thinking, rather than being controlled by collective ideologies.

By doing so, we can create a harmonious and inclusive world where all individuals are respected.

Throughout history, Muslims have made significant contributions to the field of medicine, including the establishment of hospitals and advancements in surgical techniques.

These legacies are not mere tales, but historical truths that continue to shape the medical world today. Unfortunately, there is a plot to dumb down society and keep these contributions hidden.

This agenda is driven by followers of greed who manipulate the system to distance themselves from the truth and control the minds of the weak.

By suppressing the knowledge and achievements of Muslims in medicine, these individuals seek to maintain their own power and influence.

However, it is essential to uncover and disseminate the truth so that society can acknowledge and appreciate the valuable contributions of Muslims.

Words have immense power. They can inspire, motivate, and uplift, or they can bring pain, despair, and destruction. A single word or sentence can ignite a revolution, mend a broken heart, or shatter someone's dreams.

It is astonishing how a moment of connection through eye contact can create a lasting impact. Those few seconds of connection can shape relationships, create unforgettable memories, or even spark love at first sight.

The realization that such fleeting moments can have a profound influence on the trajectory of our lives is both enchanting and unsettling.

The weight of responsibility falls upon us to choose our words carefully, for they have the potential to shape destinies, change perspectives, and alter the course of a lifetime.

It is essential to recognize that words have the power to transcend mere expression and convey the undeniable truth. Therefore, if we truly listen and pay attention to the words spoken to us, they hold the potential to transform our lives in ways we may never have imagined.

The independent and autonomous temperament refers to an individual's ability to think and act independently, making their own decisions and taking responsibility for their own actions.

This temperament allows one to break free from societal norms and expectations, paving the way for personal growth and self-discovery.

By embracing this temperament, individuals can lead their lives on fertile and fulfilling ground, pursuing their passions and goals with determination and resilience.

However, the presence of lies can have detrimental effects on both individuals and society as a whole. Lies contaminate the bearers, causing chaos and confusion, ultimately leading humanity down a path of destruction.

The spread of falsehoods undermines trust and hinders progress, making it difficult for individuals to find common ground and work towards collective goals.

It is crucial to recognize that helping those who oppress the weak is not a reflection of true humanity. The message of Jesus, for instance, emphasizes the importance of compassion, justice, and equality.

Jesus, during those times, taught the Jews who defiantly rejected him about obeying the commands of Allah.

Prophet Muhammad's teachings were centered on the restoration of justice and the empowerment of marginalized and oppressed individuals, ensuring their rights were granted.

When resources are directed towards supporting those who oppress the weak, it becomes an act of barbarism. This is true even for those who do not hold any specific faith, as every human being possesses a sense of morality and can differentiate between right and wrong.

The reasons behind such actions often defy logical explanation, as they go against the innate understanding of what is ethical and just.

Ultimately, it is crucial for individuals to strive for an independent and autonomous temperament, guided by principles of truth, justice, and compassion.

By doing so, they can contribute to the betterment of society, actively working towards dismantling oppressive systems and uplifting the marginalized.

It is through these collective efforts that humanity can progress towards a more inclusive and harmonious future.

The promotion of Islamophobia by individuals who claim religious devotion and associate Jesus with a specific ideology are directly endorsing Zionism.

It is important to note that Jesus brought the concept of monotheism to the Jewish community, rather than promoting worship of himself, which later became a key aspect of Christianity.

This ideology of Zionism originated from certain Jewish groups historically rejecting Jesus. Sadly, these individuals, who show little regard for the consequences of their actions, continue to perpetuate this legacy even in the present day.

The life of greed revolves around impulsive decisions, as they continuously navigate through each day with no regard for the future.

They rarely make long-term plans or set goals, preferring to go with the flow and embrace whatever opportunities come their way.

Whether it's deciding on a last-minute road trip, changing careers on a whim, or indulging in spontaneous adventures, leading the regions that profess chaos is leading, life is a whirlwind of uncertainty and unpredictability.

For those who live with social media as gospel truth. While some may view their behavior as reckless or irresponsible, this system thrives on the excitement that comes from living in the moment, finding joy in winnings at the loss of others.

It is disheartening to witness how they exploit the power of social media to support oppressive regimes and individuals who prey on the weak and vulnerable.

Prophet Muhammad's love for nature not only enriched the lives of his followers, but also left a lasting impact on the way Islam views the environment and our responsibility to protect it.

The act of uplifting those who are distorting the land and homes of others is inhumane, particularly considering the climate of society in the Middle East.

Instead of vilifying and oppressing others, society can strive for understanding, empathy, and cooperation to create a more harmonious coexistence for all.

The environment in the Middle East is being negatively affected by the excessive greed and manipulation, particularly regarding the control of Muslim lands and the constant changing of regimes.

This continuous upheaval and power struggle have created a lack of comprehensive and unified behavior among Muslims, resulting in further chaos and instability.

In the past, the historical Muslim empire thrived and expanded because of the firm sense of unity among its people. However, in the present situation, this unity is lacking, and its consequences are clear in the environment's degradation.

The absence of a cohesive and supportive community hinders efforts to address environmental issues, as there is a lack of collective action and cooperation.

The fragmentation and disunity among Muslims contribute to the ongoing challenges faced in managing and protecting the environment.

Allah has given humans the responsibility of being caretakers and stewards of the Earth. Various Quranic verses that highlight the significance of preserving and respecting the natural world support this concept.

Muslims have a responsibility to approach the environment with deep respect, understanding that their actions impact the fragile equilibrium of nature.

This teaching advocates for sustainability, conservation, and the ethical treatment of all living creatures, motivating Muslims to take part in environmental protection and preservation endeavors.

Sadly, in many systems, even those who did not contribute to the chaos end up suffering the consequences. This is because certain individuals' actions have caused the destruction of many lands, which can be seen as a punishment from Allah.

The continued deviation towards evil and the refusal to rectify one's actions have resulted in adverse consequences for entire communities.

However, it is essential to remember that ultimate judgment lies with Allah, as this world is temporary and fleeting.

Story of Ghaus-E- Azam a Muslim saint:

Ghaus-E-Azam, also known as Hazrat Sheikh Abdul Qadir Jilani, was a renowned Islamic saint and spiritual leader. He was born in 1077 in Gilani, Persia (now Iran). Ghaus-E-Azam dedicated his life to spreading Islam's teachings and guiding people to a righteous path.

Prophets, saints, and learned men of the past remind us of Allah's miracles and wisdom, with the revered saint being noteworthy.

Ghaus-E-Azam, was a prominent Islamic scholar and spiritual leader in the 12th century. Born in Persia, he emphasized the significance of inner spiritual development and the connection to God in one's life.

His upbringing by a single mother showcased his belief in the strength and capabilities of women in raising children and instilling important values.

With his mother's blessings, he embarked on a journey for further education, which expanded his knowledge and understanding of the world.

Ghaus-E-Azam's teachings revolved around honesty, compassion, and the importance of humanity, making him a revered figure among his followers.

He was known for his wisdom, performing miracles, and leaving a profound impact on countless individuals. Although he passed away in 1166 CE, his teachings and legacy continue to inspire and guide spiritual seekers across the globe.

The story takes place during the time of Ghaus-E-Azam, a renowned saint known for his miracles and knowledge. One day, a ruler who had heard of Ghaus-E-Azam's abilities approached him with a skeptical mind.

He challenged Ghaus-e-Azam to perform a miracle, hoping to prove that his powers were not real. Ghaus-e-Azam, confident in his faith in Allah, accepted the ruler's request.

The ruler, who lacked belief in Allah, cunningly requested an apple, knowing that it was not the season for apples. He thought that Ghaus-e-Azam would not produce the fruit, thus exposing him as a fraud.

However, with unwavering faith, Ghaus-E-Azam stretched out his hands, and to the ruler's astonishment, two ripe apples appeared in his palms.

Curious, the ruler and Ghaus-E-Azam each took one apple and split them in half to eat. As they opened the fruits, the stark contrast between the two became clear. Ghaus-E-Azam's apple was vibrant, healthy, and devoid of any flaws. The ruler's apple was infested with worms, making it inedible.

Perplexed, the ruler questioned Ghaus-E-Azam about the worms in his apple. Ghaus-E-Azam calmly responded, "Since the hands of the oppressor touched the apple, worms were born inside it."

This profound statement conveyed a powerful message - even the food consumed by those who oppress others is tainted, a symbol of the punishment they will face from Allah.

The incident serves as a reminder of the enduring presence of oppression throughout history. It emphasizes the importance of standing against oppression and upholding the truth, as Ghaus-E-Azam did.

The story conveys the belief that Allah, in His mercy, ensures that even the food consumed by oppressors is not the same as that enjoyed by those who stand against injustice.

The variations of oppression is a recurring theme throughout history, and it is a sad reality that it continues to persist in various forms.

Recent events, such as the ongoing conflict in Palestine, serve as a stark reminder of the enduring nature of oppression. However, what is truly disheartening is the lack of progress in addressing these injustices.

Those who have oppressed others, whether through their actions or their support, bear a significant responsibility for perpetuating evil.

The episode of Palestine has gained widespread attention through social media and technology, which has allowed the voices of the less fortunate to be heard.

Despite attempts to frame the situation differently, the undeniable truth remains that innocent lives are being torn apart. As Muslims, it is our duty to stand up for justice and truth, to support the oppressed, and to expose the oppressors.

Only through collective efforts can we hope to bring about positive change and put an end to the cycle of oppression.

As a land of historical and cultural significance for both Palestinians and Jews. The ongoing Israeli Palestinian conflict has resulted in the oppression and suffering of the Palestinian people, with their basic human rights being violated daily.

The world has witnessed the displacement of millions of Palestinians, the destruction of their homes and infrastructure, and imposing discriminatory laws and policies that restrict their freedom and autonomy.

Despite the clear evidence of oppression, there are still those who turn a blind eye or actively support the oppressors.

This is not only morally unacceptable, but it goes against the teachings of Allah, who calls upon believers to stand up for justice and aid those in need.

Supporting the oppression of the Palestinian people under the guise of religious belief is a grave misconception, as Jesus himself was a Palestinian Jew and a prophet who preached love, compassion, and justice for all.

It is our collective responsibility to speak out against oppression and work towards a just and peaceful resolution for the people of Palestine.

In this society, there are individuals who recognize the power and destructive nature of those who seek to oppress others.

These observant individuals understand that those who protect and enable evil actions are awaiting the inevitable disasters and harsh consequences that live within their own hearts.

While the travel to places like Palestine may be restricted, some individuals choose to volunteer and provide help, while others send funds to support the cause.

Islam does not advocate for the oppressor to torture others but encourages individuals to take a stand against oppression. The question of why Allah does not intervene to stop the oppressors is a common query that weighs on the minds of many.

Despite the toll that the deaths of innocent individuals have taken, those who have died as martyrs, firmly believing in the oneness of Allah with no partners, are still alive in a spiritual sense and hold a rank higher than anyone else.

This is a blessing and a reward for those who have endured suffering. Allah grants opportunities for the just to expose and confront evil, and it is important to remember that time is not a constraint for Allah, as His perception of time differs from that of humans.

The support provided by certain regions to fuel Islamophobia is a continuous and concerning effort. These regions not only provide financial help but also actively promote ideologies that target and discriminate against Muslims.

However, it is important to acknowledge that within these same regions, there is a significant population of individuals who are marginalized and in dire need of support.

Many people in these regions are homeless, forced to live on the streets, and struggle with poverty, hunger, and extreme weather.

Tragically, some individuals even lose their lives because of a lack of help. It is important to note that the beliefs and perspectives of individuals within any religious group can vary. While many Jews do not accept Jesus as the Messiah, it is accurate to say that most Jews reject him outright.

There are Jewish believers in Jesus, often referred to as Messianic Jews, who recognize him as the Savior.

Regarding the connection between Jesus and the Holy Land, it is significant for both Christians and Jews.

Christians believe that Jesus, as the Son of God, walked on the land and performed miracles there. For Jews, the land holds deep historical and religious significance, as it is the promised land of the Hebrew Bible.

The **Al Aqsa Mosque**, in the Old City of Jerusalem, holds immense significance for Muslims around the world.

It is the third holiest site in Islam, after the Kaaba in Mecca and the Prophet's Mosque in Medina. Prophet Muhammad undertook a miraculous night journey, known as the Isra and Miraj, from Mecca to Jerusalem, where he ascended to the heavens and received the gift of Salat (the Muslim prayer) from Allah.

The entire Muslim community received the divine gift of Salat, which made it an integral part of their religious practice.

As a result, the Al-Aqsa Mosque holds a special place in the hearts of Muslims, who consider it not only a sacred site but also a symbol of unity, faith, and the deliverance of a gift he received for his people his ummah.

If Muslims truly recognized the worth of this gift, none of them would ever forsake their Salat. Those who understand its significance would never miss the opportunity to connect with Allah.

As for the assertion that Jesus was a Palestinian Jew, it is important to understand the context of the term "Palestinian" in that time period.

During Jesus' lifetime, the region was under Roman rule, and the term "Palestinian" referred more broadly to the inhabitants of the area, regardless of religious affiliation.

Jesus was indeed born and raised in the region that is now modern-day Israel/Palestine.

However, it is not accurate to claim that Jesus practiced Islam. Islam as a distinct religion did not exist during Jesus' time, as it was founded in the 7th century by the prophet Muhammad. Jesus himself was a devout Jew and preached within the Jewish religious framework.

Just like all other prophets, Jesus brought the message of monotheism, as Islam did as well.

Allah consistently revealed the message of submission to Him, and Islam and the Quran were where the finality of this message was found. The message remains the same: worship one God, Allah, alone.

It is essential to approach religious discussions with respect and an understanding of the diversity within each faith. Different interpretations and beliefs exist within any religious group, and it is crucial to recognize and acknowledge these differences.

The Quran mentions the favor given upon the Jews as the chosen people and Israel as the favored land. However, it is important to note that the exile of the Jews from the land was a consequence of their defiance.

Despite this, Omar E Farooq, the Muslim ruler who governed Jerusalem, invited the Jews to live there. Once the truth has been realized, Islam, as a religion, does not restrict anyone from worshiping anything or anyone.

Under Muslim rule, all three religions - Judaism, Christianity, and Islam - coexisted harmoniously. In contrast, when there was Christian rule, religious warfare and turmoil were prevalent. This situation can be seen even in present times.

Throughout history, people have been drawn to America because of the freedom and independence it offers, making it an attractive destination for many.

When pursuing their own interests, it is crucial to recognize that protecting those who reject Jesus may not be justifiable.

The younger generations in Israel may not possess the same level of familiarity with Jesus as some might presume, resulting in unexpected reactions when his name is brought up.

The international community. The establishment of the State of Israel in 1948 was a response to the atrocities of the Holocaust and a way to provide a homeland for the Jewish people.

However, this has been a source of conflict with the Palestinian people who also claim the land as their own.

The two-state solution, which suggests the creation of an independent Palestinian state alongside Israel, has been proposed to address this issue and bring about peace in the region.

However, those who oppose this solution argue that it would be unjust to forcefully exile Palestinians from their homes and ask them to choose between taking only half or none of their land.

The invitation for Jews to return was not only a recognition of their historical ties to the land but also a reflection of the inclusive nature of Muslim rule.

Jewish and Palestinian people to the land remains an important foundation for seeking a just and fair resolution.

However, it is important to note that the idea of justice does not mean oppressing those who rightfully lived in their homes. Rather, it calls for a just and equitable resolution that takes into account the historical context and the needs of both communities.

The historical significance of the Muslim world and the ethical principles of Islam are not subject to negotiation or oblivion. Instead, they require constant revitalization.

Islam cannot be imposed by any regime; true understanding comes through education, not coercion.

Dementia has indeed become a leading cause of illness among the older adult population, affecting both older adults and the young.

However, it is important to note that the world should not forget the significant contributions made by Muslims throughout history. One such example is their role in providing help and support to Jews during the Holocaust.

While the Christians often overshadow it, it was the Muslims who extended a helping hand and offered refuge and help to Jews, even in the face of adversity.

They welcomed Jews into their countries and provided a haven, long before the atrocities of the Holocaust took place.

This act of compassion and solidarity is not mere rhetoric, but a well-documented part of history. It is crucial to remember and acknowledge the contributions made by Muslims in the past, as it promotes a more inclusive and accurate understanding of our shared history.

However, it is important to acknowledge that Israel's ownership is a complex and contentious one.

The establishment of Israel as a Jewish state in 1948 resulted from historical and political factors, including the Zionist movement's aim to create a homeland for Jewish people.

Many Jews around the world see Israel as their ancestral homeland, rooted in religious and cultural ties. The establishment of Israel resulted in the displacement of the Palestinians and losing their land, which cannot disregard their deep historical and ancestral connection to the land.

The Israeli Palestinian conflict remains a deeply entrenched issue with no simple resolution.

It is crucial to approach this topic with sensitivity and an understanding of the various perspectives and narratives involved.

The stretch in sensitivity becomes hypocrisy when the world is repeatedly urged to address various issues with sensitivity, yet the displacement of Palestinians is met with indifference.

Exile means no return. Foreclosure in Real Estate is when a homeowner loses their house because of financial difficulties, they cannot claim it as their home by force.

Similarly, Jews were invited by Muslims to live harmoniously, not to forcefully take land from those who were exiled by Allah.

There will be days when defiance goes beyond its limits, and this is an actual event. The irony lies in the fact that those who reject Jesus find support from those who accept him.

This displacement has occurred for centuries in order to establish a Zionist estate, a state that did not rightfully belong to those who sought to claim it.

The lack of sensitivity and concern towards the plight of the Palestinians highlights the double standards and hypocrisy in addressing global issues.

During the Muslim rule under Omar bin Khattab in Jerusalem, peace and justice were established based on Quranic law.

This period marked a stark contrast to the chaotic Roman era, which had been plagued by constant warfare and a lack of stability.

Under Muslim rule, Jerusalem flourished and experienced a golden age of progress and prosperity. During this era, scientists made significant scientific discoveries that revolutionized our understanding of the natural world.

One prominent figure was Ibn al-Haytham, also known as Alhazen, who made significant contributions to the field of optics.

His book **"Kitab al-Manazir"** (Book of Optics) revolutionized the understanding of light, refraction, and vision. Alhazen's experiments and observations paved the way for the development of the modern scientific method.

Another notable Muslim scientist was Al-Biruni, who excelled in various fields, including astronomy. He calculated the Earth's circumference using trigonometry and developed precise methods for determining the positions of celestial bodies.

Muslim scientists also made significant advancements in areas such as magnetism, mechanics, and hydrodynamics, building upon the knowledge of earlier civilizations.

Their work not only laid the foundation for modern science but also influenced future scientists in Europe during the Renaissance.

The contributions of Muslim scientists to physics and astronomy highlight the rich scientific heritage of the Islamic world and their role in shaping the progress of human knowledge.

In architecture, iconic structures were erected, showcasing innovative designs and engineering techniques. The Taj Mahal in India and the Palace of Versailles in France are just a few examples of the architectural marvels of this time.

During the dark ages in Europe, Muslims played a significant role in preserving and transmitting knowledge, particularly in literature.

Muslim scholars and intellectuals made significant contributions to various branches of literature, including poetry, philosophy, and storytelling.

They helped to translate and preserve works from ancient Greece and Rome, as well as from other cultures such as Persia and India.

These translations were instrumental in reviving interest in classical literature in Europe and played a crucial role in the intellectual revival known as the Renaissance.

Prominent Muslim figures like Avicenna, Averroes, and Ibn Rushd not only preserved the works of earlier scholars but also made notable advancements in their own right, laying the foundation for later European literary traditions.

Their struggles and dedication to knowledge dissemination during the dark ages were crucial in shaping the literary landscape of Europe.

In the world of literature, there have been renowned authors who have created exceptional works that have left a lasting impact.

Among these great writers are William Shakespeare, Miguel de Cervantes, and John Milton. Their works have brilliantly captured the essence of the human experience.

However, it is important to acknowledge that the Muslim world played a significant role in shaping the literary landscape.

Their contributions were so impactful that people from all over would travel great distances to witness their achievements and learn from them.

This demonstrated that Muslims were not only teachers but also brought humanity together in their pursuit of knowledge and excellence.

In adulterated society, it seems that the predominant focus of current events is often centered on Islamophobia.

Instead of appreciating and recognizing the diverse talents and contributions of individuals, there is a disturbing trend towards using these talents to insult Islam and provoke Muslims.

This kind of behavior does not showcase any genuine talent or worth noticing; rather, it reflects a certain level of arrogance that demeans those who lack intellect.

For example, when someone creates cartoons that depict Prophet Muhammad burning Qurans or disrespecting prayer rugs, their intention is not exercising their right to free speech, but intentionally provoking Muslims.

This act is not an expression of freedom, but a display of ignorance, hatred, and a lack of understanding towards others. Such actions only contribute to the volatility of human emotions fueled by fear, rather than promoting happiness and positive discourse.

It is essential to foster a society that values respectful dialogue and understanding, rather than perpetuating negative stereotypes and promoting division.

While acknowledging the significant contributions of Muslims to the Renaissance, as well as their philanthropy and resistance against ignorance towards others, it is crucial to note that including homosexuality in art finds its origins in Christian regions, not Muslim.

The Renaissance era in Europe saw a revival of interest in classical Greco-Roman art and culture, which often depicted same-sex relationships. Artists during this time drew inspiration from ancient Greek and Roman mythology, where homosexuality was not uncommon.

It is essential to understand that the portrayal of homosexuality in art during the Renaissance was not limited to Christian artists but reflected the broader cultural and historical context of the period.

This principle of abstaining from the depiction of human figures in Islamic art and teachings stems from the concept of tawhid, the belief in the oneness of God.

Islam strictly forbids the worship of idols or any form of polytheism, and the use of human figures in art might lead to idolatry or the deification of individuals.

To avoid any possibility of idol worship or the imitation of pagan deities, Muslims developed a unique artistic tradition that heavily relies on geometric patterns, calligraphy, and natural elements.

This style, known as Islamic geometric or arabesque art, allows Muslims to express their devotion and creativity within the boundaries set by their religious beliefs.

By focusing on non-representational art forms, Muslims prioritize the spiritual essence of their faith rather than the physical representation of individuals or deities.

The arts flourished during this period, with masterpieces created by artists like Leonardo da Vinci, Michelangelo, and Rembrandt.

These works of art continue to inspire and captivate audiences, reflecting the immense talent and creativity of the era.

Wikipedia: Other authors contend that Leonardo was actively homosexual.

Encyclopedia: Michelangelo His homosexuality was widely assumed: One man tempted the artist to accept his son as an apprentice by offering the boy's services in bed.

In ancient Rome, freeborn male citizens enjoyed a certain level of sexual freedom and autonomy. They had the liberty to engage in various sexual activities, including homosexual encounters, without facing significant social or legal consequences.

However, it is important to note that there were certain parameters and expectations that governed these relationships.

The Romans viewed sexuality hierarchically, considering the active, dominant role more socially acceptable than the passive, submissive role.

It was expected that a Roman man engaging in same sex would assume the dominant position, whether with another freeborn male or a male slave.

The age difference between partners was also a factor, with intergenerational relationships being more socially accepted.

While the concept of homosexuality itself was not taboo, societal norms emphasized power dynamics and maintaining the traditional gender roles.

The pattern of homosexuality and same-gender relationships has indeed become more prevalent and accepted in Western societies. Political regimes in these societies have played a role in promoting individuality and supporting the rights of the LGBTQ+ community.

However, it is important to note that Western societies are more individualistic and have a long history of challenging traditional norms and values.

Muslim countries have traditionally adhered to a collective society model, where societal norms and values are deeply rooted in religious beliefs and teachings. In Islamic culture, homosexuality is considered a taboo and same-gender relationships are not accepted.

These societies prioritize the preservation of traditional family structures and adhere to religious principles.

While Western societies may celebrate the freedom of expression and embrace diverse sexual orientations, Muslim countries often face challenges in reconciling these Western values with their own cultural and religious traditions.

This can lead to conflicts and tensions within these societies, as they struggle to balance modernization and preserving their cultural and religious identity.

It is important to recognize that the political, social, and cultural contexts in Muslim countries differ significantly from those in Western societies.

While Western societies may appear to be progressive, but they are backward reviving what was terminated by progressive nature of Islam.

LGBTQ+ rights are not deemed acceptable according to Islam.

The path towards acceptance and inclusion of diverse sexual orientations in these societies may require careful consideration and dialogue, considering the unique cultural and religious contexts in which they exist.

The Romans highly favored this artistic style, known as syncretism, as it allowed them to embrace and celebrate their diverse religious beliefs.

By blending elements from different religious traditions, artists could create a visual language that resonated with a wide audience.

For example, Roman sculptures often depicted figures from Greek mythology alongside biblical characters, such as Hercules and Samson.

Artists blurred the line between the divine and the heroic by depicting these figures in similar poses or with similar attributes.

This fusion of religious and mythological elements not only created visually captivating artworks, but also allowed for deeper interpretations and connections between different belief systems.

It reflected the Romans' fascination with the supernatural and the divine, as well as their desire to bridge the gap not compatible with Islam.

This unique artistic style became highly valued and sought after, influencing not only sculpture but also painting, mosaic, and other forms of artistic expression during the Roman era.

The inviting allure of Leonardo da Vinci, Michelangelo, and Rembrandt lies in their mastery of techniques and their ability to capture the human form with unparalleled realism and emotion.

Their art explores a wide range of subjects, from religious and mythological themes to portraits and landscapes.

However, it is important to note that the art of the Muslim world, particularly during the Islamic Golden Age, was in line with the beliefs and principles of Islam.

Islamic art, characterized by its intricate geometric patterns, calligraphy, and vibrant colors, often focused on depicting the beauty of the natural world and the spiritual realm.

It avoided the representation of human figures, as it was believed to be disrespectful and potentially idolatrous.

Thus, while the art of Leonardo da Vinci, Michelangelo, and Rembrandt may captivate with its realism and exploration of the human form, the art of the Muslim world followed a different aesthetic and philosophical path, reflecting the values and teachings of Islam.

Despite this, Islam played a pivotal role in fostering progress, ensuring that paintings and architecture remained free from offensive displays of nudity and homosexuality.

This intellectual exchange led to groundbreaking discoveries and inventions, such as the development of algebra, the decimal system, and advancements in astronomy.

Constantinople in 1453, fulfilling this prophecy. Sultan Mehmet II, also known as Mehmed the Conqueror, led the Ottoman Empire to the siege of Constantinople. After a long and intense battle, the city fell to the Ottoman forces on May 29, 1453.

This conquest marked a significant turning point in history, as it brought an end to the Byzantine Empire and established the Ottoman Empire as a major power in the region.

This event was foretold by Prophet Muhammad, who had prophesied that Muslims would one day rule over Constantinople. Conquering Constantinople, Sultan Mehmet II fulfilled Prophet Muhammad's prophecy, establishing the Ottoman Empire as a major power in the region.

Quran: Surah Rum: 30:2. The Romans have been defeated.

There are indeed differences between Christianity and Islam, but the Quran does highlight the commonalities and shared beliefs between the two faiths.

One verse in the Quran Surah Al-Maidah, states that among the closest to Muslims in friendship and understanding are Christians.

This verse recognizes that Christians, despite their theological differences, have a closer affinity to Muslims compared to followers of other faiths.

It is worth noting that there is a growing trend of Christians embracing Islam, which can be attributed to various factors such as personal spiritual journeys, interfaith dialogue, and a genuine interest in understanding different religions.

This phenomenon suggests that there is a level of compatibility and resonance between the teachings of Christianity and Islam that resonates with some Christians, leading them to accept Islam.

Quran: Surah Maidah: 5:82. You will surely find the most bitter towards the believers to be the Jews and polytheists and the most gracious to be those who call themselves Christian. That is because there are priests and monks among them and because they are not arrogant.

Overall, the legacy of these time periods is one of intellectual curiosity, cultural exchange, and a commitment to inclusivity and justice.

This period of Muslim rule in Jerusalem stands as a historic memorandum that highlights the positive impact of implementing Quranic principles in governance.

Although Jesus was given the Injeel (gospel), the Christian Bible and the Quran hold contrasting views on monotheism.

The confusion arising from the portrayal of monotheism in the Bible, resembling aspects of mythology and Hinduism, frequently leads individuals to turn to Islam for better understanding.

In Islam, there is no mention of God having sons or daughters, which further highlights the stark contrast in beliefs between Islam and Christianity.

In contrast, the Bible states in Genesis, that giants had sons of gods. The Quran and the Bible present different perspectives on the same subject, resulting in contrasting beliefs.

Notably, the political aspects of the Quran have remained unchanged.

Bible: KJV: Genesis: 6:4. There were giants in the earth in those days; and also, after that, when the sons of God came in unto the daughters of men, and they bear children to them, the same became mighty men which were of old, men of renown.

Quran: Surah Isra: 17:111."Praise to Allah, who has not taken a son and has had no partner in [His] dominion and has no [need of a] protector out of weakness; and glorify Him with [great] glorification."

In Islam, Allah is the one and only God, who is transcendent and beyond human comprehension. He is not a human being, but a divine being with no physical form or limitations.

According to the Quran, Allah does not have children or any offspring, as He is the eternal and self-sufficient creator of all things.

Allah is described as being free from any need for rest or sleep, as He is continuously vigilant of everything that occurs in the universe.

The concept of Allah's divine attributes and nature is central to Islamic theology and is emphasized in the teachings of the Quran and the hadiths.

CHAPTER 12
KNOWING TRUTH VERSUS FALSEHOOD

In a society that swings at full force to allocate allegations, the power dynamics are heavily skewed, and fear becomes the dominant tool used to maintain control.

Unfortunately, one of the primary sources of fear-spreading rhetoric in such societies is the Islamophobic regions.

These regions, driven by prejudice and ignorance, perpetuate a distorted and often malicious narrative about Islam and its followers.

This fear-mongering leads to a toxic environment where individuals are demonized and marginalized based on their religious beliefs, further deepening divisions and perpetuating discrimination.

Indeed, individuals have the freedom to choose their religion, and no one should be coerced into it.

While the condemnation of force may be present in certain situations, it is impossible to compel one's heart and soul to believe in something—it must arise from within.

Many individuals who find their way to Islam have gone through a deep and exhaustive search for inner peace, a respite from the turmoil within their souls.

For them, Islam offers a sense of finality and tranquility.

However, these converts often face challenges in integrating into Muslim communities or forming alliances through marriage, which can sometimes lead to divisions within their former families.

It can be an arduous task to reconcile two faiths that were once united under one roof.

Contrary to popular belief, Muslims do not fear non-Muslims; rather, it is the non-Muslims who continuously spread propaganda and exploit the situation, leading to societal ignorance.

The incessant disrespect and burning of the Quran by those who harbor hatred towards Islam only serve to further fuel the flames of animosity.

Those who exploit situations to manipulate the idea that family is more important than changing beliefs and show disrespect by crossing boundaries are individuals filled with ignorance. Islam has warned against ignorance.

They have yet to discover inner peace and harbor animosity towards those who have found it, whether they are family members or friends.

This hatred knows no limits, as Satan manipulates the closest person to become one's worst enemy. Ignorance about how the enemy can infiltrate one's life stems from a lack of understanding and faith in Islam.

Those who understand that faith comes from within cannot be coerced or swayed by the shadows of evil, which can manifest both openly in public and discreetly in the confines of homes where hatred towards Islam lives.

For believers, the enforcement of their faith over familial ties is not a dilemma, but a conviction rooted in their unwavering belief. History has shown that believers have sacrificed their lives to protect their faith, refusing to let go of the profound spiritual connection they have found in Islam.

News Reuters: Jun 29, 2023 — A man tore up and burned a Koran outside Stockholm's central mosque on Wednesday, an event that risks angering Turkey as Sweden bids to join...

News NBC: Apr 30, 2023 — The burnt cardboard box and a partially melted gas can were left behind in the stall. Worshippers in the mosque helped extinguish the flames,...

News BBC: May 16, 2024 — At least 11 worshippers have been killed and dozens of others injured after a man attacked a mosque in Nigeria's northern Kano state...

Star Tribune: May 17, 2023 — A St. Paul Mosque was heavily damaged by fire in a suspected arson Wednesday, in what would be the sixth attack on Muslim houses of worship ...

AP News: May 16, 2024 — Footage broadcast by the local TVC station showed charred walls and burned furniture in the mosque, the main place of worship for Gadan village ...

In a world where fear and hatred against Islam seem to dominate, it is important to acknowledge that this sentiment not only permeates the media but also exists within families where individuals have embraced the Islamic faith.

These individuals face ongoing abuse and discrimination from their own family members who hold a deep-seated animosity towards Islam. This fear of Islam extends beyond familial relationships, affecting personal connections as well.

However, those who have experienced this firsthand and have unwavering faith in Islam often leave these toxic environments and return even stronger, ready to help others who have faced similar challenges.

Islam, as a faith, aims to establish a framework for individuals to lead a balanced and fulfilling life. It emphasizes the importance of having a clear moral compass and a strong connection with Allah.

Islam recognizes that human beings have free will and encourages them to make choices that align with the guidance provided in the Quran. The Quran, being the last revelation from Allah, serves as a comprehensive guide for all aspects of life, addressing issues ranging from personal conduct to societal matters.

It provides a roadmap for individuals to navigate through the complexities of life and make decisions that are in line with their Creator's will.

Islam does not seek to restrict or limit an individual's life, but aims to remove the constraints that may lead to chaos and unrest.

By adhering to the principles and teachings of Islam, individuals can find peace, tranquility, and purpose, while also being accountable for their actions and behavior.

Sometimes, individuals who initially harbored hate or fear towards Islam have undergone a change of heart and found solace in the teachings of Islam themselves.

As a Muslim, it is not only important but also a religious duty to assist and guide fellow Muslims who may experience a downfall. Rather than adopting a non-judgmental stance and turning a blind eye, it is essential to offer support and redirect them towards the right path.

By neglecting this responsibility, one not only risks the displeasure of Allah, but also perpetuates the harm caused by their inaction.

It is akin to planting a tree and then neglecting to water it, leading to its eventual demise. Neglecting to help a fellow Muslim in need raises questions from Allah about one's commitment to the well-being of others.

However, it is crucial to acknowledge that despite our best efforts, the ultimate outcome is in the hands of Allah and the individual themselves. We can only do our part in guiding and supporting, leaving the outcome to Allah's divine wisdom.

It is essential to understand that Islam, as a religion, does not promote fear or hatred towards non-believers, nor does it engage in spreading propaganda.

However, Islam allows for retaliation against those who abuse Muslims, as turning the other cheek can be seen as hypocritical. Above all else, a Muslim prioritizes their faith, standing up for their beliefs and remaining steadfast in the face of adversity.

Quran: Surah Mumtahanah: 60:8. Allah does not forbid you from those who do not fight you because of religion and do not expel you from your homes—from being righteous toward them and acting justly toward them. Indeed, Allah loves those who act justly.

Justice is indeed a fundamental principle in Islam, as the Quran emphasizes the importance of standing against oneself if one is in the wrong. Hypocrisy and cowardice behavior have no place in the teachings of Islam.

While individuals may exhibit traits that do not align with their faith, the essence of Islam remains flawless and has the power to shape the lives of its followers, who truly understand and embrace its teachings.

The Quran's purpose was not only to impose limitations but also to shape and bring advantages to humanity. Allah, being all-knowing, understands the perfect timing for the delivery of His message.

Just as schools start with basic Alphabets and Numerics before progressing to more complex subjects, Allah sent the Quran as the last revelation, completing the teachings of all Abrahamic faiths, when humanity was ready.

This divine timing is a testament to Allah's wisdom.

Historically, the Muslim world has served as a center of knowledge and education, and Muslims have always encouraged sharing their wisdom with the world.

Today, the world is engaged in discussions and debates about Islam, and it is crucial for Muslims to come together in unity rather than discord to address the misconceptions and promote a better understanding of their faith.

Unity among Muslims can contribute to a more harmonious and fruitful dialogue with the rest of the world, ultimately fostering peace and mutual respect.

The consequences of this Islamophobic rhetoric are far-reaching, as it not only stigmatizes innocent individuals but also contributes to the erosion of social cohesion and the violation of human rights.

Happiness is a fleeting moment, especially for those who do not comprehend the true nature of this journey. It is not dependent on external forces, but deeply rooted in the authority of Allah. It requires observance not to be neglected.

Addressing and challenging this Islamophobia is crucial for fostering a more inclusive and tolerant society where people are valued for who they are, rather than being subjected to baseless fear and hatred.

People feared when Prophet Muhammad returned from Medina after he was driven out by his own people because they were uncertain of what his intentions and actions would be.

Many viewed his return as a potential threat to their way of life and existing power structures. They worried he would seek revenge against those who had opposed him or attempt to establish a new order that would disrupt their social, political, and economic systems.

Prophet Muhammad had gained a significant following during his time in Medina, and people were concerned about the influence he would have over his loyal supporters.

The uncertainty and fear surrounding his return created a tense atmosphere among the people.

The believers in monotheism and the polytheistic society of Mecca. The ruling elite and powerful tribes felt threatened by Prophet Muhammad's message, as it challenged their authority and the established order.

They feared losing their power, influence, and control over the people. They oppressed, persecuted, and marginalized the early Muslims.

Prophet Muhammad and his followers faced various forms of injustice and cruelty. They were subjected to verbal abuse, physical violence, and economic boycotts.

The believers were ridiculed, mocked, and ostracized from their families and communities. Many endured severe persecutions, including torture and even death.

Despite these immense challenges, Prophet Muhammad and his followers remained steadfast in their beliefs and continued to spread the message of monotheism.

It is a disservice to Islam to be born as a Muslim or to convert to Islam without truly understanding and getting to know the faith.

Islam is a vibrant and rich religion that teaches principles of justice and the consequences that follow injustice.

Sometimes it may seem like Islam has not served its purpose, but this perception often stems from those who do not fully appreciate or take the teachings of Islam seriously.

Understanding the challenges and sacrifices that Prophet Muhammad faced to establish and spread Islam should never be forgotten.

These memories should remain present for those who truly understand the value and significance of Islam. Understanding is crucial in the faith of Islam, as it remains a steadfast structure.

Following is not coerced, even for Muslims, but consequences are inevitable.

Society today shows the prevalence of disbelievers and those who harbor hatred towards Islam. Instances of disrespect towards the Quran and prayer rugs have occurred, where individuals have burned and thrown them.

The person who expresses a strong dislike for ongoing disrespectful and ignorant remarks in social media and domestic settings, along with actions that promote uninformed beliefs.

While Muslims are not obliged to retaliate in every situation, provocation can often lead to unrest because of lack of knowledge and uninformed choices.

The existence of common sense allows us to understand that if individuals who harbor hatred towards Islam did not fear its influence in the world and in households, there would be no need for them to express their hate through rudeness, dismantling, and disrespecting Islam.

News weak: May 9th 2024: Republicans warn of massive Muslim takeover.

Islamophobia is a prevalent issue in today's political landscape, with many politicians and individuals harboring unfounded fears and prejudices towards Muslims.

However, it is crucial to recognize that these fears are rooted in ignorance and misinformation.

The Muslim community has a rich history of making valuable contributions to the world. They have achieved noteworthy progress in diverse fields, including science, mathematics, art, philosophy, and more.

It is crucial to highlight the vast knowledge and teachings that Muslims have gained and continue to share; in order to address the unfounded fears some may have towards their pursuit of education.

Islamic teachings emphasize the importance of compassion, charity, and community service, which are values that Muslims actively practice.

It is important for individuals to educate themselves about Islam and engage in meaningful conversations with Muslims to dispel misconceptions and promote a more inclusive and understanding society.

Muslims are not a threat to the world; rather, they have the potential to be powerful agents of positive change and progress.

Fear and ignorance often give rise to actions such as throwing objects, destroying property, burning items or the Quran, and spreading harmful rhetoric.

Muslims have no fear of any other faith taking over because they firmly believe in the truth of Islam.

They do not seek to demolish statues of idol worshippers, the Bible, or the Torah, as they understand the importance of respecting other religions and their symbols.

Muslims follow the teachings of the Quran and prophet Muhammad, as Islam is a comprehensive belief system that encompasses both faith and knowledge.

It acknowledges the existence of hate since the time Islam became the last testament among the Abrahamic faiths.

A deep comprehension of this faith can only be attained through education. Muslims effectively challenge misconceptions and prejudices by promoting organization, fairness, and acceptance of other faiths through their knowledge and advocacy.

However, Muslims have endured far more trials than just the physical desecration of Islamic symbols. Islam lives in the hearts of those who have embraced its truth and teachings.

It is not merely a commitment to living in the same environment, but a commitment to the principles and values that Islam upholds. The endurance and visibility of faith is a testament to true commitment.

Allah is aware of those who harbor hatred, and while many Muslims have understandably reacted to this behavior, it is important to recognize that ignorance requires attention.

The education of Islam and the unity of Muslims that will address the complexity of misunderstanding Islam.

Education and understanding play crucial roles in achieving success. Remaining stagnant is a sure path to failure, while progress and enlightenment pave the way for genuine success.

Throughout history, Muslims have faced provocation and disrespect towards their faith, a trend that can be traced back to the time of Prophet Muhammad.

However, it is important to note that Allah has always provided an antidote for those who engage in such acts of hate. The consequences for those who disrespect Islam will be severe, as the result will be far worse than the initial provocation.

Monotheism has been the favored religion by Allah since the beginning of creation, and it remains a central principle of Islam. This monotheistic belief serves as a testament to the unity and oneness of Allah.

Although Islam was not initially referred to by its name, it is undeniable that monotheism is consistent with Islamic beliefs.

In a later **Surah**, Allah stated Islam is the only favored religion, because of its nature of monotheism and its recognition of all the prophets sent by Allah to the Abrahamic faiths, as they were recipients of divine revelations.

Quran: Surah Imran: 3:19. Indeed, the religion in the sight of Allah is Islam. And those who were given the scripture did not dodder except after knowledge had come to them out of jealous animosity between themselves. And whoever disbelieves in the verses of Allah, then indeed, Allah is swift in taking account.

Muslims have a responsibility to promote and protect their faith, steadfastly opposing any form of provocation or disrespect.

It is an educational duty for informed Muslims to speak out against misrepresentations and distortions of Islam in order to counteract falsehood and bring forth the truth.

The Muslims endured these injustices with patience, resilience, and unwavering faith. Over time, as the number of Muslims grew, the resistance against Prophet Muhammad also intensified.

However, it is important to note that not all individuals in Mecca opposed Prophet Muhammad's message. There were some who recognized his sincerity, integrity, and wisdom.

They acknowledged the need for reform and were attracted to the principles of monotheism and social justice that he preached.

These individuals, known as the early converts to Islam, played a crucial role in supporting and protecting the Prophet and his followers amidst the prevailing injustice.

The examples of injustice faced by Prophet Muhammad and the early Muslims serve as a reminder of the challenges faced by those who advocate for change and social justice.

It highlights the resistance and hostility that often accompany efforts to challenge established norms and power structures.

The perseverance of Prophet Muhammad and his followers ultimately led to the establishment and spread of Islam, which continues to influence millions of people worldwide.

The oppression of the Israelites by the Pharaoh in ancient Egypt is a significant event in religious history.

According to the biblical narrative, the Pharaoh enslaved the Israelites and subjected them to harsh condition.

Egypt is a prime illustration of a Muslim country, just like Israel will be, eventually. Through the rise and fall of nations, the rightful owners of the land will be revealed - those who are righteous.

Recognizing the importance of truth and its proper conveyance is essential for Muslims. Mere coexistence falls short;

The Quran sheds light on the truth regarding the exile of certain individuals, the impossibility of acquiring property or land through force, and the tragic genocide of others.

It serves as a guide for understanding the tests and trials that will shape the future.

However, it is important to note that the concept of monotheism, the belief in one supreme God, predates the formal establishment of Islam as a religion.

The idea of worshiping a singular deity can be traced back to the ancient civilizations of the world. Many ancient cultures, including the ancient Egyptians, Sumerians, and Babylonians, had beliefs centered on a supreme God or creator.

In this sense, the worship of one God can be seen as a fundamental aspect of human spirituality.

Islam, as a religion, emerged in the 7th century CE with the teachings of the Prophet Muhammad.

While the name **'Islam'** was given to this specific faith later on, the concept of worshiping one God, known as Allah in Arabic, predates the formal establishment of Islam.

The Abrahamic tradition, which includes Judaism, Judeo Christianity, and Islam, recognizes the belief in one God as a cornerstone of faith.

Therefore, while Hinduism can be one of the oldest religions, Islam can also claim a long-standing history as the first religion of humanity that worshiped one God.

Islam has contributed significantly to the spiritual and cultural heritage of humanity.

It is not to blame Islamophobia, as that would be hypocritical for Muslims. Instead, it is the fear, doubt, and sadness that distinguishes a believer from a disbeliever.

The disbeliever feels remorse and carries a heavy heart, while the believer is light-hearted and possesses a faith that surpasses imagination.

Fear is no match for a Muslim, as the power of Allah surpasses sadness, doubt, and all negativities.

When non-believers witness Muslims not behaving according to expectations, they gain control. However, it is important to note that Satan preys on the weak, not the strong.

Omar bin Khattab, a staunch believer and a convert to Islam, was feared by Satan. He held the legacy of truth and justice.

In fact, it only perpetuates the cycle of fear and misunderstanding that has plagued societies throughout history.

By stoking the flames of Islamophobia, individuals are essentially fanning the fire of prejudice and discrimination, which has never truly been extinguished.

The inclination to combat Islam with Islamophobia is not just unproductive, but it also overlooks the extensive history and varied essence of Islam as a religion.

It is the mindset of certain Muslims that contributes to no power, which is as hollow as a bow without an arrow. Life is predetermined, but so are our actions.

It is an opportunity to act and not submit to tyrants. Islam is about standing up for justice, even if it means standing alone amidst a crowd of dishonest individuals.

It can recognize that most Muslims are peaceful, law-abiding citizens who contribute positively to their communities.

Instead of perpetuating Islamophobia, it is imperative to promote dialogue, understanding, and education as an effective means to address any concerns or misconceptions surrounding Islam.

In these countries, the political arena often uses social media as a tool to instill fear and maintain control over the masses.

They manipulate information and spread false narratives to create a sense of political unrest and chaos, thus justifying their actions and suppressing any opposition.

However, this ironic situation is further compounded because these regimes are driven by greed and self-interest.

Their tactics are not aimed at benefiting the people or promoting truth, but at consolidating their power and maintaining their own wealth and privileges. As a result, the news, which is supposed to be an unbiased source of information, becomes a tool for manipulation and propaganda.

This is especially challenging for those who cannot travel or have limited access to education, as they heavily rely on television and social media for information, which is often distorted and misleading.

Therefore, the truth becomes elusive, and those who are aware of the reality struggle to find a reliable source of knowledge and understanding amidst the sea of false narratives.

Only through empathy, tolerance, and mutual respect can we hope to foster a world where people of different faiths can coexist harmoniously.

Islam is a monotheistic religion that strongly emphasizes the belief in one God, Allah. It instructs its adherents to show respect for the beliefs of others and encourages tolerance and comprehension.

The Quran highlights the significance of treating individuals with kindness and respect, irrespective of their religious convictions.

It is encouraged for Muslims to take part in dialogue and peacefully coexist with individuals of diverse religious beliefs. Going against the teachings of Islam disrespecting the faith of others can have negative repercussions in society.

It has the potential to disrupt harmony, create divisions, and lead to conflicts. To cultivate a harmonious and inclusive society, it is vital to encourage mutual respect and understanding between individuals of diverse faiths and beliefs.

Those who will endure disrespect towards Islam are lacking respect regarding their own religious beliefs. However, true believers will show respect for other faiths, even where their ideologies diverge.

This is important in our society, where social media can spread both positive and negative messages.

The lands have been home to various faiths, but coexisting under one roof with different beliefs has proven to be challenging.

Muslims in Islam are encouraged to always include Allah in their conversations, as they believe no discussion is incomplete without mentioning Him.

Israel or the Holy Land during biblical times. The history of Jerusalem is indeed complex and multifaceted.

While Islam holds great significance in the city, it is important to acknowledge that Jerusalem has been a spiritual and cultural center for multiple religions throughout its history.

Omar bin Khattab, the second caliph of Islam, did indeed grant certain rights to Jews during his rule. Islam has never failed humanity.

However, it is also essential to recognize that the establishment of the State of Israel in 1948 resulted from various factors, including Zionist aspirations for a Jewish homeland and the aftermath of the Holocaust.

The situation in Jerusalem continues to be a deeply contentious issue, with ongoing political and religious conflicts.

It is crucial to approach this topic with sensitivity, as the hypocrisy is so obvious for those who support this regime.

While some may argue that the conflict between Israel and Palestine is equivalent to a war, it is important to recognize the disparities in power dynamics.

Israel, backed by superpowers like the United States, possesses a significant advantage in terms of military capabilities and international support. Palestine lacks the same level of backing and resources, making it an uneven playing field.

This power imbalance has led to severe consequences for the Palestinian people, including displacement, loss of lives, and limited access to necessities.

Therefore, it is essential to acknowledge and address this disparity when discussing the situation in the region.

Islam does indeed have clear guidelines and rules regarding wars. According to Islamic teachings, engaging in warfare is permissible only where the rights of others are not being oppressed and there is a just cause.

However, Islam also emphasizes the importance of conducting wars in a fair and equitable manner.

It is not acceptable to wage a war against a weak and oppressed opponent who is defenseless and easily targeted, as exemplified by the situation in Palestine.

Islam calls for a just and balanced approach to warfare, where both sides have a fair chance of defending themselves and protecting their rights.

The oppression and mistreatment faced by the people of Palestine is a stark violation of these principles, as they have long been subjected to unfair treatment and violations of their basic human rights.

During times of oppression, it is crucial to address the situation with honesty and provide genuine answers. Brushing off the issue as controversial landings only perpetuates the cycle of oppression and prevents progress.

The truth never is controversial; it is a fundamental necessity in order to bring about justice and change. However, those who wish to maintain the status quo often resort to spreading lies and misinformation to divert attention from the truth.

Islam is not a religion that actively pursues proselytization or forcefully seeks converts.

Its purpose is to provide non-Muslims with an understanding of the concept of Allah, as described in the books sent and since the beginning of creation.

Allah is not a human being and will not take on the form of a human. Allah ultimately decides when someone will be guided towards the faith of Islam, deciding to embrace it is in His power.

Islam provides guidance and understanding, but the ultimate authority rests with Allah.

The invitation to embrace Islam is not imposed on anyone, but once someone willingly converts to Islam, they are expected to follow the teachings and principles of the religion.

These commands and obligations are not designed to limit or hinder individuals, but instead to promote progress and personal development.

The actions of ignorant Muslims can indeed have a profound impact on the entire ummah, as Islam emphasizes unity and collective responsibility.

When individuals within the ummah engage in misguided or ignorant actions, it not only tarnishes the reputation of Islam, but also affects the perception of Muslims as a whole.

Such actions can reinforce negative stereotypes, breed division within the ummah, and contribute to the misunderstanding and discrimination faced by Muslims worldwide.

When ignorant Muslims act contrary to the teachings of Islam, it hinders the progress and development of the ummah.

Therefore, it is crucial for Muslims to seek knowledge, practice Islam with wisdom and understanding, and strive to promote unity, tolerance, and positive contributions to society.

By doing so, the ummah can counteract the negative impact of the actions of the ignorant and present a more accurate representation of Islam to the world.

Even individuals born into the Muslim faith can occasionally stray or be enticed by the appeal of independence in specific circumstances.

Despite this, Islam presents a path that may occasionally feel confining, yet ultimately leads to spiritual liberation and enlightenment.

The path ahead necessitates certain limitations for the betterment of individuals, but it is important to acknowledge that Allah, being the creator, is not in need of anything from humanity.

With Islamophobia, there is a particular rhetoric that aims to misdirect the masses and create a climate where falsehoods about Islam and Muslims can thrive.

When lies are repeated frequently enough, people who lack knowledge on the subject may believe them, further perpetuating the cycle of oppression and discrimination.

It is essential to challenge these lies and promote the truth in order to combat oppression effectively.

Quran: Surah Fath: 48:6. Also so that He may punish hypocrite men and women and polytheistic men and women, who harbor evil thoughts of Allah. May ill fate befall them! Allah is displeased with them. He has condemned them and prepared for them Hell. What an evil!

Bible Hub: 25:46. Then Jesus said, "Those people will be punished forever. But the ones who pleased God will have eternal life." And these shall go into everlasting punishment."

Within Islam, all prophets, including Jesus, delivered the unified message of monotheism and surrendering to God's will. The Quran highlights the coherence of its message and presents itself as a direct and uncorrupted communication from God.

In contrast to other religious scriptures, the Quran does not attribute divine qualities or consider any prophet as a deity or embodiment of God.

It conveys the belief that death after judgement leads to either heaven or hell, with this current life serving as a test and a chance for people to ready themselves for the afterlife.

Muslims do not believe in the concept of eternal life on Earth in Islam, as they view death as a transition to another existence.

The focus is on recognizing and worshiping the sole creator, rather than substituting Him with other Gods.

Islam teaches that individuals who associate partners with God or veer away from the belief in one God will face consequences.

Its multiple mentions emphasize Galilee's significant religious and historical importance in the New Testament of the Bible.

It is also worth noting that Galilee is known for its picturesque landscapes, including the Sea of Galilee, which biblical accounts associate with several miracles performed by Jesus.

The region of Galilee played a crucial role in the life and ministry of Jesus, as it was where he grew up and began his teachings, gathering a group of disciples who would later become his apostles.

As it is duly noted, the different versions of the Bible are many and varied.

These versions can vary in terms of translation, interpretation, and textual sources. Some of the most well-known versions include **the King James Version (KJV), New International Version (NIV), and English Standard Version (ESV).**

There are versions that cater to specific religious denominations or academic purposes, such as the Catholic Bible, Jewish Tanakh, or the scholarly **New Revised Standard Version (NRSV).**

One Quran no authors except Allah the revealer of his words.

The variations among these versions can affect the wording, phrasing, and even the meaning of certain passages, leading to nuanced differences in understanding and interpretation.

Individuals and religious communities may choose the version that aligns most closely with their beliefs and preferences.

It is a valid viewpoint to argue that Jesus himself had no direct influence on the writings in the Bible.

Furthermore, the process of compiling the Bible involved the selection and inclusion of various texts, some of which were written by authors who were not considered prophets.

The New Testament, for instance, includes letters written by Paul and other early Christian leaders, as well as the Book of Acts, which documents the early history of the Christian movement.

The human writings influenced the final composition of the Bible, potentially diluting and altering the original revelations of the divine that Jesus himself received.

The new authors who took over the writing process mixed their own perspectives and interpretations with the core teachings of Jesus.

The question of the extent of Jesus' direct influence on the writings in the Bible continues to be a subject of scholarly debate and personal interpretation.

The gospel per Quran, known as **"Injeel,"** was given to **Isa** (Jesus) son of Mary in accordance with Islamic belief monotheism.

According to the Quran, Isa was a prophet and messenger of Allah, and the Injeel was revealed to him as guidance for the people of his time.

However, it is important to note that while Moses requested to see Allah, he could not do so because of the limitations of his human form. Islam asserts that no human being can fully comprehend or see Allah, as He is beyond human perception.

Therefore, Islam rejects the idea of Jesus walking on earth as a vessel to God, as it goes against the belief that Allah cannot be seen in His entirety.

According to the Quran and Islamic teachings, if anyone claims to have seen Allah in a human form, it is incompatible with the concept of God in Islam.

Mark Luke was a physician and a historian who wrote the Gospel of Luke and the Acts of the Apostles.

His Gospel provides a detailed account of the life, teachings, death, and resurrection of Jesus, while the Acts of the Apostles chronicles the early Christian community and the missionary journeys of Paul.

Paul was a zealous persecutor of Christians before his encounter with dreams of Jesus on the road to Damascus.

This transformative experience led him to become one of the most influential figures in the early Christian movement.

Paul, originally known as Saul, was a devout Pharisee who ardently persecuted early Christians, considering them a threat to Judaism.

He played a significant role in the stoning of Stephen, one of the first Christian martyrs. However, everything changed for Paul during his journey to Damascus.

During these encounters, Paul expressed visions that were not foretold by Jesus, challenging his behavior and revealing him as a successor.

While Jesus mentioned the truth of a voice, it was Prophet Muhammad who was specifically named as Ahmed, one of his names. However, Paul, despite playing a significant role in shaping Christendom, was not mentioned in this context.

Bible: KJV: Songs of Solomon; 5:16. His mouth is most sweet: yea, he is altogether lovely. This is my beloved, and this is my friend, O daughters of Jerusalem.

In the scripture prior to the Quran, there are several references to the mention of Prophet Muhammad.

One such mention can be found in the Bible, specifically in the Song of Solomon 5:16, where it states, "Hiko Mamittakim we kullo Muhammadim Zehdoodeh wa Zehraee Bayna Jerusalem."

This verse is interpreted by scholars as a reference to Prophet Muhammad, with "Hikko Mamittakim" meaning "the most handsome" and "Muhammadin" meaning "the praised one."

In the Mishnah Torah (Hilchot Melakhim 11:10–12), a comprehensive Jewish legal code written by the renowned scholar Maimonides, **Muhammad is indeed mentioned by name.** Maimonides states that Muhammad is the final prophet in a line of prophetic succession, indicating that no new prophets will arise after him.

This assertion aligns with the Islamic belief that Muhammad was the last and final messenger of God. The inclusion of Muhammad's name in a Jewish legal text demonstrates the recognition of his significance and influence, even within a different religious tradition.

This mention of Prophet Muhammad in the scripture prior to the Quran emphasizes his significance and presence even before the revelation of the Quran.

Islam, as revealed through the Quran, aims to provide clarity and remove any doubts or uncertainties that may exist in the minds of individuals.

It does not rely on assumptions or vague interpretations, but presents its teachings in a direct and straightforward manner.

According to the book, "The Vedas" it suggests that there are prophecies of Muhammad within Hindu scriptures, specifically the Vedas.

One such example is found in the Atharvaveda Kuntapa Sukta, known as the 'Narasamsha.' This Sukta is used to praise individuals, and within it, the word "Muhammad" is interpreted as meaning "praise." Supporters of this theory argue that the Sukta's description aligns with the prophecy of Muhammad.

The point to take home is that while the Abrahamic faiths, which include Judaism, Christianity, and Islam, are directly connected to the Quran, belief in one God has existed for centuries before these religions.

Throughout history, many prophets have emerged in various lands, teaching the principles of monotheism and spreading messages of goodness and righteousness.

However, the Abrahamic faiths specifically mention the prophets whom Allah addressed and reveal His guidance through the Quran.

These faiths emphasize the importance of following the teachings of these chosen prophets to attain spiritual enlightenment.

The Quran serves as a source of guidance, delivering its message with no ambiguity or confusion. It is like a refreshing rain that nourishes the soul, washing away any clouds of doubt and providing a clear understanding of the divine truths.

Through its clear and direct delivery, the Quran offers a profound understanding of life's purpose, the nature of God, moral values, and the path to salvation is through deeds and belief in one God.

It is a divine scripture that invites individuals to ponder, reflect, and embrace the teachings that lead to spiritual enlightenment and guidance.

Quran" Surah Aaraf: 7:33. "Say (O Muhammad): (But) the things that my Lord has indeed forbidden are Al-Fawaahish (great evil sins and every kind of unlawful sexual intercourse) whether committed openly or secretly, sins (of all kinds), unrighteous oppression, joining partners (in worship) with Allah for which He has given no authority, and saying things about Allah of which you have no knowledge"

Islam is often seen as a culmination of the Abrahamic faiths, as it acknowledges the teachings of previous prophets, including Jesus and Moses.

Jesus specifically mentioned prophet Muhammad, the final messenger in Islam, in the Quran, showing a connection between their teachings.

The Prophet Muhammad referred to Jesus as his brother, reinforcing the unity of their message.

These modifications, made by individuals, have resulted in a lack of consistency and the inability to distinguish between what was written by man and what was divinely ordained by God.

In contrast, Islam claims to have preserved the original writings with no changes or additions.

This is supported because there are no intact original scripts of the Bible available today because of the many translations, interpretations, and versions that have been produced over the centuries by various hands

The irony lies in the misconception that the doctrine of passivity within religion is an inaccurate representation of reality.

In truth, history has shown that numerous wars have been fought within Christendom, leading many of the younger generations to question the role of religion in political unrest.

However, it is important to note that religion will always remain a fundamental aspect of human existence, as faith is deeply rooted in one's convictions.

The influence of Western culture on the newer generations has further exacerbated the pursuit of material indulgence and superficial beauty, causing a decline in religious adherence.

The religion of Allah, Islam, is an eternal force that transcends the actions of individuals. Regardless of who adheres to it or strays away, Islam will persist.

This temporary exploration of alternative paths may be inherent to human nature's inclination towards self-indulgence and the creation of personal laws.

However, it is essential to recognize that the laws and regulations prescribed by Allah are immutable and superior to those devised by humans. Islam, with its steadfast commitment to monotheism, is here to stay.

The continuous stream of understanding thus highlights the challenges faced in maintaining the integrity and authenticity of the biblical text.

Muslims and Caliphs played a significant role in the spread of Islam, with figures like Omar bin Khattab, who was a prominent convert and influential leader.

However, it is important to note that throughout history, the Quran has remained unchanged, as Muslims believe it to be the literal word of Allah.

The original script of the Bible is indeed considered lost, as the earliest manuscripts we have today are copies made centuries after the events they describe.

The Bible is a compilation of different books written by numerous authors over a span of several centuries.

Understanding these distinctions between the two religions can foster dialogue and promote mutual understanding among their followers.

It allows for a deeper appreciation of the diverse perspectives on spirituality and the different ways people choose to connect with the divine.

Zionism is a political ideology that advocates for the establishment and maintenance of a Jewish state in the land of Israel.

While some argue that Zionism was a factual necessity to protect Jews from historical oppression and ensure their self-determination, it is important to recognize that blaming Zionism alone for the complexities of the Israeli-Palestinian conflict oversimplifies the issue.

The question of whether Jews would give up Israel after its establishment is not a straightforward one.

It is essential to consider various factors, including historical, religious, and cultural ties to the land, as well as the complexities of international politics and the rights and aspirations of both Jewish and Palestinian populations.

The resolution of the Israeli-Palestinian conflict requires a comprehensive and inclusive approach, taking into account the concerns and aspirations of all parties involved. While some Jews are content with the idea of Israel being under their control, it is important to note that not all Jews share the same perspective.

There are many Jews who advocate for a fair and just resolution in Palestine, recognizing the need for equal rights and opportunities for both Israelis and Palestinians.

Among these individuals, there are members of the Orthodox community and younger generations who actively acknowledge the oppression faced by Palestinians.

They understand that the concept of exile does not guarantee a permanent return to their ancestral land.

Israel and Palestine are indeed controversial, particularly for those who choose to ignore the complexities and support misleading narratives.

However, it is crucial to recognize that there is a diverse range of opinions and perspectives within the Jewish community for this complex and multifaceted issue.

The hypocrisy is so glaring that it becomes difficult for some to discuss the truth. It is much easier to direct blame solely towards Zionism, as it is a powerful force that is widely associated with oppression.

The major superpower, which claims to champion freedom and justice, is paradoxically endorsing the Christian faith as a dominant factor while advocating for mercy and turning the other cheek.

This contradictory stance raises questions about their true intentions and their support for oppressive systems.

The hypocrisy is so extinct of the super power and those who support the oppression of Palestine its barbaric.

Under the Muslim rule Israel flourished there is no question Muslims still guard the Sepulcher church knowing the support the Christian countries are providing to oppress the Palestinians who are predominantly Muslim.

Supporting them with funds revenue while their own starve many nights on the streets and die of heat and cold in harsh weather is a heartbreaking reality.

The number of homeless individuals continues to rise, exacerbating the urgency of addressing this crisis. Meanwhile, a significant portion of the revenue is being allocated to

Israel, which has been accused of oppressing Gaza, turning it into an open prison for its inhabitants.

This situation is particularly poignant as Gaza, the birthplace of Jesus in Judea, is considered a part of Palestine. Unfortunately, this historical context is often overlooked or unknown to many individuals in these regions, further adding to the complexity of the situation.

Jewish Insider: Dec 21, 2023 — The Israel on Campus Coalition survey found 81% backing for Israel's war, but Gen Z Jews are a bit less supportive.

Washington Post: Dec 21, 2023 — A poll found that more people ages 18-29 sympathized with Palestinians than with Israelis in the current conflict.

Palestine is an occupied territory and the faith that says Jesus wanted peace and preached love per Christendom is backing a society that is oppressing others. The hypocrisy of supporting those who have no backup while endorsing those with advanced destructive equipment is a grave injustice.

Many Muslim countries, for the sake of maintaining relationships and alliances with foreign lands, turn a blind eye to this injustice. However, true prosperity can only be achieved when alliances are based on truth, humanity, and justice.

Muslim countries possess significant wealth and resources that can support the oppressed and take a righteous stance. It is not only a sin to watch and do nothing, but it is also imperative to make one's voice heard.

By enjoining all Muslim countries and collectively working towards helping the oppressed, we can make a meaningful impact and bring about positive change.

To support the Jews and give them a homeland because of the harsh times they faced, it was the Muslims who extended their hand to them, particularly during the time of the Ottoman Empire.

Muslims provided a safe haven for Jews fleeing persecution and allowed them to settle in various Muslim-majority regions. However, the establishment of a Jewish homeland in Palestine through the Zionist movement led to the displacement of Palestinians from their homes.

This issue could be resolved if all parties concerned, including those who support the current regime, engage in open dialogue and address the grievances of both Palestinians and Jews.

It is important to acknowledge the historical injustices and work towards a solution that promotes equality and justice for all parties involved, allowing oppressed individuals to resist oppression while upholding principles of fairness and respect.

In the above statement, a firm opinion is expressed against a two-state solution and criticism is made towards the real estate laws and practices in various countries, specifically in relation to Gaza.

With the backing of a superpower, the argument proposes that these laws can remove and displace individuals.

The authenticity of speeches that claim to support humanity, arguing that they contribute to the establishment of homes that are later abused and result in homelessness.

The world acknowledges that real estate transactions usually require contracts and disclosures to ensure transparency and protect the rights of all parties involved.

However, in this situation, some individuals argue that engaging in such transactions supports what they deem an "evil regime" and equates it with Zionism.

Zionism, a political ideology advocating for the establishment and support of a Jewish state in the land of Israel, has been a subject of controversy and debate.

The displacement of Palestinian people is a complex and ongoing issue that has resulted in the displacement of a significant number of individuals over several decades.

While the Holocaust was a horrific event that resulted in the displacement and loss of millions of Jewish lives during World War II, it is important to recognize that the scale and circumstances of the Palestinian displacement differ significantly.

The result is the emergence of greed and the declaration of rights to a Jewish land, which has been supported by a superpower, leading to a tragic massacre. This can be seen in the ongoing conflict between Israel and Palestine.

The superpower in question, has provided significant political and financial support to Israel, bolstering its claim to the land and fueling tensions in the region.

Both sides have experienced the consequences of a cycle of violence and human suffering, because of the pursuit of national interests, combined with historical and religious narratives.

The international community continues to grapple with finding a fair and sustainable solution to this deeply complex and contentious issue. The displacement of Palestinians has resulted from various factors, including conflicts, wars, and political disputes in the region.

During the Holocaust, Muslims helped Jews escape persecution and find refuge. Muslim countries must trade with their own currency and actively work to prevent control and violence.

Losing unity in Muslim countries has become a significant dilemma, with various internal conflicts and divisions plaguing many nations.

However, Turkey stands out as a hub that has maintained unity within the Muslim world. Turkey's unique position, both geographically and historically, has allowed it to bridge the gap between different Muslim countries and foster cooperation among them.

The world is captivated by Turkey's robust economy, glittering streets, stable politics, and progressive governance, making it a symbol of hope for many Muslims aspiring for successful development and modernization. While some hope to leave Turkey, a visit from the U.S. reveals that Islam remains a core aspect of life, reflecting its Muslim identity with a diverse background and culture, emphasized by the daily call to prayer five times a day.

Despite facing challenges, Turkey has played a crucial role in diplomatic efforts, mediating conflicts, and promoting dialogue among Muslim countries, thus acting as a unifying force in the broader Muslim world.

In the pursuit of truth and justice, Muslims firmly believe in standing up for what is right, even if they are the only ones doing so. Islam emphasizes the importance of honesty, urging its followers to always speak the truth, even if it goes against their own self-interests

The principle of seeking justice and truth is not limited to the Muslim community alone but extends to all of humanity. It is crucial for Muslims and people of all backgrounds to come together as a unified human race, transcending differences and working towards a common goal.

The year 1948 holds significance in this context, as it marks the establishment of Israel, a contentious event that came at a great cost in terms of lives and suffering. To remain silent and passive observers in the face of injustice is nothing short of cruelty.

Muslims and people of conscience must strive to open their eyes, raise their voices, and actively advocate for justice and truth, regardless of the consequences. Only through collective efforts can we hope to achieve a world where justice and truth prevail.

Those who oppose Zionism claim it perpetuates injustice and the violation of human rights, particularly concerning the Palestinian people.

Therefore, they argue that taking part in real estate transactions that support the Zionist cause indirectly contributes to this perceived injustice.

While the Jewish faith does not accept Jesus as the Messiah, it is important to note that beliefs and interpretations vary among different religious traditions. Judaism, Christianity, and Islam each have their own perspectives on Jesus.

In Judaism, the awaited Messiah is believed to be from the lineage of King David, as mentioned in the Hebrew Bible. Christians consider Jesus to be the Son of God and believe that he fulfilled the prophecies of the Messiah.

A voice of reason speaks out amidst the shrill lies that perpetuate Islamophobia. Portraying the oppressed as oppressors when they defend themselves. Defending oneself after being forcibly removed from their home and tortured is not a deliberate act of evil, but rather a desperate attempt to protect their rights.

The question arises: if Allah is merciful, why does He allow the oppressed to suffer at the hands of tyrants and those who elevate Jesus to a divine status?

Or those who disobeyed Allah facing exile. Allah's timing differs from that of humans. For decades, the Israelites endured suffering until Allah drowned the main chief Pharaoh, who is now kept in the museum of Egypt, guarded and preserved.

The Quran clearly states that Allah will preserve him, if that does not satisfy the world, the country remains Muslim.

The concept is not to validate the lies of Islamophobia by disregarding the rights of Muslim countries and Muslims over the oppressed.

Islam advocates standing up for human rights. Allah holds the reward. Those who die for Allah's cause without committing suicide are still living.

The analogy in this episode is not difficult to grasp, despite the clear biblical warnings, it highlights the location and support behind the oppressor.

It confuses young minds and promotes provocative behavior, lacking morality and defense. People with limited knowledge of beliefs and moral code easily partake in what's available while claiming to defend others' rights.

One cannot safeguard others' rights without upholding the divine rights of justice and integrity in the midst of deceit and malevolence.

Those who defend the oppressors will eventually become oppressors themselves, turning against the people who supported them. Like Moses, who grew up in the Pharaoh's palace, he eventually opposed the Pharaoh and defended the Israelites.

In the same vein, individuals who prophesied Jesus regard him as either a loving god or the son of god. He offers support to these tyrannical regimes, believing they can achieve salvation with his help.

The salvation Jesus seeks is through God, as he explicitly states in the Bible that he does not know them.

It's hard to cite the Bible because the human and divine realms are in a constant battle of separation.

Unlike the Quran, this book is entirely a revelation from Allah and was completed before Prophet Muhammad passed away. The entire world reads the same book, the Quran.

"Obstacle" and "challenge" are often used interchangeably. Islam flourished in the Saudi desert despite opposing factors, with Prophet Muhammad leading the Muslims as a humble ruler and servant of Allah.

Non-Muslims who were knowledgeable spoke highly of Prophet Muhammad.

The oppressors who exploit the marginalized society's desire for salvation from Jesus are manipulative and taking advantage of people's ignorance. Just like in any faith good and bad exists.

They use the call to free Gaza as a means to deceive and manipulate the weak. However, in the modern world, the call to free Gaza is an appeal to humanity and a recognition of the suffering and difficulties faced by its inhabitants.

Gaza has become a metaphorical prison for those who face various challenges and obstacles in their daily lives. For true progression to occur, humanity must display compassion and empathy, rather than engaging in discourse that plots against the weak.

This dilemma exposes the contradictions of those who proclaim faith but are driven by greed and ignorance.

They hope Jesus will help them if they support Israel, but the truth is that Jesus' second coming, according to the Islamic perspective, will originate from a Muslim country like Syria, not Israel. This perspective challenges the notion that salvation and divine intervention are exclusive to a particular nation or faith.

It emphasizes the importance of recognizing the suffering and oppression faced by marginalized communities, such as those in Gaza, and working towards their liberation and justice with a sense of humanity and compassion.

This is a pure distortion of human rights to scream free Gaza in the decade that claims individuality from the Western society wrapped up in deceit and decoding the masses. Jesus' role in history and theology is often misrepresented by those who seek to gain control over land, such as the situation in Gaza.

To understand the true significance of Jesus, one must delve into the historical and theological context surrounding his life. Jesus was a Jewish prophet who lived in the first century in the region that is now modern-day Israel and Palestine.

His teachings emphasized the importance of caring for the marginalized and oppressed, and he challenged the oppressive systems of his time.

Jesus' mission was not about gaining control over land, but about transforming hearts and minds and bringing about a kingdom of peace and justice.

By understanding the true history and theology of Jesus, individuals can see through the misleading narrative perpetuated by those who support oppression and work towards a just resolution in the situation in Gaza.

Dec 26, 2023 — As the international community laments the devastation in Gaza, the war threatens to damage American standing in the world.

Oct 13, 2023 — The US has provided billions in military aid to Israel. What does it mean for the Gaza war?

Council on foreign relations: Increasing numbers of Jews began moving to Ottoman Palestine—a predominately Arab region—following the 1896 publication of Theodor Herzl's The Jewish State, ...

The address becomes necessary to serve humanity by providing a platform to promote kindness and uphold common morality. Regardless of nationality or faith, the focus should always be on the well-being and welfare of all individuals.

History serves as a reminder of the importance of truth and the consequences of manipulation, but the truth itself remains constant and timeless. The conditioning of minds negatively only serves as an opportunity for those seeking to manipulate and control the masses.

However, true peace can only be achieved by those who are determined to serve truth and humanity, with no bias or discrimination.

This includes actively helping those in need and standing against those who perpetrate acts of violence and immorality. Therefore, the address serves as a rallying point for individuals who are committed to promoting a compassionate and just society.

Quran; Surah Mumtahanah: 60:8. Allah does not forbid you from those who do not fight you because of religion and do not expel you from your homes - from being righteous toward them and acting justly toward them. Indeed, Allah loves those who act justly.

The explanations and descriptions in theology highlight the differences in beliefs and interpretations of various religious teachings.

CHAPTER 13
KNOWLEDGE REFUTES ARROGANCE

Waiting for something like spirituality or knowledge isn't the answer to finding fulfillment or growth. Desiring these things without taking action won't lead to any meaningful change.

Instead, actively working towards obtaining spirituality or knowledge is the antidote to experiencing true transformation and personal development.

It is through engaging in the pursuit of these goals, actively seeking and gaining spiritual insights or knowledge, that one can truly find the answers one is searching for.

By taking initiative and dedicating time and effort to areas of true interest individuals can gain new insights, enhance their self-awareness, understand the world better, and ultimately find meaning and satisfaction.

Embracing the journey of self-discovery and actively working towards personal growth is the key to experiencing the transformative power of spirituality and knowledge.

Arrogance often stems from a deep-rooted ignorance or lack of understanding. Arrogant individuals believe they know everything and have all the answers, which blinds them to their limitations and gaps in knowledge.

Arrogance serves no purpose when Allah, who is all-knowing and all-seeing, is aware of the whispers of the hearts. It is a reminder that no matter how much one may try to hide their true intentions or thoughts, Allah is fully aware of them.

The arrogance of individuals who believe they can deceive or manipulate others ultimately holds no weight in the face of Allah's knowledge.

It is a humbling realization that no matter how much power or influence one may possess; they are ultimately accountable to Allah, who can see beyond superficial appearances and into the depths of one's character.

Arrogance, therefore, is not only futile but also counterproductive in the pursuit of spiritual growth and a sincere connection with Allah.

Quran: Suran Qaaf: 50:16. Indeed, it is WE who created humankind and fully know what their souls whisper to them, and WE are closer to them than their jugular vein.

Seeking external validation is their way of masking internal insecurities, driving their need to feel superior. To enhance their self-esteem, they insult or diminish others, exposing their lack of knowledge and emotional intelligence.

Genuine success is not about what one already knows but about the dedication to perpetual learning and self-improvement.

Successful people recognize that knowledge has no limits and embrace a humble and open-minded attitude towards life. Instead of arrogance and ignorance, they view challenges as opportunities for growth and actively seek to expand their understanding.

Individuals prioritizing spiritual fulfillment prioritize intellectual equilibrium over material circumstances.

Personal growth, knowledge, and understanding are their top priorities, as they believe these contribute to their overall well-being and sense of purpose.

Those who are affected by an insecure moment of jealousy often feel overshadowed by individuals who are well-traveled, highly educated, outwardly good-looking, healthy, spiritually connected and financially secure.

While these qualities are certainly blessings, those who believe that success is solely derived from outward appearances can sometimes be perceived as internal desire still seeking solace to become whole.

Individuals who eagerly await any mistakes or failures frequently question the delicate balance between admiration and resentment to validate their insecurities.

They hold on to the notion that those who strive for success must inevitably falter, hoping to diminish the achievements of others and alleviate their feelings of inadequacy.

Experiencing knowledge and education through travel provides a level of understanding and appreciation that cannot be fully grasped through social media or history channels alone.

While these platforms can offer valuable information, they lack the immersive and sensory experience that comes with physically being in a different location or witnessing historical landmarks firsthand.

Travel allows individuals to engage with different cultures, interact with locals, and witness historical sites, which deepens their understanding and appreciation of the world around them.

It provides an opportunity to engage all the senses and develop a personal connection to the places and history being explored.

This first-hand experience fosters a more profound and comprehensive learning experience compared to passive consumption through screens.

In today's climate, individuals must recognize the role that parents play in shaping their educational journey.

Parents have a significant influence on their children's attitudes towards education and can either push them to strive for academic success or allow them to fall into the trap of unfavorable circumstances.

Mostly happens in environments where families do not find education important and survival takes precedence over using the time to study for future achievements.

Sometimes those who see others progress with knowledge education and travel become resentful not remembering the time they had was never allotted to means of success.

Surrounding oneself with a better company increases the likelihood of being positively influenced and motivated to achieve greatness. The saying "birds of a feather flock together" holds in this context.

When someone surrounds themselves with successful and driven individuals, they adopt their habits, mindset, and work ethic. The unwavering support and positive energy of an exceptional company can fuel ambition and drive towards success.

Being around accomplished individuals can offer valuable guidance, mentorship, and opportunities for growth.

Ultimately, the individuals we choose to surround ourselves with have a significant impact on our personal and professional development and selecting the right company can contribute to our success.

Travel from a young age is a teacher in itself. It allows the environment to extend beyond there is no better teacher than travel. The Quran says to travel the lands and see the history.

Traveling at a young age exposes individuals to diverse cultures, languages, and ways of life, broadening their perspectives and enhancing their capabilities.

It allows them to experience first-hand the beauty and complexity of the world, fostering a sense of curiosity and openness.

While not everyone can travel extensively, there are other ways to broaden one's horizons.

There are options to participate in cultural exchange programs, volunteer in various communities, or connect with individuals from diverse backgrounds in person and through social media.

Any situation, regardless of physical travel, can affect learning and personal development.

Some people manipulate social media to cause chaos and oppress others, intensifying unnecessary evil in our world. To correct oneself as a Muslim or believer means to enhance inner strengths and nurture the mind instead of corrupting the soul.

Apart from traveling, reading, and consulting, reliable sources are vital for broadening one's knowledge and comprehension. Accurate explanations and interpretations of Islam require consulting practicing Muslims.

Relying solely on the rhetoric propagated by Islamophobic individuals or the distorted portrayal of Islam in the media can lead to misconceptions and misunderstandings.

Only by engaging with knowledgeable practitioners of Islam can one truly grasp the depth and beauty of the religion.

It is important to acknowledge that many discussions surrounding Islam are often carried out by individuals who possess limited knowledge about the faith, perpetuating misconceptions and stereotypes.

Therefore, seeking information from authentic sources and engaging with practicing Muslims is vital for a comprehensive understanding of Islam.

When individuals heavily rely on external factors or relationships for emotional well-being and personal growth, it is known as codependency on the interior. There are different manifestations of this, which can be positive or negative.

Some individuals resist learning because they rely too heavily on others for validation and guidance. Stepping out of their comfort zone and taking responsibility for their learning process may be something they fear.

Conversely, codependency can in certain circumstances foster a positive drive for acquiring knowledge. Seeking knowledge and skills can be a way for individuals to gain approval or maintain relationship dynamics.

This upside can be problematic if it impairs their capacity to think independently or hampers their advancement. The presence of codependency internally can complicate an individual's desire to grow and gain knowledge.

In such situations, resistance becomes a defense mechanism, a way to protect oneself from the fear of failure and disappointment. However, resistance is a downplay of one's true abilities and potential.

It prevents personal growth and keeps one confined within their comfort zone, hindering their ability to explore new opportunities and reach their full potential.

Individuals need to recognize and overcome this resistance to break free from the limitations they have imposed on themselves and strive for success.

Faced with Allah's power, no nation or individual can truly flourish with an inflated ego. Throughout history, we have witnessed powerful nations rise and fall, their once mighty empires reduced to ruins.

This serves as a reminder that those who prioritize their self-interests and boast about their strength are often met with destruction.

The world is plagued by acts of violence and destruction, perpetrated by those who seek to spread evil rather than extend a helping hand.

Quran: Surah Al An 'am: 6:6. Have they not seen how many generations We destroyed before them which We had established upon the earth as We have not established you? And We sent [rain from] the sky upon them in showers and made rivers flow beneath them; then We destroyed them for their sins and brought forth after them a generation of others.

Self-reflection acts as a potent mirror, exposing one's true character and behavior. This reflection can mirror the traits and behaviors of others, including arrogance, which can influence one's own demeanor.

Arrogance can arise from either ego or disappointment in failing to meet personal expectations. Internal injuries may occur when self-esteem and self-worth are compromised through self-neglect.

Sometimes, people can make things even worse by using someone's vulnerabilities and weaknesses against them. False friendships can lead individuals to exploit vulnerabilities, manipulating and capitalizing on their weaknesses.

Bible: NIV: Matthew: 10:35. For I have come to turn "'a man against his father, a daughter against her mother, a daughter-in-law against her mother-in-law..."

Jesus highlights in the Bible that this exploitation can reach one's own family. The Bible raises questions about Jesus' statement on turning families against each other, given his mission to uphold the law of Moses for the Jews, and no other prophet advocated for breaking up families, as stated in the Bible, not the Quran.

The Bible's message is not supportive of keeping families together, as it says Jesus came to divide families.

The verse is straightforward, leaving no room for imagination.

Islam emphasizes the importance of faith over family. However, it is crucial to note that no prophet in Islam ever claimed to come and break families.

Nowadays, the bonds within families are often strained, and sometimes even friends can let you down. In such circumstances, it is best to consider Allah as the ultimate friend.

There is no disappointment in relying on Allah as your confidant, the one you turn to for your needs and share your deepest secrets with.

Allah is the one who keeps your secrets, but it is during the Day of judgment that all actions will be accounted for in Islam.

The nations and regimes, blinded by their desires and arrogance, disregarded the guidance and laws set by Allah.

They indulged in corruption, immorality, and injustice, putting their interests above the greater good. They failed to recognize the interconnectedness of their actions and the consequences they would face.

The greenery they once enjoyed, symbolizing prosperity and blessings, was gradually lost as their societies decayed. Their lands became barren, plagued by conflict, natural disasters, and societal unrest.

The wrath of Allah manifested in various forms, became evident as a reminder for humanity to strive for righteousness and adhere to the principles of Islam.

It is through comprehension of the fear of Allah and aligning one's actions with His guidance that true success can be achieved, both individually and collectively.

Understanding and acknowledging past mistakes, seeking forgiveness, and making amends are essential for personal growth and a path toward redemption.

Those who persist in living in defiance of Allah's commandments continue to witness the turmoil and destruction that befalls societies and individuals who abandon the path of righteousness. It is only by embracing the balance and wisdom that humanity can find true clarity and attain success in this world and the hereafter.

Bible: ESV: Genesis: 19:24-25. Then the LORD rained on Sodom and Gomorrah sulfur and fire from the LORD out of heaven. And he overthrew those cities, and all the valley, and all the inhabitants of the cities, and what grew on the ground.

Bible: NIV: Corinthians: 6:9. Or do you not know that wrongdoers will not inherit the kingdom of God? Do not be deceived: Neither the sexually immoral nor idolaters nor adulterers nor men who have sex with men.

The Judeo-Christian belief system explicitly emphasizes the prohibition of idol worship.

This includes the worship of gods as humans, as well as expressing them as godheads. According to the teachings of Abraham and other Abrahamic prophets, the true God is unseen and cannot be perceived by humans. Therefore, a human being cannot be a god, as they have not seen God themselves.

In these Islamophobic regions, there is a strong bias against Islam and a promotion of Christianity as the preferred faith.

The people in power who run these regions support the oppressors, hoping Jesus will come to their rescue. However, they choose to live with blinders on, ignoring the fact that a secular society is not compatible with any Abrahamic faith.

The higher-ups in these regions mask their true intentions by broadcasting messages of civility and morality, while secretly promoting their agenda behind closed doors. They aim to restrict and control what can be seen or discussed openly.

There is no need for government involvement in matters of sexuality, as both Islam and the Bible prohibit certain acts.

The subject of sexuality is forced upon humanity through social media, on western lands and those who openly indulge in promoting more **fitnah** (evil) are not a threat but a disturbance. Promoting lewd events is not allowed, and it's best to keep such matters private.

Does the Western life continue to coincide with Islam as a matter of it does not cannot be denied the morality of the culture is not in conjunction with Islamic principles.

The culture does not negotiate religion and Muslims who migrated from other lands can either keep their religion view different cultures and accept what is acceptable to them in person not excluding friendships and allowances for behavior not comprising self-awareness.

The principles of Islam are non-negotiable, but according to Islamic law, migration is encouraged in certain instances. The prophet Muhammad migrated to Medina sometime and returned after a passage of time to Mecca with victory.

However, the dilemma arises when Muslims attempt to embrace Western culture or opposing ideologies and compromise their Islamic principles in order to assimilate.

This raises the question: why do Muslims choose to travel to Western lands and settle down if Islam is not compatible with these cultures?

The issue here is not Islam itself, but self-awareness. Islam was revealed to people who were engaged in disobedience, and even Abraham, who was among the idol-worshippers alongside his father, found his true self through Allah.

It is Allah that can complement and provide opportunities for learning and teaching.

People should not be influenced by those who do not understand their own strengths. Instead, by knowing Allah and seeking balance, one can find fulfillment in any land.

After all, the entire universe, including the land, water, and sky, belongs solely to Allah and is part of His creation.

Destiny is predetermined, and individuals will navigate their paths with their destiny. It is not for ignorant people to dictate where others should go or to suggest going back home. The ultimate home is the hereafter, as this world is temporary and not the final destination.

While drifting away from one's beliefs is possible, returning can strengthen one's faith. Even the difficult and broken paths that lead us astray can ultimately guide us towards a better future.

The continual allocation of defiance in humanity can be observed throughout generations, as individuals have consistently challenged established norms and systems.

However, it is important to note that in Islam, understanding and acknowledging these acts of defiance are essential for personal and collective betterment.

Islam does not promote the passing on of such acts as a means of rebellion against God's will.

Instead, the religion emphasizes the importance of staying true to the original teachings and scriptures, without altering them to suit personal desires or illusions.

Islam survives through the adherence to these unadulterated words and the practice of sincere repentance.

Repentance is not merely a superficial act, but a genuine effort to mend oneself from within, seeking the light of goodness that can then be expressed outwardly.

It is through this process of self-restoration that humanity can be uplifted and restored to its true potential.

However, humanity is not exempt from the consequences of their actions. Their reign of ego, greed, and blame will eventually end, just like the empires before them.

In reality, it is Allah who truly rules and human rights are limited in comparison. Stepping outside the boundaries set by Allah's guidance can lead to treacherous waters, where navigating the challenges becomes increasingly difficult.

It is important to remember that opportunities for growth and success are available, but succumbing to a negative climate or surrounding oneself with a poor company can waste the potential of youth that comes around only once, and adulthood is a lengthy process.

Whether it is a deteriorating climate or a regressing climate, it is crucial to recognize the value of time and how it is spent. Regardless of age, the ability to discern between productive learning and wasteful activities becomes even more significant.

Muslim countries are currently facing significant turmoil despite the Islamic principle of just rulership.

It is indeed a challenge to find rulers who embody justice in today's climate. According to Islamic teachings, Allah may allow the appointment of destructive rulers when the actions of the nation become destructive.

One can see with their own eyes the oppressive regimes fueled by Islamophobia in these countries.

Corrupt leaders lead them astray, and their allegiance to Israel mesmerizes the masses, oblivious to the rejection of Christendom. The rejection of Jesus by the land of Israel makes funding the regime a massacre of the spirit and soul.

USA Facts: Oct 12, 2023 — The United States committed over $3.3 billion in foreign assistance to Israel in 2022, the most recent year for which data exists.

Confusion is a deliberate tactic employed by some individuals or groups with ulterior motives. The support for Israel has been a consistent bipartisan stance by the obvious supporter for decades.

Both the Democratic and Republican parties have historically shown unwavering support for Israel's security, diplomatic relations, and right to exist as a sovereign nation.

However, it is unfortunate that in recent times, there has been a rise in attempts to exploit this support for political gain and sow discord among party lines.

This divisive strategy only serves to create chaos and hinder constructive dialogue on the complex issues surrounding the Israeli-Palestinian conflict.

Instead of focusing on party affiliations, it is crucial to foster a united approach that prioritizes peace, stability, and the well-being of all parties involved.

It is perplexing and unjustifiable when people cannot comprehend the reasons behind the support for Palestine, as their struggle for self-determination and basic human rights is a legitimate cause.

However, the unwavering support given to those who advocate for Israel without question or consideration lacks logical reasoning.

The essence of injustice lies in trusting those who do not believe in the oneness of Allah or who are enemies of the belief in Allah. However, humanity is inherent in all individuals, making it a quest to seek truth.

Similarly, even in a home where Islam is despised, surviving becomes challenging for those who hold the faith, as it becomes difficult to coexist with opposing forces.

Faith overrides confusion!

It can be said that supporting those who disguise evil is akin to placing trust in those who show no regard for justice towards humanity.

Quran: Surah Mumtahanah: 60:1. O believers! Do not take My enemies and yours as trusted allies, showing them affection even though they deny what has come to you of the truth. They drove the Messenger and yourselves out of Mecca, simply for your belief in Allah your Lord. If you truly emigrated to struggle in My cause and seek My pleasure, then do not take them as allies, disclosing secrets of the believers to the pagans out of affection for them, when I know best whatever you conceal and whatever you reveal. And whoever of you does this has truly strayed from the Right Way.

Quran: Surah Burj; 85:10. Those who persecute the believing men and women and then do not repent will certainly suffer the punishment of Hell and the torment of burning.

Regardless of our differences in faith, culture, or background, it is our duty as human beings to support those who are oppressed.

There can be no excuse for turning a blind eye to the suffering of others. Whether it is because of religious persecution, racial discrimination, or any form of injustice, we must stand together and advocate for the rights and well-being of those who are oppressed.

It is not only a moral obligation but also a fundamental principle of humanity to show empathy, compassion, and solidarity towards those who are marginalized and oppressed.

By doing so, we can work towards creating a world where everyone is treated with dignity, respect, and equality, regardless of their beliefs or circumstances.

Islam has always advocated for humanity first there is no distinction in help in Islam's perspective of their religion.

Non-believers can easily sway and stray, while believers who stray can find their way back, but those who betray believers only betray themselves by confiding in non-believers.

The highest Allah has issued a warning that applies to all aspects of political and personal life, leaving no room for doubt in judgments.

If they could defy and expel the prophet Muhammad from Mecca, then ordinary individuals have little hope against the distorted beliefs passed down through generations by non-believers.

Their fear arose as he came back from Medina to Mecca with victory, believing he would retaliate. However, he displayed fairness and forgiveness, surpassing their perception of a prophet.

Quran: Surah Mumtahanah: 60:2. If they gain the upper hand over you, they would by your open enemies, unleashing their hands and tongues to harm you, and wishing that you would abandon faith.

Throughout history, arrogance has plagued those who are unjust. Prophets and wise individuals have consistently warned against the dangers of arrogance and deceit.

However, the lessons of history seem to be forgotten as arrogance and exploitation persist. Those who have been overthrown for seeking justice have faced demoralization and character assassination.

This disobedience to Allah and the rejection of justice is not sustainable. The world is not a perpetual entity like the annual cycles of nature, where flowers bloom and weather changes.

Instead, it is a transient existence, where justice will ultimately prevail. Whether it is in this life or the hereafter, justice will be served, and the arrogance of the unjust will be overthrown.

Israel serves as a prime example of peace during Muslim rule, highlighting the chaos and violation of human rights following the establishment of a Jewish state in 1948.

Force entry taking control is the worst-case scenario in any situation.

If Muslims understood the Quran, divisions among Muslim nations would cease, causing it to become their duty to actively support the oppressed instead of engaging in mere discussion.

It applies to every aspect of life. The Quran emphasizes the importance of every phase of life, as time cannot be regained.

However, Islamophobia persistently spreads lies on social media, targeting those who are unfamiliar with Islam.

The disbelievers desire the downfall of Muslims, and misery craves companionship.

The most problematic individual is someone who, even if they identify as a compromised Muslim, attempts to deceive and misguide fellow Muslims. The rationale behind considering a Muslim as the finest of all beings is straightforward: their devotion to Allah and acceptance of all His prophets with no form of discrimination, which defines a Muslim and explains why they are considered the best.

Hypocrites are those who distort faith, counting flaws and desiring more bad to occur.

Mistakes in Islam do not lead to greater evil. Islam prioritizes precaution over cure because deceivers keep reminders and secrets as assets, making those we trust potential misleaders.

While individuals can uphold ethics without faith, those with less integrity may be tempted to give up, but it's best to rely on Allah, not humanity.

It is important to recognize that supporting the cause of Israel should not blindly endorse any action or policy they take. Instead, a balanced and informed approach is needed. This approach acknowledges the complexities of the Israeli-Palestinian conflict and aims to find a fair and lasting solution for both parties involved.

The legitimacy of any position should be based on an understanding of the historical context, human rights violations, and the desire for peaceful coexistence in the region.

If the land did indeed belong to Israeli Jews in the past, who were exiled by Allah because of their disobedience despite once being favored, it cannot be solely supported by Christians hoping for Jesus to help them attain salvation through eternal life.

This lack of understanding stems from overlooking what Jesus preached to the Jews, which was monotheism.

It is important to note that it was the Muslims, particularly during the rule of Omar Bin Khattab, the second caliph of Islam, who invited the Jews back and provided them with a haven.

This historical context showcases the inclusive and tolerant nature of Islam, as well as the recognition of the Jewish connection to the land.

These nations that perpetuate Islamophobic fear have caused Muslim countries to be divided and cannot understand the consequences. Regardless of faith, humanity falls into a cycle of misunderstandings and mistakes.

However, as time passes and we approach the end times, this downfall becomes more pronounced. Israel, instead of supporting Western countries, ideologies as history tells they can eventually exploit lucrative opportunities and uses them against their supporters.

This decision can ultimately result in their own turmoil and downfall, which is quite ironic. Despite being a predominantly Christian society, the U.S, although not highly religious, hoped that this ambitious plan would save Israel.

It is interesting to note that Jesus himself was Palestinian. However, by allowing Israel to destroy Palestine, they are essentially allowing the homeland of Jesus to be destroyed.

Quran: Surah Mumtahanah: 60:04. You already have an excellent example in Abraham and those with him, when they said to their people, we dissociate ourselves from you and shun whatever idols you worship besides Allah. We reject you. The enmity and hatred that has arisen between us and you will last until you believe in Allah alone. The only exception is when Abraham said to his father, I will seek forgiveness for you, adding, but I cannot protect you from Allah at all. The believers prayed, Our Lord! In you we trust. And to you, we always turn. And to you is the final return.

Quran: Surah Mumtahanah: 60;05. Our Lord! Do not subject us to the persecution of the disbelievers. Forgive us, our Lord! You alone are truly the Almighty, All-Wise."

The Quran's language is clear, with no doubt in its examples and clarity. Only Allah can change the hearts of those who defy. Those he perceives as falsifiers are never redeemed but remain in torment.

Muslim countries, particularly Palestine, oppressed by exiled individuals, present a significant opportunity for Muslim countries to be the answer to their prayers instead of passively observing and celebrating without aiding their own.

Regardless of faith, humanity is helping anyone in need. Muslims are taught by Islam to maintain fairness and justice in all transactions, without letting religion be a barrier.

The responsibility lies with Muslims to sever ties with petrol sales and demand a shift to Muslim currency for trade, enabling them to exert influence over the masses if action is not taken for the oppressed.

Muslims possess the ability to assist and prioritizing their awareness of the Quran is crucial, as no limitations or misunderstandings can prevent a Muslim from seeking justice, regardless of their religion, color, or race.

The first democracy in the world is believed to be **Islam**. It's time to educate those who are unaware.

Politico March 25, 2024 — The U.N. Security Council passed a resolution on Monday explicitly calling for a cease-fire in the Israel-Hamas war after the U.S. declined.

CBS News: March 25, 2024. Israel says the U.S. declining to block a U.N. Security Council resolution demanding an immediate Gaza cease-fire "gives Hamas hope."

AP News: March 25, 2024, — The United Nations Security Council on Monday issued its first demand for a cease-fire in Gaza, with the U.S. angering Israel by abstaining from the vote. Israel responded by canceling a visit to Washington by a high-level delegation in the strongest public clash between the allies since the war began.

Prime Minister Benjamin Netanyahu accused the U.S. of "retreating" from a "principled position" by allowing the vote to pass without conditioning the cease-fire on the release of hostages held by Hamas.

AP News: The top United Nations court has ordered Israel to take measures including opening more land crossings to allow food, water, fuel, and other.

Reuters: Jan 16, 2024 — Saudi minister: regional peace hinges on a Palestinian state · Push for Saudi-Israel diplomatic ties derailed by Gaza war · Prince Faisal says.

Gulf News: The Saudi government stressed on Tuesday that the Kingdom will continue to play its historic and pioneering role in supporting the Palestinian people.

Saudi Arabia, as the birthplace of Islam, holds a significant position in the Muslim world.

Riyadh, the capital city, is considered the heart of the country and a symbol of Islamic values. Given this importance, it has the potential to play a crucial role in taking a stance against oppression and advocating for justice.

By using its influence and power, Saudi Arabia can actively work towards ending oppression, both within its borders and globally. It can cut ties with oppressive regimes and use its economic leverage to bring about positive change.

This act of solidarity and support would not only be a humanitarian gesture but also align with the principles of Islam, emphasizing the importance of standing together in times of need.

As **Ramadan** is a sacred month for Muslims, it carries a special significance in terms of unity, compassion, and self-reflection.

Saudi Arabia can use this auspicious time to lead by example and showcase its commitment to promoting liberation and justice for all Muslims.

This action would not just increase the nation's status but also promote a feeling of togetherness among Muslims globally. The currency of Saud makes international trade more favorable for foreign countries. It occurs because of a mix of economics and chemistry.

The economics are straightforward: foreign oil can be cheaper, even with shipping expenses, compared to domestically produced crude foreign to Middle East.

Muslim countries can halt the embargo until they resolve the issue with the Islamophobic regions supporting Israel, which is oppressing Palestine, a nation with no military or resources except their faith in God.

However, many believe martyrdom is preferable to enduring oppression.

The Old City of Jerusalem, which is one of the holiest sites in Islam. Masjid al-Aqsa holds great religious significance for Muslims worldwide, as it is believed to be the place from where the Prophet Muhammad ascended to heaven during the Night Journey.

The presence of both Muslims and Christians in Palestine highlights the diverse religious and cultural heritage of the region.

However, the ongoing Israeli-Palestinian conflict has resulted in hardships and suffering for both communities, including restrictions on access to religious sites and recurring violence that affects their daily lives.

Despite these challenges, the sacred churches in Palestine, such as the Church of the Nativity in Bethlehem and the Church of the Holy Sepulcher in Jerusalem, continue to attract pilgrims from around the world, symbolizing the enduring faith and resilience of the Christian community in the region.

The ongoing conflict in the Middle East has also led to increased regional instability and security threats. These conflicts have directly affected many Muslim countries, including Saudi Arabia, must lead to a greater sense of unity and the need for collective action.

In response to these challenges, Muslim countries must recognize the importance of joining and leveraging their collective resources and power to protect their interests. Islam has developed the world the chaos needs rest to uplift the world.

Muslim countries need to step up not step down to please the evil that surrounds the world of greed.

This unrest within Muslim regions often stems from a variety of factors, including political conflicts, religious differences, and socioeconomic disparities.

In certain cases, extremist groups manipulate these divisions in order to advance their own objectives and escalate animosity, which is largely instigated by foreign powers aiming to establish new governments that favor their businesses.

This creates a vicious cycle of animosity, where greed and a distorted sense of morality prevail over fair judgment and empathy towards those in need.

Such a climate makes it difficult to foster unity and cooperation, hindering efforts to address the pressing issues faced by Palestinians and other marginalized communities.

It is imperative to address these internal tensions and promote inclusivity to create a more conducive environment for resolving conflicts and supporting those who require help.

Muslim countries around the world are facing various challenges and crises that require attention and support from their more affluent counterparts.

While Palestine remains a key issue, other Muslim nations are also grappling with political instability, economic hardships, and social injustices.

It is crucial for the well-off Muslim countries to not only display their wealth and prosperity, but also to demonstrate how Islam has upheld justice and fairness in their societies.

By showcasing the positive impact of Islamic principles on governance, human rights, and social welfare, these countries can inspire others to learn about and embrace values Islam upholds.

It is important to break away from following policies that only lead to chaos and instead promote justice and peace, presenting Islam as a religion of compassion, harmony, and progress.

By collaborating and supporting each other, Muslim nations can work towards promoting stability, economic growth, and the well-being of their people.

The Middle East's vast reserves of natural resources, such as crude oil, provide a significant opportunity for Muslim countries to use their wealth for the development and prosperity of the region.

By harnessing their collective potential, Muslim nations can assert their influence and ensure a brighter future for the Middle East. The Middle East during the Islamic Golden Age. Muslims ruled Israel and most of the Middle East from the 7th century until the decline of the Ottoman Empire in the early 20th century.

During this period, the Muslim rulers established a relatively tolerant and inclusive society that allowed for religious freedom and cultural diversity.

People of different faiths, including Christians and Jews, could live and practice their religions without significant oppression. Muslims, Christians, and Jews coexisted peacefully and made significant advancements and friendships.

However, it is important to note that this era was not without conflicts and tensions, as power struggles and rivalries existed among dynasties and with neighboring empires. The level of oppression experienced by religious and ethnic minorities was run by Islamic regimes showing tolerance compared to later periods.

Quran: Surah Mumtahanah: 60;8. Allah does not forbid you from dealing kindly and fairly with those who have neither fought nor driven you out of your home. Surely Allah loves those who are fair.

In Islam, fairness and justice are essential principles that guide the actions and behaviors of individuals.

The religion emphasizes treating all individuals, regardless of their capabilities, with equity and respect.

It condemns any form of violence or harm towards others and promotes the protection of human dignity and rights. Although it does not deny self-defense.

Islam teaches that this world is temporary, and the outcome and judgment lie in the hands of Allah. Believers believe that the righteous will ultimately prevail, and those who forcefully occupy and engage in evil deeds will face temporary consequences.

It is important to note that human perception of time may differ from that of Allah, and although times may appear elongated, justice will prevail in due course.

Quran: Surah Mumtahanah: 60:9. Allah only forbids you from befriending those who have fought you for your faith, driven you out of your homes, or supported others in doing so. And whoever takes them as friends, then it is they who are the true wrongdoers.

This test, which transcends the boundaries of oppression, is not only for the oppressed but for all Muslims who bear witness to it. It becomes their responsibility to discern reliable sources from those who lack accountability and to seek help from those in positions of power and influence.

The intrusion of foreign lands in Muslim lands is often driven by the understanding of the infrastructure and resources that these Muslim lands possess.

Foreign powers, driven by their own interests and agendas, exploit this knowledge to employ manipulative tactics and wage wars to create chaos and maintain control over these lands.

They seek to gain access to valuable resources such as oil, gas, minerals, and strategic locations. By instigating conflicts, they create divisions among the local population, weaken indigenous governments, and establish puppet regimes that serve their own economic and political interests.

These foreign powers often use propaganda, economic sanctions, and military interventions to further their objectives, exacerbating the suffering and instability within Muslim lands.

The historical context of colonialism and imperialism has left a legacy of power struggles and geopolitical rivalries that continue to impact Muslim-majority countries today.

Despite facing many challenges, such as economic instability and political unrest, the endurance of Muslim countries remains remarkably high.

Instead of resorting to derogatory language and blaming others, it is crucial to support, and use select social media platforms to effectively spread the message.

These platforms have the potential to reach a vast audience and have a significant impact on shaping public opinion. By leveraging the power of social media, Muslim countries can promote dialogue, foster understanding, and combat misconceptions about Islam.

This approach not only strengthens the bond within the Muslim community, but also helps build bridges with people from different cultures and backgrounds.

It is through constructive communication and peaceful means that a wider audience can disseminate and understand the message of Islam, promoting harmony and unity globally.

However, it is crucial to emphasize that actual change lies in concrete actions, not distorting the truth to maintain business embargoes or succumbing to greed. Allah has blessed humanity, regardless of their faith, with abundant resources.

Therefore, Muslim countries and individuals must recognize their role as ambassadors of the world and exemplify the essence of Islam, which is the culmination of all Abrahamic faiths.

Palestine, historically, was a beautiful land with rolling landscapes adorned with lush olive trees. As Jesus himself was a Palestinian, Bethlehem, a significant town, lies on the Palestinian side.

However, over time, it has experienced massacres, destruction, and loss of its precious olive trees. These tragic events are often overlooked or unknown by those who are uneducated about the history of the region.

The Yale Review of International studies: Mar 11, 2023 — Just in November 2022, Israeli forces uprooted and destroyed 2,000 olive trees in the Palestinian village of Qarawat Bani Hassan.

In reality, Palestine flourished under Muslim rule, with thriving cities, bustling markets, and a rich cultural heritage.

It had everything, from advanced agricultural practices to impressive architectural wonders. The notion that Palestine was devoid of anything significant is a misconception that cannot acknowledge its glorious past.

Palestine, also known as Philistia, is a region in the eastern Mediterranean, bordered by Egypt to the southwest, Israel to the east, and Jordan to the east.

The name "Philistia" is derived from the ancient people known as the Philistines, who inhabited the region thousands of years ago.

The Philistines were mentioned in various historical and biblical texts, particularly about conflicts with the Israelites.

Today, Palestine is recognized as a significant geopolitical entity, with the Palestinian people seeking self-determination and statehood.

The region has been a focal point of ongoing political and territorial disputes, which have garnered international attention and efforts towards finding a peaceful resolution.

The historical significance of Israel and the surrounding areas achieving peace under Muslim rule cannot be emphasized enough.

One such momentous period was during the Islamic Golden Age, which spanned from the 8th to the 13th centuries. It was a time of great intellectual and cultural development, where Muslims, Jews, and Christians coexisted in relative harmony.

In cities like Jerusalem, Cordoba, and Baghdad, scholars from different religious backgrounds collaborated, translating and preserving ancient texts, advancing knowledge in various fields such as medicine, mathematics, astronomy, and philosophy.

This era stands as a testament to the potential for peaceful coexistence and mutual respect, which serves as an inspiration for our world today.

This raises the question of why Muslim countries are experiencing such unrest and oppression under unjust rulers.

However, it is important to note that martyrdom is a blessing in Islam, as it signifies a person's commitment to standing up for justice.

The evil regime, backed by Islamophobes, causes the deaths of countless Muslims in unstable regions where mental health issues take precedence over the revenue meant for peace.

The regimes that seek peace through sending revenue have the highest depression rates. Karma remains consistent across all religions. Martyrdom, not premeditated suicide, is the term for innocent killing.

Columbia University Department of Psychiatry: Jan 5, 2024 — 5, 2023, found the prevalence of probable PTSD, depression, and anxiety in the weeks following the attacks (29% for PTSD, 42%-44% for depression.

This is an opportunity for Muslims to rise and advocate for the rights of the oppressed. Instead of resorting to ineffective methods such as screaming and name-calling, Muslims should use their words and actions to make a meaningful impact on the world and strive for justice.

The blame placed on Muslims for the self-inflicted deaths in the name of Allah during the 9/11 attacks is a clear distortion of the truth.

It is widely recognized among Muslims that setting oneself on fire is not considered martyrdom but rather suicide, which goes against the teachings of Islam.

Despite extensive investigations and inquiries, there is still no concrete evidence to fully establish the exact events and individuals responsible for the 9/11 attacks.

However, it is alarming to observe that certain Islamophobic regimes persistently propagate false narratives and spread lies, facing no significant consequences or repercussions.

This perpetuation of falsehoods serves only to further marginalize and vilify the Muslim community, while those who propagate these lies have nothing to lose but their credibility.

News: Al Jazeera: Sep 11, 2022 — The September 11, 2001 attacks on the United States ushered in a new era of hate crimes and racism.

The Conversation: Sep 8, 2011 — Ten years ago, nineteen young Muslims commandeered passenger jets and killed themselves, taking with them 2973 people to the inferno of fire ...

The events surrounding the 9/11 terrorist attacks have been shrouded in controversy and conspiracy theories.

To note there were lies and staged elements involved in the official narrative. The discovery of Muslim passports among the debris seems suspicious and ironic, as it points towards Muslims being responsible for the attacks.

Astonishingly, the passports with Muslim names were found intact, while the bodies remained lost and undiscovered for days. This is worse than any movie that requires logical blame for allegations.

Fox 5 New York: Sep 8, 2021 — ... 9/11 — remains unsolved ... Two decades later, NYPD detectives are still trying to solve a cold case that has very few leads. ... Get breaking news ...

The alleged accusations against Muslims have forever linked them to terrorism, staining their reputation for future generations.

The terrorizing is rooted in fear of Islam, not Muslims themselves. As the timeline they fear stretches, Islam continues to attract converts who bring education and integrate with Muslim families, creating an environment where lessons of life and Islam are learned together.

Those new to Islam face challenges in learning the faith, particularly due to the distortion of teachings on social media, especially for those living in Islamophobic regions

Islam is not about impending loneliness, but rather a community of support and togetherness.

Muslims must consistently expose the truth, as failing to address false accusations is an act of dishonesty. If there's a single Muslim standing, Islam will reveal the truth. The relevance of paper passports and findings lies in their ability to expose ongoing deception.

Saying **"Allah hu Akbar"** engaging in acts of self-destruction and claiming martyrdom is contradictory to the teachings of Islam.

Those who falsify and stage also have no understanding of Islam. The empathetic Muslims were quick to extend a helping hand instead of pointing fingers, demonstrating their generous nature.

Insults are not accepted when it comes to aiding humanity. Islam is a religion that offers justice instead of hypocrisy to those who seek it.

The focus is on exposing lies, not agreeing with falsehood. The emphasis is on compassion, not aggression. It's crucial to remember that Muslim passports placed as evidence by those who staged the whole episode don't automatically imply guilt or connection to the attacks.

It makes little sense how they were found in the towering inferno. It's crucial to withhold judgment until the investigation is complete and the conclusive findings are available.

Islam unequivocally prohibits suicide and the unjust killing of innocent individuals, yet Muslims are frequently scapegoated for baseless accusations.

It is unjust to unfairly attribute the actions of a few individuals to an entire religious community. The tragedy lacks proof of Muslim involvement, except for the staged incidents.

Muslims remain loyal to the teachings of Islam and the Quran, despite being unfairly labeled as extremists. These individuals are extremists, amplifying the history of lies against Muslims and Muslim countries.

The community must unite and address this issue to help the world, rather than joining nations with no religious background or faith alignment.

Those who only seek flaws in Muslims are not friends but enemies of Islam unless it's a personal, emotional connection between two Muslims. Then it's not about Islam but about individuals.

The Muslim achievers have left an indelible mark on the history of the Western world through their groundbreaking contributions in various fields.

Their accomplishments are well-documented and supported by extensive evidence.

However, despite the abundance of proof, there are still individuals who, out of ignorance or fear, refuse to acknowledge the genuine achievements of these Muslims and instead propagate baseless conspiracy theories staging baseless accusations without full proof.

It is important to remember that any building fire is a tragedy, and someone shouting **"Allah hu Akbar"** before suicide does not imply their religious affiliation. Those who view Islam as an ignorant faith are simply conforming to ignorance.

Islam stands as the pinnacle of teachings, always progressing. Ignorance of the true faith of Islam is demonstrated by a Muslim who doesn't conform to the lies.

The unfortunate landscape of 9/11 has left countless people in a state of uncertainty, which is itself an unresolved tragedy.

Killing one self or suicide is not martyrdom in Islam. This unfounded skepticism stems from a lack of understanding and a fear of the unknown, leading some to reject the reality of these achievements and cling to misguided beliefs.

It is crucial to educate and enlighten those who are ignorant to prevent the spread of unfounded doubts and misconceptions.

Martyrdom, indeed, is not granted to everyone, as it is considered a privilege in Islam. The case of Omar bin Khattab, the strong leader, and Amirul Mumin in (Commander of the Faithful), wishing for martyrdom surprised many people, as he held a prominent position and was highly revered.

However, the status of those who attain martyrdom through the natural course of life as devout Muslims is different. Such individuals do not actively plot or seek martyrdom, but rather it is a result of their unwavering faith and dedication to their beliefs.

This type of martyrdom is seen as a noble and honorable achievement in Islamic teachings, as it demonstrates the ultimate sacrifice and commitment to Allah.

These individuals are blessed and hold a special place in the hearts of Muslims, as they have willingly given their lives for the sake of their faith. Not suicide.

Only the one who implored Allah knew the true nature of Omar's plea for martyrdom.

On the fateful day, Omar bin Khattab, the second caliph of Islam, found himself in the mosque, engrossed in prayer and contemplation.

Unbeknownst to him, a sinister disbeliever had sneaked into the holy premises, driven by hatred and malice. Armed with a menacing double-edged sword, the evil assailant lurked in the shadows, waiting for the perfect moment to strike.

As Omar was in prayers, the disbeliever seized the opportunity and launched a swift, treacherous attack. The double-edged sword cut through the air with deadly precision, piercing Omar's body and inflicting a fatal wound.

Despite the shock and pain, Omar's unwavering faith remained steadfast until his last breath, leaving behind a legacy that would forever be etched in the annals of Islamic history.

Can anyone who is killed by another be martyred when martyrdom becomes the subject? Martyrdom is exclusive to Muslims; anyone who dies with the belief in one God, Allah.

Those who deceive and replace Allah with other gods are in a state of confusion and ignorance; nothing has changed since the beginning of creation.

The Quran states that Muslims who were killed are still living, as revealed by Allah. Can a non-Muslim who doesn't believe in Allah but participates in acts of kindness towards humanity become a martyr?

Allah can choose either a believer or a disbeliever to play a role in any situation in life. Only Muslims can experience martyrdom, as the belief in Allah must come first before leaving this world.

Islam doesn't support reincarnation, making this the only opportunity. Falsifying Islam to appease the world is a sin, as Allah will not call a disbeliever to Paradise.

The rules of Islam are written and documented precisely, without any room for alterations.

The notion that a disbeliever will be welcomed to paradise for a kind act by those who say Allah the merciful will let them in is unknown. As per the prophet of Islam, there will be no door left without Islam entering, as the rules are set.

The rise of anti-Muslim rhetoric and the aftermath of 9/11 introduced a previously unknown religion to the masses. Many individuals rushed to discover the truth about Islam as false accusations were made.

The heart's compatibility with Allah, not just the regions, is why every human was created knowing the Lord.

Such comments from Muslims may recognize the claim that Islam is an extremist religion, indicating that Muslims should modify their behavior to align with societal norms and counter this perception.

Changing the Quran is beyond the audacity of any Muslim, and Allah has sworn to safeguard his final revelation. It is widely known that the previous scriptures have been changed, but the truth can still be found by those who seek it.

If a man runs in front of a tyrant to seek justice and burns himself to prove his commitment, it is suicide rather than martyrdom. Suicide is not forgiven by Allah, as martyrdom is reserved for believers, specifically Muslims.

For believers who believe in the existence of a single God named Allah. He sent prophets, not Gods, and had faith in all of them.

Allah's mercy is revealed in the Quran, which underscores that sincere individuals have opportunities for redemption until their last breath in their quest for true faith.

The belief in one God, Allah, is the creator. The monotheistic faith of a believer in all Abrahamic religions is clear in the rise and potential downfall, as seen in the restoration of faith in Constantinople, which now stands as a Muslim country.

Nothing is impossible for Allah!

According to many religious beliefs, heaven and hell are contrasting realms that are said to exist after death.

Many religious beliefs often describe heaven as a paradise, a place of eternal happiness and peace, reserved for those who have lived virtuous lives and followed the teachings of their faith.

Hell is depicted as a realm of torment and suffering, where individuals who have defied the principles of their religion and have not sought forgiveness or repented for their sins are said to be condemned.

The concept of hell serves as a deterrent, emphasizing the importance of moral conduct and the consequences of one's actions in the afterlife.

It is believed that those who die without repentance and continue to defy the principles of their faith will endure eternal punishment in hell.

Quran: Surah Hijar: 15:43. And surely hell is their destined place, all together.

Quran: Surah Hijar: 15:44. It has seven gates, to each a group of them is designated.

ABC News: Apr 23, 2022 — A person attempted to set themselves on fire outside of the U.S. Supreme Court Building in Washington, D.C., on Friday.

CNN: Apr 25, 2022 — A climate activist died this weekend after setting himself on fire on Earth Day on the plaza in front of the US Supreme Court in Washington ...

Washington Post: Feb 25, 2024 — A video shared online, which multiple officials said appeared to be posted by the man, shows him shouting "Free Palestine" as he burned ...

Al Jazeera: Dec 17, 2020 — On this day, 10 years ago, a Tunisian fruit and vegetable vendor set himself on fire in the town of Sidi Bouzid and triggered the Arab Spring.

No single scripture advises taking one's life as a heroic act in tough situations to avoid punishment.

Taking a life and claiming it was to save others is not an act of care, but self-hatred. Islam does not condone suicide or glorify individuals who die in acts of defiance; true Islam promotes benevolence and seeking truth.

Here is a history of suicide that is not relevant to Islam. The extensive evidence of disbelievers committing suicide would require many pages to expose the truth.

The acts are inhumane, however, for those grappling with inner conflict, tragedy becomes the focus, overlooking the importance of life.

Many overlook the contradiction between Islamic principles and the absence of Islamic education among new converts. Allah grants forgiveness to those who repent, rather than those who engage in evil actions or plot evil schemes.

The decision to act or not act is in your hands while on earth. Islam does not involve incorporating its laws like the previous Abrahamic faiths did with their scriptures. It won't adapt to society or the masses.

It's a combination of ignorance and arrogance. Isa, as the Messiah, will reveal his true identity to the world. Those who unlawfully take their soul, will be made to experience the pain in the same spot, with no remorse for their impulsive actions.

Such behavior goes against the principles of Islam. In Islam, it is fundamental to not act unjustly towards the loan of life granted to us.

Just like Jesus giving his life to others, if that were true does not sit with the facets and fundamentals of monotheism.

Changing scriptures will be fully paid for, not forgiven, which is how they falsely portray Muslims committing suicide in the name of Allah, even though history proves otherwise.

Bilal persevered against tyrants and ultimately became a companion of Prophet Muhammad. He was also the first Muslim to give the azan, exemplifying Islam.

Bilal, a devout believer in Allah, found himself in a harrowing situation under the rule of a tyrant who proclaimed himself as God. Bilal was the first to give Azan and call Muslims to prayers.

Despite enduring immense torture, Bilal remained steadfast in his faith and did not succumb to pressure. His strong conviction that Allah would assist those who displayed unwavering faith was evident.

The notion of martyrdom in Islam emphasizes the continued existence of those who sacrifice their lives for the sake of their faith.

And those who are killed by oppressors' believers gain martyrdom. According to the Quran, martyrs are considered to be alive in the sight of Allah, receiving rewards and blessings for their unwavering devotion.

Quran: Surah Baqarah 2:154. Never say that those martyred in the cause of Allah are dead—in fact, they are alive! But you do not perceive it.

Quran: Surah Baqarah 2:155. We will certainly test you with a touch of fear and famine and loss of property, life, and crops. Give good news to those who patiently endure.

Allah has indeed stated in the Quran that He will test humans with various needs and challenges in this life.

These tests evaluate their faith, patience, and perseverance. Life itself is a continuous test, and it is through enduring these trials that individuals develop strength of character and grow spiritually.

When faced with adversity, some people may try to use evil means to achieve their desired outcomes. However, it is important to understand that evil and good cannot exist harmoniously.

They are incompatible. Evil actions only lead to further corruption and suffering, while good deeds bring about positive change and happiness.

The only way to reconcile the conflicting forces of evil and good is by striving to meet on the mutual ground of goodness.

This means choosing the path of righteousness, compassion, and justice, even in the face of adversity. By choosing to respond to evil with goodness, individuals can contribute to the betterment of society and create a more harmonious existence.

It is through these tests and the choices we make in response to them that our true character is revealed.

Allah has provided us with the free will to choose between good and evil, and it is our responsibility to navigate these challenges with integrity and righteousness.

By doing so, we can strengthen our relationship with Allah and strive towards a world where goodness prevails over evil.

Allah's will supersedes all his creatures!

Quran: Surah Rad:13;11. Indeed, Allah will not change the condition of the people until they change what is in themselves.

The homage of those who support the regimes of Islamophobia is so constant that higher-ups within these groups are actively protecting their promises by implementing policies that discriminate or narrow the path of entry from Muslim countries.

They do so to contain the Israeli regime, as they perceive Islam as a threat. These Islamophobes not only aim to limit the influence of Muslim countries but also target individuals who dare to support the truth about the situation.

They use various means to suppress those who speak out against their ideologies, demonstrating a clear lack of justice and an alignment with evil intentions.

Oct 17, 2023 — promised on Monday that if elected president again he will bar immigrants who support Palestine from entering the U.S. and send...

Apr 28, 2023 — ... president in 2024. "I will restore my travel ban to keep radical Islamic terrorists out of our country," the twice-impeached former.

Judgment, in Islamic belief, symbolizes the bridge between the celestial realm and the earthly plane. Muslims believe that through righteous actions and devotion, they can strive to attain a favorable judgment in the afterlife.

To attract blessings and divine favor, Muslims are encouraged to cultivate a harmonious and beautiful environment, akin to a flourishing garden, and extend invitations to all people, regardless of their faith.

It is important to note that while some individuals may choose to reject the gifts and invitations of Muslims, their presence and contributions are vital for the progress and enlightenment of the world.

Without the influence of Islam, the world would have missed out on significant advancements during the Dark Ages, including the period of Enlightenment in Europe.

It is disheartening to witness the persistence of hate-filled regimes that continue to harbor prejudice towards Islam.

Islam, in its essence, represents enlightenment, compassion, and righteousness, and those who follow its teachings strive to embody the light rather than succumb to darkness.

News NBC: Since 9/11, four times as many U.S service members and veterans have died by suicide than have been killed in combat, according to a new report.

Human Rights Watch: Sep 11, 2023 — The ADC reported over six hundred September 11-related hate crimes committed against Arabs, Muslims, and those perceived to be Arab or Muslim, ...

Some Muslims, like the sun, moon, and earth, possess a sense of autonomy and grace, but they are also willing to stand up for themselves when necessary. They refuse to accept blame passively or back down from a challenge.

The believe in equal opportunities, although they may be limited. Defending the rights of truth becomes a fundamental duty for every Muslim.

In this convoluted world of Islamophobia, those who dare to resist and challenge the rhetoric of hate are often labeled as terrorists.

The hypocritical nature of these regimes is their ultimate downfall, as they allow the worst individuals to rise to power. If it weren't for the steadfastness and resilience of Muslims who refuse to bow down on these lands, they would have long been destroyed.

The ones who stage resistance movements contribute to the flourishing of their lands, as they understand the true benefit of Sujood (prostration) in strengthening their faith and resolve.

A prime example of this is seen in Palestine, where those who resist the destruction and occupation of their homeland are unjustly portrayed as terrorists. It is the deceitful who spreads havoc and creates chaos while using the guise of righteousness.

Their actions are in line with the prophecy of the end times, where deceit becomes prevalent. These individuals possess multiple personalities, embodying the call of the evil Satan.

Genuine progress is not regression; it is an internal battle for those who allow Satan to employ them as his servants.

It is important to recognize the manipulation and hypocrisy that exists within these Islamophobic narratives and stand firm against the forces that seek to divide and oppress.

The routine and consistency of Prophet Muhammad's revelations over 23 years brought wisdom and balance to not only the Muslim community but also the entire world. Islam is a faith that embraces diversity and promotes peace, justice, and compassion.

It encourages its followers to engage with the world and seek knowledge, while also upholding strong moral values.

However, some individuals harbor Islamophobia, which is an irrational fear or prejudice against Islam and Muslims.

This fear often stems from misinformation, stereotypes, and a lack of understanding about the religion. It is important to combat Islamophobia by promoting dialogue and education and fostering mutual respect and tolerance among different faiths and cultures.

Time is often referred to as the finest commodity granted by Allah, emphasizing its importance and the need to utilize it wisely.

Faced with a changing climate, it becomes imperative for individuals to prioritize their learning and engage in activities that contribute positively to their personal growth and the well-being of the planet.

Quran: Surah Qaaf: 50:18. Not a word does a person utter without having a vigilant observer ready to write it down.

Quran: Surah Qaaf: 50:23. And one's accompanying-angel will say, here is the record ready with me.

In Islam, the concept of accounting is deeply rooted in the belief that Allah is the ultimate judge and recorder of every action, thought, and intention of individuals.

Allah's accounting surpasses the accounting of any human accountant, as He has assigned angels to meticulously record every single word and action of each person.

These angels document both the good and bad deeds of individuals, ensuring that nothing escapes their watchful eyes. However, what sets the accounting of Allah apart is its inherent fairness and mercy.

If someone refrains from committing an evil deed out of fear and reverence for Allah, it is not only recorded as a neutral act but actually as a good deed.

This highlights the compassionate nature of Allah's accounting, as it encourages individuals to strive for righteousness and rewards them for their conscious efforts to avoid wrongdoing.

Ultimately, this belief in the meticulous and just accounting of Allah serves as a reminder for Muslims to lead lives filled with sincerity, piety, and constant awareness of their actions.

Social hierarchies are deeply rooted in all societies, especially in older nations, where ancestry frequently dictates one's social standing.

Affluent individuals marry others from privileged backgrounds, and well-educated individuals seek partners with similar educational backgrounds.

While some other attractions and connections exist beyond these boundaries, faith or shared spiritual beliefs often serve as the common thread that brings people together. Ultimately, the belief in true spirituality brings together individuals from varied social classes.

However, it is important to note that it is not solely society that enforces segregation, but also a long-standing understanding to remain within familiar social circles and communities.

Efforts to foster inclusivity are breaking down barriers as society evolves. Islam transcended boundaries and made faith the inherent basis for alliances, with embargoes being more fruitful among believers than non-believers.

As times change, secularism rises as the prevailing force, leaving those unfamiliar with theology to grapple with their own ideas, often struggling in the spiritual realm.

The affluent and educated have different mindsets because of their upbringing and environment.

Wealthy individuals from a young age actively look for opportunities, while those without exposure face the decision of either taking a risk or staying within their comfort zone. Success in life is influenced by the presence of consistency.

Resisting opportunities and labeling them as pressure or intensified programming stems from a mindset that believes everything good isn't true or that past failures define their capabilities. This mindset allows individuals to justify their reluctance to not succumb to pressure and challenges.

However, winners view pressure and challenges as opportune moments for growth. They understand that facing adversity is necessary to develop resilience, learn from mistakes, and ultimately achieve success.

Winners embrace pressure as a catalyst for personal and professional growth, pushing themselves to exceed their limits and seize opportunities that come their way.

They see challenges as a chance to prove themselves and demonstrate their abilities, utilizing them as steppingstones towards reaching their goals.

In this way, winners not only thrive under pressure but also leverage it to their advantage, propelling themselves towards greater achievements.

During the early days of Islam, Muslims faced numerous hardships and persecution. The Prophet Muhammad himself was driven out of his hometown of Mecca by enemies who plotted against him and his followers.

Quran: Surah Qaaf: 50:24. It will be said to both angels, throw into hell every stubborn disbeliever

Quran: Surah Qaaf: 50:25. Withholder of good, transgressor, and doubter.

Quran: Surah Qaaf: 50:26. Who set up another God with Allah. So cast them into severe punishment.

Various religions often depict hell as a fiery place of torment and punishment. The fire in hell is so intense that it can cause unbearable agony.

Hell yearns for moments of respite from its scorching heat, when the flames briefly transform into a chilling cold.

This cold is so extreme that it renders both the heat and cold equally unbearable. Hell beseeched Allah for relief, and was granted the coldness, but it is not suitable for human survival.

Repentance is preferable to the torment of the afterlife for those who believe. The alternating torment is a punishment for disbelievers who are denied relief from their suffering.

Despite the challenges and hardships, we face in this world, the faith of true believers in Prophet Muhammad and Islam remains unwavering.

Muslims have shown unwavering faith despite historical persecution and adversity. There are opportune moments for those who search for truth and understanding.

Recognizing that blending religion and secularism can result in conflicts is crucial, considering the contradictory principles and values of these two ideologies.

When the world ends, creatures and things that cannot speak, like animals and objects, will gain the ability to speak. Amidst chaos and destruction, even hell will find its voice.

In this apocalyptic scenario, even hell will be eager to condemn more transgressors and fill its fiery depths. Regrettably, the warnings and signs were intended solely for those who were attentive and heeded them seriously.

Individuals who treated the world as a mere playground and failed to ready themselves for the future will be surprised and susceptible.

Quran: Surah Qaaf: 50:30. Beware of the Day We will ask Hell, "Are you full yet?" And it will respond, "Are there any more?"

Some may question the benefit Allah would derive from punishing the humanity He formed.

With rules in place and a vast interconnected world, countless opportunities await those who seek knowledge and guidance. Islam is a faith that is not far-fetched or difficult to understand.

Quran: Surah Qaaf: 50:31. And Paradise will be brought near to the righteous, not far off.

Quran: Surah Qaaf: 50:33. who were in awe of the Most Compassionate without seeing ˹Him˺, and have come with a heart turning ˹only to Him˺.

Allah, the fairest ruler, never administers punishment without warning first. Across history, God has shown His mercy and compassion through the sending of prophets to guide and warn nations before imposing any consequences.

These chosen messengers were assigned the duty of conveying divine messages and encouraging people to pursue righteousness. Their responsibility was to teach the principles of justice, morality, and obedience to Allah's commands.

Abundant rewards await those who listen to the warnings and pursue righteousness. Various forms of rewards can be experienced, including inner peace, blessings, and the ultimate reward of Paradise in the hereafter.

Allah's justice and mercy are interconnected, as He ensures fairness and provides chances for repentance and forgiveness to sincere seekers.

Islam and Christianity have notable differences in their beliefs!

Christianity teaches that salvation can be achieved by having faith in Jesus Christ, who is believed to be the Son of God and the savior of mankind. Christians trust that Jesus' crucifixion offered redemption for sins and ensured everlasting life.

Conversely, Islam highlights the importance of personal responsibility and being accountable.

Christians believe Jesus is divine and part of the Holy Trinity, whereas Muslims strictly adhere to monotheism and do not consider any prophet or messenger, including Muhammad, as divine.

This belief system recognizes and honors all the prophets sent by Allah throughout history. Islam is unique in its unwavering belief in monotheism and the preservation of the Quran with no modifications.

The essence of the faith remains unchanged, despite the mistakes made by certain Muslims. Instead, they act as chances for believers to learn and become more devoted to Allah and His teachings.

However, despite these challenges, Prophet Muhammad and his companions mastered the trait of resilience and steadfastness in the face of pressure.

They stood firm in their belief in the oneness of God and the message of Islam, refusing to compromise their principles.

Through their unwavering dedication, they showcased the freedom of worship and the truth of Islam to the world. As a result, many people were drawn to the message of Islam and its emphasis on monotheism.

The idols and false deities that were worshipped before became a passing phase for those who understood and embraced the truth.

The winners were those who found solace and relief in knowing the truth and following the path of Islam, despite the pressure and hardships they faced.

Quran: Surah Qaaf: 50:27. One's devilish associate will say, Our Lord! I did not make them transgress. Rather, they were far astray on their own.

Quran: Surah Qaaf: 50:28. Allah will respond, do not dispute in My presence, since I have already given you a warning.

Quran: Surah Qaaf: 50:29. My word cannot be changed, nor am I unjust to My creation.

In Christianity, Satan is often depicted as a fallen angel who rebelled against God and seeks to lead humans astray. He is portrayed as the ultimate embodiment of evil and temptation, responsible for luring individuals into committing sinful acts.

The association between Satan and the serpent originates from the story of Adam and Eve in the Garden of Eden, where the serpent tempts them to eat the forbidden fruit. In the Bible.

This portrayal emphasizes Satan's deceptive nature and his role as a tempter.

In Islam, Satan is seen as a weak entity, but with a different understanding.

Muslims believe Satan is from the **Jinn** family, as mentioned in the Quran, a supernatural creation made from smokeless fire.

Satan, known as Iblis in Islam, refused to bow down to Adam as commanded by Allah, leading to his expulsion from heaven.

In Islamic teachings, Satan is considered an enemy of humanity, constantly seeking to lead people astray and divert them from the path of righteousness.

Muslims acknowledge the influence of Satan but also emphasize personal responsibility, understanding that the choice to commit sinful acts ultimately lies within the individual.

In Judaism, Satan is often referred to as the "accuser" or "adversary" rather than a malevolent tempter.

He is a celestial being who acts as a prosecutor in the heavenly court, presenting evidence against individuals to test their righteousness

Satan's role is to challenge human beings and test their faithfulness to God. In Jewish theology, Satan is not portrayed as a fallen angel or the embodiment of evil, but as a servant of God who carries out specific tasks.

Although Satan is mentioned in the Torah, there are relatively few explicit references to him compared to Christianity and Islam

However, his presence is acknowledged as a part of Jewish belief, as he has existed since before the creation of humanity.

Overall, while there are variations in the portrayal and significance of Satan across Abrahamic religions, the common thread is the recognition of a malevolent being who tempts humans to commit sinful acts. Christians associate more evil with Satan, highlighting his role as the serpent

Muslims acknowledge his influence but also emphasize personal responsibility. Jews mention Satan less prominently and focus more on the internal struggle between good and evil within individuals.

Therefore, individuals in Islam have a responsibility to take precautions during times of moral decline. Yet, pointing fingers at Satan alone won't solve our transgressions.

Many are aware that Satan employs different tactics to misguide people, but believers should not let guilt hinder them from seeking forgiveness from Allah, known for His mercy and forgiveness.

Satan's associates, commonly known as his followers or people, have a noticeable presence with a heavy aura.

It's crucial to remember that change is within reach for everyone, and there is hope for those who genuinely seek to repent and better themselves.

Some may decide to live in a non-religious setting, focusing on the temporary joys of the material realm and disregarding their spiritual health.

Yet time is finite, and in the end, their failure to prepare and fixation on worldly desires will be in vain.

Balancing spiritual and worldly pursuits is essential for believers' lives.

Education is a powerful tool that can empower individuals to overcome obstacles and achieve their fullest potential in life.

In Islam, it is important to acknowledge that Allah has bestowed power upon both believers and non-believers in His world, as He wills.

However, it is crucial to understand that injustice does not solely depend on the ruler, but lies within the souls of individuals.

Often, we witness people continuing to support and appoint the same ruler, despite recognizing the injustices present.

Islam emphasizes the concept of standing alone for what is right, but it also emphasizes the importance of justice prevailing.

A sound and righteous heart possesses the ability to discern and uphold justice in all circumstances. Thus, while Islam encourages individual responsibility and accountability, it also calls for the establishment of justice within society as a collective endeavor.

The tool of success for the materialistically rich for decades has been the environment of education. Access to quality education has been a crucial factor in their ability to accumulate wealth and achieve success.

However, education alone is not enough. The liberation and extension of travel have also played a significant role in their journey towards prosperity.

By exploring different cultures, gaining exposure to diverse perspectives, and building international networks, the materialistically rich have been able to expand their horizons and seize opportunities that might not have been available to them otherwise.

Unfortunately, travel can be quite costly in this world, limiting these experiences to only a few who can afford such luxuries. For those who can embark on these journeys, the combination of education and travel has proven to be a powerful tool for success.

Sports play a significant role in many families who aspire to their children to succeed. These activities not only provide physical exercise but also teach important life lessons.

Whether it is a game involving a ball, where players learn about teamwork, fair play, and the consequences of their actions, or a sport like fencing, where precision and strategy are paramount, the aim is always to achieve success through preparation and hard work.

In contrast, Islam emphasizes that luck and chance do not exist. Instead, it emphasizes the importance of faith, dedication, and taking responsibility for one's actions.

Islam encourages individuals to seize opportunities by being prepared and making the most of them, rather than relying on luck or chance.

Knowledge refutes arrogance. Those who possess knowledge of the Quran understand its profound message, while those who are arrogant question the relevance of a book that was revealed 600 years ago.

They cannot realize that the Quran transcends time, outliving humanity itself. Its words are divine, originating from Allah, not from any human being.

Accurate knowledge humbles a person, for arrogance is a characteristic of Satan, not of a knowledgeable or faithful individual.

CHAPTER 14
STABILIZING TRUTH IS DUTIFUL

Life is often seen as cynical by nature, with challenges and hardships at every turn.

However, Islam is the ultimate path to seek fortune, as it provides answers to the innermost questions of one's soul.

It emphasizes the importance of comprehending the sacred oath one takes when embracing Islam, which is suitable for those who truly understand its teachings. Some individuals have embraced Islam with genuine faith, but it also encourages a deeper understanding of its principles.

By doing so, one can harness the power of their mind and spirit, rather than being overwhelmed by the challenges that life presents without direction or comprehension.

Spirituality is an integral part of fulfilling the responsibilities that life entails, while also nurturing the well-being of both the body and mind.

However, it is important to adapt and embrace the positive nature of life. Having a positive attitude can be a defining aspect of one's character.

Those who find the cynicism of life to be a challenge can strive to leave behind the negative facade and instead focus on finding pleasure in the cynicism of life in a positive light.

This mindset allows one to see the light amidst the darkness and emerge as a winner.

To cultivate a bolstering mind, it is essential to counter unfamiliar thoughts with positive companionship and surround oneself with a supportive environment. Islam emphasizes the significance of choosing the right company at every crossroads in life.

It is said that the company we keep influences our progress. While stagnation occurs when we surround ourselves with stagnant individuals, those who remain curious and open-minded make progress.

Delving into my book itself signifies progress toward developing an open-minded perspective.

Those individuals who struggle with their own insecurities often find pleasure in rejecting those who exude confidence.

This act of rejection reflects their own lack of confidence. It stems from a deep-seated fear of confronting their own limitations and facing their own vulnerabilities.

By rejecting and belittling those who possess confidence, they attempt to mask their own feelings of inadequacy.

However, this behavior only perpetuates their own cycle of self-doubt and prevents them from truly conquering their own insecurities.

It's the same concept of staging Muslims as terrorists when, in reality, the ones perpetuating acts of terror are often those who seek to exert control and dominance over Muslim lands.

These individuals or groups may have ulterior motives, such as geopolitical interests, access to resources, or ideological agendas.

Muslim-majority regions often have a rich history of peace and cultural diversity, with many communities living harmoniously.

However, these peaceful lands become targets of aggression because of the desire for power, control, and influence, leading to conflict and instability.

Therefore, the portrayal of Muslims as terrorists serves as a misrepresentation that diverts attention from the root causes of violence and allows the true perpetrators to evade scrutiny.

Being depressed, doubtful, engaged with a council of disbelievers, and mocked by haters of Islam is not a sign of a believer. It is rather a sign of a confused human who has yet to understand what Islam truly is.

Stay tuned, as Islam is not just the past but also the future. It encompasses the past, present, and future, as it is a divine revelation from Allah.

This episode has not been altered by human hands, as its clarity is derived from its delivery. Only those who truly understand can appreciate the finality of Islam. As the number of believers continues to grow, it becomes essential to refine our faith and truly understand what Islam represents.

The faith of Islam provides confidence and reassurance to its believers. While the disbelievers may indulge in the pleasures of this world, a believer can have both worldly pleasures and faith in Islam.

Muslim achievements have played a significant role in shaping the world. It is important to highlight these accomplishments as a reminder that the Muslim community has contributed to the progress and development of various fields.

From advancements in science, mathematics, and medicine during the Islamic Golden Age to the preservation and translation of ancient texts, Muslims have made substantial contributions to human knowledge and understanding. It needs repetition not silence.

Those who remain silent are hypocrites, as they neither speak good nor bad. However, Islam teaches us that those who possess a knowledge of the truth but choose to remain silent are also considered hypocrites.

In Islam, it is believed that the power of one's voice lies in its ability to express clarity, rather than in silence.

The one who speaks the truth, while the other remains silent, clearly exposes the hypocrisy and doubt that prevent the heart from expressing itself. A heart that is truly connected to Allah is only afraid of Him, not of humans.

Muslims made significant contributions to the development and use of windmills, particularly during the medieval Islamic civilization.

Windmills were first recorded to be used in the 7th century in Persia (modern-day Iran) and the Middle East.

The wind is a powerful force that never shies away from expressing itself or holding back. When it arrives, it can sweep away many things, both bringing blessings and unexpectedly taking away what was stable. It is a force that Allah sends.

Muslim engineers and inventors, such as Al-Jazari, made great advancements in windmill technology by designing efficient systems for grinding grain and pumping water.

These early windmills were primarily vertical-axis windmills, which featured a vertical rotor shaft with blades radiating outwards resembling an oversized propeller.

These early windmills, typically constructed with wooden or reed sails, harnessed the power of the wind for various purposes, such as milling grain, irrigating fields, and powering machinery.

The knowledge of windmill technology percolates to other parts of the world, including Europe, during the Crusades and through trade routes.

In Islam, the wind is a powerful force that reflects the power and wisdom of Allah.

The Quran mentions the wind as a sign from Allah, reminding believers of His presence and authority.

It is believed that Allah sends the wind as a herald of His mercy, symbolizing His compassion and blessings.

The wind carries not only physical benefits, such as providing ventilation and helping in the cultivation of crops, but it also holds spiritual significance.

The ancient people used to observe the wind patterns to predict the weather and expect the changes in the days to come. This understanding of the wind's behavior allowed them to plan their activities and make necessary preparations.

The wind serves as a reminder of Allah's control over nature and His ability to provide for His creation in unexpected ways. The blessings that come with the wind are beyond human imagination, showcasing the limitless mercy and generosity of Allah.

Quran: Surah Araf: 7:57 And it is He Who sends forth winds as glad tidings in advance of His Mercy, and when they have carried a heavy-laden cloud, We drive it to a dead land, then We send down rain from it and bring forth fruits of every kind. In this manner do We raise the dead that you may take heed.

Muslim contributions played a crucial role in advancing this technology, and their expertise helped pave the way for the widespread use of windmills in different civilizations.

Today, windmills continue to be an important source of renewable energy, with modern wind turbines being much more advanced and efficient.

They are used to generate electricity on a large scale, especially in areas with high wind potential, contributing to the global efforts to reduce reliance on fossil fuels.

Muslims have made significant contributions to the progress of solar system technology, which is now widely utilized worldwide as an efficient method of conducting various tasks.

Various activities, such as generating electricity, heating water, and powering vehicles.

Muslims have been at the forefront of this technological advancement, making significant contributions in both research and implementation.

Muslim scientists, engineers, and scholars have made groundbreaking discoveries and inventions that have revolutionized the solar system technology.

For instance, in the 9th century, Muslim astronomer and mathematician Al-Farabi developed the concept of using mirrors to concentrate sunlight for heating water.

Imagine the significant contribution of the Muslim world through the years, which is still relevant and utilized by every human today.

Mirrors reflect not only our physical appearance but also our thoughts and interactions. Just as mirrors reflect our positive qualities, it is essential for us to surround ourselves with optimistic individuals who propel us forward.

Cannot overlook the roots of these advancements, as they originate from the Muslim community, providing stability and a sense of duty.

This early innovation laid the foundation for the development of solar thermal energy systems.

Muslim scientists like Ibn al-Haytham, known as the "father of modern optics," made significant contributions to the understanding of light and optics, which are fundamental to the functioning of solar panels.

Muslim-majority countries have invested heavily in solar energy infrastructure, leading to the widespread adoption of solar systems across the world.

These advancements have not only contributed to a more sustainable and efficient way of conducting various activities, but have also played a crucial role in mitigating climate change and reducing dependence on fossil fuels.

Besides windmills, Muslims have also made significant contributions to other renewable energy sources, such as the use of candles.

Islamic civilization has a rich history of advancements in various fields, including chemistry and material sciences.

Muslim scholars and inventors contributed to the development of efficient candle-making techniques, which involved using various materials like beeswax and vegetable oils.

Different cultures later adopted and further improved these techniques, leading to the widespread use of candles for illumination and decoration.

Islamic scholars like Ibn al-Haytham made significant contributions to the field of optics, which laid the foundation for the understanding of light and its interaction with different materials.

Their work on optics and the development of accurate astronomical instruments helped in the study of the solar system, contributing to our understanding of celestial bodies and the sun's energy.

In conclusion, Muslims have made notable contributions to various aspects of renewable energy, including windmills, candle-making, and the study of the solar system.

Their advancements in these fields have had a lasting impact on technology and continue to influence modern practices in harnessing renewable energy sources.

Muslims have made significant advancements in the medical field that are often overlooked.

One notable contribution is the development of forceps, which were used for procedures such as the cesarean section when it was unheard of in the medical field.

The Muslims developed forceps years later, proving that progress is unstoppable and highlighting Islamic contributions.

These forceps, designed by Muslims, revolutionized obstetrics and saved countless lives.

Muslims were pioneers in optics, creating innovative instruments that improved vision and led to the establishment of hospitals with specialized wards for different medical conditions.

In Islam, the eyes are not only seen as a physical organ but also as a window to the soul.

The Quran emphasizes the importance of guarding one's gaze and avoiding looking at anything that is forbidden or indecent.

This is because what we choose to see can have a profound impact on our thoughts, actions, and overall spiritual well-being.

Muslims are encouraged to use their eyes to seek knowledge, appreciate the beauty of Allah's creation, and show kindness and compassion towards others.

The eyes are a gift from Allah, and it is our responsibility to use them wisely and under Islamic teachings. By doing so, we can maintain the purity of our hearts and ensure that the light of faith shines through our actions and interactions with the world.

In Islam, if an unintentional gaze occurs, it is not considered a sin. Islam recognizes accidental glances can happen without one's control, and therefore, they are not held accountable for such occurrences.

However, intentional gazes and continuous negligence in looking at what is impermissible, along with the spread of evil or fitnah, are discouraged as they can have detrimental effects on the individual's heart and soul.

Islam emphasizes the importance of guarding one's eyes and avoiding indulgence in anything that may corrupt the purity of the heart.

The contamination of the heart occurs when one willingly looks at evil, as it can lead to a negative impact on one's character and behavior, promoting the propagation of evil in society. Therefore, Islam encourages believers to focus on looking at what is good and virtuous, as it contributes to the purification of the heart and the overall well-being of the individual.

Quran: Surah Imran: 3:13. Indeed, there was a sign for you in the two armies that met in battle—one fighting for the cause of Allah and the other in denial. The believers saw their enemy twice their number. But Allah supports with His victory whoever He wills.

These achievements highlight the selflessness and generosity of Muslims, as they shared their knowledge and advancements with the world, rather than keeping them exclusively for themselves.

It is crucial to remind both Muslims and the world about these contributions, as they demonstrate the immense impact that Muslim scholars and scientists have had on the field of medicine.

Muslims were the first to perform cesarean sections when the mother's life was in danger during childbirth.

This revolutionary medical procedure was described in the book "Al-Tasrif" written by the Muslim physician Al-Zahrawi in the ninth century.

Al-Zahrawi described the technique of safely delivering the baby by opening the mother's abdomen when natural birth was impossible or too risky.

This contribution to the field of obstetrics by Muslim scholars laid the foundation for modern cesarean section procedures that are still performed today to save the lives of both mothers and babies.

Muslim physicians indeed performed the first eye surgery, known as cataract surgery, during the Islamic Golden Age. In the 10th century, a Persian physician named Muhammad ibn Zakariya al-Razi developed innovative techniques for treating cataracts.

He described the use of a hollow needle to remove the cloudy lens, and then inserting a clear glass lens to restore vision. Al-Razi's significant contributions to ophthalmology laid the foundation for further developments in eye surgery by Muslim scholars, including Ibn Sina (Avicenna) and Al-Zahrawi.

Their meticulous observations and surgical techniques significantly improved the success rates of eye surgeries, setting the foundation for modern ophthalmology.

Those who have witnessed eye surgeries understand the significance of appreciating what is permissible and beautiful, rather than defying Allah.

The one who gave eyesight upon us also has the power to take it away. Those who live in darkness yearn for the light that the eyes can provide and the joy it brings. These achievements stand as a testament to the intellectual and cultural heritage of the Muslim world, showcasing a history rooted in innovation and creativity rather than destruction.

By focusing on these achievements, we can challenge the negative rhetoric and stereotypes that often overshadow the positive contributions of Muslims throughout history.

It is crucial to remind the world of the fruitful behavior and rich legacy of Muslim achievements, promoting a more inclusive and accurate narrative that recognizes the valuable contributions made by this diverse and vibrant community.

These achievements have become a practicality of comparison to understand how the concepts and perspectives of Muslim individuals differ from those of the world.

In Islam, cleanliness is not only emphasized in the physical sense but also in the spiritual and mental aspects. Muslims are encouraged to maintain cleanliness in all aspects of their lives, including personal hygiene, their homes, and their surroundings.

This includes regular washing of the hands, face, and feet before prayer, as well as performing wudu, a ritual cleansing, before each prayer.

The act of **Wudu** not only cleanses the physical body but also serves as a symbolic purification of the soul, preparing the individual for a state of spiritual connection with Allah.

Islam teaches that cleanliness is not limited to the wealthy or privileged. It is a basic requirement for all Muslims, regardless of their socio-economic status.

In the Islamic faith, prayer serves as a direct means of communication between Allah, the creator.

Salat, a ritual prayer mandated five times a day, is a method to seek guidance, forgiveness, and blessings.

An important aspect of this practice is the act of removing one's shoes before prayer, symbolizing respect and cleanliness. Believers believe one should keep the ground where they pray clean.

Prophet Muhammad established this tradition of removing shoes and holds great significance.

It is a way of acknowledging that Allah's laws are superior to any laws created by humans.

The importance of cleanliness extends beyond personal hygiene. Muslims are also encouraged to keep their homes and surroundings clean, as cleanliness is believed to be a reflection of one's faith and character.

Ultimately, the emphasis on cleanliness in Islam is not just for the sake of physical well-being but also the purification of the heart and mind.

Regularly engaging in prayer, known as Salat, serves to soften the heart and seek repentance for any mistakes or wrongdoings. It goes beyond merely cleansing the body; Salat is intended to purify the heart through spirituality.

The one who prays **Salat** does not need to speak to another about their performance. It is the actions that bring about change and make the face shine, the mind calm, the advice serene, doubts fly away, and belief sink in. Such is Salat: a one-on-one meeting with Allah.

Per Islam, clean body and mind are necessary prerequisites for a sincere and attentive connection with Allah. Arrogance and inviting others to evil are contradictory to the mindset required for engaging in Salat, as it requires humility, sincerity, and a desire for spiritual growth.

In summary, cleanliness holds great importance in Islam, encompassing physical, spiritual, and mental aspects of one's life. It is a requirement for all Muslims, regardless of their financial means, and is a reflection of one's faith and character.

Through acts of cleanliness, Muslims seek to purify their bodies, minds, and surroundings, enabling a deeper connection with Allah and fostering a sense of humility, repentance, and spiritual growth.

The faith of Islam deeply intertwines with the Muslim mind, shaping their beliefs, values, and actions.

It is important to note that these differences in thinking do not infringe upon the dominant ideologies of human concepts, but reflect the unique perspective and understanding that Muslims have.

While Muslims, like any other individuals, can make mistakes, it is crucial to recognize that their faith teaches them to strive for righteousness and avoid evil. In Islam, humans recognize their tendency to make errors and commit sins.

The mistakes cannot impede one's progress or knowledge. However, they function as an opportunity for repentance and self-improvement. Moving forward with strength is crucial for personal and collective improvement.

In Islam, it is sinful to disclose others' sins or constantly remind them of their past errors, particularly after they have sought forgiveness from Allah.

Endorsing and motivating positive change is crucial for individuals who have truly transformed.

Those who engage in conflict with Islam may experience losses, but this resilient regime has proven that its victories outweigh its setbacks.

Forgiveness is a central concept in Islam, which also emphasizes personal growth and compassion towards others.

The narrative of the Battle of Tabuk was narrated by Ka'b ibn Malik:

In the Battle of Tabuk, three people opted out of participating due to their laziness. It is important to note that these individuals were devout followers of Islam, not disbelievers.

This incident highlights the potential consequences that can befall any believer when they fail to manage their time effectively and succumb to procrastination.

Ka'b Ibn Malik, a wealthy individual, had the chance to accompany Prophet Muhammad and his fellow companions during the Battle of Tabuk.

He did not join the Muslims in the Battle of Badr, a historic win for them. Unfortunately, his laziness and tendency to procrastinate prevented him from succeeding.

When he finally approached Prophet Muhammad and admitted his laziness, the Prophet informed him that the decision was between him and Allah.

This response left him feeling even more remorseful and disappointed in himself. He sought solace by talking to his cousin, but even he turned away, leaving him to feel the weight of his own actions.

By the time he realized the gravity of his procrastination, the battle had already concluded, and the Muslims had emerged victorious.

The Battle of Tabuk, which took place in 630 AD, was a significant event for both the Muslims and Prophet Muhammad, who served as the general.

It was a crucial military expedition that aimed to confront the Byzantine Empire, which posed a threat to the emerging Muslim state.

The battle holds great importance as it marked the furthest northward expansion of the Muslim army during the lifetime of Prophet Muhammad.

It showcased the growing strength and unity of the Muslim community and showed their determination to defend their faith and territory.

Despite facing logistical challenges and harsh desert conditions, the Muslims successfully marched towards Tabuk, which sent a powerful message to neighboring tribes and empires about their military prowess.

The battle also highlighted the importance of unity and obedience to the leadership of Prophet Muhammad, as it required a large-scale mobilization of resources and troops.

The Battle of Tabuk led to the consolidation of alliances with various tribes in the region and resulted in a peaceful surrender by the Byzantines, further solidifying the influence and authority of the Muslims in the Arabian Peninsula.

Overall, the Battle of Tabuk was a pivotal moment in the history of Islam, demonstrating the strategic and leadership skills of Prophet Muhammad and the growing strength of the Muslim community.

Ka'b Ibn Malik not only disappointed Allah and the Prophet, but he also disappointed himself, as he had let an opportunity for self-growth and contribution to the Muslim community slip away.

The consequences of his inaction were far more severe than he could have imagined.

Many individuals provided excuses and displayed hypocrisy for not taking part in the Battle of Tabuk.

Prophet Muhammad accepted their excuses, took their pledge of allegiance, sought forgiveness from Allah on their behalf, and entrusted the judgment of their hidden intentions to Allah.

However, Ka'b Ibn Malik arrived with no excuses, only admitting to his procrastination.

Prophet Muhammad instructed him to await Allah's judgment. He was subsequently neglected by both the believers and the prophet.

News started circulating that Ka'b Ibn Malik is facing a boycott from his people, and a king sent him a letter offering asylum.

The people started pointing out things to him. Eventually, someone gave him a letter from the king of Ghassan.

The letter said that the king had heard that his friend, the Prophet, had mistreated him.

The king assured him that Allah would not let him live in a place where he felt inferior and where his rights were lost. The king invited him to join them and promised to console him.

His intention, as a non-Muslim, was to manipulate a Muslim into renouncing their faith and betraying their own community, despite the kindness they had shown him when he was feeling lonely.

Consumed by rage, he tossed the letter aside. Despite his genuine convictions, he succumbed to laziness and let down both himself and the prophet, as well as the Muslim community.

He was also conscious of the fact that the prophet did not interact with him.

A messenger sent by the prophet asked three men who didn't attend the battle of Tabuk to stay away from their wives.

One of the men's wives went to the prophet and pleaded that she hadn't been intimate with him because of his health, but only helped him.

She was granted permission to continue. Some people advised him to make excuses to the prophet.

Fifty days later, while standing for the morning prayers, he heard people rejoicing as the word of forgiveness had come from Allah through revelation to Prophet Muhammad.

The atmosphere in the mosque was tense as Ka'b Ibn Malik approached the Prophet with bated breath. The news of his transgression had spread like wildfire, causing a stir among the community.

Ka'b's heart raced with a mixture of hope and apprehension, unsure of how his actions would be perceived by Allah and the Prophet.

As he stood before the Prophet, his eyes downcast and his demeanor humbled, he silently pleaded for forgiveness.

Suddenly, a divine calm seemed to descend upon the gathering.

The Prophet's expression softened, and he rose to his feet, his voice carrying the weight of authority.

Every eye in the mosque was fixed on him, waiting with bated breath for his words. In that moment, it felt as if time stood still.

In a voice filled with compassion and mercy, the Prophet announced Allah had revealed a message specifically regarding Ka'b Ibn Malik.

The air seemed charged with anticipation as the community leaned in to hear what was meant for this repentant man.

The revelation spoke of Allah's infinite forgiveness and compassion.

It emphasized the importance of sincere repentance and turning back to Him after straying from the right path.

Ka'b's heart soared with relief, tears of gratitude streaming down his face. He had been forgiven by the Almighty, and this revelation was a testament to Allah's boundless love and mercy.

The news quickly spread throughout the community, and people marveled at the power of repentance and Allah's divine intervention.

Ka'b's story became an inspiration for those who had also faltered in their faith, reminding them that no matter how far they had strayed, sincere repentance and a return to the path of righteousness would always be met with Allah's forgiveness and guidance.

From that day forward, Ka'b Ibn Malik became a symbol of hope and redemption, a living testament to the transformative power of sincere repentance.

His journey served as a reminder to all believers that Allah's forgiveness knows no bounds, and that no matter how grave our mistakes may be, it is never too late to turn back to Him and seek His mercy.

He asked whether forgiveness was it from the prophet himself or from Allah. The prophet replied, "From Allah." Gratefully, he thanked Allah and declared that he would never procrastinate or lie.

Quran: Surah Taubah: 9:118. And 'Allah has also turned in mercy to' the three who had remained behind, 'whose guilt distressed them' until the earth, despite its vastness, seemed to close in on them, and their souls were torn in anguish. They knew there was no refuge from Allah except in Him. Then He turned to them in mercy so that they might repent. Surely Allah 'alone' is the Accepter of Repentance, Most Merciful.

Through many tests, he had proven his honor and became an exemplary model of truthfulness and punctuality.

Those who recognized the challenges and admonitions from Allah heeded them earnestly and passed down their experiences to those who comprehend the significance of upholding not only Allah's decree but also the values of humanity.

This individual was a man of great wealth, yet he generously contributed to charity, reserving only a small portion for himself and his family.

The verses of the Quran brought him solace and guidance, as he was among the fortunate ones who received blessings from Allah during the time of Prophet Muhammad.

Through his actions, he left behind inspiring narratives that continue to enrich and compensate our own lives.

Prophet and common people both have witnessed countless moments of devotion and repentance from both humans and animals, and these stories have left lasting memories of the profound impact that sharing can have.

May-day's Story: A Dog's Unwavering Devotion to Allah in this World:

May-day, the devoted dog to Allah, has become an inspiration for many. She was also in my first book "Delivery is Power".

Her unwavering devotion to prayer is truly exemplary.

Throughout the years, she faithfully woke up for the morning prayers, using her bark as a wake-up call for those who relied on her.

May-day, a loyal and devoted dog, had an uncanny ability to sense the five daily prayers observed by Muslims.

She would bark persistently during prayer times, serving as a gentle reminder for the attendees to fulfill their religious duties.

Despite not being allowed on the Muslim prayer rug, May-day was allowed as she would find her spot and bow her head in a gesture of respect and reverence.

Her dedication to prayer was truly remarkable, surpassing even that of many humans.

It was hard for anyone to dismiss her presence, as her unwavering loyalty and impeccable timing made her an integral part of the prayer sessions.

May-day's unwavering commitment to prayer showcased the profound and inclusive nature of devotion, transcending the boundaries of species and reminding everyone of the beauty of faith.

May-day understood that her true master was Allah, and she dedicated herself to Him seeking no affection or attention from her human owners. Her commitment and loyalty were unmatched.

As May-day has grown older, she has slowed down, no longer waking up or barking during prayer hours.

This change serves as a poignant reminder of the significance of her bark held for those who depended on her for prayer reminders.

Despite her age and physical limitations, May-day leaves behind a powerful legacy.

She has taught others the importance of prayers and the value of time. She finds solace in the place where she prayed the most, often sitting there and reflecting on the punctuality she maintained.

May-day emphasizes that procrastination is an enemy, and just as she is punctual in her prayers, she will be punctual in her departure from this world, leaving behind nothing but cherished memories and photographs of her humble posture during prayer.

May-day's story serves as a lesson about the significance of time and punctuality.

Allah chooses certain individuals, or animals like **May-day**, to become teachers and leave a lasting legacy for others to remember.

Her dedication to prayers and the value she placed on time are qualities that should inspire us all to prioritize our devotion and make the most of the time we have been given.

May-day's example reminds us that procrastination is futile, while valuing and utilizing our time wisely has immeasurable importance.

May-day, a remarkable individual, but a dog never forgot to acknowledge that her success resulted from Allah's blessings.

The story can provide some insight, but only those who witnessed her actions truly comprehend the depth of her gratitude and dedication towards her creator.

She recognized that it was Allah who provided her with the essential needs of food and health, enabling her to pursue her goals.

May-day's personality served as a constant reminder to those who overlooked the laws of the creator and underestimated their own capabilities.

She understood that the ability to achieve greatness was bestowed upon her by Allah, and she dedicated herself wholeheartedly to Him.

May-day's commitment to Allah became a gift in itself, granting her the ability to discern the truth and make righteous choices.

Despite May-day's plump appearance, she maintained good health, had a healthy appetite, and spent her time wisely. Although she shed pounds and decreased her pace, there's an extraordinary tale to recount about her wonders.

As I began to complete my story on May-day I stated there will come a day when May-Day departs from this world, her legacy will endure, immortalized on the pages that will tell her remarkable story....

May-Day has passed, leaving behind her legacy as a dog who prayed to Allah.

Reminded those who called upon Allah. She will be immortalized in the annals of history and cherished by all who knew her.

She spent 17 years focused on remembering Allah and performing Sujood at designated times with a Muslim woman. Her body was interred, not cremated.

The duty of an integral believer in Islam goes beyond simply standing for the truth. It encompasses upholding integrity and righteousness in all aspects of life, even if it means standing alone and facing opposition from the masses.

Prophet Muhammad, as the final messenger of Allah, played a crucial role in establishing the finality of faith.

If Prophet Muhammad had not stood firm in delivering the message of monotheism and truth, he would have compromised the continuity and completeness of faith gained by Adam and Eve.

It is important to note that their worship was solely directed towards Allah, and any suggestion they were not forgiven due to whispers of Satan is unfounded

Allah, in His infinite wisdom, was aware of the events that would unfold, and He gave forgiveness as a mercy upon humanity.

This serves as a reminder that, despite our shortcomings and mistakes, forgiveness is readily available to those who seek it.

Prophet Muhammad, in his teachings, emphasized the significance of time and its fleeting nature. He advised people to make the most of their youth, as it is a time of strength and vitality that should be used wisely before the onset of old age.

He also highlighted the importance of prioritizing health, as good health enables individuals to fully engage in life's opportunities and fulfill their responsibilities.

Prophet Muhammad stressed the value of wealth, urging people to appreciate and use their resources before they face financial difficulties or poverty.

However, above all, Prophet Muhammad emphasized the preciousness of time. He encouraged everyone to recognize that time is a finite and invaluable resource that can never be regained once lost.

This concept is further reinforced in the Quran, where Allah swears by time, emphasizing its significance.

This mention in the Quran serves as a reminder to humanity of the importance of valuing and making the most of each moment granted to us.

Prophet Muhammad recognized the destructive nature of procrastination and emphasized the importance of completing tasks and responsibilities promptly. He warned the people that failing to fulfill assigned tasks because of procrastination is a grave mistake.

The Quran mentions time 365 times, which is indeed significant. Time holds great significance in the teachings of Islam.

Allah has emphasized the importance of time in multiple verses, reminding believers of its value as a precious resource.

Islam motivates people to utilize their time through worship, seeking knowledge, and fulfilling obligations.

Islam promotes seizing opportunities and using time effectively, discouraging procrastination. Through valuing and wisely using time, followers of Islam can live productive and fulfilling lives.

Procrastination not only wastes time but also hinders one's ability to convey important messages or fulfill obligations.

The Prophet stressed the significance of seizing opportunities and not wasting precious time, just like the saying "the early bird catches the worm." It is not only about accomplishing tasks but also about being mindful of the spiritual aspect of life.

The Prophet highlighted the significance of waking up early for the Fajr (morning) prayer, as it is a fundamental practice for believers.

He reminded Muslims and even non-Muslims that attending to the needs of their souls is crucial.

However, facing one's inner demons and seeking repentance becomes imperative, especially when procrastination and a lack of appreciation for the blessings of life are at play.

The deceiver, Satan, often exploits pride and encourages procrastination, preventing individuals from expressing their heartfelt thoughts or taking advantage of the opportunities granted by Allah.

Those who have experienced the negative consequences of procrastination understand the wisdom in the Prophet's advice about overcoming this habit and fulfilling their responsibilities without delay.

The incident occurred when Prophet Muhammad was in the Cave of Hira, seeking solitude and contemplation.

Suddenly, the angel Gabriel appeared before him and commanded him to "Read! Initially startled by the command, Prophet Muhammad, who was unlettered and unable to read or write, experienced the incident.

However, the angel Gabriel persisted and squeezed him tightly, urging him to respond. It was then that the angel added, **"Iqra Bismi Rabuka Alaze Khaleq"** which translates to **"Read in the name of your Lord who created."**

This powerful message emphasized the importance of seeking knowledge and understanding through reading, as well as acknowledging the role of Allah as the ultimate creator and source of wisdom.

This profound encounter marked the beginning of Prophet Muhammad's divine revelation and his role as the final messenger of Islam.

Knowledge is indeed a powerful tool that allows individuals to explore and understand the world around them.

However, for seeking Allah or a higher power, simply knowing a fraction about Islam may not be enough. Genuine faith and a genuine desire to seek Allah go beyond mere intellectual understanding.

For those who genuinely seek the truth, the journey towards finding Allah is not just a matter of admiration or curiosity.

It is an inner longing, a deep yearning to connect with something greater than oneself. It is a quest for spiritual fulfillment and a desire to understand the purpose of existence.

Once individuals find the truth and embrace Islam, they realize it is not just a set of religious rules and regulations, but a comprehensive way of life that encompasses every aspect of their being.

It is then that they leave behind the confines of societal and cultural constraints and embark on a path of personal growth and self-discovery.

This journey towards finding the source that keeps Islam within close reach is not a one-time endeavor, but a lifelong commitment.

It involves continuously seeking knowledge, deepening one's understanding of the faith, and strengthening the relationship with Allah.

It is a process of self-reflection, self-improvement, and constant submission to the will of Allah.

Ultimately, those who find the truth and embark on this journey of faith experience a profound transformation.

They find solace, purpose, and guidance in Islam, and strive to live their lives under its principles. They become ambassadors of Islam, spreading the message of peace, justice, and compassion to others, and inspiring them to seek the truth as well.

In the Quran, Allah emphasizes the gravity of ridiculing Him, His revelations, and His Messenger.

Allah considers such actions as an act of disbelief **(KUFR)** committed by someone who had previously believed in Him.

Allah warns that belittling or mocking His divine guidance is a direct rejection of the faith one had embraced. This is a serious offense, as it undermines the sanctity and authority of Allah's message and shows a lack of respect for His commands.

Allah expects believers to uphold the utmost reverence and reverence for Him and His Messenger, recognizing that ridiculing them is tantamount to denying the truth and veering away from the path of faith.

Before souls came into existence 50,000 years ago, they resided in a realm where they had a direct connection with Allah, their creator. In this pre-existence, each soul acknowledged and embraced the truth of Allah's existence and oneness.

However, upon entering the earthly realm, some individuals may forget or reject this truth because of the distractions and challenges of the material world.

This topic serves as a gentle reminder for those who yearn to explore the profound and unwavering truth of the existence of one creator, Allah. It provides a means to reestablish that innate recognition and delve into the significance of this truth in one's life.

By contemplating this topic, individuals can fortify their faith and deepen their understanding of Allah's oneness, ultimately fostering a more profound and meaningful relationship with their creator.

Those who are new to Islam or Muslims who are unaware of their own faith may be tempted to make assumptions and create rules that suit their personal preferences, particularly new converts who may lack a deep understanding of Islam.

This can lead to the dangerous practice of making laws that go against the teachings of Allah, simply because they find the original laws too bothersome for the society they live in.

Actions that purposefully mock the faith of Allah can be viewed as going against the principles and teachings of Islam, which do not permit any loopholes or alterations.

It's crucial for new converts and Muslims to consult Quran and those knowledgeable of Islamic doctrine, seek guidance, and adhere to authentic teachings of Islam instead of manipulating the religion to match their own preferences.

Quran; Surah Taubah: 9:65:66. Make no excuse; you have disbelieved after you had believed. If We pardon some of you, We will punish others amongst you because they were Mujrimoon (disbelievers, polytheists, sinners, criminals, etc.)"

Quran: Surah Anam: 6:68. And when you Muhammad see those who engage in a false conversation about Our Verses of the Quran by mocking at them, stay away from them till they turn to another topic. And if Satan causes you to forget, then after the remembrance sit not you in the company of those people who are the Zalimoon polytheists and wrongdoers.

In the Quran, the concept of rules remains continuous, emphasizing the importance of the company one keeps.

It teaches that those who disbelieve after the rules have become clear are choosing to alter their path in this world and are no longer considered within the fold of Islam.

Unlike Christianity, Islam does not believe in the concept of original sin inherited from Adam and Eve.

Conversely, in Islam, individuals are solely accountable for their own actions. In Islam, a newborn child is not deemed sinful until they possess consciousness and the ability to comprehend.

Rather, it is the responsibility of parents to educate their children about Allah. In contrast to Christianity, Muslims do not view baptism as a necessary practice, as they believe per Islam children are born with purity.

Typically, Muslims allow the newborn to listen to the **Adan**, the call to prayer, as it has a calming effect.

When a child is born, they venture out of the safety of their mother's womb and start to discover and acquire knowledge, gradually taking on more responsibility as they grow up.

Muslim children usually understand more around the age of seven, and by their teenage years, many of them have already assumed important duties.

Allah places great importance on responsibility, and parents are entrusted with the task of teaching their children about Him.

Blame is not placed on others, as each person is accountable for their own deeds. Islam teaches one should strive to improve and compete against oneself, rather than competing against others.

The converts to Islam are indeed appreciated by Muslims for their decision to embrace the faith.

Islam is often seen as an easy religion to enter, as it primarily requires a belief in one God, Allah, and the acceptance of Prophet Muhammad as the final messenger. When a convert enters the fold of Islam, the takbir (the proclamation of Allah's greatness) is often recited loudly, symbolizing their new spiritual journey.

However, it is important to note that while the initial step of conversion may be relatively straightforward, the journey of learning and understanding Islam is a lifelong process.

When someone converts to Islam, it is believed that Allah completely forgives their sins and gives them a fresh start. This forgiveness is based on the belief that by accepting Islam and embracing the teachings of the Quran and Prophet Muhammad, individuals can leave their past sins behind.

Unlike other religions that have a baptism ceremony for spiritual purification, Islam does not have a specific ritual for this purpose.

Instead, the central declaration of faith, known as the Shahada, serves as the acceptance of Allah as the one God and the recognition of Prophet Muhammad as the final messenger.

By sincerely and wholeheartedly reciting the Shahada, a person officially becomes a Muslim and enters a new phase of spiritual life, with their previous wrongdoings forgiven.

Unfortunately, sometimes, the level of education and knowledge about Islamic teachings among converts may be lacking.

This can be attributed to various factors such as limited access to educational resources, cultural influences, or personal ideologies that are intertwined with their previous faiths. The environment in which a convert lives plays a significant role in their ability to deepen their understanding of Islam.

If a convert returns to the same surroundings they came from, without seeking further guidance or support, it becomes challenging for them to fully grasp the teachings of Islam.

The Muslim community must continuously provide attention, learning, and support for converts to nurture their faith. Supporting a new Muslim in their spiritual growth and understanding brings blessings to those who strive for success. While giving up is simple, it goes against the principles of a Muslim.

Marrying a convert to Islam can be viewed as a way to strengthen their faith and offer them support and guidance.

Across the ages, marriages have been utilized to strengthen religious communities and foster alliances after accepting Islam.

Within Islam, marrying a convert not only strengthens their dedication to the faith but also provides them with a supportive atmosphere to navigate their newfound religious identity.

The spouse, who is already grounded in the Islamic faith, can offer guidance, knowledge, and motivation to aid the convert in their religious development and comprehension. The alliance created by marriage has the potential to strengthen the Muslim community's unity and deepen their faith.

The company one keeps has a significant impact on the behavior of a person, regardless of whether they are converts to Islam or born and raised in the faith.

The individuals we surround ourselves with can shape our attitudes, beliefs, and actions. For converts to Islam, the company they keep can provide guidance, support, and a sense of community as they navigate their newfound faith.

To enrich their understanding and observance of Islam, individuals may choose to associate with devout and knowledgeable Muslims who can offer guidance.

Marriage serves as a potent option, as it aligns with Islamic principles and has the power to restore faith, provide stability, and promote acceptance. A notable example is Prophet Muhammad, who formed alliances and strengthened relationships through his marriages.

Similarly, for Muslims who have grown up in the faith, the company they keep can reinforce and strengthen their religious values and practices.

Being surrounded by fellow Muslims who are committed to following the teachings of Islam can serve as a source of inspiration and motivation.

Conversely, associating with individuals who do not prioritize or respect the principles of Islam can lead to deviation from religious obligations and a weakening of faith.

Therefore, it is essential for both converts and lifelong Muslims to choose their company wisely and surround themselves with individuals who encourage and uphold the values of Islam.

The person who seeks health not only goes to the gym and eats healthy but also prioritizes surrounding themselves with like-minded individuals.

They understand the importance of having a positive support system and avoiding the influence of unhealthy habits.

This person actively seeks companions who share their dedication to a healthy lifestyle, as they believe that surrounding themselves with such individuals will further motivate and inspire them.

They know that the people they spend time with greatly impact their choices and behaviors. Similarly, a dancer who engages in aerobic dancing appreciates the company of other dancers. They understand the intricacies of dance steps and the constant return to the same foundational movements.

They find comfort and camaraderie in the presence of fellow dancers who understand the physical and artistic aspects of their passion. In the same way, the person seeking personal growth and success will choose to surround themselves with individuals who inspire and challenge them to reach their full potential.

They believe that the company they keep influences their own mindset, goals, and achievements. Islam thrives with those who keep balance.

When examining the rules, laws, and regulations of Abrahamic faiths, including Judaism and Islam, there are similarities, particularly in the belief in a monotheistic God, Allah.

However, upon closer examination, it becomes evident that there are distinct differences between these faiths in terms of their doctrines and practices.

While time may have brought changes and adaptations in religious courses, the common thread of monotheism and belief in Allah remains.

For the afterlife, there are three important questions: who is your God, who is your last prophet, and what is your religion?

It is a concept that may be difficult to grasp, for some but in Islam, the answers to the questions in the grave come from the heart, not from the mind or tongue.

The test persists and questioning commences even after death, surprising many who seek peace in their final resting place.

In Islamic belief, the heart is considered the dwelling place of sincerity and true devotion.

While it may be debated that the heart is devoid of emotions and subject to the control of the mind, the Quran highlights the crucial role of maintaining a sound heart.

The verse emphasizes the importance of having a pure heart by saying, "Approach me with a sound heart," instead of focusing on the mind. With "Iman" (faith) in their heart, individuals can confidently respond to these questions and find out their identity as a Muslim.

Although the questions remain the same, they carry a weighty significance. The angel poses these questions from the grave.

Who is your Lord? Allah for a Muslim.

What is your religion? Islam for a Muslim.

Who is your prophet? Prophet Muhammad for a Muslim.

Some people may wonder why there are questions in the grave that answer simply. A person will spend more time in the grave than they did on Earth, so it is important for the grave to be a peaceful place, just like the Earth they walked on.

This concept makes perfect sense, as each phase of life is a transition, and no phase is exempt from being accounted for. It is a transitory period until the day of judgment, and Islam is clear about the significance of each phase.

Responding to these questions with unwavering conviction and genuine sincerity shows a deep faith and steadfast commitment to the principles of Islam.

Subsequently, a divine command will descend from the heavens for a Muslim. My servant speaks the truth.

Prepare Paradise's bed, dress him in Paradise's clothes, and open the doors of Paradise.

These explorations address the fact that the time spent in the grave is longer than the time spent on earth.

Understanding the details of the Quran and Islam can be transformative for those who are curious to learn.

(**Jannat's**) heaven's enchanting scent and cool breeze will adorn the grave. His vision will determine the width of the grave. Like a bridegroom, the angels will command him to rest peacefully.

The explanations provided may be overwhelming for individuals who do not hold any belief in an afterlife or those who do not believe that salvation is attained through deeds.

These individuals may find it difficult to comprehend or relate to the concepts being discussed, especially in relation to the afterlife and the significance of actions.

For those who believe that salvation is solely achieved through faith in Jesus, the comparisons made with Islam, which has a different understanding of salvation and emphasize the importance of both belief and deeds, may appear entirely different and detailed.

The contrasting beliefs and perspectives between these two faiths further highlight the complexity of religious concepts and can contribute to a sense of disconnect or confusion for those who hold different beliefs or lack a belief system altogether.

In Islamic tradition, it is believed that these angels have the duty of questioning the deceased while they are in their graves.

Munkar and Nakeer, are angels, have the duty of questioning the deceased and receiving their answers. In Islam, it is believed that every individual will be held accountable for their actions in the afterlife.

When individuals are awakened from their graves, they will be questioned by angels about how they lived their lives on Earth.

These angels are assigned by Allah to carry out this important task. Unlike humans, angels do not possess free will and simply obey the commands given to them.

This concept is exemplified by Satan, who is not considered a dark angel but a Jinn, a separate creation with the ability to make choices.

Islam emphasizes its teachings leave no room for ambiguity or imagination, providing clear guidelines and explanations for believers to understand and follow.

It encourages individuals to seek knowledge and understanding of its teachings in order to live a righteous and accountable life.

As Allah has the power to give and take life, it is effortless for Him to awaken the deceased in the grave and then return them to their deceased state after questioning.

Islam encompasses accounting for every stage of life, viewing it as a test rather than a perpetual destination.

The reason for this inquiry is to examine the departed and assess their moral character and eligibility for entry into paradise. The departed will share how they lived during their time on Earth.

Muslims will undergo questioning once they depart from this life.

The disbelievers, or those who do not believe in the existence of God, also undergo their own testing in this world and hereafter. Despite being welcomed by believers, the world operates on the principle of free choice, where individuals are free to believe or disbelieve as they choose.

However, the consequences of their disbelief become evident after they have been informed, just as any law has consequences.

In monotheistic Abrahamic faiths, God is the one and only entity. There is no concept of multiple gods or prophets evolving into becoming God.

God is believed to be eternal and unchanging, not subject to any transformation or evolution.

Disbelievers will be barred from entering paradise until the hour commences, as the gate of hell opens to engulf their grave with fire, smoke, and heat. They will remain there until the hour begins.

The penalties seem excessively severe and cruel for those who profess the mercy of God and for those who have never been exposed to the belief in a single entity.

Allah did not punish any city until he sent prophets to warn them in a language they understood.

Allah's justice is unparalleled, with swift accountability for every jurisdiction's reward and punishment. Illiteracy has no place in Islam, which welcomes all and promotes monotheistic beliefs without coercion.

Going against laws and disregarding them is not in line with Islamic principles, as every country has its own set of laws.

Allah is the ruler of all countries, as stated by the owner of this law.

Learning is a transformative experience for everyone, including those who convert to Islam and choose to remain ignorant, while others become ambassadors.

Similarly, Muslims born into this faith adapt Islamic doctrine some conform to Western society and disregard their own faith.

Restoration time cannot be avoided, but there is no opposing force. Those who spread evil and incite others face harsher punishment. In Islam, it is better to sin in private and repent than to share.

The questioning of angels and punishment in the grave. Both believers and non-believers will face the opening of either the gate of hell or paradise in their graves.

A believer's way of living in this world will protect them; nothing is free, not even this world. It's not just about enjoying the beauty of earthly pleasures, but also about preparing for the end of life.

These facts are intended to open your mind, not to coerce one into anything.

In ancient times, people either believed in a higher power or worshiped multiple deities, there was no concept of atheism or disbelief.

Being subservient to something is a part of human nature. In the modern era, humans prioritize their self-desires and lack faith because of the uncertainty caused by script alterations of previous books before the Quran.

The Quran remains unchanged and was compiled by Omar, the second caliph of Islam, completed before the passing of Prophet Muhammad.

Good actions will barricade against evil, safeguarding believers. Most practicing Muslims prioritize their own self and personal deeds.

The pillars of Islam will meet the requirements.

Salvation in Jesus serves as the ultimate foundation of belief for Christians.

The Jewish faith centers on one god and emphasizes adherence to the tenets, not greed.

While the Abrahamic religions have their differences, they all emphasize monotheism, and those deviating from this face more challenges than expected.

Education is more effective than forcing beliefs on others. Destiny is predetermined and unchangeable as humans continue on the predetermined path.

Prayers have the power to bring about change, while belief truly matters. People can believe in deities or an unseen god. However, knowledge is crucial and everyone handles their own choices.

Bible: NKJV: Romans 5:12. Therefore, just as through one man sin entered the world, and death through sin, and thus death spread to all men, because all sinned— For until the law sin was in the world, but sin is not imputed when there is no law. Nevertheless, death reigned from Adam to Moses, even over those who had not sinned according to the likeness of the transgression of Adam, who is a type of Him who was to come.

These Scriptures, such as **Romans 5:12**, tell us that when Adam and Eve disobeyed God in the Garden of Eden, death entered the world because of their sin. This original sin affected all of humanity, leading to a fallen and broken world.

The concept of original sin does not hold any significance in Islam because Allah forgives sins through individual repentance.

Adam and Eve were forgiven in Islam, and their sin did not affect humanity. If Satan had humbled himself and asked for forgiveness, he would have been forgiven. However, his arrogance got in the way, so he requested respite and it was granted to him.

When examining the contradictions between the Bible and the Quran, it is important to consider multiple factors.

To begin with, it is significant to acknowledge that the Bible comprises texts written by multiple authors over a long period, whereas the Quran is considered by Muslims to be the exact words of Allah revealed to Prophet Muhammad.

The Quran has remained unchanged because Allah swore to preserve it.

One interpretation of the biblical narrative suggests that all of humanity is affected by the consequences of Adam and Eve's disobedience in the Garden of Eden.

This notion may seem unjust or vindictive to some, as it implies that an omniscient and omnipotent God intentionally created a world where suffering and punishment are inherent. However, it is important to note that different individuals and religious communities have varying interpretations of these theological concepts.

Some argue that the story of Adam and Eve serves as an allegory or metaphorical representation of the human condition, emphasizing our capacity for both good and evil.

From this perspective, the consequences faced by humanity can be seen as a result of our own choices and actions, rather than a direct punishment inflicted by a vengeful entity. The concept of divine love, mercy, and redemption is heavily emphasized in various religious traditions.

Their suggestion implies that God's plan encompasses more than just the consequences of original sin—it also involves the provision of salvation and forgiveness through Jesus per Bible.

Both Islam and Judaism contradict the idea. According to these religions, since God is an unseen being, no prophet has ever seen Him. If God were visible or if someone had seen Him in this world, then He would not be considered God.

Therefore, monotheists believe Jesus was a preacher and a teacher, but not God, as stated in Islam, Judaism, and by many Christians.

However, there are still some Christians who associate Jesus with God, which goes against the belief in one God and leans towards polytheism.

This distinction separates Christendom from monotheistic beliefs.

Ultimately, interpreting biblical messages is subjective and deeply personal. While some may find it challenging to reconcile the concept of a loving God with the notion of original sin, others may find solace and meaning in the teachings and narratives of the Bible.

In Islam, original sin does not exist, and no child or adult is held accountable for the actions of others.

In Islam, individuals are solely accountable for their own actions, and they attain the preservation of the soul by repenting to Allah continually and before death.

It is essential to approach these discussions with an open mind, respect for differing perspectives, and a willingness to engage in thoughtful dialogue.

The comparative differences in Abrahamic faiths can foster understanding when one realizes no one can alter the ideology except oneself and the creator, who already knows the outcome.

Muslims have a rich history of resilience and growth, driven by their unwavering commitment to their faith.

Although there are Muslims who may not have a deep understanding of their history or faith, it is important to note that true learning should come from reliable sources within the Muslim community of Islam.

Relying on non-Muslims or social media for information about Islam can lead to a distorted and inaccurate understanding of the religion. It is concerning that some academic institutions in the Western world have perpetuated negative stereotypes about Islam and Muslims, often implicating them as terrorists.

The core principles and ideologies of Christianity align closely with the mythological beliefs of Hinduism, particularly in their reverence for Lord Krishna as a central figure.

In Hinduism, Lord Krishna is recognized as the eighth incarnation of Lord Vishnu, who is believed to be the guardian and preserver of the universe.

In Christianity, Jesus Christ is the divine offspring of God and is believed to have been sent to Earth to redeem humanity from sin.

Lord Krishna and Jesus Christ are both revered as divine figures, representing love, compassion, and wisdom.

Both religions stress the value of moral virtues, selfless acts, and a firm commitment to spirituality.

Despite their differing teachings, Jesus and Lord Krishna share some similarities. They were both pursued by evil forces, but ultimately remained unharmed. Jesus is often depicted as a shepherd, while Krishna is commonly portrayed as a cowherd.

However, according to the Quran, Jesus brought the same message as the other prophets, emphasizing the worship of one God rather than himself.

He made it clear to the Jews that he did not come to break the law of Moses, but to follow it.

Therefore, it contradicts the idea that he is God, rather he is considered a prophet in Judaism and Islam.

These distinctions only serve to perpetuate clarity and differences within the Abrahamic faiths. It is important to note that Jesus was a monotheist.

Allah is the highest authority in Islam and Judaism, and all prophets are humble servants of Allah. No prophet or entity can match the greatness of Allah. However, Muslims do not consider Jesus as the literal son of God or part of a divine Trinity, as this belief contradicts the concept of monotheism in Islam.

Instead, they view Jesus as a human being created by God, and reject the idea of his divinity.

In Islam, Muslims regard the belief of Jesus as the son of God as a major sin called "shirk," which means associating partners with Allah in worship.

Muslims stress the oneness of God and faithfully practice monotheism, believing that God selected Jesus, along with other prophets, to lead humanity towards righteousness and submission to His will.

Despite these differences, all three Abrahamic faiths recognize and honor the prophets sent by Allah, albeit with different narratives and tasks assigned to them.

It is important to note that although these faiths share some commonalities; they are distinct and independent from one another.

Many Jews saw Jesus as not fulfilling the criteria of this Messianic role. They did not accept him as their Messiah. Instead, they continue to await someone who aligns with their beliefs and expectations of a king-like figure.

It is crucial to approach religious beliefs with respect and understanding, recognizing the diversity and unique perspectives that exist within different faith traditions.

One significant difference in the Abrahamic faiths regarding the end times is the concept of the Messiah. While Christians believe Jesus is the Messiah who will return to save his followers, Muslims also acknowledge Jesus as the Messiah, but do not believe he will come to save those who worshiped him.

This distinction stems from the fact that Jesus himself never explicitly instructed his followers to worship him in Islamic teachings.

This difference in belief creates a notable separation between Christianity and Islam, as their core beliefs regarding the role of Jesus in the end times do not align.

However, it is important to note that, despite these differences, there are also some similarities between the two faiths, such as the belief in monotheism and the importance of righteous actions.

In Islam, the belief in destiny is deeply rooted and encompasses the past, present, and future of an individual's life.

It is believed that everything that happens is a part of Allah's divine plan and that destiny plays an active role in shaping a person's life.

However, it is crucial to understand that Islam does not promote or justify evil actions by attributing them to destiny.

Instead, evil is seen because of the whispers of Satan, who tempts individuals away from the path of righteousness. Muslims and believers of faith acknowledge the existence of both good and evil influences in life, and it is the responsibility of individuals to distinguish between the two.

The concept of destiny in Islam also highlights the importance of repentance and seeking forgiveness from Allah for any wrongdoing.

It is through repentance and turning back to Allah that individuals can find solace and redemption, as the door to repentance always remains open.

While embracing Islam is a transformative experience, it does not automatically eradicate all past habits or ingrained cultural practices.

Muslims, like followers of any other religion, are susceptible to human fallibility and can make mistakes.

This does not mean that they are deliberately falsifying the faith or promoting cultic practices. Rather, it is a reminder that individuals are on a journey of continuous learning and improvement in their understanding and practice of Islam.

It is through seeking knowledge, adhering to the true teachings of the Quran and the Prophet Muhammad, and striving for personal growth, that Muslims can align their actions with the principles and values of Islam.

The concept of Allah's forgiveness is a reminder that God is compassionate, willing to forgive sincere repentance, and guides individuals towards the right path.

The concept of forgiveness in Catholic churches is not new, and although incidents of misconduct are continuous and churches declining, it is not uncommon for the public to witness continued mishaps in the name of beliefs.

One may wonder if the sin of molestation in churches is also forgiven through the concept of blood and forgiveness, as dictated by their own ideologies, which suggest that Jesus died for all sins.

The concept of why anyone would need forgiveness when Jesus has already taken on the sins of those who believe in him can be difficult for many to grasp.

Muslims and Jews, in contrast to the Abrahamic faith, do not subscribe to this ideology. It is important to note that Jesus himself belonged to the Abrahamic faith and did not worship multiple gods or engage in pagan practices.

The Guardian: May 9th, 2024: It wasn't a big deal: secret deposition reveals how a child molester priest was shielded by his church.

Chicago Sun Times: June 4th, 2024: Augustinian Catholic order paid $2M settlement over rape...

The Guardian: July 16, 2024: Catholic priest accused of sexual misconduct and charged over child abuse images.

If these situations were to occur in Muslim facilities, they would be managed distinctly. It would never take place in a mosque.

In a mosque, there is a clear distinction between men and women, fostering an atmosphere of respect that aligns with its purpose, rather than allowing any form of disrespect.

It would be a significant outreach program if any act of evil were to occur in a mosque, which is highly unlikely.

The dissemination of selective information in regions with prevalent Islamophobia aims to instill fear in those seeking knowledge about monotheism and Muslims, but friendships persist amidst the spread of biased narratives.

The concept of salvation in human beings is often associated with religious beliefs and spiritual enlightenment.

It is a means of attaining liberation from suffering and achieving a higher state of being.

However, the idea of elevating humans to the status of Gods, as seen in Greek Mythology or the Roman Empire, is more of a cultural and mythological construct rather than a literal transformation.

The purpose of these depictions of nudity in art and architecture was to represent human beauty, strength, and vulnerability, rather than being immoral or offensive.

It is important to note that different cultures and societies have different moral standards and perceptions of nudity.

While some may find it acceptable or even appreciate the artistic value, others may view it as immodest or inappropriate.

Morality is subjective and varies across different communities and belief systems. The concept of mythology in Hinduism closely aligns with the Western religious beliefs of being polytheistic rather than monotheistic, and this statement is indeed factual.

Hinduism is a complex and diverse religion that encompasses a wide range of beliefs, practices, and deities. One of the defining characteristics of Hinduism is its belief in multiple gods and goddesses, known as devas and devis.

These deities play various roles and are associated with different aspects of life, nature, and cosmic forces. Hindu mythology is rich with stories, legends, and epics that revolve around these divine beings and their interactions with humans and the world.

This polytheistic nature of Hinduism distinguishes it from monotheistic religions like Islam, and Judaism, where there is a belief in a single supreme entity Allah.

Therefore, it is accurate to say that the concept of mythology in Hinduism reflects a polytheistic worldview, similar to the Western religious traditions.

Teachers need to uphold high moral standards and serve as role models for their students. When individuals undermine their credibility and ability to effectively teach and guide others by displaying decadence in morality to the masses.

The repetitive disrespect from educators who intentionally disregard their own teachings not only misleads the masses but also disrespects those who seek truth and knowledge.

It becomes tiresome to navigate through this and find the genuine meaning and justice of learning, which Islam provides with no contradictions, as the teachings remain preserved in the book Quran.

While it is true that mistakes can be made in private, those who exploit the privacy of others without remorse or consideration for the impact it may have on society lack integrity.

In Western societies, nudity and explicit content are often openly showcased, and this can have detrimental effects on individuals, particularly children.

The architectural displays and societal norms in these lands may inadvertently expose children to inappropriate content, conflicting with the moral code of ethics.

This discrepancy is evident when comparing these practices with Islamic concepts and the teachings of the Quran.

Unlike other religious texts that have been modified over the years, the Quran is regarded as the original word of Allah.

Individuals who show a decline in moral values and cannot conform to the teachings of the Quran are not suitable to be teachers, especially for Islam and Quran, which necessitate knowledge and learning.

The history of architecture in Western civilization has indeed depicted human figures, such as Jesus, Mary, and saints, in a manner that bears a resemblance to pagan beliefs found in Hinduism.

In Hinduism, deities like Krishna, Shiva, Rama, Sita, and Lakshmi are revered as gods, and Krishna is even said to have walked on water, a feat similar to that attributed to Jesus.

Interestingly, the Quran does not mention Jesus' walking on water, although it describes many of his miracles. One particularly mesmerizing fact mentioned in the Quran is that Jesus spoke at birth, which adds to his mystical nature as the Messiah.

While the use of statues has been removed from many churches, the belief in the Trinity, a central tenet of Christianity, remains unchanged.

Their definition of success goes beyond material wealth or societal achievements, as they believe true fulfillment comes from sharing their wisdom, experiences, and love with others.

They find solace and restoration in moments of distress by turning to their spiritual practices, connecting with their inner selves, and seeking guidance from higher powers or universal forces.

For Muslims, the universal force and commander of the world, both in this world and the next, is Allah. Allah is the one and only God, the creator and sustainer of all existence.

Allah has ultimate authority and control over everything in the universe, including the physical and spiritual realms.

He is all-knowing, all-powerful, and all-merciful, and is the source of guidance, justice, and love.

Allah is the ultimate source of all blessings and rewards, as well as the ultimate judge on the Day of judgment. Muslims strive to worship and obey Allah, recognizing that they are fallible beings who are prone to making mistakes.

Believers understand they are not perfect or indispensable, and they humbly acknowledge their shortcomings.

However, it is important to note that some individuals, driven by their insecurities and arrogance, eagerly await the mistakes of Muslims, using them to validate their negative perceptions.

These individuals cannot recognize that Muslims, like all humans, can make mistakes, but they actively seek forgiveness and strive to learn from their errors.

Muslims understand Allah is forgiving, and they endeavor not to repeat their mistakes, working towards personal growth and overcoming arrogance in their pursuit of a righteous and balanced life.

This worldview allows them to find peace, resilience, and a deeper sense of meaning in the face of challenges.

When individuals constantly criticize those who possess more knowledge, they hinder their own ability to learn and grow. This persistent criticism often stems from a shattered ego, which replaces the desire for learning with a need to assert superiority.

Instead of seeking knowledge and personal development, these individuals remain stagnant within their limited perspectives. They focus on social media platforms, where they spread news and information that aligns with their biases, particularly those originating from Islamophobic regions.

Denying history and truth is a tactic commonly employed by those who seek to manipulate and deceive in any setting.

However, it is not a simple task to manipulate the world, especially for religious beliefs. Many converts to Islam, for instance, often come from Christian backgrounds, which highlights the appeal and sincerity of the Islamic faith.

Those who criticize or attempt to undermine Islam often cannot comprehend that a rational mind naturally gravitates toward the truth. Lies and falsehoods, created to satisfy personal ego or adhere to outdated traditions, do not hold sway over the Muslim world.

If the validity of Islam depended solely on the actions and beliefs of its followers, it would have likely faded away.

However, the resilience and enduring nature of Islam stems from its inherent truth, which remains steadfast regardless of the actions of its adherents. Some argue that religion in Christendom is gradually returning to pagan ideologies, as the faith experiences a decline in influence and practice.

It is common for both young and elderly Muslims, who may lack comprehensive understanding of their faith, to interpret their compliance with societal customs as an act of defiance.

Similarly, when some people convert to Islam, they carry their pre-existing ideologies with them.

Humanity was created with imperfections, while only Allah is perfect!

However, it is important to note that no Muslim uses the word "perfection" to describe themselves, as it is understood and ingrained in every Muslim that perfection is a quality solely reserved for Allah.

Omar bin Khattab, one of the most influential and revered figures in Islamic history, left a lasting legacy through his teachings and actions. Some converts who have embraced Islam have become teachers and taken it upon themselves to carry forward the teachings of Omar bin Khattab.

These individuals recognize the immense beauty and wisdom in his name and strive to emulate his problem-solving approach in their teaching methods. They aim to be not mere critics but problem solvers, just like Omar bin Khattab himself.

This is important in mathematics, where Muslims have made significant contributions throughout history.

The mathematical prowess and logical reasoning displayed by Omar bin Khattab serve as an inspiration for these teachers as they impart knowledge of algebra and other mathematical concepts. The world continues to learn from the teachings left behind by Omar bin Khattab, and it is crucial to preserve and share his historical significance.

This interpretation highlights the continuity and fulfillment of divine messages throughout different eras and religions, as Jesus sought to convey God's teachings to his Jewish audience.

Prophet Muhammad emerged in the 7th century in Arabia, a region that was not directly under Roman control

Unlike Jesus, Muhammad peace be upon him did not have a specific group or nation to whom he was exclusively sent, but he was regarded as the final messenger of God for all of humanity.

His mission involved spreading the message of Islam, which encompasses a comprehensive code of conduct and belief system for people of all backgrounds. Muhammad's teachings and the Quran hold instructions for all people, regardless of their nationality, ethnicity, or social standing.

While Jesus' ministry was focused on the Jewish community within the Roman Empire, Prophet Muhammad's message transcended cultural and geographical boundaries, offering guidance to people from diverse backgrounds.

Both figures played significant roles in shaping religious and political landscapes, although their missions had distinct scopes and objectives.

For a comprehensive understanding of the history of individuals who may be uninformed, it is significant to recognize that Jesus, known as Isa in the Quran, is acknowledged as Jesus of Nazareth. His life and teachings are linked to the geographical location of Palestine, previously referred to as Philistine.

It is puzzling that certain individuals in countries with a predominantly Christian population are tolerating or even endorsing the atrocities committed against Palestinians.

This contradiction questions their allegiance to Jesus as their savior and their indifference towards the sacred land of Palestine, which holds immense historical and religious value.

In a society where collective thinking prevails over individualism, ignorance can be a dangerous force. When people are unaware of history or lack knowledge about certain subjects, they are more susceptible to being led astray into the waters of darkness.

Ignorance can cloud one's judgment and prevent them from seeing the truth or understanding the consequences of their actions.

However, sometimes individuals, upon gaining a deeper understanding of a topic, may choose to change their views. This transition can result from personal growth, education, or exposure to different perspectives.

Unfortunately, there are also those who, despite knowing the truth, continue to perpetuate hypocrisy because of fear of judgment or repercussions from society.

This fear of expressing their true beliefs can hinder progress and perpetuate the cycle of ignorance. Therefore, it is crucial to encourage open-mindedness, critical thinking, and the pursuit of knowledge to overcome the barriers imposed by collective thinking and combat the dangers of ignorance.

Despite growing up in a community that practiced paganism and idol worship, Ibrahim (AS) had a deep sense of contemplation and questioning about the existence of a higher power. His father, Azar, was not only a prominent member of their community but also a skilled sculptor and crafted of idols.

Ibrahim was exposed to this craftsmanship from a young age and observed the people's devotion to these idols. However, he couldn't help but question the logic and significance behind worshiping lifeless objects. This inner turmoil and curiosity would eventually lead him on a profound spiritual journey.

Despite growing up in a society steeped in idol worship, Ibrahim (AS) was a deeply thoughtful individual. He questioned the purpose and logic behind worshiping inanimate objects and felt a strong desire to seek the truth.

One night, as he gazed at the stars in the sky, Ibrahim (AS) contemplated the existence of a higher power. He realized that the stars, the moon, and the sun were all creations of Allah (SWT) and could not possibly be deities.

Determined to find the true path of monotheism, Ibrahim (AS) embarked on a journey to find Allah (SWT) and understand His divine message. He left Babylon, leaving behind his family and everything he knew, and set out on a spiritual quest that would shape the course of his life.

The consequences of committing shirk are severe, as it nullifies a person's faith and places them outside the fold of Islam.

Therefore, the Quran repeatedly warns against shirk and emphasizes the importance of pure monotheism in the worship of Allah.

However, the important aspect is that correction takes place, keeping in mind one's roots. This strategy, although amazing, does not provide a definite computation except for regrets. The verse challenges individuals to believe in Jesus as a prophet, known as Isa, who the Bible claims is the son of God.

The allure of Satan has no power over a pure soul, regardless of whether that soul is believed to be the son of God or destined to attain godhood and attain greater enlightenment

This is because Satan is merely a creation of God.

Quran: Surah Anam:104. "Certainly, clear proofs have come to you from your Lord. Whoever therefore sees (with insight), it is to his own gain, and whoever be blind, it is to his own loss; and am not a keeper over you."

It is hypocritical to blame the religion of Islam and associate it with derogatory events and political greed. This emphasis on invading and destabilizing Muslim countries, only to fail and create an environment of greed, is an obvious display of political agendas.

It is unfair to portray these countries as dangerous when Islam itself is not inherently disrespectful or extreme.

The truth must be acknowledged and prioritized. Those who claim to protect their environment in the name of Islam should not forget that Islam has a rich history of prophets and soldiers who fought for truth and left legacies.

It is inevitable to reflect on these episodes in order to progress. Knowledge is indeed power, but it must be used in the right way. Just as a Muslim would not wear a cross necklace and pretend to be Christian, true Muslims would not manipulate the Quran or disguise themselves as Muslims only to later burn the Quran.

These individuals may not go unpunished; face consequences. But repentance is open until one meets death. Injustice cannot be met with silence, but rather with attention and action.

The term "extremists of Islam" was coined by individuals who falsely promote extremism and coercion in the name of their faith.

This distortion traces back to the time of the Roman Empire, when corruption and falsehoods were introduced to incorporate a doctrine that was never endorsed by the Prophet Jesus.

Repentance is Key!

It is important to critically examine the usage of this terminology and challenge the portrayal of Muslims as extreme.

This tumultuous period of accusations, assimilations, and counterfeit ideologies has influenced the dogma and corrupted the true teachings of Jesus.

In an effort to make the beliefs more appealing to those inclined towards paganism, elements of pagan practices were incorporated. It was believed that people, who were predisposed to paganism, would find it difficult to comprehend a god or entity if their belief was not strong.

Therefore, Jesus was elevated to the status of a deity and the concept of the Trinity, with Christ as the second person, was adopted. According to this faith, the Father is the first person, and the Holy Ghost is the third. All three persons are considered to be God.

This is not a strictly monotheistic faith. Similarly, this line of thinking extends to label all Abrahamic faiths as false. The religion that was established during the Nicaea era claims to be on the path to truth, but it falls short of delivering the authentic teachings of Jesus.

This environment, which distorted his teachings for political gain, continues to persist. Islam itself is not extreme, and Muslims do not discriminate in their acts of assistance.

In fact, Muslims have historically shown solidarity with other persecuted groups, such as the Jews during the Holocaust.

It is crucial to shed light on these truths and consistently expose falsehoods in order to establish a more stable understanding of Islam. **Words fall short; only Allah can transform hearts**. Allah has clarified that no human can control the beliefs of another, emphasizing that understanding can only come from within.

According to the Quran, God is the creator and cannot be tempted by Satan or anyone else. This distinction is a major difference between the Quran and the Bible, as both Islam and Judaism are monotheistic religions.

The Quran states Jesus was not tempted and is not the son of God.

Quran: Surah Anam: 106.106. "Follow what is revealed to you from your Lord; there is no god but He; and turn away from the polytheists."

Polytheistic beliefs are incompatible with monotheism, which focuses on a single entity like Allah and does not entertain the concept of trinity or any associations with God.

The Quran provides guidance on avoiding the destructive effects of polytheism, particularly for those who cannot grasp the truth and may experience doubts. Friendships can carry on, but it is important to create a divide between beliefs to nurture the soul.

The Christian belief is that Jesus is the eternal Son of God who took on human form to save humanity through his death and resurrection.

While Hindu ideology strongly advocates for the concept of reincarnation, it is important to clarify that the belief of reincarnation in the Bible is not as straightforward.

In Hinduism, reincarnation refers to the cycle of birth, death, and rebirth, where individuals have multiple lives to learn from and evolve spiritually.

This could involve exploring and embracing the pantheon of gods and goddesses from various ancient pagan traditions such as Greek, Roman, Norse, Celtic, or Egyptian mythologies.

This approach can also involve reviving ancient rituals, ceremonies, and practices that celebrate and honor the natural world, seasons, and cycles of life, which are often key elements in pagan belief systems.

The belief in Jesus as the incarnation of God is a fundamental tenet of Christian theology.

According to Christian teachings, Jesus is not a mere mortal who is reincarnated, but rather the eternal Son of God who took on human form in the person of Jesus Christ.

This divine incarnation is a unique event in history, of Christendom through which God's love and salvation are made manifest to humanity.

In Christian thought, Jesus' unity with God is understood in terms of the doctrine of the Trinity.

This understanding of unity is distinct from the cyclical nature of reincarnation found in Hinduism, where the soul is believed to undergo multiple births and deaths in a continuous cycle of rebirth.

While the concept of Jesus evolving or progressing from son to father may be seen as reincarnation or transformation, it is important to note that this interpretation may vary among different Christian denominations and individual believers.

The idea of Jesus becoming one with the Father is often understood in terms of his divine nature and his role in the redemption and reconciliation of humanity with God.

Bible: Luke 4:2-14 ICB. where the devil tempted Jesus for 40 days. Jesus ate nothing during that time. When those days were over, he was very hungry.

Jesus exhibited various human qualities like hunger, thirst, and fatigue, but it is crucial to acknowledge that he did not possess a divine nature.

This interpretation, made by people and not by Jesus, is an essential and factual historical change that cannot be ignored. Christian theology states that Jesus possesses both human and divine nature. He is regarded as the divine Son of God sent to save humanity from sin.

The Jews never mentioned his divinity, but they rejected his claim of being born without a father as the Messiah. Pauline Christianity, a sect led by a Jewish man who never met Jesus, introduced the divine assertion after his ascension.

Who authored a new Bible with no angelic revelations, unmentioned as a prophet in scripture, with participants who were not prophets and without alterations disregarding the time of Constantine?

Jesus' mission was initially focused on the Jewish people but expanded to include all who believe in his message, including Muslims who see him as a Messiah but not divine.

Christians and Muslims share similarities yet have different theological perspectives.

The question that arises is, if Allah is the only god, then who answers the prayers of those who pray to someone other than Allah? It is a logical question.

Allah answers everyone's prayers based on the intensity of their belief. However, the answer to this questioning may lie in the afterlife, which is a longer journey compared to our current existence in this world.

Allah does not deny anyone; He answers those who call upon Him.

It's important to note that Jesus' teachings and influence have connected with people across different cultures and backgrounds over time.

Prophet Muhammad holds great reverence as the final prophet in Islam, with a message for all of humanity. It is crucial to recognize and honor the various beliefs and viewpoints of different religious traditions.

In Islam, Jesus (**Isa**) is indeed regarded as a highly revered prophet and the Messiah, but not as the son of God. Islamic belief emphasizes that God is transcendent and cannot be confined to a human form or have human qualities.

The Quran explicitly states that Jesus was created like any other human being, born to Mary through a miraculous birth.

Quran clarifies Jesus performed miracles by the permission of God, such as healing the sick and raising the dead, but these actions are seen as signs of his prophethood and not as evidence of his divinity.

The Islamic perspective emphasizes monotheism and rejects the concept of Jesus as a divine figure or part of a Trinity.

The concept that the mirror only shows the reflection of the one looking into it, remains true assuming that the entire world exists within the same mirror, is a metaphorical idea that highlights the limitations of perception.

However, it is important to acknowledge the historical contributions of Muslims to the development of mirrors. Muslims played a significant role in the advancement of optics and the creation of reflective surfaces during the Islamic Golden Age.

Scholars such as Ibn al-Haytham made significant advancements in understanding light and optics, which laid the foundation for the creation of mirrors as we know them today.

Therefore, it is a factual note that Muslims were pioneers in mirrors. This perspective questions the idea of restricting innovative thinkers, as they are the ones who have pushed the limits of knowledge and broadened our understanding.

The history of Muslims is rich and diverse, spanning over 1400 years since Islam.

Muslims have played significant roles in various fields, such as science, art, philosophy, and governance, contributing to the advancement of human civilization.

Throughout history, Muslims have continuously strived to uphold the teachings and principles of Islam while adapting to the changing world around them.

The faith of Islam encourages Muslims to seek knowledge, explore the truth, and engage with the world, as long as it is done within the boundaries and limits set by Islamic laws.

This balance between faith and worldly engagement is essential for Muslims to navigate the complexities of modern life while remaining true to their religious beliefs.

It is important to acknowledge and explain these continuous efforts of Muslims in order to understand the multifaceted nature of Islam and the diverse ways in which Muslims practice their faith while remaining connected to the broader society.

Many young and old Muslims, who may be uninformed about the intricacies of their faith, often view their adherence to societal norms and defiance.

Similarly, some converts to Islam bring their own pre-existing ideologies into their newfound belief, leading them to believe in the concept of a single god, yet continuously searching for faults in Muslims to prove that perfection does not exist within humanity.

The concept of perfection is reserved solely for Allah.

However, stability, truth, and self-dedication are closely linked to success and are imperative in Islam. It is important to assist both Muslims and converts, as well as non-Muslims, without coercing them into Islam.

Education is essential in understanding true Islam, especially in contrast to the distorted version propagated by Islamophobic regions on social media.

If someone cannot understand the essence of monotheism, which is the belief in one God, Allah, from the beginning of time, then alternative concepts like human deities, statues, myths, and personal strategies can deceive and replace the truth.

Therefore, when people suggested to the Prophets that they should preserve the remnants of their ancestors, referring to statues, the Prophets firmly declined, knowing that people might eventually start worshiping them.

Islam is a monotheistic faith that encompasses belief in every Prophet of the Abrahamic tradition, all of whom were sent to proclaim the oneness of Allah.

Despite rational explanations, aggressive social media and political regimes persist in harboring animosity towards Islam, which is ironic considering Islam's principles and policies promote truth.

Muslims value any land they live on and contribute to the land and people without discrimination is a fact. That is indeed Islam. But the haters will say then go back home if you don't like it if truth expressed has no answer from the hypocrites. '

Although friendships exist and the world is enriched with Muslim cultures, the continuous effort to shade Islam comes from the haters and aggressors, not from those who have no interference.

Some people don't even know about Islam, but they are curious and enchanted by its laws and discipline.

The answer is to reconnect with your origin and live in harmony with Allah's desires, rather than mindlessly obeying ignorant instructions from others.

It's vital to realize that Allah decides our place of residence and sustenance. God's plan for us shapes everything we do, including my writing.

CHAPTER 15
CONVERSATIONS WITH EXPRESSION INVIGORATE THE PSYCHE.

Engaging in activities that stimulate the mind and explore the concept of truth is crucial for the development and well-being of the psyche. Just as the body requires attention through exercise and nourishment, the mind also requires regular mental exercise and nourishment to thrive.

People can achieve this through various means, such as reading thought-provoking literature, engaging in deep conversations, seeking new knowledge, and critically analyzing information.

By constantly challenging our beliefs and expanding our understanding of truth, we open ourselves up to new perspectives, ideas, and personal growth.

Ignoring the mental aspect of our being can lead to stagnation, closed-mindedness, and a limited worldview. Therefore, nurturing the mind is essential for maintaining a healthy and vibrant psyche.

When engaging in educational conversations or personal discussions, it can be incredibly challenging if someone is overly sensitive and interprets everything as a personal attack.

In such cases, their mind closes off, making it difficult to have an open exchange of ideas.

However, introducing Islam brings a fresh perspective and a revival of truth. Islam does not confine itself to rigid beliefs or dogmas but offers an open and expansive approach to understanding the world.

It introduces new and enlightening ideas that may be unfamiliar to many, yet it remains firmly rooted in monotheism, a concept that has been integral to humanity since its creation.

This breath of fresh air allows for a more dynamic and open conversation, encouraging individuals to explore and embrace new concepts and perspectives.

Manners of speaking hold immense significance in Islam. The teachings in Surah Haj emphasize that those who are righteous and guided towards purity in their words and actions are the loyal followers of Islam.

It is important to note that remaining silent should not be mistaken for good manners. While the tongue holds utmost importance, in today's digital age, even our fingers, as they type our thoughts, must be guarded.

It is crucial to exercise caution with both our speech and our written words. While it is essential to provide explanations, when necessary, the key lies in ensuring that they are understood by the recipient.

Courtesy plays a vital role in Islam, and it is advised not to go overboard with explanations unless it is believed that it will genuinely assist the listener's comprehension.

However, it is essential to acknowledge that those who have lost the ability to understand may not grasp the message, regardless of whether it is conveyed through a short or long speech.

While making a point, it is unnecessary to raise one's voice or thunder. If the point being made is based on truth, it does not require volume but the essence of truthfulness.

Quran: Surah Hajj: 22.... righteous followers will ultimately triumph. Fate of the Wicked: Asserts that wrongdoers will inevitably face disgrace and suffering.

A believer's belief is that only the word "Insha'Allah" can come to mind, as the disbelievers cannot and will not win.

Prophet Muhammad engaged in playful activities with his family, but when the call to prayer (azan) was made, he promptly left to attend his worship of Allah.

It's better to prioritize prayer time instead of procrastinating. Its advantages are indescribable.

Conversations become boundless when one engages with Allah, family, romance, youth, friends, strangers. The ability to converse is truly a precious gift.

However, those who struggle to communicate effectively find themselves trapped in conversations hindered by hesitation and a lack of expression.

Therefore, the ability to speak and communicate is a divine blessing. If one possesses the skills to express themselves, it would be counterproductive and inhibiting to withhold their voice and actions.

In every relationship, conversation is vital for personal growth and development.

The conversations that Prophet Muhammad had with his people became beautiful melodies and teachings that should be treasured.

The world has so much to offer if only people realized that Allah's blessings empower them to first help themselves, and then extend that help to others. This principle is fundamental to Islam.

Understanding is the key to overcoming our fears and embracing new beginnings with a clear and open mind. Change is essential for personal growth and allows us to adapt and thrive in different stages of life.

Lies have indeed become increasingly prominent in daily life, and one contributing factor to this phenomenon is the way children are often trained to believe in and accept falsehoods by their parents.

From an early age, children are taught to believe in mythical figures such as Santa Claus or the Tooth Fairy, perpetuating the idea that lying is acceptable.

Parents often engage in this behavior intending to create magical and fun experiences for their children. However, as children grow older and develop a better understanding of reality, they may question the validity of these beliefs.

It is at this point that they realize they were misled and may question the ethics of lying.

While children learn from their parents, it is important to note that questioning later when they choose to lie is a natural consequence of their increasing cognitive development and understanding of truth and falsehood.

The authenticity of holidays like Easter and Christmas is often doubted, leading many to abandon Christianity.

These holidays, which are now fundamental to the Christian religion, were coordinated and combined with pagan traditions that have no association with the teachings of Jesus.

These holidays contradict the teachings and Jewish customs of Jesus, who himself had a Jewish background.

Incorporating pagan elements in these celebrations, casts doubt on the authentic origins and significance of these holidays.

The lack of concrete evidence supported by Jesus makes it challenging to believe in a religion with glamorous yet inauthentic holiday traditions. Evidence of alterations to the Bible has been compiled and is known globally.

If the celebrations and virtual conduct of paganism lack authenticity, it implies that Jesus the Messiah endorsed nothing that was incorporated after his ascension.

This has misled many until they delve into the historical roots that have no connection to Jesus, the son of Mary, who was not considered a god during his time on Earth.

That is precisely why the Quran was completed before the passing of Prophet Muhammad, to prevent any additions or subtractions, ensuring its preservation and originality. The Quran still prevails today, while Islam maintains its authenticity.

Over time, Easter and Christmas in the Christian world have increasingly emphasized commercialism and profits for businesses, even though these holidays hold no significance in Judaism, given that Jesus had a Jewish background rather than a Christian one.

Celebrating these holidays can be overwhelming for those facing financial difficulties.

The holidays were eventually adopted by Christendom, which emerged after Jesus' ascension, not his death according to Islam. The clarity of these distinctions aids in understanding the differences among Abrahamic faiths.

Incorporating pagan beliefs into these holidays, which Jesus did not introduce to the Jews, makes it difficult to align them with Abrahamic beliefs. Jesus was a monotheist who upheld the laws of Moses for the Jews, excluding any pagan rituals.

However, Christianity that emerged after Jesus incorporated many of these pagan elements to attract a wider audience seeking glitz and spectacle.

Exploring the true prophets of Allah and their steadfastness shows that faith does not rely on glitz, but on belief, communal gatherings, prayers, and rituals that submit to the Creator without the addition of pagan practices.

The Abrahamic faiths and the prophets who exemplified them provide examples to live by. For those who have been absent from a clear understanding of Islam, it can become a source of profound clarity and comprehension.

It is important to note that this understanding does not lead to the alienation of friendships or the assault on one's beliefs, but it brings forth a distinction and clarity of thought.

This clarity helps to stabilize one's own beliefs and allows for a deeper connection with oneself and one's spirituality. It is a process that mesmerizes the psyche and enables individuals to truly know themselves and their own beliefs.

The presentation of beliefs that align with one's soul does not impose any force, as it comes from a place of inner conviction.

In this journey of understanding, it becomes evident that Allah is the ultimate master of delivering guidance and knowledge, while humans are mere vessels and messengers since the beginning of time.

Life moves in cycles, and although they may repeat themselves, those who seek clarity and understanding will find it within the depths of their hearts.

The allure of enticing children with the myths of Easter and Christmas has remained constant, even though it involves teaching them untruths and embracing pagan beliefs that have no connection to Jesus.

Young minds are captivated by the beauty and excitement of these colorful events, despite the fact that they were not originally associated with Jesus or the Jewish traditions he was sent to.

Over time, these celebrations have become intertwined with pagan beliefs and have deeply influenced the minds of children, leading some to grow up resentful of the fact that these concepts are based on fantasies that remain untrue and lack any evidence of truthfulness.

If Christianity had not evolved to create dates that coincide with pagan holidays, there would be no events that align with Jesus' teachings.

After all, he was sent to the Jews and not meant to be matched with pagan celebrations that were later incorporated into the psyche of believers.

Christianity also relegates women to a secondary position, while the Jewish faith has historically viewed them as inferior to the extent that they were excluded from their homes during menstruation.

In Islam, menstruation is considered impure, which exempts women from participating in ritual prayers or fasting. This is because cleanliness is highly valued in Islam. However, it does not exempt women from going to homes or public places of worship during their menstrual cycle.

In Islam, women are indeed advised to refrain from sexual intimacy during their menstrual cycles. This practice is based on religious teachings that emphasize the importance of cleanliness and purity.

Menstruation is considered a natural process that requires women to maintain their hygiene and engage in acts of worship that do not involve physical intimacy with their spouse.

This temporary period of abstinence is a means of spiritual purification and a way to respect the sanctity of the marital relationship.

It is important to note that this restriction applies only during the days of menstruation. Once the menstrual period ends, sexual intimacy can resume after the completion of a ritual cleansing known as **"Ghusl."**

This practice is intended to promote a healthy and respectful approach to sexual relations within the framework of Islamic teachings.

Menstrual cycles in women are not considered a curse in Islam but rather a natural biological process. Islam highly regards women and acknowledges their physical and emotional differences from men.

The Quran and Hadiths emphasize the importance of women's health and well-being, and menstruation is a sign of fertility and a reminder of the natural cycles of life.

Islam encourages women to take care of their bodies during this time and offers guidelines for maintaining cleanliness and spiritual purity.

Therefore, rather than being viewed as a curse, menstruation is a normal part of a woman's life in Islam.

Bible: NKJV: 3:14:19. The LORD God said to the serpent: "Because you have done this, you are cursed more than all cattle, And more than every beast of the field.

Bible: ESV: Genesis: 3:16. To the woman he said, "I will surely multiply your pain in childbearing; in pain you shall bring forth children. Your desire shall be contrary to your husband, but he shall rule over you."

Genesis 3:16 contains verses that describe the woman's childbirth as being marked by intense pain. Your husband will be the object of your affection, and he will exercise dominion over you.

The mention of Eve's menstrual cycle in relation to the curse only serves to reinforce the belief that women are burdened with physical pain and suffering.

In Islam, women are not held accountable or punished for the actions of Eve or blaming her in tempting Adam.

Islam does not address the act of cursing women directly. However, the disobedience to Allah has led to the destruction of many lands and seas.

False stories and allegations also contribute to destruction.

Islam rectifies these narratives and highlights the benefits of repentance. In the Quran, the book that provides ultimate guidance, Islam explains the creation of the human body, including the formation of the embryo.

For those who wish to delve into learning about Islam, this book is the ultimate authority in understanding the religion.

Science has proven that the menstrual cycle in women is not a curse, but a fascinating and intricate process that showcases the health and regularity of the female body.

This natural cycle involves a continuous cleansing and preparation of the body, bringing forth a multitude of sensations and experiences.

Visually, the process is marked by the maturation of ovarian follicles and the stimulation of endometrial growth, creating a delicate dance within the female reproductive system.

It is a sight of intricate beauty, as the body prepares itself for the possibility of pregnancy.

Audibly, the body whispers its secrets as the fluctuations of estrogen and progesterone take center stage. These hormonal shifts create a symphony of signals, orchestrating the delicate balance required for optimal reproductive health.

The gentle whispers of these sex steroids reverberate throughout the body, influencing far more than just reproduction.

The scent of this process is subtle yet distinct, carrying a hint of life and vitality. It is a fragrance unique to each woman, a testament to her individuality and inner workings.

It lingers in the air, reminding us of the intricate biochemical processes occurring within her body.

Physically, the menstrual cycle is not just a reproductive phenomenon. It impacts various aspects of a woman's well-being, leaving its touch on her bones, cardiovascular system, lipid profile, and even her mood.

It is a tangible reminder of the complex interconnectedness between the reproductive system and overall health.

In conclusion, the menstrual cycle is a sensory journey that goes beyond its reproductive significance. It is a tapestry showcasing the intricate beauty and functionality of the female body.

Islam teaches that Adam and Eve are equally responsible for their actions and were pardoned by Allah after they sought repentance for their errors.

The pain that women go through during menstrual cycles and childbirth is not viewed as a penalty, but a normal part of being human.

This is not seen as a reflection of a woman's morality or a consequence of Eve's actions. In addition, Islam promotes gender equality by allowing women to hold positions of authority or leadership with no restrictions.

The ongoing influence of the Bible exacerbates the marginalization of women, leading to a clash and deep-seated resentment towards gender equality in Western societies.

The opposition displayed by Christianity towards women's rights further hinders the possibility of reconciliation between women and the teachings of the Bible.

Conversely, Islam emphasizes the rights of women, attracting many women who seek acceptance and equality alongside men, based on the rights bestowed upon them by Allah rather than by humanity.

Khadija, the wife of Prophet Muhammad, not only supported him but also played the role of his employer. It was she who proposed the idea of Islam to him.

In Islamic history, many women have ruled and left remarkable legacies. However, they never fought for independence or tried to become men.

They did not compromise their standards to gain acceptance. In Islam, men have a certain level of responsibility towards women, but this does not mean that women are subordinate to men.

Prophet Muhammad himself exemplified this when he stood up and offered his seat to his daughter, Fatima, when she came to visit him. This act clearly shows that Islam also emphasizes the importance of manners and recognizes the strength and fragility of women.

The Islamophobes, who are enemies of Islam, often depict Islam and women as regressive. They distort conversations by introducing false information that has no basis in truth.

They wrongly claim that the Bible dictates women should be subordinate and assert that dire consequences will occur if women hold positions of power over men.

However, what will be the fate of a society where women strive for equality in leadership roles? In the Muslim world, there are numerous instances of women in positions of authority.

Those who truly understand Islam, rather than just adhering to cultural norms, recognize that women's rights are bestowed by Allah, not by humanity.

The idea that women should not rule over men in the Bible contradicts the idea of women seeking authoritative positions and following Christendom.

Islam's teachings are dynamic and adaptable. High standards are expected of women in Islam.

Islam is the original embodiment of democracy and truth, not the corrupted systems that manipulate ideologies for their own interests.

Islam demonstrated its ability to uplift Muslim women through the example set by the Prophet of Islam.

Within the faith of Islam, it is crucial to showcase the equal status men hold and their significant level of responsibility over women, not dominance.

The portrayal of dominance in society displayed by some Muslim men is often attributed to a lack of education and a misunderstanding of Islam. It is important to note, however, that this behavior is not representative of all Muslim men or the teachings of Islam as a whole.

Islam encourages kindness, compassion, and respect towards others, regardless of gender. The Prophet Muhammad (peace be upon him) is often cited as an example of humility and gentleness towards his wives and women.

Ayub, also known as Job, is a prophet whose story is mentioned in the Quran:

Job, a prophet, belonged to the lineage of prophets in the Abrahamic faiths. He had an abundance of blessings, including good health, wealth, a prestigious lineage, and much more.

His heart was filled with purity and his belief was unwavering. The Abrahamic religions provide valuable lessons, not mere mythology or fictional holidays.

Emphasizing the importance of faith and meaningful words is of utmost importance in reminding humanity. The story of Job serves as a valuable lesson, teaching us that seeking truth holds greater significance than embracing falsehoods.

Rather than altering schemes and celebrations to appeal to our minds, it is vital to prioritize the authenticity of these celebrations, which far surpass any superficial attractiveness.

Quran: Surah Anam: 6:84. And We bestowed upon Abraham (offspring) Ishaq (Isaac) and Ya'qub (Jacob) and each of them did We guide to the right way as We had earlier guided Noah.

Devoted to God, he worshiped Him exclusively, demonstrated patience, remained steadfast, and frequently sought forgiveness.

A group of angels were overheard by Satan, who became consumed with jealousy and suppressed anger upon hearing their discussion about Job being the most virtuous man of his era.

He intended to lure Job away from righteousness and lead him into disbelief and moral decay. Satan tried to divert Job's focus from his prayers, but Job stayed strong and continued to pray with unwavering devotion and concentration.

Satan's fury grew stronger, leading him to voice his grievances to God, alleging that Job's unwavering devotion was solely due to the abundance of wealth and possessions he had been granted.

God permitted Satan and his allies to ruin Job's belongings, yet Job stayed faithful to his beliefs and recognized that God had the power to bestow or take away wealth and possessions as He saw fit.

Satan grew even more agitated and went back to God, claiming that Job was only pretending to remain faithful because he had a loving and prosperous family.

Job's home was destroyed by Satan and his accomplices, resulting in the devastating loss of all of his children as the building collapsed.

Job, once again, turned to God for comfort and accepted this arduous test without any objections.

In the form of an elderly man, Satan approached Job, concealing his identity.

The anger of Satan grew silently but burned fiercely. Upon his return to God, he reported that Job was in a good physical condition, which raised hopes for the restoration of his wealth and the addition of more children.

Satan requested consent to bring harm to Job's physical condition. Satan's third request was granted by God, but he was forbidden from harming Job's soul, heart, or intellect.

With the permission of Allah, Satan and his helpers started to afflict Job's physical being. He became nothing but a skeleton and endured excruciating suffering.

Job was afflicted with a disease that caused people to recoil from him in disgust, and his friends and family started abandoning him.

The only person who stayed by his side was his wife. Even in their destitution, she never wavered in her care and kindness towards him, taking on the role of a servant to ensure they had enough food to sustain them each day.

Despite his suffering, Job maintained unwavering faith in God. He always kept his lips and tongue hydrated with the memory of God, never losing hope or expressing discontent.

Despite the immense disaster that had struck him, he persisted in expressing gratitude to God. Faced with a dilemma, Satan couldn't figure out how to lure Job away from his loyalty to God, leading him to target Job's wife for harassment.

Taking the form of a man, he visited her and brought back memories of the good old days when life was easier for them. Job's wife couldn't hold back her tears as she confronted him, begging him to implore their Lord to relieve their suffering.

Job reminded his wife that despite their current suffering, they had been blessed by God with wealth, children, and health for 80 years.

He boldly stated that he felt embarrassed to implore God for relief from his difficulties and proceeded to reprimand his wife by threatening to inflict a hundred lashes on her if he ever regained his well-being.

The wife of Job, who loved him deeply, was heartbroken and decided to find refuge elsewhere. Overwhelmed by his circumstances, Job sought divine intervention from God, not to voice his complaints but to humbly implore for mercy.

Quran: Surah Anbiya: 21:83. And remember when Job cried out to his Lord, I have been touched with adversity and You are the most merciful of the merciful.

Quran: Surah Anbiya: 21:84. So We answered his prayer and removed his adversity, and gave him back his family, twice as many, as a mercy from Us and a lesson for the ˙devoted˙ worshippers.

Job had made a promise to his wife that if his health improved, he would discipline her for doubting God. However, he didn't actually want to harm her, especially since she had returned with joy and demonstrated her remorse and eagerness to seek God's mercy.

Job decided to honor his word, but in a way that wouldn't cause any harm. He was advised to lightly strike her with a bundle of thin grass, not with the intention of hurting her, but simply to keep his promise.

It's important to note that the act of hitting her wasn't the reason to prove his faith, but it was permitted in order to fulfill his word.

Quran: Surah Sad: 38:44. And we said to him, take in your hand a bundle of grass, and strike your wife with it and do not break your oath. We truly found him patient. What an excellent servant he was! Indeed, he constantly turned to Allah.

God restored Job's wealth as well. According to the story, there was a day when he was bathing and God unexpectedly rained down golden grasshoppers on him. His health was recovered, his family was reunited and expanded, and he regained his wealth.

Quran tells us that Job's story is a reminder for all those who worship God.(Allah).

Job's story demonstrates the importance of patience and enduring faith in a world full of trials. Although fully aware of the transitory nature of our existence, Job maintained his unwavering faith and was eventually blessed with the complete recovery of all that he had lost, and even greater abundance.

He remained true to his promises to his wife, his creator, and everyone he knew, thus upholding his own integrity. It can be challenging to maintain the patience of Job, especially when one realizes that the Creator they worship has surpassed their expectations.

The story ends with Jobs' firm conviction in the power of integrity and patience, which played a crucial role in attracting greater opportunities.

Those who have faith may encounter challenging experiences that may be difficult to endure initially, but the outcomes surpass expectations and bring greater satisfaction.

The concept of democracy in Islam goes beyond mere political parties and encompasses a broader understanding of societal dynamics. It emphasizes the continuous process of giving and exchanging that occurs in the world.

In Islam, individuals are encouraged to generously share their wealth and resources with others, viewing it as a loan given to Allah.

This act of selflessness and charity is believed to be rewarded abundantly by Allah. The Quran mentions the concept of giving to increase one's blessings and provisions in both material and spiritual aspects of life.

This principle of giving is deeply ingrained in the Islamic society, promoting a sense of collective responsibility and solidarity among its members. This democratic aspect of Islam fosters an environment where social justice, equality, and fairness are upheld, ensuring the well-being of the entire community.

According to Islamic teachings, the distribution of wealth should be done in a just and equitable manner.

Islam emphasizes the concept of economic justice and discourages the concentration of wealth in the hands of a few individuals or groups.

The Islamic economic system encourages the sharing of resources and promotes social welfare through various means such as **Zakat** (obligatory charity), **Sadaqah** (voluntary charity), and **Waqf** (endowment).

These practices aim to ensure that wealth is circulated within society and that the basic needs of all individuals are met.

Islam also encourages the concept of fair trade and prohibits exploitative practices such as usury (interest) and hoarding. Overall, Islamic teachings emphasize the importance of a balanced and equitable distribution of wealth to foster social harmony and reduce poverty.

Quran: Surah Hadid: 57:18. Indeed, those men and women who give in charity and lend to Allah a good loan will have it multiplied for them, and they will have an honorable reward.

In Islam, the concept of wealth distribution is based on the belief that Allah has given different capacities and abilities to each individual. Therefore, each person is tested according to their own capabilities and resources.

This means that not everyone will have the same level of wealth or resources, as it is part of their unique test in life. However, Islam emphasizes the importance of treating all individuals with equality and fairness, regardless of their wealth or social status.

One place where this equality is clearly evident is in the masjid, the place of worship for Muslims. In the masjid, there is no segregation based on wealth or social standing. Rich and poor, black and white, all come together as equals to worship and seek the blessings of Allah. This inclusivity and non-discrimination is one of the reasons why many people are drawn to Islam.

It is important to note that wealth in Islam is not seen as an inherently negative thing. Rather, it is considered a blessing from Allah and a means of providing for oneself and others.

However, Islam also emphasizes the importance of using wealth with dignity, integrity, and belief. Wealth should be appreciated and used in a way that benefits society and fulfills one's religious obligations, such as giving charity and helping those in need.

In summary, Islam acknowledges that wealth distribution is not equal among individuals, as each person is tested according to their own capacity. However, Islam promotes equality and inclusivity in places like the masjid, where all are treated as equals regardless of their wealth or social status.

The misinformation spread by Islamophobes on social media does not accurately represent the teachings of Islam, and this becomes apparent to those who are uninformed.

It is impossible to overlook the groundbreaking achievement of Fatima Fihri, the first Muslim woman who established the world's first university.

This serves as a powerful reminder of the capabilities and contributions of Muslim women. The United States has never had a female leader before, so it would be groundbreaking for a woman to take office, especially considering historical norms and biblical teachings that discourage female leadership.

Muslim women have been in power and continue to hold positions of authority in various countries for many years. The portrayal of Muslims and Muslim women in Islamophobic areas is a clear distortion and lack of understanding that fails to accurately represent the true essence of Islam.

That's why it's crucial to educate the general population since they can negatively influence numerous individuals.

Some examples of Muslim women who have ruled countries include:

1. Benazir Bhutto: She was the Prime Minister of Pakistan from 1988 to 1990 and then again from 1993 to 1996. Bhutto was the first woman to lead a democratic government in a Muslim-majority country.

2. Sheikh Hasina: She was the Prime Minister of Bangladesh from 2009 to 2024, and previously served as the Prime Minister from 1996 to 2001. Sheikh Hasina has been the longest-serving prime minister in the history of Bangladesh.

3. Megawati Sukarnoputri: She was the President of Indonesia from 2001 to 2004. Megawati was the first female President of Indonesia and the daughter of the country's first President, Sukarno.

4. Tansu Çiller: She served as the Prime Minister of Turkey from 1993 to 1996. Tansu Çiller was the first and, so far, the only female Prime Minister of Turkey.

5. Atifete Jahja Ga: She was the President of Kosovo from 2011 to 2016. Atifete Jahja Ga was the first female President of Kosovo and the first non-partisan candidate to hold the position.

It is important to note that while these women held prominent positions of power in their respective countries, their leadership does not represent a full range of Muslim women's involvement in politics worldwide.

Islam, from its inception, granted women various rights that were revolutionary at the time. For example, it granted women the right to own and inherit property, engage in business, seek education, and participate in social and political activities.

Islam also emphasized the equal worth and dignity of men and women, stating that they are spiritual equals in the eyes of God.

The concept of **hijab**, often misunderstood and criticized, actually serves as a symbol of empowerment and modesty for women, allowing them to be judged based on their character and intellect rather than their physical appearance.

Islam's emphasis on justice, compassion, and social welfare aligns with progressive ideals, advocating for the fair treatment of all individuals, regardless of their race, gender, or social status.

Therefore, it is essential to challenge the misleading narratives surrounding Islam and recognize its progressive contributions to society.

This is particularly ignorance considering that Islam is one of the world's major religions, with over 1.9 billion followers worldwide. Islamophobia is a prevalent issue in many parts of the world, fueled by misconceptions and a lack of understanding about the religion.

Islamophobes often propagate false information and engage in fearmongering, leading to the blacking out of the truth and the spread of lies. In such an environment, it becomes a responsibility for Muslims to share the truth about Islam.

This duty arises from the need to combat ignorance and prejudice, and to promote understanding and tolerance among people of different faiths.

Muslims have a unique opportunity to dispel misconceptions, educate others about the true teachings and principles of Islam, and encourage open dialogue. By engaging in peaceful conversations, Muslims can challenge stereotypes and build bridges of understanding, fostering a more inclusive and harmonious society.

It is a religion that promotes peace, justice, and compassion. Islam teaches its followers to treat women with respect and dignity, granting them rights and roles within society. In fact, Islam was one of the first religions to grant women property rights and the right to divorce.

The portrayal of Muslims as terrorists is not only false, but also dangerous, as it perpetuates harmful stereotypes and fuels Islamophobia.

The overwhelming majority of Muslims are peaceful individuals who contribute positively to their communities and reject any form of violence or extremism. It is crucial to challenge these misconceptions and educate others about the true teachings and values of Islam.

Remaining silent in the face of Islamophobia is not an option for those who understand the truth. It is a moral responsibility to stand up against bigotry and discrimination, and to promote understanding and acceptance.

Muslim communities have long fought for their rights and recognition as equal citizens, often facing discrimination and prejudice. It is essential to speak out against Islamophobia and work towards creating a more inclusive and tolerant society.

In conclusion, it is imperative to dispel the misconceptions surrounding Islam and Muslims. Education and open dialogue are key in challenging the negative narratives propagated by social media and other platforms.

By shedding light on the truth about Islam and Muslims, we can foster understanding, tolerance, and respect among individuals of different faiths and backgrounds.

These insecurities may show themselves in various ways, such as jealousy or the constant need to prove oneself. However, a genuine friend can see beyond these surface-level irritations and recognize the underlying qualities that make the individual confident.

They understand that these attempts to downplay their knowledge stem from a place of insecurity and are not an accurate reflection of their capabilities.

Instead of being swayed by these grains of sand, a lasting friendship with the creator focuses on supporting and uplifting each other, celebrating each other's strengths, and helping each other grow.

It is through this understanding and empathy that a deep bond can be formed, built on mutual respect and admiration.

Just like the social media accounts of Islamophobia continue to spread false narratives and stage lies, they often accuse Muslims in Syria of terrorizing those who do not believe in Islam and forcing them to convert.

However, these accusations are completely untrue and do not reflect the reality on the ground.

Islam, as a religion, does not advocate for the forced conversion of individuals. In fact, Islam stands as the only religion in the world that explicitly declares no force in matters of faith and grants individuals the liberty and freedom to follow any belief system they choose.

If any party claims terrorism, extremism, or forceful conversions to Islam, it is important to note that these actions stem from their own ideologies rather than Islam itself. Islam cannot be rewritten; it remains an unchanged document, as stated in the Quran.

In this sense, Islam can be seen as the first democracy in the world, promoting tolerance and respect for diverse religious perspectives.

The staging of Muslims as a threat on social media is indeed an ongoing effort by certain individuals or groups who perceive Islam as a potential threat because of the increasing number of Westerners converting to the religion.

These individuals or groups may have their own biases, prejudices, or misconceptions about Islam, which they perpetuate through misinformation and manipulation of social media platforms.

The importance of Syria goes beyond just its oil fields. While the region's oil reserves have attracted the attention of various global powers, including those in the Middle East, the ongoing conflict in Syria involves complex geopolitical dynamics.

The conflict is driven by a combination of factors such as political power struggles, sectarian tensions, regional rivalries, and pursuit of strategic interests.

These explanations are exclusively intended to educate those who are curious, with no intention whatsoever of coercing or luring anyone into embracing Islam.

They provide a way for curious individuals to find answers and gain clarity, ultimately promoting understanding among the knowledgeable.

Islam does not promote or condone the forced acceptance of its faith, and Muslims are not instructed to coerce others into converting. Yet, these Islamophobes persistently fabricate stories to portray Islam and Muslims as threats to the beliefs of others.

In conclusion, the comparative study of the Abrahamic faith's sheds light on the diverse beliefs and interpretations of these religions.

While they all share a common origin in the worship of one God, the variations in doctrines and interpretations highlight the rich tapestry of religious thought within the Abrahamic traditions.

The highest currency in the world is Islam. People who lack knowledge about Islam are amazed by the achievements and advancements of both women and men in the religion.

Their travels, knowledge, manners, and overall conduct leave those who are only familiar with social media and their own lifestyle questioning their own accomplishments.

Muslims believe that success is found in Islam, while other blessings may be eclipsed by deeds. Compared to other currencies, the Dinar has the highest value, and it is the currency of a Muslim nation.

The formation of a united Muslim nations can create a significant impact, leading to heightened awareness among adversaries and giving rise to historical disputes and conflicts because of concerns about the dominance of Islam.

The country's economy heavily relies on oil exports, which are backed by its plentiful reserves.

Kuwait, like other Muslim countries, has a wealth of opportunities and no taxes for its workers in Kuwait. In Muslim countries, usury is prohibited, and Muslims are blessed with wealth and knowledge to enrich the world.

Muslim countries joining is the key to solving global conflicts, just as they brought enlightenment during the Islamic golden age.

Once those who sought to exploit and envy Muslim achievements gained power and regrouped, their dictatorial inclinations towards manipulation became prominent. They placed their greed above moral ethics and education, prioritizing personal gain.

When individuals compare themselves to animals, for example, by saying "call me a leopard, I cannot change my spots," it is a cynical comment implying that those who resist personal growth and learning remain stagnant.

They argue that their ingrained habits prevent them from changing. Using the excuse that animals like leopards and tigers cannot change their physical appearance to justify being stagnant is not valid.

The animal and the human both have the capacity for change, while those who remain stagnant live with restlessness until they impose their limited thinking on others, which can only be beneficial if change occurs for the better.

Muslims are divided by distractions, but the only solution is for them to unite against falsehood.

The restlessness of the mind can indeed be channeled in various ways, as an idle mind is often considered to be a breeding ground for negative thoughts and actions.

It is commonly believed that surrounding oneself with poor company can lead to the misguidance of the masses.

This recognition of the exasperating dilemma has been relevant within the Muslim community. Those who have sought personal improvement and growth have consciously chosen to distance themselves from individuals who do not possess the intellect or desire to improve.

Instead, they have opted to spend their time in solitude, deepening their knowledge and understanding of Islamic history and events.

They have also actively invited others to participate in events that serve as educational platforms, aimed at preserving and sharing the rich history of Muslims. In order to maintain a balanced state of mind, Muslims are encouraged to engage in daily **Salat.**

This mandatory act of worship not only fosters a spiritual connection but also helps individuals find equilibrium between their worldly affairs and their spiritual well-being. Unlike multiple-choice options, mandated Salat ensures a consistent and disciplined approach to maintaining this balance.

Islam has always emphasized the importance of mental well-being and emotions, recognizing the significance of Allah's creation.

Muslims have always recognized the importance of mental health and have actively addressed it through various means. Islamic teachings emphasize the holistic well-being of individuals, including their mental, emotional, and spiritual states.

Muslims are encouraged to seek balance and inner peace through practices such as prayer, meditation, and remembrance of God.

Islamic scholars and leaders have long advocated for the importance of seeking professional help and support when dealing with mental health challenges.

Unfortunately, like any other community, there are individuals who neglect their mental health, leading to chaos in their minds. This can be because of various reasons, such as societal stigma, lack of awareness, or personal neglect.

If severe mental health issues are left unaddressed without proper help, they can persist.

Experiencing childhood trauma, such as abuse, neglect, or witnessing domestic violence, can cause various conditions, such as PTSD, depression, anxiety disorders, and borderline personality disorder.

In the same vein, individuals who have gone through toxic relationships or had a dysfunctional upbringing may develop attachment disorders, have low self-esteem, and face obstacles in establishing healthy relationships.

The misuse of substances, including alcohol and drugs, can amplify preexisting mental health conditions or give rise to new ones, such as substance-induced psychosis or comorbid disorders.

Individuals experiencing these difficulties must prioritize seeking professional help and support to tackle their mental health issues and strive for recovery. Muslims have a strong emphasis on faith and seeking guidance from Allah in all aspects of life, including mental health.

In fact, Islam places great importance on the well-being of individuals and encourages seeking help and support when facing mental health challenges.

The Prophet Muhammad (peace be upon him) himself provided guidance and advice on how to maintain good mental health and cope with stress and anxiety.

Islamic teachings emphasize the importance of self-care, reflection, and seeking solace in prayer and remembrance of Allah.

Muslims have a long history of establishing institutions such as mosques and madrasas, which not only serve as places of worship but also provide a support system for individuals facing mental health issues.

Islamic scholars and counselors are available to offer guidance and support, incorporating Islamic teachings into therapeutic interventions.

The Quran and Hadith literature contains verses and sayings that address mental well-being, encouraging Muslims to have a balanced and holistic approach to their mental health alongside their spiritual practices.

Overall, Muslims prioritize their belief in Allah and seek guidance from Him, and they were among the first to recognize the importance of addressing mental health issues within the context of their faith.

The first mental hospital for the wellness of humans was indeed established by a Muslim physician named Rhazes (also known as Muhammad ibn Zakariya al-Razi) in Baghdad, Iraq, during the 9th century.

Rhazes was a renowned scholar and polymath who made significant contributions to various fields, including medicine and psychology. He recognized the importance of mental health and believed in providing specialized care for individuals experiencing psychological distress.

Rhazes' mental hospital, known as the "Bimaristan al-Mansouri," offered a safe and supportive environment for patients, emphasizing compassionate treatment and the use of therapeutic techniques.

This historical example highlights the understanding and commitment within the Muslim community towards addressing mental health concerns and seeking professional help when needed.

It is crucial to address any misunderstandings and promote the importance of Muslims in prioritizing their mental well-being.

It is essential for them to understand that seeking professional help is not only acceptable but highly recommended, especially for seeking support from fellow Muslims.

For Muslims, every aspect of life is interconnected with their beliefs and faith. However, individuals of other faiths are free to seek help as they see fit.

Suicide is indeed considered a grave sin in Islam, as it involves taking one's own life, which directly violates the sanctity of life.

Islam places great emphasis on the preservation and protection of human life, and suicide is viewed as a severe transgression against this principle.

Martyrdom holds a revered position in Islam, as it is the ultimate sacrifice for the sake of Allah and the defense of the faith. Martyrs are believed to be granted a special place in paradise and are considered as heroes in the Islamic tradition.

It is crucial for both Muslims and non-Muslims, especially those who have recently converted to Islam and may have limited knowledge on the subject, to understand this distinction between suicide and martyrdom.

Seeking clarification and guidance from knowledgeable scholars and religious leaders is essential in order to gain a comprehensive understanding of this sensitive topic in Islam.

In Islamic teachings, it is essential to approach the understanding of Islamic concepts without imposing one's own interpretations and ideas. Islam is a doctrine that remains constant and unchanging, emphasizing stability and adherence to its principles.

Therefore, it is crucial to chase away the lies and misconceptions to gain a true understanding of Islam. One such misconception is the notion of suicide, which is strictly prohibited and considered a sinful act in Islam.

Life is a sacred gift from Allah, and it is not within the authority of any individual to take or end a life, including their own.

Islam teaches that life should be cherished and embraced, even during times of trials and difficulties. It is a fundamental belief that only Allah has the authority to give and take life, and humans must respect and uphold this divine decree.

The presence of uncertainties in decision-making does not establish a causal link in taking one's own life in Islam. It is important to address misconceptions and misunderstandings, such as the false belief that Muslims were responsible for the 9/11 attacks as suicide bombers in the name of Allah.

The case remains unsolved, and it is unfair to generalize blame onto all Muslims. Only Islamophobes, driven by hatred and fear, propagate such false narratives to perpetuate their own agenda.

Islam strictly forbids suicide, so no Muslim would ever take their own life. That Allah welcomes those who do such things is wrong, showing a lack of understanding of Islam's core beliefs. Dispelling these misconceptions requires nurturing education and fostering understanding.

ABC news: 20 years after 9/11, Islamophobia continues to haunt Muslims.

Comparing Islam to the Bible, selective verses about Jesus forgiving sins can be disputed as Jesus was a monotheist.

However, it is crucial to understand the context and overall teachings of both religions. Islam teaches that forgiveness is sought from Allah, and all prophets, including Jesus, sought forgiveness from Him. All prophets asked Allah for forgiveness.

Defiance, as well as suicide, is not considered extraordinary behavior in Islam but as acts that dishonor life and go against the teachings of the religion.

It is important to distinguish between the actions of a few individuals who may misinterpret religious teachings and the true teachings of Islam.

Bible: Hebrews: 9:14:16. So surely the blood sacrifice of Christ can do much more. Christ offered himself through the eternal Spirit[a] as a perfect sacrifice to God. His blood will make us completely clean from the evil we have done. It will give us clear consciences so that we can worship the living God.

The captivating appeal of enigmatic verses involving blood sacrifice, forgiveness, wine, and bread becomes prohibited in Islam, as this monotheistic faith, alongside Judaism, does not accept any cultic practices.

However, Muslims do not deny the prophets or selectively choose whom to elevate. It is Allah who determines and elevates one's status, not the Muslims themselves.

Song by Stealer's Wheel

I've got the feeling that something ain't right!

Here I am stuck in the middle with you!

Certain songs' lyrics can depict the current state of the world, which is often a chaotic epidemic in the Western world.

For Muslims, living in any country is insignificant; they are instructed to respect and contribute to the land they live in.

Sujood brings prosperity to any country they live in.

Muslims are not immune to being led astray. Those who are pointing fingers can often be more misguided than the person they are blaming.

Society's continuous and ineffective scapegoating of Muslims persists. Islam may seem unfamiliar or different to some individuals compared to societal norms

It is better to have knowledge of Islam than to be ignorant, as repentance holds great importance in the religion.

Action beats inaction for results!

Stagnation is not Islam, as the essence of Islam is rooted in growth, progress, and development. Islam encourages its followers to constantly seek knowledge, strive for excellence, and contribute positively to society.

The Quran, the central religious text of Islam, emphasizes the importance of seeking knowledge and understanding of the world. Muslims are encouraged to continuously educate themselves, innovate, and adapt to changing circumstances.

Stagnation goes against the core principles of Islam, as it promotes complacency and a lack of personal and societal growth. Instead, Islam encourages individuals and communities to constantly evolve, learn, and improve, in order to better themselves and the world around them.

However, it is important to recognize that the morality and ethics found within Islam often require strength in character, something that may not be clear to those who are not familiar with the religion.

Unfortunately, some actively fight against Islam and perpetuate the notion that it is backward and extreme, without fully understanding its true teachings and values. It is crucial to understand the implications and impact this has on many individuals, regardless of how Islam is portrayed or painted.

The truth about Islam can never be erased or changed, no matter how hard some may try to distort it.

The good-hearted person, upon receiving good health from Allah, embraces a life of gratitude and seeks mercy and repentance. They understand that life is fleeting and temporary and therefore strive to make the most of their time on earth by spreading positivity and helping others.

The evil person, after regaining their health, uses their time to indulge in destructive behavior. Their heart is filled with darkness, and they find satisfaction in causing harm and chaos.

They actively invite others to partake in evil and create fitnah, as the evil within them can only find contentment in doing wrong.

It may tempt one to question why Allah restored health to someone who intends to use it for harm, while a good person may leave this world.

However, the concept of life as a passing phase reminds us that our time on earth needs attendance not stagnation. It is the state of our hearts and our actions that truly matter.

Understanding the core principles of Islam is crucial because it ensures that non-Muslim influences do not dilute or distort the teachings of the faith. Islam is a comprehensive way of life, encompassing spiritual, moral, social, and legal aspects.

Therefore, it is essential for believers to have a deep knowledge of their faith in order to navigate the complexities of the world while staying true to their Islamic values.

Without this understanding, one may unknowingly compromise their beliefs and waste precious time on earth pursuing activities that do not align with the teachings of Islam.

The fortune of a believer lies in their commitment to the principles and values prescribed by Allah and the Prophet Muhammad (peace be upon him). By knowing and adhering to these principles, one can lead a purposeful and fulfilling life, in harmony with their faith and the teachings of Islam.

The evil person may appear happy, but their happiness is shallow and hollow. It is merely a facade that masks the loneliness and emptiness they feel inside. Deceiving oneself and others may provide temporary pleasure, but it does not bring true happiness.

The world is not a welcoming place for those who live in deception and seek to harm oneself and others. However, there is always a chance for repentance and redemption.

The evil person can still restore goodness to their heart, but it requires sincere efforts to rectify their actions and surround themselves with good company. Only then can they find true happiness and fulfillment in life.

The signs told in the Quran and hadiths serve as guidance for individuals who wish to restore their behavior and seek repentance, as well as for those who wish to reflect and ponder upon their actions.

Allah, being the all-knowing and all-seeing, understands the trials and tribulations faced by each individual.

Some may need to experience confinement or restriction to reflect upon their actions and seek redemption, while others may only reveal their true colors when they are granted health or freedom.

However, it is important to note that no Muslim uses the word "perfection" to describe themselves, as it is understood and ingrained in every Muslim that perfection is a quality solely reserved for Allah.

Omar bin Khattab, while not specifically known for his mathematical contributions, was renowned for his logical reasoning and problem-solving skills, which served as an inspiration for future Muslim scholars.

Their knowledge and expertise continue to inspire teachers as they impart mathematical knowledge to their students, highlighting the rich legacy of Muslim scholars in this field. The importance of history needs to be revived so that those who are unaware can learn that it all began during the Golden Age of Islam.

This interpretation highlights the continuity and fulfillment of divine messages throughout different eras and religions, as Jesus sought to convey God's teachings to his Jewish audience.

In a society where collective thinking prevails over individualism, ignorance can be a dangerous force. When people are unaware of history or lack knowledge about certain subjects, they are more susceptible to being led astray into the waters of darkness.

Ignorance can cloud one's judgment and prevent them from seeing the truth or understanding the consequences of their actions.

However, sometimes individuals, upon gaining a deeper understanding of a topic, may choose to change their views. This transition can result from personal growth, education, or exposure to different perspectives. Unfortunately, there are also those who, despite knowing the truth, continue to perpetuate hypocrisy because of fear of judgment or repercussions from society.

This fear of expressing their true beliefs can hinder progress and perpetuate the cycle of ignorance. Therefore, it is crucial to encourage open-mindedness, critical thinking, and the pursuit of knowledge in order to overcome the barriers imposed by collective thinking and combat the dangers of ignorance.

Clarification is the only way to address the contradiction and predicament of ignorance.

While some Jews may not consider Jesus as a prophet, it does not imply a lack of interest in the historical and religious significance of Nazareth.

Regarding control and access to religious sites, the situation is multifaceted. Bethlehem, where Jesus was born, is under Palestinian control, and the Church of the Nativity stands as a symbol of Christianity.

However, tensions and disputes over the control of religious sites exist, involving various stakeholders, including different Christian denominations, Muslims, and Jews.

Quran: Surah Imran: 3:64. Say, o people of the scripture, come to a word that is equitable between us and you- that we will not worship except Allah and not associate anything with Him and not take one another as lords instead of Allah. But if they turn away then say, bear witness that we are Muslims submitting to him.

Quran: Surah Imran: 3:65. O people of the book! Why do you argue about Abraham, while the Torah and the Gospel were not revealed until long after him? Do you not understand?

Quran: Surah Imran: 3:66. Here you are! You disputed about what you have little knowledge of but why do you now argue about what you do not know of? Allah knows and you do not know!

Quran: Surah Imran: 3:67. Abraham was neither a Jew nor a Christian; he was a Muslim, wholly devoted to God. And he certainly was not amongst those who associate others with Allah in his divinity.

Quran: Surah Imran: 3:69. A party of the People of the Book would fain lead you astray, whereas in truth they lead none astray except themselves, but they do not realize it.

Quran: Surah Imran: 3:70. O people of the book! Why do you reject the signs of Allah while you bear witness to their truth?

Quran: Surah Imran: 3:71. O people of the Book! Why do you mix the truth with falsehood and hide the truth knowingly?

Quran: Surah Imran: 3:71. O People of the Book! Why do you mix the truth with falsehood and hide the truth knowingly?

Quran: Surah Imran: 3:89. Except for those who repent after that and do righteous deeds. Verily Allah is oft forgiving, most merciful.

The concept of monotheism, the belief in one God, is central to the Abrahamic faiths of Islam, Christianity, and Judaism. In these religions, Allah, God, or Yahweh is the one true deity, and the idea of a trinity or multiple gods is rejected.

This shared belief in the oneness of God is emphasized in religious scriptures such as the Quran, the Bible, and the Torah.

However, in today's society, there seems to be a growing trend of losing faith and questioning religious doctrines.

The allure of the materialistic world, coupled with the influence of Western culture, has led some Muslims to adopt a more independent and defiant mindset that is not in line with the subtleties of Islamic teachings.

Despite this, there are still individuals who strive to balance their faith and the realities of the modern world.

However, it is also acknowledged that there are those who live in ignorance, unaware of or indifferent to the invitation to monotheistic beliefs and the moral teachings found in religious texts, like the Quran.

Ultimately, the invitation to truth and the belief in one God remains a central aspect of the Abrahamic faiths, as exemplified by the monotheistic beliefs of the prophet Abraham.

The Quran, as the direct word of Allah, emphasizes the mercy of Allah and consistently addresses the people of the previous scriptures who have altered the original texts and deviated from the monotheistic belief of Abraham.

Throughout history, the belief in one true God has been influenced and mixed with polytheistic beliefs.

However, it is important to note that Abraham, the revered father of all prophets, was a staunch monotheist. There is no record of Abraham ever proclaiming that Jesus would walk in the body of God, as it is understood that the sight of God cannot be perceived by any human in their limited and weak state.

This belief in Islam acknowledges the transcendence and incomprehensibility of God, making it impossible for Him to transform into a human. Humans, who carry their bodily waste within them, are considered mortal and Allah would not subject Himself to such a condition.

The constant mercy of Allah is evident in His reminders to people of other scriptures, to come to terms with their beliefs. It is acceptable in this world to acknowledge that a prophet of Allah is painted as co-equal to Allah. However, in the next world, there will be no mercy for those who join partners with Allah.

While saying that belief cannot be forced is true, it is important to understand that the terms of faith cannot be negotiated but must be sincerely expressed. Allah's mercy lies in His continuous reminders and guidance, urging individuals to recognize the true nature of faith and avoid associating partners with Allah.

However, conflicts between these denominations over control and ownership of the church often arose, leading to tensions and even violent clashes.

In fear of losing control to these internal conflicts, the Christian denominations eventually entrusted the guarding and care of the church to Muslims.

This decision was influenced by the historical role that Muslims, particularly during the time of Omar bin Khattab, had played in ensuring the protection of religious sites in Jerusalem, including the Church of the Holy Sepulcher.

Muslims were impartial custodians who could prevent further conflicts between the Christian factions and maintain the sanctity of the holy site. This unique arrangement, where Muslims have been involved in safeguarding a Christian place of worship, has persisted for centuries and continues to this day.

It is essential to approach the topic with nuance and recognize the diverse perspectives and complexities that surround the religious and political dynamics in the region.

In ancient times, Semitic peoples inhabited Palestine, with the earliest known inhabitants being the Canaanites.

They established several city-states across the region. Tradition and religious texts state that Abraham, the common ancestor of the Jews and the Arabs, migrated from the ancient city of Ur in Mesopotamia to Canaan.

This migration, known as the **"Abrahamic journey,"** holds significant religious and cultural importance for both Jews and Arabs. Scholars believe Abraham settled in various parts of Canaan, including Hebron and Shechem, and his descendants grew to form the Jewish and Arab nations.

The story of Abraham's journey and his connection to Canaan is a foundational aspect of the historical and cultural narratives of both Jewish and Arab peoples in the region.

Despite growing up in a community that practiced paganism and idol worship, Ibrahim (AS) had a deep sense of contemplation and questioning about the existence of a higher power.

His father, Azar, was not only a prominent member of their community but also a skilled sculptor and crafted of idols. Ibrahim was exposed to this craftsmanship from a young age and observed the people's devotion to these idols.

However, he couldn't help but question the logic and significance behind worshiping lifeless objects. This inner turmoil and curiosity would eventually lead him on a profound spiritual journey.

Despite growing up in a society steeped in idol worship, Ibrahim (AS) was a deeply thoughtful individual. He questioned the purpose and logic behind worshiping inanimate objects and felt a strong desire to seek the truth.

One night, as he gazed at the stars in the sky, Ibrahim (AS) contemplated the existence of a higher power.

He realized that the stars, the moon, and the sun were all creations of Allah (SWT) and could not possibly be deities. Determined to find the true path of monotheism, Ibrahim (AS) embarked on a journey to find Allah (SWT) and understand His divine message.

He left Babylon, leaving behind his family and everything he knew, and set out on a spiritual quest that would shape the course of his life.

The Bible, as we know it today, is a compilation of various texts written by multiple authors over several centuries.

These writings did not emerge immediately after Jesus' ascension, but gradually as the early Christian movement developed and spread, with different individuals, such as Matthew, Mark, Luke, and John, among others, composing them.

Various early Christian writings and traditions formed the basis of Christian belief and practice as they were preserved and incorporated into the Bible, despite the lack of definitive evidence supporting the existence of an authentic gospel directly given to Jesus by the angel Gabriel.

As the ideas of humanity evolved and different cultural influences came into play, Christianity, which originated from Judaism, underwent significant changes. While Christianity initially adhered to the monotheistic beliefs of Judaism, the concept of Jesus as the central figure and object of worship gradually emerged.

This shift occurred as various theological interpretations and philosophical ideas shaped the development of Christian doctrine.

The divinity of Jesus, his role as the savior, and his teachings on love, forgiveness, and salvation became the focal points of Christian worship, leading to a shift away from strict monotheism.

This evolution in Christian theology and the elevation of Jesus as a divine figure marked a significant departure from traditional Jewish monotheism.

However, it is important to note that different Christian denominations interpret and understand the nature of Jesus' divinity in various ways, and not all branches of Christianity have completely abandoned monotheism.

The Bible, which was written centuries before Islam, does not align with the Islamic belief in Muhammad as the final prophet. Muslims consider the Quran to be the authentic and unchanged word of God, and they rely on its teachings as the ultimate authority.

While some names of prophets may overlap between the Bible and the Quran, the narratives and stories surrounding these prophets often differ significantly.

Therefore, for the Muslim world, the authenticity of the Bible is not widely accepted unless it aligns with the teachings of the Quran. In Islamic culture, the heart holds significant symbolism and represents the core of one's being, encompassing emotions, intentions, and spirituality.

It is believed that the heart is the seat of warmth, affection, and spirit, reflecting the depth of a person's character. However, it is important to note that Muslims do not solely rely on emotions to express truth.

Islamophobia poses a challenge to expressing the factual truth, as it involves fear and prejudice against Islam and Muslims.

Muslims believe in the strength of expressing truth with clarity and honesty, without hiding behind deceit or hypocrisy.

It is through open dialogue that the true essence of Islam can be understood, breaking down stereotypes and promoting understanding among different communities.

In Islam, the concept of destiny is deeply rooted. It is believed that Allah, the ultimate authority, has predetermined the course of each individual's life. While humans possess free will, their actions and choices are ultimately guided by Allah's plan.

The Quran teaches that on the Day of Judgment, individuals will be held accountable for their deeds and will plead to be sent back to Earth to rectify any wasted time or wrongdoings.

This highlights the belief in personal responsibility and the pursuit of righteousness. Unlike in Christianity, where salvation and acceptance of Jesus Christ as the savior are emphasized, Islam focuses on individual accountability and repentance. In Islam, the concept of Tawbah (repentance) is highly emphasized.

Seeking Allah's forgiveness for sins is a direct and personal act available to everyone.

This direct connection between the individual and Allah eliminates the need for confessing sins to other humans, as Allah is seen as the ultimate judge and forgiver.

Muslims are encouraged to turn to Allah in sincere repentance, acknowledging their mistakes and seeking His mercy and guidance.

This process of repentance is a means of personal growth and spiritual development, allowing individuals to purify their hearts and strive towards a closer relationship with Allah.

In Islam, the focus is on burying one's faults and shortcomings rather than exposing them to others, as this fosters a culture of humility, respect, and compassion towards fellow believers.

In Islam, the concept of reminding others of their faults is strongly discouraged. It is believed that focusing on the flaws of others only leads to humiliation, low self-esteem, and a deteriorating sense of integrity for both the accuser and the accused.

Instead, Muslims are encouraged to promote a positive and supportive community by uplifting and encouraging one another.

This is rooted in the teachings of Islam, which emphasize forgiveness, compassion, and understanding. In fact, the act of seeking forgiveness and forgiving others is highly regarded in Islamic teachings.

Rather than seeking and exposing the faults of others, Muslims are encouraged to focus on their own self-improvement and to offer sincere advice and support to their fellow community members.

This approach fosters a sense of unity, empathy, and mutual respect among Muslims, creating a healthier and more harmonious society.

The explanation can be extended to say that while Islam is not a scientific faith, science has also gained knowledge from Islam.

The initial proposal of a theory by scientists is as a hypothesis, which is a tentative explanation or prediction based on limited evidence.

Scientists refine and develop hypotheses into theories as they gather more evidence. A scientific theory explains natural phenomena, supported by ample evidence and subjected to rigorous testing and scrutiny.

When a theory transitions into a fact, it no longer remains a theory but transforms into an established truth.

The theory of Einstein is not a hypothesis, but a proven fact. Darwin's theory is taught in academic institutions but has not been proven as fact.

Darwin engaged in debates with multiple Muslim scholars but failed to convince them, leaving with an air of arrogance.

Islam is based on scientific facts, not just theories. Keith Moore stated Muhammad could not have possessed a knowledge of embryology, which is extensively detailed in Quran.

The New Republic: Einstein Quote: Dec 4, 2013 — *"Science without religion is lame, religion without science is blind."*

Narration Of Malik Ibn Dinar: Reminder of faith.

Ibn Dinar's story serves as a powerful reminder that even in the face of uncertainty and moments of doubt, one can find their way back to their true beliefs and values.

He experienced many crossroads and temptations that led him astray from the path of Islam. However, it was his ability to overcome these challenges and return to his reality that truly left a lasting impact on those who heard his story.

It teaches us that what truly matters is not the mistakes or deviations one may have made in the past, but the journey of self-discovery and growth that one embarks on.

Ibn Dinar's story shows the importance of focusing on the present and the positive nature of personal transformation, rather than dwelling on past mistakes or regrets.

It serves as a source of inspiration for individuals who may struggle with their faith or facing uncertainties in their own lives, reminding them it is never too late to find their way back and leave a positive legacy behind.

Malik Ibn Dinar was not only known for his devotion to worship, but also for his deep understanding of Islam. He dedicated his life to studying the teachings of the Prophet Muhammad (peace be upon him) and sought knowledge from scholars who were well-versed in the true essence of the faith.

Despite making his own mistakes along the way, Malik's unwavering belief in Allah remained unshaken.

It became a common sight to find Malik Ibn Dinar at the local masjid, where he would spend hours immersed in prayer and reflection.

His sincere and profound Ibada (worship) was a source of inspiration for those who witnessed it. His devotion to Allah was so strong that it seemed to radiate from him, drawing others towards the path of righteousness.

One fateful day, as Malik was engrossed in his worship, a thief stealthily entered his home. To the thief's disappointment, he found nothing of material value worth stealing. Malik, however, saw an opportunity to offer something of far greater worth.

He approached the intruder and kindly informed him that although there was no worldly possession to take, he could offer him something invaluable for the next life.

Malik instructed the thief to perform Wudu, the ritual ablution Muslims undertake before prayer, and then joined him in offering Tahaj Jud, the voluntary night prayer.

Together, they stood in the night's darkness, seeking forgiveness and closeness to Allah. As the dawn broke, signaling the time for Fajr prayer, the thief accompanied Malik to the masjid.

The sight of the thief standing alongside Malik in prayer left the community astonished.

They had grown accustomed to seeing Malik in solitude, as he would often spend his time alone despite being capable of socializing.

Malik, with his profound wisdom, responded to their curiosity by explaining that he had initially come to steal from them, but they had unknowingly stolen his bad manners and guided him towards the path of genuine belief in Allah.

Malik Ibn Dinar's unique approach to spreading the message of Islam amazed the people.

His ability to see the potential for goodness in others, even in the most unlikely of circumstances, was a testament to his unwavering faith and compassion.

Malik's story serves as a reminder that true believers should never judge others based on their past actions, for the transformative power of belief can bring about remarkable changes in even the most hardened hearts.

Writing copies of the Quran, an important Islamic text, allowed him to generate revenue because of the high demand.

With utmost accuracy, he would meticulously replicate every page by hand. His reliable source of income came from selling these hand-copied Qurans.

However, rather than bringing the revenue back home, he would quickly spend it on food and leave the remaining amount as a deposit, not taking any money home.

A Hadith narrated in Bukhari, attributed to Prophet Muhammad, asserts that the most righteous earnings are those derived from transcribing the Quran. Even a single penny earned from writing about Allah is the most rewarding money for me.

This refers to the copies of the written Quran that are produced.

Prophet Muhammad emphasized that the greatest benefit one can derive from the written word of the Quran is through writing and spreading its teachings.

The funds received from the sale or distribution of these copies hold immense blessings, as they contribute to the practicality and accessibility of the Quran.

The peace and tranquility one attains from connecting with the truth of the Quran is an unmatched form of revenue.

It is through this process that the financial gains become intertwined with spiritual blessings, making it a truly valuable endeavor.

Ibn Dinar cautioned against boastful walking, stating that it should only occur on the battlefield, and reminded the governor of Busra to fear Allah.

The prince, adorned in exquisite robes, stood before the person and arrogantly asked, "Do you not know who I am?" Without hesitation, the person replied, their voice filled with unwavering confidence, "Yes, I know you.

Like the rest of us, you were created from a fluid and are a mere mortal. It is despicable to boast about such origins."

They continued, their words piercing through the air, "The result of pride is a lifeless corpse emitting a foul stench.

Individuals that carry their own defecation inside their bodies are not to be proud, as it is a natural bodily function that is necessary for maintaining good health.

In this story, the governor observed this and fearlessly pointed it out, highlighting the commonality of human needs.

This observation challenges accepting Jesus as a god, as it would be blasphemous to attribute bodily functions to a divine being. Unlike humans, God Allah is perfect and with no physical needs, including the need to excrete waste.

This theme is clear in various aspects of life, where humans often display their weaknesses despite the intelligence they possess. While intelligence can be a great asset, it does not guarantee the eradication of stupidity, which is a flaw that cannot be easily cured.

In this world, genuine success lies in humbly carrying the burdens of others, not in flaunting one's status or achievements." With a calm and composed demeanor, the person described themselves as someone who understands the consequences of pride and the importance of humility.

They asserted that pride had led to Satan's downfall, and it could easily lead anyone astray from the path of success.

However, they acknowledged that the timing and ultimate outcomes of one's endeavors are ultimately determined by Allah, the Divine power.

Malik Ibn Dinar, known for his reformation, led a life filled with personal struggles and challenges. Despite not being religious, he experienced a profound transformation after a dream involving his deceased daughter.

In this dream, his daughter was reciting verses from the Quran, which penetrated him.

The dream served as a powerful exchange that shifted his perspective on life. It was a wake-up call, as his daughter revealed to him that his good deeds were overshadowed by his many offensive actions.

Overwhelmed by this realization, Malik rushed to the mosque, where he was astonished to hear the muezzin reciting the same verse he had dreamt about.

This synchronicity reinforced the significance of the dream, solidifying Malik's belief that dreams can bring forth life-altering messages and insights that were previously unknown to him.

Quran: Surah Al Hadid: 57:16. Has the time not come for those who have believed that their hearts should become humbly submissive at the remembrance of Allah and what has come down of the truth?

And let them not be like those who were given the Scripture before, and a long period passed over them, so their hearts hardened; and many of them are defiantly disobedient.

The Quran presents Jesus as a prophet and messenger of Allah, while the Bible presents him as the Son of God and the Savior of humanity.

Ultimately, the belief in Jesus' divinity and his sacrifice for the sins of others is a matter of faith and interpretation.

Different religious traditions and individuals may hold varying beliefs on this matter based on their respective scriptures and teachings.

Although it is important to note the Quran denies crucifixion and history tells Pontius Pilate was holding Jesus of Nazareth and Jesus of Barabbas and they are not the same. He let go of one not the other.

Bible Study tools: Matthew: 27:26:36. Then he pardoned Barabbas. But he had Jesus whipped and then handed over for crucifixion. The soldiers assigned to the governor took Jesus

Church of Jesus Christ: Matthew: 27:26:36. Jesus is accused and condemned before Pilate—Barabbas is released—Jesus is mocked, crucified, and buried in the tomb of Joseph of Arimathea.

USCCB: Matthew: 27:26:36. Jesus Before Pilate. 1* When it was morning, all the chief priests and the elders of the people took counsel* against Jesus to put him to death.

Matthew: 27:26:36. So Pilate released Barabbas to them. He ordered Jesus flogged with a lead-tipped whip, then turned him over to the Roman soldiers to be crucified.

As a result, we can conclude that Pontius Pilate held custody of both Jesus of Nazareth and Jesus Barabbas, who were separate individuals. The crowd's demand to release Jesus but he liked Jesus' question arises which Jesus did he let go to the violent crowd.

The identity of the person he released remains a mystery, as Mary, the mother of Jesus, was summoned.

Upon seeing the face, she promptly turned away, remarking, "The face resembles my son's, but the body does not." This mysterious turn of events left everyone perplexed about the true identity of the person who was released.

If the crucifixion, which is fundamental to Christianity, is denied in Islam, how will the faith withstand the ongoing changes and the generations that question how the salvation and death of one person can bring forgiveness to another?

This complex aspect remains a strong point for both those who reject and those who embrace it. Islam rejects all of that and asserts that Allah took him back alive as he did not die for anyone's sins.

Islam sets itself apart from other Abrahamic faiths by rejecting the belief that Jesus died for the sins of others.

The Jews of that era boasted. In the Quran, it is stated that Jesus did not die to atone for the sins of others, and individuals are held accountable for their own sins.

In the biblical concepts of Christendom, there is a persistent and consistent behavior of transforming and smoothing out the strictness of the Biblical text by emphasizing the theme of love.

This trend is prevalent in today's society as well, where the focus is often on promoting love and forgiveness in relation to Jesus. However, it is important to note that the definition of a prophet does not primarily revolve around love, but discipline.

In the Bible, prophets often delivered messages of correction and warning, urging people to repent and turn away from their wrongdoing.

Contrary to the Christian perspective, in Islam, the concept of forgiveness is approached differently. While Christians may often refer to Jesus as the one who forgives, in Islam, forgiveness is sought directly from Allah.

It is believed that Allah will instruct each individual to seek forgiveness from the person they have wronged. In Islam, the wrongs committed within the heart are a matter between Allah and His creation.

This emphasizes personal responsibility and accountability for one's actions.

Muslims are taught to seek forgiveness actively from both Allah and the individuals they have harmed, rather than solely relying on the forgiveness of Jesus or any other prophet sent by Allah.

The historical Jesus, also known as the Messiah, has a complex and often unclear history because of the continuous dissemination and alterations to suit various regimes throughout history.

Historical records show that there was a letter written to Tiberius, in which Jesus was spoken highly of.

The writer of the letter, fearing an uprising of the Jews against the Romans, may have intentionally distorted the details surrounding Jesus and his role.

The historical accounts surrounding Jesus and his actions become hazy and not fully clear.

However, in the Quran, the Islamic holy book, it is explicitly stated that Jesus was taken aback or raised to the heavens, and someone else was made to resemble him, leading to confusion and different interpretations among different religious beliefs.

However, the Quran remains unchanging in its message.

It would indeed be a disturbing and contradictory event if Allah were to mock a pious family by burdening them with the sins of those who continuously sin, all under the guise of Jesus the savior having already taken away their sins.

Such a scenario would undermine the fundamental beliefs and principles of any society that adheres to a coherent religious doctrine.

It is important to note that the concept of reincarnation or fairy tales, while present in various belief systems, do not align with the teachings of Islam as conveyed in the Quran.

The Quran is regarded as the unchanging and infallible word of Allah, and any historical events that deviate from its account should be approached with caution.

The preservation of the Quran's teachings throughout history serves as a testament to its authenticity and the unchanging nature of its message.

The Trinity doctrine contradicts the Shema in Hebrew Scriptures.

Conversely, it enhances our understanding of God's nature, as revealed in both the Old Testament, where Jews also believed in monotheistic faith despite their tendency to rebel.

The Shema is a central prayer in Judaism, recited twice daily by devout Jews. It begins with the words **"Hear, O Israel: The Lord our God, the Lord is one."** This phrase, known as the Shema, affirms the belief in the oneness of God, also known as monotheism, which is a foundational belief in Judaism.

Monotheism is the belief that there is only one God, and this belief sets Judaism and Islam apart from many other ancient religions that worshiped multiple gods.

The affirmation of God's oneness in the Shema is a reminder for Jews to acknowledge and worship only one divine being, reinforcing their commitment to monotheism and their devotion to the God of Israel.

This belief in the oneness of God is not only a fundamental aspect of Jewish faith but also serves as a unifying principle that binds Jews together in their spiritual and communal lives.

Muslims and Jews are related, as they both trace their lineage back to Prophet Abraham. Both Islamic and Jewish traditions hold Abraham as the originator of monotheism, with his descendants playing a pivotal role in both faiths.

Muslims believe that Prophet Muhammad can directly trace his lineage back to Abraham through his son Ishmael, whereas Jews trace their lineage back to Abraham through his son Isaac.

Muslims and Jews have a familial bond because of their shared ancestry, highlighting their historical and spiritual connection.

Both communities, despite their differences, share a deep respect for their common heritage and teachings of their prophets.

In terms of religious history, Christianity incorporates elements from various religious traditions, including paganism. However, it is important to note that these influences do not compromise the core monotheistic nature of the faith.

Instead, they reflect the cultural context in which Christianity spread and adapted to different regions. The stories and symbols borrowed from paganism were often reinterpreted and infused with monotheistic meanings.

Jesus, a believer in one God, was sent to the Jewish people of Israel. Although Jesus shared the same message as Moses and believed in one God, Christianity deviates from monotheism by regarding Jesus as the Son of God or as part of a triune deity, thus altering its monotheistic nature.

Christianity has been shaped by the influences of different religious traditions. Has a historical link with Judaism. Judeo Christianity eventually developed into Pauline Christianity.

Evangelicals have created the stigma surrounding their beliefs and practices due to a variety of factors. One of the main reasons is their strong emphasis on proselytizing and converting others to their faith.

This can be seen as pushy or intrusive by those who do not share their beliefs, leading to the perception that evangelicals are overly zealous or judgmental.

Some evangelical leaders have been involved in controversial political movements or scandals, which have further contributed to the negative image associated with the evangelical community.

This stigma has also been perpetuated by media portrayals, which often focus on extreme or fringe elements within the evangelical movement, some represent the diverse range of beliefs and practices within the larger Christian community.

The stigma surrounding evangelicals is a multifaceted issue that is influenced by various factors.

It is crucial to acknowledge that not all evangelicals conform to the stereotypes. In fact, many of them challenge those preconceived notions and emphasize the importance of believing in Jesus for attaining eternal life.

Neither Islam nor Judaism compels individuals to convert to their faith.

While Islam is experiencing rapid growth, the challenge of maintaining truth amidst the spread of lies is evident.

HOWEVER, TRUTH WILL PREVAIL AND EXTINGUISH THE FALSEHOODS.

It is worth mentioning that Islam respects individual freedom and does not mandate or pressure people to adopt its faith.

There is no mention in the Quran of Mary having any other offspring. It is important to note that Jesus was not the son of God, but the son of Mary, as described in Surah Maryam.

The contradictions within the beliefs surrounding Jesus persist, and those who adhere to the belief in him often lack the time or inclination to explore the comprehensive meaning of Jesus and the origins of Christendom.

Jesus, a Jewish prophet and the Messiah, was ultimately rejected by many within the Jewish community.

Interestingly, Jesus never explicitly designated Paul as his successor, leaving room for confusion and disagreement.

Additionally, if Jesus was indeed the Son of God as described in the Bible, it raises questions as to why he did not communicate the details of the extended Bible or clarify its inconsistencies that may take place to his followers.

These unresolved issues contribute to the perplexing nature of the Christian faith and its interpretations.

Islam is a religion that believes in the finality of Prophet Muhammad as the last and ultimate messenger of God. The teachings and principles of Islam are considered to be complete and perfect, leaving no room for human interpretation or modification.

The Quran, is the direct word of God and is infallible. It provides guidance for all aspects of life, including social, moral, and spiritual matters.

According to Islamic belief, the Quran is a timeless and unchanging scripture, and its teachings are considered to be applicable to all times and places.

The Revised Version of the Bible was a project undertaken in the late 19th century to update and improve upon the King James Version. In order to achieve this, more than 30,000 changes were made to the text.

Reddit/Christianity: There are about 30,000 manuscripts or major portions thereof for the New Testament. All have difference but most are minor copying mistakes.

Thestandard.org UK: Apr 4, 2024 — We are told to test everything, but what if the scriptures have been changed? Research shows 64000 words changed between the KJV and NIV.

Los Angeles Times: Dec 24, 2021 — Op-Ed: A new edition of the Bible, with 20,000 revisions, should spark 20,000 thoughtful conversations.

Among these changes, over 5,000 were specifically focused on highlighting differences between the Greek text used for the Revised Version and the text that served as the basis for the King James Version.

These differences were identified and addressed to provide a more accurate and reliable translation per some sources.

Aside from the changes related to the Greek text, numerous other modifications were made in the interest of consistency and modernization.

If Muslims made significant alterations to the Quran, the news media would be quick to report on its inaccuracy. However, there is no channel in Muslim countries specifically criticizing the Bible because it is not seen as a threat to the truth of Islam.

The Quran is the direct and unaltered word of Allah, revealed to Prophet Muhammad through the Angel Gabriel. It is considered a timeless and divine message that remains consistent throughout history.

The Quran has been meticulously preserved in its original form, with the same surahs (chapters) and words, without any replication or alteration to suit the changing times.

If there were any significant changes or discrepancies in the Quran, it would undoubtedly be a subject of great controversy and scrutiny, particularly in today's Islamophobic era. However, the Quran has remained unchanged, which serves as a testament to its authenticity and divine origin.

The Quran was completed before the Prophet's passing reinforces the belief that it is a direct delivery of Allah's words to Prophet Muhammad, without any human interference. This understanding is rooted in common sense and reinforces the belief in the Quran's authenticity as a divine scripture.

Islam emphasizes the importance of intention and sincere worship, discouraging any form of deliberate harm or wrongdoing.

The pen played a significant role in Islamic history, as it was the Muslims who introduced and perfected the art of calligraphy.

During the reign of the Islamic caliphate, the craftsmen crafted the first pen for the king, emphasizing the importance of writing and knowledge in Islamic civilization.

Evident in the Quran, are artistic skill and a deep reverence for the written word.

There is a surah in the Quran known as **Surah Al-Qalam**, which translates to **The Pen**. This surah highlights the power and significance of the pen as a tool of communication and guidance, emphasizing the importance of wisdom and knowledge in the Islamic faith.

Allah ordered the pen to write the destiny of every living being, from the beginning of time until the end of days.

The pen, filled with divine wisdom and power, etched upon the cosmic parchment, recording the intricate details of each individual's life journey.

With every stroke, the pen inscribed the joys and sorrows, the triumphs and challenges that would shape the course of existence.

It meticulously chronicled the fates of countless souls, weaving a tapestry of purpose and destiny.

The pen's tip glided effortlessly, guided by Allah's omniscience and compassion, ensuring that every word written would serve a greater divine plan.

As the ink flowed, the pen carried the weight of responsibility, knowing that it held the power to shape the lives of all creation. And so, under Allah's command, the pen continued its sacred task, tirelessly documenting the unfolding story of humanity, leaving no detail untouched.

Allah has a plan for every human's life, even though the human may not be aware of it.

Therefore, it is referred to as free will, but it is important to acknowledge that the will of Allah ultimately takes precedence over the will of humans.

Muslim scholars, particularly during the Islamic Golden Age, made significant contributions to mathematics and algebra, which have had a profound impact on the world.

They built upon the existing knowledge of ancient civilizations and developed new concepts and techniques that revolutionized the field.

Their advancements in algebra, such as introducing variables and systematic equations, laid the foundation for modern mathematics and provided a framework for solving complex problems.

Muslims contributed to making the first pen with ink.

The development of the first pen with ink was influenced by Muslim scholars in the renowned Abbasid caliphate of Baghdad during the Islamic Golden Age in the 7th century.

In this period, intellectuals like Abu Hayyan al-Tawhidi and Ibn Sina (Avicenna) conducted experiments with different materials and designs to develop more effective writing tools.

Their work brought about a revolution in the traditional reed pen through structural enhancements and the use of innovative ink formulas.

The outcome was the development of a pen that is more durable and versatile, enhancing the quality of writing with smoother and more precise strokes.

The pen-making advancements of Muslim scholars played a vital role in spreading knowledge and preserving historical records, making a noteworthy contribution to the field of writing instruments.

The teachings of Muslim mathematicians not only enhanced the brainstorming process but also contributed to the development of sensible and pragmatic methodologies in various disciplines, including engineering, physics, and economics.

Their emphasis on logical reasoning and precise calculations helped refine scientific methods and fostered a more systematic approach to problem-solving.

Integrating diverse perspectives and knowledge systems, as exemplified by Muslim scholars, allows individuals to gain a more comprehensive understanding of conflicts and their underlying causes.

This holistic approach enables a more nuanced analysis of complex issues, facilitating the identification of effective strategies for conflict resolution.

The ability of Muslims to teach mathematics and algebra has not only enhanced the world's intellectual capacity but also fostered a more inclusive and interdisciplinary approach towards addressing global challenges.

In conclusion, comprehending the root causes of conflicts is essential for those seeking to become advisors or support causes related to these issues.

While the algebraic root system has its origins in Muslim contributions to mathematics, it is crucial to recognize that algebra is a universal tool that individuals from all backgrounds can use.

By incorporating algebraic thinking into conflict analysis, individuals can enhance their ability to address complex conflicts with a logical and systematic approach.

Just rants on social media do not call for support but an outcry of either support of lies needs diplomacy and platforms of the informed to support the regime of Palestine, which is mostly Muslim.

The countries to step up start with Saudi Arabia, the birthplace of Prophet Muhammad. If he was on earth, this problem would have never risen, but Hypotheticals have no place in Islam but reality.

Quran: Surah Nahl: 16:2. He sends down the angels with revelation by His command to whoever He wills of His servants, ˹stating:˺ "Warn ˹humanity˺ that there is no god ˹worthy of worship˺ except Me, so be mindful of Me ˹alone˺."

Muslims face various forms of suffering and challenges in their lives, just like any other individual. It is important to recognize that these struggles cannot be simply categorized and separated based on religious beliefs.

While being a Muslim does not exempt one from suffering, the teachings of Islam guide believers to prioritize following the rules and principles set by Allah over their desires.

However, sometimes distractions can deter Muslims and influence them to deviate from the path of righteousness.

Living in the Western world, where individual desires often take precedence, Muslims may indeed face additional challenges in maintaining their faith and values.

When a Muslim finds balance and remains steadfast in their beliefs, the true worth lies in seeking repentance and humility, rather than arrogance.

Allah is all-knowing, all-powerful, and all-merciful, and is the source of guidance, justice, and love.

Knowledge, a source of power, is un-stealable!

The story of the Jungle:

With the flames roaring and thick smoke filling the air, the once lush greenery of the jungle was engulfed. Startled by the ferocity of the fire, the animals scattered in all directions, desperately searching for safety.

In their escape from danger, the majestic lions sprinted with their flowing manes trailing behind them, propelled by their powerful strides. The agile monkeys swung from tree to tree, their shrieks echoing through the forest as they leaped to higher ground.

The graceful deer, usually calm, leaped over fallen branches and bushes, their hearts pounding in their chests. Even the mighty elephants, known for their strength and resilience, trumpeted in distress as they charged through the burning underbrush.

The heat was intense, and the animals' instinct for survival kicked in as they raced towards distant lands, hoping to find refuge from the devastating inferno that ravaged their once peaceful home.

The bird, a majestic phoenix with vibrant plumage, had witnessed the destructive power of fire many times before. It knew that every drop of water counted in extinguishing the flames that threatened to consume the surrounding forest.

With each trip to the nearby stream, the bird's determination grew stronger. The scorching heat of the fire did not deter its efforts, for it had a deep sense of purpose.

As the bird tirelessly flew back and forth, its wings beating with fervor, onlookers gathered, and marveled at its unwavering commitment. The bird became a symbol of hope and resilience, a testament to the power of taking action in the face of adversity.

And so, as the fire slowly subsided under the relentless efforts of the bird, it knew that its actions would indeed be etched into the annals of history, inspiring future generations to never give up and to always strive for change.

Drawing a parallel, the bird's story serves as a powerful metaphor for the importance of collective action and unity in times of crisis. The bird's statement resonates deeply with the Muslim community, urging them not to remain passive when confronted with challenges that threaten their faith and values.

Just as the bird refused to sit back and watch the fire consume everything in its path, Muslims are encouraged to actively engage and contribute towards the betterment of their communities and protect their beliefs.

The bird's declaration emphasizes the significance of being remembered in history for standing up and taking action. Muslims are reminded that their actions, no matter how small, can leave a lasting impact.

By enjoining together to help extinguish the metaphorical fires of injustice, discrimination, and inequality, they can contribute to a world where peace, justice, and compassion prevail.

It is a call for unity and solidarity, highlighting the importance of actively working towards positive change rather than being mere bystanders.

Therefore, the bird's story serves as a poignant reminder for Muslims to rise above complacency and actively take part in addressing the challenges that face their communities.

By doing so, they can make their mark in history as individuals who did not shy away from their responsibilities, but made a difference and strived towards a better world.

If Muslim countries come together and unite for the cause, without succumbing to the temptations of evil or the pressures to conform to the world, they have the potential to make a significant impact. Allah has blessed with abundant resources these countries, making them some of the wealthiest nations.

By pooling their resources and taking collective action, even the smallest contribution can make a difference, just like how a little water can extinguish a fire.

My stories illustrate the importance of truth for survival, emphasizing that those who simply watch without taking action are the biggest hypocrites, while those who remain silent are equally culpable.

When Muslims actively engage in providing aid and support to those in need, it sends a powerful message that resonates with people from different backgrounds.

It is a shame when others don't join in this noble cause, as expecting others to join without taking the initiative themselves is a sign of passivity.

However, by demonstrating their commitment to helping humanity, Muslims can inspire others to join in, creating a collective effort towards alleviating the suffering of those facing oppression.

Sharing stories of Islam and Muslim endeavors promotes understanding and unity among diverse communities.

In Islam, sharing knowledge is a noble act and a valuable contribution to society.

Europe and other civilizations would have been impeded if Muslims had kept the knowledge, they gained to themselves.

Muslims were instrumental in preserving and translating ancient Greek and Roman texts during the Middle Ages, which formed the basis for the Renaissance and the Enlightenment in Europe.

It's important to acknowledge and honor this historical fact. In Islam, all prophets sent by Allah are recognized and no distinction is made among them, upholding the concept of monotheism.

Islam fosters respect and reverence for all religious traditions through its inclusive approach, ensuring that no prophet is equal to Allah.

Through this understanding, Islam can bring about the articulation of truth and revitalize the human spirit, promoting a harmonious coexistence and an exploration of knowledge that goes beyond boundaries.

The boundless conversations and clarity, the allowance to converse in my writings, are a continual gift from Allah. No conversation is a myth, incident, or coincidence, but outright planning by Allah to grant permission for this conversation.

Insha'Allah, as I continue to progress and show more details, many will no longer be left behind, despite having so little time!

CHAPTER 16
ISLAM TAKES THE SPOTLIGHT, NOT A WINDING STAIRCASE.

Islam is often in the spotlight because of various reasons. One of the major factors is the media's portrayal of Islam, which often focuses on negative events or extremist individuals.

This creates a sense of fear and curiosity among the public, leading them to seek answers about this widely misunderstood religion.

The increasing number of non-Muslims converting to Islam has also brought immense attention to the faith. These individuals often find solace and happiness in their newfound beliefs, which can be a stark contrast to the lives they left behind.

This transformation can sometimes evoke resentment and hatred from their families and communities, further amplifying the spotlight on Islam.

Despite the darkness that exists in the world, Islam continues to glow as a source of guidance, peace, light and purpose for its followers

According to various studies and demographic reports, Islam is indeed considered one of the fastest-growing religions in the world. It is estimated that there are over 1.9 billion Muslims globally, and this number continues to rise steadily.

However, it is important to note that the growth of Islam cannot solely be attributed to the events of tragic 9/11. While some individuals may have been prompted to learn more about Islam and its teachings following the tragedy, the conversion of individuals to Islam is a complex and multifaceted phenomenon.

It is impossible to ignore the appeal of Islam to individuals from diverse backgrounds. The values and teachings of Islam attract many people from diverse backgrounds, who find solace and guidance in its principles of social justice, equality, and spirituality.

The accessibility of information and the ability to connect with Muslim communities through technology and social media have also facilitated the spread of Islam.

Islam's emphasis on community and the support networks provided by Muslim communities have also been influential in attracting new converts.

Many individuals find a sense of belonging and purpose within the Muslim community, which can be appealing in a rapidly changing and often isolating world.

It is crucial to recognize that the growth of Islam is not solely driven by conversions, but also by the retention of individuals born into Muslim families. The transmission of religious beliefs and practices from one generation to the next plays a significant role in the maintenance and expansion of Islam.

In conclusion, while global events, have undoubtedly sparked curiosity and interest in Islam, the growth of the religion is a complex phenomenon influenced by various factors.

It is a testament to the appeal of Islam's teachings, the strength of Muslim communities, and the demographic trends that continue to shape our world.

New York City, often referred to as the **"Big Apple,"** has indeed witnessed a significant number of converts to Islam. The diverse and cosmopolitan nature of the city, coupled with its large Muslim population, has created an environment where people from various backgrounds are exposed to and influenced by the religion.

Additionally, the presence of Islamic centers, mosques, and educational institutions in New York City has provided opportunities for individuals to learn about Islam and potentially embrace the faith.

However, it is important to recognize that conversions to any religion are a personal choice influenced by a multitude of factors, and not all converts come from New York City specifically.

The ongoing effort to sabotage Islam and Muslims is based on unfounded stereotypes and prejudices. It is unjust to label someone as a terrorist simply because they practice their faith by praying five daily prayers or adhering to the modesty of Islamic dress, such as wearing a hijab.

Modesty is a fundamental aspect of Islam, promoting self-respect and dignity for both men and women. However, these practices are often misinterpreted or sensationalized by those who seek to create a negative image of Islam.

During the time of Prophet Muhammad, the requirement for women to wear the hijab became obligatory after his marriage to Zaynab.

Hijab was not commanded by Prophet Muhammad, but rather revealed by Allah.

The claim that Muslim men oppress Muslim women for modesty is false, as it applies to both genders and is from Allah, not any prophet or Muslim.

Quran: Surah Ahzab 33:59. O Prophet! Ask your wives, daughters, and believing women to draw their cloaks over their bodies. In this way it is more likely that they will be recognized ˈas virtuousˈ and not be harassed. And Allah is All-Forgiving, Most Merciful.

Hijab is a way to promote modesty and respect for one's physical appearance. It serves the purpose of preventing any kind of misleading or inappropriate gaze from others, ensuring that one's modesty is maintained and respected.

This practice is particularly emphasized in relationships that fall under the category of mahram, which refers to individuals with whom one has a close familial bond and where there is no potential for any romantic or sexual interest.

Modesty is not required with husband and wife.

Within the mahram relationship, it is permissible to be in a relaxed state regarding the observance of hijab, as the dynamics are based on trust and familial connections.

However, outside of these relationships, it is important for both men and women to adhere to the principles of hijab to maintain modesty and uphold respect for themselves and others.

The **hijab** is not universally worn by Muslim women, particularly those in Western countries. The excuses don't render the laws breakable, only Allah has the power to guide individuals to comply with his laws, just like any other law.

While businesses must abide by regulations, Islam establishes laws based on justice rather than force for those who break them. The men must also abide by non-negotiable modesty laws.

Similarly, the portrayal of facial hair for men, which is encouraged in Islam, cannot be equated with terrorism now viewed solely as a fashion trend.

Such misconceptions only perpetuate discrimination and further marginalize the Muslim community. It is crucial to educate and promote understanding to counter these harmful narratives.

In the worst scenario, when Islam cannot be judged or held accountable for the actions of Muslims, it creates a situation where individuals or groups can act with impunity under the guise of religious belief.

This lack of accountability can lead to the exploitation of the faith for personal or political gain.

Even the best of believers can be swayed by their emotions, which can be manipulated by those with ulterior motives. Emotions, such as anger, fear, or desire, can act as a powerful catalyst, driving individuals to make choices that may not align with the true teachings of Islam.

This can cause unexpected and potentially negative outcomes, as personal interests and agendas may overshadow the principles of peace, compassion, and justice that Islam promotes.

In Islam, adhering to the teachings and principles of the faith is of utmost importance. If a Muslim finds themselves tempted to engage in sinful activities, such as premarital sexual intercourse, it is a commendable act to resist and refrain from such actions.

This act of self-control and obedience to Allah's commandments is viewed as a virtue and a step towards spiritual growth.

Muslims need to be clear about these teachings, especially in a time where disbelievers may try to manipulate or misinterpret them for their own agendas. By clearly understanding and following the teachings of Islam, Muslims can protect themselves from falling into the traps set by those who seek to exploit their vulnerabilities.

This includes avoiding not just sexual misconduct but also indulging in alcohol, drugs, porn and other harmful behaviors that can lead to moral degradation. It is crucial to address and combat the increasing prevalence of pornography in societies where boredom and easy access to explicit content exist.

Muslims should remain vigilant and stay away from such immoral acts to preserve their faith and uphold the values of Islam.

Not only did Muslims contribute to many aspects of teaching and sharing knowledge, but they also made significant contributions to introducing beauty practices that are followed by the world today, particularly in the cosmetic industry.

Muslim scholars in the medieval Islamic world were pioneers in cosmetics, developing innovative techniques and creating a wide range of beauty products.

They were known for their expertise in perfumery, creating intricate and captivating fragrances using a variety of natural ingredients.

They were skilled in the art of cosmetics, developing makeup products and techniques that are still prevalent today, such as kohl eyeliner and henna for hair and body adornment.

These contributions not only enhanced beauty practices but also influenced the global cosmetic industry, leaving a lasting impact on beauty standards and trends.

Abu al-Qasim al-Zahrawi, a renowned Muslim scholar and physician, made significant contributions to the field of cosmetics and beauty products. Besides his advancements in medicine and surgery, al-Zahrawi revolutionized the beauty industry by inventing the first solid lipstick during the 8th to 12th centuries AD.

He took perfume sticks, which were commonly used for fragrance, and ingeniously rolled them into special molds to create a more convenient and portable form of lipstick. This innovation paved the way for the widespread use of lip color and laid the foundation for the modern-day lipstick we know today.

The cosmetic field, initially pioneered by Muslims, is facing a challenge in today's changing society.

Men are now using lipstick and drag, misusing the talents that were created to enhance the beauty of women. Western countries are promoting an equation that goes against the natural order, as Allah did not create the passion for exploiting transgender individuals or give the choice of gender.

Allah created the primal being and declared it as his best creation. However, evil has infiltrated this best creation, transforming it into areas of uncertainty and doubt. Seeking satisfaction solely through outward appearance is not always enough. Humans also require inner upliftment, which is the foundation of clarity in Islam.

The Muslim world's continuous progress of learning and exploration not only affected various fields but also left an indelible mark on the fashion industry.

Islamic laws discern men from imitating women or vice versa. This includes the practice of drag, where individuals may use makeup, including lipstick, to transform their appearance. The concept of gender roles and the preservation of modesty are important within Islamic teachings.

While the use of lipstick is primarily associated with women in modern society, it is taboo for men to imitate women's appearance or adopt feminine attributes. This is based on the belief that each gender has distinct roles and characteristics, and blurring these lines goes against the principles of modesty and natural order.

However, it is important to note that interpretations of Islamic teachings can vary among different communities and individuals.

Muslim achievements have left an indelible mark on various industries throughout history. From the fields of science and mathematics to art and literature, Muslims have played a pivotal role in shaping the world.

Muslim scholars like Al-Khwarizmi made significant advancements in mathematics by introducing algebra, while Ibn al-Haytham's work on optics paved the way for the development of cameras and lenses we use today.

Cameras have become an integral part of the modern era. Even when they were unfamiliar to Muslims, they delved into discovering lenses and the art of focusing, using their minds to develop a way to capture the beauty of exploration.

Those who understand its value still pursue this passion and pass on their knowledge. It was never intended to exploit sexuality through a lens; instead, it is meant for those who seek to learn, not to contribute to the destruction of the world.

Muslim scholars made significant advancements in medicine, architecture, and navigation, among many other fields.

Their teachings and discoveries continue to influence and inspire generations of thinkers and innovators. Thus, it is crucial to highlight and celebrate these achievements constantly in order to recognize the immense contributions of Muslims to human civilization.

By showcasing their accomplishments, we not only pay homage to their legacy, but also inspire future generations to strive for excellence in all aspects of life.

The mirror, an invention attributed to Muslim scholars, serves as a poignant symbol of their intellectual contributions.

Beyond its role in reflecting outer beauty, the mirror symbolizes the potential for self-reflection and self-improvement. It reminds us that, just as we look into a mirror to see our physical appearance, we must also look inward to examine and better ourselves.

Therefore, the continuous effort to showcase Muslim achievements is not only important but also essential in ensuring that all recognize and appreciate their contributions.

Muslims have a rich history of contributing to various fields, including beauty and cosmetics.

They were the ones who first popularized the use of eyeliner, thus attributing its invention to them. Known as **"Kajal"** or "Kohl," this eye care product has been documented since ancient times.

Kohl, also referred to as **"Surma,"** is an eye preparation made from a finely processed "Kohl Stone" called galena.

Incorporating this stone with other therapeutically active ingredients creates a smooth and safe eyeliner. Its use goes beyond cosmetic purposes, as people believed it had medicinal and protective qualities for the eyes.

The invention of eyeliner by Muslims showcases their early understanding of beauty and their contributions to the development of cosmetics.

Olive oil, referred to as **Al Zaytun** olive trees in the Quran, has been used by Muslims for various purposes, including hair care and as a protectant for the body. The Quran mentions the benefits of **Zaytun oil** praising its nourishing properties.

Muslims have traditionally used olive oil to moisturize and strengthen their hair, as it is believed to promote hair growth and enhance its use.

Using olive oil, people have protected their skin from harsh environmental factors and kept it soft. Recognizing its potential, the cosmetic industry has adopted olive oil as a beauty preserve because of its natural properties and effectiveness at maintaining healthy hair and skin.

As a result, olive oil is now widely incorporated into various cosmetic products, such as shampoos, conditioners, lotions, and creams, offering individuals the benefits of this ancient beauty secret in modern formulations.

Muslim women have adorned themselves in various ways, showcasing their unique styles and cultural heritage. Their fashion choices have inspired others, not only within their own community but also in the wider society.

Modesty plays a crucial role in this behavior, as it is a virtue and a means of respecting one's own body and promoting a sense of self-worth.

In contrast, Western society often associates freedom with the ability to show skin and break societal norms of modesty, sometimes leading to objectification and exploitation of women.

This clash of values can be challenging for those women who strive for independence and self-expression while still adhering to their Christian beliefs.

The analytical nature of humans, particularly women, in the Western world, can create tension between their desire for freedom and their adherence to traditional Christian teachings.

However, it is important to note that Islam, as a religion, provides women with a wide range of rights and freedoms. In contrast, Christianity has historically suppressed the rights of women, often blaming Eve for tempting Adam and leading to the fall of humanity.

The Quran does not solely blame Eve but acknowledges both Adam and Eve's shared responsibility for their actions. This perspective from the Quran reflects a more balanced and equitable approach to understanding the roles and responsibilities of men and women.

Muslim women are often portrayed as backward in Western societies, which is ironic considering that Islam places a strong emphasis on protecting the chastity and honor of both women and men.

While living in the Western world, Muslim women may find themselves in situations they never expected.

However, it is important to note that progress does not mean conforming to Western ideals or indulging in behaviors that are not conducive to their values and beliefs. The Western society, which claims to champion women's independence, often resorts to sit-ins, parades, and the liberation of clothing to prove this independence.

However, such actions can be seen as more of a decadent display rather than a genuine pursuit of independence. In the United States, women revolted against societal norms and restrictions through various forms of protest, such as parades, sit-ins, and even symbolic acts like removing undergarments.

They also challenged traditional notions of family and relationships by choosing to have children out of wedlock and advocating for introducing birth control methods.

The concept of living together outside of marriage gained acceptance, with some even referring to these relationships as marriages by law. However, it is important to note that the laws of humans do not supersede the laws of Allah for Muslims, who remain committed to their faith.

While some Muslims are aware of the challenges they face in a society that may not fully understand or respect their beliefs, others may be ignorant of the potential consequences of prioritizing societal acceptance over pleasing Allah.

True success for any believer lies in remaining steadfast in their faith, even in the face of societal pressures and expectations.

In this society, marked by Western primordial staging of Islamophobia, observers have noticed an increasing number of individuals, both Muslim women and men, embracing Islam. Many individuals, both Muslim women and men, have embraced Islam and entered relationships as husbands and wives.

The Muslim community considers it a **Sunnah** (practice) of the Prophet Muhammad to encourage and support the marriages of converts, as they bring a unique perspective and experience.

These unions not only serve as a means of companionship and support for the converts, but also help strengthen the bond within the Muslim community by promoting understanding, acceptance, and unity.

Islam, as a religion, has spread to various countries throughout history. However, it is important to note that the chaos or peace that follows is not solely determined by Islam itself, but by a combination of factors, including political, social, and economic circumstances.

Islam, like any other faith, promotes peace, justice, and compassion. It emphasizes the importance of faith and resolute belief in God.

While wars have occurred in the name of various religions, including Islam, it is crucial to distinguish between the actions of individuals who claim to follow a faith and the teachings of the religion itself.

Hypocrisy, or the contradiction between one's beliefs and actions, is condemned in Islam. The Quran states that true believers should strive for inner peace and righteousness and that the worst form of war is the internal struggle against one's own hypocrisy.

Hypocrites, or those who pretend to be believers but do not truly uphold the values of Islam, are not inherent to the religion but a product of individual choices and actions.

During the spread of Islam on the continent of India, Muslim rulers established a firm presence in the region, leading to the formation of several powerful dynasties such as the Delhi Sultanate and the Mughal Empire.

These rulers brought with them a wealth of knowledge and expertise in trade and commerce, leading to the development of new trade networks and techniques.

They introduced innovative trading practices, including the use of coins and standardized weights and measures, which facilitated commercial transactions.

The Muslim rulers also encouraged the growth of urban centers and established marketplaces known as bazaars, which became important hubs for trade and economic activities.

They promoted long-distance trade and established diplomatic relations with neighboring regions and countries, facilitating the exchange of goods and ideas.

The architectural achievements of Muslim rulers in India were also remarkable, with the construction of magnificent monuments and structures like the Taj Mahal, Jama Masjid, and Red Fort.

These architectural marvels not only showcased the prowess of Muslim rulers but also became important tourist attractions and symbols of India's rich cultural heritage.

Overall, the Muslim rule in India left a lasting impact on the trade, commerce, and architectural landscape of the region, shaping the modern trade practices and architectural styles that continue to flourish today.

During the Muslim rule in India, which began in the 12th century, the political landscape shifted from Hindu rule to a Muslim government.

Various Muslim dynasties, including the Turks, Arabs, and Persians, migrated to India and established their reigns. This led to a cultural exchange and the introduction of new ideas, customs, and traditions.

One notable impact was the increase in trade, as the Muslim rulers promoted commerce and established trade routes. This resulted in a flourishing economy and the growth of cities as centers of commerce. Along with the political and economic changes, there was a significant influence on art and architecture.

Persian art and architectural styles, such as the use of domes, arches, and intricate designs, were adopted and flourished in India.

The fusion of indigenous and Islamic elements gave rise to a distinct Indo-Islamic style, which can be seen in various structures and monuments across the country. Overall, the Muslim rule in India brought about significant cultural, political, and artistic changes, shaping the country's history and leaving a lasting impact.

During the Mughal period, India experienced unprecedented prosperity in various aspects of its society.

The Mughal Empire, led by powerful rulers such as Akbar, Shah Jahan, and Aurangzeb, created a centralized government that fostered economic growth and stability.

They implemented efficient tax systems, encouraged trade and commerce, and promoted infrastructure development, including the construction of magnificent monuments like the Taj Mahal.

The Mughals also patronized the arts, literature, and architecture, resulting in a flourishing cultural and intellectual scene.

The empire's administration was known for its religious tolerance, allowing Hindus, Muslims, and other communities to coexist peacefully.

This era marked a golden age for Indian craftsmanship, with intricate textiles, exquisite jewelry, and delicate miniature paintings gaining international recognition.

The Mughal period left a lasting impact on India's heritage and economy, creating a legacy of wealth, dignity, and care for the entire nation. Aurangzeb, the sixth Mughal emperor of India, was known for his devout religious beliefs and his unwavering dedication to Islam.

His passion for Islam was so intense that he went to great lengths to spread and enforce its teachings.

In his zeal, he even resorted to forcing Sikhs to embrace Islam. Despite facing resistance from the Sikh community, he remained committed to his mission because of his unwavering faith in Islam.

Aurangzeb, the Mughal emperor, was indeed known for his fervent devotion to Islam and his desire to spread its teachings. However, it is important to note that his forceful approach to enlightening non-Muslims was not representative of Islam as a whole.

Islam, as a religion, emphasizes free will and encourages individuals to come to it willingly, with no coercion or force. Aurangzeb's actions were driven by his personal beliefs and his love for his faith, rather than a mandate from Islam itself.

As a convert to Islam, Aurangzeb deeply embraced his newfound faith and saw it as a source of beauty and enlightenment. He believed that by forcefully converting others, they too could benefit from the spiritual richness and guidance that Islam offered.

However, it is crucial to distinguish Aurangzeb's certain actions from the core principles of Islam. Islam does not advocate for forced conversions or imposing its beliefs on others.

Islam, in its true essence, presents itself as an invitation from Allah the Almighty. It is a personal journey of faith and submission to the will of Allah.

While humans may play a role in sharing the teachings of Islam, ultimately, it is Allah's will that determines whether one embraces Islam. Islam does not force or coerce anyone into accepting its faith; it is a choice made by individuals based on their own spiritual inclinations and understanding.

Therefore, it is inaccurate to attribute Aurangzeb's forceful actions to Islam as a religion.

His personal intensity and love for his faith influenced his approach, but it does not reflect the true teachings of Islam. Islam, at its core, respects the freedom of choice and encourages individuals to embrace the faith willingly, guided by Allah's invitation rather than human intervention.

The Sikh community eventually adopted Sikhism, blending aspects of Islam and Hinduism to form their distinct religion. It should be noted that this faith is unrelated to any Abrahamic religion.

Aurangzeb, the Mughal emperor, held firm beliefs in Allah. It is important to recognize that Islam cannot merge or incorporate into another religion, as the Quran clearly states that any religion that emerged after its delivery is false.

While this statement may come across as harsh to some, it is crucial to acknowledge that humans addressing Allah is not a matter of shyness for Muslims, but a genuine expression of their belief in the Quran as the ultimate authority.

Religion can either weaken or be influenced by human opinions, gradually losing its original essence. However, Islam is not a religion created by humans and cannot be altered. It remains steadfast, unaffected by the passage of time.

Allah will eradicate any disbelief or hypocrisy, for those to strive but the goal is to find hope and repentance. We should strive to be in the company of righteous individuals and progress, rather than regress.

Aurangzeb, the Mughal emperor, passed away, remaining steadfast in his faith as a devout Muslim. In his last moments, he humbly requested his people to place his hands outside his burial shroud, symbolizing his renunciation of worldly possessions.

This poignant act served as a reminder that despite his illustrious reign as a ruling king, he departed from this world empty-handed, taking nothing with him except the weight of his deeds and the humble soil of the earth that would eventually cover him.

Aurangzeb's last wish reflected his belief in the impermanence of material wealth and power, emphasizing the importance of leading a virtuous life and leaving behind a legacy of righteousness.

Originally, the Mughal kings were converts to Islam, who came from Central Asia to invade the Indian subcontinent. They were initially drawn to Islam because of its appeal and the influence of Islamic scholars in their homeland.

After their successful conquest, the Mughal kings embraced Islam and ruled for several generations as devout Muslims.

They established a powerful empire that blended Islamic traditions with local Indian customs, resulting in a unique cultural synthesis. The Mughal rulers patronized Islamic art, architecture, and literature, leaving behind magnificent structures such as the Taj Mahal and the Red Fort.

Their rule also witnessed the proliferation of Islamic scholarship and the spread of Sufi mysticism throughout the region.

Despite the eventual decline of the Mughal Empire, their legacy as Muslim rulers in India continues to shape the country's cultural and religious landscape.

The Mughal Empire, which ruled over India from the 16th to the 19th century, had its origins in Central Asia. Babur, the founder of the empire, was a descendant of both Timur (Tamerlane) and Genghis Khan.

He was born in present-day Uzbekistan and belonged to the Timurid dynasty, which had Turkish and Mongol roots. Babur, like many other Central Asian rulers, embraced Islam and sought to establish a powerful Muslim empire in India.

Despite their Turkish origins, the Mughals assimilated into Indian society over time and adopted Persian as their court language.

They built magnificent monuments such as the Taj Mahal and promoted a unique blend of Persian, Indian, and Islamic cultures.

The Mughal Empire played a significant role in spreading Islam in India and shaping its history, with subsequent Mughal emperors like Akbar and Aurangzeb, leaving a lasting impact on the region's religious and cultural landscape.

Akbar, the renowned Mughal emperor, revered for his unwavering devotion to Islam, embarked on a remarkable pilgrimage.

Setting aside his royal privileges, he embarked on a humble journey on foot from his opulent palace in Agra to the sacred city of Ajmer.

His destination was the revered shrine of Khwaja Moinuddin Chishti, a venerated saint, whose tomb lived within the grand mosque.

This pilgrimage was not merely a physical undertaking for Akbar; it symbolized his deep spiritual connection and reverence for the teachings of the saint.

As he traversed the rugged terrain, Akbar's heart filled with a profound sense of awe and humility as he sought spiritual solace and guidance from the blessed resting place of Khwaja Moinuddin Chishti.

The journey not only showcased Akbar's faith but also showed his commitment to experiencing firsthand the spiritual significance of his belief and the transformative power of devotion.

Ajmer, in Rajasthan, India, is important to both Muslims and Hindus.

The Dargah Sharif, the mausoleum of saint Khwaja Moinuddin Chishti, is the city's chief attraction. Each year, countless followers visit Ajmer in search of blessings and fulfilling their desires.

Muslims pray to Allah for their desires, but it's crucial to remember that Islamic teachings emphasize Allah as the sole source of blessings and fulfillment. Islamic teachings urge Muslims to establish a direct connection with Allah and actively seek His guidance and support in every aspect.

When Muslims visit Ajmer, they can go to the Dargah Sharif to pay respects and find spiritual solace. However, Muslims direct their prayers and wishes to Allah, not any saint or prophet.

In Islam, asking saints and prophets to fulfill desires is seen as shirk, a sin forbidden by Allah. Islamic teachings educate Muslims to focus their prayers and supplications only on Allah, acknowledging Him as the one and only true God.

It's crucial to understand that visiting a shrine or dargah of a saint does not equate to seeking their intercession. People visit shrines to seek blessings, and guidance, and remember the pious deceased.

In Islam, it is believed that only Allah can fulfill wishes and prayers, and it is allowed for anyone, including saints, to pray to Allah for the benefit of others. The deceased cannot pray for others in Islam.

This practice, known as seeking intercession, is considered a form of shirk or associating partners with Allah in Islam.

Muslims are instructed to direct all their prayers and supplications solely to Allah and to seek His help directly.

The concept of communicating with the deceased or asking them to fulfill wishes goes against the fundamental belief in the oneness of Allah and His exclusive power to answer prayers.

It is considered a deviation from the teachings of Islam and is classified as a bid'ah or innovation. Although this practice continues in many Muslim cultures, it is important to note that it is not endorsed or sanctioned by Islamic teachings.

Instead, Muslims are encouraged to seek closeness to Allah through acts of worship prescribed in the Quran and Sunnah, such as prayer, fasting, and charity.

This concept ensures that the focus in Islam remains solely on Allah, upholding the principle of pure monotheism.

Akbar, the Emperor of the Mughal dynasty, embarked on a spiritual journey to find solace in his prayers. In his quest for help, he turned to Allah and made his way to a Dargah, a revered shrine devoted to a saint.

According to Islamic teachings, it is acceptable to seek help from Allah, but seeking aid from departed saints is not permitted, as only Allah possesses the ability to answer prayers.

Akbar directed his pleas to Allah, not to the dargah of the saint he visited, yet he displayed reverence by paying a visit to the sacred site.

However, Akbar, with his deep faith and understanding of his creator, sought divine help through this pilgrimage to the dargah. Despite many obstacles, his unwavering determination and faith in prayer motivated him to persevere.

After weeks of walking, he finally arrived at the famous Ajmer Sharif Dargah, home to the tomb of Khwaja Moinuddin Chishti. Akbar approached the masjid with great humility and devotion, seeking the blessings of the respected saint.

With tears streaming down his face, he fervently prayed to Allah for a son, hoping to have an heir to carry on his legacy. The masjid was filled with spiritual energy as Akbar expressed his deepest desires and entrusted them to Allah.

The entire kingdom nervously expected the result of his pilgrimage, as the birth of a prince would ensure the empire's future. Akbar had a son named Jahangir. Jahangir was born on August 31, 1569, and he was the eldest surviving son of Akbar and his Rajput queen consort, Mariam-uz-Zamani.

Jahangir became the fourth Mughal emperor of India, succeeding his father's throne in 1605. His support of the arts, especially painting, and his rule ushered in a period of cultural renaissance in the Mughal Empire.

The Mughal dynasty in India was founded in 1526 by Babur, who traced his lineage back to Genghis Khan and conquered the Sultanate of Delhi. Emperor Akbar led the Mughals to expand their empire through military campaigns and alliances.

Akbar's policy fostered a peaceful coexistence of Hindus, Muslims, and people of different faiths. Artists, poets, and scholars from all over the world were drawn to the opulent and grand Mughal court.

The Taj Mahal was built by Emperor Shah Jahan as a mausoleum for his wife.

Despite this, the later Mughal rulers faced challenges such as political instability, economic decline, and conflicts with regional powers, leading to the decline of the dynasty and the British assuming control over India.

Despite this, the Mughal Empire's legacy in Indian history is defined by its architecture, art, and cultural traditions. Urdu, a language influenced by Persian, Arabic, and Turkish, originated from the cultural and linguistic fusion of the Mughal Empire.

When the Mughals invaded India in the 16th century, they brought their Central Asian Turkic language with them.

Urdu emerged as the common language of the Mughal court and the ruling elite, used for administration, trade, and communication. Urdu expanded and assimilated components from various indigenous languages across India.

Urdu is now an official language in Pakistan and is widely spoken in parts of India. Urdu has a significant impact on Indian and Pakistani culture, as seen in literature, poetry, music, and films.

The Mogul culture influenced both Hindus and Muslims, resulting in a cultural change.

The movie **"Mogul E Azam"** skillfully portrays this blend through its exquisite **Urdu dialogue** and stunning visuals. By being the language of the Moguls, Urdu enhances the film's cinematic experience with its pristine delivery. The movie portrays the opulence and grandeur of the rich Mogul culture, highlighting its artistic brilliance.

Across India and the Islamic world, the impact of the Moguls is clear, particularly in architecture and literature. The religion of Islam has thrived in many countries, notably those influenced by the Mogul Empire, shaping their culture, traditions, and way of life.

These emperors played a crucial role in shaping the Mughal Empire and leaving a lasting impact on Indian history.

Given the ongoing history and legacy of Muslims, it's hard to believe that India was once among the wealthiest nations during the Muslim rule.

History speaks, and it is possible to believe in it. Muslim-ruled lands have consistently shown tolerance and respect for all. Despite granting liberty, Islam's love for the truth made him appear less tolerant.

The Moghul empire finally met its demise, and it's important to note that intolerance in faith is not inherent to Islam. It's the actions of individuals, even if an emperor exemplifies it. Allah does not impose Islam on anyone.

Being knowledgeable about Islam allows one to make informed choices, while sharing is a duty of a Muslim, forcing is not in line with Islam.

Regardless of one's social status, frequent wars and invasions caused the depletion of the empire's treasury and resources. The economic situation worsened because of corruption and mismanagement by officials and nobles.

The Mughal Empire's bankruptcy prevented it from meeting its financial commitments and expenses. However, it made a lasting impact on India and the world, revealing its contributions to Muslim history.

The ruling party in India, with its Muslim heritage, greatly influenced both the aristocracy and the nation.

Significant influence was exerted by the dressing, jewelry, and style. While the palaces, monuments, and architectural styles still exist, their historical relevance has not been forgotten by society.

The writer's impact on the tale eventually becomes history, as humanity is not eternal and lives for a finite period, leaving a legacy and sharing knowledge. In the historical context, the Nawabs, Jagirdars, and Paigahs were the ruling classes in India when the Nizam dynasty and Sultanates were in power.

These rulers contributed to the flourishing of the lands they governed, and their presence had a positive impact on the region.

The gradual decline of India's richest county, ruled by Muslims, can be traced back to the intensifying Hindu-Muslim conflicts.

As the animosity between the two communities grew, there was a concerted effort to seize Muslim-owned lands. Many opulent palaces, once symbols of grandeur and luxury, were converted into educational institutions.

The internal divisions among Muslims have long been a vulnerability that external factors can exploit, leading to confusion and complications.

The Paigahs were a prominent noble family in India during the 18th, 19th, and 20th centuries. They were known for their immense wealth and power. They even had the authority to mint their own currency. Their vast land holdings stretched from their ancestral lands to as far as Saudia.

During their time of wealth and influence, the Paigahs, as well as other Muslims like the Nawabs, failed in effectively planning and managing their lands.

This lack of proper management led to a gradual decline in their fortunes. The mismanagement of wealth was clear in lavish parties and indulgent lifestyles, which included activities that were not permissible according to Islamic principles.

These parties often featured dancing girls, and much more which were inappropriate in Islamic culture. As the regime slipped away, some individuals in this era sought entertainment that was not worth mentioning, further straying from the teachings of Islam.

The Indian government eventually intervened, as matters were not being handled wisely. Islam teaches if respect is not upheld, a downfall is inevitable in any situation.

The Paigahs, a prominent noble family of Hyderabad, amassed a vast fortune through their shrewd legacy of wealth and Real Estate ventures, vast land holdings, and strategic alliances.

Their wealth was the envy of many, and it seemed to be an enduring legacy that could sustain future generations. However, over time, mismanagement and a growing dependence on others for the management of their assets led to unexpected losses.

The once-prosperous family faced financial hardships and struggling to maintain their lavish lifestyle.

Faced with mounting debts and dwindling resources, some members of the Paigah family made the hard decision to move away and start afresh, leaving behind the grandeur and opulence they were once accustomed to.

The Nawabs and Jagirdars faced a similar fate when migration, known as hijra, occurred and ultimately led to the downfall of the continents they governed.

The concept of old money and heritage, symbolizing a rich and prestigious lineage passed down through generations, slowly faded away as these families ventured to new places in search of fresh starts, aiming to start fresh.

The history of Islam is significant as it transcends the boundaries of Saudi Arabia and has spread across the world. Rulers and caliphs played a crucial role in spreading this faith, embracing it themselves.

Therefore, understanding its history becomes essential. Islam has made its presence felt from east to west and across the lands of Africa. There is hardly a place where Islam has not made its mark. It is up to individuals to either learn about and embrace this faith or choose to disregard it.

The question arises why some view Islam as a threat and depict it as a negative force in many parts of the world. In reality, Islam is the only faith that will endure till the end.

In Islam, the concept of wealth and its management is deeply rooted in the teachings of Allah. It is believed that Allah is the ultimate provider and sustainer of all things, including wealth.

The purpose of explaining the responsibility and importance of managing wealth in the context of families is to remind individuals of their duty to Allah and to instill a sense of gratitude and appreciation for what is given to them.

Allah has bestowed upon individuals various blessings, including financial resources, and it is essential to recognize that these blessings are not guaranteed or permanent.

Time and revenue are both transient in nature, and it is only through Allah's grace that individuals receive them. By understanding this concept, individuals are encouraged to value and respect the wealth they possess, as it ultimately belongs to Allah.

Islam emphasizes the need for individuals to exhibit certain qualities and characteristics when it comes to managing wealth. These include integrity, honesty, and fairness. It is important to handle wealth with a sense of responsibility and to ensure that it is used in a manner that aligns with the teachings of Islam.

Wealth should not be squandered, hoarded, or used for immoral purposes. Instead, it should be utilized to benefit oneself, one's family, and the community at large.

Through the example set by Allah, individuals are reminded to appreciate the blessings they have been given and to be mindful of how they manage their wealth.

By practicing gratitude and exhibiting good stewardship, individuals can fulfill their duty to Allah and contribute to the overall well-being of society. The Indian government underwent a significant transformation, resulting in a new regime that failed to cater to the aristocrats' needs.

The aristocrats were compelled to move, since a place that was under their rule could not be under someone else's rule. This resulted in leaving behind memories, servants, animals, buildings, and lands, which were a significant and drastic change.

The younger generations assimilated into the countries where their families settled, and many of them lacked a true understanding of their family's aristocratic heritage. Before long, they found themselves in the position of commoners rather than aristocrats.

Recognizing that Allah has the power to change anything reminds us to appreciate the time we have and be grateful for the blessings we receive. We can also learn important lessons about managing our wealth, health, and relationships from various stories and examples.

The government of India converted their residences into academic institutions, but provided little or no compensation to the individuals who lost their homes.

This disregard for financial management and the Islamic principle of using money wisely eventually led to the downfall of their rule.

The Paigahs also maintained their own military force in India, further solidifying their dominance.

However, their reign ended, and the compensation paid to the affected individuals, known as the heir, was often meager or nonexistent, failing to adequately compensate for the losses they incurred.

The Prime Minister of India, undertook urban development challenges, implemented an urban ceiling policy that affected lands owned by Muslims. This policy aimed to regulate land ownership and prevent excessive accumulation of urban properties.

However, there have been concerns raised regarding the compensation provided to Muslims for their lands, with some arguing that it has been inadequate or even non-existent.

This has sparked debates and protests, as it violates the rights and interests of the Muslim community. Critics argue that fair compensation should be ensured to protect the rights and livelihoods of those affected by the urban ceiling policy.

Although the Muslims held significant power during certain periods, it is important to acknowledge that within their own community, there were individuals who abused this power and used it against fellow Muslims.

This abuse of power manifested in various ways, such as political repression, economic exploitation, and social discrimination. Some Muslim rulers and elites engaged in corrupt practices, favoritism, and nepotism, which resulted in the marginalization and suffering of other Muslims.

Sectarian conflicts and power struggles within the Muslim community also led to the persecution and oppression of certain groups.

These instances of power abuse against fellow Muslims highlight the complexity and challenges faced by the Muslim community, as power dynamics and internal divisions played a significant role in shaping their history.

The Nizam in power, known for his wealth and influence, approached the Nawab with a proposal to marry his sister, seeking to strengthen the political alliance between their families.

However, the Nawab, considering various factors including their differing ideologies and the Nizam's reputation for extravagance, politely declined the proposal.

This decision did not sit well with the Nizam, who saw it as a personal insult to his status and authority. Consumed by anger and a desire to assert his dominance, the Nizam retaliated against the Nawab.

He placed under house arrest the Nawab's son, who refused his proposal for his sister, effectively confining him within his own residence. This act of confinement was accompanied by many restrictions, curtailing the brother's freedom and causing great distress to the Nawab and his family.

The consequences of this power struggle between two aristocrats would have far-reaching implications for the political landscape and the lives of those involved.

The character, of man with Turkish descent resisted the pressure and stayed resolute in his decision, refusing to succumb to the forceful scheme.

He resisted the pressure and married his sister to another Muslim. It is against Islamic principles to compel anyone into marriage against their will, and the failure of many Muslims to recognize this highlights the significance of these concerns.

Many Muslims migrated to different lands after the police action took place in 1947

Similarly, wherever Muslims have migrated or settled, their communities have often thrived, even in regions where Islamophobia exists.

The collective spirit and unity of Muslims have played a significant role in the prosperity of these communities.

Islam emphasizes the importance of togetherness, learning, and thriving together as a community. It encourages Muslims to establish strong family bonds and discourages isolation or loneliness.

Inviting both Muslims and non-Muslims to share meals is a cherished aspect of Muslim culture and a way to spread blessings and foster understanding among diverse communities.

Food holds a special place in Islam, symbolizing the unity and inclusivity that comes with breaking bread together. By opening their homes and hearts to others, Muslims embrace the teachings of Islam and promote a sense of harmony and goodwill within society.

The rich history and contributions of Islam to the world are critical aspects of learning and understanding, emphasizing the significance of embracing diversity and dispelling ignorance about religion. The British made colonies in India during the time of British rule, which lasted for nearly two centuries.

However, amidst this period, an organization led by Mahatma Gandhi and his Muslim associates emerged, determined to fight for the independence of their land.

This organization, known as the Indian National Congress (INC), played a pivotal role in advocating for the rights and freedom of the Indian people. Gandhi, a prominent leader within the (INC), employed nonviolent civil disobedience as a powerful tool to challenge British authority and demand self-rule for India.

Together with his Muslim comrades, Gandhi sought to bridge communal divides and foster unity in the fight against British imperialism. Their relentless efforts and mass movements eventually led to India's independence in 1947.

Upon Muslims and Hindus fighting in peace together with hunger strikes and making salt, they achieved independence in India from British colonial rule.

The nonviolent resistance led by figures such as Mahatma Gandhi and Maulana Azad united people from both communities in their struggle for freedom.

However, as the partition of India and Pakistan was implemented, tensions arose between Hindus and Muslims, leading to violence and displacement.

Many Muslims migrated to Pakistan, while others stayed in India. Despite the division, the shared history, culture, and cuisine of Muslims continue to be an integral part of India's diverse society.

It is important to acknowledge that amidst the domestic conflicts and acts of ignorance, there have been instances of individuals turning to Islam after witnessing the violence perpetrated against Muslims.

This highlights the power of empathy and the potential for personal transformation even amid turmoil. However, Muslims must stand up against the falsehoods and misconceptions surrounding their faith.

Islam, like any other religion, should be understood based on its core principles of peace, justice, and compassion. Muslims, regardless of the land they reside in, have a responsibility to uphold the truth and combat the misrepresentations that contribute to divisions and conflicts.

Only through promoting understanding, dialogue, and unity can the tragic cycle of violence be broken, and the true essence of Islam be embraced.

Many individuals from various parts of the world, including India, have left their homeland and settled in Western countries.

While this migration may lead to the loss of certain cultural practices and traditions, the primary concern for many Muslims is the preservation of their religious identity rather than their cultural heritage.

In Western societies, where the dominant culture differs significantly from Islamic values and principles, practicing Muslims often grapple with the challenge of maintaining their faith in an environment that may not align with their religious beliefs.

However, this exposure to different cultural norms also presents an opportunity for them to deepen their understanding of Islam and strengthen their religious convictions as they navigate through the complexities of a multicultural society.

It is important to note that this phenomenon is not exclusive to India, but is observed in many parts of the world where Muslims migrate to Western lands.

These individuals who have ventured to Western lands have not only embraced the local culture but have also contributed to it, enriching the diversity and fostering understanding between different communities.

They have been ambassadors of Islam, showcasing the values of peace, tolerance, and compassion that are integral to the religion. While some may have faced challenges or made mistakes along the way, Islam emphasizes the importance of repentance and seeking forgiveness.

Through sincere repentance and rectifying their actions, they have not only fixed any shortcomings but have also left behind legacies of positive impact, be it in academia, arts, sciences, business, or any other field they have excelled.

Their contributions have not caused turmoil but have fostered harmony and mutual respect, breaking down barriers and building bridges of understanding between different cultures and religions.

When people can get to know Muslims and their families, whether through friendships or interactions with children who come with friends, they often experience a deepening of those relationships.

Muslims, guided by their faith, place a strong emphasis on hospitality, and this extends to both Muslims and non-Muslims alike.

There is no discrimination for showing kindness and generosity. This understanding of Islam's teachings on hospitality often leaves a lasting impact on those who witness it firsthand.

These relationships, built on mutual respect and shared experiences, become a part of a preserved and shared culture, fostering friendships that can endure for a lifetime.

The bonds formed through these connections transcend religious differences and contribute to a broader understanding and appreciation of diverse cultures and traditions.

The Muslim community has a long history of leaving a positive impact on the lands they have inhabited.

Even after wars, they have made efforts to rebuild and restore, creating thriving communities. Their legacies are not mere piles of dust and destruction, but a testament to their resilience and ability to come together in times of hardship.

The Western world's interventions have often led to chaos and destabilization. Take Iraq, for example. The entry of Western powers into the country, driven by greed and political motives, resulted in immense destruction and loss of life.

The primary justification for this intervention was the search for weapons of mass destruction, which were never found. Meanwhile, the consequences for the Iraqi people were devastating. Millions of lives were lost, and the land itself was irrevocably changed.

This stark contrast highlights the difference in approach between the Muslim community and the Western world. The Muslims have consistently shown a commitment to rebuilding and preserving their communities, even in the face of adversity.

Their focus has been on creating a better future for themselves and future generations. In contrast, the Western world's actions often prioritize short-term gains and geopolitical interests, disregarding the long-term consequences for the affected nations and their populations.

It is important to recognize and learn from these historical lessons. Rather than perpetuating a cycle of intervention and chaos, it is crucial to foster understanding, cooperation, and respect among nations.

Only through such efforts can we hope to create a world where the legacies left behind are those of progress, unity, and shared prosperity.

News: Al Jazeera: Oct 18, 2021 — Before the US invasion, no weapons of mass destruction had been found in more than 70 UN site inspections. And none was found after by the US...

BBC: Mar 12, 2023 — For the US, the issue of weapons of mass destruction (WMDs), was secondary to a deeper drive to overthrow the Iraqi leader, Saddam Hussein.

The friendships between the regime and the promised promises that went unfulfilled eventually turned into deep animosity.

The regime, driven by its own agenda, began to manipulate and exploit the Muslim population, using their potential to cause destruction and instability in the country. This became second nature to them, as they understood the Middle East's vulnerabilities and sought to exploit them for their own gain.

The crucial attacks that have occurred in the region have become tiresome, as they are often staged or manipulated by social media.

It is not difficult to determine and believe, as those who perpetuate evil often blame others while pleasing the ignorant masses who believe they have accomplished something significant when in reality they have only left behind a trail of destruction and chaos.

The Islamophobic Western world in the political arena and those who follow politics through social media often seek fulfillment through perpetuating stereotypes and ignorance about the Middle East.

They are driven by their ego and a desire to assert their superiority over a region they do not understand.

Instead of seeking to learn about the rich history and resources of the Middle East, they choose to focus on their greed and desire for power. This leads to a disproportionate amount of money being spent on wars, while the needs of their lands are neglected.

The peace treaty, which could provide much-needed help to their own people, is often pushed aside in favor of sensationalized news coverage that feeds into the chaos and entertainment that the ignorant thrive on.

Unfortunately, these Islamophobic Western regions also suffer from a high level of illiteracy, with education only recently becoming a priority for the younger generation.

The promise of better jobs through education is often not fulfilled, leaving many disillusioned and perpetuating a cycle of ignorance and prejudice.

Until recently, a high school diploma was enough to get good jobs, whereas in other countries, additional education was necessary.

Education has recently gained significance in the country, which is a relatively recent development compared to older countries in contrast to a country less than three hundred years.

Education becomes less valuable when there are job prospects available that don't require any formal education.

And the consequences become apparent. However, it is important to note that not all Muslims succumb to the allure of Western culture. Many remain steadfast in their faith and values, using education to excel and contribute positively to society.

Although it is getting overly tiresome to keep hearing Muslim women being labeled as backward and their religion as male-dominated, it is important to address the misconceptions.

It is crucial to understand that Islam, like any other religion, is diverse and interpreted differently by its followers.

Challenging stereotypes, acknowledging the diversity within religious communities, and fostering a deeper understanding of women's roles and rights across various faith traditions are crucial.

The allure of freedom is captivating for most individuals, but the restrictions that accompany freedom in a society that establishes its own rules are more stringent than those who adhere to the laws and regulations set by people or Islam.

The laws in Islam perpetuate freedom, and their finality is preferable to the difficulties one encounters by attempting to circumvent the system that Allah has created.

These laws have become refined and clear, as Islam is the ultimate revelation among the Abrahamic faiths. The prophets who have come from Allah are an integral part of the Abrahamic faith.

Allah sent Muhammad to humanity as the culmination of all the prophets within the Abrahamic faiths, but Jesus will return to reveal the truth about his own identity as a prophet and the Messiah.

These individuals serve as shining examples for the rest of the world, proving that it is possible to thrive without compromising. Certain cultures not compatible with Islam may be inviting, with its perceived freedom and acceptance of everything, but it often leads to a sense of emptiness and moral ambiguity.

The presence of friendships does not affect explanations, as religion and history remain steadfast in their understanding. However, fostering harmonious relationships and promoting continuity within humanity brings about a sense of cohesion.

Muslims who have grown up with strict rules and scrutiny may find it tempting to rebel and explore the forbidden, but ultimately, they realize the hollowness that accompanies such actions.

The thriving generation in the Western regions that embraces education while strength in their faith provides hope and inspiration for others, showing that it is possible to navigate the challenges of modern society while maintaining one's moral compass.

The nature of Islam is indeed to protect the soul of a Muslim or a believer. Islam teaches that all believers, regardless of their religious background, are called to submit to the will of Allah and strive for righteousness. This includes following the example of Abraham, who is considered a believer in Islam.

Muslims often face challenges and encounters in Western environments. They may be subjected to ridicule, but they may also receive applause for their adherence to their faith. Muslims need to remember that mistakes can be made, but true repentance involves a sincere desire for change and growth.

Allah, as the ultimate judge, understands that change is possible, but it requires consistent effort and companionship with fellow Muslims.

Marriage or companionship within the Muslim community can provide a supportive environment for personal growth and the withdrawal from any evil tendencies.

By seeking the guidance of Allah and surrounding themselves with a community of believers, Muslims can strive to protect their souls and live according to the principles of Islam.

In many Islamic cultures, education is highly valued and seen as a means to gain knowledge and understanding of Allah's teachings.

The emphasis on education in Islam stems from the belief that Allah educated the Prophet Muhammad through angel Gabriel highlighting the importance of knowledge.

This can be seen in the very beginning of Muhammad's prophethood when the angel Gabriel instructed him to read **(Iqra)**. As a result, Muslims have a tradition of teaching their children to read the Quran and begin their educational journey at a young age.

It is common for Muslim children to learn the basic recitation of the Quran, such as the phrase **"Iqra Bismi Rabikallazi,"** in their fourth year as a cultural and religious practice in some Muslim cultures.

Islam highly values the role of the mother as the first teacher. It is believed that she plays a significant role in shaping her children's education, particularly in matters of faith.

Therefore, a Muslim woman needs to know about Islam so that she can effectively pass it on to her offspring, as she holds the primary responsibility for their early education, even before formal schooling begins.

Jihad, migration (hijra), and the spreading of Islam are indeed integral parts of Islamic traditions. **Jihad** refers to the struggle or effort to uphold and defend the principles of Islam, both internally and externally.

Migration, or hijra, holds significance in Islamic history as it symbolizes the movement of early Muslims from Mecca to Medina to escape persecution and establish a society based on Islamic principles. This event serves as a reminder that if circumstances allow, Muslims are encouraged to migrate to places where they can freely practice and promote their faith.

Islam, as a global religion, emphasizes the universal message of peace, justice, and submission to God.

The purpose of Islam is to encourage its followers to educate the world, welcoming people from all backgrounds exerting no force. Sharing views is beneficial, with no pressure to join the faith if one is not willing, and coercing no one to embrace Islam.

It is a matter of choice, not a forceful imposition. However, in the current climate of hatred, it is essential to educate and dispel misconceptions about Islam, which is often wrongly portrayed as backward and associated with terrorism.

Quran: Surah Baqarah: 2:256. Let there be no compulsion in religion, for the truth stands out clearly from falsehood. So whoever renounces false gods and believes in Allah has certainly grasped the firmest, unfailing hand-hold. And Allah is All-Hearing, All-Knowing.

Bible Gateway: Luke 14:23: "Then the master told his servant, 'Go out to the roads and country lanes and compel them to come in, so that my house will be full.

In Christianity, it is common to practice door knocking to invite people, but this approach is not considered logical in Islam.

Faith cannot thrive through force; however, by fostering understanding, one can accumulate significant milestones and cherished memories.

Unrequited love evolves into a tale of solidarity, honest expression, and happiness.

Two Muslims embarked on a romantic journey together. However, one of them eventually withdrew from the relationship, citing the unstable nature within and shy of Islam and the influence of individuals who spread hate in the religion's name.

Breaking the silence, he claimed that love can't be coerced, accusing her of pressuring him.

His own struggles with hypocrisy and insecurities didn't erase Islam's influence in their conversations, remaining close to his heart, despite the biased views of his opponents influencing his judgment.

Despite their contrasting approach and cultural differences, his belief in Islam outweighed their opposing viewpoints. He acknowledged her as Allah's selection, dispelling his uncertainty and embracing faith. He believed it held the key to the happiness and companionship he sought, united in their common faith.

He admitted he trusted only her!

These words made her understand that deep love exists alongside trust, and without trust, love cannot thrive. She left him alone to contemplate, as his words revealed the truth that she always sensed between the lines.

This narrative underscores the importance of trust as a bedrock for love, particularly in a shared Islamic faith. Genuine adherence to Islam requires understanding the fundamental tenets of Allah's faith and mercy.

Allah instructed them to build their relationship on mutual faith and trust for strength and survival. Their blossoming faith proved that shared beliefs transcend differences and forge strong relationships.

Therefore, it is crucial for Muslims to uplift those who seek knowledge and dispel ignorance. It is not merely a challenging task, but an essential duty, as coherence with truth is the ultimate essence of Islam.

It is unprecedented to compel individuals to fill a place of worship. God does not require humans to worship him forcibly; he already has many believers who pray to him willingly. The individuals promoting evangelism highlights its necessity rather than being a matter of preference.

However, it is important to note that Allah, as believed by Muslims, is the sustainer of all creation. He provides for both believers and non-believers alike, regardless of whether they worship Him.

Many people who do not worship Allah still lead successful worldly lives because of various factors, such as hard work, opportunity, and personal choices.

The concept of peace, according to Islamic teachings, is deeply rooted in the relationship between a believer and Allah. Muslims believe that true peace and tranquility can only be attained through submission to the will of Allah and living a life under His teachings. And gaining worldly life.

The act of worshiping Allah and recognizing Him as the creator of all things brings about a sense of peace and fulfillment in the hearts of believers.

It is important to understand that Allah, being the creator, does not need the creation the creation needs him. He is eternal and exists without a beginning or end. The prophets and the Messiah Jesus were created by Allah and were chosen to convey His message to humanity. They are not gods themselves, but human beings who were blessed with divine guidance.

In Islam, the worship of Allah is considered the ultimate purpose of human existence. It is through this worship that believers establish a direct connection with their Creator and experience the profound peace that comes from living a life under His guidance.

However, it is not for humans to question why Allah created them or the prophets. Such matters are beyond human comprehension, and it is part of faith to accept and believe in the divine wisdom of Allah.

Unlike some Christian denominations that engage in door-to-door evangelism, Islam focuses on a unique method of spreading its teachings.

Muslims frequently prioritize building connections and having meaningful discussions with individuals instead of relying only on door-to-door outreach.

Islamic outreach initiatives frequently include community events, educational programs, interfaith dialogues, and public lectures, which offer individuals a chance to learn about Islam and inquire about it in a welcoming and relaxed environment.

The focus is on fostering an atmosphere of comprehension and regard, instead of using an aggressive approach often linked with door-to-door visits. The reason Muslims must perform Salat is that consistent behavior is preferred in Islam.

Those who choose not to attend have missed out on the joy of the day, which cannot be reclaimed. Results are guaranteed when there is consistency.

Quran: Surah Anfal: 8:39. "Take on only as much as you can do of good deeds, for the best of deeds is that which is done consistently, even if it is little."

It is crucial for Muslim countries to join forces and support Palestine, guided by their moral values, rather than relying on outside help. Consistency is key for these acts to remain unchanged. Social media has the power to shape the needs of the entire human population.

The act of Muslims welcoming Jews after their exile shows an obvious display of humanity, while the current situation is driven by greed and supported by those who endorse this regime. It is the responsibility of Muslims and Muslim lands.

In Islam, the concept of justice is deeply rooted and emphasized. Islam encourages Muslims to stand up against oppression and fight for their rights, as well as the rights of others. Islam does not promote passivity when facing injustice.

Throughout history, there have been many incidents where Muslims have mobilized and fought against oppression, drawing inspiration from their faith.

These incidents compare to other struggles for rights and freedom, highlighting the universal nature of the fight against injustice. Islam encourages its followers to actively pursue justice, promote equality, and question systems that uphold oppression.

Many instances exist where the desire for power is suppressed and karma comes into play, influencing the decisions made by both the powerful and the powerless.

Muslims have consistently shown their willingness to fight for justice, not for selfish gain or to oppress the marginalized.

The principles of justice, truth, and hope are the foundation of Muslims' faith in Allah and Islam.

Many regimes have engaged in battles, but the motive behind them is for the initiator to understand and for the outcomes to become apparent, whether it results in destruction or repairing what is broken.

The free will given by Allah is akin to a loose rope, but when it is tightened, humans will inevitably face the consequences, sometimes affecting many people.

Indira Gandhi, the Prime Minister of India launched Operation Blue Star in June 1984 to remove militants from the Golden Temple complex in Amritsar, the holiest Sikh shrine.

This military action resulted in the death of many innocent Sikh civilians and the desecration of the sacred site. In retaliation, a few radical Sikh individuals formed the tyranny, seeking revenge for what they perceived as an attack on their religion and community.

Their actions included assassinating Indira Gandhi on October 31, 1984, triggering widespread anti-Sikh riots across India, where thousands of innocent Sikhs were brutally killed. The tyranny, though comprised of a small group, left a lasting impact on the Sikh community and the nation.

While some may view this as destiny or karma, it is important to acknowledge the complexities of the situation. Land ownership and religious identity is often at the heart of such conflicts, and it is crucial to find peaceful solutions.

Muslims, who form a significant population in many parts of the world, should not merely complain about the situation but actively work towards helping those in need. This responsibility falls upon all of humanity, especially Muslim countries.

One potential solution could be to change the exchange of currency to a Muslim currency, such as the dinar, to assert strength and unity. Currently, trading petrol in dollars is not beneficial for the Muslim world, as it indirectly supports Israel.

This contradicts the principles and vision of the late King Faisal, who promoted the use of Muslim countries to support humanity advocated for preventing the massacre of Palestine by regimes that lack the resources to combat Israel, which is supported by a superpower.

King Faisal's actions spoke louder than his words when he suspended the petrol trade with the U.S. temporarily. He firmly stated we have relied on dates and water in the past and we can to back to simple provisions again, but it is crucial to defend integrity, protect human rights, and support the oppressed.

Subsequently, the pursuit of profit became dominant and the Muslim country continued the trade following the guidelines established by foreign powers, failing to uphold the principles set by King Faisal.

By holding onto regions that they already possess and utilizing their resources wisely, Muslims can establish a stronger position in the global arena, guided by the principles of Islam.

During the time of Prophet Muhammad, Muslims took action and fought in wars to support justice and uphold the true cause.

They did not engage in the blame game that is prevalent today. However, in the present day, some Muslims have fallen into the trap of blaming others instead of taking responsibility for their actions.

This is hypocrisy and goes against the teachings of Islam. Instead of pointing fingers and blaming Islamophobia, Muslims should come together and support all Muslim countries, especially to help those facing oppression.

One way to make a significant impact is by changing the currency used for trading petrol, thereby reducing reliance on Western powers. It is important to note that many individuals who migrated from Western lands to the Middle East have chosen not to return, as the world is constantly evolving.

However, regardless of the circumstances, the ultimate measure remains justice. Islam teaches that even if you stand alone, you must always strive to be just.

The constant illiteracy of some individuals becomes apparent when they respond with hostility or disdain towards language or dialects they deem displeasing. In such situations, it is disheartening to witness the lack of empathy and understanding.

Instead of resorting to such narrow-mindedness, it is important to remember that the world belongs to Allah, and He guides people to migrate to lands where they can find sustenance and nourishment.

It is crucial to foster an environment of education and open-mindedness, where we strive to comprehend the circumstances of others rather than belittling or ignoring their struggles. By doing so, we can build genuine friendships and work towards a more compassionate and inclusive society.

Quran: Surah Yunus: 10:84. Moses said, O my people! If you do believe in Allah and submit to His will, then put your trust in Him.

Quran: 10:85. They replied, In Allah we trust. Our Lord! Do not subject us to the persecution of the oppressive people.

During the time of the Israelites' oppression in Egypt, they were indeed subjected to brutal torture and hardship. However, it was through Allah's intervention and guidance that Moses was chosen as a prophet to lead the Israelites out of bondage.

The story of the **Exodus** is a significant event in history, as it symbolizes liberation from oppression and the triumph of faith. It is important to note that the conversion of Egypt to Islam did not occur during the time of Moses and the Israelites.

The conversion of Egypt to Islam took place in the 7th century CE when Muslim armies conquered the region. This conquest is often attributed to the leadership of Omar Bin Khattab a companion of the Prophet Muhammad.

Prophet Muhammad predicted Omar bin Khattab, a convert who initially opposed Islam, would play a significant role in spreading the religion. Omar's conversion to Islam influenced the early growth and spread of the religion.

Omar's conversion from a staunch opponent to a committed believer had a significant influence on the Muslim community. His leadership, faith, and commitment to justice were crucial in spreading Islam. Allah is believed to select individuals for specific roles, and those guided by Allah cannot be led astray.

The conversion of Egypt to Islam is seen by Muslims as a divine sign, indicating that the land, which was once ruled by unfair and tyrannical Pharaohs, was now under the rule of Muslims

It is not a claim that the land became Jewish, but rather a recognition of the historical significance of Egypt's conversion to Islam.

Overall, the story of the Israelites' oppression in Egypt and their eventual liberation is a powerful example of how Allah intervenes in history to bring justice to the oppressed. It serves as a reminder that even in the face of oppression, there is always hope for deliverance and a better future.

And misdeeds of a few individuals should not be used to tarnish the entire religion. Just as the Byzantine Empire fell to the Ottomans, it is possible by the will of Allah that the political landscape in Israel and Palestine will change in the future.

However, it is important for those who believe in justice and freedom to actively work towards aiding those who are oppressed. Merely expressing outrage on social media is not enough; we must take concrete actions that can make a difference on a global scale.

The tyrant Pharaoh, upon receiving a warning from his magicians that a boy would overthrow him, took to killing newborns.

The boy who altered Pharaoh's path was actually raised in Pharaoh's own house, showcasing the undeniable destiny and power of Allah.

The irony of this episode lies because Pharaoh's son was later killed by a plague sent by Allah. This happened after Moses had warned Pharaoh about the consequences, but it was only then that Pharaoh believed.

It was too late for him, and his preservation serves as a lesson for others about the consequences of ignoring warnings. In Islam, punishment is not imposed on anyone until a warner is sent.

My written pieces serve as a cautionary tale for those who understand the message!

The child Moses, who was swept in a basket from the shores, arrived at the enemy's house. Muslims once ruled Israel and will do so again as peace is achieved; Islam is the only religion that has brought peace, non-discrimination, and religious freedom.

Islam prospered under Muslim governance. Israel is in chaos and experiencing daily turmoil, so it is crucial to voice our concerns and work towards a resolution.

Many Christians who view Jesus as God or the son of God hold a deep faith in Israel, making it even more important to address the situation.

It is important to note that he was a Palestinian, those who pervert justice will face injustice upon their return.

Bible KJV: 15;9. But in vain they do worship me, teaching for doctrines the commandments of men.

Bible: ESV. 7:21:23.22 On that day many will say to me, 'Lord, Lord, did we not prophesy in your name, and cast out demons in your name, and do many mighty works in your name? ' 23 And then will I declare to them, 'I never knew you; depart from me, you workers of lawlessness.

Islamic doctrine states that Jesus (Isa in Arabic) will come back to earth as a Messenger of Allah, near Syria, particularly in Damascus.

The **Mahdi**, also called the Guided One, is an Islamic eschatological figure believed to be from **Prophet Muhammad's** family. The **Mahdi** is expected to emerge in the future to establish justice and eliminate existing injustice. He is expected to usher in an era of peace, harmony, and justice, reshaping society and ensuring fair treatment for all.

The purpose of the **Mahdi** is to correct corruption and oppression that have afflicted humanity and restore balance and righteousness in all areas of life.

He aims to establish justice in all aspects - social, political, spiritual, and moral. Muslims worldwide eagerly await the arrival of the **Mahdi**, seen as a divine emissary chosen by God, to establish a just and compassionate society.

Narrated Abu Sa'Id al-Khudri: The Prophet (PBUH) said: The **Mahdi** will be of my stock, and will have a broad forehead and a prominent nose. He will fill the earth will equity and justice as it was filled with oppression and tyranny, and he will rule for seven years.

The Antichrist, also called Dajjal, will appear in this era. The Dajjal is perceived as a fraudulent messiah who will deceive people through his miracles and deceptive declarations of being divine.

When Jesus comes back, he will play a vital role in defeating the Dajjal and establishing justice and righteousness.

Hadith: Sahih Muslim: 41:7023. Jesus will slay the Antichrist and then all Jews and Christians will believe in him. Thus, there will then be one community, that of Islam. Good will triumph

Hadith: Bukhari 3:43:656. The Hour will not be established until the son of Mary. Her son Jesus descends amongst you as a just ruler, he will break the cross, kill the pig, and abolish the Jizya tax. Money will be in abundance so that nobody will accept it as charitable gifts.

The death of the **Mahdi**, who is believed to be a righteous and guided leader, will mark the beginning of a golden era of peace and justice on Earth.

During this period, known as the **"Age of Justice,"** the world will experience harmony and prosperity. However, this period will be disrupted by the emergence of **Gog and Magog**, two destructive forces that will cause chaos and corruption.

The arrival destination of Jesus is seen as the ultimate representation of understanding. Jesus, also known as Isa ibn Maryam, is coming from Damascus, Syria, a Muslim land. He will be praying behind a Mehdi, who is also a Muslim.

It's important to note that Jesus is not coming from Israel, where there is constant support for the massacre of Palestinians by those who believe they are supporting Jesus, the Messiah, in order to save themselves.

This mindset revolves around the idea of sacrificing the lives of others, which is considered a torment in both this world and the next, as Islam promotes justice. The Muslims who lose their lives in this catastrophe are considered shahid, meaning they are martyred. According to Islamic beliefs, they are still considered alive.

God will intervene and destroy **Gog and Magog**, restoring peace and order once again.

Mehdi will lead the dawn prayer when Isa Jesus ascends, and he will pray Salat behind Mehdi, following Islam's one religion.

If he were God, he wouldn't pray or lead the prayer, as he would require people to pray to him. Jesus, not being God, will pray to God during morning prayers.

Quran: Surah Imran: 3:185. Everyone is bound to taste death and you shall receive your full reward on the Day of Resurrection. Then, whoever is spared the Fire is admitted to paradise.

This clear verse of the Quran clarifies that the notion of one person dying for the sins of others contradicts the core principle of personal responsibility for one's actions.

It uses the analogy of a hunter aiming and shooting to highlight the need to accept the consequences of one's actions.

Life's balance determines the outcomes of our actions. Many consider the idea of God sacrificing his son to atone for humanity's sins as illogical and reminiscent of ancient rituals involving human sacrifices.

The historical context suggests that the belief in blood as a means of salvation is based on outdated and ritualistic perspectives, rather than a rational understanding of forgiveness and personal responsibility.

The story of Abraham the prophet:

The prophet Abraham, known for his unwavering faith and close relationship with God, was promised a long and prosperous life.

It is said that God granted him the extraordinary gift of living up to 1000 years. However, driven by his immense love and concern for his son, Abraham made a humble request to allocate 40 years of his life to be given to his beloved child.

The prophet, in his old age, reflected on the fleeting nature of human life and the importance of memory. He had forgotten that although his life on Earth was 1000 years, 40 years had been allocated to his son. However, old age had taken its toll on his memory, causing him to forget certain aspects. Those who forget cannot effectively rule.

When the angel Gabriel arrived to collect his soul, he informed him he was promised to live for 1000 years. However, he reminded him he had already given away 40 years of his life to his son.

Clearly presenting a viewpoint on the truth. In the past, prophets used to have longer lifespans, but Allah shortened the lifespan of Prophet Muhammad to only 63 years.

According to Islamic belief, Jesus did not experience death, but spent 33 years on Earth.

Islamic teachings suggest he will come back and eventually pass away, following the pattern of all prophets. No soul can die twice in Islam. On the day of judgement, Allah will bring back to life every soul, regardless of how many years or decades have passed since their death.

If Allah can bring a human into existence from nothing, then raising a human from the dead is not a challenge for Allah. Abraham appealed to Allah, asking for guidance on how to animate lifeless to life.

While he did not doubt Allah's existence, he, as a human, sought to quench his own curiosity. Abraham received a response from Allah.

Abraham was commanded by Allah to divide a bird into four pieces and scatter them in various places. When Allah summoned the bird, it returned flying to Abraham, showcasing that anything can happen when it is Allah's will.

He was the forefather of all prophets, who faced countless trials and emerged victorious in each one.

His father catapulted him, above the fire but he miraculously survived as Allah controlled the fire's temperature to keep him safe. Many pagans considered him a magician, but Allah, the creator of all, has the power to make anything possible for himself and his faithful followers.

Allah commanded him to leave his wife, Hagar, and their young child in the scorching heat of Saudi Arabia. Through a divine intervention, Hagar was bestowed with the opportunity to access the **Zam-Zam** water, which now acts as a source of healing and drinking for innumerable pilgrims in Saudi Arabia.

In the harsh desert environment, Hagar and Ishmael faced the daunting task of finding water to survive. As she ran between the mountains of **Safa and Marwa** in search of sustenance, Hagar's determination and trust in Allah's mercy became clear.

It was during this desperate search a miracle occurred. A spring of water, known as Zamzam, gushed forth from the ground, providing them with a source of life-saving hydration.

With unwavering determination, she upheld her riparian rights and selflessly shared the water with both migrating individuals and the avian inhabitants, who reveled in this divine blessing given upon her by Allah.

Only Muslims may enter Mecca to access the sacred water; non-Muslims are restricted from doing so. Some people may interpret this as a type of segregation, where certain areas have restricted certain individuals.

Admission necessitates an exclusive adherence to an established methodology and understanding of the rules. Rules are present in human environments and should not be challenged if they are from Allah.

The believer Abraham faced a challenging situation when he dreamt of sacrificing his son. The truthfulness of his faith was proven when a lamb was provided as an alternative. While there may be several instances like this, only those who comprehend the underlying meaning can use it to transform their lives

However, in places where there is a strong belief in Islam, the trials faced by individuals lie in the practice and understanding of their faith. The observance of belief becomes a source of strength and resilience for those enduring challenging circumstances.

This realization highlights the importance of memory in understanding the actions and motives of Islamophobic regimes. It becomes evident that such regimes are not genuinely concerned about the well-being of their people but are driven by greed and a desire to exploit the resources of the Middle East.

This region has always been a hub of fascination for those who see opportunities in its abundant reserves of metals, oil, and gas, as well as its strategic pipeline routes.

The sacred **Zam-Zam** healing waters and the utilization of various medicinal plants found in the Muslim world have attracted the attention of the pharmaceutical industry in the Western world.

Unfortunately, in these cases, the pursuit of profit often takes precedence over respect for the beliefs and rights of others. It is crucial to recognize that human memory holds immense power, surpassing any machinery or technological advancements.

Prophet Muhammad, the final messenger of Allah, emphasized the significance of this event by stating that, had Hagar not created a basin to contain the water, the world would have been flooded.

Hagar, recognizing her rights to this miraculous water, invited others to benefit from it while asserting her ownership over the well.

The healing properties and abundance of minerals and compounds in **Zam-Zam** water have served countless people throughout history and continue to do so.

The possession of this precious resource has attracted interest from the Western world, leading to attempts to establish pipelines for its extraction.

However, such proposals have been rejected, as **Zam-Zam** water is only reserved for use by Muslims during pilgrimage or by any Muslim who has access to it. This sacred water remains a symbol of faith, purity, and divine providence for millions of Muslims worldwide.

This event, known as the **"Qurbani," Eid Al Adha** holds significant importance during the annual pilgrimage of **Hajj**.

Muslims from all over the world commemorate Abraham's willingness to sacrifice by sacrificing animals, such as sheep, goats, or cows, and distributing the meat to their families, friends, and the less fortunate.

This act of sharing and celebrating reflects the spirit of unity, compassion, and gratitude towards Allah's blessings.

The **Qurbani** serves as a reminder that Allah does not require human sacrifice, but seeks devotion, steadfastness, and a willingness to prioritize faith over worldly attachments.

By rejecting human sacrifice, Allah emphasizes the sanctity of life and the value of mercy and compassion.

This profound lesson has had a lasting impact on Muslims, reinforcing the importance of valuing and preserving human life and rejecting violence in any form.

This act of sharing and generosity reflects the values of compassion and community in Islam.

Eid al-Adha coincides with the culmination of the **Hajj pilgrimage,** where millions of Muslims from around the world gather in Mecca to fulfill one of the Five Pillars of Islam.

The festival is a time of prayer, feasting, and spending time with loved ones, as Muslims express gratitude for the blessings bestowed upon them by Allah.

This serves as a powerful lesson for all Abrahamic faiths, emphasizing that Allah does not require human sacrifice. Instead, it highlights the importance of obedience, trust, and submission to Allah's will.

It shows that true devotion lies in following the teachings and examples set forth in religious scriptures, rather than relying on mere fairy tales. Love for one's beliefs is exemplified through acts of kindness, compassion, and adherence to the principles of the faith, rather than through gruesome sacrifices.

The continuity of belief highlights the concept of sacrifice, serves to challenge the notion that Allah would require a human to sacrifice for the entire human race.

Through the story of Abraham and his son, it becomes evident that Allah does not demand human sacrifices.

As a result, Islam refutes and rejects the concept of Jesus' sacrifice for sins, commonly referred to as salvation in Christianity.

It addresses the unfairness of expecting one individual to pay the ultimate price for the sins committed by others, especially considering that humanity constantly defies Allah's guidance.

By questioning the validity of their belief, readers are encouraged to combat skepticism and foster a deeper faith in Allah. This leads to a more personal approach to repentance.

It emphasizes that one-on-one repentance seems more logical than accepting the idea of human sacrifice, which had been previously rejected.

By challenging this concept, the story invites readers to contemplate the true nature of Allah's justice and mercy, promoting a deeper understanding of the faith.

The Hajj is one of the most significant religious pilgrimages for Muslims, taking place in Mecca, Saudi Arabia. During the Hajj, pilgrims take part in the ritual of Tawaf, which involves circling the Kaaba, the most sacred site in Islam, seven times.

It is important to note that Muslims are not worshiping the physical building itself, but engaging in a symbolic act of unity and devotion.

The circular motion of **Tawaf** signifies the eternal nature of their faith and the continuous cycle of submission to Allah. This circle has no defined end, representing the perpetual connection between the worshippers and their Creator.

During the Hajj, the dress code for men involves wearing two white, seamless clothes known as Ihram. It is customary for some men to shave their heads completely, symbolizing a state of humility and purification.

Others may simply choose to cut a strand of their hair.

Women have a different attire for Hajj. They are required to wear loose-fitting clothing that covers their entire body, known as an abaya or a long robe, usually in black or different colors.

Women may choose to cover their faces with a veil or niqab, although this is not mandated in Islam. The emphasis is on modesty and maintaining a sense of dignity and respect while performing the religious rituals of Hajj.

After completing the Hajj pilgrimage, Prophet Muhammad shaved his head as part of the ritual of Ihram. This act symbolizes the completion of the pilgrimage and the shedding of one's sins and worldly attachments.

Following the Prophet's example, many Muslims choose to shave their heads or trim their hair shortly after performing Hajj or Umrah, another pilgrimage to the holy city of Mecca.

This act of shaving the head is purification and a way to start anew, emphasizing the spiritual journey and the importance of humility and simplicity in the eyes of God.

All pilgrims use **Zam-Zam** water, which is considered the most healing and spiritually significant water during Hajj.

The water is sourced from the **Zam-Zam** well in Mecca, Saudi Arabia, and pilgrims believe it holds immense blessings and healing properties. It is customary for pilgrims to drink **Zam-Zam** water and also take some back home as a sacred souvenir.

It is truly remarkable to witness the act of giving in Saudi Arabia during Hajj.

The Saudi government and various organizations set up food tents and distribution centers across the holy sites, providing free meals and refreshments to millions of pilgrims.

The generosity is overwhelming, and pilgrims from all walks of life can enjoy nutritious meals throughout their journey.

This act of providing free food ensures that no pilgrim goes hungry and allows them to focus on their spiritual journey without worrying about necessities.

It is a testament to the grandness of the giving culture in Saudi Arabia and adds to the overall experience of **Hajj,** making it a truly unforgettable and fulfilling pilgrimage.

The pilgrims travel to Mina during **Hajj** for a specific ritual known as the **"Day of Arafah."**

This ritual takes place on the 9th day of the Islamic month of Dhul-Hijja. After spending the previous day in **Arafat,** pilgrims move to **Mina,** a small valley located a few kilometers away from Mecca. Mina serves as a temporary campsite for the pilgrims, who spend the night there before moving on to other important rituals of **Hajj.**

The purpose of staying in Mina is to symbolize the obedience and willingness to follow the footsteps of Prophet Ibrahim (Abraham), who was prepared to sacrifice his son as an act of submission to God.

The pilgrims spend their time in Mina-Muzdalifa engaged in prayers, supplications, and reflection, preparing themselves for the upcoming rituals of **Hajj.**

The pilgrims stone the devil in Mina because it is a symbolic ritual that is part of the Hajj pilgrimage in Islam. **Mina-Muzdalifa** is a specific location in **Mina, Saudi Arabia,** where pilgrims gather during the annual **Hajj pilgrimage.**

The stoning of the devil is performed by throwing pebbles at three pillars that represent Satan and his attempts to tempt Prophet Ibrahim (Abraham) to disobey God's command.

This ritual signifies the pilgrims' rejection of evil and their commitment to following the path of righteousness. It is an important act of worship that holds deep spiritual significance for Muslims taking part in the **Hajj pilgrimage.**

The three pillars that Muslims throw pebbles at during the stoning ritual are known as Jamarat.

These pillars symbolize Satan and are in Mina, near the holy city of Mecca. The stoning of the Satan ritual is an integral part of the **Hajj pilgrimage,** which is one of the **Five Pillars of Islam.**

It is performed by pilgrims as a demonstration of their faith and rejection of temptation and distractions. Each pilgrim throws seven pebbles at each of the three pillars, representing the weakness of Satan.

This act signifies their determination to stay focused on their spiritual journey and resist the influence of evil. Understanding the history and significance of Satan allows Muslims to recognize his weaknesses and reaffirm their own faith and resolve.

By participating in this ritual, pilgrims strengthen their connection to Allah and affirm their commitment to living a righteous life. The **Hajj** is a significant pilgrimage that holds great spiritual significance in Islam. It is one of the **Five Pillars of Islam** and is obligatory for every able-bodied Muslim who can afford it.

During the **Hajj,** pilgrims gather in the holy city of Mecca, where they perform a series of rituals that commemorate the actions of the Prophet Ibrahim (Abraham) and his family.

One of these rituals involves circumambulating the Kaaba, a sacred structure in the center of the **Masjid al-Haram.**

The **Kaaba** is believed to have been built by Ibrahim and his son Ismail (Ishmael) and is considered the most sacred site in Islam.

Embedded in one corner of the Kaaba is the **Hajr-e-Aswad**, also known as the Black Stone.

According to Islamic tradition, this stone was a celestial gift sent down from heaven to Ibrahim to aid him in the construction of the Kaaba.

Over time, as people's sins touched the stone, it gradually turned black. Muslims do not worship the Black Stone itself, but it holds immense reverence as a symbol of the connection between heaven and earth.

It is customary for pilgrims to kiss or touch the Black Stone during the **tawaf** (circumambulation) to emulate the actions of the Prophet Muhammad, who kissed the stone during his hajj pilgrimage.

The experience of performing the **Hajj** is transformative for those who undertake it. The pilgrimage is a journey of self-reflection, spiritual cleansing, and seeking forgiveness from Allah.

It is believed that upon completing the hajj, pilgrims emerge with a renewed sense of faith, a deeper connection to Allah, and a heightened state of purity.

The **Hajj** serves as a unifying force for Muslims worldwide, as believers from different cultures, languages, and backgrounds come together to fulfill this sacred duty.

The impact of the **Hajj** is profound, leaving a lasting impression on the hearts and minds of those who are fortunate enough to be invited by Allah to partake in this extraordinary journey.

The Saudi king, as a gesture of goodwill and in line with the traditions of Hajj, personally oversees the distribution of food to all pilgrims on the day of Hajj.

This act of generosity aims to ensure that every pilgrim, regardless of their nationality or background, is provided with nourishment and sustenance during this important religious event.

The king's efforts are carried out with meticulous planning and coordination, as a team of dedicated volunteers works tirelessly to prepare and distribute meals to millions of pilgrims gathered in the holy city of Mecca.

This act of charity reflects the Saudi king's commitment to hospitality and the well-being of all pilgrims undertaking the sacred journey of **Hajj**.

Common sense states god does not pray to himself. Christians deny evolution, but according to their indoctrinated ideology, Jesus evolving into three is nothing but evolution.

The atheist perspective is that humanity evolved, but countering their doctrine with evolution through Jesus presents a compelling case for Christendom.

The Quran and the Bible portray the outcome in contrasting manners.

Following this, Jesus (known as **Isa** in Islam) will descend from heaven to Earth. He will establish his rule and lead the people in righteousness for approximately forty years.

His reign will be characterized by justice, compassion, and the implementation of Islamic teachings. Per Islam Jesus will die a natural death during this time.

Upon his death, Muslims will perform the Salat al-Janazah, a funeral prayer, for Jesus. He will then be buried in the city of Madinah, in a space located beside the Prophet Muhammad (peace be upon him).

This act symbolizes the honor and respect Muslims hold for both Jesus and Muhammad as esteemed prophets of God. The burial of Jesus in Madinah further strengthens the connection between the two faiths and emphasizes their shared beliefs in the finality of prophethood and the unity of God.

Quran: Surah Baqarah: 2:190. Fight those who fight you do not transgress. Allah does not favor transgressors.

Quran: Surah Baqarah: 2;191. Kill them wherever you find them, expel them from wherever they have expelled you, and fitnah persecution is worse than killing. Do not fight them at Al Masjid al-Haram (Ka'ba) until they fight you there. But if they fight you them kill them. Such is the recompense of disbelievers.

Quran: Surah Baqarah: If they cease, them indeed, God is forgiving and merciful.

Al-Bukhari (3593) and Muslim (2921) narrated from the hadith of Ibn 'Umar (may Allah be pleased with him) that he said: I heard the Messenger of Allah (blessings and peace of Allah be upon him) say: The Jews will fight you and you will prevail over them, then a rock will say: 'O Muslim, here is a Jew behind me; kill him

These verses depict the events of the end times, where Muslims will emerge victorious amidst numerous trials and tribulations. Those who stumble and imitate the ways of the people of the book will face difficulties.

Prophet Muhammad has already mentioned in a hadith that if they were to enter a lizard's hole, the ignorant and those lacking Islamic knowledge would follow them, assuming it to be a symbol of independence, when in reality, Islam is not restrictive but rather liberating. It is meant for the betterment of creation, not the creator.

Those who are harming themselves by embracing the false notion of independence propagated by Western civilization are likely to experience mental health issues, loss of peace, and even contemplate suicide.

Islam requires understanding, not imposition. When Muslims turn to Allah, seeking repentance, victory, and not defeat, is the ultimate outcome, as evident in numerous verses of the Quran.

Some verses of the Quran are direct, but justice itself is devoid of harshness and instead possesses the capability to offer solace that humanity rightfully deserves.

When the oppressors and those against Islam actively hindered Muslims from praying, engaged in conflicts with them, and subjected them to oppression.

Allah's message is not to be passive, but to fight justly and avoid fighting in Mecca forbidden areas. If the opponent surrenders, it is important to accept their surrender. Fighting against the oppressed or those who are weak is forbidden.

Fairness is crucial in combat, whether it involves close-quarter combat or battles fought with swords, camels, or horses. Acting unjustly is never acceptable under any circumstances.

In the era of Prophet Muhammad, Muslims achieved victory in multiple battles, even when outnumbered by their opponents. The mercy of Allah can always prevail, manifesting in His chosen time and manner.

Many people perceive Bible verses as harsh or challenging, and churches do not frequently mention all of them.

Some verses may address difficult topics or contain powerful language, which can make them uncomfortable for some individuals.

It is crucial to acknowledge that churches often prioritize the teachings of love, mercy, and forgiveness found in the Bible.

These values align more closely with the broader message of Christianity that they choose to convey, rather than focusing on verses that challenge those seeking answers.

Islam does not shy away from any verse in the Quran and acknowledges and discusses all of them, without denying or selectively focusing on certain verses.

This approach allows for a comprehensive understanding of the Islamic faith and promotes open dialogue about the teachings of the Quran.

The intention behind offering contrasting explanations is to foster knowledge, without aiming to sway anyone's beliefs or choices. In Islam, only those who express genuine interest find their own course.

Islam will always remain in the spotlight. It is not just the theme of a winding staircase, as the climb is a straight path rather than a winding road.

Even negative publicity can be advantageous. The greater the criticism of Islam, the stronger the curiosity about Islam becomes.

Theology does not take away from, but encourages, friendships and pursuit of truth. It guides individuals in their personal endeavors and search for truth. Those who have undertaken this search know the answers.

CHAPTER 17
EMPHASIZE STRENGTH, NOT WEAKNESS.

The purpose of something didactic is to educate people, often by teaching moral lessons. Words in totalitarian societies have a didactic function. The informative Islamic doctrine emphasizes the unchanging nature of truth.

Islam emphasizes the importance of humanity, but also stresses the treatment of animals and nature as a responsibility, not to be disrespected or destroyed.

The greatest strength of a human lies in their belief in Allah, as it is this belief that clothes them, just as they were created, and guides them towards their ultimate accountability before Allah on the Day of judgment.

Unfortunately, as the influence of pagan customs persists, people are increasingly dressing immodestly, compromising their values and diminishing their faith.

They mistakenly prioritize flaunting material wealth, which holds no value in the transient moments of life.

As humans, we are merely transients in this world, destined to depart sooner rather than later. Those who have traveled the shores of life understand the fleeting nature of these moments and the importance of utilizing them wisely.

True strength lies in one's faith, for it is the richest possession that often goes unnoticed by others. Only the individual knows the immeasurable wealth they have been bestowed - the gift of faith and belief in Allah, which is truly irreplaceable.

As the faith of a human fluctuates, it is inherent in their nature. Therefore, addressing any human as a God is undeniably a theory that is difficult to accept for those who understand the indecisive nature of a human being.

Even prophets have questioned whether Allah is upset with them if the answer does not come quickly.

This is not expressing disbelief, but a concern for understanding one's own nature. Prophet Muhammad said that the faith of a human can fluctuate.

They can be a Muslim during the dawn and a disbeliever (Kafir) by dusk, but they can change again. Therefore, having a solid understanding and the right company can play a significant role in keeping one's nature in check.

In Islam, every living creature, including animals, is valuable and should be treated with kindness and compassion. In Islam, it is believed that all living beings, including animals, trees, mountains, earth, and water, pray to Allah.

The disregard of this stems from the arrogance of humans. Even angels have questioned Allah's decision to create humans, knowing that they would bring about bloodshed and chaos on earth.

However, Allah reminds the angels that they lack the knowledge He possesses about His creation. Allah has given humans with great strength, making them the most powerful among all creations.

Hence, it is perplexing how humans can be so ungrateful. This lack of gratitude arises from arrogance, ego, and a lack of self-awareness. Time passes quickly and does not show loyalty to anyone, as it takes away precious moments.

Quran: Surah Baqarah: 2:30. Remember when your Lord said to the angels, "I am going to place a successive human authority on earth." They asked Allah, "Will You place in it someone who will spread corruption there and shed blood while we glorify Your praises and proclaim Your holiness?" Allah responded, "I know what you do not know."

It serves as an obvious reminder that Satan, who belonged to the Jinn family, fought against his own people and asked Allah to live among the angels.

This is a major difference between the Quran and the Bible, as he was not portrayed as a dark angel. Unlike angels who lack free will and simply follow orders, Satan had the freedom to disobey.

Just as the Jinn caused chaos on earth before humans, humans are now doing even worse. However, Allah, being the creator, possesses the ultimate knowledge and clarity.

This should inspire humans to better themselves, as Allah has demonstrated the strength and uniqueness of his creation countless times.

Quran: Surah Tin: 95:4."Indeed, We created humans in the best form".

The arrogance of Jinn Satan, also known as Iblis, led to his expulsion from heaven. His animosity towards humans, which he believed was the reason for his expulsion, stemmed from his true nature of arrogance and deceit.

His first act of mischief was to strip Adam and Eve, who were subsequently cast down to earth and covered themselves with leaves.

However, all they did was repent, and Allah forgave them.

In Islam, Allah is the forgiver, known as **Ar-Rahman**, and he forgives those who repent. His strength surpasses human imagination, and therefore, no human or prophet can be considered a God or take on the form of God.

It is important to note that humans were not created in Allah's image, as he does not possess a physical form. He is the light behind the veil, and no one has laid eyes on him.

The unfortunate situation in this incident involving Satan that requires attention is that Satan had more than he realized before he destroyed himself because of his inflated ego and arrogance.

His strength was not as powerful as he thought, and his weakness overshadowed his judgment.

This is a common trait among many people who fail in life—they cannot recognize the strength within themselves.

Allah has stated that among all his creations, humans are the best. However, humans have often failed to acknowledge this precious gift, just like Satan. Repentance is a solid path for those who believe in change. Transformation can indeed occur through belief.

Some humans have been incredibly ungrateful, to where they undermine their own prayers. They cannot acknowledge that their prayers were actually answered and, in their ungratefulness, they forget the true essence of prayer.

This behavior only leads them down a path of self-destruction. However, if Allah shows mercy to that person, He may send a warner to guide them.

The story is about a man who was blessed by Allah with a beautiful garden and unimaginable wealth.

However, his arrogance and pride led to the destruction of the entire garden and wealth. It was then that he realized that pride and arrogance are not meant for him, but for Allah.

He understood that as a human, he depends solely on the mercy of Allah, even though he should never give up striving without the taint of arrogance and pride.

Quran: Surah Qaaf: 18:33. Both the vineyards yielded abundant produce without failure and We caused a stream to flow in their midst.

Quran: Surah Qaaf: 18:34. And he had fruit, so he said to his companion while he was conversing with him, I am greater than you in wealth and mightier in [numbers of] men.

Quran: Surah Qaaf: 18:35. Then he entered his vine-yard and said, wronging himself: Surely, I do not believe that all this will ever perish.

Quran: Surah Qaaf: 18:36. Nor do I believe that the Hour of Resurrection will ever come to pass. And even if I am returned to my Lord, I shall find a better place than this.

Quran: Surah Qaaf: 18:37. While conversing with him his neighbor exclaimed: Do you deny Him Who created you out of dust, then out of a drop of sperm, and then fashioned you into a complete man?

Quran: Surah Qaaf: 18:38. As for myself, Allah alone is my Lord, and I associate none with my Lord in His Divinity.

As the listener explained, the only one he relied on was the Lord of Abraham, Allah. However, the executioner, who believed he was defending himself, was left with nothing. The man who believed in Allah had everything. The strongest thing a believer can hold on to is their faith.

Some arrogant individuals, including Satan, require the destructive forces of Allah to dismantle their pride, arrogance, and defiance.

However, those who believe in the strength within themselves find it empowers them rather than weakening them. It is the belief that drives all convictions, even when it seems impossible, Allah has the power to make it possible.

Other creations of Allah, such as Jinn, do not require an address. There are both good and bad jinn who remain invisible to the human eye. However, they can reveal themselves to those whom they choose, as Allah has given unique abilities to all of His creations.

Animals also have their own distinct roles and relationships with humans, with some relying on humans while others assist humans.

In today's world, animals are not only used for detection of robbers but also for a wide range of purposes that benefit humans. One notable example is the use of therapy animals to assist older adults and sick.

These animals, often trained specifically for this purpose, provide comfort, companionship, and emotional support to individuals in hospitals, nursing homes, and rehabilitation centers.

Animals have possessed a unique bond with humans, and there have been instances throughout history where prophets and spiritual leaders were believed to can communicate with them.

One such example is the biblical figure Solomon, who was said to have possessed the ability to understand and speak the language of animals.

Similarly, the Islamic prophet Muhammad is believed to have had incidents where animals approached him with their pleas and concerns, reflecting a deep connection and communication between humans and the animal kingdom.

These stories highlight the enduring belief in the extraordinary abilities of certain individuals to connect with and understand animals, emphasizing the profound relationship between humans and the animal world.

Animals possess an instinctual connection to the natural world that allows them to perceive and sense things beyond human comprehension. This innate nature enables animals to communicate through their behaviors, body language, and instincts, providing valuable insights to those who have developed a deep understanding of them.

For instance, animals have exhibited unusual behaviors or display signs of distress or unease in the presence of imminent danger or impending natural disasters.

Many pet owners have experienced instances where their animals have displayed a remarkable ability to detect illness or predict the onset of a medical condition before any visible symptoms manifest in humans.

This intuitive connection between animals and the world around them serves as a reminder of their profound sensitivity and connection to the mysteries of life and death.

By attuning ourselves to their language and observing their instincts, we can gain valuable knowledge and potentially avert or prepare for future events that may affect our lives.

The strength of a powerful tool needs to be harnessed and used effectively, while weaknesses should be acknowledged and minimized in order to allow the stronger aspects to shine through, whether it be in humans or animals.

Strength is indeed a real and tangible attribute that exists, but its manifestation depends on the training and conditioning of both the individual and their environment.

An individual's environment plays a crucial role in shaping their strengths, as it can provide the resources, opportunities, and challenges to develop and enhance specific abilities.

Similarly, self-discipline, perseverance, and focused training are vital in honing one's strengths and overcoming weaknesses.

By recognizing and leveraging their strengths, individuals and animals can tap into their full potential and excel in their respective domains.

The story of Umm Habiba showcases how her strength outweighs her weaknesses.

The story of Umm Habiba is incredibly relevant in understanding the challenges and tests that individuals of faith face amid turbulence and hardship in any episode of life.

Faith is truly put to the test when it becomes a barrier between a person, their loved ones, and their possessions, revealing what truly matters in one's actions.

Umm Habiba's journey begins with her marriage to her first husband, Ubayd Ibn Jahsh.

It was when Prophet Muhammad declared the message of Islam that she wholeheartedly embraced the faith. Alongside her husband, she embarked on the hijra to Ethiopia, escaping the persecution faced by early Muslims.

Her pregnancy didn't hinder her from making the Hijra journey in seclusion with her husband, finding solace and comfort in her faith in Islam and Allah.

Umm Habiba deeply loved her husband, who was initially a Christian but later converted to Islam. However, during their journey, she had a dream that revealed her husband's wavering non commitment to Islam.

She witnessed her husband's disobedience to Allah when he confessed to her that he was returning to his Christian faith. He urged her to follow his apostasy, but she tried to convince him otherwise.

She even warned him about a dream she had, but he paid no attention and became addicted to alcohol.

Confronting him, she discovered her dream had come true - although he had accepted Islam, he ultimately returned to Christianity.

This powerful experience serves as a reminder that Allah often communicates with his chosen people through dreams, providing them with guidance and answers.

Umm Habiba's story: is a testament to the unwavering faith and resilience that individuals must possess, particularly reverts, as they navigate the complexities of family dynamics and the challenges that arise within the realm of faith.

Eventually, her husband after fair warnings died in a state of disbelief and alcoholism. Throughout this difficult time, she was also being tested in her loyalty to him, but she remained steadfast in her faith in Islam.

Prophet Muhammad once said that there is no obedience to people when it goes against the will of Allah. Allah tests us to see who we love more - our love for other people, material things, or Allah Himself.

She fervently prayed to Allah to keep her steadfast, and soon enough, she had another dream. In this dream, she was addressed as **"Ya Umm Ul Momineen,"** a title reserved for the wives of Prophet Muhammad. Not as Umm Habiba.

Can a Muslim imagine being referred to as the mother of believers? That was how the Prophet's wives were called **"Umm Ul Momineen."** As she woke up from her dream, she felt a sense of peace and purpose.

The dreams of a faithful Muslim are true. Sometimes they are awaited but the truth lies for those who believe.

As soon as she woke up from the dream, a messenger from the king of Habsha arrived with a message. It was revealed that the Prophet Muhammad had discovered her husband's apostasy, as he had abandoned her and her faith was her only shield.

The messenger brought a marriage proposal on behalf of the Prophet Muhammad. Overwhelmed with awe and reverence, she immediately removed her silver jewelry and presented it to the messenger as a token of her acceptance.

In Islam, dreams hold a special significance, as it is believed that they are a divine means of communication. The Prophet Muhammad himself stated that the dream of a believer is a 47th part of prophethood, emphasizing the importance and authenticity of such dreams.

It is firmly believed that no dream from Allah can be false, thus reinforcing the believer's unwavering trust in these divine signs. Despite the skepticism of others, the believer who witnesses such dreams transcends the limitations of human doubts and embraces the profound connection with the divine.

No matter how dark life appears, if Allah is with his believers, it is enough to say that one is with Allah and following the opposition of Islam is not a core belief of Muslims. The **Rahma** (mercy) of Allah is abundant, and the belief in Him gives **Taw Akul** (reliance on Allah). In this belief, Allah is sufficient for a person's needs.

In the historical context, during the time of Prophet Muhammad, there was a king known as Najashi (Negus) who conducted a wedding. Sayed Al was the **Wali** (guardian) of the bride, Habiba.

Prophet Muhammad did not marry out of personal desires; rather, he married as Allah directed him. Everything Prophet Muhammad did had a purpose and a plan from Allah.

Habiba was a sincere believer and she was the first to perform hijra (migration) for the sake of her faith. This act required her to leave her homeland and endure the hardships and loneliness of a foreign land, as her husband left her. However, she remained steadfast in her faith, which is a testament to the beauty of faith in Allah.

Abu Sufyan, a prominent figure in Mecca, and the brother of Umm Habiba, named Abdullah ibn Jahsh, also accepted Islam during the later days of the faith.

Inspired by their newfound belief, **Umm Habiba** embarked on another **hijra** (migration) to Medina, following Prophet Muhammad and the other early Muslims after her marriage to Prophet Muhammad PBUH.

This migration was a significant step towards establishing a Muslim community in Medina and escaping persecution in Mecca. Umm Habiba's journey to Medina exemplified her unwavering trust in Allah (the Arabic word for God) as Al Qadir (the All-Powerful).

It demonstrated her reliance on **Taw Akul** (placing complete trust in God) as she left behind her hometown and embraced a new life in a foreign land. While in Medina, Umm Habiba had the privilege of spending a small amount of time with Prophet Muhammad before he passed away.

During this period, she eagerly absorbed his teachings and learned about the principles of Islam. Umm Habiba's thirst for knowledge led her to not only memorize the Prophet's sayings but also write some of the hadiths (traditions and teachings of Prophet Muhammad).

Her dedication to preserving the knowledge of Islam through writing played a crucial role in transmitting the Prophet's teachings to future generations.

Allah explicitly states in the Quran that one should not merely claim to be a Muslim and assume they will not face any trials.

She also experienced the passing of Prophet Muhammad, which left her feeling lonely. She rarely left her home. One day, while she was in a carriage, an enemy approached and peered inside, describing her appearance.

He then exposed her aura. In response, she made a dua against him, being a devout woman. As a result, his hand was severed by supporters who struck him with a sword. The blow landed on his left hand and exposed his aura.

This man had violated her privacy, but Allah ensured he faced the consequences, not her. Allah safeguards both believing men and women and reveals the true nature of hypocrites.

When a believer prays for another believer, their words are heard. If there is a delay in the answer, there is a reason, and a believer should not question it, for the source is more powerful than the one who seeks.

After returning from Damascus, where she had visited her brother, she called for Aisha, the youngest wife of Prophet Muhammad and sincerely apologized if there was any tension between them.

She prayed for Aisha and expressed her desire to maintain positive relationships with everyone. Seeking to resolve any misunderstandings, she also called for **Umm Salma** and asked if there were any ill feelings.

She acknowledged that polygamy was prevalent during the time of Prophet Muhammad, but emphasized the importance of respect.

She believed that the reason for striving towards peace between oneself and their Lord was not overshadowed by any practices. This mindset reflected the strength of the believers, as their strength lies in their unity rather than their weaknesses.

She prayed for all Muslims to drink the water that Prophet Muhammad will serve to the believers in the next life. She also prayed for a pure heart (**Qalb Al Saleem**) for herself and all Muslims.

After her passing, she left behind a legacy for believers to reflect upon. Such is the way of the believers.

Prophet Muhammad's camel Qaswa and the vital roles animals play in stories:

The story of **Qaswa** highlights the importance of animals in Islam and the responsibility humans have towards them. Prophet Muhammad treated Qaswa with the utmost care and kindness, recognizing the value and contributions of animals in the world.

This story serves as a reminder to Muslims of the importance of treating animals with compassion and respect.

Besides Qaswa, the camel of prophet Muhammad other animals mentioned in Islamic literature have also played significant roles.

For instance, in the story of Prophet Solomon (Sulaiman), a bird named **Hudhud** (hoopoe) played a crucial role in bringing a message to Solomon about the queen of Sheba's idolatrous practices.

This shows that animals can be messengers and convey important information to humans.

Animals are mentioned in various instances in the Quran and Hadiths, illustrating their significance in Islamic teachings.

The ant, for example, is mentioned in the story of Solomon, where it warns other ants to retreat to their homes to avoid being trampled by Solomon's approaching army.

This story highlights the importance of unity and cooperation, even among the smallest of creatures. Allah can use the smallest creatures to show the examples that resonate with believers.

Qaswa, the camel of Prophet Muhammad, holds great significance in Islamic history and teachings. Not only was **Qaswa** known for its physical strength, but it also possessed exceptional character traits that are highly valued in Islam.

Qaswa the camel exemplifies the importance of resilience, determination, and loyalty, which are essential qualities for Muslims to emulate in their own lives.

Qaswa's unwavering support and unwavering dedication to the Prophet during critical moments, such as the migration from Mecca to Medina, showcases the importance of trust and steadfastness. He rode on **Qaswa.**

This theological context of **Qaswa's** strength and character serves as a powerful lesson for Muslims, reminding them of the need to cultivate these virtues in their own lives. It emphasizes the idea that strength of character is not limited to humans but can also be found in animals, highlighting the interconnectedness and harmony of all creation in Islam.

The camel purchased by Abu Bakr was a beautiful and strong animal, known for its endurance and speed. It had a sleek coat of brown and white, with elegant humps that stood tall and proud.

Prophet Muhammad, peace be upon him, paid a sum of four hundred dirhams to gain a camel named **Qaswa.**

However, instead of accepting it as a gift, he insisted on making the purchase. **Qaswa** was got as a young camel when he reached an age where he had to separate from his mother.

Prophet Muhammad immediately formed a strong bond with the camel, treating him with kindness and care. He would often ride on **Qaswa** during his journeys, and the camel proved to be a loyal companion, never faltering in its duty

Qaswa quickly became famous among the Muslims, admired for his strength and reliability. His name became synonymous with loyalty and steadfastness, serving as a symbol of the values upheld by the followers of Islam.

The animal purchased by Prophet Muhammad came with the name **Qaswa.** He highlighted the importance of choosing fitting names in Islam, as it is believed that a name holds great power in shaping the character and future of an individual or creature.

The prophet was often seen riding Qaswa during his journey from Mecca to Medina.

Upon the arrival in Medina, of Prophet Muhammad riding Qaswa many people rushed forward to grab the reins of Qaswa, eager to be part of this blessed event.

However, Prophet Muhammad advised them to leave **Qaswa** alone, as he said that Allah was guiding this camel. **Qaswa** eventually sat down at a particular spot, which marked the location where the beloved Masjid-e-Nabawi (Prophet's Mosque) was later constructed.

To this day, the entrance that the Imam uses to enter the mosque is at the place where **Qaswa** sat down.

This serves as a significant reminder of the historical event and symbolizes the profound connection between Prophet Muhammad, **Qaswa**, and the establishment of the Masjid-e-Nabawi. Ruqbah, from the tribe of Quraish, emerged as one of the most vehement enemies of Islam during the time of Prophet Muhammad.

Known for his extreme hostility towards the Prophet and his followers, Ruqbah resorted to despicable acts to undermine and threaten the Islamic faith. One such incident involved him throwing the entrails of an animal on the Prophet, a deeply disrespectful and offensive act.

Besides these actions, Ruqbah also composed a poem, which epitomized his antagonism towards Prophet Muhammad. The poem, directed at the Prophet, contained the lines, "Oh you who is riding on **Qaswa**, in a short period I will come with my armor and emerge victorious against the one who is riding **Qaswa**."

This poem served as a direct threat to the Prophet's life and was a manifestation of Ruqbah's determination to harm and defeat him.

The Islamic prophet faced threats from enemies, so it is not surprising that Islam and Muslims often have adversaries. Those who have no enemies may also have nothing to contribute.

The Victory of Badr was a significant battle in Islamic history that took place in the month of Ramadan in the second year of Hijrah.

The Prophet Muhammad led a small army of around 313 Muslims against a much larger force of the Quraysh tribe. During the battle, Prophet Muhammad rode on his trusted camel named **Qaswa**, which played a crucial role in the events that unfolded.

After the victory, the Prophet Muhammad, in accordance with his forgiving nature, pardoned all those who had fought against Islam except for a few individuals.

Among them were Ruqbah, Abu Jahl, and approximately 70 others who were considered the staunchest enemies of Islam. They were killed during the battle.

Zaid Ibn Haritha, a close companion of the Prophet Muhammad, was chosen to deliver the good news of the victory to the people of Mecca.

He rode on **Qaswa** and embarked on the journey, filled with excitement. However, in his enthusiasm, Zaid started chanting the names of the enemies who were defeated and killed during the Battle of Badr.

Realizing his mistake, Zaid calmed down and delivered the full story of the battle and the victory to the people of Mecca. His narration of the events led many people to embrace the triumph and acknowledge the power of Islam.

Another incident involving **Qaswa** occurred when bandits stole the camel along with a Muslim woman who was riding it. However, during the night, the woman managed to free herself and heard the other animals refusing to let her ride on them. **Qaswa**, however, allowed her to ride back to safety.

Grateful for her escape, the woman made a vow to Allah that she would slaughter the animal in His name and distribute its meat to those in need. When she later discovered that **Qaswa** belonged to Prophet Muhammad, she informed him of her promise.

The Prophet, known for his sense of humor, playfully remarked that she wanted to kill the very animal that had aided her in her escape.

However, he then explained that a promise could only be made with something one owns and that she could not carry out her vow as **Qaswa** did not belong to her. This incident is documented in **Sahih Hadith**, emphasizing the importance of fulfilling promises and respecting the ownership of others.

Qaswa, the cherished racing camel of Prophet Muhammad, gained fame not only for his swiftness and grace but also for his unwavering devotion to the Prophet.

Qaswa's loss in the race not only saddened the people but also deeply upset them, as they viewed her as a representation of the Prophet's integrity and love. Prophet Muhammad provided solace to the people by reminding them it is Allah who gives abilities and achievements upon individuals and creatures.

He highlighted the fact that it is solely Allah's prerogative to withdraw these blessings. The recognition of this brought solace to the hearts filled with sorrow, as it reminded them that nobody's status or triumphs are assured, and in the end, everything is owned by Allah.

Qaswa's defeat in the race was a powerful reminder to the people that true greatness and respect come from acknowledging and submitting to the supreme authority of Allah.

The narration of **Qaswa**, the beloved camel of Prophet Muhammad, holds significant lessons for Muslims. When **Qaswa** went missing, Prophet Muhammad sent people to search for him, demonstrating his concern for his camel.

However, his enemies used this opportunity to mock him, questioning how he could claim to deliver Allah's word while not knowing the whereabouts of his own animal.

In response, the **angel Jibril** appeared to the Prophet and informed him that **Qaswa** was stuck in the rain, unable to free himself from his harness.

This incident highlighted the Prophet's reliance on Allah's guidance and the fact that he only knew what Allah revealed to him.

Another instance where **Qaswa** played a significant role was during the **Treaty of Hudaibiya. Qaswa** sat down, causing frustration and annoyance among the people.

Little did they know that this was a sign from Allah, as the treaty was about to be established.

It was during this time that the Quranic revelations, including Surah Al-Fath (The Victory) and **Surah Al-Maidah** (The Table Spread), were received by the Prophet on Qaswa. The power and strength of these revelations were so profound that even **Qaswa**, the humble camel, responded to them by sitting down.

The impact of these revelations and the beauty of the Quran are still felt by Muslims today. When reading the Quran, believers often tremble, their hearts soften, and their eyes tear up. This is a testament to the profound faith and connection to Allah that the Quran instills within them.

Prophet Muhammad's return to Mecca after the victories of the Muslims serves as a reminder of the numerous battles, hardships, and oppression that they faced. Despite these challenges, the Muslims emerged victorious, and their success was attributed to their unwavering faith in Allah.

The Prophet displayed a humble demeanor as he rode on **Qaswa**, his head bowed down in humility to Allah. With gratitude for the triumphs and unity of the Muslim community, he returned to Mecca victorious.

Even in this moment of triumph, the Prophet showed no arrogance, keeping his head bowed low on Qaswa. As a sign of victory, the Muslims chanted "Allah Hu Akbar takbir," while Mecca was filled with the genuine belief that enveloped the city in a symphony of sounds.

In times of victory, it is often pride that takes over, but not for the Prophet.

It is crucial for Muslims to understand the history and teachings of Islam to resist the allure of Western culture and its false promises of independence. In this battle against external and internal challenges, Muslims face the constant temptation to indulge in worldly desires and deviate from the path prescribed by Allah.

The struggle is not just about resisting external influences that may lead them astray, but also about conquering their own inner struggles and desires.

By adhering to the teachings of the Quran and following the commandments of Allah, Muslims find the strength and guidance to overcome these obstacles. The Quran serves as a source of inspiration, providing Muslims with the wisdom and clarity needed to navigate through life's challenges.

It reminds them of the consequences of deviating from the path of righteousness and encourages them to seek forgiveness and repentance

Prophet Muhammad's first **Umrah Tawaf and Hajj Atul Wida** took place in the month of Dhu al-Qi'dah in the 8th year of the Hijra (630 CE). The Prophet and his followers had faced many challenges and opposition throughout their journey to spread the message of Islam.

This pilgrimage was a momentous occasion as it marked the first time the Prophet could perform the rituals of Umrah in the sacred city of Mecca since the migration from Mecca to Medina.

The presence of both believers and **mushrikun**, or polytheists, during this pilgrimage was significant. This pilgrimage became an important milestone in the history of Islam.

From this year onwards, entry to the Ka'ba was restricted to Muslims only. When the prophet touched the idols on **Qaswa**, they all crumbled to pieces. Islam unequivocally affirms its monotheistic beliefs and firmly rejects the presence of idols within its religious framework.

One of the most remarkable aspects of this pilgrimage was the fact that the Prophet performed it on **Qaswa**, his beloved camel. Qaswa had been with the Prophet on various expeditions and journeys, and it held great sentimental value to him.

The choice to perform his first and final pilgrimage on Qaswa further added to the significance of the event.

The pilgrimage, known as **Hajj Atul Wida** or the **Farewell Pilgrimage**, was a farewell to the sacred city of Mecca and the last pilgrimage performed by the Prophet. During this pilgrimage, the Prophet delivered his famous sermon at Mount Arafat, where he emphasized the importance of unity, equality, and justice among the believers.

This sermon, known as the Farewell Sermon, contained profound guidance and teachings that continue to resonate with Muslims to this day.

Abu Bakr, known for his unwavering loyalty and dedication to Prophet Muhammad, was chosen to convey the message of victory and propagate Islam following the Battle of Hunayn.

However, as he witnessed Ali, the beloved son-in-law of Prophet Muhammad, riding on **Qaswa,** the Prophet's cherished camel, he was taken aback and began to doubt his position.

Concerned that he might be replaced, Abu Bakr yearned for clarification. In response, he was instructed to publicly recite Surah Taubah, a chapter from the Quran that emphasized the core principles of unity, loyalty, and unwavering commitment to Islam.

By reciting this powerful surah, Abu Bakr's doubts were dispelled, and his faith in his role as a trusted companion of the Prophet was reaffirmed.

In his final days, Prophet Muhammad delivered a sermon and recited Surah An-Nasr (Iza Jaa Nasirul Lahi Wal Fath) which translates to "When the victory of Allah has come and the conquest, and you see the people entering into the religion of Allah in multitudes."

This sermon indicated that his time on Earth was coming to an end, as he knew he had only a few weeks left to live.

Following the passing away of Prophet Muhammad, Qaswa, his loyal camel, was deeply affected. Qaswa cried so much that he eventually went blind and stopped eating. After a month, he passed away, symbolizing the profound bond between the Prophet and his faithful companion.

In this story, the importance of both humans and creatures is emphasized, as they are valued and significant to Allah. It is the duty of individuals to acknowledge and value this importance.

These stories act as valuable lessons that can improve and enrich the lives of those who genuinely comprehend and appreciate their teachings. Muslims have always displayed immense strength and resilience in the face challenges. They have never been hesitant to share their skills and knowledge with the world, contributing to various fields.

These stories are not just simple deliveries; they are profound truths and compelling examples that we should contemplate. If the Quran was not important, Allah would not have revealed it.

This book has the power to bring about change, yet it remains preserved, allowing us to learn from the stories and examples it contains, regardless of the decade.

It is important to note that Muslims did not originally use a beverage like coffee to gain energy from caffeine to start their day. Instead, it was used to stay awake during prayer, as their devotion to Allah took precedence over sleep.

Coffee, a popular beverage enjoyed by people all over the world, has a rich history with its origins rooted in the Muslim world. The discovery of coffee can be attributed to the Muslims, specifically in the 9th century.

Legend has it that a Yemeni shepherd noticed his goats became more energetic and alert after consuming the berries from a certain tree.

Intrigued, he shared this observation with the local monks, who then began experimenting with the berries. They soon discovered that by roasting and grinding them, they could create a flavorful and stimulating drink.

This discovery spread throughout the Muslim world, and coffeehouses became popular gathering places for scholars, intellectuals, and traders.

From there, coffee made its way to Europe and the rest of the world, becoming an integral part of many cultures and lifestyles. So, it is evident that Muslims played a significant role in introducing coffee to the world and shaping its global popularity.

The tradition of using coffee to stay awake for prayer and devotion to Allah originated in the Muslim world. The practice of drinking black coffee with cubes of sugar, known as Qahwah, became popular among Muslims.

This unique way of consuming coffee was later adapted by the Western society and became known as espresso. However, it is important to note that the contributions of Muslims extend beyond coffee.

Coffee has gained attention for its potential to aid in weight loss and boost metabolism. Several studies have suggested that caffeine, a key component of coffee, can stimulate the central nervous system and increase thermogenesis, leading to a higher calorie expenditure.

Coffee has been found to suppress appetite and improve fat oxidation, making it a popular choice among those trying to shed extra pounds. However, it is important to note that the effects of coffee on weight loss may vary among individuals and should be combined with a balanced diet and regular exercise for optimal results.

Islam emphasizes the importance of moderation in all aspects of life, including food consumption.

Prophet Muhammad set an example by advising his followers to fill their stomachs with one-third of food, one-third with water, and leave one-third empty for easier digestion.

Mediterranean diet is suited best for health.

In contrast to countries that promote the use of hormones and inhumane methods for slaughtering animals to meet the demands of their excessive population, Islam promotes a different approach.

Islam emphasizes the importance of consuming halal meat, which refers to food that is prepared in a permissible manner according to Islamic law.

The halal way of killing an animal involves ensuring that it is healthy and fit for consumption, rather than being sick or older.

This not only ensures the quality and safety of the meat but also takes into consideration the welfare and ethical treatment of the animal. Islamic teachings emphasize the need for mercy and compassion towards all creatures, including animals, and encourage the preservation of their well-being throughout the entire process of slaughter.

The blood suppression inside the body of the animal during the halal slaughter is done swiftly and skillfully, minimizing any suffering or pain experienced by the animal. This approach to slaughter aligns with Islamic principles of ensuring the health and well-being of both humans and animals.

The consumption of halal meat has gained popularity among individuals who have realized the negative health effects associated with the consumption of hormone-treated and artificially preserved food products.

Many countries with beautifully stocked shelves of food products often contain hidden dangers as hormones and artificial preservatives. As a result, maintaining a healthy diet in such countries can be more expensive than opting for unhealthy alternatives.

It is easy to observe that certain populations in these countries are facing widespread health issues, despite being considered well-off. The prevalence of health, depression and various diseases among these populations shows the detrimental effects of consuming unhealthy food.

Those who realize the detrimental effects of unhealthy lifestyles and eating habits on their overall well-being often seek ways to change and alter their habits.

Many individuals find solace and guidance in Islam, as it emphasizes the importance of maintaining a healthy body and mind.

However, merely adopting Islam is not sufficient; it is crucial to actively follow the teachings and principles of the faith.

Taking positive steps towards a healthier lifestyle, such as incorporating regular exercise, consuming nutritious foods, and seeking mental wellness, is essential for long-term change.

Prophet Muhammad promoted engagement in various physical activities to maintain a healthy lifestyle.

Swimming was one sport that he specifically mentioned. Muhammad peace up upon him identified swimming as a one-of-a-kind sport that requires the coordinated movement of every body part, making it an exceptional activity for improving overall fitness.

He emphasized the importance of maintaining one's physical well-being and encouraged his followers to swim regularly to stay active and maintain good health.

Prophet Muhammad's encouragement emphasizes the importance of swimming as a well-rounded activity that promotes physical and mental well-being.

Not only did he swim and walk extensively, but he also refrained from asking his followers to do anything he himself didn't do to enhance their physical and spiritual lives.

While expansion and conflicts occurred, they were driven by a desire to defend their faith and protect themselves from persecution, rather than a greed-driven agenda to seize what did not rightfully belong to them.

It is important to recognize the complex history of Muslim countries under Ottoman rule, where periods of prosperity and cultural exchange coexisted with external pressures and conflicts.

The recent destruction and chaos witnessed can be attributed to the interference and greed of external powers. The Mediterranean diet, followed by Muslims, expanded as

Muslim rule extended to countries that later took back territories, such as Spain, Portugal, and Europe.

The empire of Muslims spread across various regions, including North Africa, the Middle East, and parts of Europe, during the medieval period.

This expansion facilitated the dissemination of the Mediterranean diet, which is characterized by a high consumption of fruits, vegetables, whole grains, legumes, and olive oil, along with moderate intake of fish, poultry, and dairy products.

The Muslim influence in these territories left a lasting impact on their culinary traditions, incorporating flavors, ingredients, and cooking techniques from the Mediterranean diet into their own cuisines.

This cultural exchange contributed to the diversity and richness of the culinary heritage in Spain, Portugal, and other European countries.

Had Muslim rule continued, the region may have experienced less chaos and destruction. However, the greed of the Romans and subsequent colonial powers led to the devastation of many Muslim lands.

These actions resulted in the formation of newer countries, some of which are less than three hundred years old, and they continue to perpetuate damage and pollution in these areas.

The consequences of excessive urbanization and deforestation have taken a toll on the environment, causing suffering for trees and animals. As habitats are destroyed to make way for buildings, animals are left without proper residences.

There are instances where historical structures from the Golden Age of Islam and even from the time of Prophet Muhammad have been destroyed or damaged by both natural and human causes.

During the time of Prophet Muhammad, the Muslims faced intense persecution from the non-believers in Mecca. Prophet Muhammad himself suffered immense losses, including the death of his beloved wife, Khadijah and his uncle Abu Talib.

However, he remained steadfast in his mission and never wavered in spreading the message of Islam.

Omar bin Khattab also displayed immense generosity by providing pensions to the wives of Prophet Muhammad, setting a precedent that was later adopted by Western societies.

This text emphasizes the important role of pensions in Islam and how it influenced western cultures and the rest of the world. Islam was the first Omar bin Khattab to implement pensions, which had a lasting impact.

Without Islam, the world would still be in the dark ages. Even those who are unfamiliar with Islam may think they are modern, but they are actually still stuck in the dark ages. Islam emerged from the dark ages 600 years ago, and it is not just the advancements in technology that determine modernity. Rather, it is the continuous pursuit of knowledge and progress that defines a modern society.

However, despite the success of the Muslim empire, there have always been individuals within the Muslim community who lack knowledge and understanding of their faith.

Ignorance and jealousy can often overshadow the true teachings of Islam, and it is crucial for Muslims to continuously seek knowledge and understand the principles and values that their faith upholds.

This loss of cultural and historical heritage is a matter of concern and highlights the need for preservation and conservation efforts.

They have made significant contributions to various aspects of life, including the establishment of the world's first university. The University of al-Qarawiyyin, founded in Fez, Morocco in 859 CE, is recognized as the oldest existing degree-granting university in the world.

Muslims have also enriched the world with their culinary delicacies, art, literature, and scientific advancements throughout history. In Islam, philanthropy is not limited to Muslims alone. It is a universal concept that encourages individuals, regardless of their religious beliefs, to contribute to the betterment of society.

However, for the best use of one's wealth, Islam emphasizes the importance of earning money through lawful means and using it in ways that align with Islamic principles.

This means that the revenue generated from spreading and promoting knowledge about Islam holds a special significance. Such funds are clean, as they are earned with honesty and integrity, with no boundaries or falsehood.

In Islam, giving is a means of receiving blessings and rewards from Allah.

Zakat, which is one of the five pillars of Islam, is a compulsory form of giving that involves donating **2.5%** of one's wealth to those in need.

However, it is important to note that Zakat is only required from those who can afford it, ensuring that the burden of giving is not placed on those who are struggling financially.

This aspect of Islam highlights its fairness and consideration for the well-being of its followers.

In contrast, other Abrahamic faiths may have novel concepts and practices regarding giving and charity, as they may not have the same specific guidelines and requirements as Zakat in Islam.

If Allah desired a single religion, He would have imposed it forcefully. However, choices in this world enable believers in the God of Adam and Eve, the first creation and the father of all Abrahamic faiths, to comprehend that nothing has changed.

Religions may emerge and disappear, but Islam will remain unaltered as it represents the religion of the original creation and serves as the last revelation for humanity.

However, Christian-based countries supporting those who engage in violence against individuals such as in Palestine, is a complex and controversial issue.

The situation in Palestine, particularly regarding the coexistence of Christians and Muslims, is not controversial; lies and misinformation are propagated. But Islam has co-existed with all Abrahamic faiths in peace with Muslim rulers.

The rule of non-Muslims has fueled the factional separation between faiths and chaos in the Middle East. It has led to the dismantling of homes, the separation of friendships, and the emergence of evil that was absent during the Muslim regime when Muslims ruled Israel.

It's truly unfortunate that Muslim countries don't unite to help the world. Instead, the temptation of greed and glamor often corrupts even the most well-intentioned individuals. However, if they were to come to a mutual understanding within themselves, they have the power to positively impact global issues.

True peace existed back then, and nothing will change until the Muslim rule gains strength, not to mistreat those who mistreated them, but to show the duality and choices that Allah has presented, which cannot be taken away.

It is up to each individual to discern between right and wrong, and destiny has already been planned. In the end, only the righteous will possess the lands of Allah.

This apparent lengthy chaos will only change according to the timing set by Allah, when Muslims redirect their path towards the formidable truth taught by Prophet Muhammad, instead of falling into the trap of worldly allure.

Muslims must remain steadfast in understanding that this world is only temporary.

However, if the truth is upheld and factual information is shared, there should be no room for controversy. It is important to recognize that a significant portion of both Christian and Muslim communities reside in Palestine, and their well-being and help in times of need should be a matter of concern for all.

This is not a matter of conjecture, but a call for empathy and support for those who are facing difficult circumstances. It is crucial to promote understanding, dialogue, and humanitarian aid in order to help alleviate the hardships faced by the people of Palestine, regardless of their religious affiliation.

It is also worth mentioning that different Christian denominations and individuals hold varying views on the Israeli-Palestinian conflict.

Some Christians advocate for peaceful coexistence and support efforts to find a just resolution, while others may have different perspectives shaped by their political, cultural, or theological understandings.

Islam is a religion that emphasizes the principles of justice, dignity, and the preservation of justice for all of humanity, regardless of whether they are Muslim or non-Muslim. In Islam, it is not only encouraged but also mandated to stand against oneself and speak the truth, even if it is against one's own interests.

The concept of justice in Islam surpasses religious boundaries and is rooted in the teachings of the Quran. Muslims are called upon to be just and fair to all of humanity, irrespective of their race, ethnicity, or religious beliefs.

Islam promotes equality and fairness, and it rejects any form of discrimination or prejudice based on religion or any other factor. Therefore, Muslims are guided to treat all individuals with justice and respect, recognizing their common humanity and inherent dignity.

Islam promotes the idea of using one's skills and knowledge to generate wealth and contribute to philanthropic causes and earnings. The exchange of resources and expertise in this manner benefits all parties involved, creating a fruitful and harmonious environment for everyone.

The exception of giving is indeed a complex concept that extends beyond the realm of traditional notions of good and evil.

While some individuals, particularly musicians associated with satanic imagery, themes, and music that arouses many use their talent and influence to spread messages that may have negative consequences, it is crucial to acknowledge that even in these situations, giving still occurs.

However, it is important to remember that their giving is driven by self-serving agendas and aims to promote the evil they believe in. Those who believe in their creator, Allah, understand that every act of giving holds value and cannot be diminished, whether it is as revenue, knowledge, a smile, or a kind word.

These musicians give their time, energy, and creativity to create art that resonates with certain audiences. However, the impact of their message can be controversial and potentially harmful, leading some listeners down destructive paths, such as drug overdose or self-destructive behavior.

In regions that claim independence, the struggle for self-determination often involves a battle against societal norms and moral expectations.

People in these regions may prioritize their personal desires and lifestyles over traditional morality, not seeking solace and forgiveness through religious beliefs.

According to a recent German study, which adds to the existing body of literature on the topic, it has been reaffirmed that Muslims are the most satisfied with their lives. The study highlights that this high level of satisfaction is primarily attributed to their firm sense of "oneness."

Muslims often experience a profound connection with their faith, community, and a higher power, which contributes significantly to their overall well-being.

This feeling of oneness provides them with a sense of purpose, belonging, and inner peace, leading to a higher level of life satisfaction compared to other religious or non-religious groups.

The study's findings shed light on the positive psychological impact that religious practices and beliefs can have on individuals' overall happiness and contentment.

In Western societies, the emphasis on sexuality as a force of love and the promotion of expressing oneself and physically engaging in relationships are widely accepted norms. Spreading like wild fire.

However, this perspective on intimacy and relationships can create challenges for individuals who follow the teachings of Islam.

For young Muslims who are exploring their identities and seeking meaningful connections, the prevalent culture of casual relationships and frequent breakups can be disheartening.

Many find themselves feeling empty and unfulfilled after going through multiple failed relationships. Some may even choose to enter into official relationships out of a sense of rebellion or defiance towards Allah, which only serves as a constant reminder of their internal conflict between their desires and their religious beliefs.

This struggle highlights the difficulty faced by Muslims who strive to practice Islam while navigating a society that often undermines their values and ideals.

There is no denying that temptation exists in all aspects of life, regardless of age or sexuality. Attractions and desires have often been the cause of many struggles that individuals try to resist.

However, in today's Western society and in many societies where acceptance of various human behaviors is prevalent, the idea of giving in to these temptations has become more prevalent.

This can sometimes oversimplify matters that do not align with the teachings of Islam.

Islam places a strong emphasis on maintaining self-restraint and adhering to moral guidelines, which may not always align with the prevailing attitudes and values in modern society. As a result, individuals who follow Islam may face additional challenges in resisting these temptations and staying true to their faith.

However, it is important to recognize that each individual's journey is unique, and finding a balance between societal acceptance and religious values is a personal struggle that many Muslims face.

Alcohol consumption and the desire to fit into society can create a sense of apprehension for individuals seeking societal acceptance. The pressure to conform to societal norms and expectations often leads people to prioritize fitting in over challenging established rules.

For many years, alcohol was widely accepted and permissible in various cultures. However, in Islam, there came a point where a complete halt was put on the consumption of alcohol. This decision was made in order to simplify cognitive behavior and prevent the defiance of Islamic teachings regarding alcohol.

Alcohol is a potent drink created from the fermentation of various substances, such as grains or fruits. While it is widely consumed and enjoyed by many, it is important to acknowledge the potential destructive effects it can have on the brain.

The damage caused by alcohol cannot be simplified, as it affects different individuals in various ways. Human behavior undergoes significant changes after alcohol consumption, impairing judgment, coordination, and cognitive function.

Prolonged and excessive alcohol consumption can lead to serious brain damage, including memory loss, reduced cognitive abilities, and even neurological disorders such as Wernicke-Korsakoff syndrome.

It is crucial to understand the complexities and risks associated with alcohol consumption to make informed decisions about its use.

Alcohol consumption has been a topic of debate in various societies and religions. In Islam, the prohibition of alcohol is a command from Allah to protect humanity from harm.

While some may argue that Allah gains nothing from stopping humanity from consuming alcohol, it is important to understand the underlying reasons behind this prohibition.

First, Allah, being the creator of humanity, knows what is beneficial and what is harmful for His creation. Alcohol has been proven to have detrimental effects on both the brain and behavior.

Excessive alcohol consumption can lead to a range of health issues, including liver disease, cardiovascular problems, and addiction. Long-term alcohol use has been linked to the development of Alzheimer's disease, as it destroys brain cells and contributes to memory loss.

Celebrations in societies that do not follow Islam often involve the consumption of alcohol. These celebrations are often seen as defiance against Allah's teachings.

By abstaining from alcohol, Muslims aim to maintain their spiritual and moral integrity, avoiding the pitfalls that excessive drinking can lead to, such as impaired judgment, violence, and other negative consequences.

It is important to note that warnings against alcohol are not meant for all individuals, as some may have the knowledge and understanding to make informed decisions about their consumption.

However, the prohibition serves as a reminder for those who may be prone to the harmful effects of alcohol or who may be easily swayed by societal pressures.

In summary, the prohibition of alcohol in Islam is not about Allah gaining anything, but about protecting humanity from harm.

It is a command based on the understanding of what is productive for human survival and the potential damage that alcohol can cause to the brain, demeanor, and overall well-being.

By adhering to this prohibition, most Muslims strive to maintain their physical, mental, and spiritual health, while also upholding their commitment to Allah's teachings.

Jesus drank wine, and bread in the Bible is not part of the Quran. If Jesus was drinking wine, then why did Allah forbid wine in the Bible remains a logical question.

Most devout Christians don't drink wine or any alcohol, clearly stating the Bible forbids it. The mixed beliefs can concoct to the brain. Islam clearly rejects the consumption of alcohol.

Quran: Surah Baqarah: 2:219. They ask you about wine and gambling. Say, "In them is great sin and [yet, some] benefit for people. But their sin is greater than their benefit."

In the Quran, alcohol is entirely prohibited, even though people used to drink it. The Quran marked the declaration of things that were previously not strongly rejected as impermissible.

Therefore, when imparting knowledge and providing materials, a positive and meaningful approach is essential. It is crucial for readers to comprehend the delivery, and for recipients to utilize the materials in ways that benefit themselves and others.

It is crucial to understand that the act of giving itself is not limited to positive or negative intentions. The distribution of ideas and influences, whether they are beneficial or detrimental, can still be seen as giving.

The key lies in discerning the difference between just causes and the spread of evil. Those who possess a keen awareness can distinguish between messages that contribute to the betterment of society and those that perpetuate harm.

Ultimately, the exception of giving challenges us to critically analyze the intentions and consequences behind the actions of individuals, even when their contributions may be controversial or negative.

By understanding the complex nature of giving, we can become more discerning consumers of ideas and influences, making conscious choices that align with our own values and contribute positively to the world.

Gift giving is deeply ingrained in Muslim culture and holds great significance. Muslims view it to show appreciation, mend relationships, and express love and gratitude towards one another.

The practice of gift giving has its roots in the teachings and actions of Prophet Muhammad. He sent gifts to people, including dates, grains, and meat, as a gesture of kindness and goodwill.

These gifts were gladly accepted by those who received them, as they symbolized the Prophet's care and concern for others. Inspired by his example, Muslims continue to exchange gifts on various occasions, such as Eid, weddings, and other special events, fostering bonds of friendship and strengthening social connections within the community.

The Satan, also known as **Iblis**, is a Jinn created out of fire. His goal is to lead people astray and distance them from receiving blessings and guidance that would be beneficial to their lives. He employs various tactics to deceive individuals, particularly those who claim to be believers.

His cunning nature allows him to manipulate their thoughts and beliefs, making them believe they are on the right path while subtly steering them towards destruction.

Muslims, like any other human beings, are not exempt from making mistakes. However, what sets them apart is their awareness of these mishaps and their commitment to repentance. They understand that their faith is a lifelong journey, and that they may stumble along the way.

Yet, they strive to learn from their errors and seek forgiveness from Allah. Instead of forming a council of Allah, some individuals choose to live in doubt, questioning the teachings of Islam and finding flaws in Muslims.

They cannot comprehend the chaos that emanates from their own disbelief and instead succumb to the temptations of evil, often driven by Satanic invitations.

It is crucial to recognize that Muslims are not perfect, but their faith guides them to acknowledge their mistakes and work towards rectifying them, ultimately seeking a closer connection with Allah.

In Islam, believers are encouraged to have compassion, understanding, and forgiveness towards one another. It is believed that Satan, or Shaytan, seeks to create division and discord among Muslims by constantly reminding them of their mistakes or flaws.

However, a genuine believer who is knowledgeable about Islam would not engage in this behavior. Instead, they would strive to remind their fellow Muslims of the teachings of Islam in a gentle and respectful manner, intending to guide them back to the right path.

It is important to differentiate between genuine reminders that come from a place of sincere concern and those that should belittle or harm others.

The negative forces of the satanic cult undoubtedly influenced the latter, which seeks to sow seeds of doubt and discord within the Muslim community.

In Islam, the approach to reflecting on others differs from that of Christianity. While Christians often use rhetoric spreaders to convey the message of Jesus's love and forgiveness, Muslims do not have a similar practice for Prophet Muhammad or Allah.

The concept of forgiveness in Islam is deeply personal and between an individual and Allah. It is believed that only Allah knows who is truly forgiven, and seeking repentance is a fundamental requirement in Islam.

Reminding others of their past mistakes or spreading gossip is strongly discouraged in Islam, as it goes against the principles of unity, forgiveness, and respect for one another.

Muslims are encouraged to focus on their own actions, seek forgiveness from Allah, and no judge or gossiping about others.

In the eyes of those who perceive life as a mere illusion and a test, the transient nature of this world becomes clear. They believe that those who consider worldly pursuits as the goal are misguided and caught up in the trivialities of existence.

Some individuals, as they grow older, become more entrenched in their negative behaviors, while others undergo a transformation after enduring the trials and tribulations of their youth.

Within the depths of the soul lies the genuine dilemma of human personality, as the battle between good and evil, faith and doubt, rages on.

The current state of society, particularly in Western regions, is disconcerting for those who observe a shift towards secularism. The erosion of moral values that once held faith communities together is a cause for concern.

The erosion and false belief that westernization grants independence and that Islam conforms to it is untrue.

Contrary to this notion, the rates of depression and suicide are higher in societies that promote false individualism, where even movie stars and the wealthy have taken their own lives.

This widespread rhetoric has permeated throughout the world, leading many to believe that Islam was forced upon them during childhood, causing them to rebel and do the opposite.

However, in Islam, there are rules and parents are instructed to guide and direct their children, rather than leaving them to decide on their own. If despite this guidance, individuals go astray, then no parent can be held responsible as it is considered their destiny in Islam.

It is still a question why the laws created by humans are mandatory from childhood, while the laws of gods are burdensome in a world filled with conflict.

Bible: NIV: John 16:11. New International Version... and about judgment, because the prince of this world now stands condemned.

The Quran never refers to Satan as the Prince of the world. Only Allah granted Satan's request to deceive the humanity he created. Allah trusted the believers and established repentance.

Believers in Satan's deception are weak, mirroring his weakness. Satan lacks both princely status and power. He doesn't reign over this world, as Allah, according to Islam, possesses dominion over the present and future.

Quran: Surah Nisa: 4:76. Those who believe do battle for the cause of Allah; and those who disbelieve do battle for the cause of idols. So, fight the minions of the devil. Lo! the devil's strategy is ever weak.

In the realm of Christianity, it is believed that Satan was appointed as the ruler and king of this world.

Islam rejects this idea and encourages believers to understand that Satan is weak and incapable of imposing his beliefs on them. The whispers of Satan hold no power over a steadfast believer who knows the truth.

This deliberate distortion is akin to the plot of Satan, as he knows that if he were to only tell outright lies, no one would believe him. However, by mixing truth with falsehood, he can sow confusion and mislead people who lack a proper understanding of Islam.

Therefore, it is the responsibility of knowledgeable Muslims to diligently educate the masses and counter the continuous spread of misinformation and ignorance.

This epidemic of ignorance must be addressed and countered to prevent its contamination of society at large.

The symbolism of Islam is indeed powerful, as it emphasizes the concept of monotheism, which is deeply ingrained in human nature.

Continual mistakes and flaws do not negate one's belief, as faith is an ongoing process. It is crucial to foster a supportive environment that encourages learning, growth, and understanding, rather than focusing on the shortcomings of others.

Ultimately, the belief and practice of Islam should be a personal and continuous journey towards strengthening one's faith.

In Islam, there is a deep understanding of the power of humility and the dangers of pride.

The teachings of the religion emphasize the importance of remaining humble and recognizing our own shortcomings. This is often exemplified through stories and parables that warn against the perils of arrogance.

One such story is that of the Pharaoh in ancient Egypt. Despite his great power and achievements, his arrogance and refusal to acknowledge the existence of a higher power led to his downfall. His end was far worse than his beginning, as he suffered divine punishment and was ultimately defeated.

This story serves as a reminder that pride and arrogance can lead to one's downfall, while humility and recognition of one's mistakes can lead to personal growth and spiritual enlightenment.

While communal support and facilities can provide a supportive environment for individuals to strengthen their faith and seek guidance, they are not meant to create dependency or reliance on human beings or institutions.

The emphasis is on personal responsibility and accountability to Allah.

There may be individuals who, out of jealousy or insecurity, may accuse and insult others who are striving to live according to Islamic principles. However, it is important for believers to remain steadfast in their faith and not be swayed by such negative influences.

Islam teaches that breaking rules and indulging in sinful behavior is not a sign of independence, but a deviation from the path of righteousness.

The role of Satan, known as Shaytan in Islam, is to tempt and mislead individuals away from the straight path, but it is the responsibility of believers to resist his influence and seek refuge in Allah's protection.

In Christianity, the role of Satan is often seen as a fallen angel who tempts individuals to sin and opposes God's will.

While there may be differences in the interpretations of Satan's role between Islam and Christianity, both religions emphasize the importance of resisting evil and seeking guidance from a higher power to overcome challenges and maintain spiritual well-being.

The Quran offers a unique perspective on **Shaytan,** unlike any other religious text. It details the reason **Shaytan,** a Jinn, was permitted to mislead humanity: his unwavering devotion and worship of Allah.

His arrogance led to his downfall. Allah recognizes those who are familiar with Shaytan will recognize his deception.

However, his pride and arrogance led him to disobey Allah's command and refuse to bow before Adam. He became the embodiment of evil and temptation, constantly luring humans towards sin and misguidance.

The role of Jinn in this world and the next is explained in Islamic teachings.

Jinn, like humans, can choose between good and evil. They coexist with humans on earth and can influence their actions, either positively or negatively.

Jinn are believed to possess various powers and abilities, including the ability to shape-shift, possess individuals, and communicate with humans through mediums.

In the hereafter the Jinn will be held accountable for their actions, just like humans. They will face the consequences of their choices and be judged accordingly.

Quran: Surah Fatir: 35:6. Indeed, Satan is an enemy to you, so take him as an enemy. He only invites his party to be among the companions of the blaze.

In Islam, the companions of evil are known as Shaya teen or devils. They constantly seek to exploit the weaknesses or flaws of believers, enticing them to turn away from righteousness and follow their path.

These whispers of evil are often loud and recognizable to a true believer, as they go against the teachings of Islam.

It is important to note that in Islam, Allah is all-knowing and understands the struggles and temptations faced by humans. However, this does not mean that committing sins is justified or permissible.

Islam teaches that believers should strive to resist the temptations of Shaya teen and maintain their faith and righteousness.

Bible NIV: Timothy 6:10. For the love of money is a root of all kinds of evil. Some people, eager for money, have wandered from the faith and pierced themselves with many griefs.

This verse emphasizes the dangers of greed and the negative consequences that can arise from an excessive attachment to wealth.

Quran: Surah Baqarah: 2:177.Righteousness is not that you turn your faces toward the east or the west, but [true] righteousness is [in] one who believes in Allah , the Last Day, the angels, the Book, and the prophets and gives wealth, in spite of love for it, to relatives, orphans, the needy, the traveler, those who ask [for help], and for freeing slaves; [and who] establishes prayer and gives Zakah; [those who] fulfill their promise when they promise; and [those who] are patient in poverty and hardship and during battle. Those are the ones who have been true, and it is those who are the righteous.

Islam has a different perspective on money. While it acknowledges the potential for greed and the misuse of wealth, Islam does not consider money inherently evil.

In fact, Islam encourages believers to strive for financial success and prosperity through lawful means.

Both the receiver and the giver depend ultimately on Allah's will. It is crucial to cultivate gratitude and appreciation for the opportunity to give, as it is through this act of selflessness that we can truly understand the beauty of giving with no expectations.

The stories in the Quran serve not only as moral lessons but also as historical accounts. One such example is the story of Pharaoh and his wealth.

The Quran describes the immense riches and opulence of Pharaoh, which cannot be compared to the regimes of today. These stories provide a visual representation of the past, allowing us to understand the magnitude of the wealth and power that existed during that time.

Those who have traveled to Egypt can witness the remnants of this history firsthand. The pyramids, museums, and ancient buildings serve as tangible reminders of the wealth that once belonged to Pharaoh.

Only by understanding the deeper complexities of power and injustice can we work towards a more equitable and just society.

Bible Gateway: Exodus: 2:11:15. Moses Commits Murder and Flees to Midian - In the course of time Moses grew up. Then he went to ⌊ see ⌋ his own people and watched them suffering under.

Bible NIV: Deuteronomy: 19:11-13. But if out of hate someone lies in wait, assaults and kills a neighbor, and then flees to one of these cities, the killer shall be sent for by the town elders, be brought back from the city, and be handed over to the avenger of blood to die. Show no pity. You must purge from Israel the guilt of shedding innocent blood, so that it may go well with you.

Bible NIV: Exodus. 2:1:12.One day, after Moses had grown up, he went out to where his own people were and watched them at their hard labor. He saw an Egyptian beating a Hebrew, one of his own people. Looking this way and that and seeing no one, he killed the Egyptian and hid him in the sand.

The storyline of most prophets in the Bible and the Quran differs drastically, making it impossible to believe prophets who are portrayed as murderers or lacking in character. When the credibility of these stories is tested, belief becomes slim.

Quran: Surah Fus Silat: 41:34. and who gave you all you asked for. Were you to count the favors of Allah you shall never be able to encompass them. Verily man is highly unjust, exceedingly ungrateful.

Accepting the ten commandments from a murderer would be extremely difficult, especially since murderers are not even accepted in this world, let alone as prophets.

Blaming and constantly finding flaws is a habit of those who blame. Islam views Moses differently, highlighting the prophet's strength and the forgiveness granted by Allah for the person who unintentionally caused his death

He not only forgave him but also elevated him to a high position and spoke to him personally.

Humans have tampered with the Bible, causing an ongoing clash between its followers and those who wish to challenge its restrictions. The fight for freedom has expanded to include the propagation of Islam, a belief system that is unfamiliar to many.

It is important to remember that Christianity, too, emerged from Judaism and underwent various reforms and modifications.

Islam has less compatibility between the ideologies of Judaism or Christianity. The reason the term "Abrahamic faiths" is used is because of their shared prophets, although the Quran depicts these prophets' stories in unique ways.

Some Muslims and individuals who lack knowledge mistakenly believe that all religions are identical, but this is not true.

The emergence of Islam was driven by the goal of reclaiming the truth, rather than aligning with narratives that were manipulated by regimes to manipulate people's beliefs according to their own agendas.

However, as the cultural landscape changed, Gen X, born between 1965 and 1980, began to question and challenge traditional religious ideologies.

Then came millennials and Gen Z, who also failed to grasp the waning influence of Christendom on Western society. Evangelicals, while advocating for their own beliefs, often disregarded the hypocrisy when their proposed ideologies contradicted their own actions.

This led to a rise in influence from new and intellectually vibrant groups that questioned the relevance of longstanding laws not aligned with their progressive mindset.

This generation disregarded biblical teachings and instead embraced their own ideologies, gradually losing touch with key concepts from the Bible. This decay further spread with the certain Muslims, who found this newfound independence and open-mindedness more accepting.

It permeated regions where Islam is already prevalent to establish sinking concepts of Westernization in the facade of independence.

However, it is important to note that this cannot be compared to regimes like political arenas, which forcefully impose a distorted version of Islam in territories where it lacks genuine authority.

The only influence Islam has is through the upbringing of children by Muslim parents. This responsibility cannot be underestimated, as it is a duty that Allah himself questions and cannot be neglected.

Christianity has been progressively declining and has influenced other faiths to believe that they are all the same. The Biblical laws that treat women as subordinate to men have caused many issues and have wrongly portrayed Islam in their fictional interpretations of the Quran.

Pew Research Center: Sept 2022: Large numbers of people in the U.S who practice Christianity are declining.

The New York Times: Aug 23, 2023 — "American Christianity is in crisis," Moore writes in his new book, "Losing Our Religion." "The church is a scandal in all the worst ways."

The Guardian: Jan 23, 2023 — As the US adjusts to an increasingly non-religious population, thousands of churches are closing each year

Katie Couric Media: According to the Public Religion Research Institute, 56 percent of respondents said they left their faith because they just stopped believing in its teachings.

BBC: Islam is currently the world's second largest religion after Christianity, but this could change if trends continue.

Weekly Blitz: 20, 2023 — Recently, Muslims in Buffalo bought Saint Ann Catholic Church and Shrine, built in 1886 by German immigrants just with US $250,000.

BBC: Jul 10, 2020 — Built 1,500 years ago as an Orthodox Christian cathedral, Hagia Sophia was converted into a mosque after the Ottoman conquest in 1453. In 1934.

The blame game has become deeply entrenched and shows no signs of fading away. Unfortunately, one of the most targeted groups in this blame game are Muslims, as Islamophobia continues to fuel prejudice and discrimination.

This blame game has become an inherent force, perpetuating a cycle of scapegoating and division within Western societies.

"Prophet Muhammad was known for his business dealings and honesty; they called him Al-Amin, meaning 'the trustworthy.' His example set the standard for ethical business practices in Islam.

Islamic principles emphasize the importance of honesty, fairness, transparency, and accountability in all business transactions. Muslims are mandated to conduct their business with integrity, regardless of the faith or color of the individuals involved.

Quora: Jan 7, 2018 — Over 100, 000,000 after inquisitions, Christian on Christian wars, persecution of Jews, maintaining feudalism, genocides, mass murders, and purges...

Prophet Soloman the prophet and a king was a giver in Islamic doctrine. Not only did he hold kingship he had abundant gifts from Allah which he used wisely. He married the Queen of Sheba and converted her to Islam by permission of Allah. He named her Bilquis.

Allah has given many examples of the impossible become possible!

The skills of Soloman are so many he could speak to animals and had his own open zoo without restrictions he was a disciple he could speak to Jinn and he controlled the Jinn. He also controlled the wind.

The depiction of Solomon in the Bible and the Quran does differ in certain aspects. While both texts recognize Solomon as a wise and prosperous king, the Bible specifically mentions his many wives and concubines, totaling 700.

This aspect of Solomon's life can be seen as contradictory to the teachings of the Bible, which emphasize monogamy and fidelity in marriage.

As a result, it becomes challenging to hold the prophets in the Bible in high regard, as many stories highlight their character flaws. Many Bible readers overlook the historical context, and the changes made to fit the timeline of those who lived in the Roman Empire. The assertion that this faith came from the Western land is erroneous.

Bible: KJV: 11:1-3 And he *had* seven hundred *wives*, princesses, and three hundred *concubines*: and his *wives* turned away his heart.

Islamic prophets have indeed left behind legendary stories that serve as examples to humanity. These prophets, including Solomon, were sent by Allah as guides and role models for people to follow.

While the Bible mentions that Solomon had 700 wives and concubines, it is important to understand that these accounts are not mentioned in the Quran.

In fact, the Quran does not encourage polygamy, but it allows it under certain specific circumstances. The main purpose of these stories is to highlight the wisdom, leadership, and spiritual guidance of the prophets,

Islam, as a religion, emphasizes the importance of monogamy and the equitable treatment of spouses. It recognizes that polygamy is not beneficial for everyone and must be practiced responsibly and with proper consideration for all parties involved.

The values and teachings of Islam are complex and require a deep understanding of its method and thinking. Relying on surface-level knowledge can lead to misunderstandings and misinterpretations.

Becoming a teacher without a solid foundation in Islamic teachings can perpetuate ignorance rather than promote true learning.

Quran: Surah Nahl: 16:1. The command of Allah is at hand, so do not hasten it. Glorified and Exalted is He above what they associate with Him in worship.

Quran: Surah Nisa: 4:19. O believers! It is not permissible for you to inherit women against their willl or mistreat them to make them return some of the dowry 'as a ransom for divorce'—unless they are found guilty of adultery. Treat them fairly. If you happen to dislike them, you may hate something which Allah turns into a great blessing.

The concept of adjustments among Muslim beliefs varies, but the Quran remains unchanged. Similar to other Abrahamic faiths, Muslims sometimes adopt practices without fully understanding them, leading to misinterpretations.

For example, Christians, and Jews referred to as the "people of the book," certain Christians believe that Jesus allows blessing the food before eating, pork or any food despite him explicitly forbidding pork to the Jews is defiance.

There is a debate surrounding the prohibition of wine, known as **Qamar**, in Islam. Some argue that Islam only forbids certain types of alcohol, not all. Those who deviate from the truth are defiant. It is important to note that adjusting Islam to suit one's own desires is not in line with the principles of the religion.

Similarly, the Jews altered their faith to meet their own needs, but it is crucial to remember that the wrath of Allah is not something to be taken lightly. It is subservient to His commands, as this world and the next belong to Allah.

In Islam, the consumption of pork is strictly forbidden. However, there are certain exceptions where it may be allowed under specific circumstances. For instance, in cases of severe hunger or life-threatening situations, consuming pork to save a life can be permissible.

Zina (sexual intercourse) is prohibited in Islam, regardless of whether it is with a girlfriend, fiancée, or outside of marriage.

Quran: Surah Nisa: 4:4. And give to the women (whom you marry) their Mahr (obligatory bridal money given by the husband to his wife at the time of marriage) with a good heart, but if they, of their own good pleasure, remit any part of it to you, take it, and enjoy it without fear of any harm (as Allah has made it lawful).

Quran: Surah Nisa: 443. O you who have believed, indeed, intoxicants (Khamar), gambling, [sacrificing on] stone altars [to other than God], and divining arrows are but defilement from the work of Satan, so avoid it you may be successful.

Pork prohibited in Surah Baqarah Verse 173; Surah Maida Verse 3; Surah Anam Verse 145, and Surah Nahl 16:115.

Quran: Surah Isra 17:32: "Do not go near adultery. It is truly a shameful deed and an evil way"

Quran: Surah Nur 3: Forbids male fornicators from marrying anyone but a female fornicator or idolatress, and vice versa

Knowledge serves no purpose if it isn't shared; knowledge becomes meaningless when foolish actions dominate.

When truth is spoken, it is impossible for a Muslim to remain passive while lies are challenged through hypocrisy or sarcasm.

Advocate for truth, as it underscores strength instead of weakness!

CHAPTER 18
VIBRATIONS AND EXPECTATIONS

This phenomenon of vibration at a microscopic level is known as molecular motion.

Within the human body, cells constantly undergo various processes such as metabolism, respiration, and cell division, which involve the movement of molecules and ions.

These movements create vibrations that propagate throughout the body, contributing to the overall vibrational frequency of the human body.

At a more macroscopic level, organs and tissues within the body also exhibit their own unique frequencies of vibration. For instance, the heart beats at a specific rhythm, generating vibrations that can be felt as pulses. Similarly, the respiratory system produces vibrations during breathing.

Thoughts, emotions, and energy flows within the body also contribute to its vibrational frequency. Everything in the universe comprises atoms, which are essentially vibrations.

These vibrations can be constant or fluctuating, and they determine the frequency at which things exist.

When these vibrations are at a high frequency, there is a sense of happiness and gratitude. Low-frequency vibrations are associated with negative feelings such as guilt and shame.

Interestingly, this concept of vibration and frequency applies to everything, including religion. In Islam, for example, connecting with Allah through a practice called dhikr, or remembrance of Allah, elevates one's frequency.

Those who do not remember Allah, however, have a lower frequency.

This can be observed through the expression of frequency obtained by doing tasbih, prayer using beads, to Allah. Quantum physics even supports this notion of vibrating frequencies, as seen in high-frequency vibrating birds.

Humans, who vibrate on the land, can expand their frequency by remembering Allah. By doing tasbih and uttering the simple phrase "la Ilaaha Illa Allah" (there is no god but Allah), the frequency increases.

The mercy of Allah encompasses all of creation, and the key to accessing this frequency and power lies in awareness and acknowledgment. Therefore, some people's presence is more significant and noticeable than others.

It is essential to let go of the past and embrace the breath of life, as breath is a symbol of awareness in Islam. By breathing life into our bodies, we can expand our awareness of Islam and the frequencies it offers.

There are many ways in which Muslims engage in spiritual practices and connect with their faith.

One such practice is the recitation of tasbih, which involves repeating phrases such as **"Subhan Allah"** (glory be to Allah), **"alhamdulillah"** (praise be to Allah), **"la Ilaaha Illa Allah"** (there is no god but Allah), and **"Allah hu Akbar"** (Allah is the greatest).

The concept of vibration extends beyond spiritual practices. Engaging in physical exercise can also be seen as vibration, as it energizes the body and mind, promoting overall well-being.

Similarly, engaging in meaningful conversations and travel experiences can create a vibrational connection with others and the world, fostering a sense of unity and understanding.

Moreover, **Dhikr** is also considered a form of therapy and healing for believers. It acts as a means to alleviate stress, anxiety, and emotional burdens.

By turning to Allah and seeking solace in His remembrance, Muslims can find comfort and relief from the challenges of life. **Dhikr** serves as a source of spiritual healing, allowing individuals to surrender their worries and trust in Allah's guidance and mercy.

In summary, **Dhikr** of Allah is an integral part of a Muslim's life, providing a constant connection to Allah and enhancing one's spiritual journey.

The human body is a complex system of interconnected cells, vibrating and conducting electricity, with the heart as its key organ. Our body's largest organ is the skin. There are three primary layers that make up the skin: the epidermis, dermis, and subcutis. The condition of our skin reflects our overall health.

The hadith tells the story of Alqamah and his mother:

Alqamah, a righteous man, followed all the teachings of Islam except when it came to his mother. He showed disrespect towards and harsh words.

He believed he didn't need to be respectful to his mother and mistreated her by responding disrespectfully and disregarding anything she said. His mother held onto these hurtful words, and eventually, she couldn't bring herself to forgive him.

The narrative underscores the value of abstaining from harsh words in Islam, particularly when directed at one's mother, who has lovingly raised and nurtured them.

Transitioning from positive to negative vibrations in one's actions can cause avoidable negative outcomes. It is undeniable that an exit is inevitable, and Allah will provide for those who seek him, disregarding the desires of any human including the mother if she stands between her desires and Islam.

In Alqamah's case, he prioritized his wife over his mother, disrespecting her, when he could have avoided conflict and continued with his plans.

However, Alqamah emitted negative vibrations despite initially presenting himself with a positive vibration in the presence of Allah. The concept of frequency suggests that the vibrations should align and maintain a balance, although they can never be completely matched.

The good should outweigh the bad. When the time came for Alqamah to depart, to everyone's surprise, he could not recite the Shahada.

Although he was known as a pious man, he had one flaw - he mistreated his mother to agree with his wife and treated his mother with harsh words, dismissing her. Allah observed all of his actions, and as he struggled on his deathbed, Prophet Muhammad called his mother and asked her if he was a dutiful son.

She replied, "Yes, he was a good man, but he always dismissed me for his wife. His harsh words silenced my own, and there was no kindness. I cannot forgive him."

Prophet Muhammad, in his moment of struggle, urged the people to gather wood for a funeral pyre, as he believed Allah would not take his soul back.

However, unable to bear the sight, she exclaimed, **"I forgive him!"** Understanding the gravity of the situation, the prophet declared that the pains of the grave and the afterlife would surpass any suffering he experienced in this world.

With conviction, he uttered his **Shahada** the creed of Islam and peacefully passed away.

In Islam, the rights of individuals are valued and respected. However, it is generally advised to peacefully part ways if disagreements arise, in order to avoid any disrespect towards the religion and unintentional support for its oppressors.

Some individuals may choose to distance themselves from family members who are opposed to Islam, to showcase their personal transformation. It is important to emphasize the need for respect towards one's mother

While Allah takes precedence over everything else, it is crucial to maintain respect for both parents. In AL Qamas' story, he demonstrated his utmost respect for Allah, but unfortunately, he was disrespectful towards his mother. It is essential to follow Allah's teachings and respect the beliefs of others, while also refraining from using harsh words that go against the principles of Islam.

It is impossible to cohabitate with those who disrespect Islam. However, it is also disrespectful to be a Muslim and disrespect one's mother in order to please one's wife. Both situations can be managed, as Islam teaches harmony instead of promoting evil.

Hadith: Muslim: Omar Bin Khattab reported:

The questionnaire role is played by the visitor, and Prophet Muhammad takes on the role of the answerer in this story.

A visitor joined the gathering unexpectedly. His eyes were piercing and filled with wisdom, captivating everyone in the gathering. The man's noble demeanor and aura of tranquility made it evident that he was no ordinary traveler.

He was dressed in pristine white garments, appearing as if they were impeccably pressed without a single crease. His remarkable appearance immediately drew the attention of everyone in the room.

As he approached Prophet Muhammad, peace be upon him, a sense of awe and reverence filled the air. The companions of the Prophet, curious and intrigued, couldn't help but steal glances at this mysterious visitor.

Some whispered amongst themselves, wondering about the identity of this remarkable individual. His steps were graceful, and his presence commanded respect and admiration. It was as if he carried the secrets of the universe within him, yet humbly concealed them beneath his humble exterior.

As he sat down in the company of the Prophet, his radiant smile and gentle demeanor immediately put everyone at ease. The atmosphere became charged with anticipation, as everyone eagerly awaited the conversation that was about to unfold with this extraordinary guest.

Prophet Muhammad (PBUH), upon hearing the question, turned his attention to the man sitting next to him. The man's appearance was unfamiliar, and his voice carried a sense of authority.

His question was "O Muhammad, tell me about Islam"

Prophet Muhammad (PBUH) acknowledged him with a gentle smile and began explaining the essence of Islam.

With a serene expression, he delved into the fundamental principles of the faith, emphasizing the importance of submission to the will of Allah, the worship of the One true God, and the significance of maintaining a righteous and just lifestyle.

As the man listened intently, his stern expression gradually softened, and his curiosity seemed to be replaced with a deep understanding of the profound teachings being imparted to him.

The prophet Muhammad, peace be upon him, imparted profound wisdom to the man about the pillars of Islam.

He explained that these pillars are the foundational principles and practices that every Muslim should uphold.

These include the declaration of faith (**Shahada**), performing the five daily prayers (**Salat**), giving to charity (**Zakat**), fasting during Ramadan (**Sawm**), and undertaking the pilgrimage to Mecca (**Hajj**) for those who are able.

The man, deeply moved by the prophet's words, expressed his gratitude and proclaimed, "You have spoken the truth." He recognized the significance of these pillars and pledged to embrace and follow them wholeheartedly.

The man's words hung in the air, and the gathering grew curious as they awaited his next question. With a sense of anticipation, he turned to the group and said,

"Tell Me About Imaan" faith

His tone was earnest, revealing a genuine desire to delve deeper into the concept of faith and belief. The atmosphere in the room shifted, as the attendees recognized the weightiness of the question.

They exchanged glances, silently acknowledging the significance of the topic at hand. It was clear that this was a moment to share profound insights and reflections on matters of the heart and soul.

He said that believing in Allah means acknowledging His existence and recognizing His supreme authority. It involves having faith in His angels, who are His divine messengers and carry out His commands.

Believing in His Books refers to accepting and revering the scriptures He has revealed to guide humanity, such as the Quran, the Torah, and the Bible.

Belief in His Messengers entails acknowledging and accepting the prophethood of individuals like Prophet Muhammad, Moses, Jesus, and others who were sent to convey Allah's message to humanity.

The concept of the Last Day encompasses believing in the resurrection, judgment, and the ultimate accountability of all beings. Lastly, believing in Al-Qadr, the divine will and decree, means understanding that everything that occurs, whether good or bad, happens by the will and knowledge of Allah.

It requires acknowledging that He has complete control over all aspects of creation and that everything happens according to His plan. Prophet Muhammad explained to the questioner that Imaan, which translates to "faith" in Islam, is a fundamental aspect of a Muslim's belief system.

He described Imaan as a deep conviction and unwavering trust in Allah (God), His Prophets, the revealed scriptures, the angels, the Day of Judgment, and divine destiny.

The Prophet emphasized Imaan is not just a mere belief, but also entails sincere actions and deeds that reflect one's faith. He elaborated on the importance of Imaan in shaping a Muslim's character, guiding their moral compass, and instilling a sense of purpose and connection with Allah.

Prophet Muhammad emphasized Imaan is not stagnant but can fluctuate in strength, and it requires continuous effort to strengthen and protect it.

He also highlighted the significance of seeking knowledge, practicing patience, and maintaining good company to enhance one's Imaan and maintain solidarity with fellow believers.

Through his answers, Prophet Muhammad provided a comprehensive understanding of Imaan and its vital role in the life of a Muslim.

In this conversation, the person being addressed spoke the truth, which was acknowledged by the speaker. Following that, the speaker inquired to be educated on "Ihsan," a concept connected to worship.

He said "tell me about Ihsaan" Indebted

The response given was that Ihsan means indebted worshiping Allah as if one can see Him, even though He cannot be seen.

The significance of this is that although humans cannot physically see Allah, they should maintain the awareness that Allah can see them. This understanding of Ihsan encourages individuals to strive for excellence in their worship, as if they were in the presence of Allah.

It fosters a sense of mindfulness and devotion in the worshiper's actions and intentions.

Ihsaan, which means gratitude and excellence, encompasses not only expressing thankfulness to those who have taught us Islam but also refraining from demeaning them by counting their mistakes.

In Islam, Allah does not hold us accountable for unintentional errors but offers us the opportunity for repentance and the strength to improve ourselves.

To truly embody Ihsan, (Kindness, Beneficence, Highest level of Iman) striving to become stronger and better individuals, constantly seeking a deeper understanding of our faith is progress. The illustration of Ihsan lies in expressing gratitude to those who have guided us on the path of Islam, regardless of who they may be.

The one who has shown us the way holds an irreplaceable position in our lives, as nothing holds more value than our faith.

It is crucial to not focus on the faults of those who have introduced us to Islam, as this would undermine the essence of Ihsan.

A prime example of this is Prophet Muhammad, who holds the highest reverence for Muslims, as he showed and taught the faith of Islam, even though its existence predates him, dating back to the creation of humanity and the worship of one God. Islam was the finality of all Abrahamic faiths.

He said: "Then tell me about its signs"

This statement, often attributed to Prophet Muhammad, is a powerful and thought-provoking prophecy. It suggests a reversal of social hierarchies, where a slave-girl will give birth to her mistress.

This phrase symbolizes a shift in power dynamics, where those who were previously oppressed or marginalized will rise to positions of authority and influence.

The prophecy foretells a time when even the most impoverished and humble individuals, represented by barefoot, naked, and destitute herdsmen, will compete in constructing impressive and towering buildings.

This highlights the potential for societal transformation, where the underprivileged will take part in and contribute to remarkable advancements and achievements.

Overall, this prophecy serves as a reminder that the future holds unpredictable changes and surprises, challenging conventional expectations and notions of social order.

He said: "Tell me about the Hour."

The questioner was curious about the concept of the Hour, referring to the Day of Judgment or the end of the world. In response, the person prophet Muhammad being asked humbly admitted that he did not possess any additional knowledge about it compared to the one asking.

This statement highlights the universal nature of this eschatological event, showing that no individual holds exclusive knowledge regarding its exact timing or the events surrounding it.

Jibreel, also known as Gabriel, is an important figure in Islamic tradition and is believed to be the angel who brought revelations from Allah to Prophet Muhammad. In this incident, Jibril had come as a man to ask Prophet Muhammad a series of questions.

After witnessing this encounter, the people present were amazed at the depth and clarity of the questions and the wisdom with which Prophet Muhammad answered them.

It was only after Jibril departed that Prophet Muhammad revealed to his companion Omar the true identity of the questioner.

This revelation left Omar in awe, realizing that it was Jibril, the trusted angel of Allah, who imparted divine knowledge and teachings to the prophets.

This incident served as a reminder to the believers of the importance and significance of their religion, and the role played by Jibril in delivering Allah's message to Prophet Muhammad and, subsequently, to the Muslim community.

Islam is a monotheistic religion that emphasizes the belief in one God, Allah, and recognizes all the prophets sent by Him.

Islam teaches that Allah is the sole creator and sustainer of the universe and that no prophet should be worshiped or considered divine.

It is through the exchange of knowledge and ideas that friendships can be strengthened, as individuals who value learning recognize the importance of embracing diverse viewpoints and supporting the pursuit of knowledge.

Islam, as a constitution, has its own set of immutable laws and regulations that are not subject to human alteration. While previous scriptures may have adapted to the changing times, the laws of Islam remain steadfast and unchangeable.

Islam is a living religion, relevant and enduring, and it will continue to thrive in the present and shape the future.

Iman, or faith, is an essential aspect of Islam that goes beyond the outward expressions and actions of a person.

It is a deeply personal and spiritual connection with Allah, rooted in the belief and acceptance of the Six Articles of Faith.

The first article, Tawheed, focuses on the belief in the oneness of Allah, acknowledging Him as the one and only God. The second article emphasizes the belief in the angels of Allah, unseen beings created by Allah to carry out His commands.

Third article emphasizes the belief in all the prophets of Allah, including but not limited to Prophet Muhammad (peace be upon him. Fourth article emphasizes the belief in the Books of Allah, including the Quran, as the last revelation.

The fifth article emphasizes that believers have a belief in the Last Day and the Day of Judgment, where all individuals will be held accountable for their actions. The sixth article emphasizes the belief in Divine Destiny (**Qadr**), understanding that everything that happens, both good and bad, is ultimately decreed by Allah.

While a person may identify as a Muslim and practice the outward rituals, Allah is the only one who can know true faith and Iman, which live in the heart.

Those who are sincere in their search for truth will find solace and enlightenment in the Quran's unyielding message.

The love of Dunya, referring to the temporary world and its materialistic attractions, is often embraced by those who prioritize artificial pleasures over seeking a genuine connection with their Creator.

They may claim to worship and follow the teachings of the Lord, but their actions betray multiple identities and contradictory behaviors. Although they may make mistakes along the way, it is not the mistakes themselves that define them, but their secretive actions that eventually come to light.

Continuous fear and guilt eventually compel them to reveal their true selves, just as Satan and his deceivers operate. Like Satan, they use deceit and manipulation to lure others into their web of falsehood and superficiality.

Quran: Surah Hijar: 15:88. Do not let your eyes crave the fleeting pleasures We have provided for some of the disbelievers, not grieve for them. And be gracious to the believers.

The jealousy of material possessions is indeed wasteful, as it often leads to greed and discontentment. Knowledge is a true blessing, particularly for understanding and studying the Quran.

They cannot deceive themselves or others about their faith, for the light of truth shines through their actions. Islam discourages the act of pointing fingers or constantly reminding others of their faults. Instead, it emphasizes the importance of communication with Allah and seeking repentance for personal growth and resolving internal struggles.

Christians believe Jesus was born in Bethlehem, which is indeed part of Palestine, historically known as the region of Judea. Bethlehem, in the West Bank, is currently under the control of the Palestinian Authority. However, it is important to note that the political and territorial dynamics of the region have evolved over time.

The modern-day state of Israel was established in 1948, and since then, Bethlehem has been subject to various political and administrative changes.

The recognition of Bethlehem as part of Israel by some nations is a complex geopolitical issue, with differing perspectives on the Israeli-Palestinian conflict and the status of the territories.

However, the Quran does not mention the specific location where Jesus was born. It focuses more on emphasizing his divine credentials and the miraculous nature of his birth as a prophet. In one verse, it describes Mary going away to a distant place and experiencing labor pains, during which she sought solace by a palm tree.

This type of deception not only perpetuates prejudice and stereotypes but also undermines the principles of unity and tolerance that Islam promotes. Non-Muslims who truly understand the faith recognize that if the principles of Islam were to govern the world, there would be a significant reduction in the evils of injustice.

An example of a Muslim ruler who brought peace and justice during his reign is Omar bin Khattab, who ruled Jerusalem. However, unfortunately, many people are unaware of the positive contributions made by Muslim leaders throughout history.

Instead, they mistakenly believe that peace existed before 1948, as a reminder it was only during the Muslim rule. When the establishment of Zionism, driven by Western countries, led to the displacement and suffering of the predominantly Muslim Palestinian population.

It is disheartening to witness how those who were once educators and bearers of knowledge have become victims of those who have exploited and abused the system.

They have strategically positioned themselves in the region not to assist or contribute positively but rather to serve their own selfish agendas and perpetuate lies about Islam.

The United Nations, as an international organization, closely monitors the situation in Israel where individuals are being displaced from their homes with the backing of a superpower. It is important to note that those who solely rely on watching news media or have limited access to social media become hate spreaders rather than agents of reform.

The excessive drama and fear mongering surrounding these events only serve to further divide and polarize communities. It is crucial to find a more constructive approach that amplifies the voices of those who resonate their voices and speak to the world.

The Zionist movement, which aimed to establish a Jewish homeland in Palestine, gained momentum during this time. In 1948, following the end of the British mandate, the State of

Israel was declared, leading to a series of conflicts and wars between Israel and its neighboring Arab states.

Quran: Surah Anam: 16:65. For it is He Who has appointed you vicegerent over the earth, and has exalted some of you over others in rank that He may try you in what He has bestowed is upon you. Indeed your Lord is swift in retribution, and He is certainly All-Forgiving, All-Compassionate.

Quran: Surah Araf: 7:31. "O Children of Adam! Take your adornment to every masjid, and eat and drink, but waste not by extravagance, certainly He (Allah) likes not the wasteful."

These events have had a profound impact on the modern history of the Muslim world and continue to shape the political dynamics in the region.

Israel belonged to the Muslims and was run by Omar bin Khattab it was the Muslims who invited the Jews and the Jews handed over the keys to Jerusalem is a written history.

The ongoing subject of Palestine is a complex issue that requires a deep understanding of its historical context. Relying solely on social media and the views of Islamophobia will not lead to a true understanding of the situation.

To truly grasp the history of the Muslim empire and the Ottoman reign, it is important to seek knowledge from diverse sources, including scholars and historians who have studied the subject extensively.

While a Muslim perspective may provide insights into the splendor and flourishing of the Muslim empire, it is equally important to approach history with an open mind and consider multiple perspectives.

Prophet Muhammad expressed his words by conveying and asked Allah that those who were not present in his time could understand them better than those who were absent.

It is a misconception to assume that Muslims and non-Muslims have inherently different thinking patterns. While individuals may have different beliefs and perspectives, religious affiliation does not limit the capacity for empathy, critical thinking, and understanding.

The pursuit of knowledge should go beyond religious boundaries, and a shared commitment to uncovering the truth should guide individuals.

Unfortunately, sometimes people wrongly label individuals who practice Islam or adhere to its principles as extremists or terrorists because of Islamophobia.

These variations in belief arise from different interpretations of religious texts, cultural contexts, and theological traditions. Ultimately, the understanding of God's responsiveness to human prayers and calls is shaped by the specific theological framework and beliefs within each Abrahamic faith and outside of this meridian.

The concept of justice is often associated with the notion that it will not be fully realized until the end of time. This idea suggests that while injustices may prevail in the present, ultimate justice will be served.

When we delve deeper into this understanding, we realize it highlights the fundamental belief in the oneness of God. Throughout history, various religions and belief systems have emerged, each with its perception of a divine entity.

However, the underlying truth that emerges is that there has always been only one true God, the creator of all existence.

Regardless of who individuals call out to or worship, it is ultimately God who answers every sincere invocation. This notion emphasizes the unity of humanity and the shared connection we have with the divine.

The Prophet Muhammad himself did not remain silent in the face of injustice; he spoke out and took action. When belief is strong and unwavering, even the strength of a small bird can be enough to achieve victory in the cause.

Muslims, Christians, and Jews lived side by side in peace and harmony, with individuals from different faiths freely interacting and engaging in trade and cultural exchanges. Only peace was under Muslim law.

This period of peace and tolerance lasted for several centuries under the Islamic rule of various dynasties. However, the dynamics of the region changed over time, and conflicts arose because of various political, religious, and territorial disputes

The occupation of Palestine and Israel is a complex issue that involves multiple factors and historical events, including the establishment of the State of Israel in 1948 and subsequent conflicts.

From the iconic Dome of the Rock in Jerusalem to the majestic palaces of Damascus, their architectural achievements are a testament to their influence. Their rule brought about significant changes in governance, trade, and social structures, shaping the region's history.

While history channels and television programs provide valuable insights, truly understanding the depth and complexity of this rich history requires immersing oneself in the vibrant streets, markets, and ancient ruins that still exist today.

However, when Omar bin Khattab, the second caliph of the Rashidun Caliphate, took over Jerusalem in 638 CE, he recognized the historical and religious significance of the mosque.

With great reverence and respect, Omar oversaw the cleaning and restoration of the Masjid al-Aqsa. This act symbolized the restoration of the mosque's sanctity and marked the beginning of a new era of Muslim rule in Jerusalem.

Omar's efforts not only revived the spiritual significance of the mosque, but also set a precedent for the preservation and protection of Islamic holy sites for future generations.

Muslims lit the lights of Cordoba, a city in Spain, during a time when Europe was engulfed in the darkness of the Middle Ages.

With their advanced knowledge and appreciation for art, architecture, and science, they transformed Cordoba into a beacon of enlightenment. The streets were adorned with beautiful trees, casting a mesmerizing glow upon the city.

The Great Mosque of Cordoba, with its intricate geometric patterns and stunning archways, stood as a testament to the Muslim influence on the development of European architecture. Scholars, poets, and scientists flocked to Cordoba, drawn by the vibrant intellectual atmosphere that thrived within its walls.

It was a time of cultural exchange and innovation, where ideas from various disciplines were cultivated and shared. The Muslims of Cordoba truly illuminated the European continent, igniting a spark of knowledge and progress that would eventually spread throughout the world.

As Muslims have illuminated both the streets and minds, it is perplexing to see some individuals embracing paganistic ideologies and mindsets instead of enlightening the masses with intelligence and combating the darkness that is once again descending upon the world.

The resurgence of pagan rituals under the guise of modernization is nothing but a facade, and the world is now being inundated with behaviors that stem from a loss of morality, corrupting and misleading the impressionable youth into thinking that expressing themselves inappropriately is their right, unaware that such expressions have already been discredited and replaced with new ideologies.

The oppression and words of the suffering may be intense for some, but it's crucial to realize that what you desire is also seeking you.

Those who aid tyrants in diminishing independence and remain unapologetically indifferent. Those who enter this turmoil experience the same vibrations; depression, cancer, obesity, and more. Hormone-packed food becomes an answer for aggression, but unfortunately, some feel the ricochet while others feel nothing.

This is disheartening for those who have strayed from the practices of Islam yet still identify as Muslims, either culturally or nominally.

Islam, in its essence, does not support the abandonment of its teachings.

Quran: Surah Anfal: 8:26:27. "And remember when you were few and were reckoned weak in the land, and were afraid that men might kidnap you, but He provided a safe place for you, strengthened you with His help, and provided you with good things (for livelihood) so that you might be grateful. O you who believe! Betray not Allah and His Messenger, nor betray knowingly your Amanat (things entrusted to you)."

Come together and focus on the important issues at hand. The land and space that we have been given is a trust, a responsibility that we must uphold. It is our duty to take care of the environment and preserve it for future generations. Similarly, showing respect for Islam is not just a choice, but an unpaid debt that we owe to our faith.

Imam Ibn-Ul-Qayyim (Rahmatullah) stated:

"Time wasting is more serious than death because time wasting cuts you off from Allah and the home of the afterlife, whereas death cuts you off from the worldly life and its people."

CHAPTER 19
THE MIND CANNOT BE MITIGATED BY AUTHORITY EXCEPT BY THE WILL OF ALLAH.

The mind, enveloped in a realm of thoughts, remains impervious to any external authority, its resilience tethered solely to the divine will of Allah.

The mind, like a vast labyrinthine network, intricately weaves together the tapestry of our thoughts, emotions, perceptions, and memories. It resonates with the symphony of sights, from vibrant colors to breathtaking vistas, and echoes with the harmonies of sounds, from gentle whispers to thunderous roars.

The mind dances with the fragrant melodies of scents, from the sweet aroma of blooming flowers to the invigorating scent of freshly brewed coffee.

It delicately touches the fabric of our being, feeling the warmth of a loving embrace and the coolness of a gentle breeze. In its complexity, the mind is the master conductor of our inner world, orchestrating the symphony of our existence.

It encompasses a range of cognitive abilities, including reasoning, problem-solving, decision-making, and creativity.

The function of the mind is crucial in shaping our perception of reality and influencing our behavior. It plays a central role in our ability to learn, adapt, and navigate the world.

Understanding the functioning of the mind is essential to comprehend the challenges individuals encounter, such as mental health issues, cognitive limitations, and the impact of external factors on our thoughts and behaviors.

By gaining insight into the workings of the mind, we can better address these challenges and promote mental well-being. There are two parts of the brain that are important to note: the cerebral cortex and the limbic system.

The cerebral cortex, also known as the neocortex, handles higher cognitive functions such as thinking and problem-solving. The cerebral cortex, also known as the neocortex, divides into four lobes: the frontal lobe, parietal lobe, temporal lobe, and occipital lobe.

Each lobe has specific functions, such as the frontal lobe being involved in decision-making and the parietal lobe in sensory perception.

The limbic system plays a crucial role in emotions, memory, and motivation. It includes structures like the amygdala, hippocampus, and hypothalamus. These two parts of the brain work together to regulate and control various aspects of human behavior and functioning.

The cortex of the brain that bends down and puts the head on the ground while Muslims go into Sujood prostration plays a crucial role in activating the frontal cortex and recharging it.

When the forehead touches the ground during **Sujood**, it creates pressure on specific areas of the frontal cortex, responsible for higher cognitive functions such as decision-making, reasoning, and problem-solving.

This pressure stimulates blood flow to these regions, enhancing oxygen and nutrient supply to the brain.

As a result, revitalizing the frontal cortex improves cognitive function, mental clarity, and overall well-being. The act of Sujood also promotes relaxation, reduces stress levels, and encourages mindfulness, contributing to a balanced and rejuvenated mind.

During the act of **Sujood in Salat,** a Muslim finds a profound sense of humility and submission to Allah.

This physical posture, where one fully bends down and places their forehead on the ground, symbolizes complete surrender to the will of God.

Their deep faith and spiritual connection with Allah drive their devotion to prayer. They prioritize their relationship with the divine above all else, including their own well-being or the desire to please others.

This sincere prayer allows them to find strength, guidance, and inner peace, enabling them to navigate challenges and difficult situations with courage and conviction.

They understand that their ultimate purpose is to submit to the will of Allah and seek His pleasure, which gives them the confidence to stand firm in their beliefs and values, regardless of external pressures or expectations.

In Islam, it is important to remember that everyone, including Muslims, is prone to making mistakes.

It is not under Islamic teachings to eagerly anticipate and draw attention to the mistakes or blunders of others. Allah warns believers to conceal the sins of others and not discuss them, as forgiveness ultimately lies in the hands of Allah for those who genuinely repent.

This message is reiterated multiple times, but gossiping remains a prevalent human tendency. To eradicate such behaviors, it is necessary to address the issue and avoid engaging in gossip when the topic of conversation does not involve it.

The mind can cloak wisdom in distractions or intentional actions, while also preserving innocence. The path ahead may be uncertain, but Allah, who already knows the choices a human will make, predetermines the future.

Various situations and circumstances shape our personal journey through life. It is our responsibility, as the ones inhabiting these bodies and experiencing our own souls, to comprehend that the way we live our lives is shaping our ultimate destiny in the hereafter.

The Satan thrives on manipulating human desires and exploiting vulnerabilities. It preys on our deepest insecurities and temptations, using them as leverage to ensnare us in a never-ending cycle of indulgence and self-destruction.

Whether it's enticing us with the allure of illicit pleasures or fueling our insatiable need for power and control, Satan and his people's goal is to keep us trapped in a state of constant craving and dissatisfaction.

It thrives on our inability to practice moderation and preys on our weaknesses, pushing us further into the depths of our obsessions and addictions. By harnessing the forces of greed and avarice, Satan ensures we remain shackled to our vices, unable to break free and find true contentment.

The Muslim countries are indeed many, with a rich diversity of cultures and landscapes. Some notable ones include Saudi Arabia, home to the holy cities of Mecca and Medina and a leader in the Islamic world.

Egypt, with its rich history and ancient wonders, such as the Pyramids of Giza and the Nile River. Iran, known for its vibrant culture, beautiful mosques, and historical sites like Persepolis. Indonesia, the world's largest Muslim country, is known for its stunning beaches and diverse wildlife.

Malaysia, with its modern cities and lush rainforests. Pakistan, with its breathtaking mountain ranges like the Karakoram and the vibrant city of Lahore. These countries, along with many others, have the potential to come together and contribute towards the betterment of the Muslim world if they unite in their efforts to help rather than destroy.

Qatar is indeed one of the richest countries in the world, known for its abundant oil and gas reserves. It has a unique taxation system where there is no personal income tax, making it an attractive destination for expatriates and entrepreneurs.

The Qatari currency, the Qatari riyal, is one of the highest-valued currencies globally, further contributing to the country's prosperity. Iran is a country that often stands up and voices its opinions on various global issues. It has expressed its views openly, especially on matters concerning the Middle East and international relations.

However, its outspoken nature has garnered some disapproval from Western countries, who may have differing perspectives and interests in the region.

Moving on to Iraq, it is a nation that has experienced significant destruction due to Western invasion and subsequent conflicts.

Maldives, with its stunning white sand beaches and crystal-clear waters, attracts travelers from all over the world.

Mauritania offers a unique desert experience, with vast stretches of sand dunes and nomadic traditions.

Somalia, facing many challenges, relies on support from other Muslim countries to overcome its hardships.

Tunisia, a popular tourist destination, boasts a diverse mix of Mediterranean and Arab influences. Afghanistan, despite facing foreign invasion, is renowned for its natural resources, including medicinal plants used in pharmaceuticals.

Morocco, with its vibrant markets and ancient cities, captivates visitors with its rich heritage.

Comoros, Palestine, Jordan, Libya, Sudan, Azerbaijan, Pakistan, Senegal, Gambia, Kosovo, Mali, Bangladesh, Egypt, Mayotte, Sudan, Azerbaijan, and Western Sahara are all examples of Muslim countries that hold significant cultural and historical importance.

By uniting and working together, these nations have the potential to create positive change and make a difference in the world.

The spread of knowledge is indeed crucial for the development and progress of any society.

It is important to note that Islamophobia, which refers to the fear or hatred of Islam and Muslims, does not contribute to the dissemination of knowledge.

Islamophobes often rely on biased and distorted information from news sources, which can perpetuate stereotypes and misconceptions about Islam and its followers.

In contrast, spreading knowledge involves promoting understanding, tolerance, and empathy. It encourages individuals to engage in critical thinking, independent research, and firsthand experiences rather than solely relying on news sources.

By actively seeking knowledge through diverse channels, such as literature, academic studies, and interactions with people from different backgrounds, one can gain a more comprehensive understanding of the world.

It is important for countries, including Muslim-majority nations, to prioritize the well-being of their own citizens.

While international cooperation and support are essential, a nation must first address its internal challenges and ensure the welfare of its people.

Only by strengthening their own societies can countries effectively contribute to the betterment of the world.

Taking a proactive stance, rather than resorting to threats or violence, is crucial in addressing societal issues.

By promoting dialogue, peaceful resolutions, and constructive actions, individuals and nations can make a meaningful impact. Merely observing chaos without taking steps to alleviate it is indeed futile.

In summary, the spread of knowledge is not hindered by Islamophobes but rather by reliance on biased news sources and lack of personal experiences.

It is crucial for countries to prioritize their own citizens' well-being while also contributing to the greater good. Taking a proactive and constructive stance is essential in addressing societal challenges.

Muslims around the world have been blessed with many countries and resources by Allah.

However, it is disheartening to see that some Muslims do not actively engage in enjoining good and supporting those in need.

Instead, they live lavish lifestyles, wasting material funds on unnecessary luxuries while others suffer.

Omar bin Khattab extended his efforts towards justice for both Muslims and non-Muslims alike.

He actively sought to adapt the principles of justice and fairness to accommodate the needs and rights of all individuals within the Islamic state.

His commitment to creating a just society remains a testament to his leadership and dedication.

Omar bin Khattab, a renowned Islamic caliph, indeed conquered many cities during his reign. His military campaigns expanded the Islamic empire across vast territories.

However, it is important to note that for Jerusalem; force did not take the city. In 637 CE, Omar bin Khattab arrived at the gates of Jerusalem, which was under Byzantine control.

The Christian Patriarch Sophronius surrendered the keys to the city to Omar, recognizing his authority. This act of surrender was significant as it showed the respect and tolerance that Omar and the Islamic forces showed towards the inhabitants of Jerusalem.

Omar bin Khattab's conquest left a lasting impact on the city, establishing a Muslim presence and starting a period of religious coexistence in Jerusalem.

Jerusalem, a city of historical significance and religious importance, has indeed experienced periods of turmoil and conflict. Over the years, various groups have fought for control, leading to destruction and displacement.

While it is true that Muslims have supported certain factions for Jews gaining entry to the lands they were exiled from, it is important to note Omar the second Caliph played an important role in welcoming them back.

The region, who supports this evil is heavily influenced by evangelicals unfortunately, has also seen the sale of arms as a means of compensation and survival amidst the ongoing conflicts.

It is essential to recognize that both Orthodox Jews and Muslims who understand the truth and advocate for peace and justice often face opposition from those driven by defense and greed.

There are individuals who strive to establish Jerusalem as a Jewish state, and they may receive support from external sources that supply arms and financial aid.

However, it is crucial to remember that such actions do not represent the entire Jewish community or its beliefs.

In Islamic doctrine, the concept of destiny is known as **Qadr**. It is believed that destiny is predestined by Allah and everything that occurs in life is part of His divine plan. However, individuals have been granted free will to make choices and decisions.

The **Qadr**, which is also known as predestination or divine decree, holds a significant place in Islamic theology. It signifies the belief that Allah possesses complete knowledge and control over all events in the universe.

According to Muslims, everything that happens, whether good or bad, is ultimately determined by Allah's will. This concept is derived from the Quran, which emphasizes Allah as the ultimate planner and controller of destiny.

Muslims are advised to accept and submit to the **Qadr,** understanding that it is a part of Allah's wisdom and that humans may not always comprehend the reasons behind certain occurrences.

The belief in **Qadr** offers solace and reassurance to Muslims, as they have faith that Allah's plan is flawless and ultimately leads to their spiritual growth and well-being.

It promotes humility and gratitude, as individuals acknowledge that their successes and blessings result from Allah's favor, while hardships and challenges serve as tests and opportunities for personal development.

Ultimately, the belief in **Qadr** shapes the worldview of Muslims and influences their attitudes towards life's uncertainties and challenges.

When Moses finally emerged as the leader destined to rescue the Israelites from slavery, it marked a personal triumph for the son of Pharaoh.

It's challenging to accept the portrayal of Jesus as a Jewish prophet in light of Islam's contrasting viewpoint.

Bible: John 12:3. Mary then took a pound of very costly perfume of pure nard, and anointed the feet of Jesus and wiped His feet with her hair; and the house was filled with the fragrance of the perfume.

Bible: Luke 8:2: "Mary called Magdalene, out of whom went seven devils" Mark 16: Also mentions that Jesus drove seven demons out of Mary Magdalene.

Bible: John: 20:17. In the Gnostic text Gospel of Philip, we read, "And the companion of the Mary Magdalene. He loved her more than all the disciples, and used to kiss her ...

These practices appear more cultic than monotheism.

The verse unambiguously states that Mary Magdalene was possessed by evil spirits, and Jesus kissed her, as is reiterated in several verses.

The behavior of the Jewish women raises doubts about the prophet who came to teach them, as he is engaging in actions that most Jews openly condemn, like kissing women openly.

The allegations involve adding occult practices to monotheistic beliefs, which is captivating the Western society that is currently trending towards acceptance of such practices, as Jesus, the leader, is setting a different trend compared to other prophets.

Mary Magdalene, a possessed woman, is chosen as a confidant, making it hard to understand her judgment or messages.

The preservation of Jesus' temperament is not a match with the Quran and the Bible which rose years after the ascension of Jesus. The Quran was finished during the lifetime of the prophet Muhammad in 23 years.

The practices that remain occult and close to paganism cannot be discarded. Since God is infinite, he does not gain wisdom.

If Jesus were his son, he would not require nurturing or be carried in a woman's womb, nor would he grow in wisdom. God embodies wisdom, compassion, and mercy. He does not improve with time.

While the Quran mentions the ascension of Jesus and his eventual return, it is important to acknowledge that the Quran and the Bible have different theological perspectives.

While Christendom adheres to the ten commandments, it is important to note that neither Moses nor the commandments explicitly expressed belief in Jesus as God or the idea of God evolving into Jesus or God having an offspring.

The commandments establish the basis for all prophets, including Jesus, sent by Allah, emphasizing that there is no God but Him, and no other deities or idols.

In a society tainted by adultery, the absence of moral laws is evident through the losses experienced, raising doubts about morality and ethics.

Therefore, a reminder about the importance of moral ethics becomes imperative.

Moses is acknowledged as a prophet who received direct instructions from Allah, underscoring the importance of these divine commandments without any intermediaries.

In Christianity, the notion of sin revolves around the belief that every person is born with original sin as a result of Adam and Eve's disobedience in the Garden of Eden.

Jesus' sacrifice and redemption bring forgiveness and salvation to Christians. Grasping this concept might pose difficulties for certain people, but it is the central tenet of Christian theology.

While Islam differs in its understanding of original sin, it underscores the importance of repentance and seeking forgiveness from Allah.

Islam provides a clear and easily understandable path to faith that appeals to a wide range of individuals.

To sum up, the apparent inconsistencies between the Bible and the Quran can lead to uncertainty in certain people. It is crucial to consider the historical and theological backgrounds when interpreting these texts.

The spiritual aspect of **Akhil** is incomplete without the other intelligence. All individuals possess intelligence given by Allah; the accurate measure of intelligence lies in the balance between the heart and mind, not neglecting one for the other.

Physical intelligence can comprehend the body, but spiritual alignment is essential for genuine harmony and balance.

Establishing a connection between the body, mind, heart, and soul is crucial. It's complete happiness. The plea of a Muslim is for Allah to unveil the truth and not remain oblivious. The spiritual intelligence of Iman cannot be learned; it is innate.

Islam teaches that without balance, a spiritually bankrupt life and physical fitness cannot compensate for each other

. Allah has the power to grant physical fitness and a curious mind that explores the unknown, but genuine success lies in achieving a spiritual balance between body, mind, and heart.

When the body is in balance and free from evil, and when one has hope in Allah's mercy and feels his closeness without seeing him in a human form, the mind is only relieved by truth. Allah's balance is a gift to his creation.

Alhamdulillah, for blessings and Insha'Allah for new findings.

CHAPTER 20
THE IRREPLACEABLE WEALTH LIES IN THE MODULE OF TIME

No matter how it is explained, those who are ignorant of the value of time refuse to embrace the truth. Instead, they choose to remain entangled in the complexities and superficialities of life, missing out on the time allocated to everyone, regardless of wealth or status.

It cannot be denied that each person is given a specific amount of time.

Allah describes those who have been blessed with everything: the seas were parted, twelve springs emerged, and the dead were brought back to life.

Yet, despite receiving such abundant blessings, their hearts remain in turmoil. They are like someone who receives good health but is constantly afraid of death, and perform worse acts after health is restored. As a result, their health deteriorates even further.

The answer lies in the heart's hardening. Those who defy and rebel against the truth are the ones who suffer from a hardened heart.

Only they truly understand the pain and turmoil that come with it. They often evade happiness and seek out others who carry the burden of a hardened heart, as if they are drawn to it.

The greatest symptom of a hard heart is when you are reminded of Allah or when correction in actions is needed. The person becomes deviant and surpasses boundaries, as if there is no sign of correction. Such a person is suffering from a hard heart.

The burden of constantly hearing about Allah weighs heavy on the hard heart. It resents engaging in discussions about dhikr, conversations about Allah and His prophets, as if every topic must somehow relate back to Allah.

It yearns for a different subject, uninterested in these matters. This mindset reflects a heedless Muslim, or even a non-Muslim. Having a hard heart is a torment in its own right, as it seeks only superficiality instead of the fulfillment of the soul.

The person is not experiencing any enjoyment during the time of worship. Overly concerned with the opinions of others. Rather than feeling grateful, these individuals choose to bring negative news about the house of Allah when they attend worship.

Prayer doesn't captivate their attention, they frequently space out, even when it fits within the allocated time. The habits of worship become monotonous and the enjoyment is gone, these are symptoms that need attention and Astaghfar (I seek forgiveness from Allah).

The advice of disbelievers becomes more important to them than attending to Allah and fulfilling their spiritual needs.

The tender heart finds joy in connecting with a devoted believer, a Muslim, and appreciates listening to the Quran, the stories, and the recitation.

The hardened heart resists those who possess a kind heart, feeling threatened by its own insecurities. Despite projecting a sense of self-importance and satisfaction, this heart is actually empty, constantly seeking solace in worldly desires rather than finding contentment in the pleasure of Allah.

A person with a hardened heart not only frequently engages in sinful behavior, but also allows it to become a way of life. What's even more concerning is that when they commit these sins, they feel no remorse or concern, as if it doesn't even matter.

This indifference towards their actions is even worse than committing a sin while being completely unaware. If confronted about their behavior, they deflect and avoid taking any corrective actions. Such a person can be described as having a hardened heart.

The sinner who repents has hope, but one who lacks remorse and consciousness within himself, or if someone reminds them and they remain clear-minded and apathetic, becomes susceptible to the mother of all diseases: hardness of the heart.

The indifference is like a prowler, deceiving himself while pointing out the sins of others without correcting their own.

There are many diseases that can be cured, while others result in departure from this world due to lack of a cure. However, addressing and repenting for the hardness of the heart is necessary before departing, as it is the root of evil and can lead to facing many judgments.

If someone is a new convert, undermining their choices can potentially cause a rebellion among the weak. Islam, though impervious to assault, can only be liberated through the softness of the heart.

Repentance is required to overcome the hardness of the heart, and seeking a new environment offers hope for those seeking rectification.

Various units and systems measure time, such as seconds, minutes, hours, days, weeks, months, and years. The most commonly used unit of time is the second, which is defined as the duration of 9,192,631,770 periods of the radiation corresponding to the transition between two hyperfine levels of the ground state of the cesium-133 atom.

This standard unit is used to derive other time measurements, such as minutes (60 seconds), hours (60 minutes), and so on.

Fajr (pre-dawn prayer), Duhr (midday prayer), Asr (afternoon prayer), Maghrib (evening prayer), and Isha (night prayer).

These clocks were often placed in mosques and other prominent locations to ensure that the Muslim community could easily access and adhere to the prayer timings, which are essential for the practice of Islam.

Ibn Khalaf al-Muradi, a Muslim engineer and inventor, made significant contributions to the field of timekeeping in Islamic Iberia during the 11th century.

He is credited with creating a revolutionary device known as the first geared clock. This clock was a mechanical marvel, featuring a complex system of gears and mechanisms that allowed for precise timekeeping.

It marked a significant advancement in the science of horology, as it provided a more accurate and reliable means of measuring time compared to previous methods.

Ibn Khalaf al-Muradi's geared clock paved the way for further developments in timekeeping technology and had a profound impact on the progression of Islamic science and civilization.

The water clock, also known as a clepsydra, was an ancient timekeeping device that used the flow of water to measure time. Various cultures, including ancient Egypt, Greece, and China, widely used the water clock, also known as a clepsydra.

However, it was the medieval Islamic engineer Ismail al-Jazari who created a remarkable innovation with his invention of the elephant clock.

The water clock, also known as the "castle clock," was a remarkable invention designed by the brilliant Turkish engineer Ibn al-Razza al-Jazari. Born in 1136 and living until 1206, Al Jazari was a prolific inventor and engineer during the Islamic Golden Age.

Around the year 1200, he created the water clock, a sophisticated timekeeping device that relied on the flow of water to measure hours and minutes.

The clock featured a series of interconnected vessels and floats, which regulated the flow of water and showed the passage of time. This revolutionary invention not only gave a precise way to measure time but also demonstrated Al Jazari's creativity and skill.

In his book, The Book of Knowledge of Ingenious Mechanical Devices, Ismail al-Jazari provided a detailed description of this intricate and ingenious device, which was a model of a water clock.

The elephant clock incorporated various mechanisms and features, such as automated figures, water-driven gears, and a complex hydraulic system. It not only served as a timekeeping device but also as an elaborate display of art and engineering.

Ismail al-Jazari's contributions to the field of mechanical engineering and his invention of the elephant clock highlight the advancements made by Muslim scholars during the medieval Islamic era. Muslims have a deep passion for clocks, as they play a significant role in their daily lives and religious practices.

Time is the most valued in Islam!

One notable example is the clock tower in Saudi Arabia's holy city of Mecca. This clock tower, known as the **Abraj Al-Bait Clock Tower**, stands tall at a height of 601 meters and is one of the most iconic landmarks in the city. It features the largest clock face in the world, measuring a staggering 43 meters in diameter.

The clock tower holds immense importance for Muslims, as it helps to regulate their daily prayers and serves as a reminder of the time for various religious rituals. Its presence in Mecca symbolizes the unity and devotion of Muslims worldwide, who flock to the city each year for the sacred pilgrimage of Hajj.

Muslims have a deep understanding of the importance of time and the need to make the most of it. Muslims recognize the importance of time and the need to make the most of it, as symbolized by creating the elephant clock, a remarkable timekeeping device.

They believed in utilizing every moment to advance in all aspects of life, not only for themselves but also for the betterment of society. Muslims have left a lasting impact wherever they have gone, contributing to the fields of science, medicine, art, and philosophy.

Their contributions have enriched civilizations, leaving behind legacies of progress and knowledge. Unlike those who seek to exploit and destroy, Muslims have historically shown a sense of responsibility and a commitment to improving the world around them.

Quran's account of the elephant story:

During the time of Abraha, the ruler of Yemen, he aimed to destroy the Kaaba, the sacred Islamic shrine in Mecca. The Muslims, in fear and desperation, turned to Allah and made heartfelt prayers, seeking His protection and intervention.

They put their complete trust in Allah's power and timing. In response to their prayers, Allah, who holds the ultimate power over all things, unleashed His divine retribution.

A flock of birds, known as Ababil, descended upon Abraha's army, showering them with small stones and destroying their forces.

This miraculous event not only protected the Kaaba but also served as a powerful demonstration of Allah's might and the victory of the believers.

It serves as a reminder that Allah's justice is swift and on time, and He has the power to use any means to protect His faith and those who oppose it. The Muslims, through their unwavering faith and reliance on Allah, emerged triumphant.

The Muslims, led by their leader Abdul-Muttalib, were outnumbered and lacked the military strength to defend against Abraha's formidable army. However, they had faith in Allah's protection and sought solace in the sacredness of the Ka'ba.

As Abraha and his troops approached the holy city of Mecca, a miraculous event unfolded. Allah sent a flock of birds, known as Ababil, carrying small stones in their beaks and claws.

These birds descended upon the army of Abraha, showering them with the stones. The stones struck with such force and accuracy that they annihilated Abraha's forces and decimated his powerful elephants.

The birds that Allah used were unique and majestic. Their bright yellow bodies stood out against their sleek black head, while their beaks were a vibrant shade of red.

It was truly a sight to behold as these birds descended from the sky, each carrying three pebbles in their beaks. The Muslims, in awe of this divine spectacle, watched as the birds arrived over sixty thousand people.

It was a powerful reminder of Allah's might and the importance of faith. Allah had sent these birds to destroy those who had gone astray, demonstrating that nothing is too difficult for Him.

These miracles served as a testament to the believers, showcasing the vastness of Allah's power and the countless wonders that He is capable of.

The Muslims witnessed this divine intervention and were saved from certain destruction. This event, known as the Year of the Elephant, serves as a reminder of Allah's power and the significance of the Ka'ba to the Islamic faith.

It also stands as a testament to the consequences of disobedience, pride, and arrogance in the face of Allah's authority.

After the demise of the bodies that came with the army, the water from the rain poured down relentlessly, washing away the remnants of the fallen soldiers.

It was a scene of both sorrow and relief, as the earth absorbed the traces of the battle and cleansed itself. Amid this aftermath, Surah Al-Fil from the Quran captures the awe-inspiring nature of this event with its vivid description.

The surah beautifully portrays the power and mercy of Allah as it narrates the story of the miraculous intervention that protected the holy Kaaba from the army of Abraha.

Not only does the rain following the destruction of the enemy forces symbolize the cleansing of physical remains, but it also represents the purification of the land from the oppression and aggression that had endangered the sacred sanctuary.

The imagery evoked by Surah Al-Fil serves as a reminder of the divine intervention and the ultimate triumph of righteousness over evil. Abraha, a powerful ruler from Yemen, sought to challenge the authority of Allah and the sanctity of the Kaaba in Mecca.

He constructed a grand cathedral in Yemen, known as the Church of the Abyssinians, in an attempt to divert the pilgrimage and worship away from the Kaaba.

Abraha believed that his cathedral was superior and that people should worship there instead. However, Allah had other plans. As Abraha marched towards Mecca with a massive army, intending to destroy the Kaaba, Allah sent a flock of birds carrying small stones to strike down Abraha's forces.

The stones rained down on the invaders, annihilating them and protecting the holy sanctuary.

This event, known as the Year of the Elephant, serves as a powerful reminder that Allah will not allow anyone to disrespect what He has honored and that His protection extends to the Muslim Ummah and the sacred places of worship.

Quran: Surah Fil: 1-5. Have you not seen ʿO Prophetʾ how your Lord dealt with the Army of the Elephant. Did He not frustrate their scheme? For He sent against them flocks of birds, that pelted them with stones of baked clay, leaving them like chewed up straw.

The illustrations of Allah's mercy, justice, and anger continue to illuminate those in search of answers.

The story that involves a mosquito, King Nimrod, and his army in Mesopotamia:

The story of Nimrod's encounter with the power of Allah's weakest soldier is fascinating. Despite many debates and arguments with the Prophet Ibrahim, Nimrod remained steadfast in his disbelief in Allah. In response to Ibrahim's assertion that Allah would demonstrate His power through His weakest creation, a remarkable event unfolded.

Allah, in His infinite wisdom, sent forth a dense cloud of mosquitoes to descend upon Nimrod and his people. These tiny yet relentless insects swarmed the air, causing great discomfort and distress to all present.

Amidst the chaos, one mosquito found its way into Nimrod's head.

The mosquito's relentless torment caused excruciating agony to Nimrod, as it relentlessly bit and stung him. Despite his wealth and power, Nimrod could not escape the torment inflicted by this seemingly insignificant creature.

Eventually, the relentless torture proved too much for Nimrod to bear, and he succumbed to his painful demise. This event serves as a powerful reminder of the strength and sovereignty of Allah, even as His weakest creation.

Quran: Surah Baqarah: 2:26. Surely Allah does not shy away from using the parable of a mosquito or what is even smaller. As for the believers, they know that it is the truth from their Lord. And as for the disbelievers, they argue, "What does Allah mean by such a parable?" Through this ˈtestˈ, He leaves many to stray, and guides many. And He leaves none to stray except the rebellious—

Quran: Surah Baqarah: 2:258. And ˈrememberˈ when We said, "Enter this city and eat freely from wherever you please; enter the gate with humility, saying, 'Absolve us.' We will forgive your sins and multiply the reward for the good-doers."

The Red Sea, in Egypt, holds significant religious and historical importance for Muslims. The people of Madyan were engulfed by the earth in their tale.

This story serves as a warning from Allah to humans not to disobey on Earth and to stay away from idolatry, immorality, and rejection of divine teachings.

The people of Madyan were living in a society that had deviated from the path of righteousness.

They not only worshiped trees as gods, but also indulged in immoral practices that went against the teachings of Allah. Despite the warnings and guidance provided by the Prophet Shuaib, they persisted in their disobedience.

To rectify this, Allah sent a powerful earthquake as a punishment. The earthquake was so intense that it caused the ground to shake violently, seizing the people of Madyan and bringing them down to the ground in a state of complete destruction.

Those who had rejected the Prophet and continued in their sinful ways were obliterated, as if they had never even lived in that place.

This story serves as a reminder that the consequences of disobeying Allah and engaging in immoral behavior can be severe and that it is essential for humans to heed the divine guidance and stay away from such actions.

Quran: Surah As Shura: 26:178. I am truly a trustworthy messenger to you.

26;180. I do not ask you for any reward for this ˈmessageˈ. My reward is only from the Lord of all worlds.

26;183. And do not defraud people of their property. Nor go about spreading corruption in the land.

26:197. Was it not sufficient proof for the deniers that it has been recognized by the knowledgeable among the Children of Israel?

26:201. They will not believe in it until they see the painful punishment.

26:202. which will take them by surprise when they least expect ˈitˈ.

26:203. Then they will cry, "Can we be allowed more time?"

26; 208. We have never destroyed a society without warner.

26:221. Shall I inform you of whom the devils ˈactuallyˈ descend upon?

26:222. They descend upon every sinful liar,

26:227. Except those who believe, do good, remember Allah often, and ʿpoeticallyʾ avenge ʿthe believersʾ after being wrongfully slandered. The wrongdoers will come to know what ʿevilʾ end they will meet.

Surah Ashura, also known as Surah Al-Isra, highlights the treachery and deceit that people can engage in, and how Allah deals with them.

It emphasizes that Allah only punishes them after sending warnings to guide them towards the right path.

However, despite these warnings, many individuals persist in their egotistical defiance. It is important to note that Allah's concept of time is not limited to our human understanding of time.

As the people of Palestine and various Muslim countries endure suffering, it is a test of Allah.

He is granting Muslims an opportunity to unite, support one another, and rectify their behavior. It is crucial not to fall into the trap of Satan, who seeks to mirror the pagan practices of medieval times under the guise of modernization. It is crucial to recognize that such practices do not align with the teachings of Islam.

The angels Harut and Marut were sent to Earth to evaluate humans' ability to obey and resist temptation:

The story of Harut and Marut is mentioned in Islamic literature, particularly in the Quran:

According to the narrative, these two angels were sent down to Babylon, which is in modern-day Iraq. This event predates the time of Ibrahim (Abraham) and other prophets.

The purpose of their arrival was to assess the human ability to resist temptation and obey God's commands.

In Babylon, Harut and Marut presented themselves to the people and offered to teach them magic and how to work with the evil jinn.

However, they explicitly warned the humans that by accepting this knowledge, they would only harm themselves.

The Quran highlights that while alcohol **(Khamar)** may have some benefits, magic held no true benefit for the individuals except for forfeiting their afterlife **(Akhirah)** The angels emphasized that the next world, which is eternal, holds more significance than this temporary earthly existence.

Despite the angels' warning, there were individuals who did not prioritize their future afterlife and willingly volunteered to learn magic.

It is important to note that the angels did not suggest or encourage them to learn magic; rather, they were a test for the humans to see if they would resist the temptation.

During the time of Solomon, also known as Sulaiman in Arabic, the era was characterized by great prosperity and power.

Solomon was not only a wise and just ruler but also a prophet of Allah. He was blessed with immense knowledge and understanding of the world, and his deep faith in Allah guided his every decision.

As humans, we often question the reasons behind certain occurrences, but the answers may lie in the sources we seek, such as the Quran.

Allah, in His infinite wisdom, has granted the ability to comprehend His teachings to those who sincerely seek guidance.

It is through the gift of Iman, or faith, that one finds true peace and richness in their lives.

Quran: Surah Baqarah: 2102 And they followed [instead] what the devils had recited during the reign of Solomon. It was not Solomon who disbelieved, but the devils disbelieved, teaching people magic and that which was revealed to the two angels at Babylon, Harut and Marut. But the two angels do not teach anyone unless they say, "We are a trial, so do not disbelieve [by practicing magic]." And [yet] they learn from them that by which they cause separation between a man and his wife. But they do not harm anyone through it except by permission of Allah. And the people learn what harms them and does not benefit them. But the Children of Israel certainly knew that whoever purchased the magic would not have in the Hereafter any share. And wretched is that for which they sold themselves, if they only knew.

The Church of Satan, founded in 1966 by Anton Lavey, is a religious organization based in the United States. While there are individuals who deny the existence of witchcraft and Satanism, these practices and beliefs do exist and have followers around the world.

The Church of Satan, often misunderstood because of its name, is a nontheistic organization that promotes individualism, self-empowerment, and skepticism.

They reject supernatural beliefs and instead focus on rationality and the exploration of the human condition.

Despite the controversy surrounding it, the Church of Satan has gained recognition as a legitimate religious entity and continues to advocate for the freedom of thought and expression.

There are numerous essays and articles on the subject of Satanism and occultism. Anton Lavey, the founder of the Church of Satan, was a prolific writer and his works played a significant role in shaping the philosophy and practices of the Satanic movement.

The Satanic Bible, published in 1969, is considered one of his most influential works, outlining the core beliefs and rituals of Satanism.

The Satanic Rituals delves deeper into the ceremonial practices of the Church of Satan, while The Satanic Witch explores the role of women in Satanism and offers advice on how to use seduction as a tool of empowerment.

The Devil's Notebook and Satan Speaks! are collections of Lavey's essays, observations, on a variety of topics related to Satanism, magic, and human nature. These writings continue to be studied and discussed by both followers and critics of Satanism.

Occult practices have a way of reaching individuals who may not be aware of or intentionally following cultic ways and practices.

In Islamic beliefs, some individuals may seek answers or help from jinn, supernatural beings created from smokeless fire. However, jinn cannot know everything and are restricted from accessing the higher realms of the heavens.

They may attempt to eavesdrop on the conversations of angels but are prevented from reaching the knowledge that resides in the seven heavens, as ordained by Allah.

When jinn relay information, they can only provide a partial truth mixed with falsehoods. This deceptive nature is often exploited by those involved in satanic cults or magic practices to attract and manipulate individuals.

The historical accounts, such as the story of Pharaoh in the Quran, highlight the undeniable existence and usage of magic for evil purposes.

Islam teaches that magic is inherently evil and serves as a test for individuals to resist its allure and prioritize the eternal rewards of the afterlife over transient worldly pleasures.

The choices we make determine whether we wish to learn and grow or remain stagnant. It is crucial to understand that Islam is a dynamic faith that constantly evolves and cannot be emphasized enough.

Fath Al-Bari, Hadith: 6304: Every prophet was given one dua which was guaranteed to be asked and it will be answered. Most prophets use their dua prayer to curse the people who disobeyed them.

Apart from Prophet Muhammad, who prayed for his ummah (his community), he said, "My Ummati (my people), it is a harsh truth that after knowing all this, Muslims need endurance to understand the faith that originated in the deserts of Saudi Arabia will ultimately is prevailing worldwide.

This is a factual reality, as it is the faith of Allah and the last revelation.

Everything is now revealed and disclosed. The disclosures have been made, and the warnings are clear. It is now up to Muslims to educate themselves and share this knowledge with others."

Dua's of other prophets that passed away shed light on their asking.

Quran: Surah Nuh: 71;26 O Allah do not leave a single non believer on earth.

Quran: Surah Sad: 38:35. He said: "My Lord, forgive me and bestow upon me a kingdom such as none other after me will deserve. Surely You are the Bounteous Giver."

Quran: Surah Maidah: 5:78. Cursed were those who disbelieved among the Children of Israel by the tongue of David and of Jesus, the son of Mary. That was because they disobeyed and [habitually] transgressed.

Quran: Surah Yunus: 10:88. And Moses said, "Our Lord, indeed You have given Pharaoh and his establishment splendor and wealth in the worldly life, our Lord, that they may lead [men] astray from Your way. Our Lord, obliterate their wealth and harden their hearts so that they will not believe until they see the painful punishment."

Sahih Bukhari, Hadith: 6304-6305.: Every Prophet made a du'a' that was accepted. I have reserved mine to intercede for my Ummah on the day of Qiyyama.

Other countries, leading to the establishment of the state of Israel. However, it is important to acknowledge that the Muslim empire of the Ottomans played a significant role in the flourishing of the land.

This diverse array of beliefs adds further complexity to the already intricate religious and geopolitical dynamics surrounding this issue.

The affirmation of the Philistine, which is Palestine, rests on the rich and diverse history of Muslim rule in Jerusalem.

Throughout centuries, various Muslim dynasties have governed the region, leaving a lasting impact on its culture, architecture, and religious significance. The name Palestine originates from the ancient Philistines, who inhabited the coastal areas.

The region earned the name Judea, derived from the biblical tribe of Judah. However, it gained its utmost significance as the Holy Land because of its association with Jesus known as Isa.

This reflects a consistent trend and continuity among all prophets, as they all preached the belief in one God.

Therefore, according to Islam and Judaism, Jesus cannot disrupt the pattern of monotheism and claim divinity, which only occurred later after he gained attention from the people.

The land has since become a focal point for Christians worldwide, attracting pilgrims and believers seeking to connect with their faith and the historical roots of Christianity.

This prophet referred to none other than Muhammad, the deliverer of Islam the final closure to Abrahamic faiths the Quran.

Jesus clarified he had much more to say, but he had to depart in order to send the comforter, who would be none other than the awaited prophet, Muhammad.

This migration, known as the "Abrahamic journey," holds significant religious and cultural importance for both Jews and Arabs. Scholars believe Abraham settled in various parts of Canaan, including Hebron and Shechem, and his descendants grew to form the Jewish and Arab nations.

The story of Abraham's journey and his connection to Canaan is a foundational aspect of the historical and cultural narratives of both Jewish and Arab peoples in the region.

The trials and struggles faced by the people of Palestine continue to persist, but according to Islamic beliefs, Islam is the only religion that will survive in this world.

The lands of Allah will be allocated to the righteous, and ultimately, this staged world and the test it presents for humans, the creatures of Allah, will end.

Time is a powerful force, as prophecies continue to come true. Shamelessness, deceit, fires, earthquakes, greed, academia, materialism, fornication, music, alcohol, same-sex and bisexual relationships – these actions are primitive and are often revived by Western regimes who still follow occult practices.

Islam acknowledges the importance of time and does not deny that the doubtful may follow the arrogant. However, restoration lies in understanding time, which cannot be combatted.

Quran: Al Kauthar: Surah 108. Title of Surah is great abundance.

108:1: "Indeed, We have granted you abundant goodness"

108:2: "So pray and sacrifice to your Lord ʹaloneʺ"

108:3: "Only the one who hates you is truly cut off 'from any goodness'"

Those who understand the value of time know that it cannot be emphasized enough.

Understanding faith does not entail adhering to it. Knowledge has the potential to transcend belief, yet those whom Allah selects possess both the steadfastness of knowledgeable faith and the accuracy of timing.

It is important to acknowledge that flaws are presented before Allah, not before humanity, for Allah perceives what humans cannot comprehend.

This is precisely why **Astaghfar**, seeking repentance, is an essential practice for Muslims, providing us with solace and solitude.

Expressing gratitude to Allah Alhamdullilah for His continuous blessings, seeking forgiveness with Astaghfirullah, and hoping for what is coming, God willing.

Insha Allah!

CHAPTER 21
THE WELL-BEING OF THE HEART, SOUL, AND MIND.

The well-being of the heart and soul is a constant reminder of its importance in leading a fulfilling and meaningful life.

Unfortunately, many people overlook the significance of nurturing their soul and mind. However, it is crucial to maintain the integrity of these aspects of oneself, as they play a significant role in shaping one's overall well-being.

When we prioritize our soul, our body responds in a consistent and durable manner, reciprocating the care and attentiveness. The hadith, Prophet Muhammad (peace be upon him) emphasizes the significance of the heart in relation to the overall well-being of the body.

He states that within the body lies a piece of flesh, often referred to as the heart. If this heart becomes corrupted or diseased, it has the potential to affect the entire body.

This statement serves as a metaphorical reminder that the spiritual and moral state of a person's heart has a profound impact on their actions, character, and overall righteousness. Just as a healthy heart pumps pure blood throughout the body, a pure and righteous heart leads to virtuous actions and a righteous life.

Conversely, if the heart becomes corrupted with negative traits such as envy, greed, or arrogance, it can lead to sinful behavior and a detrimental impact on one's spiritual and physical well-being.

Therefore, the hadith underscores the importance of purifying and safeguarding the heart from moral and spiritual diseases in order to maintain a healthy and righteous life. Teaching children or new converts to Islam should focus on the concept of Allah's mercy rather than solely emphasizing His wrath.

Islam is a religion that encourages believers to purify their hearts and establish a strong connection with Allah. The first encounters of **Prophet Muhammad,** as recounted are **Angel Jibril** cleansing his heart.

It was not initially about the rules of what is halal (permissible) and haram (forbidden). When the heart is not deeply attached to Allah and doubts surround it, it becomes easier to engage in forbidden actions (haram).

Therefore, cleansing the heart is crucial as it influences our thoughts and actions, ultimately affecting the overall health of our body and soul. The heart of Prophet Muhammad (peace be upon him) was cleansed from impurities since his childhood, serving as a powerful reminder for those who may not fully grasp the significance of this extraordinary attribute.

From a young age, Prophet Muhammad showed exceptional qualities of honesty, integrity, compassion, and a deep connection with the divine. His heart was free from the corrupting influences of greed, jealousy, and arrogance that often plague human beings.

This purity of heart allowed him to receive divine revelations and guidance with utmost clarity, enabling him to fulfill his role as the final messenger of Allah.

The cleansing of his heart highlights the divine favor given upon him and serves as a profound lesson for all believers to strive for spiritual purification and sincerity in their own lives.

It emphasizes the importance of nurturing a heart free from negative traits and filling it with love, humility, and devotion to Allah first then His creation.

Through Prophet Muhammad's example, we are reminded of the immense blessings and guidance that can flow from a pure heart, and the transformative impact it can have on individuals and societies alike.

Prophet Muhammad, peace be upon him, warned Muslims about the dangers of greed and excessive attachment to the materialistic world, known as the Dunya.

Despite this, Prophet Muhammad did not complain about Allah or question why such mistreatment had befallen him. He maintained his unwavering faith and turned to Allah with his heart, seeking guidance and strength.

This serves as a remarkable example of true faith, as many people complain about Allah or question His wisdom when faced with adversity.

However, Prophet Muhammad's steadfastness and lack of complaints show his profound trust in Allah's plan, even during times of distress.

This serves as a lesson for believers, reminding them to have faith and seek clarity in Islam when faced with difficulties, rather than questioning Allah's wisdom.

The Quran emphasizes the importance of the heart by mentioning it 132 times, showing its significance in shaping one's spiritual and moral state. It distinguishes between various types of hearts, reflecting the diverse conditions of human beings.

The heart of a believer is described as illuminated by a blazing torch, symbolizing faith and guidance. The heart of a disbeliever is depicted as encased, implying a hardness and resistance to the truth.

The heart of a hypocrite is said to be inverted, signifying a person's knowledge of the truth but their deliberate rejection or deception. Some individuals possess a heart with two urges, torn between believing and hypocrisy, illustrating the inner struggle within them.

Prophet Muhammad emphasized the importance of maintaining a balanced approach to faith.

He recognized that faith is not a stagnant state, but something that requires constant effort and attention. To effectively express and live out their beliefs, one must have a peaceful heart.

Prophet Muhammad warned against the danger of losing faith if belief is abandoned or neglected. He taught that spirituality should be a daily practice, as it is essential in maintaining a strong connection with Allah.

The Prophet also highlighted the significance of treating others with kindness and respect. He gave the example of a woman who would pray regularly, but abused her neighbors, stating that such behavior does not reflect true worship.

There is a defined need to address the concerns and challenges faced by converts who embrace Islam while still wanting to maintain connections with their previous life and contacts that compromised their character traits.

It is important to understand that accepting Islam is not just a mere change in faith, but a comprehensive way of life that requires continuous learning, sharing, and caring for others.

The decision to enter Islam cannot be taken lightly, as it is ultimately up to Allah to grant permission for someone to embrace the faith. Neglecting Islam after accepting it goes beyond neglect; it is a failure to uphold the principles and teachings of the religion.

Islam emphasizes the importance of change and growth, rather than stagnation. As Muslims, we should not only focus on our own spiritual development but also actively encourage and support newcomers to the faith.

While it is true that only Allah invites someone to His faith, it is our responsibility as Muslims to assist and guide those who are sincere in their acceptance of Islam.

This can include providing assistance, support, and even considering marriage if the person's acceptance is genuine and valid. By actively engaging with and supporting converts, we can help them navigate their new faith and ensure that Islam flourishes in their lives.

These young Muslims, who were raised in Islam but have limited knowledge or find it burdensome to practice their faith in western societies, face unique challenges.

They are often caught between the traditional teachings of Islam and the allure of a more liberal and secular lifestyle.

It is crucial to address their concerns and struggles in a compassionate and understanding manner. Instead of simply instilling fear of punishment in Hell, it is important to emphasize that Islamic rules and teachings benefit humanity as a whole, rather than solely serving Allah.

After all, the creator of humans understands the potential benefits that can be derived from following certain guidelines and principles. By providing a comprehensive understanding of the reasons behind Islamic teachings, we can help young Muslims navigate the complexities of their faith while living in western regions.

This illustrates the holistic nature of Islam, where both spiritual devotion and compassionate engagement with humanity are emphasized.

The act of prayer, known as Salat, was not imposed as a burden, but given to Prophet Muhammad as a gift during his miraculous journey of the **Night Journey (Miraj).**

It is indeed unfortunate for Muslims to view this gift as a burden, as it is a means of attaining closeness to Allah and finding inner peace.

In Islam, sins are not viewed as equal in severity. While all sins are discouraged, some sins hold higher consequences and are considered more detrimental to one's faith. Zina, which refers to engaging in sexual intercourse relations outside of marriage, is a grave sin that leads to the erosion of one's faith.

As a person continues to commit **Zina** and lives in defiance of Islamic teachings, their faith gradually diminishes, much like a building whose roof is gradually collapsing.

Similarly, consuming alcohol is strictly prohibited in Islam because of the shamelessness and harmful consequences it can lead to. The fleeting moments of indulgence and display are outweighed by the deep moral and spiritual degradation it entails.

As we review the prohibition of consuming pork in the Islamic faith, it is important to note that this restriction is in place to prioritize the well-being of the creation as the creator is aware of his creation.

Many health hazards and diseases have been associated with pork. Scientific studies have found that pork can carry parasites, bacteria, and viruses, causing illnesses such as trichinosis, tapeworm infection, and swine flu. Eating pork can lead to a higher risk of high cholesterol levels, heart disease, and certain types of cancer.

It's not about one specific address, but about comprehending how quantum physics relates to the heart and soul, and how all of Allah's addresses and rules bring benefits to humanity.

Islam encompasses various definitions and aspects, including modesty. However, its core values revolve around humanity, emphasizing the importance of structured justice, discipline, progression, and continuous self-education.

Islam also promotes the idea of assisting those who can benefit from our help. It reminds us that this world is temporary and transient, urging us to focus on the bigger picture rather than being stagnant.

However, it is important to note that Allah is merciful. Through repeated acts of repentance and a commitment to avoid continuously falling into the same sins, individuals can repair and strengthen their core and soul that lives within.

Salat, also known as the Islamic ritual prayer, is a fundamental practice that lies between belief and unbelief. It is an act of worship that serves as a physical and spiritual manifestation of one's faith and submission to Allah. It's repeated often as this act has no excuses.

Through performing **Salat**, believers establish a direct connection with their Creator, seeking His guidance, forgiveness, and blessings. While belief in Allah is essential for Salat, it also serves to strengthen and reinforce one's faith.

However, **Tahaj Jud**, an additional voluntary prayer, goes beyond the regular Salat. It is a special form of worship reserved for those who have reached a higher level of spiritual closeness to Allah.

These individuals wake up in the middle of the night, forsaking sleep, to engage in Tahaj Jud. It is a time when the world is quiet, and distractions are minimal, allowing them to focus solely on their devotion to Allah.

Tahaj Jud is a deeply intimate and personal prayer, where individuals can seek solace, repentance, and draw closer to Allah, experiencing a profound sense of spiritual awakening and enlightenment.

In this verse, Allah emphasizes the importance of seeking His presence and guidance during the quiet hours of the night. This act of waking up from slumber and engaging in prayer shows a deep level of commitment and sincerity in one's faith.

It is not about indulging in worldly pleasures during the night, but about finding solace in solitude and strengthening one's (Iman) through prayer and reflection.

This verse encourages believers to prioritize their spiritual growth and connection with Allah above all else, recognizing the value of dedicating time to worship and seeking His blessings and mercy.

When believers, including Prophet Muhammad himself, have implored Allah to strengthen their faith, it is an acknowledgment of the constant need for spiritual growth and guidance.

Despite the Prophet's unwavering faith, he humbly encouraged his followers to emulate his example, recognizing that even he could strive for improvement.

This humility, along with his honesty, sincerity, and even sense of humor, made him relatable and approachable, qualities that inspire personal growth and self-improvement in others.

Hypocrisy is a fear that believers may experience, and Islam emphasizes the importance of sincerity and truthfulness. The Quran teaches that understanding and implementing its teachings in one's life are essential for true faith.

Faith, **Iman**, is considered a gift for a believer, and without it, their spirituality can feel empty. Many people focus solely on their physical appearance, neglecting their spiritual well-being, which can lead to discontentment.

The story of the lady who diligently sewed every day, only to undo her work. People perceive her as crazy if they abandon their faith and lose the honor and integrity that they had gained through their good deeds and demeanor can also serve as another example of loss of time.

It is crucial to cherish and nurture one's faith, as it is the foundation for a fulfilling spiritual journey.

Prophet Muhammad, in his dream, observed a gathering of people where he noticed that the shirts they were wearing came in various sizes. This symbolized the diverse range of individuals who embraced Islam, regardless of their backgrounds and differences.

However, what caught the Prophet's attention was the attire of Omar bin Khattab, which dragged on the ground because of its length. Prophet Muhammad interpreted this as a manifestation of Omar's unwavering faith and his firm commitment to Islam.

The Prophet recognized Omar would play a crucial role in fortifying the foundations of the religion and spreading its message. Omar's heart was filled to the brim with faith, and he possessed an unyielding belief in Allah.

Such was the strength of his conviction that even Satan could not approach him or sway him from the path of righteousness. This unwavering faith is a testament to the power of belief and the impact it can have on an individual's life.

If I were to write a book about a person, focusing solely on their human qualities rather than their prophethood. Omar bin Khattab, the devoted convert to Islam, would undoubtedly be the protagonist.

His resolute acceptance of Islam with no doubts or hesitations serves as an inspiration for believers to maintain steadfastness in their faith. He was the second Caliph of Islamic world.

In Islam, the concept of truthfulness and keeping one's word holds great importance. Muslims are taught to be truthful in their words and actions, as lying and failing to uphold promises are sins.

If one's faith is truly present, it should reflect in their words and deeds, becoming an integral part of their spirituality.

The movement of the heart is constant, just like the beating of a heart. If one's heart is not settled with spirituality, they may go through the motions of reciting the Quran, but fail to truly implement its teachings in their daily lives.

Prophet Muhammad emphasized the importance of not only reading and reciting the Quran, but also understanding its message and applying it in practical ways.

Allah does not force belief upon His creation; rather, He wants them to comprehend and internalize His words.

Allah cautions against emulating the previous book's people who treated time as transient and altered scriptures to fit their preferences. The timeless nature of Islam and the Quran can bring order to any era.

The difference in time with Omar's belief before accepting Islam is a powerful testament to the transformative nature of the Quran and the mercy of Allah. Initially, Omar's mindset was filled with anger and the idea of killing Prophet Muhammad.

However, when he heard the Quran being recited, something within him stirred. It was when he discovered that his own sister had embraced Islam that he seized the opportunity to explore further.

Using his time as a catalyst for change, Omar took it upon himself to read Surah Taha, a chapter from the Quran.

The words resonated deeply within him, and he was overcome with a profound sense of conviction. Without hesitation, he rushed to Prophet Muhammad and openly declared his acceptance of Islam.

Once Omar embraced Islam, his doubts vanished, and he became steadfast in his faith. His experience serves as a reminder that those who are born into Islam or those who convert to it may not fully comprehend the true value of this faith.

Omar's unwavering belief and his pivotal role in the early days of Islam have earned him a place in history, and his story continues to inspire generations.

The concept of time as a catalyst in Omar's journey is significant. It demonstrates how Allah intervenes to protect individuals from committing grave sins.

Allah, out of His infinite mercy, prevents those nearing transgression to protect their hearts and souls. The reason He doesn't do this for everyone is simple: He knows the intentions of their hearts.

Omar's story serves as a powerful reminder of the transformative power of faith, the mercy of Allah, and the importance of seizing opportunities for spiritual growth.

It highlights the immense value of Islam as a guiding light for those who embrace it and the potential for profound change in the hearts of individuals.

The believers may continue to sin, but it is crucial for them to control their sinful desires and prioritize what Allah would say over the opinions of others.

It is a constant struggle for a believer to maintain their faith (Iman) in every aspect of life. However, it is disheartening when someone who claims to believe repeatedly betrays themselves by indulging in sinful behavior despite being warned repeatedly.

The narrative revolves around a mother and her son. The son who adopted Islam as his faith:

The mother, exerted her force and power as a mother to compel her middle-aged son, who lived with her, to give up Islam.

He was a Christian who reverted to Islam. She resorted to discarding his belongings, which he had received as gifts upon accepting Islam.

The clash between her faith of Christendom and his conversion to Islam enraged her, showcasing her authority and serving as a reminder of her kindness in raising him.

Her advanced age added to her influence, as she used it as a source of intimidation.

Despite his involvement with Muslims and his desire for marriage, she remained steadfast, erecting walls and barriers to shield him from the faith he had embraced.

He rebelled against Islam without understanding why she had more influence over his beliefs.

He engaged in actions that contradicted Islam, returning to his bad habits, which pleased her more than the peace he found in Islam.

His unwavering support stemmed from a Muslim, not his environment. It was a test of faith, not only for him but also for the Muslim helping him.

Would surrendering be an easier path than clinging to Allah's guidance? It was Allah's will that brought these two together, despite all obstacles.

Allah held the power, not his creation. This was a test of his faith, through which he would eventually realize the significance of his choices.

It is important not to underestimate the value of any human being.

As the years passed, his well-being and inner contentment suffered, becoming at odds with the enemy of Islam that his mother represented.

She cared little for his loss, as long as she could please herself and maintain their impoverished conditions. His health and values were compromised to fulfill her wishes.

The turmoil was witnessed by Allah as another Muslim prayed for him, recognizing his sincerity in accepting and facing the backlash for his actions.

Allah listened to the Muslims, as no disbeliever can weaken the faith of a Muslim.

Allah comes first, then family or friends. It is not meant to disrespect, but the one who created cannot be equated with idols and deities.

The environment felt cursed, as it seemed wrong to deny a Muslim the right to pray, making a rescue necessary. Support was essential, not scorn.

Driven by the burden of doubt, he embarked on a tumultuous quest for truth, eventually finding solace and certainty in Islam, his heart already convinced of its validity.

Allah rescued him from his own evil and turmoil, seeing that his heart was true upon accepting Islam.

Despite the environmental attempts to stop him, he showed to the disbelievers that Allah's choice and worship cannot be hindered by anyone, including the womb or any disbeliever.

He continued to be kind and helpful, as Islam teaches respect, not disrespect. He flourished, and the disbelievers became jealous.

After years, he returned to his choices and finally gained respect from them.

Undermining the choice to follow disbelievers does not gain further respect; it only distorts respect, as they feel they are in control, just as Pharaoh did.

He was so arrogant that he asked Haman to bring a ladder to see the god of Moses. The animosity happened then and is happening now.

Making the right choices and caring for the heart and soul can bring respect, peace, and unity within oneself. Finally, he married a Muslim woman and embraced Islam, solidifying his commitment to his choices.

The story concludes with joyful outcomes and the protagonist's embrace of his faith, ultimately bringing happiness to his heart and pleasing Allah.

The identity of those who obstruct belief, regardless of who they may be, is insignificant compared to the priority of Allah, the creator, followed by the creation, as taught in Islam.

His tale highlights the undeniable inner strength he possesses, culminating in his marriage to a Muslim woman, which deepens his faith and personal life. Those who had previously disagreed with his decisions ultimately accepted them, understanding the power he held over truth not fear.

He married as Allah ordained, and his commitment to Islam served as evidence of his belief. Though doubts may arise, a believer's faith endures.

His relationship was special because Allah divinely ordained it. Their love for Islam brought them more blessings than they could have imagined.

Finding solace in Islam, they found their happiness in the understanding that life in this world is fleeting. When Islam unites two hearts, their bond is unbreakable.

Anyone seeking to sever it will only discover Islam's finality for all humanity.

Most people who turn against Islam turn to Islam.

Dhul Qarnayn, also known as the Two-Horned, was a legendary figure mentioned in the Quran. Although his exact identity remains uncertain, to some but the Quran mentions him which leaves no doubt of his kingdom and knowledge he is often associated with the historical figures Alexander the Great or Cyrus the Great.

. It is incorrect per Islamic doctrine Dhul Qarnayn's title, Two-Horned, is believed to represent his dual leadership over the Roman and Persian empires. As a ruler, he was known for his righteousness and just governance, guided by his profound knowledge and wisdom.

He understood that true power, bestowed by Allah, comes with responsibility and should not be used to satisfy one's ego. Instead, he approached his leadership with humility and sought to justify his actions as a faithful believer.

Dhul Qarnayn's reign serves as an example of how knowledge, combined with divine guidance, can lead to a just and humble governance. The renowned philosopher Aristotle did indeed tutor Alexander III of Macedon, historically known as Alexander the Great.

It's crucial to mention that there is no proof linking him to Alexander the Great, which contradicts the existence of Dhul Qarnayn and erroneously associates his identity with someone unrelated.

In Islamic doctrine, Dhul Qarnayn is a virtuous figure, whereas Alexander the Great was a pagan leader. Their religious beliefs do not align nor do stories and presentations with Islamic doctrine.

Dhul Qarnayn's life and actions are not explicitly detailed, but he was known as a pious, knowledgeable, and just ruler. His name is Al Khidr.

The narratives and stories of Dhul Qarnayn because of their profound understanding of the Islamic version and teachings. Approaching non-Muslim interpretations with caution is crucial, as they may have manipulated the stories to serve their interests.

The Quran acknowledges Dhul Qarnayn's wisdom and righteous rule as a significant figure in Islam. Dhul Qarnayn, mentioned in the Quran, is described as a righteous and knowledgeable man who was granted special abilities by Allah.

According to the Quran, he embarked on a journey and reached a place where the sun appeared to be setting in a body of water with different venues - one muddy and the other clear.

While the exact location and nature of these lands are not fully described, it is believed that Dhul Qarnayn possessed the power and capability given to him by Allah to navigate and explore these extraordinary terrains.

This message is unequivocal: Islam remains steadfast in its monotheistic beliefs, regardless of any travel or exploration.

The answer becomes even more apparent when one considers the vastness of the world. It is only logical to conclude that such a magnificent creation can only be the work of one creator, Allah, and not multiple deities. Islam emphasizes the oneness of Allah and the unity of all creation, rejecting the notion of polytheism or the worship of any other gods.

This fundamental principal guides Muslims in their understanding of the world and their devotion to Allah. Regardless of the diversities and complexities encountered during travel, the core belief in the oneness of Allah remains unwavering.

The story of Dhul Qarnayn is mentioned in the Quran in Surah Al-Qaaf (Chapter 18). Dhul Qarnayn was a righteous and just king who was granted great power and authority by Allah.

He embarked on a journey to a distant land, where he encountered a tribe that was oppressed and living in chaos because of the influence of Gog and Magog, who were corrupt and destructive beings.

Most Christians may not be familiar with or give much importance to the concept of Gog and Magog, whereas in Islam, the story of Gog and Magog is mentioned in the Quran and is well-known among Muslims.

As the individual continued his journey, he eventually came across two mountains where the sun appeared to set. He then traveled to a distant and sparsely populated land, where the level of civilization was minimal, and the people spoke a language unfamiliar to him.

In Islamic eschatology, Gog and Magog are believed to be two tribes or nations that will wreak havoc on the earth before the Day of judgment.

The Quran describes them as a destructive force that will be unleashed upon the world, causing chaos and destruction. Muslims are encouraged to be aware of this prophecy and to seek protection from Allah against the mischief caused by Gog and Magog.

While the concept of Gog and Magog is not central to Christian theology, there may be some Christians who are familiar with the biblical references to them, primarily found in the book of Revelation.

However, the level of knowledge and importance attributed to Gog and Magog may vary among individual Christians based on their specific religious beliefs and interpretations. Dhul Qarnayn, a wise and just ruler, listened attentively to the concerns of the tribe. Intrigued by their plea for help, he sought further information about Yajuj and Majuj.

The tribe explained how these malevolent beings were causing havoc in their community, spreading chaos and destruction wherever they went.

During their communication, the people conveyed to him the significance and nature of Yajuj and Majuj, also known as Gog and Magog.

Although the Quran does not offer an exhaustive account of this encounter, it provides precise and direct information to ensure clarity and comprehension for the reader. They revealed tales of plundering, pillaging, and the relentless torment inflicted upon innocent villagers.

Deeply moved by their plight, Dhul Qarnayn expressed his empathy and resolve to help. Rejecting their offer of payment, he humbly stated that the blessings given to him by Allah far surpassed any material wealth.

Recognizing his duty as a responsible leader, he assured the tribe that he would construct a formidable wall to protect them from the evil that had befallen their lands. This wall would serve as a barrier, shielding the tribe from the destructive forces of Yajuj and Majuj, restoring peace and security to their community.

Quran: Surah Qaaf: 18:04. They pleaded, O Dhul Qharnayn! Surely Gog and Magog are spreading corruption throughout the land. Should we pay you tribute, provided that you build a wall between us and them?'

Quran: Surah Qaaf: 18:95. He responded, what my Lord has provided for me is far better. But assist me with resources, and I will build a barrier between you and them.

Quran: Surah Qaaf: 18:96. Bring me blocks of iron! Then, when he had filled up the gap between the two mountains he ordered. Blow! When the iron became red hot, he said, bring me molten copper to pour over it.

Quran: Surah Qaaf: 18:98. He declared, this is a mercy from my Lord. But when the promise of my Lord comes to pass, He will level it to the ground. And my Lord's promise is ever true.

The land referred to here is beyond the comprehension of humans, and only Allah possesses knowledge of its true meaning and destination unseen by humanity who lives in present times. It is a distant and mysterious place, unlike any known wall in the present day.

Dhul Qarnayn, with the help of Allah, intervened and aided the tribe in overcoming evil and restoring peace and order. This episode teaches us the importance of standing up against injustice and using our power and resources to help those in need.

The Quran emphasizes the significance of travel to acquire knowledge and wisdom. However, the Quran goes beyond mere travel and highlights the importance of understanding and reflecting on its teachings.

To fully benefit from the Quran, it requires more than just reading the words. It requires a deep understanding of the heart and mind, where one ponders and reflects upon the teachings. By contemplating the messages and lessons within the Quran, believers can gain spiritual enlightenment and guidance in their lives.

Some have referred to this wall as the Great Wall of China which is false. The Great Wall of China was constructed of different materials. Therefore, it is a baseless claim with no historical support. The Great Wall of China is not enclosed.

Many sections of the wall are open to tourists and visitors, allowing them to experience its magnificence and historical significance firsthand. He acknowledged that building such a massive wall required not only physical labor but also specialized skills and knowledge.

He recognized the tribe's plea for help and he believed that their involvement would guarantee the wall's durability and effectiveness. Together, they began Recognizing the enormity of the task.

Dhul Qarnayn realized that his army alone would not complete such a colossal project because of the vast distance that needed to be covered. To construct the wall, combining their resources, manpower, and expertise to accomplish this monumental task and team work was involved. They agreed to work together and complete the task.

With a combined effort, they were able to build the wall in record time. The wall was an immense success and still stands today. Most don't know the location but it's in a faraway land as the universe of Allah is incomprehensible to the human mind.

While the Great Wall of China is an impressive structure, those who have climbed it truly understand the breathtaking beauty and vastness of the surrounding scenery. However, it is important to note that the wall built by Dhul Qarnayn is distinct from the Great Wall of China.

Some individuals have proposed it's the Great Wall of China which is untrue by Islamic doctrine. However, these claims are unfounded and lack substantial evidence.

The Great Wall of China is indeed a colossal structure that stretches across thousands of miles, constructed mainly using stone, brick, and wood. It was built over centuries by various Chinese dynasties, with the labor of millions of workers, including soldiers, peasants, and prisoners.

The Tang Dynasty during the 7th century. Known as the Great Mosque of Xi'an, it is located in the city of Xi'an, the capital of Shaanxi province. The mosque showcases a unique blend of Chinese and Islamic architectural styles, with intricate carvings, colorful tiles, and traditional Chinese pagoda-like structures.

It stands as a testament to the long-standing presence of Islam in China and the cultural exchange that occurred between the Chinese and Muslim communities. Today, China is home to a significant Muslim population, with vibrant Muslim communities and mosques found throughout the country.

Chinese Muslims have made valuable contributions in various fields, including science, art, and literature, and have much to offer in terms of knowledge and wisdom.

According to Islamic teachings, the Quran encourages believers to seek knowledge and expand their horizons by traveling to various lands.

In one verse, it states, "Travel through the land and observe how He began creation. Then Allah will produce the last creation. Indeed, Allah, over all things, is competent"

Quran: Surah Anaka 'but: 29:20. Say, O Muhammad. Travel through the land and observe how He began creation. Then Allah will produce the final creation. Indeed Allah, over all things, is competent.

This verse emphasizes the importance of exploration and observation to gain understanding and wisdom. The Hadith, which are the sayings and actions of the Prophet Muhammad (peace be upon him), further emphasize the value of seeking knowledge from different cultures and civilizations.

In Islamic tradition, he is not regarded as a prophet, but as a righteous wise figure and a ruler. To gather the narrative and consider him the legend who plays a major role. He arrived in a faraway land.

Some speculate that this might suggest that the inhabitants of this land did not wear clothes, showing a lack of civilization or cultural norms as perceived by narration. However, the Quran does not provide a full description or explanation of this land.

While the narrative uncovers more details about how it occurred, but the location remains undisclosed. Some aspects of Allah's creation are beyond human comprehension and remain veiled. It is often narrated that the Prophet Muhammad encouraged his followers to seek knowledge, even if it meant traveling to distant lands like China (known as "the Chin" during that time).

This highlights the Quranic principle of acquiring knowledge through exploration and learning from diverse sources, ultimately fostering intellectual growth and understanding. While maintaining a monotheistic facade and not blending polytheism.

Surah Gha Shiyah is the 88th chapter of the Quran. It discusses various themes, including the Day of judgment, the consequences of people's actions, and the rewards and punishments in the afterlife.

The Quran focuses on imparting moral and spiritual guidance, rather than providing detailed geographical or historical information of travel. It emphasizes the importance of faith, righteousness, and the worship of Allah, rather than specific travel destinations.

In several verses, the Quran encourages believers to seek knowledge and reflect upon the signs of Allah's creation. It emphasizes that knowledge is not restricted to a particular group or region but can be found in all corners of the world.

The mention of the Chin in Islamic doctrine can be seen as a symbol of the vastness and diversity of knowledge that exists beyond one's immediate surroundings.

It encourages believers to expand their horizons, engage with different cultures, and learn from sources that may be unfamiliar or distant.

By doing so, individuals can gain a broader perspective and a deeper understanding of the world, its people, and their diverse ways of life. This emphasis on seeking knowledge from various sources is a powerful reminder of the Quran's universal message of learning, tolerance, and appreciation for the diversity of human experiences.

However, instead of just constructing a wall, Dhul Qarnayn proposed to build something even stronger. He asked the people to bring pieces of iron, which he would use to build a dam that would imprison the evil Gog and Magog in a distant land.

The iron was heated and molded into shape, with the fire blazing and the iron becoming molten hot. Dhul Qarnayn then instructed for copper to be poured onto the iron, further reinforcing its strength. It is important to note that he possessed insight, known as "Ilhaan" in Arabic, which is a gift from Allah that grants deep understanding and wisdom to righteous individuals.

Gog and Magog found themselves trapped between two mountains, with a wall made of molten iron and copper blocking their escape. They could not climb or dig. They have been imprisoned for many years.

Despite their daily efforts to dig their way out, the job is frustrating and leaves them unfulfilled, unable to escape the wall's confinement. Allah's mercy is evident in this. They make another attempt the following day, and by the next day, the small hole in the wall is filled.

According to Islamic tradition, Prophet Muhammad stated that during his lifetime, a small hole was made in a barrier that was separating the world from the mystical creatures known as Gog and Magog. While this prophecy may seem distant and fantastical to some, it is important to note that the Quran does not contain fictional tales.

In fact, the Quran serves as a confirmation and correction of previous scriptures that had been tampered with or altered by previous generations. Thus, the warning of the escape of Gog and Magog serves as a reminder of the consequences that may arise from altering or doubting divine scriptures.

Gog and Magog, two powerful and destructive people of the tribe, are engaged in a relentless struggle behind the immense wall constructed by Dhul Qarnayn the soldiers and the tribe of Gog and Magog who feared their evil.

This wall was specifically built to enclose them at the request of the tribe and prevent their chaotic influence from spreading throughout the world.

As the end times draw nearer, the intensity of their conflict grows, and the consequences of their release would be catastrophic. The land encompassed by this wall is vast, extending far beyond what is visible to humans in the present day.

Its expansiveness is unseen by humanity. Allah can utilize any part of this unseen land, serving as a realm for divine intervention as the world approaches its ultimate fate.

Prophet Muhammad, peace be upon him, warned the Muslims about their eventual descent upon the Earth. The small hole, the size of a grain of a pea, through which they are currently confined, is said to have been opened during his lifetime as a reminder to those who have seen the changes in the world attitude and morality shift constantly becomes imperative to gain knowledge.

However, it remains protected for now. As time passes and evil spreads, the day of their release draws closer.

Descriptions of Gog and Magog portray them as having small eyes and hammered faces. They are believed to originate from the Far East and are said to wear clothing made from wool and fir.

The sheer number of Gog and Magog is overwhelming, and it is said that their thirst will drive them to drink all the water from the Taberiye Golu, also known as the Sea of Galilee in Israel.

This event symbolizes their destructive nature and the havoc they will wreak upon the world. As believers await the fulfillment of this prophecy, it serves as a reminder of the fleeting nature of life and the importance of preparing oneself spiritually for the challenges that lie ahead.

One day, they will declare **"Insha'Allah"** and create an opening to escape. The Quran mentions the power of **Insha'Allah.**

Moses told Al Khidr, who was known as Dhul Qarnayn, that he would be patient if Allah would do it. Surah Qaaf mentions Insha'Allah. Muslims rely on the phrase "Insha'Allah" to signify their reliance on divine will for both positive and negative outcomes.

Upon Gog and Magog uttering "Insha'Allah," their long-awaited liberation from years of attempting to escape will finally come to pass, by the grace of God. With the power of Insha'Allah, anything is possible. This word holds great strength, as Muslims firmly believe.

Without the belief in Insha'Allah, nothing is deemed possible. Those who understand the power behind this word never surrender and live their lives with unwavering faith and trust. The Quranic text says they will be set free before the day of judgment.

Quran: Surah Anbiya 96:97. "Until, when Ya'jooj and Ma'jooj are let loose (from their barrier), and they swiftly swarm from every mound. And the true promise (Day of Resurrection) shall draw near (to fulfillment)...

Allah has given the authority for Isa Jesus to kill the Dajjal but not Gog and Magog Jesus will take his followers to the mountain and pray to Allah for mercy from the evil of the tribe of Gog and Magog he is aware of the issues he will be facing followed by peace in the end.

Everything that has evil must come down and good prevails the evil

When Gog and Magog are released, they will emerge with immense power and will bring chaos and destruction to the world.

They will engage in widespread killing and violence, causing immense suffering and death to most of the world's inhabitants. Their victory will seem inevitable as they unleash unimaginable havoc upon the Earth.

The world's circumstances have led people to wonder if the tribe has already emerged, although Islam mentions physical traits that are not yet apparent. The current events mirror the prophesied description.

In a deceptive move, Gog and Magog will shoot arrows towards the sky, which will miraculously return, stained with what appears to be blood.

This illusion will lead them to believe that they have successfully exterminated all of humanity. However, during this tumultuous period, Prophet Isa (Jesus) will be with his followers on a mountain, seeking mercy from Allah.

It is important to note that the spread of falsehoods and evil is condemned in Islam. Those who distort the truth and promote evil actions will have no redemption or penance except for perpetuating a society of wickedness.

The story of Gog and Magog serves as a reminder of the ultimate test of faith, the consequences of straying from the righteous path, and the importance of seeking mercy and guidance from Allah in times of tribulation.

The story of Gog and Magog is a perfect example of the scrutiny the world will undergo, where individuals given a second chance may either choose to repent and improve their behavior, or continue down a path of evil and corruption. This long-awaited freedom of Gog and Magog serves as a significant event in the history of this temporary world, signifying the finality and consequences of our actions.

Ultimately, it is up to everyone to take heed of the signs and make the choice to seek repentance or reflect upon their behavior.

While the biblical and Islamic narratives differ in some aspects, both convey the significance of understanding and preparing for the events of the end times.

The purpose of learning about Gog and Magog in Islam is to remind individuals to stay vigilant, uphold their faith, and strive for righteousness in the face of adversity. It serves as a precautionary reminder to protect oneself from the temptations and trials that may arise during this tumultuous period.

By studying these prophecies and teachings, individuals are encouraged to strengthen their relationship with God and maintain their moral compass amidst the challenges of the end times. The Quran is clear of their identity as evil known as fitnah.

In the prevailing force will be the absence of hatred and division, as Islam advocates for unity and peace. The detailed account provided in the Quran adds to the intrigue and mystery surrounding Gog and Magog, fueling further debate and speculation about its true nature and origins. The Quran remains constant and precise.

The Quran is the divine word of Allah, encompassing complete guidance and clarification on different aspects of life, including future events. Gog and Magog are mentioned in various verses, including **Surah Al-Qaaf and Surah Al-Anbiya.**

These verses reveal information about Gog and Magog, their mischief, and their ultimate downfall. There is no ambiguity or speculation in the Quran's descriptions, as they are presented with clarity and precision.

The Quran's description of the events leading to the end times is final and not up for debate or interpretation by Muslims. However, some interpretations of Bible draw a link between Gog and Magog and the descendants of Noah, specifically the nations that emerged from his sons, Japheth and Ham.

These interpretations suggest that Gog and Magog represent a coalition of nations that will rise against God's people in the end times.

The Quran indeed describes Gog and Magog as a distinct tribe from a faraway land, but it does not establish any direct connection between them and the family of the prophet, Noah. While Noah's son chose not to join him on the ark, there is no explicit mention in the Quran linking Gog and Magog to this disobedient son.

Contrary to popular belief, the Quran does not offer any information about the origins or lineage of Gog and Magog. The Quran simply states that Gog and Magog will be a corrupt and destructive force unleashed upon the world near the end of time.

The Quran teaches while parents can guide and teach their children, ultimately, individuals handle their actions and choices. Even the most devoted and righteous parents cannot control or dictate every action of their offspring.

By studying these prophecies and teachings, individuals are encouraged to strengthen their relationship with God and maintain their moral compass amidst the challenges of the end times.

The hadith, a collection of sayings and actions of Prophet Muhammad, provides further clarification on the events that will unfold before the end times.

It states that the stench of the corpses of disbelievers and Gog and Magog will get a disease and die; it will be so repulsive that animals will feed on their bodies and become well-fed. Subsequently, Allah will send birds to dispose of their remains. Jesus and his followers will emerge freely, and the world will embrace Islam as the only religion.

This means that there will be a unified worship of one God, bringing about the happiest and most content times for the people.

In the prevailing force will be the absence of hatred and division, as Islam advocates for unity and peace. Islam holds a unique position as the only monotheistic faith that has remained unchanged throughout history, transmitting the stories and teachings of Prophet Muhammad to those who possess an open mind and a willingness to believe.

Individuals who lack belief or have not yet embraced faith are regarded as disbelievers, although circumstances can always change.

Although other scriptures discuss apocalyptic events, the Quran leaves no room for doubt. The detailed account provided in the Quran adds to the intrigue and mystery surrounding Gog and Magog, fueling further debate and speculation about its true nature and origins.

The Quran remains constant and precise.

The Quran is the divine word of Allah, encompassing complete guidance and clarification on different aspects of life, including future events.

These verses reveal information about Gog and Magog, their mischief, and their ultimate downfall. There is no ambiguity or speculation in the Quran's descriptions, as they are presented with clarity and precision.

The Quran's description of the events leading to the end times is final and not up for debate or interpretation by Muslims.

Bibe: KJV: 20:7-10. And when the thousand years expire, Satan shall be loosed out of his prison. And shall go out to deceive the nations which are in the four quarters of the earth, Gog and Magog, to gather them together to battle: the number of whom is as the sand of the sea. And they went up on the breadth of the earth, and compassed the camp of the saints about, and the beloved city: and fire came down from God out of heaven, and devoured them. And the devil that deceived them was cast into the lake of fire and brimstone, where the beast and the false prophet are, and shall be tormented day and night forever and ever.

Satan is only confined during Ramadan, not throughout the year, which is a fact.

These religions, often referred to as cults, have existed for decades and have a continuous practice of pagan worship.

Every mishap has the potential to teach those who change direction.

\In conclusion, while the friendships between Muslims and Christians, or any other Abrahamic faiths, may not determine the theological truth of their beliefs, it is important to foster mutual respect and understanding among different religious communities.

Lack of knowledge does not equate to hypocrisy; it may simply show a desire to avoid misrepresenting or misinterpreting religious teachings.

Prophet Muhammad extensively discussed religion during his lifetime, leaving behind a rich legacy for Muslims and non-Muslims alike. However, it is important to note that not everyone possesses the same capabilities or responsibilities as a prophet.

Each person's role in society is unique, and their approach to discussing religion may differ based on their circumstances.

By embracing dialogue and understanding, we can create an environment where individuals feel comfortable engaging in religious discussions without fear of judgment or misunderstanding.

Islamophobes, who lack knowledge of both Christendom and Islam, often make sweeping generalizations and stereotypes about Muslims. They fail to understand that Islamic practices, although they may falter at times, are based on a deep education and understanding of the religion.

However, Islamophobes tend to label all Muslims as terrorists, disregarding the fact that they may engage in acts of terror, both internally and externally.

Islam is an organized religion with a comprehensive doctrine that includes laws and regulations. These laws, far from overriding the importance of love, emphasize the significance of respect and self-control.

In the Islamic tradition, love is not merely driven by sexual desires, but rather it is a profound connection that is rooted in respect and admiration.

The Prophet Muhammad, for instance, was initially revered for his admirable qualities before love for him grew among his followers.

Islam encourages individuals to curb their appetites and align themselves with the guidelines and principles outlined in its laws. This inherent force within Islam fosters a sense of discipline and self-control for those who adhere to its teachings.

These episodes do not provide any lessons, except for highlighting Jesus' temperament, which is inconsistent with the Quran and the Bible which were written years after his ascension.

The Quran was completed by Prophet Muhammad within 23 years.

The practices closely related to paganism, which remain hidden, should not be dismissed. With churches declining, Islam emerges as the world's fastest-growing religion.

Quran: Surah Mumtahanah: 60:9. Allah only forbids you from those who fight you because of religion and expel you from your homes and aid in your expulsion- forbids

The individuals who hold power in these regimes often exhibit deep-rooted Islamophobia, which is clear in their actions and statements. They continue to support these oppressive regimes despite the clear evidence of these governments looting and causing suffering in other countries.

It is perplexing how they can justify this support, especially when it contradicts the very principles of humanity that should guide their decisions.

Islamic texts state that Jesus, the Messiah, will come from Syria, specifically Damascus, where the prophet Muhammad traded. Answers are clear in Islam. The significance of this lies in the connection between Jesus's arrival and Muslim lands, rather than Israel. Jesus is expected to unite with and pray behind the Mehdi, the guided leader of the Muslim community, as per belief.

His arrival is scheduled to coincide with the Fajr morning prayer, making this event even more significant. Although Jesus is revered as a prophet in Islam, he will show his humility by praying behind the Mehdi, acknowledging his leadership but prays behind a Muslim.

He preaches Islam not Christendom is a clarity and difference in Abrahamic faiths also not aligning with Judaism the final revelation Islam will continue as it began with one God one worship Allah.

It's important to highlight that Jesus, similar to other prophets, is a believer in monotheism and will abide by the message of worshiping only Allah. This aspect underscores how the divine message remains unified and continuous across time.

Their misguided support is fueled by belief that salvation can be found through Jesus, a figure who is native to Palestine, not Israel.

This shows a lack of understanding of the historical and cultural context of the region. It is disheartening to witness such ignorance and blatant disregard for the suffering of others.

The forgetfulness that comes with old age is a natural occurrence, but it becomes clear as individuals grow older. However, it is important to note that deceit can also fuel this forgetfulness. Sometimes individuals may use deceit to gain power and control.

They oppress and manipulate others, disregarding the rights and well-being of those they rule over. It is worth mentioning that Allah has allowed these tyrants to come into power, and they will eventually face consequences for their actions.

Just as the Pharaoh in ancient Egypt oppressed the Israelites, they too will face a similar fate. The Pharaoh's oppressive regime ended when he drowned, serving as a powerful example for all.

Egypt, as a predominantly Muslim nation, showcases the remnants of pagan beliefs and pyramids, serving as a testament to Allah's justice and the ultimate triumph of Islam. In conclusion, winners thrive under pressure, regardless of their religious or cultural background.

It is their ability to handle and excel in challenging situations that sets them apart. It is important to acknowledge the achievements and resilience of individuals from all walks of life, rather than making generalizations based on stereotypes.

The notion of a semblance of tranquility being worse than an open and frank discussion can be seen in the ongoing conflict between Israel and Palestine.

Maintaining a false peace or avoiding tough conversations only perpetuates the underlying issues. This is relevant for addressing Islamophobia, as some individuals and groups have long perpetuated rhetoric, blaming Islam for societal problems.

However, simply taking homes and implementing a two-state solution without open dialogue and understanding is not the answer either. Just as Islamophobic lies spreaders would not accept having their homes forcibly taken away, Palestinians also have legitimate concerns about their rights and land.

Supporting Palestine and spreading awareness about the situation there may provide a sense of compensation to individuals who feel a need to make a difference. However, true and meaningful help for Palestine can only come through concrete actions and exposure to effective means of support.

The biblical context of the extraordinary support for the belief in Jesus's eventual destruction of the disbelievers, particularly among evangelical Christians, is rooted in various passages in the New Testament.

It is believed by Christendom during the end times, those who have rejected Jesus will face judgment and be separated from those who have accepted him. This belief is not exclusive to evangelicals but is shared by many Christians who adhere to a literal interpretation of the Bible.

It is important to note that this support is not driven by any desire to control the masses or bring Jews together. Their beliefs dictate that if this happens, Armageddon will take place and Jesus will come to save the Christians, although he has an original plan as stated in the Quran.

Quran: Surah Hujurat: 49:13. "O mankind! We have created you from a male and a female, and made you nations and tribes that you may know one another. Surely the most noble of you in the sight of Allah is the most righteous among you. Allah is truly All-knowing, All-Aware.

Understanding that life is a test is crucial, as Allah could have easily made everyone follow one religion and have the same status. Humanity is not created equal, and neither is their status or faith. Some trials are cautionary tales, demonstrating paths we should avoid. Many questions find their answers in certain individuals.

Regardless of physical beauty, material wealth, spiritual richness, or varying levels of health, one universal truth remains: every individual has the same access to Allah In Islam, the concept of equality is deeply rooted, emphasizing that all believers, regardless of their worldly attributes, have an equal opportunity to connect with their Creator.

While external qualities may differ among individuals, the path to Allah lies in the sincerity and devotion of the heart. The key factor in accessing Allah is not based on the superficial aspects of life, but on one's intentions, actions, and pursuit of spiritual growth.

It is through faith, prayer, and righteous deeds that individuals can strive towards a closer relationship with Allah, transcending any disparities that exist in the world.

The pursuit of knowledge and learning never ends for those who seek answers or are curious about Muslims. Allah does not possess human characteristics. Knowing the faith, you choose is a journey that requires dedication and time, just like any job or talent.

All prophets sent by Allah adhere to monotheistic beliefs. Any alteration in the method of delivery is a departure from monotheism. Yet, fostering familiarity is a cornerstone of this enduring world, and education, not coercion, is the means to deliver truth.

In the evangelical faith, Armageddon holds a significant place, as it is considered a crucial aspect of their beliefs.

While both Muslims and Christians expect the return of Jesus, their perceptions of this event differ significantly. Despite these differences, there is a shared belief between the two faiths in the ultimate return of Jesus to Earth, marking the culmination and conclusion of the world.

Within evangelical beliefs, there is a perception of favoritism towards Zionism, where the idea of a superpower assisting the Zionist cause aligns with their own beliefs

Bible: Matthew 1:21 that "he (Jesus) will save his people from their sins".

As a religious group, Jews hold their own set of beliefs that differ from those of Christendom. It is important to note that the interpretations of the Messiah concept vary between Jewish and Christian traditions. While Christianity can be seen as an extension of Judeo-Christianity, it is crucial to understand that Islam emerged to rectify misconceptions rather than simply copying previous scriptures.

It is important to stress that this support is driven by desire to unite the Jews. Their beliefs state that, in the event of such situations, Armageddon will occur, and Jesus will come to save the Christians.

This belief is not explicitly mentioned in the Quran, although there is a unique plan in Islam where Jesus, as the Messiah, clarifies that he is not God or the son of God.

In Islam, Jesus (known as Isa) is highly revered as a prophet and is believed to play a significant role in the end times. Muslims believe that after a period of hardship and battle, Jesus will return and bring about peace on earth.

In conclusion, it is crucial to seek advice from individuals who have a broader understanding of global dynamics and who are not confined by limited perspectives and controlled narratives.

The chosen prophet Muhammad, peace be upon him, possessed a remarkable combination of skills and qualities that went far beyond his role as a spiritual leader for Muslims.

His finesse and diplomacy allowed him to navigate complex social and political challenges, forging alliances and resolving conflicts peacefully.

Prophet Muhammad's intelligence was evident in his ability to govern and administer a rapidly expanding state, establishing a fair and just society that valued knowledge, education, and the pursuit of wisdom.

Moreover, he left behind a rich legacy of the Sunnah, which encompasses his teachings, actions,

Quran: Surah Maidah: 5:78. The disbelievers among the children of Israel were condemned in the revelations of David and Jesus, son of Mary. That was for their disobedience and violations.

Jerusalem, a city of immense significance, will flourish once again, but it will be under the governance of righteous leaders, who are not the Zionist regime, Jews, or Christians. Throughout history, Islam has played a pivotal role in shaping the lives of countless individuals and societies.

From the time of its inception, it has provided guidance, moral values, and a framework for social justice. The faith of humanity has always been intertwined with the principles of Islam, as it calls for compassion, justice, and the well-being of all people. Muslims, as followers of this faith, are no strangers to trials and tribulations.

They have faced persecution, discrimination, and oppression throughout different periods and regions of the world. However, their unwavering faith and determination have enabled them to overcome these challenges and emerge stronger.

The closure of lands, resolving conflicts, and the establishment of justice and fairness lie in the hands of Muslims who prioritize the rights of all humanity.

They understand that genuine victory comes through upholding the values of Islam and striving for the betterment of society. Just as rain cannot fall until the clouds gather, Muslims will undoubtedly face many challenges before their ultimate triumph.

These trials will test their faith, resilience, and commitment to the principles of Islam. In this process, they will encounter both good and evil, but it is through these trials that their faith and resolve will be strengthened.

The journey may be arduous, but the unwavering belief in the principles of Islam will guide Muslims toward a future of justice, compassion, and harmony for all of humanity. The prophets, except for Moses, received direct revelations from Allah with no intermediary, other prophets were given a multitude of revelations through Angel Gabriel.

Jesus denounced the Pharisees and scribes for their legalistic approach to the Law and their failure to understand its true meaning. However, it is important to note that Jesus, being Jewish himself, based his teachings on the Jewish scriptures and traditions.

Jesus was not Christian and he is connected to Christendom he would deny it he is a literal Muslim meaning monotheistic born from the descent of a Jewish mother only no father the reason he connected to Muslims is Muslim means one who follows the will of Allah, not his own will and that is Jesus.

Usury, the practice of charging excessive interest rates on loans, is not a complex topic, but attributing its origins solely to Jews is not accurate. While the Jewish community played a significant role in the early development of usury, it is important to acknowledge that other cultures and religions, including Christianity, also adopted and practiced usury.

Ancient civilizations such as Mesopotamia and Greece traced back to usury, where they charged interest on loans. However, it was during the medieval period that usury became a prominent issue, with Jewish moneylenders being frequently associated with the practice.

Hence, it is crucial to recognize the broader historical context and the involvement of various cultures and religions in the development and evolution of usury practices, while we cannot negate the early association between Jews and usury.

Usury is the operating principle of the system, except in Muslim countries and for practicing Muslims. Christians declare their faith in Jesus, who strongly opposed usury. However, the practice of charging interest is a significant influence in countries that claim to follow Christianity.

The high interest rates on loans have led to many individuals losing their homes, as they cannot keep up with the payments. The enduring symbol of Jesus' love in Christianity is often used to justify the belief that the prophet who punished the Jews for practicing usury is a significant influence in countries and powerful nations that adhere to Christianity, leading to the distress of individuals who cannot repay borrowed money without interest.

The hypocrisy cannot be negated, but it brings to the forefront how the laws in the Bible have changed to accommodate the system of humans, rather than following the Biblical laws that have been lost for decades.

Although Christianity did not exist during Jesus' time, he shares a connection with Islamic beliefs as all prophets, including Jesus, believed in one God, a belief that has been present since Adam and Eve. Jesus' teachings and life are deeply connected to Judaism, as he was born to a Jewish mother, Mary.

He preached the message of monotheism and following the will of God, which aligns with the principles of many religions, including Islam. But Christianity professes love and compassion and Jesus forgives

However, it is important to note that Jesus' own identity and beliefs are not explicitly stated in historical records. Therefore, it would be speculative to categorize him as anything except Jewish heritage and a monotheist.

Islamic principles prohibit usury.

Quran: Surah Baqarah: 2:276. Allah has made interest fruitless and charity fruitful. Allah does not like any ungrateful evildoer.

Hadith: Ahmad Ibn Maja: Abu Huraira related: Prophet Muhammad said: On the night of the Miraj I came upon a group of people whose bellies were like houses. They were full of snakes which could be seen from outside their bellies. I asked Gabriel who they were, and he told me that they were the people who had practiced RIBA interest.

Hadith Bukhari: Abu Huraira narrated that Prophet Muhammad said: A time will come upon the people when one will not care how one gains one's money, legally or illegally.

Bible Hub: Deuteronomy: 23:21Thou mayest lend on usury to a stranger, but to thy brother thou shalt not lend on usury; that the Lord thy God may bless thee in all thy works upon the land,
…

Bible NIV: Exodus 22:24. "Whoever steals an ox or a sheep and slaughters it or sells it must pay back five heads of cattle for the ox and four sheep.

Bible: Exodus: 22:22:24. Do not take advantage of the widow or the fatherless. If you do and they cry out to me, I will certainly hear their cry. My anger will be aroused, and I will kill you with the sword: your wives will become widows and your children fatherless.

Usury is against Islamic principles.

Islamophobia is a prevalent issue in many societies today, fueled by ignorance, stereotypes, and fear. It is important to educate and explain the differences between the Abrahamic faiths to combat this prejudice.

While reason and logic are valuable tools in understanding and analyzing religious beliefs, they often cannot capture the deep emotional and spiritual connections that individuals have with their faith.

The heart, with its capacity for love, compassion, and faith, often transcends the limitations of reason. It is crucial to recognize that the teachings and practices of Islam, Christianity, and Judaism have unique aspects that are deeply rooted in their respective traditions.

By shedding light on these differences, we can foster understanding, promote tolerance, and challenge the prejudices that perpetuate Islamophobia.

Many scholars and theologians find the decline of Christendom within the Abrahamic faith and the emergence of polytheistic beliefs to be a fascinating subject.

It is vital to recall that Jesus never endorsed usury or any form of polytheism, and he did not see himself as a divine being.

The land of Palestine has a deep historical significance, with evidence of human habitation dating back thousands of years. It has been home to various civilizations, including the Canaanites, Israelites, Philistines, Assyrians, Babylonians, Persians, Greeks, Romans, and Byzantines.

Throughout history, Palestine has witnessed beauty before neglect.

Neglecting to acknowledge this narrative not only disregards the rights and aspirations of the Palestinian people but also perpetuates an incomplete understanding of the region's history.

Winners love pressure because it pushes them to perform at their best and brings out their true potential. In challenging situations, they thrive and use pressure as a catalyst for growth and success.

This means that they will take on the responsibilities, work diligently, and strive for excellence.

They know that success often requires making sacrifices and pushing themselves beyond their comfort zones. Recognizing that meeting expectations entails long hours of hard work, continuous learning, and adapting to new challenges.

Not afraid to step up and take ownership of their tasks, knowing that it is through these efforts that they can achieve their desired outcomes.

The recognition and embracing of demands and expectations also entails being open to feedback and constructive criticism, as it provides valuable insights for growth and improvement.

By acknowledging and embracing these demands and expectations, individuals show their commitment and determination to reach their goals.

Amidst the ongoing turmoil and conflicts, people often question the struggles endured by both Muslims and Christians.

Yet, it is important to acknowledge that most of the population in Palestine is Muslim, and their connection to this land is deeply rooted in their faith.

In the same vein, it is important to acknowledge that the land of Israel cannot be owned by those who oppose Allah's commandments. Palestine, which holds significance for Jesus and is predominantly Muslim, has unfortunately witnessed atrocities committed by individuals who bear the burden of their actions.

Those who aid in this malevolence should be held accountable. Palestine is home to both Christians and Muslims, with the Muslim population being the majority.

Geopolitical interests often motivate the superpower that is providing protection and sending funds, rather than purely altruistic reasons.

While a portion of Christians occupy Gaza and may have a desire to support the land where Jesus came from, the primary motive for the superpower's involvement is likely to ensure stability in their own unfounded truth to help the region and maintain influence over strategic territories.

Helping Israel, despite their rejection of the Christian Bible or the belief in the prophet Isa, can be seen as supporting Zionism. The concept of Jewish lands refers to the declaration of the territory as historically belonging to the Jewish people.

While there may be disagreements among Orthodox Jews, a small portion of the community, many of them fear the loss of a homeland, which was reinforced by Western support.

The Muslim rule in Jerusalem historically brought a sense of peace and stability, rather than chaos. Muslims, as rulers, seek justification for their actions irrespective of religion or race. Islam, as a democratic faith, has the potential to bring positive change and fix global issues.

The superpower that is projecting a negative image internationally while still maintaining diplomatic relationships with various stakeholders in the Middle East is the ability to manipulate perception.

With this superpower, an individual could selectively control how different audiences around the world perceive them.

By strategically presenting themselves as a strong and uncompromising force, they could deter potential adversaries from taking actions that could harm diplomatic relations.

Simultaneously, they could maintain positive relationships with Middle Eastern countries by utilizing their superpower to project a more favorable and cooperative image.

This would involve presenting themselves as a reliable partner

By manipulating their image, this superpower would enable the individual to navigate complex international dynamics and achieve their diplomatic objectives in the Middle East.

The statement presents a perspective that Jesus' salvation depends on Allah, rather than on Jesus himself.

It argues that Jesus did not create himself, and if he were truly God, he would not have needed to be created.

This view asserts that humans altered the biblical texts, implying that they may not accurately reflect the original teachings of Jesus. The argument contradicts itself by criticizing the mention of supporting Israeli forces for denying Jesus.

It claims that Jesus brought a message of truth, but the Romans altered his identity, who worshiped humans as gods. The argument mentions that including nudity in Roman architecture is corruption, likening it to a Muslim empire.

Quran: Surah Raa'd: 13:11. For each one there are successive angels before and behind, protecting them by Allah's command. Indeed, Allah would never change a people's state ˹of favor˺ until they change their own state ˹of faith˺. And if it is Allah's Will to torment a people, it can never be averted, nor can they find a protector other than Him.

Islam is a religion that emphasizes personal responsibility and accountability.

In **Surah Raa'd,** it is clarified that Allah does not change a person's circumstances unless they will change themselves.

This emphasizes how important it is to work on yourself and take initiative to improve. Allah is a merciful God who responds to those who alter their behavior for their own benefit. The concept of belief and faith is crucial in Islam.

When two Muslims or believers engage in conversation, Allah's mention is integral to the discussion, as it solidifies their shared belief and strengthens their faith.

Quran; Surah Raa'd: 13:14. Calling upon Him ˹alone˺ is the truth. But those ˹idols˺ the pagans invoke besides Him ˹can˺ never respond to them in any way. ˹It is˺ just like someone who stretches out their hands to water, ˹asking it˺ to reach their mouths, but it can never do so. The calls of the disbelievers are only in vain.

Despite religious differences, people can still connect and show care. Understanding various religious beliefs, cultures, and stories can help ease the ongoing chaos in the world, which has been expected. Humanity's arrival on Earth was straightforward yet fruitful, although losses have also been significant.

CHAPTER 22
GRASPING THE ULTIMATE END OF OUR EXISTENCE AND THE VITALITY OF LIFE.

The ultimate existence in this world goes beyond the mundane tasks of attending to worldly affairs and accomplishing work for oneself and others.

It is a journey filled with personal battles, challenges, and growth. However, amidst the trials, there comes a significant person who has the power to transform the entire course of one's life.

Parents have a crucial role in raising children with righteousness, and the mother, being the first teacher, bears a significant responsibility in providing diligent guidance while never neglecting the teachings of Islam, which hold utmost priority.

This is not merely a cultural expectation, but a fundamental requirement of Islam that should be instilled from a young age.

The father leads by example, while the mother nurtures and educates, as she typically spends the most time with the child in today's ever-changing world.

The pursuit of knowledge is never-ending, as certain individuals continue to learn and grow. This individual may fulfill various roles, such as a teacher, mentor, partner, or even a friend, offering profound wisdom and guidance.

It is through the collective efforts of those who stand up against o

While faith and belief in a higher power may offer solace and guidance, it is ultimately the responsibility of individuals to work towards justice and create a more inclusive and equitable society.

The overwhelming and all-encompassing emotions that erase all traces of rationality and result in crazy actions can be seen in various situations throughout history.

One such example is the greed and passion for belief in helping evil, which ultimately leads to catastrophic outcomes. Regardless of one's faith, all humans possess a certain level of rationality and humanity.

The folly of going separate ways without exploring the possibilities of taking the same path lies in missed opportunities for unity and understanding.

By refusing to consider the potential outcomes of setting aside differences and pursuing common goals, divisions only deepen and misunderstandings prevail. Allah's understanding of human capabilities surpasses that of humans themselves. He does not burden any individual with more than they can handle.

Quran; Surah Baqarah: 2:286. Allah does not lay a responsibility on anyone beyond his capacity.[338] In his favor shall be whatever good each one does, and against him whatever evil he does.[339] (Believers! Pray thus to your Lord): "Our Lord! Take us not to task if we forget or commit mistakes.

The connection between Allah and humanity is profound and incomprehensible to those who do not fully understand themselves.

Through the practice of Salat meditation, one can delve into their innermost being and find their true essence. However, it is essential to establish personal boundaries and adhere to them.

When these boundaries are disregarded, one's self-respect becomes distant, and others, particularly Muslims, may lose respect for them if this defiance persists. But Allah forgives whom he wills. While Allah is the ultimate forgiver, people's perception of an individual's respect and sincerity may change.

Without the truth, people are left adrift, navigating a world of illusions and falsehoods. Therefore, embracing the truth, no matter how uncomfortable it may be, is essential for a genuine and meaningful existence.

Quran: Surah Imran: 3:139. Do not falter or grieve, for you will have the upper hand, if you are true believers.

Quran: Surah Imran: 3;144. Muhammad is no more than a messenger: other messengers have gone before him. If he were to die or be killed, would you regress into disbelief? Those who do so will not harm Allah whatsoever. Allah will reward those who are grateful.

The Quran's clarification highlights the importance of listening to the prophet, who receives revelations from God but does not replace God. The prophet himself, being a servant of Allah, has emphasized this multiple times.

This is a factual dilemma that arises when considering the beliefs of Christians who follow the teachings of the Bible with alterations known to the world.

Quran: Surah An-Nisa 19: "Give those you have consummated marriage with their due dowries".

Gifts hold great significance in Islam as appreciation. Prophet Muhammad himself sent many gifts as tokens of appreciation, and the Mahr is also considered as a gift.

In the case of Ali and Fatima, the Prophet Muhammad's daughter, he suggested that Ali sell his shield to cover the mahr. While mahr can be negotiated and agreed upon by both parties and their families, it should not be dismissed or altered without proper consideration.

Some Muslims who claim to be academically engaged may attempt to modify the laws of Islam, but it is important to remember that the laws of Islam are not negotiable. Any alteration goes against the teachings of Islam, which emphasize the importance of fulfilling obligations and respecting the laws set by Allah.

Only time laws have resistance when a life can be saved. In Islam, no gift, regardless of its size, is refused, as it is seen as a gesture demanded by Allah.

Quran: 2:284: All that is in the heavens[333] and the earth belongs to Allah.[334] Whether you disclose whatever is in your hearts or conceal it,[335] Allah will call you to account for it, and will then forgive whomsoever He wills, and will chastise whomsoever He wills. Allah has power over everything.

However, it is crucial for the new convert and strayed Muslims to find a balance between their faith and their previous life and beliefs. This may require some seclusion or time for personal reflection, but it does not mean complete isolation from their family or community.

The growth of a convert in Islam can be facilitated through education and understanding, by inviting them to take part in religious activities and providing them with resources to deepen their knowledge and practice.

Building bridges of communication and fostering dialogue can also help break down any barriers and misconceptions about Islam.

Ultimately, the key to supporting a convert is to create an environment of acceptance, where their choices and boundaries are respected, and they are encouraged to grow and flourish in their newfound faith.

In Islam, interfaith marriages can be seen as attractive initially, but the importance of preserving one's faith becomes paramount. Islam does not allow for negotiation or compromise for the religious upbringing of children in such marriages.

Therefore, it is crucial to establish boundaries and discuss these matters beforehand. If a person has to negotiate their Islamic beliefs, it may show a weak foundation in the relationship from the beginning.

For those who prioritize their faith in Islam above all else, the role of Islam is to guide their actions and decisions. This stance may seem harsh to some, but the reality of life can be harsh, and Allah has provided rules and guidance to ensure the well-being and truthfulness of humanity.

The Quran is the word of God and is unchangeable.

However, understanding its message requires deep study, reflection, and interpretation within the framework of Islamic scholarship and guidance.

Making up one's own rules or disregarding the established principles of Islam would blur the distinction between Islam and previous faiths.

Therefore, education plays a vital role in promoting a proper understanding of Islam. It enables individuals to grasp the true essence of the faith, appreciate its rich teachings, and apply them in their lives.

It is important to note that no faith should be disrespected.

Islam, as a religion, emphasizes the importance of learning and sharing knowledge. It arrived as a final revelation of the Abrahamic faith, but it did not abandon the fundamental principle of monotheism and the worship of one God, Allah.

Taking advice from those who have accomplished nothing themselves can be detrimental, as their lack of success and understanding can hinder progress and destroy forward motion.

Quran: Surah Anam: 6:116. O Prophet! If you were to obey most of those on earth, they would lead you away from Allah's way. They follow nothing but assumptions and do nothing but lie.

Islam holds individuals accountable for their actions. The conflicting views on Jesus as the forgiver and the path to redemption create a divide in the concepts of beliefs between Christianity and Islam.

No sentence in the Bible, even with alterations, directly states that Jesus declares himself to be God. The trinity's existence is solely based on a political vote, with no other grounds to believe in it.

Christians learning about Islam wonder what the Islamic concept of God looks like, given that Jesus is represented in various forms in Christianity, which is blasphemous in Islam as he is a prophet.

Quran: Surah Maidah: 5:65. Had the People of the Book only been faithful and mindful of Allah`, We would have certainly absolved them of their sins and admitted them into the Gardens of Bliss.

Quran: Surah Maidah: 5:68. Say, O Prophet, O People of the Book! You have nothing to stand on unless you observe the Torah, the Gospel, and what has been revealed to you from your Lord. And your Lord's revelation to you `O Prophet` will only cause many of them to increase in wickedness and disbelief. So do not grieve for the people who disbelieve.

The prophets of the Abrahamic faiths were undoubtedly sent the previous scriptures by Allah. Jesus, the presumed triune God, did not receive the gospel directly from him, but God sent the books and revelations to all prophets, except Moses who received revelations directly with no intermediary.

Prophet Muhammad ensured justice through their scriptures for people of the book Jews and Christians.

Subsequently, the books adopted a revised edition that aimed to bring humanity together, contradicting their complete adherence to the word of God.

These historical changes are documented in previous scriptures, except for the Quran remains intact.

The concept of end times holds significance in understanding the differences in beliefs regarding the end times in Abrahamic faiths, particularly in relation to Jesus, the prophet and Messiah, son of Mary, who is shared among them.

It is reported that Jesus will not recognize those who worshiped him, as he himself was a monotheist and never instructed Jews to worship him.

These differences in belief systems within the Abrahamic faith have led to questioning among those who have traditionally prayed to Jesus as God, as opposed to those who pray to Allah in the monotheistic faiths of Judaism and Islam.

One question that arises is why Muslims claim the Quran is the last testament of the Abrahamic faith, yet God did not deliver Islam as the starting point and the ultimate revelation in the beginning. This question is often pondered by individuals with a curious nature.

The concept of the finality of the Quran and the role of Islam as a culmination of the Abrahamic tradition may seem contradictory or puzzling to those seeking without a deeper understanding of these religious beliefs.

As the final chapter of my delivery, it becomes necessary to touch on all sensitive subjects. In Islamic theology, Allah is the one true God, and Islam is regarded as the only accepted religion.

Quran: Surah Imran: 3;19. Certainly, Allah's only Way is Islam. Those who were given the Scripture did not dispute `among themselves` out of mutual envy until knowledge came to them. Whoever denies Allah's signs, then surely Allah is swift in reckoning.

The finality of the Quran was revealed by Allah when he deemed his creation was ready to receive it. The creator understands all limits of their creation.

The recap of each chapter is restated to ensure that falsehoods do not overshadow the truth.

TRUTH RULES LIES FAIL.

Ultimately, it is only Allah who can grant the true understanding, and believers implore Allah to provide them with the comprehension to fully grasp the divine message.

This constant seeking of understanding and connection with Allah is at the core of the Islamic faith.

This raises the question of what will happen to those who believe in deities and worship the Prophet Jesus, not considering him to be a mortal rather a divine figure not recognized in Islam.

It is worth mentioning that this concern has been a subject of debate among scholars and theologians throughout history.

Throughout history, scholars and theologians in Islamic belief have debated that judgment, not salvation, ultimately lies in the hands of Allah, who is both just and merciful.

The focus is on repentance for one's actions, rather than relying on others or external factors, and on improving oneself through self-reliance and faith in a single deity.

The beauty of Islam lies in its inclusivity, as anyone, even an underage child, can teach and correct misconceptions or explain Islam through Dawa.

It does not require a specific scholarly background or priesthood, unlike other Abrahamic faiths. In Islam, the pursuit of knowledge and understanding is paramount. Learning the Quran is accessible to everyone, and education is a lifelong journey.

Those who remain stagnant cannot improve, as Islam itself is not stagnant. It has revealed knowledge that was previously unknown to humanity, offering a vast realm of exploration for those who are knowledgeable.

The question of what happened to Adam and Eve and all the prophets who did not accept Jesus as the savior is complex.

It is truly astonishing to comprehend how one human being can possess such immense power, especially when Allah has imparted teachings to prophets like Moses, Jonah, Noah, and Prophet Muhammad, emphasizing that He alone is the ultimate source of empowerment.

While the existence of mythology has always been present, it is important to note that monotheism is not a recent concept but has existed since the very beginning of creation. Thus, it is illogical for the human mind to perceive any individual as divine, as it goes against the principles of theology of Islam.

In Islam, forgiveness is sought directly from Allah through sincere repentance and good deeds. The concept of original sin, which is central to Christian theology, is also rejected in Islam.

This fundamental difference in beliefs between Islam and Christianity regarding the role of Jesus and the concept of salvation creates a stark contrast in the understanding of forgiveness and redemption between the two faiths

One reason for the Jews and rejection was their disbelief in the concept of Jesus being born to a virgin mother, Mary. In their perspective, this concept challenged the notion of Mary's chastity, which they believed was necessary for the divinity of Allah.

The defiance they displayed was not something novel; they discovered ways to circumvent and attempted to outwit the laws. Christians adhered to the concept of creation in order to establish new laws based on no evidence.

Unwavering faith in Allah's capabilities is deeply rooted in the teachings of the Quran and the Hadiths (sayings and actions of the Prophet Muhammad) Miracles, which are extraordinary events that defy the laws of nature, serve as a demonstration of Allah's omnipotence and are considered as signs of His divine presence and intervention.

Thus, defiance, disbelief, or questioning the miracles of Allah is not only discouraged but also contradicts the core principles of Islamic faith.

However, it was not solely the Roman Empire that played a role in solidifying the belief in Jesus' divinity.

The Roman Empire's adoption of Christianity as the state religion under Emperor Constantine in the 4th century certainly contributed to its widespread acceptance and influence.

The exploration of faith requires a deep understanding of its distinct principles, teachings, and beliefs.

Islam considers this belief as a form of associating partners with God **(shirk)**, which is strictly forbidden. It is an unforgivable sin in Islam.

Islam acknowledges the previous scriptures, such as the Torah, Gospel, and Psalms, as divine revelations, but believes that they have been altered or corrupted over time.

The Quran, as the last revelation, is the comprehensive and unaltered guidance for humanity. Islam presents its teachings with clarity and leaves the decision regarding faith and salvation to each individual, ultimately to be determined on the Day of judgment.

The prophets, including Jesus, were messengers who brought a consistent message from God. If God were to constantly change his message, he would not be considered truly divine.

Allah sent Prophet Muhammad as the final prophet is a recognition of his unique abilities and role in the world.

Prophet Muhammad was chosen to bring the message of Islam during his time, and he is the only prophet hailing from Saudi Arabia.

His prophethood and the establishment of Islam as a faith during his time were significant events in the history of religion. The number of Muslims continues to grow, and many argue that those who oppose Islam inadvertently contribute to its promotion.

However, it is crucial to approach discussions with respect and understanding, rather than resorting to rhetoric or labeling others as extremists. Individuals who choose to convert to Islam should be supported, rather than judged or disapproved of.

In Islam, the company one keeps is given great importance, as it has the power to shape an individual's character and faith. By recognizing Allah as our primary source and abiding by His teachings, we can navigate the challenges and complexities of self-employment with integrity and righteousness.

KJV: Colossians: 3:17. And whatsoever ye do in word or deed, do all in the name of the Lord Jesus, giving thanks to God and the Father by him.

It is believed that each individual's destiny is predetermined, as humans are given the freedom to choose their own paths, which Allah has already written.

The Quran also mentions that if humans were to plead for another chance and be sent back, they would likely repeat the same actions and choices.

Unlike previous miracles that were limited to a particular time and place, the Quran's message is timeless and universal, addressing the spiritual and moral needs of people throughout history.

Its language, eloquence, and profound teachings continue to resonate with individuals from diverse backgrounds and cultures.

Physical copies of the Quran may be removed, but Allah will ensure that the pages are erased before doomsday, preserving His book.

The true essence of this divine revelation lives in the hearts and minds of those who have memorized its words. The memorization of the Quran is considered a remarkable accomplishment and a source of immense spiritual reward for Muslims.

Bible: ESV: Colossians: 3:17. And whatever you do, in word or deed, do everything in the name of the Lord Jesus, giving thanks to God the Father through him.

Bible: Colossians: 3:18. Wives, submit yourselves to your husbands, as is fitting in the Lord.

The concept of wives submitting to their husbands, as described in the Bible, has been a topic of interpretation and discussion for centuries. While some individuals and religious groups adhere strictly to this belief, many others have evolved their understanding of gender roles and relationships.

In Western societies, the fight for equality is driven by a desire to ensure equal rights, opportunities, and treatment for all individuals, regardless of gender.

This movement seeks to challenge and dismantle traditional gender norms and stereotypes, recognizing that women should have the freedom to make their own choices and have agency over their lives.

While some may choose to follow the teachings of the Bible, others believe in forging a more egalitarian society where both men and women can thrive and have equal opportunities.

Ultimately, the interpretation and application of religious texts are complex and multifaceted.

While some may find it challenging to reconcile certain passages with their pursuit of equality, others strive to reinterpret, contextualize, and prioritize the core values of justice, compassion, and respect for all individuals within their religious traditions.

A Muslim cannot alter the rules outlined in these sacred texts but have the choice to conform to them or seek repentance if one deviates from them. Life is not a series of interchangeable events, but a journey of progress and growth. It is only through sincere efforts to understand and grasp the message of truth that genuine progress can be achieved.

Opportunity and opportunists can indeed be seen as the elusive illusion of success, as they often represent individuals who take advantage of favorable circumstances to further their own interests.

The treatment of those who are less fortunate with kindness, compassion, and justice is strongly emphasized in Islam. From: Those who are in positions of power have a responsibility to protect and support the weak and vulnerable members of society, according to Islam.

Islam not only condemns taking advantage of the less fortunate but also considers it a violation of basic human rights.

Islam promotes a fair and just society where power is not used to oppress or exploit the weak. Muslims strongly discourage hypocrisy and encourage fighting for justice and equality, standing up against any form of injustice or abuse of power.

Islam teaches that true strength lies in helping and uplifting those who are less powerful, rather than using power to destroy or oppress them This faith refers to Islam, which has played a significant role in shaping the history and development of societies. The Golden Age of Islam, which occurred during the 8th to 14th centuries, witnessed remarkable advancements.

Islamic scholars and thinkers made important contributions that continue to shape our understanding today.

Without the opportunities provided by this faith, these historical achievements would not have been possible. It is crucial to recognize the importance of education in countering illiteracy and misinformation, especially in the age of social media.

While social media can be a valuable tool for education, it is also important to promote critical thinking and discernment to prevent the spread of false information.

By availing education and embracing tolerance, we can learn from the legacy of winners and teachers, ensuring a better future for all.

Through the unfolding chapters, I present thought-provoking perspectives that can only resonate with individuals who approach them with an open mind.

As the truth gradually unravels before their eyes, it becomes an undeniable force, captivating their consciousness. While some may perceive it as a mere tabloid event, seeking simplistic answers, those who yearn for a deeper understanding find themselves drawn towards exploring the ultimate scripture of the Quran.

Quran: Surah Hijar: 15:26. Indeed, We created man from sounding clay molded from black mud.

Allah, in the Quran, has provided detailed descriptions of the composition and nature of the Jinn, shedding light on the paranormal world that often intrigues humans.

The Jinn existed on Earth before the creation of humans, inhabiting a realm that has captivated the human imagination.

However, the Quran clarifies that while humans cannot perceive the Jinn family; the Jinn can see and observe humans from a realm that is beyond human perception.

Quran: 15:27. As for the jinn, We created them earlier from smokeless fire.

Islam that emphasizes the belief in the oneness of God, known as monotheism. It teaches that individuals should worship and submit to Allah, the one true God.

While Islam does not force its beliefs onto others, it emphasizes the consequences of one's actions. In Islam, it is believed that those who are unaware of its teachings cannot be blamed or punished for not following them.

Deliberately choosing not to learn the Quran, especially for a Muslim, and ignoring it is not an excuse; rather, it hinders personal growth and deprives oneself of valuable knowledge

. The concept of accountability in Islam is considered superior to human systems, as Allah's accounting is believed to be more just and fair.

As a Muslim, it is an honor to explain and share the teachings of Islam with others. When someone grasps the message and excels in life, it is a splendid achievement.

Wasting time on trivial pursuits such as loud workshops, nightclubs, alcohol, and sinful acts only leads to the decay of life and valuable time.

The believers pray to Allah, the one and only God in Islam, seeking His protection and guidance.

They implore Allah not to let the disbelievers gain power, wealth, or any other means that would enable them to falsely believe they are right. It is understood among those who have knowledge of Islam that having the upper hand is preferable to being subjugated by the falsehoods propagated by tyrants.

Some names include Al-Rahman (The Most Merciful), Al-Wadud (The Loving), Al-Hakim (The Wise), Al-Adl (The Just), and Al-Qadir (The All-Powerful).

Most non-Muslims read my book **"DELIVERY IS POWER"** and the future is with **"POWER IS TRUTH"** because my writings offer a unique perspective on the power of education and open-mindedness.

Those who are open-minded and eager to learn have always captivated me; they are the finest individuals.

Friendships help ventures, and those interested in Islam read, learn, and form their own opinions through positive learning environments that focus on education rather than coercion.

These readers, especially U.S have been exposed to Islamophobia, appreciated the opportunity to learn and support the concept of educating minds without forcing beliefs.

The positive reviews and widespread interest in my words are a testament to the curiosity and open-mindedness of people throughout the world.

I am grateful to Allah for his mercy and to humanity for their support. Those who fear humanity and try to control it are ultimately losing, as true power lies in embracing diversity and empowering individuals to shape their own values.

Islam views destiny as a predetermined course of events, where the outcome is already planned. However, those who constantly fear others and their abilities cannot truly succeed as the rightful successor.

The true successor fears only the highest power, not the lowest human. It is important to remember that humans were created from a clinging substance, and the first creation was made from dirt.

Muslims have a responsibility to speak out for justice and fairness for all of humanity, as Islam is a religion founded on justice and fairness.

Islam is a comprehensive faith that allows individuals to embrace the world with one hand while holding Allah in their hearts.

In doing so, there is nothing to lose but everything to gain. By seeking knowledge and engaging in dialogue, Muslims aim to challenge these prejudices.

It needs more accurate understanding of Islam and its followers.

These private individuals who hold friendships with Muslims understand the importance of learning and accepting cultural exchange.

They genuinely appreciate the rich Muslim culture, including its cuisine and mannerisms.

Social media plays a significant role in influencing the masses, particularly those who are less educated or have never traveled to Muslim lands.

Economic conditions, health issues, or fear of entering Muslim countries may prevent some individuals from experiencing the beauty of these cultures firsthand.

The genuine friendships formed between private individuals and Muslims serve as a testament to the positive impact of cultural understanding and acceptance.

Differences in faith should not be a barrier to forming friendships, but an opportunity to learn and understand each other better.

When we encounter someone who practices a different faith, such as Islam, it can open our eyes to a whole new world of beliefs, traditions, and values.

Rather than assuming or relying on stereotypes, engaging in meaningful conversations about Islam can help dispel misconceptions and foster mutual respect.

By seeking to understand what Islam truly is, we can cultivate a deeper appreciation for the rich diversity of human beliefs and ultimately build stronger connections based on empathy and understanding.

In Islam, time is considered a precious gift from Allah, and it is emphasized that every moment should be utilized wisely.

The Quran mentions the significance of time in **Surah Al-Asr**, where Allah swears by it, highlighting its importance.

This surah serves as a profound reminder of the fleeting nature of time and the urgency to make the most of it. As I reflect on the moments shared with those who encountered my passion, I realize how these experiences shaped me and taught me valuable lessons.

Whether it was the joyous celebrations or the challenging times we faced together, each moment holds a special place in my heart.

The memories created during these moments have become the most treasured and unforgettable adventures of our lives. Cherishing and appreciating these shared experiences is a reminder of the brevity of time and how they contribute to our personal growth and spiritual development.

The beauty lies because even if only one surah were to be included in the Quran to emphasize the importance of time, **Surah Al-Asr** would suffice in capturing its essence.

The prayer of Prophet Musa (Moses) reflects his desire for ease in communication understandings.

Similarly, I hope that our discussions have allowed for a greater understanding of Islam, free from any misconceptions or biases.

Throughout our conversations, we have delved into various subjects, such as the pillars of Islam, the importance of prayer, the concept of jihad, and the role of women in Islam.

By examining these topics, we have been able to highlight the unique aspects of Islam within the broader context of the Abrahamic faiths.

Just as Musa prayed for his words to be understood, I too have strived to present Islam in a clear and comprehensive manner, shedding light on its beauty and teachings.

Although the comparison is present without no human compares to any prophet.

In Abrahamic faiths, there are contrasting views that aim to highlight the distinctions and commonalities of belief in one Go These views are not intended to promote hostility or prejudice, but to foster understanding.

The notable contrast is the difference in the stature of Jesus in Islam compared to Christianity.

Despite these differences, friendships can still exist among adherents of these faiths, as learning about each other's beliefs can lead to knowledge and open one's eyes to different perspectives.

For example, Muslim women may find Islam liberating rather than confining, as they perceive the rules and regulations as beneficial to humanity rather than restrictive Muslims believe God owns everything visible and beyond, and His knowledge surpasses that of His creation.

As humans continue to study and understand themselves, it is important to use time wisely, as Islam teaches that success is achieved by making the most of the time we have been given.

Each person handles their choices and actions, and they will be held accountable for them in the Hereafter.

Islam teaches everyone has free will and the ability to make their own decisions, and therefore, they handle the consequences of those decisions.

This concept of individual accountability is emphasized throughout the Quran and the teachings of Prophet Muhammad (peace be upon him).

It promotes personal responsibility, self-reflection, and the importance of seeking forgiveness and repentance for one's own transgressions

One Surah that holds great significance and serves as a profound reminder is **Surah Al-Asr** from the Quran. **Al-Asr, meaning "The Declining Day," is the 103rd Surah in the Quran.**

Despite its brevity, it carries a profound message about the value of time and the path to endurance, repentance and stability from all that Allah has given in this world most precious is time.

In just three concise verses, it emphasizes the importance of faith, righteous actions, and mutual reminders for guidance and time.

The **Surah** serves as a reminder to humanity that time is a precious resource, and we must utilize it wisely by seeking knowledge, performing good deeds, and encouraging one another towards righteousness.

Its timeless message resonates across generations, serving as a constant reminder of the importance of living a purposeful and fulfilling life.

Surah Asr:

103:0. In the name of Allah, the Entirely Merciful, the Especially Merciful. 103:1. By time,

103:2. Indeed, mankind is in loss, 103:3. Except for those who have believed and done righteous deeds and advised each other to truth and advised each other to patience.

Throughout our time together, we have experienced countless moments of deep connection. Our shared curiosity has led us to explore and engage with the world around us, igniting our senses and fueling our thirst for knowledge.

As we part ways, I want to emphasize the value and importance of time. Time is a precious resource that we must cherish and utilize wisely. It is through the passage of time that we grow, learn, and evolve.

Everything in this world has a definite start and finish, even though it may appear as an everlasting saga filled with countless tales.

From Allah we come and to Allah we return!

Every entity that embarks upon a journey has an inevitable conclusion. Those fortunate enough to witness the genesis are also destined to witness the ultimate conclusion

The inherent nature of creation, carefully crafted by the divine creator, calls for us to be mindful of the fleeting nature of time and to seize every moment.

Seizing every opportunity that comes our way and finding purpose in every step is progress. **Insha'Allah**, those who tread the path with determination will be filled with abundance, and those who strive to distinguish right from wrong are rewarded.

As the creation of Allah embarks on this transcendent journey through life, I extend my sincerest wishes to you.

Each of my chapters delivers meaningful insights and sparks curiosity for those unfamiliar with Islam and its position as the final Abrahamic faith.

The legacy and conclusion of all religions is to acknowledge Allah as the only creator, with forgiveness granted through repentance, and laws created to ensure fulfillment on earth and water.

In my discussions and presentations about Islam, there is no implication of encouragement for anyone to convert to Islam.

In fact, embracing Islam or practicing it as a Muslim is considered the highest level of learning and applying principles of stability and conformity in one's life. That invite can only come from Allah.

It is hypocritical to fear other human beings or hold prejudices, as humans are mere creations and not the creators themselves.

The only one who deserves our fear and reverence is the creator, Allah. We can expect great things from Him, and whenever we raise our hands to seek His help, they are never empty.

Allah is the benevolent provider and forgiver of His creation. Life lacks flavor for those who never discovered and embraced the essence of knowing Allah.

The truth is essential for the vitality of existence, and Muslims should never hesitate to convey it. I see it as a privilege, and comparing with other Abrahamic faiths only strengthens the adherence to Allah's last message.

Understanding the true essence of Jesus, a shared prophet, is crucial, just as acknowledging prophet Muhammad as the last prophet and bearer of truth Every follower of a religion firmly believes in the correctness of their faith.

Undoubtedly, the truest religion of all is the belief in one God, known as Allah. Regardless of the name one may use to refer to Him, Allah stands as the sole creator and owner of the world.

I express my deepest gratitude and thanks to Allah for granting me the ability to write about him. May Allah accept my efforts, **Insha'Allah**. I plead with him to pardon any unintentional errors I made during my delivery.

The best conversation and delivery of words is the **dhikr** (remembrance) of Allah. It is through this constant remembrance of **Allah** I find my solitude and peace.

Insha'Allah (God willing), I hope that my words have conveyed the privilege and honor I feel in being able to address Allah and discuss His greatness. The knowledge that we are here to worship and serve Allah alone underscores every event and aspect of our lives.

May Allah grant me and those who seek him the ability to constantly remember Him and seek His forgiveness. Also for any shortcomings in my efforts to convey His message.

Allah reveals that He found Prophet Muhammad when he was lost and guided him. Similarly, if Allah chooses, He can guide anyone He wishes.

I seek Allah's guidance to use my words in aiding those who can benefit. I seek help from Allah alone for myself.

Quran: Surah Ad Duha: 93:7. "And He found you lost and guided you"

Kind Regards,
As-Salamu Alaykum!

 Peace be upon you!

Shazadi Baig

Shazadi Baig

SUMMARY

The only estimate of this world is time, for it is through the passing of moments that we witness the ebb and flow of life's experiences.

With a heart subservient to Allah, I find solace and guidance in His divine presence, allowing His teachings to shape my character and actions.

My mind, aligned with His wisdom, seeks to comprehend the intricacies of existence and unravel the mysteries that lie within.

Education and knowledge are essential for making informed decisions. The Christian and Islamic faiths have different interpretations of Jesus.

While Judaism mostly rejects Jesus as the Messiah. Knowledge alone cannot alter a person's faith, only their desire for spiritual fulfillment can.

Through my writing, I strive for precision, handpicking words that convey my thoughts and beliefs with clarity and purpose. My aim is to craft every sentence, intending to inspire myself and others and ignite a thirst for knowledge and truth.

In my delivery, I am mindful of the impact my words may have, ensuring that they resonate with sincerity and authenticity.

I embark on a constant exploration of truth, seeking to broaden my understanding of the world and the divine principles that govern it.

Time becomes my measuring tool, reminding me of the fleeting nature of this earthly existence and the importance of using it wisely to fulfill my purpose and leave a positive impact on those around me.

Quran: Surah Al Asr: Indeed, mankind is in loss. Except for those who have believed and done righteous deeds and advised each other to truth and advised each other to patience.

If **Surah Al-Asr** was the only surah in the Quran, it would still be sufficient. This surah emphasizes the significance of time and the importance of sharing advice based on truth and patience.

If one truly comprehends its value, this surah has the potential to transform the life of anyone seeking truth.

Whether in times of distress or happiness, this surah can serve as a meaningful and invaluable companion.

The intricate contrasts of faith are implications of understanding there is only one God Allah since humanity was created is of utmost importance to share in the irresistible climate of today that sways minds in many directions.

In my writing, I often find that my thoughts flow freely and spontaneously, with no preconceived plan or structure.

Each chapter seems to unfold naturally, guided by the deep emotions that resonate within my heart.

However, amidst this seemingly unplanned process, I am constantly reminded of the importance of clarity and the knowledge that I have gained throughout my life's journey.

I am immensely grateful to Allah, who has given upon me the talents and abilities to express myself and share my thoughts with the world. Talents cannot be shunned, but expressed and shared.

Knowledge, smiles, revenue, food - all are gifts, and it's alright to give and take if it's for Allah's sake.

This gratitude stems not only from a sense of submissiveness, but from a profound recognition of Allah's divinity and the role of His prophets in shaping the lives of Muslims today.

Unfortunately, in the current world, Islamophobia and prejudiced attitudes prevail, fueled by ignorance and fear. It is this lack of understanding and doubts that often leads humanity astray.

However, for those who seek solace and truth, the pursuit of knowledge can serve as a beacon of hope, offering a glimpse of the eternal bliss that awaits them.

The concept of seeking a creator and finding solace in an unseen God transcends generations. It is a universal desire that drives both the old and new generations.

While different religions may have varying interpretations and beliefs about God, the underlying motivation remains the same – the longing to connect with something greater than ourselves.

In Islam, the belief in Allah as the ultimate knower of hearts provides a sense of clarity and understanding. By acknowledging Him as the creator of both this world and the next, I express gratitude towards Allah.

My journey of self-discovery and spiritual growth is reflected in my books, **"Delivery is Power" and "POWER IS TRUTH."**

The titles emphasize the importance of embracing the truth and rejecting falsehoods. The conclusion is with gratitude towards the reader for taking the time to engage with their thoughts and expresses a hope for future encounters.

Physical presence and spirituality balance humanity. I prioritize a balanced life by attending to both. **Memories linger, hoping they stay with you as intended!**

Quran: Surah Imran: 3:149. O you who have believed, if you obey those who disbelieve, they will turn you back on your heels, you will then become losers.

Quran: Surah Nisa: 4:135. O you who have believed. Stand out firmly for justice, as witnesses to Allah, even though it be against yourselves, or your parents, or your kin, be he rich or poor, Allah is a better protector to both than you. So, follow not the lusts of your heartlets you may avoid justice, and if you distort your witness or refuse to give it, verily Allah is Ever Well-Acquainted with what you do.

In my conclusion, I want to express my gratitude for the privilege granted by Allah to write about Him, His prophets, and the truth of His affairs.

It is a great honor to be allowed to speak about Him to the world, and I am humbled by this responsibility.

Through my studies of the Golden Age of Islam and beyond, I realized that the stagnation of humanity is often a result of close-mindedness and a failure to learn from history.

Ignorance can sometimes lead to arrogance, but expanding one's knowledge can lead to personal growth, regardless of religious affiliation.

I am thankful for the "has Anath" blessings that flow through my writing, resonating within my heart and yours.

This connection creates a lasting and profound effect.

While truth should always be the guiding principle in delivering our message, friendship extends beyond theological events, and justice in Islam encompasses all of humanity, regardless of faith.

It is crucial to emphasize that this book does not aim to convert or guide anyone towards Islam; only Allah can guide a person to their faith.

This is an invitation to learn and explore the Abrahamic faiths, including their differences, comparisons, history, and present conditions.

Allah's knowledge surpasses all, and He knows best the preparations required for His subjects. As I share my words, rooted in the contract of Islamic theology, history, and current events, I trust in His guidance and pray that those who receive them may understand my words.

We discover treasures in our hands and hearts!

Muslims must protect and speak for the oppressed. I support the measures of true Palestine, the land where Jesus walked as a Palestinian Jew, as a Muslim woman and humanitarian.

When truth is revealed, competition becomes insignificant.

OPT for truth, not blame. "POWER IS TRUTH".